THE PENTAGON AND THE PRESIDENCY

THE PENTAGON AND THE PRESIDENCY

CIVIL-MILITARY RELATIONS FROM FDR TO GEORGE W. BUSH

DALE R. HERSPRING

UNIVERSITY PRESS OF KANSAS

Published by the University Press of Kansas (Lawrence, Kansas 66049), which was organized by the Kansas Board of Regents and is operated and funded by Emporia State University, Fort Hays State University, Kansas State University, Pittsburg State University, the University of Kansas, and Wichita State University

Library of Congress Cataloging-in-Publication Data

Herspring, Dale R. (Dale Roy)
The Pentagon and the presidency : civil-military relations from FDR to George W. Bush/ Dale R. Herspring.
p. cm. — (Modern war studies)
Includes bibliographical references and index.
ISBN 0-7006-1355-2 (cloth : alk. paper)
1. United States—History, Military—20th century. 2. United States—History, Military—21st century. 3. Presidents—United States—History—20th century. 4. Presidents—United States—History—21st century. 5. Generals—United States—History—20th century. 6. Generals—United States—History—21st century. 7. Civil-military relations—United States—History—20th century. 8. Civil-military relations—United States—History—21st century. 9. Political leadership—United States—Case studies. 10. Command of troops—Case studies. I. Title. II. Series.
E745.H47 2005
322′.5′09730904—dc22 2004025537

British Library Cataloguing-in-Publication Data is available.

Printed in the United States of America

10 9 8 7 6 5 4 3 2 1

The paper used in this publication meets the minimum requirements of the American National Standard for Permanence of Paper for Printed Library Materials Z39.48–1984.

To the men and women
who have proudly worn the uniform
of the United States military

Civilian authority must scrupulously respect the integrity,
the intellectual honesty, of its officer corps. Any effort to force
unanimity of view, to compel adherence to some politico-military
"party line" against the honestly expressed view of
a responsible officer . . . is a pernicious practice that jeopardizes
rather than protects the integrity of the military profession.

—*Sam C. Sarkesian*

CONTENTS

PREFACE

The idea for this book came to me after I spent many years crossing back and forth between the civilian and military worlds. I grew familiar with the mind-set of the civilian world when I served the Department of State as a foreign service officer in Washington, D.C., and in various U.S. embassies. In Washington, I ran the Office of Security Affairs, and in Moscow I was responsible for political-military affairs—both of which involved considerable contact with military officers. I also was twice assigned to the Pentagon, once in the office of the secretary of defense, and once on the staff of the chief of naval operations. This experience was further enriched by the two years I spent teaching at the National War College. Needless to say, I witnessed the interaction between military officers and civilians on a daily basis. Finally, I gained additional firsthand knowledge of the military's differing mind-set when I wore the uniform of the U.S. Navy, both active and reserve, for a total of thirty-two years, beginning as a seaman recruit and ending as a captain. During that time, I had numerous opportunities to discuss with senior military and naval officers some of the issues addressed in this book.

One thing that became clear to me as I crossed from one world to the other and back again was the extent to which the two spheres misunderstood each other. Unfortunately, this was especially true of the civilian world. I can remember case after case in which my civilian colleagues could not understand why the military simply did not do what the administration wanted. And when the relationship seemed marked by conflict, the reaction was invariably the same—the military is getting out of line again. I soon began to understand, however, that the relationship was far more complex than many of my civilian friends realized. Indeed, I quickly realized that the way to ensure a rocky relationship between those in uniform and those in civilian clothes was to ignore military concerns or assume military leaders were there only to serve the current policy interests of the executive.

As I surveyed the literature on civil-military relations in the United States, I was struck by the constant emphasis on "control." A common theme was that the United States had to guard against any effort by the American military to assert its will on the rest of the country. In fact, I am aware of only one case in which a senior military officer disobeyed a direct order, and in that single case, the officer's behavior was condemned by his colleagues. At this point I decided that a perspective other than that of civilians was necessary, because addressing any issue from only one side always provides a shortsighted and often misleading view. I believed the viewpoint of those in uniform would be useful. Although there have been a few memoirs written by retired officers and biographies written about senior officers, I could not find a serious study from the vantage point of the "controlled." Thus, I decided to write this book. Recognizing that the relationship between the military and the president was never entirely free of conflict, I wondered why some administrations experienced far more civil-military conflict than others. My hope is that the following examination of the problem from the standpoint of the military will contribute to a better understanding of the dynamics of civil-military relations.

Covering the period from 1940 to the present was not easy—especially for someone who is neither a trained historian nor a specialist on U.S. military history. But I was lucky to have the assistance of a number of individuals who read all or part of the manuscript and provided insightful and helpful comments. First and foremost, I want to thank Mike Briggs from the University Press of Kansas, who played a key role in the preparation of this book. I am also deeply indebted to Adm. Dennis Blair, USN (Ret.), who read the entire manuscript and provided the kind of insightful feedback that can come only from someone who has dealt daily with many of the problems discussed herein. I should also single out Col. Andrew Bacevich, USA (Ret.), who went far beyond the call of duty in pushing me to develop my ideas, even though he disagreed with them.

Others who provided much-needed help include Joe Aistrup, Laurie Bagby, David Barrett, Kisangani Emizet, Peter Feaver, LTC Paul Gardner, USA, Jack Holl, Don Mrozek, LTC Timothy Muchmore, USA (Ret.), Jeffery Pickering, William Richter, and students from my civil-military relations course who read and commented on the book while it was still in draft. Their incisive comments and criticism were critical, and there were times when they disagreed with my conclusions. I alone bear responsibility for the opinions expressed in this book.

Finally, I would like to take this opportunity to say a word of thanks to the president of Kansas State University, Dr. Jon Wefald, a distinguished military historian in his own right, for his support over the years. I must also express my thanks and appreciation to my wife for reading and criticizing parts of the book, and for putting up with my constant absences over eighteen months while I worked on this project. Finally, however, I dedicate this book to the men and women who have proudly worn the uniform of the United States over the years, especially my son-in-law, Maj. John Payne, who spent twelve years on active duty with the U.S. Army before leaving for graduate school and the Kansas National Guard; my daughter, Larissa Payne, who served in the U.S. Army as a JAG officer; and my son, Kurt, a graduate of the U.S. Naval Academy and a surface warfare officer. As Churchill said of the Royal Air Force, "Never have so many owed so much to so few."

1
THE MILITARY, THE PRESIDENT, AND CIVIL-MILITARY RELATIONS

There is no place in a democratic state for the attitude that would elevate each military hero above public reproach simply because he did the job he has been trained for and is paid to do.
—General of the Army Omar N. Bradley

This book is about the military and presidential leadership in the United States. Instead of focusing on civil-military relations primarily from the perspective of the political leadership working to impose its will on a reluctant military, this book examines the issue from the viewpoint of military officers in the United States. I have in mind individuals who have sworn to serve and be subordinate to civil authority and who are prepared to put their lives on the line if necessary in defense of the American nation. In other words, this book will look at the relationship between senior political authorities and military officers from the perspective of the "controlled" rather than from that of the "controllers." This is not to suggest that the political leadership does not play a critical role in this drama; indeed, it does.

I will argue that a major change has taken place in civil-military relations in the United States. *To begin with, in contrast to the interwar period, the U.S. military is no longer apolitical.* One may rue the day that happened, but the military is now a bureaucratic interest group much like others in Washington. *As a result, the definition of "subordination to civilian control" has changed.* In the mid-war period there was little doubt in the minds of senior military officers that they worked almost exclusively for the president. That too has changed. Beginning with the Truman administration, senior military officers began to look to the Congress as well as the media as vehicles for countering efforts by the president to be the single arbiter over the fate of their services, strategies, and programs.

Increased political activity by senior military officers inevitably raises the question, What is to be done to ameliorate conflict between the executive and the military? This book argues that while conflict between the president, senior ranks of the military, and Congress is inevitable over issues like resources or foreign policy options, one way for the president to minimize conflict is by working within the framework of military culture when he deals with senior military officers. *In essence, the greater the degree to which presidential leadership style coincides with and respects prevailing service/military culture, the less will be the degree of conflict. Similarly, the greater the degree to which presidential leadership style does not provide leadership and clashes with the prevailing military culture, the greater will be the probability and intensify of conflict.* This is not to suggest that the military believes it is above or on an equal standing with the president. Military officers are trained to take and follow orders even when they do not like them. If the president orders the military to do something, it will. However, senior military officers will not blindly acquiesce if the president proposes a strategy opposed to the one they believe is most appropriate for carrying out their missions. They will utilize Congress and the media like other bureaucracies to defend themselves.

This study focuses on the military and only indirectly examines the twelve different presidents who were in office from Franklin Roosevelt to the present. One of the purposes of this study is to understand how senior military officers thought and behaved toward the different occupants of the White House. One of the reasons why they have been critical of some of the presidents is because the country's senior military officers believed that the particular commander in chief being discussed was violating service culture or military culture. In a normative sense the generals may have been wrong, and the president right. But that is an issue for a different kind of book.

Before looking at civil-military relations from the viewpoint of the military, however, a review of the conceptual frameworks suggested by six writers on the topic is appropriate. The first four individuals, Carl von Clausewitz, Herbert Lasswell, Samuel Huntington, and Morris Janowitz, have had the greatest impact on the study of civil-military relations over the past fifty-odd years. Furthermore, in contrast to this study, they demonstrate why placing primary focus on the problem of "civilian control" tells only half of the story. They helped create the perception that when political authorities issue a direct order, officers will (or should) salute and carry it out whether they like it or not. But they also maintained that military leaders try to gain as much autonomy as possible in order to effectively carry out their difficult tasks. The fifth author,

Peter Feaver, is included because his work is both one of the newest and most comprehensive efforts by a political scientist to apply the rational-actor model to the study of civil-military relations. He points out the serious limitations of studies that focus almost entirely on civilian efforts to control the military. The sixth author, Eliot Cohen, does an excellent job of showing the role of politics in civil-military relations in a number of polities. Conflict between civilian and military authorities is not always a result of civilian efforts to control the military; rather, it is a consequence of the nature of presidential leadership and a cultural clash between civilians and military professionals, factors that many authors have tended to overlook.

THEORISTS OF CIVIL-MILITARY RELATIONS

Carl von Clausewitz

Any discussion of civil-military relations must begin with Carl von Clausewitz, the famous theorist and military officer who stressed the political importance of war and conflict at a time when his native Prussia, like most of Europe, considered war a matter for the army and the army alone.[1] Having seen firsthand the impact of the French Revolution on France's new mass army, Clausewitz recognized that a "revolutionary" change was taking place in the way wars were being fought.[2] No longer was war the exclusive province of soldiers—the vast majority of whom were either professionals or mercenaries—who fought for financial gain.

From Clausewitz's perspective there was a new element in warfare: the mass army, which was motivated in part by ideology. Thus Europe confronted a new form of military structure, one that Napoleon had mastered and used to conquer most of the continent. The majority of Clausewitz's colleagues both in Prussia and abroad seemed unable to grasp the implications of these changes. A government now had to appeal to the citizenry and realize that these new military forces had serious implications for both war and civil-military relations; to fail to do so would undermine the military effectiveness of its forces. In writing that "the political object—the original motive for the war—will thus determine both the military objective to be reached and the amount of effort it requires," Clausewitz meant that the motivation behind the military's actions would be political—not a surprising conclusion, because in his mind, the goal of every war was always political. This belief led to his most famous statement: "We see therefore, that war is not merely an act of policy but a true political instrument, a continuation of political intercourse carried on by other means.

What remains peculiar to war is simply the nature of its means. War in general, and the commander in any specific instance, is entitled to require that the trend and designs of policy not be inconsistent with these means."[3]

Over the years, many scholars have taken Clausewitz's statements to suggest that military officers are merely implementers of political decisions, regardless of how silly, self-defeating, or dangerous those decisions may be. The assumption is that there "should" not be conflict between civilians and military officers. There may be tension between the two, but in the end, soldiers must obey the orders issued by their civilian masters. Clausewitz, however, understood that war was more complex and that soldiers had to be able to do their job without undue political influence; he wrote, "Policy, of course, will not extend its influence to operational details. Political considerations do not determine the posting of guards or the employment of patrols. But they are more influential in the planning of war, of the campaign and often the battle." Clausewitz added another critical qualification to his discussion of the primacy of politics when he observed that "the statesmen often issue orders that defeat the purpose they are meant to serve. Time and again this has happened which demonstrates that a certain grasp of military affairs is vital for those in charge of general policy."[4]

Clausewitz's approach is problematic. To begin with, he ignored the issue of when and why the military might attempt to assert itself vis-à-vis political authorities. He admitted that tension will exist between the two, but he made little effort to understand the dynamics of civilian interactions with the military. One may easily say that generals and admirals must ultimately recognize the primacy of politics in matters concerning war, but such a statement ignores the question of why the process of civil-military relations in a country such as the United States works smoothly at one time and is conflict ridden at another. To suggest that a harmonious relationship results when the military gets everything it wants from civilian authorities and that conflict arises when the military steps out of line grossly oversimplifies reality. The process is much more nuanced than Clausewitz suggests, especially in a country where the military has become a bureaucratic interest group.

Harold D. Lasswell

Many scholars consider Harold Lasswell to be one of the greatest social scientists of the twentieth century. He wrote across disciplines, producing in the process some of the most important works in each of them. I suspect, however, that one of his most influential pieces was an article he wrote about civil-military relations titled "The Garrison State."[5] Indeed, Raymond Aron called the article a "developmental construct."[6]

Lasswell was concerned with the rise of what he called the supremacy of the "specialists on violence," who were replacing specialists on bargaining. He feared that instead of a world dominated by businessmen, society could possibly be overtaken by the "supremacy of the soldier." In the garrison state, the military would use modern technology to ensure its rule. In particular, Lasswell believed that the new elite would rely heavily on "the manipulation of symbols in the interest of morale and public relations," to gain and keep the loyalty of the populace.[7] The government's influence would be further enhanced during periods of prolonged international tension. In this kind of state, the government and society's "preparation for war becomes overriding." As a consequence, the population would be subjected to military-like discipline in preparation for these wars. The key rule of life would become "obey or die" as the state's propaganda machine saturated the country with the government's message. The state would become a military entity in which the individual would be required "to obey, to serve the state, to work," and all "social change would be translated into battle potential."[8] If such a state were created, drawing a line between the civil and military spheres or worrying about conflict between the two would serve little purpose because the military would be running the country to the point that the civil sector would disappear; thus, there would be no conflict.

Fortunately, Lasswell's warning has not come to pass, certainly not in the United States. The U.S. military has become a bureaucratic interest group but it has not tried to take over the country; indeed, in critical situations it generally has willingly complied with orders, even those it has opposed. Lasswell says little or nothing about how the military will react to efforts to militarize society, focusing instead on the need for civilian control of the military.

Samuel Huntington

Few contemporary political scientists have had a greater impact on the study of civil-military relations in the United States, and in the world in general, than Professor Samuel Huntington. Peter Feaver said it best when he asserted that "Huntington's theory, outlined in *The Soldier and the State,* remains the dominant theoretical paradigm in civil-military relations, especially the study of American civil-military relations."[9]

The key to understanding Huntington's deductive paradigm is his concept of professionalism. First, he maintained that contemporary officers possess special expertise. In an earlier time period, military officers and civilians were interchangeable because war was not a complex undertaking; anyone who could ride a horse, handle a saber, and perform well on a battlefield was a qualified soldier. With the rise of technical forms of warfare (e.g., artillery and engineering), however, war became increasingly complex. Being courageous, riding a horse, and handling a saber were no longer sufficient. Specialized training in areas such as mathematics, physics, chemistry, and management gradually became prerequisites for someone hoping to become an officer, especially for artillery and engineering officers. "No longer was it possible to master this skill while still remaining competent in many other fields."[10] Huntington argued that the basic institutions of professionalism were in place in Europe by 1875, fifty-some years after Clausewitz had noted them.

In addition to a high degree of expertise, Huntington also singled out institutional autonomy as a key component of professionalism. Paraphrasing Clausewitz, he argued that "the fact that war has its own grammar requires that the military professionals be permitted to develop their own expertise at this grammar without interference."[11] Military officers must also be subordinate to politicians, but to be effective, a military organization must be permitted considerable autonomy in managing its own affairs. Having civilians looking over officers' shoulders makes the conduct of war more difficult, intensifies internal conflict, and could lead to defeat. After all, the soldiers, not the civilians, were experts in the "management of violence."

Huntington conceptualized two kinds of civilian control that were aimed at ameliorating conflict. Under the first, which he called subjective civilian control, civilian authorities devised a whole series of intrusive control measures to minimize conflict and ensure civilian control of the armed forces. The implication was that the military was unreliable and that conflict was a major problem. Among the control measures were the commissars who were widely utilized in the early years of the Soviet Union to ensure the military's loyalty. They made certain that former Czarist officers did what the Communist Party wanted them to do. Holding families hostage made it clear to the former Czarist soldiers that if they went over to the other side, or even failed to carry out an order, their families would pay the price. Conflict was the order of the day.[12]

Nonetheless, subjective control measures were incompatible with Huntington's concept of military professionalism. Because they were intrusive and created conflict, they interfered with military autonomy, and, therefore, military efficiency. "Subjective control achieves its end by civilianizing the military, making them mirror the state. The essence of subjective civilian control is the denial of an independent military sphere."[13] For example, the Soviet use of political commissars to constantly oversee the actions of line officers resulted in conflict between the two. The latter, in particular, were concerned about constant interference in military matters by "political hacks" who knew little or nothing about how to operate an army. And not surprisingly, the political commissar resented the disdain in which the line officer held him.

Huntington believed that subjective civilian control was less effective than objective civilian control, whose essence "was the recognition of autonomous military professionalism."[14] Under objective control, the military would run itself and conflict between soldiers and senior politicians would be minimized. Issues such as personnel, training, and military doctrine would remain the military's prerogative, although Huntington admitted that military and civilians would become involved in issues of doctrine if they impacted on the overall conduct of a war. Most observers believe that he was right in suggesting that militaries would fight better if they were left alone. As Eliot Cohen argued, "There is good news here: soldiers not only respect the bounds of democratic politics when subject to objective control, they also fight more effectively. When politicians leave purely military matters to officers, and when they draw clear distinctions between their activities and those of civilians, outstanding military organizations emerge."[15]

Significantly, Huntington argued that a professional military controlled by objective control measures would not pose a political problem because such a fighting force was apolitical by definition, unlike a subjectively controlled military, which would be unreliable. Feaver summarized the argument thusly: "Autonomy leads to professionalism, which leads to political neutrality and voluntary subordination, which leads to secure civilian control."[16] Conflict would therefore be minimalized. Thus, in contrast to Lasswell's military that would seize on technology to maintain its hold on power, in Huntington's mind, the rise of an increasingly technical military would have the opposite effect. The military would not attempt to interfere in civil-military affairs.

While Huntington's paradigm represents a step forward in that he tried to understand military behavior, his primary focus was on control of the military. But there is more to civil-military relations than creating an apolitical military. In any case, the existence of an apolitical military is, in itself, an illusion. The military will always be political if political action is defined as a struggle for resources, autonomy, and influence in Washington. Such a contest inevitably leads to conflict between military officers and civilians. To quote Richard Kohn, "The critical issue is where, and how, to distinguish between military and civilian responsibility. With war increasingly dangerous, civilians want more control to ensure congruence with political purpose; with weapons and operations becoming ever more technical and complex, military officers want more independence to achieve success with the least cost in blood and treasure."[17] All national security issues have both a political and military component. An officer who disobeys a direct order is easily condemned, as are civilians who become involved in disciplinary practices or training policies.

Huntington failed to explain the presence of conflict when the military has accepted the regime's basic values and no longer needs to be managed with subjective control measures. The military's decision to sometimes support and other times oppose the administration is not just a question of group autonomy, as he implied, although that is an important consideration from the military's perspective. Unfortunately, he focused only on one part of the equation—that of the civilians. Furthermore, the history of civil-military relations in the United States from 1940 to the present suggests that it has become an influential bureaucratic interest group—not an apolitical entity.

Morris Janowitz

Morris Janowtiz was another major figure in the evolution of civil-military literature. Where Huntington argued that the military and the civilians who sought to control them belonged to separate categories, Janowitz expanded upon an ascendant, late–1940s theory that the military profession was losing its uniqueness because modern technology was leading to a convergence of military and civilian occupational categories. As he explained, "The new tasks of the military require that the professional officer develop more and more of the skills and orientations common to civilian administrators and civilian leaders."[18] As a result, the distinction between civilian and military has become increasingly blurred. In fact, in contrast to Huntington, who saw professionalism as a way of making the military apolitical, Janowitz suggested that it could have the opposite effect because the professional military was becoming more civilianized, while civilians actually knew less and less about the military. Since those in the services are the only ones who understand the complexities of military technology, civilians are increasingly dependent on them to explain what weapons can and cannot do and what kind of strategies and doctrines will and will not work.[19]

As a result, Janowitz believed it was senseless to talk of a division of labor between the military and civilians: there was no such thing as a distinctly professional military in the Huntingtonian sense. Furthermore, the risk of nuclear war that accompanied the development of atomic weapons prevented the superpowers from using military force to break their standoff during the cold war. As a consequence, Janowitz saw the military moving closer to what he called a "constabulary concept," primarily because it "is continuously prepared to act, committed to the minimum use of force"; his was a logical deduction since the idea of victory in the traditional sense of a total defeat of the other side was no longer a reasonable strategy.[20] As Feaver quoted Janowitz saying, "[T]he military draws its inspiration more from the image of a police officer than the warrior."[21]

If one accepts Janowitz's major premise, then the dividing line between civilian authorities and the military should be diminishing. He was correct in arguing that occupational skills, especially in high-tech services such as the air force and navy, are becoming more interchangeable with civilian occupational categories. But it does not follow that the cultural divide between the two has evaporated, or that generals and admirals do not look first and foremost on themselves as military professionals and see the world through such a prism. Sailors, soldiers, Marines, and aviators still consider themselves members of a tightly organized group to a far greater degree than Janowitz implied.

Like Huntington, Janowitz's primary concern was keeping the military out of politics. He believed that the teaching of military ethics, an inherent part of military professionalism, helps convince military officers to limit their forays into politics. Yet many officers would argue in the postwar period that they have an ethical requirement to function as a bureaucratic interest group, if for no other reason than to ensure that they will be able to carry out whatever mission is assigned to them.

Peter Feaver

Peter Feaver is the author of a new major work on civil-military relations in the United States. In his pioneering work, *Armed Servants,* Feaver constructs a deductive framework to replace Huntington's paradigm. The model, which he calls "Agency Theory," focuses on "strategic interaction between civilian principals and military agents." It attempts to specify "the conditions under which we would expect civilians to monitor the military intrusively or nonintrusively and conditions under which we would expect the military to work or shirk."[22]

Feaver argues that regardless of how much power the military may enjoy, *de jure* authority favors civilians. In contrast to Janowitz and Huntington, he argues that this is true in a democracy even if civilians are not competent from a technical standpoint. "In the civil-military context, this means that even if the military is best able to identify the threat and the appropriate responses to that threat for a given level of risk, only the civilian can set the level of acceptable risk for society." In short, relying on his understanding of democratic theory, Feaver argues that civilian control is a prerequisite, regardless of the politician's knowledge, competence, or intentions. He further explains:

> In sum, civil-military relations is a game of strategic interaction. The "players" are civilian leaders and military agents. Each makes "moves" based on his own preferences over outcomes and its expectations of how the other side is likely to act. The game is influenced by exogenous factors, for instance the intensity of the external threat facing the state comprised of the players. The game is also influenced by uncertainties. The civilians cannot be sure that the military will do what they want; the military cannot be sure that the civilians will catch and punish them if they misbehave.

Feaver's theory thus makes several assumptions. First, there are two sets of actors, the military and civilians. Second, their behavior is rational. Third, the military accepts civilian supremacy. Fourth, the civilians attempt to control the military, first by monitoring its conduct (sometimes in an intrusive manner), then by instituting a policy of rewards and punishments. The strategic interaction model Feaver builds from these assumptions results in real hypotheses and findings. "What is striking about agency theory is that factors that emerge as so obviously central from the deductive logic of the model—the costs of monitoring, the expectations of punishment, the strategic calculus of the actors—are nevertheless essentially absent in traditional civil-military relations theory."[23]

From a conceptual standpoint, Feaver's paradigm certainly marks a step forward in comparison with those of Huntington and Janowitz. It provides a rational approach within which one can observe civil-military interactions. However, Feaver (like Kohn) focuses primarily on the macro-level. At the micro-level in a country like the United States, the relationship between civilians and the military depends upon more than rewards and punishments to convince officers that they cannot or should not get away with disobedience. Feaver is correct in assuming that a reward (promotion) for a compliant officer will probably lead to his or her compliance with the wishes of a senior civilian official, just as it is fair to assume that the threat of a punishment (loss of a promotion) may deter him from "shirking," to use Feaver's term. The task is not to eliminate conflict, which he see as being inevitable, but to control it. And as Feaver is aware, examples abound of carefully selected officers refusing to comply with a civilian superior even though the officers realize that they will suffer a punishment. Instead, they put their own service or the military as a whole ahead of the wishes of their civilian superior.

What Feaver's model does not pretend to answer is the "why" of conflict on the micro-level. He argues that conflict is a result of "different preferences (gaps in preferences), intrusive monitoring, shirking and punishment shirking."[24] He is correct in assuming that all of these can easily lead to conflict. This writer would argue, however, that there is another factor that helps determine the intensity of conflict on the micro-level: the existence of a fundamental difference in culture between military and political officials. While I will discuss this issue further in detail below, my point is that service and military culture are fundamental factors that lead to conflict.

Where Feaver's model is especially helpful is focusing attention on military behavior—on the nuts and bolts of politics—the decision-making process. The problem, however, is that it focuses primarily on the relationship between the president and the military. Yet Congress is now playing a major role, indeed, in many cases, a decisive role.

Eliot Cohen

Eliot Cohen's insightful look into the dynamics of political leadership during wartime persuasively demonstrated the various problems that have resulted from Huntington's basic thesis (i.e., that the military that fights best is the one that is left alone by the political leadership to carry out military tasks).[25] Cohen argued that there is no arbitrary line separating the civil from the military in national security decision making; rather, the line shifts back and forth depending on the situation. In making his case, Cohen focused on four political leaders—Abraham Lincoln, Georges Clemenceau, Winston Churchill, and David Ben-Gurion—and maintained that all were effective leaders because they showed strong leadership in dealing with their armed forces during wartime. All of them understood both the broader concepts of a war, as well as many of the details involved in fighting it. When necessary, they were also prepared to stand up to their generals and admirals and overrule them, and even fire them if that became necessary. On occasion, these individuals changed major strategic battle plans and even became involved in the minutiae of tactics or weapons design. Cohen also demonstrated the importance of clear and strong guidance in fighting a war. Soldiers, at least those in the United States, would prefer to avoid political authorities unsure of their policy goals; they much prefer strong policy guidance identifying clear limitations that may affect the conduct of the war. Although the officers are prepared to be overridden, they expect to be respected and listened to by their leaders, as Cohen demonstrated was the case with Lincoln, Clemenceau, and Churchill.

Cohen's book marks an important step forward because his case studies showed that politics are always present in military affairs and that a strong political leader is an important part of the civil-military equation. There are limitations, however, to his analysis. To begin with, comparing Lincoln, Clemenceau, Churchill, and Ben-Gurion and then applying those lessons to the post–World War II U.S. military raises serious methodological problems. For example, Lincoln, the sole American studied, was not dealing with the same kind of military force that recent presidents have. For the last sixty-odd years, the U.S. armed forces have been run by professional military officers, the majority of whom were graduates of U.S. military academies. Lincoln's military, as Cohen demonstrated, was composed of professionals, retired military, civilians, and younger officers who rose through the ranks because of their courage during the war. Furthermore, Lincoln was dealing with a low-tech military, not one marked by emphasis on high technology.

The same was true of Ben-Gurion's experience. His brilliance came in his ability to weld together disparate guerilla and military forces at a time when Israel was fighting for its very existence. He did a remarkable job and is justifiably considered an Israeli hero, but the relevance of his experience to the post–World War II American military is questionable.

Finally, comparing the United States to the other nations that Cohen analyzed is also problematic. Churchill was a very important political leader, but he was also dealing with a military that was far less political than the American armed forces have become since the end of World War II. The same can be said of Clemenceau, since the World War I French Army operated in a political environment that was far different from the one that has existed in the United States in the recent past. In short, trying to draw cross-national comparisons during the same time period is difficult enough; trying to draw them over different time periods is even more difficult. Cohen did not demonstrate the applicability of these four cases to the U.S. experience.

So where does this leave us? Cohen was right in demonstrating that assertive political leadership played an important role in the four cases discussed in his book. The fact, however, is that in the United States the armed forces have become an important bureaucratic interest group. The Congress is often as much involved as the president in resolving military-related issues, and the military is prepared to play one off against the other when it is in its interest. With this in mind, I believe there is another way to view civil-military relations in the United States during the past sixty years, one that will help the reader understand why some conflicts between the executive and the military are so intense.

AN ALTERNATIVE APPROACH: FOCUS ON THE PROCESS

My approach builds upon Feaver's model and agrees with Cohen's argument that political leaders have interfered successfully in strategic affairs during wartime (and even in operational and tactical matters as well). However, instead of examining the macro-level, or broad picture, it will focus on the micro-level. In particular, my approach seeks to explain why conflict between senior military and political officials is intense on some occasions, while mild on others. Conflict is built into the American system, but there are occasions when generals and the White House conduct bitter battles, and others when they cooperate. I will argue that service or military culture plays a critical role in civil-military relations. The American military is structured very differently from other governmental groups in the United States, and its members tend to be very loyal to their service and organization as well as to the political leadership. Soldiers, sailors, Marines, and aviators share many attributes with their civilian friends and colleagues, but those who lead them and make the key decisions, the senior officers, continue to view the political world through the lens of a military professional.

Military professionals look to their chain of command for guidance. In the United States this means the president, who is their commander in chief, and civilian authorities such as the secretary of defense. Officers expect the president or appropriate civilian official to take the lead and provide them with guidance and, when necessary, orders they *must* carry out. Each of the twelve presidents since the beginning of World War II has dealt with the military in a different fashion. In some cases, the relationship was cooperative, in others it was characterized by a high degree of conflict. Why? At this point a distinction between the terms "service culture" and "military culture" is in order.

Service and Military Culture

Service culture and military culture are alike in that they share the same general characteristics. However, service culture dictates that members of the military owe primary loyalty to their individual service, not only psychologically, but operationally as well. The term "military culture," in contrast, suggests that the armed forces are operating in a joint fashion. The idiosyncrasies of service culture recede into the background, although they never completely disappear.

The distinction creates a double-edged sword for civil-military relations. A military that is primarily marked by service culture will show the inefficiencies that result from the four services operating separately. However, from a political standpoint, it will be easier for a president "to divide and conquer" the services, to play one service off against another. Military culture means that the armed forces enjoy the increased efficiency that accompanies more "jointness," but it also means that the Joint Chiefs of Staff (cited hereafter as the Chiefs) will be better able to resist efforts by the executive to split them and get them to fight against each other.

Importantly, like political culture, service and military cultures are constantly changing. At one point in time, the military may resist an effort to force them to fight jointly, while at another such cooperation may seem natural. Similarly, acceptance of minorities or women may change. At one point they may be considered second-class citizens, as blacks were in World War II, only to play a critical role in later years.

Defending Service and Military Culture

How does the military respond to efforts to change or ignore its service or military culture? Do the Chiefs interact only with the president in opposing change, or do they invoke a larger political community when they believe the president is trying to force them to do something that violates their service or military culture? To what degree do they involve other institutions in their battle with the president ? Do they consider such action legitimate?

The military is a conservative institution and often *resists* change; indeed, it is probably one of the most conservative institutions in the United States. The occurrence of change in the military is not a critical factor for this study; what is critical is the manner in which the president introduces that change to the leaders of the armed forces. To repeat, *I am not suggesting that a president should bow to the wishes of his generals and admirals to avoid conflict. On the contrary, civilian leadership is critical in a democracy, and the military expects it, but each president has a choice to make—if he or she fails to provide leadership and violates military culture, conflict will result and potentially intensify.* The change imposed by the executive (e.g., racial integration or joint operations) and the resulting conflict may have a positive impact on the military; however, the manner in which the change is implemented determines to a certain extent the degree of conflict it creates.

From the military's perspective, concurrence with military service culture or military culture can be evaluated using the characteristics outlined below.

I. Presidential Leadership Style

By presidential leadership style, I have in mind the interactions between the president and the armed forces, as well as the structures and procedures that the president implements to facilitate those interactions. The military expects strong political leadership; however, in the process of being led, the country's senior military officers expect to be consulted by the president and to be granted access to him or her. The president's leadership style may be evaluated in a number of ways, including the extent to which the Chiefs are given a meaningful input into the decision-making process, regardless of whether the issue is the military budget or the application of force. Does the president delegate authority to the secretary of defense, and if so, does the latter involve the military in the decision-making process? Does the president show respect for them and the office they hold? Senior military officers fully understand that each administration will be run differently, and they are prepared to adapt to varied leadership styles, but they do not expect to be ignored, disrespected, or micromanaged.

II. Service and Military Culture

The concept of service and military culture is often amorphous.[26] This study examines four prominent issues related to service and military culture that often arise when the military and civilian authorities interact. It is on the basis of these issues that the military evaluates the president's leadership.

1. The Use of Force

When the military is called upon to use force, it prefers a situation in which the following are present:

A. A Clear Chain of Command

The military is a hierarchical organization that works on the basis of orders given and received. It is therefore important that orders pass through a clear chain of command, ideally from the president to the secretary of defense, then to the responsible officers. Carrying out instructions is very difficult when the recipient is unsure of who sent them. Orders that come from the president (or one of his senior civilian officials) and bypass the normal chain of command can create consternation and hostility within the military. Attempts to violate the chain of command are viewed as violations of military culture.

B. Clear and Unambiguous Orders
Although the military leadership understands that there will be occasions when orders cannot be completely unambiguous, the greater the degree to which they are clear and unambiguous, the more efficiently the military will be able to achieve the goal desired by political authorities. This is true both of operational orders as well as instructions on topics such as strategy or doctrine. If the president does not provide leadership in this area, the military will look elsewhere for direction, and confusion is likely to result.

C. Strategic Decision-Making
Senior military officers *expect* civilians to be involved in deciding strategic goals and policy. Military officers, who may sometimes be uncomfortable in making such decisions on their own, look to the president or his senior associates to provide critical guidance in this area. However, they expect to be consulted on purely military matters (e.g., how many and what kind of forces will be needed to fight two and a half wars simultaneously).[27]

D. Operational and Tactical Autonomy
The military and its branches welcome civilian involvement at the strategic level, but share less willingly command authority at the operational and tactical levels. The military expects to have its plans approved by senior civilian officials, but it strongly opposes any attempt by civilians to interfere at the levels in which military expertise is the highest. Persuasion is unlikely to overcome service hostility to outside interference.

2. Roles, Missions, and Resources
The military must clearly understand it roles and missions and have the resources necessary to carry them out. The Chiefs believe that the military's ability to fulfill its duties will be enhanced to the degree that the president possesses the following attributes:

A. Respect for Military Expertise
The military is fully aware that for a variety of reasons the White House will want to change force structure as well as roles and missions from time to time. The key to presidential leadership in this area is for the president to convince the Chiefs that he respects their military expertise. Presidential persuasion may have an important impact, but only if the military leadership believes the president recognizes its special, technical knowledge. The Chiefs expect to be tasked with organizing battle plans based on the strategic

plans and goals to be decided by senior civilian authorities. They will, however, resent civilian interference in the planning process if such actions impinge on technical military matters. With input from both the executive and Congress, the Chiefs also expect to play a major role in designing roles and missions.

3. Personnel Policies

   The military is a closed institution and expects civilians to have minimal impact on personnel appointments or internal policies.

   A. Personnel Appointments

      The military recognizes that the White House and secretary of defense will significantly influence appointments to the most senior military positions. However, if the White House abuses this privilege and begins to politicize these appointments, the military will object.

   B. Internal Policies

      The Chiefs are very protective of the military's right to determine internal military policies, such as those concerning discipline or promotions. They will also object strongly to efforts by politicians to determine internal policies on topics such as race, gender, or sexual orientation. Rightly or wrongly, the military believes it knows better than outsiders how such social issues affect the armed forces.

4. Responsibility and Honor

   Personal responsibility and a sense of honor are very important to the military. Indeed, ideas such as "duty, honor, country" go to the heart of the military oath.

   A. Assumption of Personal Responsibility

      Because the president is the commander in chief, the military expects him to assume personal responsibility for the outcome of military operations (both positive and negative), just as the senior military officer in command is expected to assume responsibility for the actions of his subordinates. Attempts by senior civilian officials, including the president, to deflect criticism for a failed military action will cause the military to lose respect for him.

   B. Code of Conduct

      Because the military regards the president as the commander in chief, they expect him or her to conform to the same code of conduct they live by. Although some discretion is involved, gross violations of the code of conduct will lead to a loss of respect for the president. A loss of respect will undermine the president's authority over the military.

Importance of Leadership Style

As the commander in chief, the president can issue orders on any topic to the Joint Chiefs of Staff. However, as anyone who has spent time in a bureaucracy knows, receiving the willing cooperation and compliance of the military requires more than simply issuing an order. Feaver, for example, argued that one of the main considerations in the minds of military officers when they choose to disobey is whether or not they think they can get away with such behavior. I do not deny that such considerations may play an important, if not major role; indeed, one cannot rule out the possibility that an officer will refuse to obey the president, or at least comply with minimal effort, as illustrated by a number of examples of such behavior since 1940. The president may decide to punish that individual. However, I argue that a more critical consideration is the style of presidential leadership. Conflict between the president and the Chiefs is exacerbated by the administration's refusal to respect military culture, even if the president's policy may be a wise decision in the long run, as it was with the integration of African Americans into the military. In a nutshell, in spite of policy disagreements between the Chiefs and the president, *the less the degree to which his or her relationship with the Chiefs coincides with the characteristics outlined above, the greater the degree of conflict will be between the two.* The president does not have to act in accordance with all or any one of these characteristics, but a clear violation of several of them will increase the possibility of conflict and undermine his effectiveness in achieving his goal.[28]

The Military and Congress

In understanding military behavior, it is important to remember that in the post–World War II world many of the country's generals and admirals hold the fundamental belief that they work for two different institutions. The military's subordination to the president is widely understood; however, the military also works for the United States Congress. The problem, from the military's standpoint, is that the nature of these relationships, as specified in the Constitution, is at best ambiguous. For example, although the Constitution explicitly delegated to the president the authority as the commander in chief to nominate officers for appointment and promotion, the Congress was given the power to confirm or deny them. Similarly, while military officers must obey the president's orders, the House has the power of the purse, and Congress has the authority to declare war as well as "to raise and support armies . . . to make rules" for them. As a result, viewed from the perspective of the military, the lines of authority are often unclear; more often than not, military officers are thus placed in a situation where conflict with political authorities is the order of the day. To quote Thomas Parrish,

> Thus the Constitution not only failed to provide for any clear-cut civilian control of the military but also guaranteed that the U.S. government would experience continual internal confrontation in a tug of war between the Congress and the president with the legislative attempting to expand its own territory and curb the executive, while the president strove for room for maneuver.[29]

The truth is, as Kohn pointed out, that the balance between those various institutions is a delicate one, something the founding fathers fully understood.[30] Because the relationship between these institutions changes over time, the position of the military (and its role) within this institutional "balance of power" also changes. Hence, Congress's power and its relationships with the Chiefs will have a major impact on the military's ability to influence critical aspects of the national security decision-making process.

The Line between Civil and Military

Cohen was right in arguing that any effort to determine or define once and for all the location of the dividing line between the civilian and military worlds is a senseless undertaking. Its location depends on the institutional balance of power at a particular point in time. The military's past behavior is important, but is not determinant, and in some cases may not be relevant. In other words, an area that has traditionally been considered the province of civilians could someday become an area where military influence is more significant.

Although most observers have argued that the implementation of defense-related policy is enhanced when the military has considerable autonomy, few have supported the military's involvement in the formulation of policy. Kemp and Hudlin noted that "the military are to be policy implementers, not policy makers," and Kohn commented, "The central assumption behind civilian supremacy is the abstinence by the military from intervention in political life."[31] To some, this means that the military is supposed to wait for civilians to tell it what to do—"Attack here" or "Bomb that target"—and then carry out the task at hand. Such a perception is problematic.

In many cases the political objectives outlined by senior political leaders are ambiguous and contradictory. As Cohen explained, "It is one of the greatest sources of frustration for soldiers that their political masters find it difficult (or what is worse from their point of view, merely inconvenient) to fully elaborate in advance the purposes for which they have invoked military action, or the conditions under which they intend to limit or terminate it."[32] Expecting the military to remain solely on the implementation side of the process makes no more sense than expecting civilians to remain solely on the formulation side of the process. Although the extent of the military's involvement in policy formulation will vary, the result will be a greater understanding of the policy that is to be implemented.

SOME NOTES ON THIS STUDY

In an effort to better understand the military's relationship to a variety of presidents, this study takes a historical approach to examine at the military's perception of its relationship with each American president from Franklin D. Roosevelt to George W. Bush. Each has dealt with the military under a variety of circumstances. To the degree possible, the primary focus will be on the use of military force, a critical issue in the military-civilian interface. Because the goal of this study is to identify how presidential leadership affects military culture, evaluation of the "rightness" or "wrongness" of such actions will be left to other normative studies.

Definitions

When it comes to defining various aspects of civil-military relations, I agree with the observation that "like pornography, we can't always define it, but each generation surely knows it when it sees or hears it.[33] Nevertheless, some basic definitions are in order. In a sense, the military leadership is simply those career military officers who have reached the top ranks of the armed forces. I have in mind not only the Joint Chiefs of Staff, but other four-star-level officers within the military and, on occasion, some lower-ranking officers who find themselves having an important impact on policy. These key decision makers speak not only for their individual services (or all the services), but also interact with senior political officials. I am, of course, not suggesting that all military professionals necessarily share the views of these officers who sit atop the hierarchical military institution.

As the reader may have noted, throughout the first section of this book I have referred to senior civilian officials or the political leadership. The reason is simple. The civilian bureaucracy, whether it refers to professionals in the civil service, the Foreign Service, or organizations like the FBI or Drug Enforcement Agency, does not make the key decisions that affect the military unless that institution is serving at the direction of a senior civilian or a political official. In this regard, I have in mind officials who deal directly with the senior military officers noted above. They include the president, the secretaries of defense and state, members of Congress, the national security advisor, and other individuals who have a direct impact on military policy. While I recognize that this definition is somewhat loose, authority in this regard is derivative. This means, for example, that a senior political appointee (or civil service employee) in the Department of Defense may be a key player in the civil-military interface because he or she was appointed by a senior political appointee to carry out a task with major implications for the military. As is the case with senior military officers, however, I do not intend to generalize in terms of the views of all politicians, only those who are key players in the politico-military process.

Sources

This study relies on three different types of sources, the memoirs of key decision makers, histories of civil-military relations, and a variety of newspaper and journal articles. The latter were often very useful in filling in many of the blanks. As one of the reviewers pointed out to me, there is a danger in relying on secondary sources, which do not always present a balanced view of these often emotional issues. He was right. However, because I am focusing on the military perception of the problem over a lengthy period of time, I believe the sources available are sufficient to provide the reader with an idea of how the military leadership has reacted to twelve different types of presidential leadership since the end of World War II. I must admit a tremendous obligation to the many journalists, historians, political scientists, and others who have written about these many events. I make no claim of being an expert on any of these presidents or time periods, and any failure to note a particular source was unintentional. From a historical standpoint, this book is totally dependent on the work done by others. Without their efforts, it would have never been written. The purpose of this book was not to break new ground from a historical standpoint. I will leave that work to the many others who are cited in this book.

Structure of This Study

The remainder of this book is divided into twelve chapters and a conclusion. Each of the chapters focuses on one of the postwar presidents in chronological order and begins by examining the leadership style of the president concerned. In addition, each chapter also discusses other significant personalities and contains from one to three case studies showing the military's reaction to the president's leadership style. These case studies are not meant to be exhaustive; clearly the military and the various presidents interacted far more often than discussed here, but for reasons of space, it was not possible to delve into all of the presidencies in detail.

Each chapter closes with two questions: First, to what degree did the president's leadership style mirror or violate service or military culture, and how did that style affect civil-military relations? Second, did service or military culture change at a fundamental level or use new methods to oppose those changes?

Finally, the conclusion will draw together the findings of the various chapters. For example, which president had the best relations with the military, and which the worst? To what degree did the interaction between military culture and presidential leadership style play a critical role in the area of civil-military relations. Assuming that the role was critical, are there certain characteristics that ensure a cooperative relationship (in spite of policy differences)? Similarly, do other characteristics guarantee a relationship characterized by conflict? What can we learn about civil-military relations in the United States by examining military culture and presidential leadership style?

2
THE MILITARY AND FRANKLIN ROOSEVELT

A great politician is not of necessity a great military leader.
—General George S. Patton

From the military's standpoint, its relationship with Franklin Roosevelt was a positive experience. Indeed, given some of the disagreements that would occur later, the era of the Roosevelt administration might be considered one of the golden ages of U.S. civil-military relations when cooperation was the order of the day, and Roosevelt left almost all internal military decisions to the country's admirals and generals. It was also a period in which the relationship between the lines of authority between the president and his senior military leaders was vague at best.

PRESIDENTIAL LEADERSHIP STYLE

Unlike his successors, Franklin Roosevelt relied far more on personal relationships than on highly structured organizations in order to govern. Indeed, one author characterized Roosevelt's administration as a "famously chaotic organization."[1] The structure may have been chaotic, but there was a certain logic to the president's style of governance—especially in regard to his relationship with the country's admirals and generals during World War II.

Roosevelt had served as assistant secretary of the navy earlier in his career and understood the military better than many presidents. He knew how to evaluate personnel and had a good eye for picking top military officers to fill key positions; the best known, of course, was his choice of Gen. George A. Marshall to serve as army chief of staff. Although he relied heavily on Marshall, he also surrounded himself with other officers whose judgment he trusted, individuals with whom he felt comfortable disagreeing. Indeed, he expected them to stand up to him—and they did.

As had been the case in other administrations, the president's style significantly affected civil-military relations. Characterizing Roosevelt's overall leadership style within the White House, George Edwards and Stephen Wayne emphasized the flexibility and ambiguity that he built into it: "The President ran the staff operation himself, making assignments, receiving reports, and generally coordinating activities. Presidential assistants were expected to be anonymous. They were given general responsibilities. . . . Lines of authority were purposely blurred and assignments overlapped." In essence, Roosevelt's "White House was a prescription for personal control."[2] This was certainly true of his relations with the country's military leaders. He could exercise his power whenever he wanted, which he did.

Richard Neustadt argued that Roosevelt relied heavily on competition between his subordinates as a mechanism for keeping them off balance and under control. "Competing personalities mixed with competing jurisdictions was Roosevelt's formula for putting pressure on himself, for making his subordinates push up to him the choices they could not take for themselves."[3] The president may have relied upon competition to deal with other members of the government, but he did not do so with the military. His chief of staff, the heads of the various services, and a senior officer who served as his liaison to the Joint Chiefs would sometimes disagree, and on occasion he would overrule them, but very little "competition" existed for his attention. Roosevelt was more interested in winning World War II than in pitting one group of military officers against another. He also went out of his way to establish good relations with each of the Chiefs, an effort that paid off when he decided to use his persuasive powers—even when they disagreed with him.

Roosevelt and the Chiefs

When Roosevelt became president the country lacked a Joint Chiefs of Staff (JCS); for all practical purposes, the army and navy were independent services. As was typical of his approach to such problems, Roosevelt ignored the normal bureaucratic practice. He did not even issue a formal order when he created the executive body; instead, Washington woke up one day to find that the country had the JCS. As one author explained, "When they finally drifted into being—and 'drifted is the only word' . . . they were never formally established; no executive order creating them was issued."[4] The same was true of Roosevelt's decision to appoint Admiral William Leahy as his chief of staff. No precedent existed for such a position, and Leahy's powers were never formally articulated. Indeed, in a press conference, Roosevelt described him as "a sort of leg man."[5] In practice, he served as a conduit between Roosevelt and the Chiefs.

THE MILITARY BEFORE WORLD WAR II

The U.S. military was in horrible shape before World War II. For example, when Gen. George Marshall became chief of staff of the army, the military service "ranked seventeenth in the world, numbering some 174,000 men with an authorized strength of 210,000." Marshall called the army "ineffective." Troops were spread around the world in 130 different posts, and the army held almost no exercises involving large units until it conducted the 1941 maneuvers in Louisiana. As one writer observed, "[T]he Army in its dispositions had changed little from the old Indian fighting force that had suddenly found itself called on in 1898 to go to war with Spain."[6] Its equipment was increasingly obsolescent because Congress insisted that the army use up the surplus from World War I before purchasing new weapons. Indeed, the only major technological achievement within the army during the interwar period was the development of the M-1 Garand, the rifle that would become the mainstay of the U.S. infantryman throughout World War II. The situation was so bad that soldiers were often forced to use sticks to mimic machine guns, while trucks were painted with the word "tank" to enable the army to practice maneuvers. In a certain sense the U.S. Army was seriously unprepared for the war that would descend upon it in the aftermath of the Japanese attack on Pearl Harbor.

The situation in the navy was somewhat better only because some members of Congress, under the influence of the famed naval strategist Rear Adm. Alfred Thayer Mahan, regarded the service as the United States' primary protector against foreign aggression as well as its main force in diplomacy. If problems arose abroad, most people assumed that the United States would send the navy and its Marines to set things right.

Interservice Rivalry

Rivalry between the army and navy was a serious problem that inevitably affected civil-military relations. On the one hand, such competition permitted the president to divide and conquer when dealing with the two services (the

Marines were considered part of the navy at that time), while on the other it degraded the ability of the U.S. military to fight a war effectively.

At the Pentagon, it was sometimes said (and only half in jest) that the problem with the U.S. Navy was that it had yet to recognize the sovereignty of the U.S. government. An overstatement perhaps, but one that contained more than a grain of truth and extended to a lesser degree to the U.S. Army. Furthermore, before World War II, the two services dealt with each other on an irregular basis. For example, during the 1920s they communicated through a joint army-navy committee. According to one author, this group "was no more than a pro forma bow to a coordinated command."[7] In fact, both services went their own way, paying only lip service to this "joint" body.

In 1939 President Roosevelt transferred the Joint Board, as it was then known, as well as the Joint Army-Navy Munitions Board, to his own executive office. The reorganization was a major event in civil-military relations. Prior to 1939 the first of the two boards was an interdepartmental consultative agency that advised service secretaries and tried to adjudicate disagreements between "matters of joint interest to the War and Navy Departments."[8] Roosevelt's 1939 order raised the Joint Board above the departmental level. "By placing the Chiefs in a special relationship to the President, it made them in some sort independent of their immediate superiors on the secretarial level."[9] In practice this meant that the Joint Board was directly subordinate to the president. As far as the secretaries of war and the navy were concerned, however, they remained heads of their departments—at least in principle. In reality, however, their "military subordinates now reported directly to the President over their heads."[10] More often than not, the secretaries had to rely on the good graces of their military subordinates to keep them apprised of major military decisions.

The change in the status of the Joint Board also led to a modification in its focus. Instead of worrying just about issues related to interservice rivalry, the board now began to concern itself "with questions of national, rather than service, strategy, and produced in their prewar studies some of the basic plans that were to influence our wartime role."[11] In addition to refocusing the services on the "big picture," the reorganization also provided Roosevelt with a structure that enabled him to direct American strategy: the board now worked directly for him. And he used that power when he believed it was necessary. For example, he brushed aside the Chiefs' concerns about providing aid to the British, and he "ignored General Marshall's sharp warning that his plans were 'contrary to the considered judgement' of his military advisers. The Presidential decision was accepted, under protest."[12]

Speak Out? Never!

During the prewar period the constitutional balance of power was very clear in the minds of military officers: they worked for the president, the commander in chief, while superficially respecting the power of Congress. In carrying out its obligation to serve the president, the military was an apolitical institution. Many, if not most, soldiers did not even vote (fearing that casting a ballot would be seen as a political act), and senior military officers made clear to Congress that as far as they were concerned, the armed forces worked for the president.[13] Senior military officers did not believe they had a right to lobby Congress for more funds than the president had approved. For example, note the following exchange between senior army officers and members of Congress in 1924:

> Ques: "Would it prevent the War Department from presenting its needs before this committee?"
>
> General Walker (Chief of Army Finance): "I think it would. I think when the budget has once been approved by the President and transmitted to Congress, it is his budget estimate and no officer or official of the War Department would have any right to come up here and attempt to get a single dollar more than . . . contained in the estimate."

A year later, on December 8, 1925, General Nolan, who was deputy chief of the army staff, appeared before Congress.

> Ques: "If you do not get all you need is that because you do not ask or it?"
>
> General Nolan: "Oh yes, we ask for it."
>
> Congressman: "Well, you ask for the budget and they do not give you the money nor does Congress?"
>
> General Nolan: "But we are prohibited by law from asking Congress for anything except the amount that is allowed in the Budget."[14]

Although members of Congress may not have liked this arrangement, they apparently accepted it.

The unacceptability of senior officers speaking out against the president's policies was so deeply ingrained in the military mind that in 1939, despite

Marshall's desperate fight for budgetary increases to build up the army in the face of Roosevelt's insistence that scarce resources be allocated to helping the British in their fight against Hitler's Germany, Marshall explicitly instructed senior officers to support the president's position: "Accordingly, the Chief of Staff desires that this attitude be clearly maintained by all representatives of the War Department who may be called upon to testify."[15] It was perhaps because of their apolitical approach to policy issues that individuals like Marshall gained great respect from members of Congress. When asked during the war why his word counted for so much on the Hill, Marshall listed a number of factors: "his lack of 'ulterior motive,' the beginning of Congressional trust in his judgment, and most important, the fact that his advocacy of certain measures could remove partisan labels."[16]

Marshall was careful to avoid making any statements that went against presidential policies, but he felt no such inhibition from criticizing Congress and other groups that he believed undermined the executive's efforts to increase military preparedness. For example, in addressing the American Legion on September 15, 1940, Marshall emphasized his view at the time that he owed his primary loyalty to the president when he took on members of the Hill:

> I submit to you men of the Legion the impossibility of developing an efficient army if decisions which are purely military in nature are continually subjected to investigation, cross examination, debate, ridicule, and public discussion by pressure groups, and by individuals with only a superficial knowledge of military matters, or the actual facts in the particular case. I submit that there is a clear line of demarcation between the democratic freedom of discussion which we are determined to preserve and a destructive procedure which promotes discontent and destroys confidence in the army.[17]

Later, in speaking to the American Historical Association, he claimed that the "army was less than 25 percent ready to fight. Some weeks later, in a radio address urging preparedness, he warned that time was running out for America."[18] He eventually created a political firestorm during the war when he blasted labor unions that were threatening to strike. He "declared that strikes might literally cost hundreds of thousands of American lives."[19] Needless to say, union leaders responded vigorously to this attack by the army chief of staff.

In essence, Marshall's view of "speaking out" was simple. He worked for the president, and he believed that a responsible officer had the right both to question a policy he considered wrong or mistaken and to discuss thoroughly a proposal. And he did exactly that. Even when he was still a brigadier general and the issue of whether he would become chief of staff was still undecided, Marshall stood up to the president. Two examples illustrate his forthrightness.

To begin with, Marshall was appalled at the situation in the U.S. Army. He believed it was critical for the United States to develop a balanced military force—both services needed to be modernized in order to handle the coming conflict. But the president had other ideas. One of Roosevelt's primary interests lay in strengthening the air force to counter Hitler's imposing fleet of aircraft. At a meeting in the White House, Roosevelt pushed his plan of building ten thousand planes a year—the majority of which would go to the British.

> As the proceedings drew to a close, Roosevelt summing up, turned to Marshall, whom he scarcely knew, and said, "Don't you think so George?" Marshall replied: "I am sorry, Mr. President, but I don't agree with that at all." He got a startled look from his Commander in Chief and, as they were leaving, expressions of sympathy from the others at so quick an ending to so promising a tour of duty in Washington.[20]

Five months later, the president "reached thirty-four names down the rank list of senior generals and asked George Catlett Marshall, Jr., to become the next Chief of Staff of the U.S. Army."[21] Furthermore, when he was called to the White House to be told by the president that he would become the next chief of staff, he informed the president that he wanted the right to say what he thought "and that it would often be unpleasant." "Is that all right?" "Yes, said Roosevelt."[22] Roosevelt certainly had no inhibitions about having his generals argue with him, which they would do on numerous occasions during World War II. They respected him highly for his willingness to hear their points of view, even if he decided to move in another direction.

Finally, in addition to believing that senior military officers had a right and an obligation to speak openly with the president, Marshall also ardently defended free speech within the military. When the president demanded that a news magazine be banned from the army for publishing an article he believed to be "scurrilous," Marshall answered the president "dramatically and furiously: 'I won't obey that order unless I get it in writing, and if I do, it will come back with my resignation as Chief of Staff.' "[23]

Working with the British

At the Arcadia Conference in Washington, immediately following the Japanese attack on Pearl Harbor, the UK and the United States created what would be called the Combined Chiefs of Staff "to shape their coalition strategy and conduct their coalition war efforts."[24] Although this staff was supposed to have operational control over joint operations around the globe, the Pacific soon became largely an American operation, so the organization primarily focused on the war in Europe. In terms of structure, the Combined Chiefs included representatives of the three British services, who were permanently stationed in Washington, as well as the chiefs of the U.S. services: General Marshall for the army, Gen. "Hap" Arnold for the army air forces, and Adm. Ernest King for the navy. In addition to being irritated that the air forces were trying to become an independent arm, King was extremely sensitive to the possibility that the navy would always be outvoted by the two "army" services. Consequently, Admiral Leahy was added to the group as a fourth member when he became the president's chief of staff. The task for the Americans now would be to reach consensus on a strategy for working with the British.

Doing so would not be easy, because the American chiefs delegated authority to two different units: an army team and a navy team (and even the latter would be further split into two units). In contrast, the British were carefully integrated under the direction of Brig. L. C. Hollis, who was close to Churchill. "Unlike the American group, this team had not been hastily formed but had been working together for some considerable time—a comparison that could accurately be made between any of the British groups and its American counterpart."[25] Furthermore, the British side included the air force as a separate unit.

The U.S. military branches' lack of experience in dealing with each other created a major problem. Field Marshal Sir John Dill, the senior British officer assigned to Washington, was shocked at American inexperience in working in a joint environment and commented that "the whole organization belongs to the days of George Washington."[26] Indeed, when Winston Churchill and his staff visited Washington during the Arcadia Conference, the need for changes became obvious. The American board had to be given more power if it was to deal effectively with the British (who were not fully trusted by many American officers). The U.S. side was in vital need of being able to reach general agreement not only between the services but with the president in advance of any future meetings with representatives from the UK. Such a need was one of the primary factors behind the president's decision to create the Joint Chiefs of Staff in 1942. The Chiefs held their first meeting on February 9. Significantly, Gen. "Hap" Arnold, head of U.S. Army Air Forces, was raised to full membership so that the U.S. model would parallel the British structure.

U.S. Military Autonomy

The military's independence typified the way in which Roosevelt operated—without any special organizational format, a style that would irritate several of the country's senior military officers. As one author noted with regard to the JCS, "It was consultative, and advisory to the Commander in Chief, not executive, and positive action came only when it was required."[27] Marshall tried repeatedly to get the president to behave in a more systematic "military" fashion, to consider matters in a more structured manner, but the latter refused in order to keep his lines of authority flexible and unfettered by bureaucratic procedures.

In terms of American military structure in World War II, cooperation between the services was almost nonexistent, and the military chiefs worked directly for the president. According to Admiral Leahy this meant that during World War II the Chiefs were "under no civilian control whatsoever"—the exception being, of course, the president.[28] It was Admiral Leahy who, as the president's chief of staff, became the primary liaison between the White House and the Chiefs. As he explained, "It was my job to pass on to the Joint Chiefs of Staff the basic thinking of the President on all war plans and strategy. In turn, I brought back from the Joint Chiefs a consensus of their thinking."[29]

In conducting the war, Roosevelt relied almost entirely on the military to make major decisions. Consequently, the Chiefs were in the catbird seat when it came to military, diplomatic, and sometimes political decision making. However, when major strategic decisions arose, Roosevelt was prepared to intervene, and on at least one major occasion he overruled the Chiefs, even though his decision put him at odds with them.

WORLD WAR II

Operation Torch

Of all the decisions made by the Americans during World War II, none was more hotly debated nor caused greater disagreement between Roosevelt and his military advisors than the issue of where to attack the Germans during 1942. Like London, Washington was very sensitive to Stalin's call for a second front. After all, the Russians were carrying the brunt of the war in Europe at that time, and America's military leaders worried about the prospect of a Russian collapse. Such an event would have not only freed up German troops for action elsewhere, it would have had catastrophic implications for the West's ability to fight effectively a two-front war. The question of where to attack thus had major political implications.

George Marshall, who was by far the most influential of the country's senior military leaders, believed that a direct attack on the European continent was the only way to defeat Germany. As Gen. Omar Bradley recalled, "To smash Germany's offensive power, he argued, it would be necessary to close with the Wehrmacht and destroy it."[30] The only way to achieve that goal was a cross-Channel invasion. In fact, Marshall was most insistent in advocating his position. General Marshall flew to London in mid-1942 to present the plan to very skeptical British military and political leaders. After arriving, he met with Eisenhower and others in London and convinced them of the appropriateness of his plan; one of General Eisenhower's aides noted in his diary, "By Sunday morning, opinion crystallized in favor of an attack on the Cherbourg Peninsula. General Marshall is to see the British war leaders today and recommend immediate preparations for an attack in September, if conditions then appear favorable."[31] Much to Marshall's surprise, the British accepted his plan. What he did not know was that they did so because they saw his plan as a way to keep the United States tied to the UK and its prioritization of the European theater over the war in the Pacific. They feared that if they rejected Marshall's idea, the United States could turn its attention to the latter theater, leaving the UK to fight the European war on its own. Indeed, once having agreed to Marshall's plan they "almost immediately began working on Roosevelt to shift back to North Africa," where they believed the West stood a better chance of success.[32]

In retrospect, London's pessimism was well founded. First, the British did not believe that this American army that had been using sticks for guns and trucks for tanks would be in any position to fight the battle-hardened German armies in 1942; indeed, the initial performance of American troops in the North Africa campaign would demonstrate that their allies had good reason to be skeptical. Furthermore, the British did not see how they would be able to provide most of the troops, "while American units were still making their way across the Atlantic."[33] With the vast majority of British forces already fighting, where would these additional troops be found? Finally, there was the problem of landing craft, which were essentially nonexistent. London did not believe a sufficient number of them could be produced in time for a major attack in 1942.

Churchill's position was strengthened when the British Parliament formally came out against a 1942 cross-Channel attack. Churchill also claimed that "he can't find an admiral or a general to support it."[34] The British viewed a second front in Europe as "too risky and too unlikely really to help the Russians."[35] Thus, America's key ally, whose territory would be used to launch the invasion, would not agree to Marshall's plan, effectively vetoing it. However, the JCS would not take no for an answer. Nor would Eisenhower, who "became almost obsessed by the threat of 'scatteration'; of failure to focus on one goal and bend every effort in its direction."[36] Many Americans became convinced that Britain's reluctance represented a case of British "duplicity."[37]

In the meantime, the situation in the Middle East had become desperate. Tobruk, Libya, fell to the Germans, and Gen. Erwin Rommel threatened to smash his way into Egypt, which, in Marshall's words, would "lead to complete collapse in the Middle East, the loss of the Suez Canal and the vital oil supply in the vicinity of Abadan."[38] Furthermore, the Russians appeared to be on the ropes, as the Germans were closing in on Sevastopol. It was at this point that Roosevelt called in Marshall and obtained his agreement to send new Sherman tanks—ones that were just coming into production—to the beleaguered British troops, an action that helped save El Alamein from the Germans and turn the tide against Rommel and his Afrika Korps in Northern Africa.

Marshall remained convinced of the need for a cross-Channel invasion, believing that a massive attack on Europe was the only realistic means of drawing German troops away from the Russian front. In the end, however, a number of factors torpedoed Marshall's efforts to attack directly the German bastion in Europe. To begin with, Eisenhower himself recognized the Allies' inability to assemble enough troops and equipment in time to launch Marshall's attack. "There was no hope of beginning a major invasion of Europe until America could produce the necessary land, sea, and air power to participate in the initial operation on at least an equal basis and be prepared, thereafter, to provide the great bulk of the ground and air units that would be needed."[39] The British were also correct about the shortage of specialized equipment needed to carry out the attack, including the elusive landing craft, which were now at a premium because of amphibious operations in the Pacific. Almost all of this equipment would have to be produced by American factories. Eisenhower claimed that the American command in Great Britain communicated this view to the Joint Chiefs in Washington.[40] Indeed, the more he studied the issue, the more he understood that mounting a cross-Channel invasion would be impossible until 1944.

FDR himself was not about to act against his British allies on an issue they felt so strongly about. Yet pressure continued to mount for some sort of action by the Western Allies. According to General Bradley, "Roosevelt insisted that the Allies could not sit by until the summer of 1943. Even a shoestring venture, he declared, would be better than none at all."[41] The president believed this was a strategic issue of the highest importance. Frustrated at Marshall's continued opposition to an attack on North Africa, Roosevelt stepped in on July 25, 1942, and informed both his senior military advisors and Churchill that the United States would invade North Africa. That ended all further discussion between Roosevelt and his military advisors. Their opposition, to use Elliott Cohen's phrase, was "muted."[42] To drive home his point, FDR summoned his lieutenants to the White House on July 30 and announced that, because he was commander in chief, his decision was final. North Africa was "now our final objective."[43] Although military leaders such as Marshall would throw themselves fully into executing Operation Torch, he and many of his colleagues were crushed by Roosevelt's decision. They did not question his right to make such a decision, and they recognized their duty to carry out his order. Nevertheless, in Marshall's mind, "Roosevelt had followed the advice of a British prime minister, not that offered by his own chief military adviser."[44]

Marshall was not a political neophyte, but the experience taught him a great deal about domestic and international politics, destroying in the process the apolitical attitude that had marked the American military during the 1930s. On the domestic front, more than a year and a half had passed since Pearl Harbor, and Americans were impatiently wondering when Washington would avenge the attack by striking the Axis with a hard-hitting counter-blow. Furthermore, the midterm elections that were scheduled for November would "provide a referendum on Roosevelt's war leadership."[45] With one-third of the Senate and the entire House of Representatives up for reelection, the establishment of a second front just prior to election day might help salvage the Democrats' image. In fact, for a number of reasons, the invasion took place several days after the election (the Democrats lost seats). As far as Marshall was concerned, he admitted that "we failed to see that the leader in a democracy must keep the people entertained. That may sound like the wrong word, but it conveys the thought. . . . People demand action."[46] In the future, the country's generals and admirals would work hard to take such factors into consideration. As Field Marshal Dill observed about Marshall, "During the war he was in many ways a supremely political general, following Wavell's advice 'to understand the ways of politics without becoming involved in them.' "[47]

Although Roosevelt intervened in major strategic decisions like Operation Torch, he refused to micromanage the military operation itself. Indeed, had he ordered the armed forces to follow his political schedule, rather than their own military schedule, the Democrats might have won more seats in the election. Instead, having made the basic strategic decision, he delegated as many decisions as possible to his subordinates.

President Franklin D. Roosevelt with Winston Churchill and their chiefs of staff at Casablanca, January 1943. (Franklin Delano Roosevelt Presidential Library and Museum)

The Casablanca Conference, January 1943

The decision to invade North Africa represented a turning point in the evolution of civil-military relations under Roosevelt. Once the decision had been made, the question of where the Allies should attack next once again became a key issue. Not surprisingly, the Americans returned to the cross-Channel idea that Marshall had fought so hard for before Operation Torch. Roosevelt told the Chiefs well in advance of the January 1943 Casablanca Conference that they should devise a carefully crafted strategy for the next step in World War II, but they failed to heed his advice. (In his sole planning session with them prior to the conference with Churchill, he failed to communicate any strongly held views on the subject.) Consequently, the Chiefs arrived at the conference without a commonly held position. They had an "inclination," as one writer deemed it; the British, in contrast, had a "plan" for hitting Hitler's soft underbelly.[48] As a result, the president soon found himself embarrassed.

"The British Chiefs of Staff Committee had done its homework, knew it, and even lorded it over the Americans."[49] They asked, for example, what kind of weapons and equipment the Americans could provide for a cross-Channel invasion. No one on the American side knew. They asked about training mechanisms the Americans would use in preparation for an attack on the European mainland. "Sorry, the JCS answered, that hasn't been determined. The British officers were amused, Leahy, King and Marshall were humiliated."[50] The British won a complete victory when the group decided that the next point of attack would be Italy. As General Wedemeyer quipped, "We came, we listened and we were conquered."[51] The Chiefs had learned their lesson. The British would never do the same thing to them again. "Casablanca, like the Africa campaign as a whole, was part of the American coming of age, a hinge on which world history would swing for the next half century."[52]

To worsen matters, the president said nothing to the Chiefs about his plan to demand "unconditional surrender" at the conference. He believed that "the elimination of German, Japanese and Italian war power means the unconditional surrender of Germany, Italy and Japan."[53] His stance completely surprised the Chiefs and drove presidential-JCS relations to their lowest point thus far.

Using the Military for Diplomacy

Perhaps to a far greater extent than any of his successors, Roosevelt relied on his senior military officers in the world of diplomacy. As one writer has suggested, Roosevelt did not "create complementary organizations and officials to provide a robust civilian perspective in planning and directing the war. The chiefs filled every inch of this vacuum. They became the president's military, diplomatic, political and intelligence officers."[54] Their expanded role was evident at the diplomatic conferences in Tehran and Yalta.

In preparation for the November 1943 conference in Tehran, Marshall in particular played a critical role in setting American strategy. As usual, the British, under Churchill's prodding, were pushing the Americans toward something that neither Roosevelt nor the JCS agreed with: in this case, the so-called "Balkan strategy." At a preliminary conference in Cairo, Marshall responded to another of Churchill's entreaties by bursting out that "not one American soldier is going to die on that God dammed beach."[55] Leahy, who was also present at these meetings, noted that "the British bulldog tenacity did not like to let go of a desire to retain a controlling hold on the Mediterranean in the Near East. The American Chiefs followed their instructions from

Roosevelt not to agree to the diversion of any useful forces from Operation OVERLORD."[56] Roosevelt took the lead at the Tehran meeting with Stalin and Churchill, but his senior military officers accompanied him to support his position and provide consultation as necessary. Importantly, the hard line taken by the Americans, with strong support from Josef Stalin, stopped Churchill in his tracks. All attention now focused on the invasion of Western Europe.

Roosevelt's consultation with his military advisors also played a major role at the Yalta Conference in February 1944. The Chiefs not only participated in the preliminary meetings with the president, but they joined him as well when he met with Stalin. In addition, they conducted a number of meetings alone with their British and Russian military counterparts.

Admiral Leahy appears to have played a particularly key role at these conferences. For example, he noted that "before we went into the main meeting, Roosevelt again reminded me to be sure to attend all of the political conferences in order that there might be an American participant in whom he had confidence who would have a continuous memory of the discussions and the decisions reached." Furthermore, Leahy could speak openly with the president about even nonmilitary issues. As he explained, "As soon as I could talk with the President after the plenary session closed, I warned him about the possible difficulties back in the United States that would result from his agreeing to give the Soviets more votes in the proposed United Nations Assembly than we had. I felt this would be received very badly and meet with serious objection in Congress." Leahy apparently even felt free to question the president's decisions during the plenary sessions. As he noted, "When the issue of making Darien [the Chinese port in Manchuria] a free port came up, I leaned over to Roosevelt and said, 'Mr. President, you are going to lose out on Hong Kong if you give the Russians half of Darien.' He shook his head in resignation and said, 'Well, Bill, I can't help it.' " Another example of Leahy's lack of inhibition was his dismissal of Russian guarantees that the new Polish government would be democratic. "I handed the paper back to Roosevelt and said, 'Mr. President, this is so elastic that the Russians can stretch it all the way from Yalta to Washington without technically breaking it.' The President replied, 'I know, Bill—I know it. But it's the best I can do for Poland at this time.' "[57] The point here is not to exaggerate the role played by Marshall or especially Leahy, but to note both Roosevelt's openness to advice from senior military professionals on diplomatic topics and his trust in them when making some of his most important diplomatic decisions. In contrast to the State Department perspective, Roosevelt believed that "generals and admirals are trained to present themselves as brisk pragmatists who receive an assignment and then go back to their offices and devise ways of carrying it out—unlike civilians professionals who tend to wrinkle their brows, pull out their pipes and begin presenting objections to a proposed line of action."[58]

ROOSEVELT AND INTERNAL MILITARY DECISION MAKING

Roosevelt Remains Aloof

Given the lack of a cooperative relationship between the services, Roosevelt's decision to leave major decisions to his military leaders disastrously affected the conduct of the war, especially in the Pacific. The Japanese attack on Pearl Harbor provides an excellent example.

Prior to World War II, the United States had four commands in the Pacific. The army and the navy each had one in Hawaii and the Philippines that were, for all practical purposes, independent of each other. Joint operations barely existed. In fact, the navy and army did a poor job of communicating with each other in the days before the attack on Pearl Harbor. As one analyst characterized the situation,

> Nominally there are two top commanders: Lieutenant General Walter C. Short commanding the Hawaiian Department of the Army; Admiral Husband E. Kimmel commanding the Pacific Fleet. . . . [T]hese two were not in any real sense "opposite numbers" having equivalent duties and responsibilities. The Fleet's assignment is "far flung and offensive," the Army's is "local and defensive"; and there is no machinery for meshing the two commands into anything approaching a single directing unit. The coordination of Army and Navy activities, to the extent it exists, largely depends upon, and derives from, the voluntary cooperation of the two nominally supreme commanders.[59]

To make matters even worse, both the commandant of the Fourteenth Naval District and the army were responsible for the defense of Pearl Harbor. Technically, the commandant worked both for Kimmel and the Navy Department in Washington, but he outranked Kimmel, making it difficult for Kimmel to control him. The idea of employing liaison officers between these various entities was foreign to their way of thinking. Admiral Kimmel and General Short met from time to time and that was thought to be enough. Ultimately, however, neither service was in a position to work with the other in the event of hostilities.

The situation was further complicated by poor communications between Washington and Hawaii. Take, for example, Washington's attempt to warn Pearl Harbor of a possible attack. On December 5, the U.S. government intercepted thirteen paragraphs of a message sent by the Japanese government to its embassy in Washington. Neither Marshall nor Adm. Kelly Turner, who was in charge of navy war plans, saw the message.[60] When the fourteenth paragraph of the Japanese cable finally arrived, Marshall was out on his customary Sunday horse ride, and no one could reach him until he returned. Once he arrived at his office and noted that the message indicated that Tokyo no longer believed that an agreement was possible and that "the hope of peaceful cooperation was finally abandoned," he called Admiral Harold Stark (the chief of naval operations) and asked if Washington shouldn't warn Pearl Harbor of these latest developments. Stark replied that he thought there had been enough war scares and that another one would be unnecessary. Why add to the problem with another warning?[61] Marshall was still worried by the final paragraph of the message: it called on the Japanese ambassador to deliver Tokyo's response at 1300 on December 7. Because he feared that the intercepted communication might presage a Japanese attack on Pearl Harbor (or even more likely the Philippines), Marshall decided to send a warning to the Hawaiian base. A cable was drafted and sent to the message center. However, the center could not reach Hawaii through its normal means of communication because of static, so it decided to send the warning via Western Union. The telegram arrived in Hawaii and "was given to a messenger boy a few minutes before the first bombs fell. The boy spent the next two hours hiding in a ditch, and the telegram was not decoded and delivered to Short's adjutant general . . . [until] a little over seven hours after the raid began."[62] Although historians have debated and will continue to discuss the impact that a timely delivery of Marshall's message might have had on U.S. preparedness on that fateful morning, the fact remains that the divided commands made communication more difficult. The army and navy did not talk to each other. If they had, they might have noticed the numerous signs that the Japanese were planning an attack. A higher level of alert, combined with closer cooperation between the two services both in Pearl Harbor and the Philippines, could have saved hundreds, if not thousands, of lives.

The bottom line was that Washington—and the rest of the U.S. military's world—was afflicted with a most serious disease, that of service independence and interservice rivalry, which undermined the war effort. Britain's air marshal, Sir John Slessor, saw it firsthand on more than one occasion, noting, "The violence of interservice rivalry in the United States had to be seen to be believed and was an appreciable handicap to their war effort."[63]

Throughout the war in the Pacific, such rivalry between various forces would pose a major problem. First and foremost was the issue of who was in charge of the Pacific. Unfortunately, the command remained split because personalities in the Pacific combined with Roosevelt's decision not to throw around his weight regarding operational matters. To many, the question of who should command American forces in the Pacific was a simple matter of logic: the Pacific was a large ocean where the navy was the major actor. Unfortunately, those who felt this way had not considered the personality of Gen. Douglas MacArthur.

The larger-than-life MacArthur had previously served as army chief of staff and then as commander of U.S. and Filipino troops fighting the Japanese until he was ordered to leave his island fortress of Corregidor and travel to Australia, first by PT boat and subsequently by submarine. With an ego as big as the Pacific Ocean, MacArthur was not about to cede command of the Eastern Theater to the navy.

Admiral King, however, was just as determined to have the navy play the primary role in the Pacific. And he was not only in a key position, he was as stubborn and willful as MacArthur, who complained,

> Admiral King claimed the Pacific as the rightful domain of the Navy; he seemed to regard the operations there as almost his own private war; he apparently felt that the only way to remove the blot on the Navy disaster at Pearl Harbor was to have the Navy command a great victory over Japan; he was adamant in his refusal to allow any major fleet to be under other command than that of naval officers although maintaining that naval officers were competent to command ground or air forces.[64]

In addition to the tremendous egos involved, serious substantive differences existed between the army and the navy in regard to operating forces in the Pacific. From the navy's perspective, the idea of placing navy assets under the command of an army general was ludicrous. For example, the role to be played by aircraft carriers proved to be a contentious issue. From MacArthur's standpoint, the ships' primary function was to provide air cover for amphibious operations until army troops could secure landing fields ashore, thereby permitting army air corps planes to take over the job of protecting the troops on the ground. The navy, however, viewed the aircraft carrier as a potent offensive weapon. Instead of being confined to areas near shore—where they could be attacked by the enemy—they should be deployed at sea where they could maneuver and avoid the enemy while delivering devastating attacks on his ships. Using the carriers to cover the landing of troops, a job the navy

President Roosevelt with General Douglas MacArthur and Admiral Chester Nimitz on the USS *Baltimore* at Pearl Harbor, July 1944. (Franklin Delano Roosevelt Presidential Library and Museum)

would rather leave to the army air force units, was considered to be a waste of a valuable resource.

How could the United States fight a war when its services were at loggerheads? The answer came during a March 1942 meeting in Washington with the adoption of the "Pope's Line," the line drawn along the 159th east meridian northward to the equator. "Thus the Eastern Solomons, including Tulagi and Guadalcanal, were inside the South Pacific Area." Everything east of the line went to MacArthur, while everything west of it belonged to Adm. Chester Nimitz, the senior navy officer in the Pacific (and a much more accommodating and diplomatic officer). In addition, Gen. Hap Arnold was given command of the Twentieth Air Force, "a strategic air command that operated its own particular kind of war from Washington, literally half a world away."[65] MacArthur and Nimitz reported to the JCS through their respective service chiefs, while the air forces in the Pacific were directed from Washington. "That meant a military committee, becoming 'in effect a supreme command,' directed Pacific operations."[66] This ersatz arrangement was typical of the Roosevelt administration, and while it provided a way out of the personality conflicts, it did nothing to resolve interservice rivalry. As James Locher observed, "This decision doomed the Pacific theater to four decades of discord among the services and under-achievement or failure on the battlefield."[67]

Holland "Mad" Smith

If ever an example of interservice rivalry in the Pacific had serious postwar implications, it was the fight that broke out between Lt. Gen. Holland Smith, USMC, and Lt. Gen. Robert Richardson, USA. General Smith was in command of operations in and around Saipan. One of the key units was the army's 165th Regiment and, according to Smith, it was not doing its job.

> I was very dissatisfied with the regiment's lack of offensive spirit; it was preposterous that a small Japanese force could delay the capture of Makin three days. It probably was not the fault of the men. The 165th was not too well officered. When I returned to Pearl Harbor, I reported to Admiral Nimitz that had Ralph Smith [the regimental commander] been a Marine I would have relieved him of his command on the spot. His conduct of operations did not measure up to my expectations at all.[68]

Smith's unhappiness with the army commander continued. Trying to persuade him to be more aggressive, he talked to him, but to no avail. Finally, he believed something had to be done. He went to see Vice Adm. Raymond Spruance, who was in overall command. Holland Smith laid out the facts and argued that a change in command was necessary. "He asked me what should be done. 'Ralph Smith has shown that he lacks aggressive spirit,' I replied, 'and his division is slowing down our advance. He should be relieved.' " Spruance agreed, ordering, "You are authorized and directed to relieve Major General Ralph Smith from command of the Twenty-Seventh Division, U.S. Army, and place Major General Jarman in command of this division. This action is taken in order that the offensive on Saipan may proceed in accordance with the plans and orders of the Commander, Northern Troops and Landing Force."[69] Smith's action in relieving an army officer infuriated Lieutenant General Richardson, who was the War Department's senior representative in the Pacific. He approached General Smith, arguing "you had no right to relieve Ralph Smith. . . . The Twenty-Seventh is one of the best trained divisions in the Pacific. I trained it myself. You discriminated against the Army in favor of the Marines. I want you to know you can't push the Army around the way you have been doing." He continued, "You and your Corps commanders aren't as well qualified to lead large bodies of troops as general officers in the Army. . . . We've had more experience in handling troops than you have and you dare," he almost screamed, "to remove one of my Generals."[70] Richardson did everything possible to have Smith removed, including the launching of an investigation, but was unsuccessful (Holland Smith continued to play a major role in marine operations throughout the Pacific). When Smith complained to Nimitz, the admiral listened but did nothing, hoping to avoid a confrontation.

The spat between Smith and Richardson reflected the deep split between the services. Because the president was not about to get involved in issues concerning operations or, in this case, tactics (e.g., how to fight a war on an island such as Saipan), and because each service essentially worked for its own commander, such incidents could and did get out of hand. In 1942, for example, MacArthur wanted to be in charge of an offensive move to capture the major Japanese base at Rabaul on New Britain, arguing that it was in his area of operations. The navy, however, wanted it under Nimitz's command "because it would be 'primarily amphibious in character.' "[71] The JCS debated the issue for a week. An outraged King suggested he would order Nimitz to use navy and Marine Corps assets to take the base. Eventually, Marshall defused the conflict by proposing a suitable compromise.

In 1943 Nimitz and MacArthur battled yet again, this time over the direction U.S. attacks should take against the Japanese. Nimitz wanted to move westward across the Pacific to Formosa through the Gilbert, Marshall, Carolina, and Mariana Islands. His plan would have meant bypassing the Philippine island of Luzon and, in the process, placing MacArthur in the backwater of the fighting in the Pacific. Needless to say, MacArthur complained about Nimitz's plan, maintaining that he had to return to the Philippines in order "to eradicate the memory of the stinging defeat of 1942 and rebuild U.S. prestige in the area." Because no supreme authority existed to decide the matter, "the JCS from mid-1943 to mid-1944 essentially compromised and postponed action by endorsing both sets of offensive plans."[72]

Then came the disastrous battle of Leyte Gulf. Almost all observers, including MacArthur, believed the heavy American losses resulted from the sin of divided command. To quote the general, "I have never ascribed the unfortunate incidents of this naval battle to faulty judgment on the part of any of the commanders involved. The near disaster can be placed squarely at the door of Washington. In the naval action, two key American commanders were independent of each other, one under me, and the other under Admiral Nimitz 5,000 miles away, both operating in the same waters and in the same battle."[73] E. B. Potter, Nimitz's well-known biographer, agreed. "Though two separate fleets, the beefed up Seventh and the stripped down Third, were to support the invasion, there would be no overall commander at the scene. Admiral Thomas Kinkaid, Commander, U.S. Seventh Fleet, took his orders from General MacArthur, who would be present, and General MacArthur took his orders from the Joint Chiefs of Staff in Washington. Admiral William Halsey, Commander, U.S. Third Fleet, took his orders from Admiral Nimitz, who would be at Pearl Harbor"[74] In sum, most observers agreed that none of the many errors that marked this battle would have happened if command had been in the hands of a single officer—regardless of whether he was from the navy or army.

The consequences of this divided command would have been even worse if the United States had been forced to invade Japan. The invasion plans represented yet another service compromise. "MacArthur would command the land campaign, Nimitz would direct the sea battle, and General Henry H. Arnold, commanding general of the Army Air Forces, would command the Twentieth Air Force's bombers as an executive agent of the JCS."[75] In the meantime, the JCS "ordered MacArthur and Nimitz to complete their current campaigns under the old command structure."[76] Fortunately, the Americans never had to carry out the planned invasion.

Roosevelt and Personnel Decisions

As with strategic matters, Roosevelt became involved in personnel matters only at the highest level (i.e., selecting officers to work directly with him), and even then he proceeded carefully. The best-known example of Roosevelt's involvement in such an instance concerns the appointment of an officer to command Operation Overlord.

Most observers believed that George Marshall would be appointed commander of any attack on continental Europe. In fact, Churchill had suggested several times that Marshall be given the command of a cross-Channel invasion, which now clearly would be directed by an American because the United States held the preponderance of troops. Despite their past disagreements, Churchill felt comfortable with Marshall.

But appointing Marshall to a position that every professional military officer dreamed of would not be easy. Leahy stated his belief that Roosevelt wanted to give the assignment to Marshall but was worried about domestic reaction in the United States. General John Pershing had called on the president to keep Marshall in Washington, and Roosevelt's political opponents accused him of trying to send Marshall to Europe "to get rid of [him] in order to control Army contracts."[77] To complicate matters, senior military officers (including members of the Joint Chiefs) and many members of Congress expressed concern that Marshall was simply too valuable to be spared from Washington. He was the one military officer who could talk to the media and testify before Congress with total credibility. Some expressed concern that Operation Overlord was too small a command for someone of Marshall's stature, but the British strongly resisted any efforts to broaden the command because they would have had to bear the brunt of the additional burden.[78]

Still, Roosevelt seems to have seriously played with the idea of appointing Marshall anyway.

> At his meeting with Eisenhower at Carthage in November, Roosevelt had gone through one of those disarming changes of mind which were so characteristic of him. He told Eisenhower that he had come to the conclusion that Marshall must be Supreme Commander of OVERLORD. He spoke of how chiefs of staff were always forgotten. Who, for example, could remember the names of the chiefs of staff under Lincoln? He was concerned that Marshall's name be remembered. He explained that Eisenhower would be recalled to take Marshall's place in Washington. Eisenhower was confused. From King and Arnold he had heard a contrary story, while Harry Hopkins was reasonably sure that Marshall would be leaving Washington shortly for London.[79]

At Tehran, Stalin insisted that the United States appoint a commander for Overlord as a way of ensuring that the operation take place in the near future, and he made clear that he favored Marshall. Given strong Russian and British support, everyone expected that Marshall would be named to the position in spite of Roosevelt's domestic concerns.

Roosevelt relied heavily on tact and his persuasive powers in making clear to Marshall that the command was really his if he wanted it, but he just as carefully made clear that he would prefer to keep him in Washington where, Roosevelt argued, he was invaluable. The president knew Marshall well, and he was well aware that being the good soldier he was, Marshall would readily agree to stay in Washington, which he did.[80] Consequently, Eisenhower found himself in charge of Operation Overlord, a command that would eventually lead him to the White House.

The Patton Story

There was no more colorful, competent, indispensable, and difficult officer for Eisenhower to control than George W. Patton III. When it came to combat, Patton was unequaled. He accomplished feats that other officers could only dream of; indeed, from the German standpoint, he was America's most feared general. Stephen Ambrose called him "an erratic genius, given to great outbursts of energy and flashes of brilliant insight."[81] He also relied heavily on his intuition,[82] unlike Eisenhower, an officer who took a more systematic approach to problems and believed that the key to winning wars was good planning. For Patton, however, leadership was key. As he put it, "Victory in the next war will depend on EXECUTION not PLANS."[83] In the area of execution, Patton would turn out to be a genius: "To think like a corps commander is an unusual gift . . . and to think like an Army is a rarity itself. Patton could think like an Army. When the occasion required, he could turn it on a dime, and this raises him high above the rest of Allied generals."[84] Both generals were correct, and during the war each would excel in their special areas. Furthermore, in spite of their many differences, Eisenhower and Patton were close friends. Patton helped Ike with his studies at the Command and General Staff School at Fort Leavenworth by providing him with a copy of the notes he had taken the year before.[85] In addition, in contrast to many of their peers, they had shared a deep dedication to the role of tanks; between the First and Second World War, a time when most of the army's attention was focused elsewhere, the two men argued that the weapons were the wave of the future.

The friendship between Patton and Eisenhower paid off in 1943 when, after the disastrous showing by the U.S. Army at the Battle of Kasserine Pass in Tunisia, Eisenhower brought in Major General Patton to take command of the battered II Corps. "He told Patton to restore morale, raise the image of American troops in British eyes by winning a victory or two."[86] Patton immediately set to work, drilling them hard, making them dress meticulously regardless of where they were—in fact forcing them to train far longer and more frequently than was the case with most other generals. They became effective troops in short order. His reward was command of the invasion of Sicily.

Patton set the Germans and Italians reeling as his forces roared across the island to the city of Palermo, an action that "left the British, especially General Bernard Montgomery, awestruck."[87] That was quite an accomplishment given the low regard the British had at the time for the fighting capabilities of the U.S. Army. And then it happened.

On August 10, 1943, Patton visited an evacuation hospital to talk to and encourage soldiers who had been wounded. When he asked a young man why he was in the hospital, the soldier responded that it was his nerves. Patton exploded. From his perspective, battle fatigue and shell shock were synonyms for cowardice. He then yelled at the young man, "Your nerves, hell, you are just a goddamn coward, you yellow son of a bitch." He then hit the soldier twice, knocking off his helmet liner.[88] Within a week, a report of the incident made its way to Eisenhower's headquarters, and shortly thereafter into the public domain.

When the president was asked about the issue, he dismissed it by recalling "Lincoln's response when told Grant drank too much, and only slightly misquoted: 'It must be a damn good brand of liquor.' "[89] Instead of making the decision himself, Roosevelt believed the matter should be resolved by the military. As a result, the question of what should be done with Patton fell into Eisenhower's lap. As General Bradley noted, "It would have been easy for Eisenhower to dump Patton now that the heat was on, but he chose to keep him."[90] However, Eisenhower severely reprimanded Patton.

> I determined to keep Patton. I first wrote him a sharp letter of reprimand in which I informed him that repetition of such an offense would be cause for his instant relief. I informed him, also, that his retention as a commander in my theater would be contingent upon his offering an apology to the two men whom he had insulted. I demanded that he apologize to all the personnel of the hospital present at the time of the incident. Finally, I required that he appear before the officers and representative groups of enlisted men of each of his divisions to assure them that he had given way to impulse and respected their positions as fighting soldiers of a democratic nation.[91]

Patton swallowed his pride and complied with Eisenhower's order.

When Eisenhower was appointed supreme commander of Operation Overlord, he decided to take Patton along, in spite of some misgivings on the part of Marshall. After all, Ike's task was to win a war, and no general in the U.S. Army could hold a candle to Patton when it came to killing Germans. So Patton moved to England to prepare for the cross-Channel invasion. Once again, however, he was unable to control himself.

On April 25, 1944, Patton was invited to the opening of a club that had been set up for the growing number of American troops stationed in Knutsford. He had been warned to avoid press conferences and public statements by Eisenhower, who felt that Patton "had a genius for explosive statements and rarely failed to startle his hearers."[92] Nevertheless, he used the opportunity to spark another firestorm. Patton spoke about the importance of Anglo-American unity, "since it is the evident destiny of the British and Americans to rule the world, [and] the better we know each other the better job we will do."[93] A journalist picked up on his statement, which soon spread across the wires. The press was indignant, and the Russians were furious. So that was what this war was all about! The Americans and British out to rule the world—what about the Russians who were bearing the brunt of the German attack? If anything, Patton's comment only served to confirm some Soviets' belief that the United States' primary goal was to get the Russians and Germans to annihilate each other so that Washington would be the sole major power remaining after the war. How could such a man be permitted to command an American army?

Cables flew back and forth between Eisenhower's command and the War Department over what to do with Patton. According to Eisenhower, "as usual the Secretary and the Chief of Staff left the final decision to me, to be based completely on my judgement as to the needs of battle."[94] Ike decided to keep Patton, telling him that he owed his superior officer some victories. Patton would uphold his end of the bargain.

In mid-July, shortly after the Normandy Invasion, Patton's Third Army was driving across France at a hectic pace. When Bastogne was surrounded, Patton's forces were the ones that were called upon to provide relief to the city—and they did so in record time. Patton was also the first to cross the Rhine. Soon the war came to an end, and Patton was assigned to be the military governor of Bavaria. Again, however, he blundered.

Patton informed Eisenhower on several occasions that he failed to see how the government in Bavaria could be run without the use of former Nazis. After all, they had the technical expertise needed to operate the machinery of government. Eisenhower, viscerally opposed to Nazis, did not want to see them used in any capacity. Nevertheless, when a journalist at a September 22, 1945, press conference asked Patton why reactionaries were still in power in Bavaria, he responded, " 'Reactionaries!' . . . 'Do you want a lot of communists?' After a pause, he said: 'I don't know anything about parties. . . . The Nazi thing is just like a Democratic and Republican election fight.' "[95] Again, believing that the military had the responsibility for addressing the problem, Roosevelt left Patton's fate up to Eisenhower. Ike, whose patience had finally been exhausted, ordered America's most colorful (and many would say most successful) general to report to him in Frankfurt. Patton complied, and after a rather acrimonious discussion in Eisenhower's office, Patton left and was relieved by Eisenhower of his governorship a few days later. He died the following December after an automobile accident.

CONCLUSION

Presidential Leadership Style

Roosevelt was a strong president. He took one of the most important steps in civil-military relations for a president when he made clear from the very beginning that he was commander in chief and was prepared to step in and countermand military proposals or suggestions when he believed the situation required him to do so. However, such a statement must be qualified, because Roosevelt exerted his influence in a way that minimized friction between himself and the Chiefs, primarily by limiting his involvement to strategic matters.

The president's aloof style created difficulties for the military at a time when the armed forces needed a strong unifying leader. The battle between Generals Smith and Richardson was indicative of an interservice problem that surfaced during Roosevelt's tenure: the issue of the U.S. Marine Corps. During the interwar period the Corps had been a small expeditionary force, spread all over the world from China to Nicaragua. In World War II, however, the Marines had grown exponentially and played a major role in the Pacific. The army resented the situation, as illustrated by General Richardson's one-sided investigation of the relief of the army general by his Marine superior. But the best that could be done at the time was to try to sweep matters under the rug, which Nimitz attempted to do when General Smith complained to him. Clearly, this dispute had touched a sensitive nerve, one that would figure prominently during Truman's time in office.[96]

In Europe, where the show was primarily put on by the U.S. Army, the situation was much better. The U.S. Navy, to the degree it had a presence in the theater, knew it worked for the army. Furthermore, Eisenhower was the supreme commander, and Marshall permitted him almost total autonomy in carrying out his duties. Interservice relations worked well, as long as one service overwhelmingly predominated. But Roosevelt understood that becoming personally involved in the matter of interservice cooperation would have probably led to even worse interservice rivalry, which may have been why he restrained himself.

Violations of Service/Military Culture?

Did Roosevelt's leadership style violate service/military culture? In a word, no. With the exception of personnel matters (namely the selection of a supreme commander for Operation Overlord), Roosevelt made only limited intrusions into those areas the military tends to hold sacred. His primary concern was at the strategic level. For example, he overruled the Chiefs on Operation Torch, the attack on Burma, and, later, the firing of General Joseph Stilwell as Chiang Kai-shek's chief of staff. Like Churchill, he believed that diplomatic relations with a critical country were strategic matters, and he reserved the right to interfere when he considered it necessary, especially when the policies of the United States toward its British allies were involved. At the same time, he readily involved senior military officers even in areas normally considered to be the province of civilians. One could argue that Admiral Leahy was the most important advisor to the president at both the Tehran and Yalta conferences.

Military culture places critical importance on the Joint Chiefs' perception as to whether the president genuinely respects them, their values, and opinions. Leahy remarked, for example, that

> As we worked in close liaison with the Chiefs of the British armed forces, there was more than one occasion when we felt that our British colleagues were loyally supporting the views of their defense minister only because it was their duty and because they were carrying out orders. On our side, we never labored under any such handicap. There were differences of opinion, of course, but due to the mutual confidence and daily contact between the president and his military chiefs, these differences never became serious.[97]

Key indicators of Roosevelt's respect for his military subordinates were the access he provided them and the willingness he showed in listening to their viewpoints. This respect became readily apparent at an early stage, as when Marshall told the president he did not agree with his position on issues as important as the invasion of Europe, or when he informed the president that he would resign rather than permit anyone to abridge the right of soldiers to read whatever they chose. The country's senior military leadership did not feel inhibited about raising problems and concerns or disagreeing with the president; disagreements, however, were always raised in private. The president refrained from making any public attacks on his senior military officers, yet another trait of critical importance to military culture.

Still, Roosevelt's leadership style frustrated the military at times. Indeed, the military craves a clear chain of command and unambiguous orders. Thanks to the role played by Admiral Leahy as the president's chief of staff, the armed forces knew "more or less" where they stood. They also understood their orders and appreciated the fact that the president largely permitted them to run the war.

Changes in Service/Military Culture?

During the Roosevelt administration, military culture changed in at least two important ways. First, among the lessons the Chiefs learned from the war was that politics was very much a part of national security policies. Their effort to insulate themselves from politics prior to World War II and focus only on military matters was a thing of the past. Operation Torch, the decision on the cross-Channel invasion, Marshall's decision to turn down the assignment to London, all made clear to the Joint Chiefs the importance of both domestic and international politics. In addition, the Chiefs were permitted to play a significant role at the summits with foreign leaders, certainly a heavy dose of politics. The bottom line was that *Roosevelt and World War II drew the JCS into the political arena.* Furthermore, in the postwar period, the heads of the armed services (especially the navy and Marine Corps) would quickly discover that they worked for Congress as well as the executive. Their assertive use of that connection would have a profound impact on the nature of civil-military relations in the United States.

Second, some of the military, especially those in the U.S. Army, were beginning to comprehend that interservice rivalry was a luxury they could not afford. As Roosevelt's successor would quickly learn, the view was not unanimous; but beginning with Pearl Harbor and continuing on to Holland Smith and the constant bickering between King and MacArthur, it was becoming clear that the services' strong parochial attitude had to change. Bringing about such a transformation, however, would be a very painful process.

3
THE MILITARY AND HARRY TRUMAN

Some of our seniors are forgetting that they have a commander-in-chief.
—*General Dwight D. Eisenhower*

The military initially enjoyed a positive relationship with Harry Truman, but conflict quickly developed. Indeed, World War II had hardly ended when battles between Truman and the services erupted. Most important, the services started playing bureaucratic politics behind the scenes in an effort to protect themselves. From this point on, the executive would never be able to change military plans without taking into consideration the Chiefs' position vis-à-vis Congress. An indecisive president like Truman would have difficulty forcing the military to do what he wanted unless he had congressional support.

Truman and the Chiefs would engage in major battles with each other, and in the end the president would win, but not without considerable delay and effort. On questions such as unification, roles and missions, and integration, the various chiefs adopted differing stances toward Truman, depending on which branch of the service each man represented. The navy would fight unification to the end, while the army significantly obstructed the integration of blacks into the armed forces. Truman would try persuasion in a number of cases, but it was not enough. In both of the preceding instances, he was forced to order the military to take the steps he advocated. But when the question of MacArthur's dismissal arose, the president was the one who hesitated, not the Chiefs. They wished that Truman had fired the general a year or so earlier.

PRESIDENTIAL LEADERSHIP STYLE

Alexander George and Eric Stern labeled Truman's leadership style the "formalistic" approach.[1] This model casts the president in the role of chairman of the board. When addressing problems, he listens to what the heads of the various departments (i.e, the secretary of defense, the JCS, or the services) have to say, and after hearing their opinions synthesizes them, makes a decision, and then leaves implementation of the solution up to them. He functions within bureaucratic channels. Two other presidential scholars called Truman "a systematic administrator."[2] Recognizing the importance of bureaucratic structure, Truman wouldn't think of talking with a subordinate without informing his superior ahead of time. His systematic approach was exemplified by his support for the creation of the National Security Council (NSC) as a vehicle "to coordinate foreign policy advice to the president and assist him in arriving at coherent and cohesive foreign policy judgments."[3]

Truman also was a pragmatist who was prepared to compromise, as illustrated by his support for the Marshall Plan in the face of isolationist Republican senators.[4] Or as another observer commented, "[H]e does appear to have been shrewd and generally successful at the art of the possible. He assessed situations intelligently, defined priorities accordingly, and at times used defeats . . . to consolidate his electoral coalition."[5] Rather than advancing a specific agenda, however, Truman more often reacted to situations, as evidenced by his responses to North Korean aggression, pressure from the black community to desegregate the military, and MacArthur's repeated insubordination. Importantly, Truman would eventually make decisions and willingly accept responsibility for his actions. He did not welcome conflict, but he was prepared to respond, even when that meant going out on a limb, such as sending American troops to Korea. When trouble arose he acted, albeit reluctantly and hesitantly; thus, he tolerated insubordination by the navy, his secretary of army, and MacArthur much longer than many believed he should have.

From the military's standpoint, Truman possessed severable favorable traits, among them his willingness to meet as needed with Admirals William Leahy and Sidney Souers. Thus, regardless of what course the president ultimately chose to follow, he would first hear the military's views and recommendations. The Chiefs also appreciated the degree to which the president relied upon one of their own former members. As one writer noted, "Truman revered . . . George C. Marshall, as he did no other man in public life."[6]

TRUMAN BECOMES PRESIDENT

No one was more surprised to become president than Harry S. Truman. In the summer of 1944 he found himself on the presidential ticket with Franklin Roosevelt. Roosevelt, however, would serve only eighty-two days of his fourth term. On April 12, 1945, Roosevelt died and Truman was suddenly commander in chief. He was soon off to Europe to meet with Churchill and Stalin at Potsdam, and like his predecessor, he relied heavily on senior military officers at the conference, most notably George Marshall and William Leahy. Leahy in particular would play a major role at Potsdam, just as he had at Yalta and Tehran.[7]

Shortly after becoming president, Truman learned for the first time about one of the most important events of World War II—the development of the atomic bomb. Confronting him was the question of what should be done with it. Should the weapon be used against the Japanese? Dependent as he was on military advice, Truman "went into immediate consultation with James Byrnes, Henry Stimson, Admiral Leahy, General Marshall, General Arnold, General Eisenhower, and Admiral King. [He] asked for their opinions whether the bomb should be used."[8] This was a major strategic decision that had critical ramifications for the future of not only the United States but the world as well. On this important occasion, Truman relied primarily on his military advisors, one of whom (Eisenhower) argued against the bomb's use. It is also worth noting that after World War II Truman frequently named senior military officers to what would normally be considered civilian positions. For example, he selected Walter Bedell Smith as ambassador to the Soviet Union and then as director of the Central Intelligence Agency; Lucius Clay as the military governor of Germany; Douglas MacArthur as governor of Japan; "Brigadier General Charles E. Saltzman as assistant secretary of state; Major General William H. Draper as undersecretary for the army; Admiral Alan G. Kirk as ambassador to Belgium; General Frank T. Hines as ambassador to Panama; and General Thomas Holcomb as ambassador to South Africa."[9] And, of course, Marshall served as secretary of defense, Omar Bradley as head of Veterans Affairs, and Admiral Leahy retained for several years his position as chief of staff to the president. In the days soon after World War II, Truman felt comfortable being advised by former senior military officers.

THE FIGHT OVER UNIFICATION

Because of Franklin Roosevelt's particular leadership style, the military services—and indeed the whole defense effort—had been held together by personalities and arrangements that one writer called "haphazard and jerry-rigged."[10] As long as the war lasted, the informal relationships worked. However, they could not substitute for a structured, institutionalized arrangement, in spite of the joint work of JCS committees; consequently, these highly per-

President Harry S. Truman meets with senior defense advisors, some of whom have just returned from the Far East, where they met with General Douglas MacArthur. General Omar Bradley, chairman of the Joint Chiefs of Staff, is standing on Truman's left. (Harry S. Truman Library)

sonalized arrangements were bound to break down as soon as the war ended and "normalcy" returned to Washington. Truman would have to institutionalize relationships and reconcile differences between the services. The task would not be easy: "The War and Navy Departments . . . found it difficult to meet a presidential request for a comprehensive plan on the overall size and composition of the postwar military establishment, in large part because their planning kept faltering on the overlapping roles and missions of the armed forces in such areas as anti-submarine warfare, over-water reconnaissance, and the protection of shipping."[11] If he hoped to exercise power, the president needed bureaucratic structures, institutionalized forms of power sharing. A greater degree of "jointness" seemed to be the best approach.

Efforts toward joint planning had begun during World War II. For example, in the aftermath of the bureaucratic beating the JCS took at Casablanca from the much better organized British, General Marshall ordered a "comprehensive reappraisal and reorganization of the support structure of the Joint Chiefs of Staff."[12] As the war progressed, this reorganization led to the creation of a number of joint committees on topics such as intelligence, civil affairs, postwar policy, and industrial production.

The primary obstacle to unification was resistance from the navy. When Marshall proposed (with the support of General Arnold) as early as November 1943 that the JCS adopt his proposal to combine the War Department and Navy Department into a single Department of War, Admirals King and Leahy adamantly refused to agree "even in principle."[13] The idea was sent to a study group, Washington's way to kill the issue or at least delay its serious consideration for the indefinite future.

Meanwhile, six months after the end of the war in Europe, Marshall handed in his resignation as chief of staff of the army. In his place Truman appointed Dwight Eisenhower. For Eisenhower, the appointment was quite a comedown. He had been at the head of U.S. forces in their conquest of Nazi Germany before being in charge of occupation forces there. Now, however, he was being asked to assume one of the worst jobs imaginable. Not only did he have to deal with problems associated with demobilization, he would battle the other Chiefs on everything from integrating the armed forces to determining roles and missions. No longer "in command," he was now "one among equals in power within the JCS, and . . . a supplicant in his dealings with Congress."[14] For example, in September 1946 Eisenhower suggested a plan outlining the roles of the JCS as well as those of unified and component commanders. He soon learned, however, that he couldn't even keep his plan alive without making concessions to the other services.[15]

Eisenhower's relationship with Truman was "formal."[16] In contrast to the very close relationship that Roosevelt had with Marshall, Truman did not seek out Eisenhower for advice, even "on the most major decisions of his Presidency, decisions that had crucial military implications."[17]

Among the major issues that Eisenhower faced as army chief of staff was the integration of atomic weapons into the American arsenal. The United States did not yet understand the full implications of this new technology, which had already destroyed two Japanese cities and helped win the war. What role would it play relative to conventional weapons systems? The country's military leaders shared a widespread concern that the public would look upon nuclear bombs as "wonder weapons." They feared that "public sentiment . . . held that atomic bombs made armies and navies obsolete, and that possession of the atomic monopoly by the United States constituted a sufficient defense policy by itself."[18]

Eisenhower also had to address the question of unification. Many, especially Truman, increasingly believed that unification of the services would strengthen their combat readiness. Eisenhower agreed, arguing that unification would "promote efficiency" and "avoid unconscionable duplication."[19] In fact, he went so far as to propose that the services have a single uniform and that cadets from West Point and midshipmen from Annapolis swap schools in their third year of study. His goal, one of his biographers argued, was "to break the power of the West Point and Annapolis cliques, to make the armed services more democratic."[20]

The navy, however, was dead set against unification, because the admirals saw it as a no-win proposition. The idea that airmen or soldiers could be put in a position to direct naval assets was an anathema. Furthermore, the country's senior admirals were convinced that they would always be outvoted in any unified arrangement because the army and the army air force occupied key JCS positions. The Marine Corps, however was a part of the navy and thus did not have a seat on the JCS. The navy had resolved the problem during the war by ensuring that the JCS chairman was a navy officer, but the admirals could not assume that arrangement would continue in the future. If and when an army or army air force officer became chairman, the admirals feared that the navy would quickly find itself in a second-class position.

The navy and the Marine Corps had good reason to be concerned over their role within the JCS and the defense establishment in general. To begin with, many in Washington believed that Roosevelt was pro-navy. He had been assistant secretary of the navy during World War I, and in the minds of many had always had a soft spot in his heart for the navy, which showed in his policies. Truman, however, took great pride in his service as an artillery captain during the First World War in the Missouri National Guard, and by all appearances he made no effort to hide his pro-army bias. For example, shortly after he had been sworn in, "a close friend told a Missouri audience, during the Roosevelt administration the White House was a Navy wardroom: we're going to fix that."[21] Furthermore, Truman clearly had little use for the Marine Corps. As he put it in a letter to a congressman, "The Marine Corps is the Navy's police force and as long as I am President that is what it will remain. They have a propaganda machine that is almost the equal of Stalin."[22] On policy issues Truman almost always sided with the army. Finally, the upper ranks of the navy feared that the army air force would do its best to get rid of naval aviation. The possibility was very threatening. Fast carriers of World War II had replaced the battleship as the "queen" of the sea, and any effort to undermine the carriers' utility would severely hurt the navy.

The navy also viewed Eisenhower first and foremost as an army general, despite his service as a joint commander in World War II. And insofar as service unification was concerned, he thought like an army officer, a trait only too prominent in the minds of navy and Marine Corps officers. Indeed, the Marine Corps was convinced (correctly) that Ike was out to eliminate its branch of the service, or at least prune it so severely as to render it irrelevant from a military standpoint. Eisenhower wrote in a confidential memorandum that "the conduct of land warfare is a responsibility of the Army" and added that "operationally, the Navy does not belong on the land, it belongs on the sea."[23]

The army air force was even more outspoken in attacking the navy. On November 9, 1945, Lt. Gen. James Doolittle appeared before the Senate Military Affairs Committee to testify in favor of service unification. In the process, he let loose a blast at the navy, claiming that airpower was the first line of defense for the United States, and then observed, "Admiral Nimitz and Admiral Mitscher are great commanders, . . . but this war was won by teamwork. . . . I do feel very strongly that it was not sea power that compelled Japan to sue for peace, and that it was not carrier strength that won the war. Our B-29 boys are resting uneasily in their graves as a result of these two comments." He further insisted that carriers were becoming obsolete because they were too easily sunk. Besides, once the range of aircraft were sufficiently increased, "we will not need carriers."[24]

Not surprisingly, the navy's response to talk of unification was to circle the wagons. If its admirals could not torpedo the idea, they could at least water it down to the point that it did minimal damage to the navy's ability to act independently, not only in terms of operations, but in procurement and force structure as well. The admirals were determined to keep whatever structure that was adopted as decentralized as possible, one that would have a weak secretary of defense whose authority would be limited to *coordination* rather than administration or control. After all, during World War II the JCS had operated on the basis of compromise. No one service was strong enough to force its will on another.

Faced with pressure from the army and the White House to accept unification, the secretary of the navy convinced investment banker Ferdinand Eberstadt, a protégé of Secretary of the Navy James Forrestal, to head a committee to devise an institutional arrangement that de-emphasized centralization. And he did just that. The Eberstadt Commission's report would have "safeguarded the Navy against the dangers of centralization by ruling out a single department of defense with a single civilian secretary and military chief of staff."[25]

Truman, however, remained committed to unification. In December 1945 he urged Congress to unify the services, creating a single military establishment. Just as the navy had feared, his proposal came down clearly on the side of the army, arguing in favor of greater centralization. Truman's concern was greater efficiency, and he believed this was the way to achieve it. Negotiations between the War Department and Navy Department soon followed, with the navy continuing to fight for administrative autonomy and the army pressing to merge the services. "The Navy wanted the individual service chiefs to retain their current powers and work collaboratively in the Joint Chiefs of Staff; the Army envisioned a single chief of staff with his own general staff and substantial authority."[26]

At this point, naval officers decided to speak out. The navy's leaders had professed their loyalty to Truman, their commander in chief; however, they were deeply upset at what they saw as an attack on their service's roles and missions. Consequently, they turned to Congress (for whom they also worked). In doing so, they maintained correctly that they had an obligation to answer questions honestly and openly if requested. Politicking by the admirals had apparently "sandbagged" Truman, who could hardly argue that they should not give honest answers to congressional inquiries.

> Reluctant to instruct military leaders to withhold information from the legislative branch, the president found himself maneuvered into a position where he had to tolerate something close to naval mutiny against his authority as commander-in-chief—the first of many challenges that eventually established for the military a new degree of independence from presidential control.[27]

Much to the president's chagrin, the admirals not only leaked information to the press, but also lobbied Congress for a more decentralized command structure. Truman was furious and "warned that unless the Navy's official leaders 'got into line,' he might have 'to alter the situation.' "[28]

Testifying before Congress, Secretary of the Navy Forrestal publicly argued that while the navy supported the president's desire for unification, it was opposed to a single military chief of staff and any restrictions on the Marine Corps or naval aviation. Adm. Chester Nimitz went even further, arguing that "he personally believed that 'the ultimate ambition of the Army Air Force [is] to absorb naval aviation in its entirety and set up one large air force.' "[29] To protect the navy against unwarranted attacks on its role within the Defense Department, the admirals insisted that any unification bill clearly and carefully define the roles that the various services would play. Otherwise, they feared that the army and air force would soon renew their attacks on naval aviation and the Marine Corps.

Faced with the navy's opposition (and the recognition that no bill was likely to get through Congress as long as the navy was vehemently opposed to it), Truman called a conference at the White House to discuss the matter on May

31, 1946. The president was upset. He told the conferees that interservice fighting was undermining his efforts to get a defense bill and a balanced force structure adopted. Despite this "hard line" from the president, the fact was that he "had been reduced to a supplicant, pleading with the Army and Navy for support."[30]

The issue of naval aviation would not go away. At one point it was proposed that all of the navy's land-based planes be given to the army air force. The navy's carrier admirals counterattacked, claiming that the army air force was either unwilling or unable to carry out over-water reconnaissance or protect shipping. They further argued that land-based aircraft were critical in carrying out naval operations. Again, they insisted that any unification bill must carefully detail the functions to be carried out by naval aviation and the Marine Corps.

During the course of the congressional hearings on the passage of a National Security Act, Admiral Nimitz made an especially interesting observation in his answer to a question posed by New Hampshire senator Styles Bridges about the role of the military.

> Senator, it is my impression that the Constitution of the United States charges the Congress with the furnishing of armed forces. It charges the president with their use.
>
> The Congress, in the furnishing of the armed forces, is entitled to every bit of information that it needs, and I perceive no objection whatever in the writing into this bill of the kind of safeguards you have in mind; because it is the Congress that makes provision for the armed forces and they should certainly have the right to every bit of information that they think they need in making appropriations.[31]

What is interesting about Nimitz's comment is his observation that Congress (in cooperation with or in opposition to the president) has a right and a role in determining the roles and missions of the armed forces. As far as Nimitz and the navy were concerned, civilian control over the military was a shared responsibility. Nimitz's testimony was only the first of many efforts by the services to draw Congress into their disputes with the president.

It is also worth noting that throughout the unification battle of the 1940s, Secretary Forrestal openly used the navy's public relations organization to spread its message. In addition, he repeatedly threatened to resign if legislation harmful to the navy's interests became law. "He also tried to outflank the President by working through Wall Street friends with close ties to the War Department."[32] The bottom line was that Forrestal's outspoken opposition "reflected . . . the views of the preponderant majority of high naval officers, all of whom could not be dismissed and replaced."[33]

The incredibly bitter battle pitted not only the navy against the army, but, to a certain degree, the army against the army air force, which wanted to be a service of its own. "The prospect of an independent air force 'engendered fear and dismay in the Navy and Marine Corps.' "[34] Giving independence to the U.S. Army Air Corps, which wanted to get rid of the Marine Corps, would threaten the existence of the Marines. An army air force officer probably put it best when he remarked that the air force would "be the predominant force in war and peace and 'is going to run the show.' Calling the Marines, 'a small bitched-up army talking navy lingo,' he said, 'We are going to put those Marines in the Regular Army and make efficient soldiers of them.' "[35] Given such comments, as well as the World War II experience between the two services, the Marines believed this was nothing less than a battle for the Corps' very existence. As a result senior Marine officers lobbied vigorously with members of Congress to ensure the Corps' continued survival.

In June and July, a number of navy fliers testified in opposition to the creation of an independent air force, expressing their concern that it would institutionalize the kind of strategic bombing campaigns common to World War II. Admiral Radford testified,

> I just feel that World War III is going to be different, and I would hate to see our new organization patterned after the organization of World War II. I think that this is trouble, the basic trouble with this bill. It is setting up permanently the pattern established by World War II. That is usually, historically, the way we work. We organize for the next war by following the pattern of the last one.[36]

From the navy's standpoint, strategic bombing could best be carried out by smaller, faster, more evasive aircraft launched from aircraft carriers close to the opponents' shorelines. "In short, the admirals were beginning their longer-term campaign against the theory of strategic bombardment applied by the large high-level bombers, on which the Army Air Forces were at this point striking their claim for separation and would later base their claim for the lion's share of the military budget."[37]

Given how bitter and fundamental the role and mission dispute was, it should come as no surprise that professional naval officers and their civilian secretary continued to fight publicly for what they considered to be the navy's vital interests, regardless of how the president felt. In essence, Truman was cornered. He wanted a National Security Act, but he was up against a determined and politically sophisticated opposition that relied on Article 1 of the Constitution (which delegates power to Congress). As a result, he agreed to several compromises.

First, the 1947 act created a Department of Defense and established an independent air force "coequal with the Army and the Navy."[38] However, the secretary of defense, who was given neither a department nor sufficient staff to support him, would be forced to rely on cooperation and assistance from the services. In addition, the navy's land-based aircraft were protected from an air force takeover. Furthermore, the Joint Chiefs had no control over the budget, nor did they have independent access to the president to discuss strategy and military policy. They had to go through the new secretary of defense. The JCS also did not have a chief to oversee their proceedings and represent the body when dealing with the president. Most important, from the standpoint of the Marines, the Corps "finally came out of unification not only without its World War II combatant functions curtailed but also with those functions enshrined for the first time in statutory language that would presumably protect the Corps against Army campaigns for its emasculation."[39]

Eisenhower recognized that the solution was imperfect, writing, "In that battle the lessons were lost, tradition won. The three service departments were but loosely joined. The entire structure . . . was little more than a weak confederation of sovereign military units. Few powers were vested in the new secretary of defense. All others were reserved to three separated executive departments."[40] The act did nothing to change the nature of the military organizations (except to create the air force), nor did it define the relationship between the service secretaries and the secretary of defense. His lack of authority meant that he would have to call upon his persuasive powers when dealing with military officers who were incredibly protective of their bureaucratic interests. Furthermore, the new arrangement meant that nothing really had changed—the JCS would continue to work on the basis of compromise. As Locher noted, "It left the military side unreformed and gave statutory legitimacy to a dysfunctional, service-dominated JCS."[41]

Those who believed that the new act would help resolve interservice debates and acrimony would be sorely disappointed. Indeed, one could argue that, if anything, the enmity between the air force and navy would only intensify, growing even more bitter as a consequence of their fundamental and deep-seated battle. Fueling the fires were two factors: the question of nuclear weapons and Truman's determination to maintain a balanced budget.

In an effort to iron out differences between the three services, Forrestal, who was now secretary of defense, held a March 1948 meeting in Key West, Florida. He realized that he had to find a way to overcome the bitterness of the past and get the services to agree on a road map for the future. The navy left the meeting believing it had won both the right to keep the Marine Corps and the ability to provide close air support for Corps operations. In addition, the navy was told it could carry out over-water air operations (e.g., antisubmarine warfare). Despite being prohibited from developing a separate strategic air force, the navy was not prohibited from using the atomic bomb. For its part, the air force agreed to give the army airlift assistance and close ground support. Although a settlement apparently had been reached, concern over roles and missions was so deep that interservice disputes would continue to plague the military.

Forrestal also announced at Key West that he and the president had approved the construction of a prototype 80,000-ton flush-deck carrier—the navy's favorite project; the Chiefs agreed with the president's decision. Nevertheless, as Paul Hammond noted, a major disagreement arose over what exactly had been decided. General Hoyt Vandenberg, chief of staff of the air force, would claim that the Key West Conference did not agree to the construction of the carrier. However, Forrestal and the chief of naval operations, Adm. Louis Denfeld, believed that such an agreement had been reached. In fact, Forrestal stated as much in a press conference.[42]

The most contentious issues facing the military, particularly the question of which service would handle nuclear weapons, were swept under the rug at Key West. Nothing was decided about who would have responsibility for the awesome new weapon; as General Bradley noted, "It was the Navy's only hope of getting its hands on atomic bombs."[43]

The air force's dream was the creation of seventy groups of aircraft that would include strategic bombers capable of carrying atomic bombs and dropping them on the USSR. Budgetary problems meant that this kind of an air force could be created only at the expense of another service—in this case, the navy and its desire for a flush-deck carrier. Indeed, Secretary of the Air Force Stuart Symington went so far as to promote the seventy-group structure as the "minimum air defense."[44] Needless to say, Forrestal was furious; this was a recipe for interservice war.

Persistent budgetary restrictions would continue to drive military planning and construction. For example, the navy argued that it needed twelve aircraft carriers, while the army and the air force maintained that the carriers were unnecessary. When Forrestal agreed that the navy would have to scrap some carriers, the navy refused to go along and instead continued its attack on the air force. In fact, a propaganda war was well under way. Toward this end the navy's side employed the language of an internal navy memo that had been leaked to columnist Drew Pearson in May 1948. The memo maintained that the air force could not carry out strategic bombing and that its mission should be limited to defending the continental United States. In a meeting with Forrestal and the JCS, Denfeld stated that "the Navy has honest and sincere misgivings as to the ability of the Air Force successfully to deliver the [atomic] weapon by means of unescorted missions flown by present-day bombers, deep into enemy territory in the face of strong Soviet air defenses, and to drop it on targets whose locations are not accurately known."[45] The belief that only navy carriers were up to the task was not mere propaganda. The navy had formed heavy attack squadrons that could carry heavier bombs than the planes usually deployed. The Skywarrior, the second aircraft for the heavy attack squadrons, required larger aircraft carriers. Consequently, the navy believed not only that it should keep the twelve carriers already in operation, but that it should have a new, larger class of carriers as well.

Toward the end of 1948 Forrestal told the JCS they would have to agree to a budget of $14.4 billion, a figure far below what they believed was necessary. Forrestal insisted that the Chiefs decide how to divide these funds, something they were unable to do. The army agreed to a figure of $4.9 billion, and the air force accepted $5.1 billion. The navy, however, would not agree to $4.4 billion before undertaking a study to determine the budget's overall impact on operations.

Compounding the problem was Forrestal's lack of a clear conception of roles and missions; he did not know which responsibilities should be allocated to the navy, the army, or the air force. Without a detailed division of labor, allocating the budget would prove impossible. Even if Forrestal had a clear idea of what kind of a military he wanted, he could not force his will on the reluctant Chiefs.

Forrestal went to Truman and asked him for more authority. Not surprisingly, the army and the air force supported him. The navy, however, reacted bitterly. "It was his urging of amendments to strengthen the hand of the Secretary of Defense that cost him the remaining support and loyalty of many of his former friends and colleagues in the navy. . . ."[46] Deeply distressed by his inability to get the chiefs to agree, Forrestal gave up the battle on March 2, 1949, when he submitted his resignation to the president. He committed suicide shortly thereafter.

Partly as a result of Forrestal's lobbying and partly because he believed he had to do something on his own, Truman called on Congress on March 5, 1949, to make changes in the National Security Act. Congress responded by creating a chairman for the JCS but did not give him the power to vote in their decision making. As finally approved, "the Chairman's duties included serving as presiding officer of the Joint Chiefs; providing the agenda for JCS meetings and assisting the Joint Chiefs 'to prosecute their business as promptly as practicable;' and informing the Secretary of Defense and the President as appropriate, of issues when the Chiefs could not agree."[47] Thus, the chairman's job would be "to coordinate the work of the group," and toward that end the JCS staff was increased from 100 officers to 210.[48] The navy believed this new arrangement was a disaster. "Top naval officers had constantly opposed the appointment of such a high-level official and had won the first round of the debate back in 1947, when the National Security Act was drafted. Now, however, the Navy was not only stuck with a JCS chairman, it was in danger of losing its vaunted supercarrier."[49]

On the civilian side, the secretary of defense received greater authority. For example, he was allotted a deputy secretary and three assistant secretaries, one of whom was given budgetary responsibility. The secretary of defense now had authority over the service's budgets.

Forrestal was succeeded by Louis Johnson, an acerbic former army officer and under secretary of the army. Appointed by Truman with a mandate to cut the defense budget, he soon asked the JCS for its opinion on the super carrier. The Chiefs voted two-to-one against construction of the ship, arguing that it duplicated the tasks assigned to the air force. Johnson then asked Eisenhower, who at this point was a consultant to the secretary of defense, for his opinion. He also agreed that the carrier should be cancelled. Indeed, he told one of his friends that "our present Navy can scarcely be justified on the basis of the naval strength of any potential enemy."[50] He believed that the super carrier would only provide a super target. Johnson then informed CNO Denfeld on April 23, 1949, five days after the ship's keel was laid, that he was cancelling construction of the carrier.[51] Secretary of the Navy John Sullivan, who was in Texas when he heard the news, hurried back to Washington and submitted his resignation in protest. The admirals were not ready to give up so easily, however. Admiral Radford called Johnson's action the "straw that broke the camel's back."[52]

The Revolt of the Admirals

The Revolt of the Admirals began when Capt. John G. Crommelin released the confidential comments of three admirals. He called reporters to his home on September 10 and told them that an effort was under way to "gradually, but intentionally" eliminate the U.S. Navy.[53] In their comments, the admirals criticized defense management in general and claimed the administration favored the B-36 over naval aviation. They argued that the navy was being castrated—stripped of its offensive power. In response, the House Armed Services Committee initiated hearings that began on August 9. The air force testified in favor of the B-36, using the argument that the plane could fly at 40,000 feet, deliver atomic weapons 4,000 miles away, and, with the help of refueling, return to the base from which it originally departed.

Despite orders to the contrary from the new secretary of the navy, Francis P. Matthews, the admirals went public. The navy's star witness was Admiral Radford, who at that time was stationed in Hawaii as commander in chief of U.S. forces in the Pacific (CINCPAC). He maintained that a number of younger air force pilots had told him that the B-36 was not a good plane. He claimed that the B-36, "under any theory of war, is a bad gamble with national security. Should an enemy force an atomic war upon us, the B-36 would be useless defensively and inadequate offensively."[54] Its only value, he believed, would be in carrying out a policy of saturation bombing, an unlikely tactic in the event of a nuclear war. As a result, he called the aircraft "a billion dollar blunder."[55] His bottom line was that air force strategy simply would not work, and even more damaging, he argued that the air force had misled the American people. Furthermore, he criticized the air force for "endangering national security by neglecting tactical aircraft and fighters."[56] Radford also pointed out that propeller-driven bombers stood little chance against Moscow's jet fighters.

For his part, Admiral Denfeld had told the Senate Armed Services Committee a month after the flush-deck carrier had been cancelled that "the full JCS had approved the carrier, that it was necessary in order to accommodate newer aircraft, and that it was essential for national security."[57] In his later testimony to Congress, he showed his frustration by firing a broadside at both the air force and Secretary Johnson. He blasted the former for the cancellation of the super carrier and the approval of more B-36s; he accused Johnson of violating the spirit of unification, "criticized him for cancelling the supercarrier; and said that 'uniformed and arbitrary decisions' had grievously weakened the Navy."[58]

Not surprisingly, the Marine Corps also took shots at its primary nemesis: the army. The commandant, Gen. Clifton B. Gates, claimed that the army was trying to take over the Marines' amphibious operations and doing its best to eliminate the Corps. He argued for greater Marine representation "in higher councils of the Defense Department," and he "insisted Congress had set up the Marine Corps, not as subsidiary of the Navy comparable to a Navy Bureau or an Army Corps, but as a separate service."[59]

The air force struck back in the person of Secretary of the Air Force Stuart Symington, who turned out to be an excellent witness. Maintaining that the JCS had assigned strategic bombing to the air force, he blasted the navy for undermining national security:

> It was bad enough to have given a possible aggressor technical and operating details of our newest and latest equipment. In my opinion, it is far worse to have opened up to him in such detail the military doctrines of how this country would be defended. We have now given the military leaders of any aggressor nations a further advantage in developing their strategic play by telling them so much about our own.[60]

Bitterness permeated the atmosphere. The navy felt it had been treated badly, while others believed the admirals were completely out of line in terms of civil-military relations. As General Bradley explained,

> Never in our military history has there been anything comparable—not even the Billy Mitchell rebellion in the 1920s. A complete breakdown in discipline occurred. Neither Mathews nor Denfeld could control his subordinates. Most naval officers despised Mathews. Denfeld, in my judgement, had abandoned, or at least grossly neglected, his disciplinary responsibilities in an apparent, and unwise, effort to straddle the fence. Denfeld gave lip service to unification, yet he allowed his admirals to run amok. It was utterly disgraceful.[61]

Bradley also called the admirals " 'Fancy Dans' who won't hit the line with all they have . . . unless they can call the signals."[62]

The president was sick and tired of the whole mess. Congress sided with the air force against the navy, and Truman responded by firing Denfeld for his outspokenness and inability to control subordinates. Denfeld refused the offer of another command and retired. Many years would pass before the bitterness and hatred between the navy and the Marine Corps and the other services evaporated—indeed, many senior naval officers today still remember the way the navy was treated by the army and, especially, the air force during the late forties.

INTEGRATING THE ARMED FORCES

The navy may have been the odd man out insofar as service unification was concerned, but the army would occupy the hot seat on the issue of racial integration. In the army during World War II, almost all Negroes—as they were then called—were organized into segregated units led by a majority of white officers. Believing they had shown themselves to be patriotic and loyal "in the hope that their efforts would be rewarded," the African American troops harbored considerable bitterness toward the "separate but equal" way they had been treated. The army, conversely, had maintained as early as October 1940 that segregation "had proven satisfactorily over a long period of years."[63]

During the latter years of World War II, some African American soldiers were assigned to white units because of manpower shortages. And they apparently performed well: "General George S. Patton approved of the mixed units under his command and told a Negro correspondent that he was thinking about recommending a continuation of mixed units in the Army."[64]

In contrast to the army, the navy, which had the most restrictive racial policies of all the services when the war began, had adopted a policy of integration by the hostilities' end. After 1942, ratings other than messmen were opened up to Negroes, and one of Forrestal's first acts as secretary of the navy was the integration of twenty-five auxiliary ships' crews. On February 27, 1947, the following order was sent to all navy commands: "Effective immediately, all restrictions governing the types of assignments for which Negro naval personnel are eligible are hereby lifted. Henceforth, they shall be eligible for all types of assignments in all ratings in all activities and all ships of the Naval Service. . . . In the utilization of housing, messing and other facilities, no special or unusual provisions will be made for the accommodation of Negroes."[65] The situation in the navy was far from satisfactory, but the fact remained that integration was the order of the day, in contrast to the army, where unit segregation remained the rule.

To better understand the role and status of African Americans in the army, General Marshall appointed a board under the chairmanship of Lt. Gen. Alvan C. Gillem to investigate the situation and report back to him. The so-called Gillem Board convened on October 1, 1945. Board members listened to a variety of witnesses and then issued their findings in April 1946. They argued that African Americans had a right and obligation to serve in the armed forces and stated that the army had an interest in using them efficiently, something the board maintained that the army had not done during the war. The board then recommended that

> Negroes should be integrated in duty assignments in special and overhead units (post housekeeping and administrative jobs); Negroes should form 10 percent of the population; a special staff group should be formed within the War Department to see that Negro policy was implemented; Negro officers should be accorded equal opportunities for

> advancement and assignment; groupings should be made of smaller Negro units with larger white units in "composite organizations"; War Department policy that the use of post recreational facilities must be without regard to race should continue; and commanders of Negro troops should be fully cognizant of the Army's Negro policy.[66]

Although the board made a significant effort to improve the lot of African American enlistees, it did not question the traditional army approach of segregation. Integration would not happen until some point in the future, if ever. In the meantime, the stipulated quota of 10 percent would be a major factor in limiting the number of African Americans serving in the army.

The Gillem Board's findings accorded with the views of the vast majority of army officers, who did only what was absolutely necessary in implementing this policy. As Gen. Jacob L. Devers, who was serving as commanding general of army ground forces, explained in 1946, "We are going to put colored battalions in white divisions. This is purely business—the social side will not be brought into it."[67] Consequently, African Americans' status in the army changed little between 1946 and 1948.

The election of 1948 served as an important turning point. Truman needed the African American vote if he hoped to win the election. Recognizing their widespread dissatisfaction with their treatment by the army, the president gave a speech on February 2, 1948, in which he discussed civil rights. Truman stated that he had "instructed the Secretary of Defense to take steps to have the remaining instances of discrimination in the armed forces eliminated as rapidly as possible. The personnel policies and practices of all the Services in this regard will be made consistent."[68] Although recognizing that change was in the air, the army did everything possible to ignore the president's directive. For example, Secretary of the Army Kenneth C. Royall commented that the army would continue to follow the recommendations of the Gillem Board.

In 1948 the state of New Jersey raised the question of its National Guard units' treatment of African American members. The New Jersey legislature had passed a law that forbade the state from segregating its militia. In response, "the Army General Staff, including Chief of Staff, General Dwight Eisenhower, agreed that federal recognition should be withdrawn from those National Guard units which integrated Negroes into white units."[69] And Eisenhower was not alone. General Bradley, for example, argued that "from the military point of view, I still think that any integration of Negroes . . . in the National Guard will create problems which may have serious consequences in the case of national mobilization of those units."[70] In the end, however, it was the civilian head of the army, Secretary Royall, who led the battle against integration. In his opinion, 1948 was not the right time, as he told a conference of African American leaders.[71]

Enough was enough, or so decided A. Philip Randolph. He announced the creation of the League for Non-Violent Civil Disobedience against Military Segregation. He further informed President Truman that if he did not issue an order ending segregation in the armed forces by August 16, 1948, the date the new conscription law took effect, the league would ask African Americans to refuse to register. Truman got the message; after all, he wanted both to be elected president and to pass selective service legislation.

With these goals in mind, on the eve of a special session of the Republican-held Eightieth Congress, Truman issued Executive Order 9981. The July 26, 1948, order vaguely called for "equality of treatment and opportunity" but did not mention the word "segregation" or its abolishment. Although Secretary Royall expressed support for Truman's order, it immediately became apparent that the army was not on board. For example, the day after the order was issued, General Bradley stated that the army was no place for social experiments. Furthermore, he argued that "desegregation would come to the Army only when it was a fact in the rest of the United States."[72] As far as the army was concerned, equality of treatment and opportunity did not necessitate an end to segregation.

The army soon found itself confronting a new difficulty, however. The draft, reimposed in 1948, was inducting far more African American soldiers of low mental aptitude than a segregated army could absorb. The navy and air force avoided having to deal with the problem by arguing that their greater number of volunteer enlistments and more technical requirements made them less dependent on the draft and much less able to handle individuals with minimal educational skills. Consequently, "thousands of Negroes, less skilled and with little education, were therefore eligible for service in the Army although they were excluded from the Navy and the Air Force."[73] Even racial integration resulted in interservice conflict: it was an army problem.

The army did not give up easily. On December 2, Royall proposed an interservice experiment. A number of units would be created that would contain both combat and service components. Both the navy and the air force were opposed. The air force believed the new arrangement would upset an already functioning system of racial integration, while the navy felt that its policy of gradually moving toward greater integration worked well and rested "on a sound and permanent basis without concomitant problems of morale and discipline."[74] Not only was Royall's proposal dead on delivery, it had been conceived as a stalling tactic to hold off integration as long as possible.

Faced with continuing obstacles to bringing about integration, the president asked the Fahy Committee (the Committee on Equality of Treatment and Opportunity in the Armed Forces) to examine the issue and attempt to devise a policy for all of the services. The committee held its first meeting on January 13, 1949, and discovered at an early stage that the key problem was convincing the army of the practical need for integration. Many army officials were personally convinced African Americans had performed poorly in the last two wars, a belief that disqualified them from participating in the army's current missions. When General Bradley was asked if a 15-percent African American army would be less efficient, he replied, "[F]rom our experience in the past I think the time might come when it wouldn't, but the average educational standards of these men would not be up to the average of the white soldier. In modern combat a man is thrown very much on his own initiative."[75] Furthermore, the high percentage of southerners in the army heightened concern that African Americans would not be accepted. How would white soldiers react if given orders by nonwhite officers? As far as the other two services were concerned, navy officers not only argued that integration improved the navy's combat efficiency, they openly admitted problems with the perennial problem of the steward's rating, largely an African American position (African Americans represented two-thirds of the stewards but only five of the forty-five thousand active-duty officers).[76] The air force held a similar position, which, like the navy's, impressed the Fahy Committee.

Still, the army resisted on the grounds of combat efficiency and the best use of available manpower. Furthermore, the army refused to accept claims of discrimination against African Americans. True, they were in separate units, but the army maintained that they had equal opportunities and equal facilities. In fact, some argued that given the soldiers' poor educational status, segregation "has been the thing that has given the Negro far greater opportunity than any business profession in the United States can point to."[77]

In response to the Fahy Committee's study, Secretary Johnson issued an order declaring that all Department of Defense personnel would be treated equally and considered "on the basis of individual merit and ability for enlistment, attendance at schools, promotion, and assignment. . . . "[78] Because the Department of the Army was subordinate to the secretary of defense, his decree ended the formal policy of segregation. Though still the de facto practice in many areas, segregation no longer had a legal justification.

Nevertheless, the army continued to fight—in spite of the orders that had been issued by Truman and Johnson. For example, Royall repeated his claim that the army provided equal opportunity, even though the Fahy Committee had found otherwise. The committee issued a statement that the Gillem Board's racial quota of 10 percent should be abandoned in favor of a system based on aptitude and qualifications. Toward this end, the committee came out against all racial considerations, regardless of whether they related to schools, promotions, or assignments.

Finally, the new secretary of the army, Gordon Gray, went to the president with the following proposal. The army would drop its racial quota under one condition: "If, as a result of a fair trial of this new system, there ensues a disproportionate balance of racial strength in the Army, it is my understanding that I have your authority to return to a system which will, in effect, control enlistments by race."[79] Truman agreed, and an order opening recruitment to all races (without a quota) was sent out on March 27, 1950.

Following his leadership style, Truman looked to his subordinates to implement the new policy. He knew well that it would meet with considerable resistance, but in his mind, that was an issue for the Department of Defense, not the White House. "In effect, the President was guaranteeing the services the freedom to put their own houses in order."[80]

The real catalyst for racial integration was not governmental policy, but the Korean War. The army doubled in size within five months of the outbreak of hostilities. By June 1951 the army numbered 1.6 million, with 230,000 men serving in Korea in the Eighth Army. Realistically, quotas and segregation would keep the army from maintaining this rapidly expanding force. African American recruits flooded army training installations; indeed, predicting the number of each race that would arrive was impossible. "By April 1951, black units throughout the Army were reporting large overstrengths, some as much as 60 percent over their authorized organizational tables."[81] Faced with the need to employ soldiers, many commanders did not wait for an official change in policy. Rather, they started assigning desperately needed replacements to units without regard to race.

The policy of segregation in the Far East met its decisive end when General Matthew Ridgway took over from General MacArthur. As Ridgway told it, Gen. William Kean approached him, arguing "that both from a human and a military point of view it was wholly inefficient, not to say improper to segregate soldiers in this way." Ridgway discussed the issue with Secretary of Defense Marshall and made a formal request to the army staff to fully integrate units in Korea. "The plan was ultimately approved and I promptly executed it in my theater. After that, the entire United States Army adopted this long-overdue reform, with all the beneficial results we had foreseen—in morale as well as in civilian acceptance."[82] The army had come around, slowly to be sure and primarily out of necessity. One suspects that the army would have eventually embraced integration on its own, but the process probably would have taken a few more years or a more assertive secretary of defense had it not been for the Korean War.

MACARTHUR AND THE KOREAN WAR

The North Korean attack on the South was as much a surprise to Gen. Douglas MacArthur as it was to President Truman. In 1948 the Joint Chiefs sent Truman a memorandum recommending that "the United States should not become so irrevocably involved in the Korean situation that an action taken by any faction in Korea or by any other power in Korea could be considered a 'casus belli' for the United States."[83] Their reasoning was simple—the United States was moving into the cold war, and the Chiefs, like most observers, believed that any war with the Communists would develop into a world war. If that happened, American forces would be more badly needed elsewhere, namely in Europe. MacArthur, who was commander in chief of U.S. Far Eastern Forces, agreed. As a consequence, in 1948 the State Department assumed responsibility for Korea, and that included supervision of Washington's military advisors, who were all that remained after the withdrawal of U.S. forces from Korea in the summer of 1949.

Unfortunately, U.S. military forces were in horrible condition. Truman was pushing the Chiefs to tighten the defense budget, and Congress agreed with him. To make matters worse, senior military officers perceived that Secretary of Defense Johnson was prepared not only to scrap the navy's super carrier, but to make widespread cuts as well. He was determined to eliminate $2 billion from the defense budget up until to the day the North Koreans attacked in 1950. " 'On the twenty-fifth of June, five days before the end of the fiscal year, he did some horrible things,' according to General Lemnitzer. 'He was closing hospitals, closing stations, cutting back the forces, stretching out procurement programs and so forth. And he got his two billion dollars.' "[84]

In fact, the soldiers who had to fight the war Johnson had "unprepared" them for rejoiced when he was fired a short time later. An artillery officer on a ship bound for Korea recalled later that

> cheers broke out all over the ship. Soldiers slapped each other on the back and clapped. . . . We hated Louis Johnson. We hated that man with the hatred of a blood feud. We damned him day and night. We damned anyone anywhere who would not damn him. He had cut the Army to the bone and then scraped the bone to the quick. . . . To us a simple

> proposition presented itself. We were apt to get killed—because that man cut our strength so much.[85]

Not all the blame lay with Johnson, however. On January 12, 1950, Dean Acheson had given a National Press Club speech in which he repeated what MacArthur had noted a year previously. He stated that Washington's "defensive perimeter runs along the Aleutians to Japan and then goes to the Ryukus. . . . [It] runs from the Ryukus to the Philippine Islands. . . . So far as the military security of other areas in the Pacific is concerned, it must be clear that no person can guarantee those areas against attack."[86] Such public statements that South Korea was essentially outside America's defensive perimeter, not to mention the deplorable state of the U.S. Army and the wretched condition of the South Korea military (which then was more of a police force than an army), led Stalin to believe that the Americans would not resist North Korean aggression. The Soviet leader thus gave the North the green light.

When the North Koreans attacked on June 25, Truman was in Independence, Missouri. Acheson telephoned the president, informed him of what happened, and suggested that the United States ask for a special meeting of the United Nations Security Council. Truman decided that the United States would go to war. "I felt certain that if South Korea was allowed to fall, Communist leaders would be emboldened to override nations closer to their own shores. . . . If this was allowed to go unchallenged, it would mean a third world war."[87] Fortunately for the United States, the USSR was boycotting the UN for refusing to seat the People's Republic of China. As a result, the UN voted to support the use of military force to stop the North Koreans.

The Soviet-trained and -equipped North Koreans were slicing through the South Koreans like a hot knife through butter. Their success stemmed partly from an earlier U.S. decision to withhold modern military weapons from the South Koreans: "in order to avoid provocations of the Communists we were careful to keep out of South Korean hands any weapons that would encourage them to make good their frequently voided threat to attack north."[88] John Foster Dulles was visiting MacArthur at the time and found him so despondent that he told the president that he should withdraw him then and there. However, Truman, ever the politician, felt he had no alternative but to stick with MacArthur, a military hero. He told Dulles that because the general was "involved politically in this country . . . he could not recall MacArthur without causing a tremendous reaction."[89]

As early as June 25 the Joint Chiefs authorized the use of both U.S. air and naval power. One high-ranking officer boasted, "Turn the Air Force loose and we'll stop those tanks."[90] The problem, however, was that instead of stopping all of the North Korean tanks, they only managed to destroy perhaps two or three out of a column of sixty. MacArthur visited Korea on June 29 and, seeing the magnitude of the disaster, ordered bombing north of the thirty-eight parallel (on his own authority) and decided that major assistance by the United States was necessary. He warned, "The Korean Army is entirely incapable of counter action, and there is grave danger of a further breakthrough. . . . The only assurance for the holding of the present line, and the ability to regain later the lost ground, is through the introduction of U.S. ground combat forces into the Korean battle area."[91] Truman responded at 0500 on June 30 by deciding to send in ground troops, at first believing that one reinforced battalion would be sufficient. Although most of the Chiefs agreed, Bradley was worried that the war was a no-win proposition and famously commented that "Korea is the wrong war, at the wrong time, in the wrong place."[92] Wrong or not, it was war.

On June 27, Chiang Kai-shek offered to send 33,000 Nationalist Chinese combat troops to Korea. An elated MacArthur raised the issue with Washington. At first, Truman was tempted to accept the offer, but the JCS made clear that these forces would require reequipping and training; besides, as Secretary of State Dean Acheson noted, their use would also raise a number of political questions, most obviously the United States' continued support at the UN.[93] MacArthur was selected to be commanding general of UN forces, "at the recommendation of the Joint Chiefs of Staff."[94]

In spite of the UN resolution to halt the North's aggression, the situation in Korea was going from bad to worse. American troops were holding on by their fingernails to an enclave known as the Pusan perimeter. Many feared that U.S. troops would soon be thrown into the sea. But it was at this point that MacArthur pulled what many consider to have been one of the most impressive military maneuvers of the twentieth century.

Faced with an enemy whose lines of communication were clearly overextended, MacArthur came up with the idea of outflanking the North Koreans by an amphibious assault on the city of Inchon, 150 miles north of Pusan, near Seoul on the Yellow Sea. If successfully carried out, the operation would provide an opportunity to hit the enemy hard far in the rear, disrupt if not destroy his supply lines, and force him to fight a war on two fronts. On July 7 MacArthur communicated his plan to the JCS. He argued that a counteroffensive was the last thing the enemy expected.

While the North Koreans would have been surprised to know that MacArthur was considering such a daring operation, the Joint Chiefs were astounded. "I was simply too astonished at the mention of Inchon, where one narrow channel was easily blocked and the high tides necessary to bring assault waves ashore occurred only a few times a month."[95] The navy expressed its concerns, as did the army, which worried that the operation could turn into another Anzio. As a result, the JCS sent Gen. J. Lawton Collins, the army's chief of staff, and Adm. Forest Sherman, the chief of naval operations, to attempt to talk MacArthur out of what one author called a "harebrained scheme."[96] The meeting took place from August 6 to 8. According to General Ridgway, it "was a personal triumph for MacArthur."[97] He made a two-and-a-half hour presentation outlining his master plan for Korea. "When he had finished he had won us all over to his views. I know that after this brilliant exposition, and after I had studied the plans for Operation Chromite, the Inchon landing, my own doubts were largely dissolved."[98] In the end, the JCS went to President Truman, obtained his approval, and told MacArthur to proceed, even though some of its members continued to have serious doubts. "Even Sherman had second thoughts. Within twenty-four hours of his Tokyo briefing, he confided in Collins: 'I wish I had that man's optimism.' Collins concurred but went even further, calling the landing a '500 to 1 shot.' "[99]

Armed with Washington's approval, MacArthur's troops landed on September 17 and won an overwhelming victory. The North Koreans were on the run. By September 27 the UN forces had recaptured the South Korean capital of Seoul, which MacArthur handed over to Syngman Rhee, the South's erstwhile president. The American general had been vindicated in much the same way that Hitler had in World War II when he attacked Czechoslovakia despite his generals' warnings and won an overwhelming victory. The only negative aspect of the operation was that approximately 40,000 North Koreans escaped to the North. Still, the North Korean Army had been destroyed and would never again be considered a serious military threat throughout the remainder of the war.

The question arose of what to do next. Should the American and South Korean armies continue on to the Yalu River, thereby ousting the Communists from Korea? MacArthur made clear his intentions: on July 13 he told Collins that he was out to destroy all of North Korea. Subsequently, Truman informed MacArthur on September 15 that he "was to conduct the necessary military operations either to force the North Koreans behind the 38th Parallel or to destroy their forces."[100] However, the president placed one important restriction on MacArthur that would create major conflict between the two men—cease ground operations if either the Soviet or Communist Chinese enter the fray. On September 29, General Marshall sent MacArthur a cable he would soon regret. It stated: "We want you to feel unhampered strategically and tactically to proceed north of the 38th parallel."[101] By October 9 U.S.

forces had crossed the thirty-eighth parallel. Republican senator William Knowland politicized the issue by demanding a total military defeat as well as a total political settlement. Only in this manner would the American people be able to accept the sacrifices the war had demanded.

MacArthur intended to pursue the North Koreans and liberate the rest of the peninsula. However, much to his displeasure, the JCS had sent him a message on September 27, ordering him to "submit your plan for future operations north of the 38th parallel to the JCS for approval."[102] MacArthur considered these instructions nothing less than a case of unwarranted political interference in his command. He was the commander on the scene, and the army's leaders had enjoyed a long tradition of not being told by Washington how to fight their wars. In any case, the Chiefs were well aware that MacArthur would undoubtedly interpret whatever orders he received "liberally, not literally." Furthermore, Ridgway believed that MacArthur's tendency would always be to widen the war.[103]

Despite Washington's interference, MacArthur believed that his forces would prevail. Indeed, "complete victory seemed now in view—a golden apple that would handsomely symbolize the crowning effort of a brilliant military career. Once in reach of this prize, MacArthur would not allow himself to be delayed or admonished. Instead, he plunged northward in pursuit of a vanishing enemy, and changed his plans from week to week to accelerate the advance, without regard for dark hints of possible danger."[104] MacArthur strongly opposed the imposition of any restrictions by Washington. For example, he was told he could not pursue enemy aircraft into Chinese airspace (which thus became a sanctuary) and that he could not bomb hydroelectric plants on the Chinese border. He was also forbidden to bomb the city of Racin on the Soviet border.

Truman, feeling the heat of attacks from the far right, decided to meet privately with MacArthur. A meeting would show that the president and the general were on the same wavelength, which, if nothing else, would help Truman win votes for the upcoming midterm election. On October 15, 1950, the president and his senior commander met on Wake Island with no special agenda. MacArthur used the opportunity to assure the president that the Chinese would *not* intervene and that U.S. troops could well be home by Thanksgiving.[105]

The previous day, however, Chinese "volunteers" had begun to move en masse across the North Korean border undetected. On October 19, MacArthur launched a major offensive, taking Pyongyang. On October 24, he ordered his subordinates to "drive forward with all speed and full utilization of their forces."[106] The Chiefs reacted by informing MacArthur that he was violating

President Truman meets with General Douglas MacArthur on Wake Island. (Harry S. Truman Library)

instructions clearly stating that only Korean forces could approach the Chinese border. MacArthur pointed to Marshall's September 29 message that he should feel unhampered in his operations. General Collins was furious. He told Bradley that MacArthur's actions were nothing less than a violation of his orders. "Bradley agreed: MacArthur was stretching the limits of his responsibility; he was playing with politics and taking actions designed to bring China into the war."[107] Nevertheless, the Chiefs did nothing. They were dealing with a saint, a national hero, a winner, and everyone was afraid of moving against him.

Then the Chinese struck. On October 25, massive numbers of well-trained and -led Communist Chinese troops defeated several major South Korean units. Worried by reports of Chinese troops in Korea, the JCS asked MacArthur for his evaluation. On November 4 he downplayed the Chinese presence, suggesting that they were probably sent there to protect what was left of the North Korean state. His optimistic analysis contributed to allegations that he did nothing to prepare for a possible Chinese intervention. One could even argue that he provoked their involvement.[108] One of the most bitter comments about MacArthur's lack of military leadership in this context came from a Marine who was part of the division trapped at the Chosin Reservoir.

> [The] 1st Marine Division was pushed up onto the Chosin plateau at the onset of winter in the face of incontrovertible evidence that China had entered the war in force and that the original parameters of the conflict no longer applied. Chosin was not a gamble; it was criminal stupidity. You do not sacrifice your elite force without overpowering justification. What purpose was served by stringing out 1st Marine Division in the mountains of North Korea in winter?[109]

On November 6 MacArthur ordered air force lieutenant general E. G. Stratemeyer to take out Yalu River bridges that the Chinese used to send supplies and troops into Korea. Stratemeyer advised the Pentagon of the order. The Chiefs met and reaffirmed their prohibition of military action against the Yalu bridges. MacArthur was furious. He warned that failure to bomb these spans would be a "calamity" and that this inaction would threaten the "destruction of the forces under my command."[110] Truman overruled the Joint Chiefs and authorized MacArthur to bomb *only* the Korean halves of the bridges (almost a military impossibility). In any case, the idea of bombing the bridges was by then a useless idea, as the Yalu had frozen and the Chinese were crossing on the ice.

On November 29, MacArthur again repeated his request for Washington to accept Chiang's offer of thirty-three thousand Nationalist Chinese troops. Truman told the JCS to tell MacArthur that the matter was still under study. By December 3, MacArthur was describing the situation facing the Eighth Army as "increasingly critical." He argued that his ability to stop the Chinese was being hampered by both the terrain and the restrictions placed on him by Washington. At this point, General Ridgway asked General Vandenberg, the air force's chief of staff, why the JCS did not simply tell MacArthur what to do. "Vandenberg responded, 'What good would that do? He wouldn't obey orders. What can we do?' " To that comment, Ridgway replied, "You can relieve any commander who won't obey orders, can't you?"[111]

Defiance of Washington's military orders was not MacArthur's only sin. On August 17 he sent to the Veterans of Foreign Wars a message stating that "with Formosa, United States air power could dominate 'every Asiatic port from Vladivostok to Singapore.' "[112] Truman was furious, although MacArthur later apologized and assured him that it would not happen again. But it did.

> On November 28 he sent a message to Ray Henle of the *Three-Star Extra* news broadcast explaining his position on the thirtieth, another to Arthur Krock of the *New York Times* justifying his march north; and on December 1 he gave an interview to *U.S. News and World Report* in which he said that orders forbidding him to strike at Communist forces across the Manchurian border had put UN forces under "an enormous handicap, without precedent in military history." Others followed to the United Press, International News Service, the *London Daily Mail* and the Tokyo press corps.[113]

Not surprisingly, MacArthur's continued discussions with the press further infuriated Truman. In response, he ordered a moratorium on government speeches on foreign or military affairs, and "he had Secretary Marshall and me [Dean Acheson] direct, on presidential authority, that military commanders and diplomatic representatives abroad must cease 'direct communication on military or foreign policy with newspapers, magazines or other publicity in the United States.' "[114] In his memoirs, Truman admitted that "I should have relieved [MacArthur] then and there."[115]

On December 29, the JCS sent MacArthur a new set of instructions informing him that he would not receive any more troops and would instead have to make do with those he had. The United States had no intention of expanding this limited war into one with far greater consequences: "Therefore . . . your directive now is to defend in successive positions, subject to safety of your troops as your primary consideration, inflicting as much damage to hostile forces in Korea as is possible."[116] MacArthur, interpreting Washington's order as "a loss of the 'will to win' in Korea," remarked that "President Truman's resolute determination to free and unify that threatened land had now deteriorated almost into defeatism."[117]

Needless to say, MacArthur's message was not well received in Washington. On January 9, the JCS again rejected MacArthur's suggestion of a retaliatory campaign against China and his plan to use Nationalist Chinese troops against China. Only if U.S. forces were attacked outside of Korea would MacArthur be allowed to proceed with the two options. He sent back an especially gloomy reply. He claimed that morale was low because of shameful propaganda and further stated that battle efficiency would be severely impaired "unless the political basis upon which they are to trade life for time is clearly delineated, fully understood and so impelling that the hazards of battle are accepted cheerfully."[118] Simply put, he was trying to force Washington to change policy by unleashing him from the restrictions. The effect, however, was an almost complete rupture of relations between MacArthur and the Joint Chiefs.

By the end of February Truman believed that MacArthur's effort to reconquer North Korea was leading nowhere. The Chinese had unlimited reserves of manpower. MacArthur should have understood the writing on the wall, but he did not. He was still planning for a campaign to throw the Chinese out of North Korea.

> MacArthur intended to first regain the Seoul line as a base of operations. He would then destroy the enemy's rear by massive air strikes along the top of North Korea. If still not permitted to bomb enemy reinforcements in Manchuria, as he anticipated, MacArthur intended to lay vast fields of radioactive wastes across all major enemy supply lines in North Korea. Then using American and Nationalist Chinese reinforcements, he would launch simultaneous airborne and amphibious strikes against both the east and west coasts of North Korea.[119]

MacArthur then decided that his only hope of influencing policy was to go public. On March 15, in open defiance of the president's December 6 order, he gave an interview to Hugh Bailie, the president of United Press. In the interview he criticized the decision to stop the resurgent Eighth Army's advance at the thirty-eighth parallel, and he condemned any policy less than the reunification of Korea. Then, on March 24, he released what he called his "Military Appraisal" of the situation in Korea. In it, he argued that the new peace approach being planned—which he had been informed of by the JCS—was unnecessary. It would undermine Washington's efforts to get peace negotiations started with the Chinese and North Koreans. Once again, Truman was livid: "By this act, MacArthur left me no choice—I could no longer tolerate his insubordination."[120]

The final straw was MacArthur's letter to Joe Martin, the House Republican leader. On February 12 Martin had accused the administration of preventing the Chinese Nationalists from invading China, saying, "There is good reason to believe that General MacArthur favours such an operation."[121] Martin then wrote to MacArthur soliciting his views. MacArthur responded by stating he believed in "meeting force with maximum counter-force." He also came out in favor of Martin's suggestion that the Chinese Nationalists should be allowed to open a second front in Asia and concluded with his now-famous statement "There is no substitute for victory."[122] On April 5, 1951, Martin made MacArthur's letter public. The letter "showed that the general was not only in disagreement with the policy of the government but was challenging this policy in open insubordination to his Commander in Chief."[123]

On April 6, Truman asked Marshall for the views of the Joint Chiefs of Staff with regard to relieving MacArthur. Marshall met on April 9 with the Chiefs, who were unanimous in recommending the immediate relief of General MacArthur from his command. For his part, Bradley stated that after reading the Pentagon files, he came to the conclusion that MacArthur should have been fired two years before. As far as the other chiefs were concerned, General Bradley listed three reasons for recommending that MacArthur be fired: "First, the general's official communications and public statements indicated a lack of sympathy with the limited war policy in Korea; second, MacArthur had violated the President's directive relative to clearly public statements; third, The Joint Chiefs of staff, have felt and feel now that the military *must be controlled by civilian authority in this country.*"[124] Other military officers concurred. Eisenhower said that he believed Truman was justified in firing the general: "You know when you put on a uniform you impose certain restrictions on yourself."[125] Matthew Ridgway, despite his considerable respect for MacArthur and his military abilities, was especially critical of the controversial general's attempt to legitimize his actions by claiming that soldiers take an oath to the Constitution and not to a particular individual or policy:

> The concept of duty, in military service, has been elevated to extreme importance, and obedience to properly constituted authority is primal. No man in uniform, be he private or five-star general, may decide for himself whether an order is consonant with his personal views. While the loyalty he owes his superiors is reciprocated with equal force in the loyalty owed him from above, the authority of his superiors is not open to question.[126]

Ridgway succeeded MacArthur and drove the Chinese out of South Korea.

After his relief and retirement, the soldier who defied his commander in chief more openly than any of his successors criticized Truman in testimony before Congress, but then dropped out of view—insofar as wearing a uniform and exercising command were concerned. As he said, echoing an old army ballad, "Old soldiers never die, they just fade away."

CONCLUSION

Presidential Leadership Style

Truman's biggest problem in dealing with the military was that contrary to his popular image, he was both weak and indecisive. Following in the footsteps of FDR would be a challenge for anyone, but Truman failed to face down his opponents. Rather than forcing his will on reluctant admirals and generals, he relied on his subordinates to enact policy.

The navy openly defied the president on the issue of service unification, yet he did little until he fired Admiral Denfeld toward the end of 1949. He did not want to get in the middle of a service battle over roles and missions, although he clearly sided more with the army than the navy and Marine Corps. If nothing else, Truman's leadership style convinced senior officers that they were free to openly criticize the president's actions. By doing so, they risked retribution, but only if they lost.

One can understand Truman's concern with domestic politics, but as far as the Chiefs were concerned, he was too hesitant in dealing with racial integration. Thus the conflict between the president and the army, navy, and air force was longer and more intense than it would have been if he had dismissed Secretary of the Army Royall and made clear to his successor that he wanted immediate change. Secretary of Defense Forrestal was on board, but Royall, one of Truman's key civilian subordinates, did everything possible to undermine efforts to integrate the army. Interestingly, an outside group, the Fahy Committee, did the most to move matters forward. Furthermore, the new secretary of the army, Gordon Gray, came to the president and agreed to the idea of integration, "on one condition": if a disproportionate racial imbalance developed in the military, Truman would permit him to cancel the experiment. Truman agreed. The idea of any service going to the president and agreeing to carry out his instructions "on one condition" was unheard of. One cannot help but wonder whether the plan would have been fully implemented if it were not for the Korean War.

The issue of MacArthur's insubordination probably best represents Truman's indecisive approach to dealing with the military. Although the president left operational matters in the military's hands, he involved himself on the strategic level and reviewed all major military decisions. However, when confronted with the problem of MacArthur, he followed the chain of command, relying primarily on the JCS. Even when Truman met directly with MacArthur at Wake Island, the latter won a psychological victory; the president was forced to travel farther than the general, who said he could not be away from the war long enough to travel to the continental United States.

MacArthur's behavior became increasingly outrageous. When the Communist Chinese intervened, he disobeyed his orders by sending U.S. forces to the Chinese border. Then he tried to get the air force to bomb bridges on the Yalu, in defiance of specific orders. MacArthur also publicly criticized Truman's policies on numerous occasions. He finally became involved in domestic politics in the United States, a transgression that forced Truman's hand. Although Dean Acheson was correct when he told Truman that "if you relieve MacArthur . . . you will have the biggest fight of your administration," the fact was that the Chiefs thought he should have done so much earlier.[127] One can empathize with Truman's hesitation in taking on a living icon, but from the military's perspective, his failure to dismiss MacArthur gave the impression that he was weak.

Changes in Service/Military Culture?

A sea change occurred in service/military culture under Truman. Prior to Truman, most officers believed that allegiance to the president was their overriding concern. They dealt with Congress as necessary, but their first loyalty in the political process was to the executive. This aspect of their culture changed dramatically during Truman's administration. When senior military leaders felt attacked, they turned to their allies on the Hill to help override what they perceived to be a weak president. One can decry this action, but like it or not, a new, powerful player had entered the civil-military arena in Washington. From this point on, the individual services, and even the military as a whole, would enlist the aid of Congress in an effort to protect their bureaucratic prerogatives. In addition, the military began to employ the media and the infamous "anonymous leak" as admirals attempted to defend the navy's position against the army and air force. No longer a bilateral affair between the president and the military, civil-military relations had evolved into a three-way interaction that would make such relations stormier and more difficult to control. Henceforth, the president would have greater difficulty when trying to change military culture.

The National Security Act that was passed and amended during Truman's tenure began the long, slow, and often difficult process of bringing the services together. In that sense, it marked a major move away from a totally "service" culture toward a more "military" or joint one.

4

THE MILITARY AND DWIGHT EISENHOWER

I think the tendency, which was manifest many times during my tenure as Chief of Staff, of civilian secretaries making decisions on a basis of political considerations constitutes a danger to this country.
—*General Matthew Ridgway*

Eisenhower had a difficult relationship with the military. Although many senior officers respected him both as president of the United States and as a former military officer, his presidency did not benefit their cause as they had anticipated. Indeed, during most of his tenure, the commander in chief and his senior subordinates fought over the budget and over roles and missions. The military officers, more than ready to criticize him in public as well as in private, made extensive use of their allies on the Hill. By the end of Eisenhower's administration, the military had become very adept at using the media and leaks for its own purpose.

When Eisenhower changed senior military officers in an effort to find individuals with whom he could work more easily, he discovered much to his chagrin that the new men considered themselves officers of the army, navy, Marines, and air force and were prepared to protect their service cultures at all costs, even if it meant going head to head with the president.

EISENHOWER'S LEADERSHIP STYLE

Not surprisingly, Eisenhower's leadership style owed much to his many years in the army. Understanding bureaucratic politics all too well, he realized that if he did not take appropriate steps, he ran the danger of being drawn into every inter-bureaucratic dispute in the U.S. government. To avoid this pitfall, he adopted two related approaches.

First, like Truman, Eisenhower believed in formal lines of authority. He expected his subordinates to address and solve problems on their own. Toward this end, he relied heavily on the National Security Council on a regular basis. To quote Fred Greenstein, "Eisenhower viewed the NSC as a mechanism for engaging his national security team in sharply focused debate on issues bearing on the nation's global policies."[1] He expected NSC members to hash out most of their differences and leave the more difficult and seemingly intractable issues for him to decide. Most often, he made such decisions at his regularly scheduled weekly NSC meetings. And unlike some presidents, he welcomed different points of view. According to Robert Cutler, his NSC advisor at the time, " 'nothing was to be swept under the rug or compromised or glossed over.' Cutler also noted that the NSC meetings were lively: 'The President likes a good debate. . . . He wished to hear frank assertions of differing views, if they existed; for from such interchanges might emerge a resolution which reasonable men could support.' "[2] If nothing else, Eisenhower used the NSC as a tool to "identify policy disagreements so that they could be resolved at higher levels and to monitor implementation of policy decisions."[3] The kind of debate that took place in the NSC was so important to him that he reportedly told Kennedy that his NSC meetings were the most important weekly meetings he held in the White House.[4] The bottom line was that Eisenhower did not like yes-men. However, as in the military, he expected dissent to take place in private, behind closed doors, not in public.

Eisenhower also met weekly with his cabinet, in contrast with some of his successors. He wanted his department heads to know that he was interested in what transpired in their areas of responsibility. At the same time, the meetings provided him with an opportunity to hear what the various secretaries had to say about important issues of the day. George and Stern referred to this arrangement as a modified "formalistic" model, a leadership style that "encompassed advocacy and disagreement at lower levels of the policy making system, even though he wanted subordinates eventually to achieve agreement, if possible, on recommendations for his consideration."[5]

Second, Eisenhower streamlined the bureaucracy. He wanted a clear chain of command that "ran from the president through a chief of staff who reported directly to him to the rest of the president's team, and back again."[6] Indeed, he was the first to have a chief of staff to funnel information to the executive.[7] This arrangement permitted him to remain "above politics," and it relieved him of "minor burdens, allowing him to concentrate on major issues. "[8] In this sense, the structure of the White House, and the government in general, was more hierarchical and formal than it had been under Roosevelt.

President Dwight Eisenhower with Admiral Arthur W. Radford, chairman of the Joint Chiefs of Staff. (Dwight D. Eisenhower Library)

Despite the clear structure, Eisenhower believed that he should primarily work behind the scenes, casting himself in a role that one presidential scholar has called the "hidden hand."[9] To the greatest extent possible, "He desired to set general policy and then work behind the scenes to build political support for it."[10] To achieve his goals Eisenhower favored persuasion over confrontation, an approach that was most evident in his handling of the Joe McCarthy affair; he believed that a public battle with the senator from Wisconsin would only hurt the presidency, telling his brother on one occasion, "I will not get into a pissing contest with a skunk."[11] Instead, he worked with congressional allies and the media to undermine McCarthy's reputation. Eisenhower also believed that his subordinates should and must obey the instructions of the country's leader. After all, he was the president. However, in contrast to several of his successors, he believed in the military axiom "Praise in public, criticize privately." Eisenhower's desire to work behind the scenes should not be exaggerated. He was not afraid of a fight, and he learned that he would have to confront the services on several occasions when persuasion did not work.

Eisenhower also did not believe that domestic and international/security affairs matters could be separated. They were intimately tied together. This was especially evident in his belief in the intimate relationship between economics and military affairs: "[O]ur military strength and our economic strength are truly one—neither can sensibly be purchased at the price of destroying the other."[12] Thus, the government's task was to "discover a reasonable and respectable posture of defense . . . without bankrupting the nation."[13] The basis of a sound military was a sound economy, and the key to a sound economy was a sound budget. Eisenhower was fully aware he would face obstacles in simultaneously addressing military strength and economic vitality: conflict was inevitable. Indeed, he noted the inherent difficulties in tying these two elements together as early as 1948, when he testified before Congress about the need to reconcile the "conflict" between the "mission of the armed forces" and the "economic capacity of the Nation."[14]

Eisenhower and the Military

Many of the country's general and admirals were excited when Eisenhower won the election. Now the Oval Office would be occupied by one of their own, a man who understood far better than a civilian the importance of national security to the country's survival. Such knowledge was especially important in light of what they saw as the rising Soviet threat. The casualties the United States suffered in the opening days of the Korean War demonstrated very clearly (or so they believed) that the United States could not again ignore its military as it had in the immediate aftermath of World War II.

The problem, however, was that the generals and admirals did not agree with Eisenhower's thinking on the relationship between the defense budget and economic growth. He believed that the only way the country could successfully achieve a healthy military and robust economy was through a long-term strategy, not a quick fix. In his mind, a temporary solution would only bankrupt the nation, because every time a crisis arose, the country would have to allocate more and more money to the armed forces, which would result in increasingly larger deficits. Eisenhower would have to devise what his spokesmen would call the "Great Equation."[15]

The New Secretary of Defense

Charles E. Wilson, Eisenhower's secretary of defense, faced two major problems: First, he was working for a president who knew and understood the Pentagon like few others. Second, he was dealing with a group of admirals and generals who had cut their military teeth while fighting World War II or Korea, and from the beginning they did not take this laid-back former president of General Motors seriously. They knew that Wilson possessed little understanding of military affairs, especially the kinds of problems that they would face when Eisenhower decided to cut the military budget.

Given his leadership style, Eisenhower preferred not to deal directly with the military—that was Wilson's job. Recognizing Wilson's lack of a military background, Eisenhower tried to buttress the secretary's position when he reorganized the Pentagon on July 1, 1953. Wilson's authority was strengthened, as the number of assistant secretaries increased from three to nine. In a bow to the military, the president also gave the chairman of the Joint Chiefs the authority to manage the joint staff and approve the selection of those who were to serve on it. Eisenhower wanted the chairman to recruit officers who would focus not just on the interests of their own service, but on "national planning for the overall common defense."[16] Despite the added authority, Eisenhower would soon decide that Wilson was not forceful enough as a manager or a leader. Consequently, in contrast to other departments whose leaders were given considerable leeway in solving problems, Eisenhower took a special interest in the Department of Defense. Furthermore, while he did not want to micromanage the Pentagon, the more he watched Wilson operate, the more he became convinced that he had to involve himself directly. "The Eisenhower Library files are replete with presidential directives specifying a particular Defense Department policy or procedure. These directives were not, as was usually the case even when Eisenhower meant to tell a subordinate what to do, worded as suggestions. They were orders."[17] This inevitably brought the president into direct contact—and often conflict—with the country's senior officers.

Eisenhower and the Chiefs

Eisenhower understood the Chiefs very well. He had known them during World War II, and he was convinced that he had to do something with them if he hoped to have his policies enacted. When he came into office it was like old times, as many of the Chiefs had worked under him. He assumed that he would be able to work with them; they knew and understood him, and he knew their needs. Unfortunately, the relationship would turn out to be a rocky one from Eisenhower's perspective.

THE MILITARY BUDGET

When Eisenhower won the 1952 election, the United States was still mired in Korea, fighting a war that appeared to be going nowhere. True to his election promise, on November 29, 1952, he flew to Korea on a fact-finding mission of his own. Gen. Mark Clark, commander in chief of U.S. forces there, had worked out a new battle plan, the goal of which was to drive the Chinese out of Korea and thereby unify the beleaguered country. When the two men met, Clark tried to present his plan to the president-elect, but Eisenhower did not give him an opportunity. Instead, Ike spent three days touring frontline units to see the situation for himself. He was not pleased with what he saw. He decided that Gen. Omar Bradley had been right all along: Korea really was the wrong war in the wrong place at the wrong time. In some cases, it was almost impossible to move forces in the mountains and valleys of Korea without walking straight into an ambush. Indeed, after Ike later took the opportunity to review Clark's plan he remarked that he considered any strategy calling "for an all-out assault as bordering on madness." In view of the strength of the positions the Chinese had developed, he wrote, "it was obvious that any frontal attack would present great difficulties."[18] Soon, however, the Chinese Communists made a major concession on the question of prisoners of war—the issue that had deadlocked the negotiations—and the two sides gradually moved toward an armistice and an end to the war.

Another challenge facing Eisenhower at an early stage in his presidency was the defense budget. Truman left behind a budget proposal for fiscal year 1954 that called for spending $46.3 billion on the military. However, the Bureau of the Budget argued that such an expenditure would create a deficit of $9.9 billion, something that flew in the face of Eisenhower's strongly held belief in a balanced budget.[19] During January and February the newly appointed secretary of the treasury, George Humphrey, and the director of the Bureau of the Budget, Joseph Dodge, insisted that the federal deficit that had been carried over from the Truman administration (due in large part to the Korean War) had to be reduced. Humphrey wanted to cut Truman's budget by 50 percent by 1959.[20] Needless to say, major military cutbacks would be required, which caused great concern to the country's generals and admirals; they knew that any savings would come out of their services' hides.

Just before he left office, Truman approved NSC 141, a study that argued that between sixty-five and eighty-five of "the atomic bombs launched by the USSR could be delivered on target in the United States."[21] To deal with this "critical" situation, the paper argued that the United States would have to allocate even more money to defense, especially to air defense, civil defense, and an early warning system. Other papers prepared for the administration reached similar conclusions. Eisenhower understood these problems, but he was also aware that the country had to avoid bankrupting itself in dealing with the Soviet threat. He was hopeful that the JCS would agree with him and his desire to protect the country's economic security, upon which everything else depended.

Instead of agreeing to a cheaper approach for ensuring the country's military security, the JCS did the opposite. They pushed for a continental defense system (to make the country less vulnerable to nuclear attack) and then argued that the country's armed forces were taxed to the limit. Not only were they stretched too thin, argued the Chiefs, the services needed additional money to fund new programs for fulfilling tasks assigned by the 1954 Joint Outline War Plan. But Dodge informed the president that the administration's fiscal problems made it impossible to fund the kind of forces the Chiefs were demanding. Eisenhower decided that if funds were insufficient to pay for the current strategy, he would have to come up with a new one. Before he could turn to that task, however, he and the Chiefs would have to agree on a budget for FY 1954.

On March 4, 1953, Dodge began his effort to bring the defense budget under fiscal control when he proposed that $4.3 billion be cut from Truman's proposed FY 1954 defense budget, bringing it down to $41.2 billion. Then he suggested that the Pentagon absorb an additional $9.4 billion decrease the following year, thereby creating a balanced budget by FY 1955. The president's special assistant for national security affairs, Robert Cutler, asked Wilson to ask the JCS to take a look at how such a cut would affect military programs. The JCS responded shortly thereafter, noting that the limits suggested by Dodge "would so increase the risk to the United States as to pose a grave threat to the survival of our allies and the security of this nation." Military forces would suffer severe cuts: the army would have to shrink from twenty to twelve divisions, and the air force would have to go from ninety-eight to seventy-nine wings, while only the navy "could hold its own." The bottom line was that the American military would lose the capacity to carry out the "minimum military tasks in the event of a general war."[22] The JCS presented its case to an NSC meeting that Eisenhower attended on March 25. They reiterated the points they had previously made to Dodge, but Eisenhower would have none of their opposition to budget cuts. Wilson then infuriated the president by giving his qualified support to the Chiefs. Eisenhower ended the meeting by asking "them to trim costs and support personnel, not combat forces. No decision would be made on the military budget, the president instructed, until Wilson provided the NSC with a list of 'economies.' "[23]

In the end, Wilson recommended a cut of $5 billion from Truman's FY 1954 budget, a decrease down to $36 billion. He suggested that reductions should continue until the budget fell to $33 billion in 1957.[24] The army would receive a slight increase because of the ongoing Korean War, and the navy would take a slight cut. The air force would be the big loser.

Not surprisingly, the military and the air force especially were furious. One air force general claimed that "Wilson is fiddling with our national security," while another remarked, "[Y]ou can't make across the board cuts without hurting the whole armed services."[25] Furthermore, other senior military officers claimed that this budget was the result of a recommendation by Wilson "with little help from or consultation with the Truman Joint Chiefs" (referring, of course, to the Chiefs who held their positions when Eisenhower assumed the presidency).[26] When Eisenhower submitted his budget to Congress, Democrats teamed up with senior air force officers to fight the cuts. Senator Stuart Symington (a former secretary of the air force), for example, claimed that the defense cuts were dangerous, and in April he argued that the president was sacrificing national security for the sake of a balanced budget. Even former president Truman joined in criticizing the president's budgetary proposal. In a clear challenge to both Wilson and the president, an air force general told a congressman in May that the air force required a minimum of 143 wings to ensure the country's national security.[27] U.S. Air Force Chief of Staff Hoyt Vandenberg, who "was in an absolute fury," then testified that the 143-wing force was critical in light of the buildup of Soviet forces. He accused Eisenhower of trying to foist a "second class" air force on the United States. He also claimed that the Chiefs did not play any part in designing the budget: it was all Wilson's work. In fact, Vandenberg had not even had the opportunity to see the budget until May 7.[28]

Eisenhower was not about to yield to the Democrats and the air force. "He told Republican legislative leaders, who gathered regularly at the White House, that they should not believe those Air Force officers who said they could not carry out their responsibilities if they did not get their 143 wings. 'I'm damn tired of Air Force sales programs,' he said." In the end, the president was able to rally Republicans in Congress and pass his budget. In the meantime, faced with their open defiance of his efforts to cut the budget, Eisenhower decided that he would have to do something about the Chiefs.

He was convinced that they would never be able to adjust to the new world of military sufficiency and economic prosperity. He needed JCS men who understood that they worked for him. Eisenhower also realized that if he hoped to implement the kind of fiscal program he believed was critical to the country's well-being, he would have to develop a new military strategy, one that would both protect the country and avoid putting it into bankruptcy.

Eisenhower Sacks the Old Chiefs

To deal with what seemed to him to be a revolt on the part of the Chiefs, Eisenhower decided to change them en masse. He appointed Adm. Arthur Radford to replace Gen. Omar Bradley as chairman of the Joint Chiefs. On one hand, Radford's appointment came as a surprise; after all, he had led the charge against Truman's cancellation of the super carrier during the Revolt of the Admirals! On the other hand, when Radford accompanied Eisenhower to Korea just after the election, the two men spent considerable time together and got to know one another. Radford had told the president that he believed that America's ground forces, stationed around the world, were overextended. He argued that if a war broke out, they would be "ineffective." His comment came as music to Eisenhower's ears. "The logical thing to do was to emphasize America's nuclear striking power and to rely on indigenous ground forces as a first line of defense against local aggression. American forces should be redeployed to the United States where they would be reorganized to form a smaller, highly mobile strategic reserve that could come to the aid of our allies in the event of a war."[29] Radford had another endearing quality insofar as Eisenhower was concerned: he was a pilot and thus understood the role of strategic airpower better than most naval officers.

When Eisenhower had met the new chiefs a month before he took office, he asked them to review U.S. military strategy with an eye toward making some major changes. As Gerald Clarfield explained, "Ike was calling for a break with the past, one that would provide a fresh view as to the best balance and most effective use and deployment of our armed forces, under existing circumstances."[30] Radford indicated that "President Eisenhower asked the service chiefs to concentrate on the larger aspects of the job; their roles as members of the JCS. He said at one meeting that he was certain they could organize their offices so that their vice chiefs could take care of the service details, freeing them for 'national planning.' "[31] Indeed, when the president met with the Chiefs at the White House, he asked each of them if they were certain they could carry out this task. They all agreed that they could. The relationship between the executive and his handpicked subordinates appeared to be starting on the right foot. Eisenhower was sure he could work with them, and they appeared to be ready to work with him. Unfortunately for the president, grand strategy was not the Chiefs' primary interest.

Searching for a New Strategy

A May 9, 1953, meeting held in the White House's Solarium Room gave the search for a new strategy its name: Operation Solarium. The exercise postulated three different approaches that the United States could use against the USSR. One group considered the implications of a continuation of the current policy of containment. The second group focused on the possibility that the United States would use any means, including nuclear weapons, to break up the Soviet bloc. Finally, the third group assumed an increasing Soviet threat and decided that the only way to confront it was by considerably increasing the U.S. military budget. The NSC, chaired by the president, met on July 30, 1953, and decided that Operation Solarium would serve as the starting point for a new military doctrine. Eisenhower considered it useful food for thought, but he understood that the details remained to be worked out.[32]

As far as the president was concerned, several key issues had to be considered in devising a new strategy. To begin, the United States had to realize that its relations with the Communist world were fraught with protracted dangers that would not disappear in the foreseeable future; indeed, they could increase significantly. Thus the United States should plan for such contingencies. How? By ensuring that its economy was strong and that its military resources were used in the most efficient manner possible. Or as Eisenhower explained at a press conference, the nation intended to obtain "the maximum military strength within economic capacities."[33] The United States would have to cut its military budget to achieve a balanced budget, which in turn was the only way to ensure a strong economy. Finally, because he believed that any conflict between Washington and Moscow would quickly result in a nuclear exchange, the United States must concentrate on developing its nuclear forces, even if at the expense of its conventional army and navy forces.[34]

After meeting with the Chiefs, however, Radford immediately recognized that the president's new approach to the JCS was falling on deaf ears. He wrote: "The service chiefs did not want to give up their service responsibilities. They enjoyed them. It was the broader planning and national aspects of their jobs that they appeared willing to delegate. Among ourselves we would agree that the President had to say such things, but they felt he knew how they actually had to operate."[35] Still, the president had ordered them to formulate a new strategy, one that would eliminate overlap and waste. His charge to them was made more difficult by the fact that whatever they decided would directly affect all three (four, if the Marines were included) services. Faced with such serious implications for the future of their services, they did what any good bureaucrat would do—they sidestepped the issues. The Chiefs discussed the issues but were unable to make the hard decisions the president was expecting from them. Admiral Robert Carney and General Ridgway in particular were strongly opposed to any change in roles and missions, and because the Chiefs tended to work on the principle of unanimity, nothing was decided.

At this point in time, service parochialism continued to be a major issue, a problem Eisenhower understood very well. For his part, he believed that the only hope for more discipline and less conflict among the services was greater unification. The primary problem was institutional authority: each service chief considered himself first and foremost to be a representative of his own service. Loyalty to the JCS, the Department of Defense, and, to some degree, even to the president were distant seconds, as Eisenhower was reminded by his dealings with the newly created air force (which was now going its own way), the Revolt of the Admirals, and the 1954 budgetary battles he had just finished. Ike realized that he had to do something to bring the various services together under central control if he hoped to impose a unified strategy upon them. But progress on that front would have to wait. Now he needed to persuade them to agree to a strategy that would justify major cuts in defense budgets.

Faced with seeming intransigence by the JCS, Radford decided to take matters into his own hands. He invited (i.e., ordered) each of the Chiefs to join him aboard the secretary of the navy's yacht, the *Sequoia*. He also decided that they would remain onboard until they had produced a strategy paper:

> I asked Secretary of the Navy, Robert Anderson if I could borrow his yacht *Sequoia* and take my colleagues to sea, keeping them there until we could agree on an answer to the President's memorandum. He agreed and a date was set, not without grumbling from the others. Some thought that at least we should come back to Washington every night. But I was adamant. Thursday morning 6 August we set for departure. Only the chiefs would be aboard, with two enlisted secretaries. *Sequoia* provisioned for an indefinite stay in the lower Potomac.[36]

Radford was successful. By August 8 he had a report signed by all of the Chiefs. The report did not make specific recommendations; rather, it contained suggestions for the U.S. government to consider. "It foresaw no new weapons to enhance overall military power, 'except perhaps in the atomic field.'" There was no movement on the very difficult and sensitive question of a force structure mix, and, in fact, both Carney and Ridgway were concerned by the report's emphasis on the importance of air assets in a future war. The report simply noted that the Chiefs had not had sufficient time to examine the question. The document did make two recommendations: First, it called for a clear policy on the use of nuclear weapons. When, and under what circumstances, did the United States plan to use them? Second, it argued that American military forces were overextended. As a remedy, the United States should scale back its overseas commitments and instead place "first priority [on] the essential military protection of our continental U.S. vitals and the capability for delivering swift and powerful retaliatory blows."[37] Radford took a copy of the report and flew to Denver, where the president was vacationing. After reading it over several times, Eisenhower expressed his pleasure and had it placed on the agenda for the August 27 NSC meeting.

At the meeting, which took place prior to the president's return to Washington, Radford made the main presentation. He convinced the NSC that redeployment would have to be part of any future strategy. Not surprisingly Secretary of the Treasury Humphrey, who was already calculating the money that could be saved by bringing troops back home, enthusiastically supported him. Air Force Chief of Staff Nathan Twining, who also saw the writing on the wall (i.e., more importance being assigned to airpower), went so far as to note that he agreed with "everything Admiral Radford had stated."[38] The question of limited wars was not considered. Both Admiral Carney and General Ridgway objected to the direction the discussions were taking. Carney hedged by hinting that once the navy had time to carefully examine the paper and its ramifications, it might turn out to be unacceptable, while Ridgway maintained that the report was not an official recommendation, but merely a study of the problem. Besides, how could the United States hope to fight a war using only one part of its arsenal? He "could not possibly subscribe to any theory that you can prevent war though the deterrent effect of any single arm."[39] He also made clear that he would not support the withdrawal of U.S. troops from abroad. Secretary of State John Foster Dulles also criticized the withdrawal idea, believing that such an action would be read as a return to isolation and "Fortress America." The president listened to the secretary's warning that the psychological blow to the military's psyche would be considerable and decided to hold off on a final decision. In the meantime, Dulles agreed with the Chiefs by arguing that the United States should spend more money both on continental defense to counter the Soviet threat and on the development of thermonuclear weapons and guided missiles.

The Joint Chiefs of Staff, chaired by General Nathan Twining, who succeeded Admiral Radford. From left to right: General Maxwell Taylor, Admiral Arleigh Burke, Twining, General Thomas White, and General Randolph Pate. (Dwight D. Eisenhower Library)

In spite of Carney's and Ridgway's reservations, the president was "ecstatic" when he received NSC 162/2 (as the doctrinal statement was labeled), believing that "it appeared that the JCS had come up with the answer to his 'dilemma,' by placing emphasis on the need for a robust offensive nuclear striking power."[40] In reality, however, the report provoked as much disagreement as it did agreement. In a September 30 meeting, the Chiefs argued that "while admitting the eventual need for the partial withdrawal of U.S. troops from overseas theaters, they did not believe that the United States should undertake this 'under present conditions,' and proposed instead 'continued study of U.S. global strategy.' At the same time, NSC 162/2 recommended that troop withdrawals begin 'reasonably soon.'"[41] For his part, Wilson again angered Eisenhower by defending the Chiefs' adoption of Dulles's line that the United States could not simply withdraw our troops overnight without serious political ramifications. In the end, the document followed the Chiefs' contention that overseas reductions should not take place at that time. Most important, the document's failure to state clearly how and when nuclear weapons would be used, together with its inaction on the redeployment of troops, would continue to haunt the Eisenhower administration.

Back to the Budgetary Battle

No sooner had NSC 162/2 been agreed upon when another problem appeared—the budget for FY 1955. Treasury and the Budget Bureau estimated that the Eisenhower administration was facing a deficit of $8.7 billion. The situation was so bad that the administration had to ask Congress to increase the federal debt limit to $290 billion. Seeking a remedy, Humphrey demanded that the military absorb an additional cut of $10 billion. Wilson reacted strongly, arguing that such a drastic decrease would turn the military budget upside down. He noted that because 162/2 included neither a firm commitment to redeploy forces nor a clear statement that nuclear weapons would be used in both large and small conflicts, the Defense Department was not prepared to accept such major surgery.[42] The secretary argued that "we could not change our military posture overnight."[43]

Despite a plea from the president for more austerity, and in spite of the Korean War having come to a close, when the budget issue was raised in October, the Chiefs called for an increase of 135,000 men, which would bring military strength up to 3.5 million. Such an expansion would leave the army at twenty divisions, provide the navy with a large Forrestal carrier, and permit the air force to grow from 114 to 120 wings.[44] Needless to say, both Humphrey and Dodge were horrified. They had just pointed out the need for cuts in the defense budget, yet here was the JCS demanding more troops, more weapons, and more money! However, the Chiefs could not rationally plan a force structure without a clear statement on how nuclear weapons were to be used, what kind of war the United States was to fight, and how many deployments were to take place. Besides, they believed any force structure should be balanced. As a result, the JCS tabled their objection to the Planning Board's draft of September 30, arguing that the words "a strong military posture to include" should preface the provision on retaliatory strikes.[45] The NSC agreed; however, the president disagreed. In place of the JCS language, he preferred "with emphasis on," regardless of complaints from the JCS.

In addition to Ridgway's predictable objection that the draft document failed to address conventional military forces, Admiral Carney weighed in, arguing that the president's language was not only premature, it "was bound to affect the character and composition of our forces."[46] Eisenhower responded that he was more interested in deterring a war than in winning one. Cutler then suggested that the JCS be permitted to take a footnote.[47] A displeased Eisenhower refused. Although he did not expect the Chiefs to be overjoyed about the new direction American military strategy was taking, and while he understood that $10 billion was a lot of money, he assumed they would get on board and at least make a good faith effort to introduce some cuts. But here they were demanding more money. The American economy simply could not absorb a defense budget of $42 billion.

Faced with the military's seeming intransigence, Eisenhower ordered Wilson and Radford to go back to the drawing board and find weapons and forces to cut, even if it meant banging the Chiefs' heads together. He wanted them to come up with a completely new approach, one that avoided cutting combat units, but instead focused on "fat" in support units and on areas of service redundancy. As a consequence, on October 16 Wilson ordered the Chiefs to provide him with recommendations on military strategy as well as "the size and composition of the armed forces for FY 1955, 1956 and 1957."[48] To draft recommendations, the Chiefs established a committee with two officers from each service and Lt. Gen. F. E. Everest as its chair.

In its report, the committee argued in favor of massive retaliation as a deterrent and recommended the construction of a continental defense system. Troops would be withdrawn from Korea and Japan to form a mobile reserve. The Chiefs agreed to decrease troop strength to 2.8 million by FY 1957, a cut of 600,000 men over the next three years. The army would shrink by a third and the navy by about 15 percent, while the air force, which would play the major role in implementing a massive strategy of retaliation, would receive 60,000 additional personnel.[49] Two of the Chiefs (Radford and Air Force Chief of Staff Twining) supported this proposed force-structure; both Ridgway and Carney opposed it.

Ridgway was upset over the cuts the army would have to absorb, believing that the plan put too much emphasis on airpower. Carney, who shared Ridgway's view about the plan's overemphasis on air power, also seized on the president's focus on the nuclear option when he sent a memorandum to the other Chiefs, warning that "if we base our strategy upon a predetermined concept of enemy intentions, and in consequence circumscribe our military capability by building forces capable of countering only one predetermined enemy course of action, we invite disaster."[50] The defeat of the French by conventional and guerrilla forces at Dien Bien Phu in Vietnam suggested that he knew what he was talking about. Ridgway also warned that an emphasis on nuclear weapons would weaken his service to the point that "the Army could no longer carry out its missions."[51] When Ridgway's concerns were relayed to the president, Eisenhower listened, but decided to ignore them. When the administration claimed that the committee's report had been unanimously supported by all the Chiefs, Ridgway expressed his anger to the House Appropriations Committee.[52] He wrote in his memoirs,

> As one member of the Joint Chiefs of Staff who most emphatically had not concurred in the 1955 military program as it was presented to the people, I was nonplused by the statement. The fact is the 1955 budget was a "directed verdict," as were the Army budgets for 1956 and '57. The force levels provided in all three were not primarily based on military needs. They were not based on the freely reached conclusions of the Joint Chiefs of Staff. They were squeezed between the framework of arbitrary manpower and fiscal limits, a complete inversion of the normal process.[53]

Once again the Chiefs were prepared to play the congressional card when they believed the president's actions would negatively affect their services. If the president thought that this new group of senior officers would "behave" better than their predecessors, he was in for a rude awakening. Ridgway in particular would soon publicly expose the extent of his disagreement with his commander in chief.

The New Look Goes Public

The first time the phrase "New Look" was used officially to describe Eisenhower's strategy in public was on December 14, 1953, in a speech by Admiral Radford before the National Press Club: "That brings me to what you have called the 'New Look.' First, let me give you my description. A New Look assessment of our strategic and logistic capabilities in the light of foreseeable deployments, certain technological advances, the world situation today, and with considerable estimating of future trends and developments. It is a searching review of this nation's military requirements for security."[54] He stressed the importance of planning over the "long haul," echoing what Eisenhower had stressed since he became president: he did not intend to work on the basis of a year-to-year budget. Instead, he intended to come up with a long-term strategy, one that would aid both the country's economy and military planning. Not forgetting the position of the JCS, Radford was careful to note that the Chiefs continued to believe in the importance of balanced and mobile forces. With Ridgway's concerns in mind, he also emphasized the importance of being prepared for local conflicts as well as for a major war.

Secretary of State Dulles followed up with a speech to the Council on Foreign Relations in January 1954. He sent a draft of the talk to Eisenhower, who rewrote parts of it. The revised speech, which contained the first public mention of "massive retaliation," emphasized the concept of striking back: "The way to deter aggression is for the *free community* to be willing and able to respond *vigorously* and at places with means of its own choosing."[55] To Eisenhower, this meant having enough military force to totally destroy the other side's military, political, and social institutions, not to mention its population. Such a response would be so devastating that the other side would think twice before attacking the United States. For economic reasons, the president wanted just enough strategic weapons, and no more or no less, to accomplish this task.

Not surprisingly, the concept of massive retaliation provoked a significant amount of public debate, beginning with civilian academics. As General Maxwell Taylor explained in his 1959 book, *The Uncertain Trumpet,* "Such articles from unofficial sources represented the first public questioning of the validity of the New Look policy of Massive Retaliation and I welcomed them warmly. Their acuity was the more remarkable from the fact that the authors did not have access to complete information with regard to atomic weapons' effects."[56] Army and navy officers in particular were cheering on critics of the government's new approach, which would benefit the air force at the other services' expense.

Renewing the Budget Battle

The ever-present budgetary problems once again came to the fore on May 10, 1954, when the new budget director, Rowland Hughes, informed the president that the 1956 budget would be out of balance by $6.8 billion. The gap for 1957 would be only a bit lower at $5.9 billion. Under certain circumstances, he warned, the deficit would be even higher, up to $9.7 billion in 1956 and $12 billion in 1957.[57] In Hughes's view, the only way to balance the budget was to cut national security programs.

The issue was referred to the NSC's Planning Board. The JCS had a twofold position. First, the Chiefs argued that U.S. foreign policy since World War II had been a failure. The Communists were clearly on the march, and the West was not keeping pace militarily. Second, the Chiefs believed more emphasis should be placed on conventional forces. They argued that the

United States should develop new programs "to increase the striking power of all U.S. force which can be brought to bear on the enemy" (155). Given Washington's overreliance on nuclear weapons, the Chiefs were worried that the United States could soon find the Communists gradually taking parts of the world through a series of local aggressions; although such actions would not warrant the use of nuclear weapons, they would have the effect of placing one new state after another under the Kremlin's control. The Planning Board, agreeing with the Chiefs, sent a report to the president on June 14 indicating that the world situation had "changed for the worse" (151). An additional cause of the worsening situation was Communist China, which represented a major threat in Asia.

Secretary Wilson also agreed with the military's contention that the worldwide military situation was deteriorating. He agreed that there should be slight increases in the troop strength of the army, navy, and Marines, modest budgetary increases for FY 1956, and extra funding for the air force. Wilson made these proposals to an NSC board meeting on July 30. Hughes was shocked when Wilson confirmed that the services would keep 150,000 more men than originally planned. The Chiefs' final numbers for 1956 were $37.4 billion in new money (155).

Then, in November, the JCS sent the NSC what one writer called a "doomsday" paper. In it, the Chiefs argued that if the United States did not do something quickly, it would find itself "isolated from the rest of the free world" (156). Admiral Radford told the NSC that given the balance of nuclear forces that existed between the United States and the USSR, the U.S. military could no longer ensure victory in a war with the Soviets. Indeed, the JCS was not only asking for more money; it was asking for action. Radford did not actually call for a preventive war, but his presentation certainly implied the idea.

The Joint Chiefs were not alone in their desire for a more aggressive foreign policy, one that would be backed up by a larger and more robust military establishment. Eisenhower's special assistant for national security affairs, Robert Cutler, made clear that some members of the board believed that, absent such a policy, the Soviets would be able to avoid nuclear war and "nibble the free world to death piece by piece." The United States, board members argued, should have the capability to fight limited wars without recourse to the use of atomic weapons (156). As a result, the JCS again called for an expansion of conventional forces, which were deemed indispensable if Washington intended to counter the Soviets. The military needed more, not less money.

Eisenhower resented the Chiefs' criticism of his foreign policy, which, in his mind accomplished the number one priority of deterring an attack by the other side on the United States. As far as local wars were concerned, he did not want another Korea, an endless war that soaked up countless American resources. If other countries were threatened, they would have to bear the brunt of their own defense. The army's role would be homeland defense and the preservation of order in the United States in the event of a nuclear war. Eisenhower believed that army forces overseas should primarily serve as a "trip wire" in the event of a Soviet attack. Once they had been run over, the United States would respond with nuclear weapons. Needless to say, this strategy did not endear Eisenhower to the army.

When Wilson and Radford met with the president in December 1954 they poured oil on a hot fire, again arguing for a significant increase in military spending. The army would expand to twenty-eight divisions, the navy would receive two new Forrestal aircraft carriers, and the Marine Corps would get more men. The president flatly rejected their FY 1957 budget proposals and insisted that the administration would stay with the figures for 1956 with one exception. To save money, all of the changes that were supposed to be completed in three years would now have to be completed in two. In the end, the military ended up with $5 billion less than it requested.

Looking for Fresh Blood

Frustrated with the Chiefs' opposition to his policies, especially that of Ridgway, Eisenhower began to look around for fresh blood. On February 18, 1955, Army Secretary Robert Stevens telephoned Gen. Maxwell Taylor, who was serving as commander in chief of U.S. Forces, Far East, and ordered him to return at once to Washington. When Taylor arrived he met with Stevens, who was evasive concerning the reason for his order to return. Taylor was then ordered to see Secretary Wilson the next day. After some diplomatic foreplay, Wilson got down to the purpose of the meeting. As Taylor remembered,

> He then began to cross-examine me on my readiness to carry out civilian orders even when contrary to my own views. After thirty-seven years of service without evidence of insubordination, I had no difficulty of conscience in reassuring him, but I must say I was surprised to be put through such a loyalty test. . . .
>
> Apparently, I passed this test because later he told me to call on the President at 2:30 P.M., February 24. This I did. It was my first meeting with my old wartime commander since he had become President. He greeted me with his customary warmth but there were serious matters on his mind. He wished to be sure of the attitude of the prospective

> Chief of Staff. He went over essentially the same ground as Mr. Wilson with regard to loyalty to civilian leadership. His manner of expression was different but the purport the same. Again I had no trouble in responding without reservations. Again I apparently passed the test—still hardly knowing why it had been given. As I left, the President indicated his intention to nominate me to succeed General Ridgway after a short tour of duty in General Hull's post of Commander in Chief, Far East.[58]

The lengthy quote by Taylor illustrates how careful both Wilson and the president were in trying to find an agreeable army chief of staff, one who would become part of the Eisenhower "team." What neither of them realized, however, was that almost any officer would stand up for his own particular service when asked to make major modifications in the roles and missions of the military branches. Although the Chiefs believed in obedience to civilian authority, as evidenced by their response to Truman's firing of MacArthur, they were not about to sit still and permit the services to which they had devoted their lives to be destroyed or at least neutered by anyone, even if the president had been a military hero.

Eisenhower also decided to replace Carney. Although he had kept his opposition to the New Look strategy "in house" and avoided public comment, Carney had a major run-in with his boss, the secretary of the navy, who resented Carney's refusal to consult him when making senior naval appointments. Carney believed that such decisions should be made by professional naval officers, not civilian politicians, who had neither the professional nor the technical competency to make such judgments. Arleigh Burke, a relatively junior admiral, was appointed to replace Carney.

According to Burke, when he was called to the Pentagon, Secretary of the Navy Charles Thomas and Under Secretary of the Navy Thomas Gates informed him that "there had been differences of opinion" with Carney and that "they felt they could no longer work together as an efficient team."[59] Burke, who was only a two-star admiral, was offered the four-star job. He was "startled." He hesitated, arguing that Carney was an officer he highly respected, and pointed out that he was too junior for the job, but Thomas was insistent. Burke then spoke with Wilson and the president, with the latter telling him, "I am very much annoyed at the habit that seems to be springing up of a man seeking, or inadvertently finding, opportunities to talk on the outside. That habit might belong to a bunch of politicians, not to the military." Eisenhower told him that if he could not agree to keep his views within the administration or was not prepared to give the president the best advice possible regardless of service loyalty, he should not take the job.[60] Burke accepted the position.

Carney retired quietly, unlike Ridgway, who sent a memorandum to Wilson that he intentionally did not classify. In it, he noted all of the problems he found with the president's policy regarding the military, especially the army. Wilson quickly classified the memo, but it was leaked to the *New York Times* a few days later. The departure of Carney and Ridgway may have led Eisenhower to believe that military opposition to changes in roles and missions would cease. Now he had Burke and Gen. Mark Clark, who, he was convinced, would work as part of his team. In fact, both would be as outspoken in private and in public as their predecessors.

In May 1955, during their May Day celebrations, the Soviets showed the West their new Bison bombers, planes that bore a strong resemblance to the American B-52 bomber. Needless to say, the Chiefs were very upset. The United States had fewer than twenty operational B-52 bombers, and here the Soviets were with a comparable model. Eisenhower responded by asking Congress for a $436 million supplemental appropriation to speed up production of more B-52s and the F-100 interceptor. Senator Stuart Symington seized on the news of the Bison to argue that the United States had lost control of the air to the Soviets. He blasted the secretary of defense, arguing that "throughout his tenure in office, Mr. Wilson has underestimated the strength of the Communists and their ability to produce modern arms. Nor has he taken the steps necessary to obtain adequate arms for the country."[61]

A few days later, Gen. Nathan Twining, the air force chief of staff, jumped into the fray, maintaining that although the United States was ahead of the Soviet Union at that time, he could not guarantee how long the nation's lead would last. Then followed a statement by air force general Thomas Power that the USSR had "the largest air force."[62] He spoke plainly of a "bomber gap" between the United States and USSR, with the latter having the advantage.

Rejecting the idea of a bomber gap as nonsense, Eisenhower was infuriated by the military's criticism. He had made important concessions to the military on the FY 1957 budget. To wit, after considerable negotiating with the Chiefs, the administration had come up with a budget (including carryover funds) of $35.7 billion. Although less than the services requested, the amount was $3 billion more than Congress had approved in 1956 and $2 billion more than Eisenhower had planned to give the military.[63] Where was their gratitude?

The next blow came when excerpts of Ridgway's new book appeared in the *Saturday Evening Post*. *Soldier* was a very hard-hitting indictment of the Eisenhower administration's national security policies. For example, Ridgway charged that for fiscal reasons, Wilson had repeatedly made decisions that hurt military preparedness in order to keep voter support for the administration. He also claimed that Wilson's politically motivated actions constituted a serious danger to the United States.[64] Then Trevor Gardner, assistant secretary of the air force for research and development, resigned, claiming that the Eisenhower administration was not doing enough to fund research and development of missiles.

Radford presented the president with another unwelcome memorandum when the Chiefs returned from a week-long retreat in Puerto Rico. In the memo, the Chiefs continued to argue that U.S. foreign policy had been a dismal failure: "The deterioration of the free world position leads the Joint Chiefs of Staff to the conclusion that either the programs for general strategy have not been resolutely implemented or that the general strategy is inadequate to cope with the situation now confronting the United States as leader of the free world."[65] They also blasted the administration on military spending. The only way the United States could meet the challenges facing it was to increase spending from "$38 billion to $40 billion for the years 1958 to 1960, exclusive of the aid to America's allies."[66] To make matters worse, it was at this point that a statement by the army's chief of staff, Maxwell Taylor, was leaked to the media. He reportedly stated that " 'we are going full-out on the 1,500 mile missile.' Wilson was immediately phoned by the president and ordered to tell the General that 'this is the kind of thing that need not be known.' "[67]

Eisenhower then called both Wilson and Radford to the White House for a "chat," during which the president said that he did not agree with the JCS paper. If their depiction of events was correct, he maintained, "we should go to field conditions, declare an emergency, increase the military budget and even to a garrison state."[68] The president told Wilson and Radford that he would not accept the paper and told them to tell the Chiefs that he expected them to come up with a more positive analysis, one that would also highlight the positive steps his administration had taken on the military front. He also opposed the Chiefs' plea for more military spending. Wilson, however, objected. He told the president that the services had their backs to the wall. Inflation, worn-out weapons systems, and budgetary tricks would no longer suffice. The military had to have more money and that was all there was to it.[69]

In an effort to break the logjam with the Chiefs, Eisenhower met with them on March 13, 1956. He told them he understood and agreed with their concerns; he knew they were out of money and that they were operating on a spartan basis. However, he also expected them to resist pressures from Congress to raise spending, and he spoke to them as if they were players on an army football team: "Everyone in the Defense establishment should nail their flag to the staff of the United States of America, and think in terms of the whole."[70] If they did not do as he asked, he would become personally involved. After warning Twining that he would not put up with continued air force sniping at the navy, he offered the Chiefs a carrot. Knowing how unhappy they were and well aware of the support they had on the Hill, the president said he would give the Chiefs $36.5 billion for the years 1958 through 1960, only $1.5 billion below what they had requested. Furthermore, he stated he would approve the 1956 budgetary supplement for more B-52s (178).

Congress Steps In

Despite his best efforts, Eisenhower's efforts to get the Chiefs back in line failed again. Senator Stuart Symington's subcommittee held its first hearing on April 16, 1956. Rather than repeating Eisenhower's suggestion that all was well when he was asked to testify about weaknesses in the air force, Twining proceeded to recite a whole list of what he considered to be significant weaknesses. They included "among other things an inadequate supply of officers and enlisted personnel with technical skills, insufficient research funds, and, above all, a serious need for more B-52s." He then claimed that the administration had ignored his request for three hundred additional B-52s (179). Other senior air force officers adopted similar positions. General Curtis LeMay, commander of the Strategic Air Command, was especially outspoken in his demand for more funds: "The United States could still win a war against Russia, but not 'without this country receiving very serious damage. Five years ago we could have won the war without the country receiving very serious damage.' " Turning to the so-called bomber gap, he argued that "this means that by 1960, 'the Soviet Air Force will have substantially more Bisons and Bears than we will have B-52s. . . . I can only conclude then that they will have a greater striking power than we will have."[71] As a consequence, Congress added one billion dollars (a significant amount at that time) to the air force budget, an action that greatly displeased Eisenhower. Ultimately, however, Secretary of Defense Wilson sequestered the additional money given to the air force.

More Jointness?

The battle with the air force convinced Eisenhower that the Defense Department was in critical need of additional reforms if he were to gain control of it. The services spent most of their time fighting with each other, and when they weren't fighting with each other, they were fighting with the president by leaking material to the media or going to Congress to circumvent him. The turf battle over roles and missions was especially out of control, with the army fighting the air force over the relationship between long-range artillery and surface-to-surface missiles. Each argued that it should have control over the missiles.[72] Then there was the question of whether the army should be permitted to have aviation units. Generals Taylor and James Gavin publicly argued that the army had a critical need for such assets, but the air force considered their argument to be heretical. By the beginning of 1956, the battle between the army and air force had devolved into a major public-relations war. The air force drew up plans for a two-year public-relations campaign called "A Decade of Security through Global Air Power." In response, the army launched its own campaign. Secretary of the Army Wilbur Brucker defended the army's NIKE antiaircraft missile as one of the finest in the world. Then General Gavin proclaimed that the system "can destroy any airplane present or planned regardless of great height or speed."[73]

In January 1956 Taylor directly attacked the president's idea of massive retaliation, arguing that it was not a sound policy. A month later he blasted the " 'confused thinking' that had 'obscured defense matters since World War II.' "[74] Like other army officers he maintained that no war would be won by any single service. As Taylor saw things,

> massive retaliation strategy had "reached a dead end" and should be replaced by what was later called "flexible response," whereby the United States should be equipped with the capability "to react across the entire spectrum of possible challenge." When during 1953–1954, nuclear weapons had little impact on the army's strategic thinking, by 1956 army leaders became alert to the possibility of utilizing nuclear tactical weapons not only in limited wars but also in general war.[75]

Taylor argued that the United States must be in a position to respond to aggression in a variety of ways. Although the nation would retaliate with equal force in the event of a full-scale nuclear attack on the country, the possibility of such an attack seemed highly unlikely to him. A small-scale action that resulted in the loss of a small amount of territory was much more likely, and such an attack was best addressed by the army, which would need the forces to meet such challenges.

The air force responded in kind, and the situation worsened to the point that in April 1956 Radford urged Eisenhower to take some action. Given his leadership style, Eisenhower did not want to get involved, especially after holding fruitless discussion with the Chiefs in the past. Nevertheless, he met with them again in March. He told the army that he would not support their claims for aviation or missile development. Then he made a big play for joint cooperation between the services, pleading with the Chiefs to think beyond their institutional loyalties. Once again, Eisenhower was wasting his time.

The navy sided with the army, although not openly. One of the attributes that Admiral Burke brought to the position of chief of naval operations (CNO) was a keen understanding of strategic matters. He thus decided at an early stage that the navy should have more to offer than the nuclear weapons carried aboard aircraft carriers. Faced with air force opposition to the development of a seagoing missile, Burke turned to the army, and the services agreed to work together (at the army's Redstone Arsenal) to develop an intermediate range ballistic missile (IRBM).[76] Eisenhower gave the undertaking his "enthusiastic backing," thereby making the project "the highest priority" by mid-1957.[77] The navy was now thoroughly embroiled in the strategic retaliation business. When it came to the battle between the other two services, the CNO kept his head down.

Relations between the army and the air force deteriorated to the point that a group of middle-level army officers went public during the so-called "Revolt of the Colonels." They provided a copy of a paper they had written on the army's role in a future war to the *New York Times.* After obtaining the air force's perspective, the *Times* then published both papers. The government's dirty laundry was now being laundered in public. Eisenhower was livid. At a press conference he said that "while debate and disagreement among the services were to be expected, he would not tolerate revolt" (186). He began to think again of ways to unify the services so that he could get a handle on these never-ending battles over roles and missions.

Aware of how upset the president was, Wilson decided it was also high time that he took control of the Chiefs. In November he issued an order stating that the army would have responsibility for "point defense" and thus could have missiles, but only those with a 100-mile range. He also clearly expressed his opposition to the creation of a separate air force in the army. Wilson's orders were ignored: almost no one in the Pentagon paid any attention to him. The army continued to buy more aircraft and refused to end its war with the air force.

The army also pressed ahead in its battle over the deployment of nuclear weapons. Taylor and Twining met with the president in May. According to Taylor, there were major differences of opinion on how to interpret the president's New Look policy. Taylor's opponents believed that any war with the

Soviets would inevitably escalate into a large-scale nuclear exchange. Among those holding this view were the other Chiefs, who also believed that nuclear weapons should be available for use in all kinds of conflicts, whether large or small. Eisenhower himself flatly disagreed with Taylor: a war with the Soviet Union would become nuclear whether the United States liked it or not. He also felt that local conflicts were best left to indigenous forces, although the United States would back them up with air and naval forces. The president maintained that tactical nuclear weapons were part and parcel of a modern military and would be used against smaller targets when appropriate (190). Thus the Chiefs had their guidance from the president: nuclear weapons would be used from the very beginning of a general war.

When to Use Nukes

The Chiefs remained stymied by the lack of clear directions on how and when nuclear weapons were to be used. If the president intended to employ them in local conflicts, for example, cutbacks in army forces would not be so painful. Then there was the issue of release authority: Should the authority to use these weapons be delegated in advance to the Chiefs? Should they be able to use tactical nuclear weapons just like any other battlefield weapon without first getting the president's permission? Would the United States actually use the atomic bomb? Eisenhower's answer was vague: "We must make plans to use the atom bomb if we become involved in a war."[78] The United States would avoid hasty decisions on the use of nuclear weapons, but the other side should have no illusions. If push came to shove, the United States would use these weapons. For the time being, release authority would remain in the White House. Only the president could decide when and where atomic weapons would be employed.

Eisenhower valued massive retaliation as a means of deterrence. As long as the Soviets or anyone else understood that an attack on the United States would lead to the most disastrous consequences, he believed they would hesitate to attack. In an NSC meeting in December 1953, he had stated:

> Our only chance of victory . . . would be to paralyze the enemy at the outset of the war. Since we cannot keep the United States an armed camp or a garrison state, we must make plans to use the atom bomb if we become involved in a war. We are *not* going to provoke the war. . . . If war comes, the other fellow must have started it. Otherwise,

> we would not be a position to use the weapon, and we have got to be in a position to use that weapon if we are to preserve our institutions in peace and win the victory in war.[79]

As one might expect, General Ridgway refused to accept this new strategy. What if the Soviets launched a conventional attack on the West—could we morally justify using nuclear weapons? Furthermore, as Andrew Bacevich has pointed out, the new strategy of reliance on nuclear weapons "made war inconceivable and the military profession unnecessary" (particularly the army).[80] Admiral Carney shared Ridgway's concerns. However, the president simply repeated his earlier statement: he would be the one to make the final decision on whether or not to use nuclear weapons—a response that did not answer Ridgway's question. How could the JCS plan for contingencies if they did not know under what circumstances nuclear weapons were likely to be employed?

In the meantime, Soviet missiles were becoming more accurate. Radford warned the president that by 1958 the Soviets would probably have an ICBM with a thermonuclear warhead that would enable them to "force a showdown" with the United States.[81] Thus, he believed it was critical that the United States spend more money to develop more accurate missiles to keep the United States ahead of the Soviets. Frankly, the Chiefs were totally dissatisfied with the president's approach to strategy issues, and they were not bashful about letting him know it. As Ambrose wrote, "So strongly, and so often did the Chiefs—all of them—object to the New Look that Eisenhower was nearly driven to distraction."[82] Eisenhower argued that the idea of "absolute defense" that the Chiefs seemed to be seeking was nonsense. The United States could spend itself into bankruptcy, and never reach the point where it would be 100 percent secure. The Chiefs had to be realistic.

The question of when nuclear weapons were to be used continued to be a matter of concern. Did Eisenhower mean that he would only use them in response to a full-scale attack by the Soviets on the United States? Or did he plan to use them anywhere in the world and at any time in local conflicts? Was he prepared to challenge Communist adventurism anywhere—even in Africa, for example? In this context, the NSC, the JCS, and even the secretary of state argued for a more vigorous battle against Communism, "as evidenced by the number of times in 1954 they urged the President to launch an atomic strike against China."[83] He refused, maintaining that he would only use nuclear weapons if the Russians invaded Western Europe or launched a nuclear attack on the United States. He made clear, however, that he would not oppose having the CIA carry out a covert war against Communism around the world.

The Budget—Again

In late 1956, with the most recent election behind him, Eisenhower again faced the question of the military budget. He had gone over the FY 1958 budget line by line with Wilson and had cut $500 million of the $39 billion. Then, in yet another effort to gain the Chiefs' support, the president met with them on December 20. They argued that U.S. involvement in a local, conventional war had become more likely in the aftermath of the Hungarian Uprising and the Suez Crisis. Eisenhower disagreed. A few days later during an NSC discussion of the budget, Eisenhower listened to each of the services and then made clear that they would simply have to live with the lower figure. Within a week, a rebellion seemed imminent. Eisenhower then sent his staff secretary, Gen. Andrew Goodpaster, to see the Chiefs. Each man was asked to sign a document stating that he agreed that the president's budget was "well balanced and satisfactory" and that he was prepared to give the president "his whole hearted support." They all signed. The president was pleased.

Then came news that the economy was weakening, followed by a warning from Wilson that the military budgetary situation was worsening as well because of inflation, overspending by the air force, and research and development costs. He asked if it might not be possible to raise the $38 billion spending limit the president had imposed. Eisenhower refused. Consequently, when the president sent his January 16, 1957, budget message to Congress, he announced that "the Air Force, which had just achieved its long sought after goal of 137 wings, would drop to 128 wings by mid-1958 while the Army would be cut from 19 to 17 divisions. Similar cuts would be made in the Navy and Marine Corps." In the end, Congress cut the budget even further, down to $33.8 billion, $15 billion below what the Chiefs had requested.[84]

Sputnik

Few events have had a more important impact on American military policy than the Soviet Union's launching of the *Sputnik* satellite on October 4, 1957. It was followed shortly thereafter by the launching of *Sputnik 2,* which carried a dog. These spacecraft not only raised serious questions about American technological superiority, they also brought into question the security of the United States. If the Russians were this far ahead in satellites and the ability to put such heavy payloads into orbit, one could only imagine how great their lead must be in the development of ICBMs. As David Snead put it,

> The Soviet launch of Sputnik I in October and Sputnik II in November raised serious questions of the vulnerability of the United States. While it was much easier to launch a rocket into space than to hit a target with a nuclear weapon thousands of miles away, the Soviet satellites seemed to indicate that country's nuclear superiority over the United States. Khrushchev's claims that his country possessed this capability only heightened concerns.[85]

The Chiefs tried to use the *Sputnik* launches to argue for a larger budget. Appearing before Congress, U.S. Army Secretary Brucker pushed the Nike Zeus missile-defense program, and Taylor expressed his dissatisfaction with the current situation in the army, despite comments by the administration that the situation was satisfactory. Also complaining was General Gavin, who "was even more outspoken in his criticism of his executive superiors . . . claiming that insufficient funding for the Army as a whole had forced the service to sacrifice the long-overdue modernization of its equipment to the furtherance of its missile program; furthermore, he charged . . . that the lack of money for research and development had been so severe that the balance of military power was finally shifting against the United States."[86] The air force complained as well, asking for immediate steps to give the service the weapons it needed to carry out its job. Then the navy weighed in. Burke emphasized the value of the Polaris missile system, calling it the best strategic weapon available to the United States. He also supported the army (and Marines) by arguing that the United States needed to do more in preparing for limited wars. Finally, "he alleged that administration harassment ('continuous review and review and review') had forced the Navy to submit smaller budget requests (in the order of three to four billion dollars) than it believed necessary."[87]

A Change of Command

In October 1957, Neil McElroy, the former head of Procter and Gamble, succeeded Wilson as secretary of defense. McElroy, who knew almost nothing about either the military establishment or how the Pentagon functioned, would need on-the-job training. His first task was the FY 1958 budget, which the White House insisted should not surpass $38 billion. Eisenhower suggested to McElroy that unification offered a means of reining in the budget, because he was certain that the services would once again come forth with requests for more money that would exceed the limit he had set. However, the new secretary ignored the president's proposal, suggesting instead that the Pentagon adopt a go-slow approach.

Meanwhile, behind the scenes, the president met with Nelson Rockefeller, who presented a service unification plan that the president found very attractive. The proposals were forwarded to McElroy. who immediately formed a group to review them. Eisenhower then listed defense reorganization as his number one priority in his State of the Union Address in January 1958; unification would now be a focal point of civil-military relations. Indeed, when Eisenhower sent his proposal to Congress, he stated that

> Separate ground, sea and air warfare is gone forever. If ever again we should be involved in war; we will fight it in all elements, with all services, as one single concentrated effort. Peacetime preparatory and organizational activity must conform to this fact. Strategic and tactical planning must be completely unified, combat forces organized into unified commands, each equipped with the most efficient weapons systems that science can develop, singly led and prepared to fight as one, regardless of service.[88]

The JCS soon entered the fray. On one hand, the army generally agreed with Eisenhower's plan. General Lemnitzer said, "We in the Army are not generally opposed to the reorganization plan, assuming of course that some common sense will be used in administering it."[89] On the other hand, the navy and Marine Corps were especially opposed to making the chairman of the Joint Chiefs first among equals. The Marines, still smarting over their past treatment by the army, were worried that if the secretary of defense wielded too much power, he might decide at some future date to reduce or, as the army wished, even exterminate the Corps. Speaking for the navy at a National Press Club luncheon, Burke defended the status quo, arguing that "it assures reality . . . it avoids the fatal ivory tower." He continued, "There are proposals . . . all leading in one way or the other toward more and more concentration of power, more and more autocracy by military policy and military decision, more and more suppression of differences of judgment, and more and more of what is described as 'swift efficiency of decision' as a substitute for debate and discussion of the military aspects of national policy."[90] And he would not back down. In spite of a warning from McElroy that the president expected him to support his reorganization policy, he testified before the Senate Armed Forces Committee in June 1958 that he continued to oppose giving greater power to the secretary of defense and taking the service secretaries out of the chain of command. A day later, McElroy told a press conference that he was disappointed in Burke's testimony.

Eisenhower did not get everything he requested from Congress, but he did enjoy some limited success. For example, the secretary of defense was given more power. The new law clearly stipulated that the services, "though 'separately organized,' operated under the 'direction, authority and control of the Secretary of Defense.' Service secretaries no longer had any basis upon which to oppose or place obstacles in the way of policies decided upon at a higher level. They had become mere administrators with no role to play in policy formulation."[91] The secretary's authority was further enhanced by the creation of unified commanders. In addition, Congress created the position of director of research and engineering "to supervise and direct all research that required central direction."[92] To prevent duplication of effort, the director had the power to decide both which projects would be undertaken and which service would be in charge.

Despite such gains, the issue of limited warfare continued to haunt Eisenhower. After the Marines were deployed to Lebanon in 1958, the navy and the Marines argued in favor of the army's request for more money to deal with such contingencies. Even the State Department was on board. Both John Foster Dulles and his successor, Christian Herter, agreed "that a revision of basic national security policy had become essential."[93] Then Eisenhower came under criticism for his handling of the Soviet blockade of Berlin, which led Senate Majority Leader Lyndon Johnson to complain that the Eisenhower administration was "not doing enough, fast enough or thoroughly enough," to keep the nation strong. Admiral Radford also expressed his concern about an overemphasis on a general nuclear war to the detriment of limited conflicts.[94] Neither the army nor the navy ever fully accepted Eisenhower's New Look policy.

By the time he left office, Eisenhower had witnessed a generational change in the JCS. As Stephen Ambrose noted, "The JCS were no longer his contemporaries, as Bradley and Radford had been in the early years, but relatively junior officers from World War II, men who could not impress him."[95]

CONCLUSION

Presidential Leadership Style

Eisenhower established a clear chain of command, and he tried to work with the Chiefs. He was respected because of his war record, but he appointed first one and then a second secretary of defense who knew little about the military. Both his "hidden-hand" efforts to deal with the Chiefs and his "pep talks" to them were ineffectual. In retrospect, one could argue that given the kind of changes the president was attempting to impose, he should have involved himself more closely in the process and appointed a secretary of defense who understood the military. (Even had Eisenhower done so, he still would have needed the cooperation of Congress.) It may be stretching matters, but one gets the impression that as a professional military officer he may have believed that the Chiefs would have been more willing to follow the directives of their commander in chief.

Violations of Service/Military Culture?

From the Chiefs' perspective, Eisenhower's "New Look" strategy violated their service and military culture. It meant nothing less than a major overhaul of the military, particularly the army. Eisenhower asked for the Chiefs' views, and they came back with a package that they believed was the minimum their services required in order to keep up with the Russians. Eisenhower, however, ignored their proposals. If nothing else, the infuriated Chiefs considered this a lack of respect for their expertise. They believed they were the ones who knew what was needed. Besides, from their perspective, Eisenhower failed to recognize the need for an integrated, overall strategy. In their minds, he was trying to buy security on the "cheap." Nuclear weapons were relatively inexpensive when compared to large conventional forces, but what about the need to deal with low-level conflicts? How did he expect them to fight such a war if their conventional forces were insufficient?

To make matters worse, the Chiefs believed that not only was Eisenhower trying to force his preferred strategy on them, he was attempting to make changes that had major implications for their roles and missions, as well as their operational and tactical autonomy. Indeed, one of the interesting aspects of Eisenhower's dealings with the military was that his radical changes frequently united them against him at a time when they were often at each others' throats.

When Eisenhower grew tired of the Chiefs' belligerency and their refusal to obey him, he fired them, which accomplished nothing. Their replacements were just as prepared to disagree with him as had been their predecessors. Consequently, presidential authority over the Chiefs dwindled. He could give them direct orders, but even when he had decided upon and articulated a policy, they would interpret his comments in a manner that was beneficial to the needs of their respective services. Attempts at persuasion proved equally useless. From the military's perspective, if the president was out to destroy their services, then they were prepared to use Congress to set things right.

Changes in Service/Military Culture?

To defend themselves against Eisenhower's introduction of his new military strategy, the military moved further in the direction of involving Congress (e.g., Twining's testimony before Senator Symington's committee). The military, which worked for the legislature as well as the executive, was not supposed to lie when asked questions by members of Congress. So, if military leaders believed that the president's strategy endangered the army's ability to fight a conventional war, they had an obligation to say so.

More ominous, however, was the Chiefs' belief that they had a right to go to the media with their complaints against the president and his secretary of defense. No longer did they limit themselves to the Hill as a launching pad for disagreements with the executive. Generals Ridgway, Gavin, and Taylor showed that the military was prepared to make its case in the public arena as well. The "art of leaking" on the part of senior military officers reached a new high, which angered Eisenhower, who considered such acts to be clear violations of the military code of ethics. But the rules of the game had changed, and the Chiefs employed both Congress and the media as tools to "protect" themselves from radical changes.

Finally, Eisenhower tried hard to drive home the importance of "jointness" to the Chiefs. They should not look upon themselves as servants of a particular service, but as members of a common national-defense team. He reorganized the Pentagon in 1953, which strengthened Wilson's position as secretary of defense, but he accomplished little in the way of creating a common military culture.

5
THE MILITARY AND JOHN F. KENNEDY

There is no question of resisting civilian authority. However, it is very proper for the military commander to point out to civilian authorities the military risks of military decisions.
—*Admiral George Anderson*

Kennedy experienced difficult relations with the military, primarily because of his leadership style, which presented his senior officers with more challenges than had Eisenhower's. Furthermore, the Chiefs perceived that the new president had far less understanding than his predecessor of how the military functioned. Yet Kennedy clashed with the military over roles and missions only once: he lost the battle in his struggle to introduce special operations into the army. His defeat would have serious long-term implications for the military's relationship with future presidents, especially his successor.

Kennedy confronted major military issues on three separate occasions: the Bay of Pigs, the Cuban Missile Crisis, and the beginning of American military involvement in Vietnam. In the first instance, he wrongly assumed the military would speak up during his policy seminars and provide him with critical advice as needed. He learned that the military normally provided advice only when requested to do so and when the Chiefs assumed they had responsibility for the mission at hand. Thus, the military played a very peripheral role in the decision-making process during the Bay of Pigs, much to Kennedy's chagrin.

The Cuban Missile Crisis was different, with the military playing key roles in the decision-making process and in the implementation of the naval quarantine. During the confrontation, the Chiefs resisted and resented the tendency of the president and the secretary of defense to interfere in operational matters. Having been chastised by Kennedy for not speaking up during the Bay of Pigs, several of the chiefs readily—and eagerly—expressed their opinions on how best to respond to Soviet missiles in Cuba; however, the president found their advice useless.

The slide into the Vietnamese quagmire that began in earnest during Kennedy's tenure put him and his secretary of defense partially at odds with the military (particularly the army) over the proper way to deal with that country. Many in the upper ranks of the army resisted the president's effort to introduce a new military doctrine and instead tried to fight the Viet Cong as if they were the North Koreans or Chinese. Kennedy's failure to clearly define the mission in Vietnam also led to constant confusion on the part of the generals.

KENNEDY'S LEADERSHIP STYLE

Kennedy's leadership style could not have contrasted more with Eisenhower's approach to working with the military. While Eisenhower believed in the chain of command, with everything handled in formal bureaucratic channels and every participant assigned particular responsibilities, Kennedy ran the government more like a university seminar. Not surprisingly, George and Stern labeled Kennedy's style the "collegial model."[1] As they explained, "He did not find personally congenial the highly formal procedures, the large meetings, and the relatively aloof presidential role characteristic of Eisenhower's system." Key to the new president's style of decision making was group problem-solving, with the president's advisors working as a "debate team," and the expectation that every person present (regardless of special expertise) would provide his or her frank opinion. Furthermore, the president often gave overlapping assignments.[2] Kennedy, who considered the hierarchy favored by Eisenhower to be obstructive in nature, wanted a wide range of options and did not care where the ideas came from. He did not even hold regular staff meetings, which created problems for the more bureaucratic, regimented military. Gen. Maxwell Taylor recalled that "the President would have little of my feeble effort at regimentation and found it far more stimulating to acquire information from the give-and-take of impromptu discussion."[3] Unfortunately, the latter approach "produced few clear and properly considered recommendations."[4] Participants often were not certain of their responsibilities, nor were decisions made in a clear and unambiguous fashion. According to one source, "Eschewing a hierarchical staff system, Kennedy described himself as the hub of a wheel with a series of spokes, his assistants. In fact not all had equal influence."[5] It was a form of regulated chaos. Taylor, who served as the president's special assistant for national security affairs,

> was shocked at the disorderly and careless ways of the new White House. I found that I could walk into almost any office, request and receive a sheaf of top secret papers, and depart without signing a receipt or making any record of transaction. There was little perceptible method in the assignment of duties within the staff, although I had to admit that the work did get done, largely through the individual initiative of its members.[6]

The NSC rarely met. Instead, the council was the president's private organization, and its members "became advocates, rather than brokers, of national security policy."[7] Often Kennedy's own assistants, not to mention the generals and admirals, were left in the dark: they knew neither where they stood nor what was expected from them. This nonbureaucratic relationship was similar to Roosevelt's personalized style. However, in contrast to Roosevelt's willingness to delegate authority, Kennedy interfered in operations. And when crises arose, JFK lacked Eisenhower's more formal relationships, a critical type of structure during such events. Having one leader issuing unambiguous orders to a distinct chain of command was of vital importance.[8]

Finally, Kennedy was not ideological. Indeed, one of the best-known presidential scholars criticized him on those grounds with regard to the Cuban Missile Crisis, noting that "Kennedy showed an impressive capacity to empathize with his Soviet counterpart once that confrontation was under way. A clearer sense of direction might have made it unnecessary to put his crisis management skills to use."[9]

Kennedy and the Military

The military initially responded to Kennedy in a very positive manner. Army and navy officers found him appealing as a presidential candidate because he criticized Eisenhower for cutting conventional forces in order to fortify the country's strategic nuclear deterrent. Kennedy questioned the value of Eisenhower's massive retaliation strategy, repeating an argument that had been made by Generals Lemnitzer and Taylor—namely that nuclear deterrence did little good in areas where the Communists relied primarily on local insurrections, coups, political appeals, political subversion, and internal revolution. The only way to effectively resolve such situations was to have "military capabilities across the whole spectrum."[10] In essence this meant that in addition to a credible nuclear capability, the United States critically needed stronger conventional forces for limited military operations and a meaningful civil-defense program.

On March 28, 1961, Kennedy restated his dedication to a balanced force structure in his first speech on defense since taking office:

> "Our defense posture," he said, "must be both flexible and determined. Any potential aggressor contemplating an attack on any part of the free world with any kind of weapons, conventional or nuclear, must know that our response will be suitable, selective, swift and effective." In the same message, the new president reaffirmed also the need for a wider range of *usable* military power. "Diplomacy and defense are no longer distinct alternatives, one to be used when the other fails—but must complement each other."[11]

The United States could not fight wars using only nuclear weapons; indeed, the nation had to have the ability to fight conventionally as well so that small conflicts would not mushroom into a nuclear holocaust.

Of all the actions that Kennedy took, none would so strongly affect civil-military relations during and after his presidency as his decision to appoint Robert McNamara as secretary of defense. Kennedy's main reason for appointing this former executive from Ford Motor Company was his hope that he could and would introduce modern management techniques to the Pentagon as well as create a better climate for civil-military relations than had existed under Eisenhower. The problem, however, was that McNamara had little respect for the military or their expertise. As Lawrence Freedman explained, "The military appeared as amateurs in his presence, fumbling for answers to questions that had never been asked before, expected to explain their programs without recourse to the normal slogans or a sense of what the political marketplace would bear."[12]

McNamara arrived in Washington with his so-called "Whiz Kids," the majority of whom came from places like the Rand Corporation, where they had relied on analytical frameworks such as systems analysis to understand and address defense issues. The most notable of those he brought was Alain C. Enthoven, who became deputy assistant secretary for systems analysis. Although many military officers liked him and found him interesting, he and his similarly minded colleagues were determined to apply quantitative methods to military problems as much as possible. To quote McNamara, "I am sure that no significant military problem will be wholly susceptible to purely quantitative analysis. But every piece of the total problem that can be quantitatively analyzed removes one piece of uncertainty from our process of making a choice."[13] Among the other changes introduced by the new secretary of defense was an emphasis on "cost effectiveness," which became the Pentagon's pet phrase.

President John F. Kennedy with Secretary of Defense Robert McNamara (center) and General Maxwell Taylor, chairman of the Joint Chiefs of Staff. (John F. Kennedy Library)

Indeed, the new budgeting system that was created, the Planning-Programming-Budgeting System (PPBS), led to a reorganization of the Defense Department. Unfortunately, the transformation was enacted with little concern for service sensitivities or culture. For example, military forces were divided into strategic offensive and defensive forces and general purpose forces. Hence, the services were mixed together: the Polaris missile systems and the air force's missiles and bombers would come under one heading, as would the army and the Marine Corps—a guaranteed recipe for interservice rivalry and service irritation with the PPBS system.

The Chiefs became concerned that these amateurs would take over their function in designing and building weapons systems and in determining the mix of such systems. Every general and admiral would openly admit that cost effectiveness was an important consideration, but they rebelled at efforts by

McNamara and his Whiz Kids to make it the top priority. The resulting clash of cultures would lead to one problem after another.

The Whiz Kids proceeded from the assumption that "military people were border-line literate at best and communicated by animal noises."[14] A *New York Times* correspondent called them "downyfaced lads who seek pretentiously to ladle the fog of war with mathematically precise measuring cups."[15] And the generals responded in kind. To quote General LeMay, "The Kennedy Administration came in and right from the start we got the back of the hand. Get out of our way. We think nothing of you and your opinions. We don't like you as people. We have no respect for you. Don't bother us." The disdainful attitude was held not only by the Whiz Kids, but by McNamara himself. "We [The Joint Chiefs] started off trying to talk to him. It was like talking to a brick wall. We got nowhere. Finally it was just a waste of time and effort. We could state opinions when we had a chance. That was all."[16] Another well-informed observer noted that McNamara "ignored or dismissed military advice, disparaged military experience and expertise, and circumvented or sacked generals and admirals who opposed him. The warfare inside the Pentagon was intense and vicious."[17] Indeed, the problem was so serious that Maxwell Taylor found it necessary to urge Kennedy to rely primarily upon the Chiefs for military advice, and not upon the Whiz Kids.[18]

THE BAY OF PIGS

The Kennedy administration was haunted by a fear that it would be seen to be soft on Communism. The cold war was at its height, and most Americans would not accept the idea of a Communist regime only ninety miles from Florida. In 1956, for example, President Eisenhower approved a statement that read, "If a Latin American state should establish with the Soviet bloc, close ties of such a nature as seriously to prejudice our vital interests . . . [the United States must] be prepared to diminish Government economic and financial cooperation with that country and to take any other policy, economic or military actions deemed appropriate."[19] Subsequently, on November 5, 1959, Acting Secretary of State Christian Herter suggested that Eisenhower encourage opposition to Castro with the goal of replacing him with a democratically elected regime. By January of the following year, Eisenhower decided to try to overthrow the Castro regime, and by March the CIA had developed a plan. "That included assembling and training in the United States a paramilitary force capable of covert operations." The cadres would be deployed in Cuba "to organize, train and lead resistance forces recruited there both before and after the establishment of one or more centers of resistance."[20] The president approved the plan and put the CIA in charge. Attached to the Eisenhower administration's approval was a very important qualification: U.S. military personnel could not be part of combat units. By December 1960 the idea had developed to the point that the U.S. government was planning to infiltrate sixty or eighty men into Cuba, assuming that the Cuban masses would rise up and join these "Cuban volunteers" to throw out their oppressors. "With the uprising and probable chaos in Havana, the United States would be able to recognize a provisional government and send in a pacification force. The idea of supporting an amphibious operation involving Cuban rebels run by the CIA left the Pentagon deeply unimpressed, but Eisenhower appeared enthusiastic."[21]

Thus, when Kennedy took office he was presented with an ongoing program that had received strong support from Eisenhower before developing a life of its own. The day prior to the inauguration, Ike told Kennedy about the guerillas who were currently being trained in Guatemala and the plan to land them in Cuba; he asked the president-elect to support the operation "to the utmost" and urged "that this effort be continued and accelerated."[22] Kennedy's freedom to maneuver had been severely limited.

The CIA had been placed in charge of the plan because of its ability to run covert operations. There was nothing intrinsically wrong with that arrangement, but it would have important long-term implications. In the military, when someone supervises an operation, he or she takes control of it, runs it, and accepts responsibility for it. However, if the operation is under nonmilitary control and the military officer is not in the chain of command, he or she stays out of the way and permits the individual in charge to run the show. Because the president had placed the CIA in charge, therefore, the Chiefs did not consider the overthrow attempt to be the military's business. Richard Bissell Jr., the CIA official who was in charge of the Bay of Pigs, maintained in his memoirs that he "always thought that the Joint Chiefs were mainly influenced by their sense that the operation as a whole wasn't theirs. They didn't dream it up, they weren't in charge of it, they didn't plan it, and they were called in later to pass judgment on somebody else's idea."[23] Furthermore, the CIA was obsessed with secrecy. The JCS never received any written documents regarding the operation. Normally, such matters would be handled on paper, albeit tightly, so that very busy senior officers would have time to focus on the topic when their schedules permitted. Indeed, on more than one occasion, the JCS asked the CIA for such documentation but were turned down.[24] The military was further removed from the operation by Eisenhower's earlier decision to keep U.S. military personnel out of combat. The undertaking would be run by "spooks," not the military. Even though the Chiefs had a senior officer assigned to follow events closely, they were often kept in the dark with regard to what was happening.

Finally, the military was also pushed to the sidelines by the atmosphere that McNamara and his colleagues created upon their arrival in the Pentagon. The message the Chiefs received was that McNamara was in charge and that they would be asked for their opinion only when he desired to hear it. As a rule, he was not especially interested in learning their views. Meanwhile the president failed to explain clearly to senior officers that he expected them to be outspoken about military-related aspects of an invasion of Cuba.

The Joint Chiefs were formally apprised of plans to overthrow Castro on January 11, 1961, when Brig. Gen. David W. Gray, who was chief of the JCS's Joint Subsidiary Activities Division, was briefed by the CIA. Gray was not given anything in writing, but he prepared a report based on the meeting that reflected JCS views. He believed that directly involving the U.S. military with Cuban volunteer troops was key.[25] The Cubans could not carry out such an operation on their own.

On January 28 Kennedy presided over a meeting on Cuba that was attended by Vice President Lyndon B. Johnson; Secretary of State Dean Rusk; Secretary of Defense Robert McNamara; McGeorge Bundy, who was the president's special assistant for national security affairs; Paul Nitze, assistant secretary for international security affairs; General Lemnitzer; and CIA Director Allen Dulles—a gathering of national security stars. The president listened to a very optimistic CIA report and then asked the Defense Department to take "a hard look at the CIA's military conception." In addition, the president stipulated that Eisenhower's ban on U.S. participation in any operation against Castro would remain in force.[26]

On January 31 CIA operatives again briefed General Gray, who was appointed the JCS contact for all matters related to the effort to topple Castro. The CIA plan "called for a diversionary attack elsewhere and an air-sea assault on Trinidad area beaches a day after B-26 bombers had attacked Castro's airfields, patrol vessels, communications centers, and tank and artillery parks. . . . The object would be to establish a beachhead and attract local support in an area in which there was considerable anti-Castro activity."[27] The JCS response stated that success depended upon an uprising by the Cuban populace or outside (i.e., American military) assistance. Indeed, the Chiefs believed that unless the Cuban people rose up, Castro's army would eventually drive the invading volunteers into the sea. In the end, the JCS document stated that "despite the shortcomings pointed out in the assessment, the Joint

Chiefs of Staff consider that timely execution of this plan has a fair chance of ultimate success."[28] Unfortunately, few civilians, including the president, understood that the Joint Chiefs used the term "fair" to mean only a 30 percent chance of success!

Discordant voices were raised, however. Admiral Burke, in particular, argued that the CIA proposal was "weak" and "sloppy." "Burke had little faith in a military concept that came from men who had no military command experience."[29] According to Mark Perry, Gen. David Shoup, the commandant of the Marine Corps, thought the plan "was the height of stupidity."[30] But neither Burke nor Shoup attended many of the key meetings with Kennedy; even if they had, military protocol at the time suggested that they spoke only if asked to by the president, the chairman, or some other very senior official. Compounding their reluctance to voice their concerns was the president's own lack of overt enthusiasm. "General Gray argues that if the president had said 'We're going to go' a little more intensity would have gone into it."[31] Perhaps if the chiefs had believed that the president really intended to invade Cuba, they would have become more deeply involved and been more outspoken in expressing their misgivings.

After the president asked the Joint Chiefs to take another look at the CIA plan in February, General Gray sent three colonels to Guatemala to inspect the Cuban force. Despite some misgivings about Cuban airpower's potential to inflict damage on an invasion force, the Joint Chiefs stated that the invasion would "achieve initial success." But as they had in the past, they argued that success of the overall operation would ultimately depend on an uprising in Cuba. In addition, the Chiefs also argued that surprise was critical. "Without surprise, 'it is most likely that the air mission will fail,' and with it the whole operation."[32] Although the Chiefs were less than forceful in raising their concerns, a careful reading of their statements demonstrates that they were not enthusiastic about the operation.

At a key meeting in the White House on March 11, the CIA argued that no alternative existed to using the brigade of Cuban volunteers to topple Castro. Kennedy feared he would run serious domestic political risks if he decided to cancel the invasion idea: Cuban exiles would blast him, and Republicans would jump all over him. He had to do something. Yet he also worried that the CIA plan would turn out to be too spectacular. With the Soviet invasion of Hungary fresh on his mind, he did not want to be accused of "invading" another country, an action that would undermine Washington's relations with Latin America. As a consequence, after listening to Bissell's presentation of the Trinidad proposal, he said that "this is too much like a World War II invasion." Instead, he asked the CIA to come up with "quiet" landing somewhere else.[33]

President Kennedy with the Joint Chiefs of Staff. General Lyman Lemnitzer, chairman of the Joint Chiefs, is on the president's right. (John F. Kennedy Library)

On March 14 the CIA gave the JCS's Interdirectorate Working Group five new proposals for evaluation. The group came out in favor of a place called Zapata because of its airstrip, which would permit Cuban volunteers to bring in needed supplies, and because of its swamp, which would make it more difficult for Castro's troops to attack. Although they accepted Zapata (the Bay of Pigs), the JCS also noted that they still preferred the old site, Trinidad.[34] General Gray, who believed that moving the landing site reduced the chances for success to 20 percent, later commented that he should have recommended to the Chiefs that the operation be cancelled.[35] But the Chiefs approved the findings of the working group in less than twenty minutes and then passed them on to McNamara. Unfortunately, both the president and McNamara mistakenly believed that the Chiefs preferred the Zapata plan, which called for air and ground troops to make night landings, over the earlier Trinidad scenario. On March 16 the president told the CIA to go ahead with the Zapata attack, but he warned them that he was prepared to cancel the operation up to twenty-four hours prior to the actual invasion.

The Chiefs committed a major mistake when they decided to support the Zapata plan even though several of them had serious misgivings. Lemnitzer commented later, "Probably no JCS paper of this period proved more controversial and surely none did greater damage to JCS reputations."[36] The paper put the Chiefs on record in favor of the invasion, something they would live to regret. The Chiefs erred further when they, like the president, accepted the CIA's assurances that Cuban volunteers could simply melt into the countryside and become guerillas if the worst happened. As one writer noted, "Nobody pointed out until after the event that no guerrillas had operated in the Zapata during the twentieth century and that even trained guerrillas find it hard to escape helicopters."[37] To make matters worse, General Gray had begun to realize by the end of March that the CIA had not lived up to its promise to create a viable subversive movement in Cuba "as they had promised"; once again he regretted not pushing the Chiefs to call for a cancellation of the invasion.[38]

On April 4 the president presided over a meeting at the State Department. Kennedy decided that the invasion would take place on either April 15 or 17. Lemnitzer claimed that he "argued vigorously" against the Zapata plan with Thomas Mann, who was the assistant secretary of state for inter-American affairs. Mann, however, told him that discussing such subjects was a waste of time because the president had made up his mind. Given his military background, Lemnitzer decided not to raise the issue again with the president. Now that the president had made his decision, Lemnitzer's job as a good soldier was to carry it out, not to question it.[39]

Although the Chiefs were willing to do whatever the president requested, they felt excluded from the process. They were not in operational control—they had only been asked to comment on another agency's operational plan. To quote Peter Wyden,

> General Lemnitzer, the Chairman of the Joint Chiefs of Staff, was not unsympathetic when Fulbright pointed out how difficult it would be to disavow U.S. sponsorship of the operation, but the general noted to himself that disavowal was now his trade, and that he could make no contribution on the subject. Admiral Burke, the normally outspoken Chief of Naval Operations, thought that so much time had been given to presentations by Messrs. Bissell and Fulbright that none was left for more military details. When the President again expressed concern that the operation would look too much like a World War II invasion, General Gray, sitting on his left, assured him that the landings had been shifted from daytime to night and that there would now be relatively small assaults spread over four separate beaches. This seemed to make

> the President feel easier. Otherwise, contributions to the meeting by the military were minor. Secretary McNamara merely cast an affirmative vote.[40]

To be fair to the Chiefs and General Gray in particular, the latter pushed the CIA hard to provide the president with a briefing on the military aspects of the proposed invasion. For example, at a meeting in early April, Gray spoke with Tracy Barnes, who was representing the CIA. " 'For Christ's sake, Tracy, this is the last chance,' he said. He was still keeping after Barnes to set up a 'full-scale military briefing' for the President. Again Barnes assured him that a briefing would be held. It never was."[41]

On the way to an April 12 meeting at the White House, Gray pressed both Lemnitzer and McNamara to emphasize to the president the critical importance of air supremacy to a successful operation. Without it, he feared that the Cuban volunteers would be destroyed from the air. Bissell's presentation, according to Gray, was "stellar. . . . but he never gave the complete briefing we had begged for and never once mentioned the air strikes."[42] Unfortunately, neither Lemnitzer nor McNamara raised the issue, thereby giving the president the impression that the military was not concerned about the issue. "Gray left the meeting feeling frustrated: too much time was being spent on political problems, not enough on military necessity."[43]

The president formally approved the operation on April 16, the day before the main attack was to occur. In fact, the invasion had already begun. On April 15, eight B-26s of World War II vintage had bombed and strafed three Cuban airfields. The attacks were claimed to have destroyed over 70 percent of the Cuban air force, a highly inaccurate estimate; of Castro's thirty-seven combat aircraft and fifteen transport planes, only five had been destroyed. In addition, 160 members of the Cuban Brigade were supposed to have launched a diversionary attack thirty miles from the U.S. naval base at Guantanamo. Unfortunately, the operation was a disaster from the beginning. The diversionary force never landed; instead, they aborted "when they saw a jeep and two trucks on the shore."[44]

The operation was further compromised on the evening prior to the invasion when Kennedy, fearing that U.S. involvement with the operation might become public, cancelled the air strike that had been scheduled for the next morning. The original purpose of the strike was to knock out Castro's remaining air force. Now, a new plan called for air strikes to be delayed until the brigade had captured the airstrip at Zapata. Planes could then be flown in under the guise of being part of the brigade's efforts to topple Castro.

Realizing the profound implications of the president's decision, CIA

Deputy Director Charles Cabell, an air force general, went with Bissell to see Secretary of State Dean Rusk, who had been instrumental in getting the president to call off the air operation. They asked Rusk's permission to launch a second strike. Rusk responded, "I told them I couldn't authorize that strike. They persisted, and I invited them to call President Kennedy and ask him personally. They elected not to do so, but later claimed that had the strike gone ahead, Castro's planes would not have hit the landing ships."[45]

Most agree that the Chiefs were neither consulted nor given prior notification of the president's decision to call off the air strikes. In fact, this decision was made at a meeting that neither McNamara nor Lemnitzer attended. When the latter learned about the president's decision, he became very upset. According to one source,

> In Fort Meyer, near the Pentagon, Generals Wheeler and Gray rang General Lemnitzer's doorbell about 2 A.M.
>
> The Chairman of the Joint Chiefs, sleepy and in his bathrobe, inquired, "How did things go?"
>
> "They cancelled the air strike!"
>
> Lemnitzer "couldn't believe it." It sounded so unbelievable that he called the JCS situation room to confirm it. "Pulling out the rug" like this was "absolutely reprehensible, almost criminal."[46]

Lemnitzer was not the only senior military officer who was outraged by the decision. General Shoup later remarked, "I want to tell you this right now. Had I as an individual heard that they were going to call off the air strikes I'd have asked that the commander in chief be informed. I'd have called him myself because it was absolutely essential to success." For his part, Gen. Thomas White, the air force chief of staff, later said that the decision to call off these air strikes was "a very key factor" in Castro's halting of the invasion.[47]

The invasion landing was bungled from the beginning as well. A member of the local police spotted the invaders and sounded the alarm, bringing the attack to Castro's attention by 3:15 A.M. At dawn, Castro's surviving air force, primarily T-33s (small jet trainers that carried two machine guns and rockets), wreaked havoc on the brigade and its ships and supplies. The landing craft experienced problems, and the green troops fired their weapons at such a rate that the brigade soon found itself out of ammunition. Furthermore, the uprisings that Bissell had promised never materialized. Unfortunately, the swamp that surrounded the volunteers seriously hindered their attempts to melt into the countryside and thus escape the fire they were taking from Soviet-made tanks and artillery. Besides, the guerilla movement's home in the Escambray Mountains was over eighty miles away.

The second day into the invasion, Kennedy met with his senior advisors, including Admiral Burke and Lemnitzer. Burke, as well as Bissell, argued very strongly for the use of aircraft from the USS *Essex*, which was in the region, to destroy the T-33s. Kennedy compromised and told the Chiefs he would authorize a jet escort to defend the B-26s attacking ground targets. Even this effort failed, however. The B-26s passed overhead the next morning while the navy's jets were lined up on the *Essex* waiting for them, but the two squadrons had gotten the time mixed up. The B-26s were on Nicaraguan time, while the *Essex* was in another time zone. By the time the navy scrambled its jets, two of the B-26s had been shot down and the others had returned to Nicaragua. Soon the brigade commander, Pepe San Roman, sent a distressing message: "We are out of ammo and fighting on the beach. Please send help. We cannot hold."[48] By nightfall, resistance had ended. The comedy of errors was over. Of the 1,400 men who landed at the Bay of Pigs, 114 were killed and 1,189 were captured, including San Roman.[49]

In retrospect, the operation had been severely handicapped by the secretive nature in which important details were withheld from the military. For example, during the last week of March, Rear Adm. John Clark was called to the office of Adm. Dennis Dennison, commander of U.S. Forces, Atlantic. A captain from Washington told Clark about the possibility of an invasion of Cuba by Cuban volunteers. Clark was told to take his staff aboard the carrier *Essex*, which would take onboard a special squadron of AD-4 Skyhawk jet fighters. The *Essex,* with five destroyers, was to escort five of the Cuban Brigade's ships to a point near the Bay of Pigs. To ensure secrecy, the hull numbers on the destroyers were to be painted out. Two of the destroyers would then escort the brigade's ships to the beaches. "Clark's job was to make sure that the Cubans got safely to the beaches. This would be highly unlikely to create problems, because Castro's air force would be destroyed. He was not to allow a shot to be fired by an American vessel or aircraft unless absolutely necessary in self-defense."[50]

Even though Dennison had been told about the operation and provided rules of engagement, the CIA refused to let him see the invasion plan. As a consequence, the navy was unable to make the kind of contingency plans necessary to rescue the Cuban Brigade if something went wrong. "Not surprisingly, in common with other orthodox military men, the alarmed Admiral concluded that the whole Cuban project should have functioned directly under his own centralized control rather than that of the CIA in Washington."[51] And he was right, because the navy and Marine Corps understood the problems associated with amphibious warfare far better than the CIA. They would have known that the poorly maintained aluminum boats would have major problems when they approached the beaches at the Bay of Pigs. Logistics would also prove to be a disaster, because the various items carried on the ships had not been loaded properly.

When the invaders were attacked by Castro's fighters, Dennison and Clark could do nothing, despite being only twenty miles away. With its hands tied by Washington, the navy was forced to sit by and watch as the massacre of the brigade proceeded. Three times Admiral Clark asked Washington for permission to help the invaders, and three times he was told no. "It was agonizing, just like ignoring a man dying of thirst begging for a drink of water." Having difficulty believing that the U.S. Navy would simply leave, he later recalled, "It's just too cold-blooded and brutal to say, 'OK fellows, this isn't working, goodbye now.' "[52] At his Norfolk headquarters, Admiral Dennison responded with a deep sense of frustration, if not betrayal, when he read the message from Washington. "He shook his head and reddened. 'Do not seek air combat,' it said. And: 'Do not attack ground targets.' What was the point? How can you protect somebody if you can't shoot? It was 'ridiculous.' 'Bumpy Road,' the Navy's code for the operation, should have been called 'Quagmire.' "[53] When the time came to evacuate the surviving invaders, Dennison and Clark learned that the CIA had drawn up secret plans for such an evacuation but had not bothered to let the navy in on them. Dennison complained, "When we were called upon to start the rescue operation, we didn't know how many men were in there, what particular beaches they'd be landing on, where they were likely to be, or any information of this sort."[54]

Kennedy joined the CIA in arousing the ire of the military. Although senior officers accepted the president's authority, they were upset by his interference in operational and tactical matters. During the day of the invasion, for example, the president seemed "stunned" and confused, lacking a clear idea of what to do and how to do it. Admiral Burke, who was the senior military officer on the scene, was "pressing for every yard of ground he could get in the direction of more American participation by American forces in at least limiting the damage." Kennedy kept saying no. He even went so far as to demand that navy ships stay over the horizon so they could not be seen from Cuba. One participant in the day's events "watched a 'stricken look' cross Admiral Burke's face when the President picked up one of the little magnetic destroyer models and moved it over the horizon. It clearly pained the admiral to see the President bypass all channels of command—and all tradition." And in one of the worst criticisms of Kennedy's actions, Harlan Cleveland, the State Department's assistant secretary for international organizations, "was chagrined to see how obvious it was that the President's only executive experience had been as commander of a PT boat."[55]

The Bay of Pigs fiasco significantly damaged the Chiefs' relationship with the White House. The president felt they had "disappointed him."[56] He was reportedly "angry at himself for having signed on to what in retrospect seemed like such an unworkable plan but also at the CIA and the Chiefs for having misled him."[57] In fact, he was more than disappointed. He was angry.

> The President was especially wistful about his own branch of service, the Navy, and its chief. "Arleigh Burke sat right across from me, . . . I've been reading about 'Thirty-knot Burke.' He was terrific! I was a lieutenant on a PT boat! You should have seen how impressive it was to see the Joint Chiefs of Staff show up with all that fruit salad. . . . And they'd have colonels carrying pointers and maps." The president told Powers he had asked Burke, "Will this plan work?" And Burke had said, "As far as we've been able to check it out, the plan is good."[58]

After the Bay of Pigs experience, the president began to question the Chiefs' professional competence. If they were going to let him down on something this important, how could he trust them on other issues? Similarly, in a development that would have major implications when the Vietnam conflict began to heat up, McNamara "became reluctant to take military opinions at face value without checking the data upon which they were based."[59] General Taylor probably put it best when he remarked that "there is a time when you can't advise by innuendos and suggestions. You have to look him in the eye and say, 'I think it's a lousy idea, Mr. President. The chances of our succeeding are about one in ten.' And nobody said that."[60]

To Kennedy's credit, he realized in the aftermath of the Bay of Pigs that he needed to improve his relationship with the military. On May 27 he went to the Pentagon to meet with the Chiefs. He began by telling them that he considered them his principal military advisors and wanted to hear their views "directly and unfiltered." The president also informed them that he expected them to provide the country "dynamic and imaginative leadership in contributing to the success of military and paramilitary aspects of Cold War programs." Third, he expected the Chiefs to present the military's view "in such a way as to ensure that military factors are clearly understood before decisions are reached." Finally, he observed, "While I look to the Chiefs to present the military factor without reserve or hesitation, I regard them to be more than military men and expect their help in fitting military requirements into the overall context of any situation, recognizing that the most difficult problem in government is to combine all assets in a unified, effective pattern."[61]

Kennedy's manner of making military-related decisions may have been questionable, but one should not underestimate the importance of his decision on May 27 to go to the Chiefs, rather than demand they come to him, something he could have easily done. It was a clear signal to the Chiefs that he wanted them to participate in the decision-making process. In a certain sense, this would be a new experience for them, because the majority of them did not understand the world of political-military decision making. Even fewer realized just how soon their advice would be required in this arena.

TAYLOR BECOMES MILITARY CZAR

Despite his visit to the Pentagon, Kennedy remained aloof toward the military. He knew he needed military advice, but he did not want to rely too much on senior military officers he did not trust. Kennedy thus turned to the author of flexible response, Gen. Maxwell Taylor, who was recalled to active duty on July 1, 1961, to become the president's special assistant for national security affairs in the White House. The recall order made clear that Taylor did not have any command authority, but the political reality was that he was closer to the president than any of the Chiefs. And in Washington, proximity is power. As a result, Taylor's appointment raised serious questions about the status of the JCS. Lemnitzer rationalized Taylor's appointment, suggesting that it was necessary because of the president's limited experience with military affairs. But Taylor did far more than fill gaps in the president's knowledge of military issues. And in spite of the efforts by both Lemnitzer and Taylor to put the best face possible on the arrangement (and the latter's willingness to swear undying devotion to cooperation with the Chiefs), the balance of power had changed. Henceforth, all papers sent from the JCS to the White House went through Taylor's hands and then to the president. To think that Taylor would not put his stamp on military policies or at least provide private comments to the president would be naive at best. Taylor essentially became another JCS chairman, and a far more influential one at that, especially given the close relationship he developed with Kennedy's inner circle. Indeed, he and Bobby Kennedy became so close that the latter named his new son "Maxwell." From the Chiefs' standpoint, the primary benefit of Taylor's appointment was that they now had someone between McNamara and the president: "Taylor was not awed by McNamara's power and treated him as if he [Taylor] were at least his equal and even his mentor."[62]

THE CUBAN MISSILE CRISIS

Few events in the post–World War II history of the United States would be more important to both the country and the nature of civil-military relations than the Cuban Missile Crisis. If nothing else, the showdown exposed the greater willingness of the military to speak out, as the president had requested, on issues of critical political-military importance. However, the military officers' lack of political-military experience was only too obvious; in fact, their hawkish approach scared the president. Indeed, one could argue that the combined impact of the Bay of Pigs and the Cuban Missile Crisis was to make Kennedy very wary of listening to the Chiefs on any issue. Consequently, Maxwell Taylor's authority and power increased significantly in the aftermath of the crisis. As the one officer the president genuinely trusted, Taylor would be appointed by Kennedy to succeed Lemnitzer as chairman of the Joint Chiefs when the latter's tour of duty ended in October 1962. In addition, the Cuban Missile Crisis once again illustrated just how sensitive and resistant the military was to civilian interference in operational matters.

The Bay of Pigs fiasco had only increased the pressure on Kennedy to remove Castro from power. Try as the new president's administration might, it could not hide the fact that it had failed to carry out Eisenhower's plan. Castro was still in Havana, while more than a thousand Cuban "volunteers" sat in his jails. Hence, "at this juncture the President could scarcely afford any further unfavorable developments in Cuba, which might tie Cuba still more closely to Soviet Communism or make Castro seem still more of a threat to the stability of the rest of the hemisphere or to the composure of the United States."[63]

American intelligence officials were fully aware that the Soviet Union was supplying Cuba with weapons in the aftermath of the failed invasion. The Soviet ambassador to the UN stated that the weapons were for "self-defense," which made sense, even if Washington was not happy about the arms shipments. However, by 1962 the volume of Russian military supplies increased substantially, and the American intelligence community began to focus greater attention on what was happening in Cuba. The primary vehicle for tracking Soviet weapons to Cuba was the U-2, a spy plane capable of flying at high altitudes while taking pictures of both Cuba and of Soviet vessels traveling to that island nation.

According to General Taylor, between July and September 1962 about "seventy shiploads of war material had arrived in Cuban ports." These ships brought a wide variety of weapons—artillery, tanks, MIG fighters, Komar missile boats, and surface-to-air (SAM) missiles. In addition, the number of Soviet military technicians on the island increased from a few hundred to around four thousand. Still, the United States was unsure of what the Soviets were doing.[64]

The breakthrough came on October 14, when a U-2 took photographs showing that the Soviets were deploying missiles capable of carrying nuclear warheads. As Schlesinger put it, "By Monday afternoon, reading the obscure and intricate markings, they identified a launching pad, a series of buildings for ballistic missiles and even one missile on the ground at San Cristobal."[65] On October 15 an extremely upset president was shown the pictures. Soviet officials had personally assured him that they were only supplying Cuba with defensive weapons, and here was indisputable evidence of offensive weapons—weapons that could be aimed only at the United States. If these missiles were allowed to remain, not only would serious questions arise about the president's ability to stand up to Moscow, but those who criticized his handling of the Bay of Pigs affair would gain additional ammunition. Kennedy could hear it now: "a weak President was being pushed around not only by Nikita Khrushchev, but by Fidel Castro as well."[66]

On Tuesday, October 16, the president told his brother and close confidant, Robert, about the photos. According to Robert, most top government officials believed that the only course of action open to the United States was an air strike against the missile sites.[67] For their part, the Chiefs, according to McNamara, were " 'strongly opposed to [a] limited air attack. [They are thinking not of] twenty or fifty sorties or a hundred sorties, but probably several hundred sorties.' 'Such an assault on Cuba,' the Defense Secretary acknowledged, almost certainly, 'will lead to a Soviet military response of some type someplace in the world. It may well be worth the price.' "[68] The Chiefs felt that these missiles represented such a serious threat to the United States that they should be attacked even if they became operational (and thereby could launch missiles against the United States). McNamara added that he thought the United States should mobilize its military forces.

By Wednesday additional photographic evidence indicated that other sites existed with "at least sixteen and possibly thirty two missiles of over a thousand mile range."[69] Analysts estimated that these missiles could be operational within a week. The Chiefs continued to argue for a massive air strike combined with a naval blockade. To the air force, and especially Gen. Curtis LeMay, who was the service's chief of staff and an advocate of strategic bombing in World War II, the idea of limited strikes made no sense. And the military's position was not without merit. The Chiefs insisted that unless "Castro's planes, the artillery batteries opposite the American base at Guantanamo, [and] the nuclear storage sites" were eliminated with the first strike, the Russians would be able to offer serious military opposition.[70]

In spite of these logical arguments, the Chiefs often gave the impression that all they wanted was a war. Indeed, Robert Kennedy referred to LeMay when he spoke of "the many times I heard the military take positions, which, if wrong, had the advantage that no one would be around at the end to know."[71] The president may have been upset at the military's refusal to say what it thought during Bay of Pigs crisis, but during the Cuban Missile Crisis, military officers (especially those like LeMay) were not only outspoken, but rather blunt and in some cases disrespectful. For example, when Robert Kennedy informed LeMay that he would not be permitted to brief the White House, the latter observed, "What a dumb shit."[72]

The Chiefs continued to push hard for a full-scale air strike. On October 18 General LeMay told the president that a military attack was critical. Kennedy looked skeptically at LeMay and asked about the potential Russian response. "They, no more than we, can't let these things go by without doing something. They can't, after all their statements, permit us to take out their missiles, kill a lot of Russians, and then do nothing. If they don't take action in Cuba, they certainly will in Berlin."[73] LeMay was certainly the most anxious of the Chiefs to start a war, but his outbursts did the Chiefs little good in Kennedy's eyes. First, Kennedy went through a period in which the Chiefs said almost nothing, and now he was faced with a fire-breathing general who was prepared to bomb Cuba regardless of the implications for U.S. security. Importantly, the various Chiefs held differing opinions, and they never made a recommendation as a group to invade Cuba; nonetheless, they strongly advocated that the United States prepare to launch an invasion should one become necessary.[74] The outspoken Chiefs continually increased the number of planes they believed would be necessary to attack Cuba and eliminate the missiles. Indeed, the increasingly harder line they took alarmed Taylor to the point that he warned them, "You are defeating yourselves with your own cleverness, Gentlemen."[75] The president was growing tired of having them devise one scenario after another in which each was worse than its predecessor and required the commitment of more resources from the United States.[76]

To clarify the issue of a full-scale air attack, the president called in Lt. Gen. Walter C. Sweeny Jr., who, as commander of the Tactical Air Command, would be responsible if the United States launched an attack on the missiles in Cuba. When asked by the president about such an operation, Sweeny informed Kennedy that he intended to launch 100 sorties to knock out the five SAM sites and the three MIG airfields. He would follow up with 250 sorties against the missile launchers at the eight or nine known missile sites, while sending another 150 sorties against Cuban airfields to make certain all of the MIGs and IL-28s had been destroyed.[77] Sweeny told the president that he was certain the strikes would be successful, but when the president asked what that meant, Sweeney "readily conceded that any such attack could not guarantee the destruction or neutralization of all the missiles."[78] His response convinced the president that an air strike was not the correct answer.[79]

Kennedy then decided on a blockade. On October 21 Adm. George Anderson told Kennedy that each Soviet ship would be asked to stop; if it did not, a shot would be fired across its bow. If the ship continued on its course, a shot would be fired into its rudder, thereby disabling the vessel. Kennedy asked Anderson if he was certain that the navy could successfully carry out such interdictions. Anderson responded, "Yes, Sir!"[80]

On October 22, the president made his historic speech to the nation concerning events in Cuba. Noting that Nikita Khrushchev had been caught red-handed in his efforts to place offensive strategic missiles in Cuba, he proclaimed a quarantine around Cuba of "all offensive military equipment under shipment to Cuba." Second, he ordered the military to continue close surveillance of Cuba and directed that the "Armed Forces . . . prepare for any eventualities." Kennedy then stated that any missile launched from Cuba would be viewed as a Soviet attack on the United States. Finally, he called upon Khrushchev to remove the offending missiles.[81]

The Joint Chiefs of Staff were ordered to contact personally the relevant senior military officers and provide them with instructions.

> In brief, the President's decision announced in his speech of October 22 initiated a vast concentration of ground, air, and amphibious forces complete with the supplies necessary for an invasion of Cuba. At the same time it initiated actions to protect the continental United States from air attack; to deter a possible nuclear strike on the United States or any of our allies; and to mount a blockade of Cuba on the terms laid down by the President. In the course of discharging these tasks, the responsible commanders established and maintained a partial blockade of Cuba from October 24 to November 20. They assembled invasion forces totaling roughly a quarter million men during the period from October 17 to October 31, held them in readiness to invade Cuba until November 31, and thereafter held them in standby readiness until December 20.[82]

The navy's plan was to stop Russian ships before they sailed within range of Cuban jets. However, on October 22, the British ambassador suggested to President Kennedy that he make the interception point much closer to Cuba, thereby giving Khrushchev more time to make a decision. Kennedy immediately agreed, despite protests by the navy, which did not want to put its ships and planes in harm's way.

The quarantine became effective on October 24. In implementing it, Kennedy worried that the navy might become overly aggressive and begin shooting at Soviet ships if they acted suspiciously; the president insisted that only the minimal amount of force necessary be used so that the Soviet ships would be disabled, not sunk. He asked McNamara to check into matters. McNamara, who also believed that Admiral Anderson had failed to provide him with important information, went to see him at about ten o'clock that evening. He reportedly stormed into Flag Plot (the navy's command center) "like a madman" and started chewing out one officer after another until Anderson appeared.[83]

> The encounter started badly. McNamara spotted a marker showing an American ship off by itself on the vast ocean, far away from the interception area. "What's it doing there?" he asked. Anderson did not answer directly because—as he later explained—too many others were listening. Eventually, he drew McNamara aside and explained that the lone ship was sitting on top of a Soviet submarine. McNamara asked about the first interception: exactly what would the Navy do? Anderson replied there was no need to discuss the issue; the Navy had known all there was to know about running a blockade since the days of John Paul Jones. But McNamara was not to be put off. "We must discuss it."[84]

McNamara explained that the president wanted to be sure that the United States did not humiliate the Russians. Kennedy wanted to leave them a way out. "Khrushchev must somehow be persuaded to pull back, rather than be goaded into retaliation." The secretary of defense then proceeded to go over all the details of the intercepts with the chief of naval operations, an unprecedented move. "No Secretary of Defense had ever spoken that way to a member of the Joint Chiefs of Staff."[85] The incident ended with Anderson commenting to McNamara, " 'Now Mr. Secretary, if you and your deputy will go back to your offices, the Navy will run the blockade.' Making no reply, McNamara walked out," noting to his deputy, "That's the end of Anderson." (In 1963 Kennedy sent the admiral to Portugal as ambassador.)[86]

Anderson discussed this encounter some years later. He, like General LeMay, had clearly favored a more aggressive policy toward the Soviets. "My personal view was that the missile crisis offered the United States the opportunity to rid itself of Castro and his communist regime in Cuba." Having said that, he also claimed that he tried to stay out of policy issues: "I was very careful not to involve the military in the determination of national policy." Anderson viewed his encounter with McNamara in light of what had happened at the Bay of Pigs, where civilian intervention in military matters was rampant. "I endeavored to do everything possible to ensure that the navy kept the president fully informed of every aspect of the naval blockade while precluding the interference into military operations by civilian authorities, who had a tendency to bypass the normal military chain of command."[87] In other words, McNamara's "grilling" of Anderson was neither welcome nor appropriate in the admiral's opinion.

On October 23, as a Russian ship neared the quarantine line, it turned back. Ironically, the vessel may have turned around less in fear of causing an international incident than out of concern that the Americans might gain access to Soviet missile secrets. In the end, Khrushchev agreed to dismantle the missiles, thus removing one of the greatest threats to American national security since World War II.

GETTING INTO VIETNAM

Like the Bay of Pigs, U.S. involvement in Vietnam dated from the Eisenhower administration. When the 1954 Geneva Agreements split Vietnam along the seventeenth parallel, President Eisenhower wrote South Vietnam's prime minister, Ngo Dinh Diem, assuring him of U.S. support "to assist the Government of Viet-Nam in developing and maintaining a strong, viable state, capable of resisting attempted subversion or aggression through military means."[88] As the originator of the domino theory, Eisenhower worried that if Indochina adopted Communism, the rest of Southeast Asia would follow suit very quickly. His successor, Kennedy, feared that Republicans would thus make an issue out of U.S. influence in Asia. As Phillip Davidson observed, "Ever since 1949, when the Republicans had branded Harry Truman as 'the man who lost China,' Democratic hearts quailed at the thought of another defeat in Asia under a Democratic president. . . . A Democratic president could not see Vietnam fall to communism without inviting a devastating political attack at home."[89] Just as Kennedy's hands had been tied during the Bay of Pigs and the Cuban Missile Crisis, he could not simply sit by and watch Vietnam become a Communist nation, at least not without paying a very heavy price on the domestic political front.

Kennedy believed that the new doctrine of flexible response provided the answer to the Vietnam insurgency. When he spoke of flexible response, he had counterinsurgency in mind. Thus he favored the special forces—small units capable of fighting Communists behind enemy lines and of winning the hearts and minds of the population to inspire them to fight for a cause, even if they lived in poor societies. "One of the first questions he is reported to have asked was 'What are we doing about guerilla warfare?' "[90] The answer he received was simple: not much. The Special Warfare School at Fort Bragg, North Carolina, was training fewer than a thousand soldiers, far too few to do the job Kennedy had in mind. As a result he called a special meeting with the Joint Chiefs in which he pushed them to upgrade the status of the special forces within the army, and then he ordered McNamara to divert $100 million from his budget to train soldiers to fight guerilla wars. In January 1962 he created a new interagency group to coordinate such activities.

Kennedy confronted an obstacle, however. Special forces ran contrary to American army doctrine. U.S. generals had been trained to fight wars in which heavy armor, backed up by massive amounts of artillery and infantry, broke through enemy lines and annihilated or captured the other side's soldiers in the process. This was the heart of a conventional war: occupy territory and either kill or imprison the enemy. Indeed, for many senior military officers, Vietnam appeared to be just another Korea or World War II. Counterinsurgency was fine, but it was not mainstream. (It certainly was not the right career path for an enterprising young officer who hoped to become a general.) Besides, the army did not come up with the doctrine; rather, it was the idea of the latest politician, whose primary military expertise came from running a torpedo boat. In coming years, senior army officers would repeatedly resist the president's effort to see Vietnam through the prism of counterinsurgency. For many of them, the conflict was a military problem best solved by traditional military means.

In 1961, the key problem facing the Kennedy administration in Vietnam was Diem, an unusual individual. Not only was he a Vietnamese patriot, but he was also an especially devout Roman Catholic who lived a celibate life. Politically, Diem was authoritarian and refused to hold the elections called for by the 1954 Geneva Agreements. His popularity began waning by 1957, as evidenced by an assassination attempt, which he survived. Then, in 1960, he withstood an attempted coup by the army, which left him very suspicious of the military. He worried that if the armed forces became too strong, they might again move to oust him. Furthermore, he was not the kind of individual who was sympathetic to efforts to win the hearts and minds of the Vietnamese people. His primary concern was to keep himself and his nefarious family in power, which, according to one source, was limited to only 40 percent of the territory of South Vietnam.[91]

On May 10, 1961, the JCS issued their first formal proposal addressing the

Vietnam question. They proposed sending U.S. combat troops to Vietnam: "The objective would be to deter the North Vietnamese and Chinese while impressing Asian nations generally with American resolve."[92] The Chiefs wanted only a limited deployment, believing that it could be augmented at a later date if necessary.

That same month, Kennedy sent Vice President Lyndon Johnson to Saigon to obtain a sense of the situation on the ground. "The Vice President found Diem 'remote from the people' and 'surrounded by persons less admirable than he.' "[93] Johnson and the American ambassador pushed Diem to accept democratic reforms, and Diem hinted that he would do so. Suspicious of Diem's sincerity, the vice president nonetheless realized, as had most other observers, that the United States had no alternative to the South Vietnamese leader. In the meantime, Diem asked for more American aid, primarily in the military sphere. On August 4, the president agreed to help finance an expansion of the South Vietnamese army to 200,000 troops.

Unfortunately, the situation on the ground did not improve. The Viet Cong grew increasingly stronger. In fact, on September 18, they overran a provincial capital only fifty-five miles from Saigon, "beheaded the province chief, loaded up the arms and ammunition they had captured, and departed before a relief force arrived."[94] Morale in South Vietnam sank even lower. Diem immediately requested a further increase in aid from the United States. In response, Kennedy sent General Taylor and White House staffer Walt Rostow to Saigon on a fact-finding mission.

In Arthur Schlesinger's opinion, the fact that Taylor, a general, headed the visit sent an important signal. "The effect was to color future thinking about Vietnam in both Saigon and Washington with the unavowed assumption that Vietnam was primarily a military rather than a political problem."[95] Taylor raised the issue of U.S. combat troops for Vietnam with Diem, who "avoided the subject until near the end of the interview and then dealt with it with deliberate ambiguity."[96] He clearly wanted the help of the Seventh Fleet to seal the country's approaches from the sea, but said that he did not want foreign troops in his country at that time. In his report, Taylor recommended that the United States provide the South Vietnamese with weapons and equipment, including helicopters to give them the kind of mobility they needed to fight the Viet Cong. He also recommended sending a logistical task force, which the Department of Defense estimated would require about 8,000 troops. The JCS agreed with Taylor, but expressed several reservations. First, they believed that the fall of Vietnam was inevitable unless substantial numbers of U.S. troops were introduced. Second, the Chiefs believed that given the stakes, the U.S. government had to think long and hard before becoming directly involved. Was the nation ready to pay the potentially high price of direct involvement? Most important, however, was the Chiefs' belief that the United States should avoid a policy of gradualism, in which the number of troops and amount of force deployed would slowly increase. If the United States decided to use force in Vietnam, then the undertaking should be carried out on an all-or-nothing basis.[97] The last of these three reservations would haunt the U.S. government and lead to numerous clashes between the Chiefs and senior politicians for years to come. In the end, the president agreed to most of Taylor's suggestions, with the exception of sending U.S. combat troops.

At this time, Washington made a major personnel decision that, despite the scant attention it drew, would have major implications for the United States. The top U.S. general in Vietnam, Lt. Gen. Lionel McGarr, was finishing his tour, and an obvious choice for his replacement was Brig. Gen. William P. Yarborough, a special forces officer who was thoroughly familiar with counterinsurgency warfare. Unfortunately, at Taylor's suggestion and urging, the president appointed (and promoted) Gen. Paul D. Harkins. In fact, "Kennedy could hardly have chosen a general less qualified than Harkins. In terms of the billet to which he was appointed, Harkins's military career was remarkable in two respects: he had no experience with insurgency warfare, and he had a close association with Maxwell Taylor."[98] Harkins began by doing exactly what the president did not want him to do: he corrupted the intelligence reports the army was sending to Washington. Prior to his arrival, intelligence reporting had been fairly accurate, but he soon let it be known that Saigon would send Washington only positive information. Field officers who attempted to file accurate (and thus negative) reports found their careers in jeopardy. Unfortunately, the precedent set by Harkins would significantly influence the U.S. Army's future reports from South Vietnam.

In addition to Harkins's rosy reporting, a major discrepancy also existed between what the president wanted done in Vietnam and the advice the army was giving the South Vietnamese military. The army continued to believe the problem was essentially military in nature. After troops had moved in to clear an area and sent the Viet Cong running, they would hand the area over to the civil guard, and thus theoretically permit economic, social, and political reform to take place. The first targets would be close to Saigon, but as they were "liberated," the military would expand the circle wider and wider.

Senior army officers considered the concept of winning the hearts and minds of the population to be a "fashionable idea."[99] Men's lives were at stake, and the army could not risk experiments on some new ideas that might or might not work. The old approach worked; Korea showed that. The problem was that in contrast to the North Koreans or Chinese Communists in Korea, the Viet Cong faded into the countryside when the South Vietnamese army appeared and then reemerged once the battle ended. Pushing the guerillas out of a particular region might make the army feel good, but it hardly changed matters. By training the South Vietnamese army along traditional military lines, the U.S. Army played into the Viet Cong's hands even further. Instead of providing security for the population, the army carried out military maneuvers that barely affected the situation on the ground. "Despite the presence of U.S. advisers at the province level who observed firsthand the inadequacies of the program, the generals in Saigon preferred the bogus statistics of success offered up by the GVN [Government of Viet Nam]. It was certainly a convenient arrangement for MACV [U.S. Military Assistance Command Vietnam]; so long as strategic hamlets were a success, the Army could continue developing the ARVN [Army of the Republic of Vietnam] into an effective strike force based on firepower and air mobility."[100]

In January 1962 the tension between McNamara and the Chiefs worsened. On January 13 they provided him with a memo taking issue with the president's decision to avoid combat in Vietnam. They argued that U.S. forces would have to be sent to South Vietnam if the current arrangement did not produce positive results. McNamara sent the memo on to Kennedy, noting however, that he did not agree with it.

Just as the Joint Chiefs and the secretary of defense found themselves increasingly at odds, the cracks continued to open in the facade of the South Vietnamese government. The Americans might consider Diem to be the only game in town, but by 1963 he was losing power. Consequently, those whom he promoted in both the political and military spheres tended to be those who pledged to him their political loyalty, which was his overriding concern. Unfortunately, loyalty frequently trumped merit. By mid-1963, Diem also faced unrest among the country's majority Buddhists and the failure of the strategic hamlet program. The United States found itself confronting a key decision: it could continue to support him in spite of his problems or pull the rug out from under him by backing a military coup.

Gen. Earle Wheeler, the army chief of staff, returned from his early–1963 visit to Vietnam with a "relatively favorable" report for the JCS on the ability of the United States to bring the insurgency under control by 1965. Shortly after coming back, he met with the president to discuss the situation in Vietnam. Unfortunately, according to Robert Dallek, he overemphasized the positive aspects of the situation in Vietnam. At the meeting "Wheeler frustrated and irritated Kennedy with a report Forrestal described as 'rosy euphoria' and a 'complete waste of . . . time.' "[101] The picture he painted, however, illustrated some "disquieting" factors as well, including the South Vietnamese army's shortage of noncommissioned officers (NCOs) and junior officers and "the continuous build-up of the Viet-Cong in strength and quality of the[ir] weapons."[102] Wheeler recommended continuing military support at its existing level.

On May 8 government forces reportedly fired on a group of Buddhist demonstrators in Hue. Several were killed and others were wounded. As a result, Vietnam was rocked by a large number of demonstrations. The Chiefs sided with Diem, fearing that any move to replace him would undermine the war effort, while a group of State Department officials argued that unless he was replaced, any hope of gaining the support of the Vietnamese population as a whole would never succeed. Then, on August 21, demonstrations and riots broke out when Diem's police raided several pagodas in Saigon. The recalcitrant leader continued to ignore American advice to work toward reconciliation with the Buddhists.

Upset by Diem's repressive policies, a State Department group took advantage of several key officials' absence from Washington and sent a cable to the U.S. Embassy in Saigon. The message informed Henry Cabot Lodge, the newly appointed U.S. ambassador, that he "should urgently examine all possible alternative leadership and make detailed plans as to how we might bring about Diem's replacement if this should become necessary."[103] The advisors who met with the president on August 26 were furious that a major change in policy had been engineered while they were out of town. It did not smell good. The culprit was Assistant Secretary for Far Eastern Affairs Roger Hilsman, who, despite having only recently assumed his Department of State position, had taken advantage of Kennedy's undisciplined and somewhat chaotic decision-making process to send out the cable. Taylor, arguing against support for a coup, asked for time to consult with the Chiefs.

Kennedy met with his senior advisors on September 3 to discuss once again how to proceed in regard to Diem. Taylor brought with him an upbeat evaluation from the Chiefs that noted "favorable trends in all military activities, despite Saigon's preoccupation with the unstable political situation."[104] Thus, the cable that was sent to Lodge after the meeting emphasized persuasion over force. The president wanted the embassy to continue pushing Diem toward liberalization while avoiding any actions that could be misinterpreted as U.S. support for his overthrow.

Because of continued questioning of the Chiefs' assertion that the war could be won with Diem in power, Gen. Victor Krulak was sent to Vietnam on another whirlwind trip. When he returned on September 10, Krulak submitted a report that repeated the standard JCS line: the war was going well and the impact of internal political problems was minimal. Interestingly, the report from the State Department official who accompanied General Krulak took the opposite point of view, leading Kennedy to ask the two men if they had been on the same trip. At the same time, Ambassador Lodge weighed in, arguing in favor of supporting a coup. The result was a cable to Lodge instructing him to begin a dialogue with Diem to see if he could get some movement on the political front.

Kennedy then sent McNamara and Taylor to Vietnam on another fact-finding mission. In his meeting with McNamara, Diem "dismissed the American suggestion that there was a serious political crisis, [and he] took no note of warnings about the effect of public opinion on the American ability to support his government."[105] Needless to say, McNamara was not impressed. When they returned to the United States, McNamara and Taylor issued a report that enthusiastically supported the military campaign but expressed concern over the internal political situation.[106] They suggested that future aid be dependent on better performance by the Diem government in meeting political and military objectives. As far as the idea of a coup was concerned, Taylor repeatedly warned that it would only serve to slow down the military effort, a view that was shared not only by the Chiefs, but by General Harkins, who was still the senior military officer in South Vietnam.

On November 1, a few hours after meeting with Ambassador Lodge, who supported the coup, Diem and his brother were murdered. Power now rested in the hands of a group of Vietnamese generals who had been worried about where Diem had been leading the country. As Schlesinger put it, "What lay behind the coup was not the meddling of Americans, quiet or ugly, but the long history of Vietnamese military resentment against Diem, compounded by the fear that Nhu, with his admiration for totalitarian methods of organization, might try to transform South Vietnam into a police state."[107] With the South Vietnamese army now in charge, one would be forced to admit that Vietnam was a military problem that was most efficiently solved by military force. From a policy standpoint, Diem's assassination meant that the U.S. military, especially the army, would become the key vehicle for addressing the situation in Saigon. Equally important, the military would assume the key roles of framing the issues and fleshing them out with the necessary information. Both the Viet Cong and the North Vietnamese took advantage of the resulting instability. Less than three weeks after Diem's assassination, Kennedy was gunned down in Dallas.

CONCLUSION

Presidential Leadership Style

The Chiefs were not hostile to Kennedy when he took office; in fact, they initially welcomed him as a breath of fresh air. Unfortunately, they were never able to adjust to his collegial style of leadership, and he never understood how they thought and operated. His relationship with them was complicated by McNamara and his "Whiz Kids," who infuriated the Chiefs. Not only did the analysts understand very little about fighting a war, they had no respect for the military, believing instead that their slide rulers would solve all of the country's problems.

The Bay of Pigs fiasco illustrated perfectly the problems that Kennedy's leadership style created for the Chiefs. Although Kennedy's frustration with his senior officers in the aftermath of the invasion was understandable, they believed they had done their job for a president whose crisis-management techniques stood in stark contrast to Eisenhower's. Kennedy had relied not on a traditional decision-making structure, but on seminar-like meetings, which the Chiefs viewed as an invitation to chaos. They would listen to the president and believe he had made a decision only to learn later that the issue had not been settled and was instead still open to discussion.

Furthermore, the Kennedy administration had moved the military to the sidelines and given the CIA responsibility for what the Chiefs believed was a military operation. (Despite not being in charge of the invasion, they probably should have been more critical of the CIA's plan, or at least articulated more clearly that the term "fair," which was their assessment of the operation's likelihood of success, meant only a 30 percent chance.) The plan changed constantly, and nothing was put in writing. And how could they be expected to give the kind of advice that the president wanted if he did not even consult them on something as important as cancelling the second air strike? Then there was the issue of speaking up, of providing the president with "political-military" advice, of not limiting themselves to issues that were strictly military. Hitherto, the administration sent out signals that the Chiefs were to restrict their focus to military issues. For example, McNamara's office had cancelled a speech by Admiral Burke because of its political nature. " 'As a result,' the chairman recalled, 'during National Security Council discussions, the JCS members were reluctant to volunteer opinions on matters beyond their own professional cognizance.' "[108]

Finally, the military—especially the navy—was not accustomed to having politicians not only place limitations on how it conducted operations, but even interfere in operational matters once they were under way. The military relied on the chain of command, atop which sat the officer on the spot. Furthermore, the idea of abandoning troops, even if they were Cuban volunteers, went against everything senior military officers had been taught all their lives.

After the Bay of Pigs, the Cuban Missile Crisis revealed that the military's working relationship with the president had improved little. When asked to do so by Kennedy, the Chiefs spoke out on critical military issues, believing that the president and his brother possessed only a sophomoric understanding of the matters at hand. For his part, Kennedy was appalled at what appeared to be the officers' willingness to plunge the country into a third world war. Military leaders always seemed to assume that the enemy was only too ready to back down in a crisis. Indeed, the president perceived that they had no concern for the possible political consequences of decisions they favored. As Robert Kennedy observed,

> President Kennedy was disturbed by this inability to look beyond the limited military field. When we talked about this later, he said we had to remember that they were trained to fight and wage war—that was their life. Perhaps we would feel more concerned if they were always opposed to using arms or military means—for if they would not be willing, who would be? But this experience pointed out for us all the importance of civilian direction and control and the importance of raising probing questions to military recommendations.[109]

Kennedy's experience with the Chiefs during the Cuban Missile Crisis strengthened his trust in McNamara's judgment. As the president noted, "An invasion would have been a mistake—a wrong use of our power. But the military are mad. They wanted to do this. It's lucky we have McNamara over there."[110]

Violations of Service/Military Culture?

Kennedy's relations with the Chiefs were never good, largely because of a culture clash. The president failed to understand the Chiefs and how they operated, and the Chiefs could not adapt to a very different kind of president with a leadership style at odds with their own culture. From their perspective, Kennedy constantly violated military culture, especially during the Bay of Pigs and the Cuban Missile Crisis: he would not let the officers do their job; he criticized them when they tried to provide advice; and he confused them with his seminar-like decision-making process. The president further violated the culture when he appointed General Taylor as his trusted advisor. Thereafter, both McNamara and Taylor filtered the Chiefs' communication to the president. Although many of them liked and trusted Taylor, this additional layer of separation was insulting.

The military, particularly the navy, was appalled at the administration's efforts to micromanage military operations. To senior officers, the overzealous meddling in their internal affairs stemmed from the Ivy League brain trust's militarily naïveté, rather than the administration's concern over the political implications of military decisions. The idea of politicians telling senior military officers not only how to handle operational matters but when and how to drive ships completely countered naval tradition.

From the president's perspective, the military failed to provide him with valuable counsel. When the Chiefs tried to become the kind of political-military advisors the president wanted, it became painfully obvious that their past isolation from such spheres precluded them from knowing what kind of advice to provide. Too often they came across as political Neanderthals unequipped to function in the world of politics and diplomacy.

Changes in Service/Military Culture?

Kennedy would have loved nothing more than to have been able to transform the U.S. Army's idea of how to fight the war in Vietnam. One can only imagine what would have happened had he not been assassinated. He understood the value of unconventional warfare, and one suspects that he also knew that joint operations were important. As it was, he got the idea of such warfare off the ground, but he was not able to live long enough to see significant adoption of the various tactics involved.

Importantly, McNamara endeavored to break down service parochialism. For example, he forced the navy and the air force to develop a joint-strike fighter—the TFX. But both of these services tried in vain to explain to McNamara that they needed very different kinds of planes. The navy's required a much stronger airframe because of the beating it took when landing upon and taking off from aircraft carriers. The Chiefs argued repeatedly that one aircraft would not satisfy the needs of both services, but McNamara insisted. Ultimately, the failure and cancellation of the TFX project further diminished the Chiefs' respect for McNamara and exacerbated their relationship with him and the president.

6
THE MILITARY AND LYNDON JOHNSON

Maybe we military men were all weak. Maybe we should have stood up and pounded the table. . . . I was part of it and I'm sort of ashamed of myself too.

At times I wonder, "Why did I go along with this kind of stuff?"
—*Admiral David McDonald*

Of all the presidents discussed in this study, Lyndon Johnson had the worst relationship with the American military; indeed, post–World War II civil-military relations reached their nadir under his administration. Against a background of organizational chaos, Johnson ignored the Chiefs (and most other senior military officers), failed to provide them with clear policy guidance, personally insulted them on more than one occasion, and patronized them on others. Robert McNamara, whom the president retained as secretary of defense, misled and occasionally lied to the Chiefs—all the while expecting them to win a war in Vietnam, a war on which their counsel counted for little. In the past, senior military officers had often been frustrated by the presidents they served. But in such cases, such as Ridgway and Taylor under Eisenhower and Anderson and LeMay under Kennedy, the presidents gave the impression of respecting their officers, and the officers reciprocated. The situation under Johnson, however, was far different. He made no secret of his contempt for the military, and as time passed, their lack of respect for him became an open secret. Indeed, the situation became so bad that, for the first and only time from 1940 to the present, the Chiefs came very close to resigning.

JOHNSON'S LEADERSHIP STYLE

At first glance, the decision by George and Stern to omit Lyndon Johnson from their study of presidential management styles seems odd. They discuss John Kennedy, but then skip ahead to Richard Nixon. The only other president omitted was Gerald Ford, presumably because of his short tenure.[1] Johnson may have been omitted from the study because he had no systematic approach to managing foreign policy issues. As Fred Greenstein observed: "Johnson inherited a free-form White House from Kennedy and made no effort to institute rigorous procedures for assessing policy options. Kennedy's alertness and interest in policy enabled him to make the most of his fluid advisory system, but its lack of built-in structure made it ill suited for Johnson, who was erratic about calling meetings and dominated those he did convene."[2] The closest he came to a managerial form was his Tuesday luncheons. "Each week almost without exception, the president and his senior advisers gathered for lunch and deliberation in the president's Dining Room on the Second Floor of the White House."[3] But the list of those who attended varied, and key military decisions were sometimes made with no military officer present (the latter problem would not be rectified until October 1967, in the immediate aftermath of the Chiefs' threat to resign). Johnson's belief that Secretary of Defense McNamara's presence was sufficient meant that military views were often ignored. In any case, Johnson was secretive and did not like to hear opinions that differed from his own strongly held views. Johnson biographer Doris Kearns probably put it best when she remarked, "Under siege . . . [Johnson's] operational style closed in and insulated him in the White House, where discussion was confined to those who offered no disagreement."[4] He attempted to keep as much power in his hands as possible and treated the delegation of responsibility as a foreign concept.[5] To make matters worse, like Kennedy he seldom used the NSC; when the body did meet, it was primarily used to brief attendees.

As far as organizational structure was concerned, there was none. As John Burke noted, "Members of Johnson's circle of advisers held a broad spectrum of views, yet the advisory process was so disorderly and Johnson's management of the process so haphazard that they never were channeled into focused debate."[6] And even if he had permitted debate, his advisors knew that he was not interested in criticisms of his proposed policies. The NSC members were policy implementers, he was the policy formulator. Consequently, the lack of open discussion hurt him, particularly on the issue of Vietnam. He did not want to hear suggestions that the war was not going well. Chester Cooper, who was a White House assistant, "has written that President Johnson often polled his foreign policy advisers one at a time to hear their views on the Vietnam War. Each would respond 'I agree,' although Cooper, and undoubtedly others, did *not* agree. Cooper even dreamed of answering no, but he never did."[7] The president punished those who disagreed with him, especially on Vietnam, by forcing them to leave the administration. Because of Johnson's disinterest in other views and the disorganized nature of his administration, his decisions "were not the product of focused and organized deliberations and clear-cut choices."[8]

The Generals and Johnson

From the military's standpoint, Johnson would turn out to be a bureaucratic disaster. Senior officers had to deal with an unpredictable and chaotic form of presidential decision making and a president who was not only disrespectful of them but deeply suspicious as well. He thought that many of them were "arrogant," that they were "contemptuous of new ideas, mean and thoughtless in dealing with those below them." In addition, he thought they did not understand the political ramifications of military decisions and that their understanding of problems was consequently often too narrow. In short, "Johnson could be merciless when he talked about the generals."[9] And they were well aware of his feelings. "It was well known among the JCS staff that the president . . . mistrusted the high command, an attitude that wasn't lost on JCS officers."[10] Just two days after he took office, he called a meeting at the White House that included McNamara, Secretary of State Dean Rusk, Ambassador Henry Cabot Lodge, CIA Director John McCone, and Presidential Assistant McGeorge Bundy—but omitted the JCS.

JOHNSON AND MCNAMARA ON VIETNAM

If members of the new Johnson administration could agree upon one point, it was that the United States faced major problems in Vietnam. The Kennedy administration's strategic hamlet program and counterinsurgency techniques were not working, nor were the CIA's attempts to run covert military operations in North Vietnam. Rather than bringing about a revolution, individuals sent north were always captured, almost as soon as they landed.

When Johnson assumed the presidency, he knew only that he wanted the war to be limited. He did not want the conflict to interfere with his plans to

President Lyndon B. Johnson meeting with the Joint Chiefs of Staff at Johnson's ranch in Texas. Secretary of Defense Robert McNamara is to the president's left, and General Earle Wheeler, chairman of the Joint Chiefs of Staff, is opposite the president and leaning forward. (LBJ Library)

build the "Great Society." Being the good politician he was, he also did not want to place undue strains on the economy. Discussing the South Vietnamese, he quipped, "I want 'em to leave me alone, because I've got some bigger things to do right here at home."[11] Lyndon Johnson sincerely wanted to win the war in Vietnam, and he wanted to do so convincingly, but it was a sidebar, a war he did not understand, an event that stood in the way of his attempt to change the face of American society.

As far as Johnson was concerned, McNamara was in charge—or at least the president wanted a world in which McNamara took care of the war and left him alone to work on his domestic agenda. Allowing the secretary of defense (and his civilian Whiz Kids) to run the show profoundly influenced how the war was fought. To begin, McNamara did not ask the Chiefs for an overall strategy for Vietnam. Instead, he imposed his own approach, one he believed provided the president with what he wanted. And he approached the problem from a civilian standpoint. In fact, one could argue that his approach, in which the military was "told" to follow his orders, was structured along the lines of a civilian industrial plant—not surprising given his background in the Ford Motor Corporation, where he had worked for many years prior to becoming secretary of defense.

McNamara's strategy comprised three major components. First, he believed in the idea of graduated response. In essence, this approach was aimed "not at imposing one's will on the enemy but to communicate with him."[12] If the United States showed its resolve and gradually increased pressure on the Vietcong and especially the North Vietnamese, in time the latter would come to recognize that battle against the mighty United States was a futile undertaking. Johnson preferred this approach because it would not undermine his domestic agenda; unfortunately, it did not work. Graduated response was fine, but it could not be so completely refined that the other side remained oblivious to the message or dismissed it as insignificant, which is exactly what happened throughout the Vietnam conflict. For example, General William Westmoreland complained: "Operations began on December 14, 1964. Known as BARREL ROLL, the flights involved only two missions a week, each with four aircraft, so that it was hardly surprising that the North Vietnamese failed to discern that a new program was underway."[13]

The second component in McNamara's strategy was quantification: the secretary of defense was obsessed by numbers. In his mind, the military had to be monitored, just as processes had been at the Ford Company; thus, believing that an emphasis on numbers was the only reasonable means of measuring success in Vietnam, McNamara argued "there are things you cannot quantify; honor and beauty, for example. But things you can count, you ought to count."[14] Among the "things" that could be counted were bodies, which led to the infamous body counts in the mistaken belief that the more VC the United States killed, the more likely the enemy was to negotiate an end to the war or simply give up. At one point McNamara claimed that Westmoreland said that it was the only way one could operationalize McNamara's graduated response strategy. The secretary argued that Westmoreland, who took over command of MACV in January 1964, was responsible for the idea, having maintained that at some point the VC and the North Vietnamese would reach a position where their losses were greater than their ability to provide replacements. The fact is that it fit in very nicely with McNamara's own approach to the war. What better way than a body count to show the president that the United States was winning on the battlefield!

The generals were appalled at McNamara's insistence on body counts.[15] From their perspective, the process made no sense. To begin, the South Vietnamese repeatedly inflated the numbers in an effort to make themselves look good. Furthermore, although numerous American military officers tried to play the game fairly, others exaggerated numbers. And even if officers in the field reported the numbers accurately, they would probably be inflated as they moved up the chain of command. Everyone wanted the general to be happy, and the higher the numbers, the happier he would be. Then there was the question of identifying VC members. Often they dressed like civilians, which meant that even simple villagers who were wounded or killed were often counted as VC casualties if there was any doubt as to their status. And when a military unit could not return to the battleground because the VC retained the upper hand, the Americans could only estimate how many had been killed.[16] As a former army officer who served in Vietnam explained,

> Most conscientious commanders tried to make a valid count. For example, they would insist that the enemy weapons captured be matched with the body count. An infantry commander had better have a powerful explanation for a discrepancy such as a body count of one hundred and a weapons count of five, when a ratio of enemy bodies to weapons ran generally at three to one in that given area of operations. In an effort to improve accuracy of count, there evolved. . . . a complex set of ground rules governing the reporting of enemy casualties. Nevertheless, the majority of senior United States ground commanders. . . . felt the enemy body count to be exaggerated.[17]

McNamara was fully aware that the military constantly criticized him behind his back over such measures as the body count. " 'This guy McNamara,' they said, 'he tries to quantify everything.' " But he defended such quantification, arguing that it was necessary "when you are fighting a war of attrition."[18]

Going far beyond his insistence on body counts, McNamara's obsession with numbers was part and parcel of his approach to running the war. At one point, for example, he told General Westmoreland that his objectives were "to increase the percentage of VC/NVA base areas denied the Viet Cong from 10–20% to 40–50%. He is to increase critical roads and railroads open for use from 30 to 50%, and to increase population in secure areas from 50 to 60%."[19] Such numbers were meaningless because they bore no relation to reality.

In operationalizing McNamara's goal of taking control of territory away from the enemy, General Westmoreland utilized a "search and destroy" strategy. According to Westmoreland this "was nothing more than the infantry's traditional attack mission: locate the enemy, try to bring him to battle, and either destroy him or force his surrender." To Westmoreland, it was "an operational term for a tactic."[20] An attack would be preceded by heavy bombing, artillery fire, and heliborne machine-gun attacks. The tactic met with little success. More often than not, the Americans would find nothing—the VC or North Vietnamese forces would have vanished into the jungle. Indeed, finding the enemy turned out to be much more difficult than McNamara or the president realized:

> Almost always VC/NVA troops had ample warnings of coming American operations. United States troop movements took time to plan, and the massive preparations were visible to the hundreds of Vietnamese civilians who did the menial labor on the American bases. The preparatory air strikes and ground attacks often had to be coordinated with South Vietnamese military and civilian hierarchy, and this structure had been penetrated by Communist agents.[21]

Even when American forces were successful in killing a large number of the enemy, resulting in correspondingly high body counts, the VC would wait until the Americans left the area and then return. The use of search and destroy rested on the assumption that the VC and the North Vietnamese had only a certain number of fighters and that once they had been decimated, the war would end. Unfortunately, that did not turn out to be the case.

To make matters even worse from the military standpoint, McNamara involved his hated Whiz Kids in the war-fighting process. For example, every time Westmoreland requested more troops, McNamara would turn to his civilian analysts, who knew little or nothing about military matters, something the civilians were only too aware of. For example, Deputy Assistant Secretary for Systems Analysis Enthoven noted in 1965, "I don't know anything about it [the situation in Vietnam]. If I barged into an area where I knew nothing, I would be attacked. I was under attack already from many fronts. I was vulnerable."[22]

Needless to say, the Chiefs were strongly opposed to McNamara's strategy. With the Korean experience fresh in their minds (many of them had fought there), they did not want a repeat situation in which troops were chewed up and victory denied while the politicians sat around and talked. In short, they believed that the options were clear: the United States could plunge in with both feet and fight for a victory or get out. The idea of graduated response was nonsense as far as the Chiefs were concerned. Indeed, their feelings were so strong that Admiral Thomas Moorer remarked years later that, had the military been allowed to handle the conflict its way, "we could have polished those clowns off in six months."[23] General Andrew Goodpaster also was critical when he protested to McNamara in the fall of 1964, " 'Sir you are trying to program the enemy and that is one thing that we must never try to do. We can't do his thinking for him.' Goodpaster's words fell on deaf ears."[24]

One of the first steps Johnson took on Vietnam was to send McNamara and General Taylor there in December 1963 to get a firsthand view of the conflict. Upon their return, they reported that "the situation is very disturbing."[25] In fact, that was an understatement. Internecine warfare seemed to be the primary occupation of South Vietnamese generals, and as far as the battlefield was concerned, the South Vietnamese army was proving itself to be grossly incompetent. McNamara, in particular, was upset by what he recognized as General Harkins's overly optimistic reports on the military situation. The reports proved to him that he could just not trust the U.S. military. Journalists, who were getting their information from more junior officers in the field, understood the war far better than did the Joint Chiefs, who were prisoners of Harkins's reporting. As a result, much to the Chiefs' chagrin, McNamara began to rely more heavily on his civilian analysts.

The Chiefs were not about to back down, however. On January 22, 1964, they sent a proposal to McNamara calling for more forceful actions in Vietnam. "They argued that in order to achieve . . . victory, the Joint Chiefs of Staff are of the opinion that the United States must be permitted to put aside many of the self-imposed restrictions which now limit our efforts, and to undertake bolder actions which may embody greater risks."[26] The restrictions the Chiefs were referring to included keeping the war inside South Vietnam and the refusal to involve U.S. combat troops. The Chiefs wanted permission to bomb North Vietnam and to deploy U.S. combat forces. McNamara brought up the Chiefs' request with both Dean Rusk and Johnson, who asked them to elaborate. They did so, arguing that the United States should hit the Ho Chi Minh Trail, which was being used to bring weapons, ammunition, and supplies to the South. They also downplayed the administration's concern that bombing of the North could bring the Chinese into the war, as in Korea. McNamara claimed that he and President Johnson were concerned that if the Chiefs got their way, the situation could escalate into a nuclear war, something no one wanted.

The next month the VC bombed a theater in Saigon frequented by American soldiers, killing three of them and wounding fifty. As a consequence, on February 18, 1964, the infuriated Chiefs again sent a plan to McNamara calling for a series of escalatory steps against North Vietnam, but nothing came of it. Gen. Wallace M. Greene, the commandant of the Marine Corps, "believed that the time had come to 'either pull out of South Vietnam or stay there and win.' He told his colleagues that the Marine Corps' position was that victory ought to 'be pursued with the full concerted power of U.S. resources.'"[27] He then went on a speaking tour of military staff colleges, where he argued in favor of greater military power as a means for solving the Vietnam problem.

President Johnson and the Joint Chiefs of Staff on the White House lawn. (LBJ Library)

The frustrated Chiefs wanted action, even if they were often unable to agree on a specific plan among themselves because of parochial service reasons.

McNamara had little time for or patience with military procedures. For example, he met with the Chiefs on March 2, 1964, just prior to the trip he made with Taylor to Vietnam. He told them that he would ensure that the Chiefs saw and had a chance to comment on his latest policy memorandum before it became official policy, thereby giving them the impression that he had not yet made up his mind. That same day, copies of the draft document were circulated. The plan called for a "tit for tat graduated military pressure" on the North. Three days later the second draft of the document was sent to the president. "The Chiefs did not receive a copy of the Draft Presidential Memorandum (DPM) until after McNamara and Taylor returned from Saigon on March 13."[28] Needless to say, the idea that the country's most senior military officers would be cut out of such an important decision-making process did not go down well.

The Johnson administration's hesitation to escalate the use of force and its unwillingness to rely upon senior officers for advice represented only two of the most obvious problems the military encountered. For example, General

Westmoreland, who replaced General Harkins as the senior U.S. military officer in Vietnam at a time when the internal situation was worsening, complained about Washington's micromanagement. He observed that "a major problem in those early days, as through the entire war, was that Washington policy decisions forced us to fight with one hand." Initially, the most crippling restriction was the Operation Farmgate program, which hindered the use of U.S. military aircraft: American pilots could provide air support only with a Vietnamese pilot aboard, ostensibly executing a training mission.[29]

The president met with the Chiefs on March 4, 1964, and was somewhat taken back when Generals Greene and LeMay told him that it was time to "either get in or get out." Johnson was not about to agree to a major escalatory action until after the upcoming election in November had passed. And when the Chiefs finally got a chance to see McNamara's memo, which recommended his favored policy of graduated response and had previously been seen only by General Taylor, who was chairman, Greene argued that "half measures won't win in South Vietnam." General Wheeler, who was the army's chief of staff, maintained that the actions recommended in McNamara's paper were inadequate. Admiral McDonald, the chief of naval operations, claimed that the paper "did not go far enough" and argued that the United States must "take stronger action." For his part, LeMay later accused both Taylor (who, many senior officers believed, had become as much a civilian policy maker as a representative of the military) and McNamara of not properly representing their views to the president; at the time, he maintained that the Chiefs should send their own memo, one that would clearly state their concerns to the president. Taylor toned down the memo that LeMay wanted to send before passing it on to McNamara, who refused to pass it on to Johnson. Then Taylor, who was the only military representative present at a March 17, 1964, NSC meeting, sided with McNamara, claiming that the Chiefs "supported the McNamara report," which was only partially accurate.[30]

Discontent among the Chiefs was rampant. In fact, McDonald, Greene, and LeMay complained to General Chester Clifton, the president's military aide, that their views had been misrepresented. Clifton went to the president, telling him that they were calling the McNamara plan an "Asian Bay of Pigs" and were "carefully recording their dissent." He added that he saw "a potentially difficult and even dangerous situation in the Joint Chiefs of Staff."[31] In response, Johnson extended the outspoken LeMay as the air force chief of staff for a year (better to have him as part of the administration than outside criticizing with an upcoming election) but did little to bring the Chiefs into the policy-making arena.

McNamara decided to cut all lines of communication between the Chiefs and the president. He would be the one and only conduit. He also ended back-channel communications between the Chiefs and General Clifton. When they subsequently tried to use this connection in a issue not related to Vietnam, McNamara came down hard on them, and President Johnson supported him, informing the military that "all military requests for appointment or decisions" were to "come through the McNamara channel."[32] As a consequence, McNamara had a stranglehold on policy recommendations to the White House: the president would see only those proposals McNamara approved of. The Chiefs' contacts with McNamara became meaningless. To quote General Harold Johnson, conferring with McNamara was like "a mating dance of the turkeys," in which participants "went through certain set procedures" but "solved no problems."

Symbolizing to many a major break with the past, General Wheeler took over as the new JCS chairman in July 1964. He was a man who had limited combat experience, having risen to the top via staff jobs. In the words of Mark Perry, his appointment marked "an end to the age of heroes." More of a politician than a combat military officer, Wheeler "was strictly a manager, an officer who was not only inexperienced at running a war, but actually incapable of doing so."[33]

The Gulf of Tonkin Incident

The Gulf of Tonkin incident became one of the key turning points in the Vietnam War. On August 2, the USS *Maddox* was attacked by North Vietnamese PT boats while in international waters twenty-five miles from the North Vietnamese coast. The *Maddox* was attempting to track North Vietnamese efforts to infiltrate men and supplies into South Vietnam by sea. The ship did not report any injuries or damage, but there was little doubt that an attack had occurred because crew members found a North Vietnamese shell fragment on the deck.

According to President Johnson's memoirs, General Wheeler and Secretary Rusk decided that "an overeager North Vietnamese boat commander might have been at fault or that a shore station had miscalculated. So we decided against retaliation."[34] However, two days later another North Vietnamese attack was reported, this time on two American destroyers: the *Maddox* and the USS *Turner Joy*. Both ships reported that they had spotted enemy ships on their radar and that both of them appeared to be taking hostile actions. They subsequently reported that they were being attacked and that they were returning fire.

To this day no one is certain exactly what happened. It is possible, for example, that the two American ships were seeing shadows on their radar screens. On the other hand, intercepts of North Vietnamese communications "indicated that the enemy *decided* to begin a hostile action against the American ships." Furthermore, the North Vietnamese indirectly confirmed the second attack by establishing August 5 as North Vietnamese Navy Day, when "one of our torpedo squadrons chased the USS *Maddox* from our coastal waters, our first victory over the U.S. Navy."[35] According to McNamara, to ascertain that an attack had taken place, he had Lt. Gen. David A. Burchinal, who was director of the Joint Staff, call Admiral U. S. Grant Sharp in Hawaii for his assessment. The latter responded that "no doubt now existed that an attack on the destroyers had been carried out."[36]

Having decided that a retaliatory strike was in order, Johnson asked McNamara to present some options. As Johnson fumed, "Now I'll tell you want I want. I not only want those patrol boats that attacked the Maddox destroyed; I want everything at that harbor destroyed; I want the whole works destroyed. I want to give them a real dose." Although the Chiefs believed that they and the president were on the same wavelength when they returned to the Pentagon to devise a list of possible actions, the fact was that McNamara was again playing a two-sided game. While the Chiefs endeavored to come up with a list they thought appropriate, McNamara "retired to his office with Vance, Bundy, Rusk and Marshall Green, assistant to William Bundy." They came up with three options: (1) Sharp, limited strikes against PT boats, PT bases, etc.; (2) continued pressure on the North Vietnamese, i.e., mining the North Vietnamese coast; or (3) a combination of both. When the Chiefs got wind of what McNamara was doing, they asked General Burchinal to make clear that they continued to favor a hard line against the North. In contrast to McNamara's "limited response," they wanted a "heavy effort" to "establish an 'outer perimeter' of how far the United States was willing to go should North Vietnam continue to undertake actions hostile to the United States."[37] Once again Johnson sided with McNamara. He decided to authorize a limited strike against PT boats at five North Vietnamese ports and at the oil depot at Vinh, believing that this limited response would sit better with American voters in the midst of a campaign than the more robust option favored by the Chiefs. In addition, the president met with members of Congress and convinced them to pass a resolution supporting his action. The operative part of the Tonkin Gulf Resolution stated that "the United States is, therefore, prepared, as the President determines, to take all necessary steps, including the use of armed force, to assist any member or protocol state of the Southeast Asia Collective Defense Treaty requesting assistance in defense of its freedom." In effect,

Congress gave the president a blank check to fight the war in Vietnam. McNamara had no doubt "that Congress understood the resolution's vast grant of power to the President."[38]

The Chiefs and Decision Making

Johnson's exclusion of the Chiefs from the decision-making process was an open secret in Washington. During the 1964 presidential campaign, Barry Goldwater blasted Johnson for ignoring his senior officers. But in Johnson's mind, Vietnam was not primarily a national security problem; it was a nuisance issue—something that he was determined to keep out of the election campaign. The less said about Vietnam, the better. Consequently, the Chiefs, who viewed the conflict as a major military problem, were a potential threat to Johnson's reelection. If they were successful in getting the Gulf of Tonkin incident on the front pages of the nation's newspapers, they could sidetrack Johnson's attempts to appear as a peacemaker.

Increasingly, the Chiefs became aware that they would be unsuccessful in convincing the president to change his strategy for dealing with the North. Johnson would never approve the kind of full-scale attack on the North that the Chiefs believed was critical if the United States hoped to stop what they considered to be North Vietnamese aggression. They were frustrated by the limits that had been placed upon them. However, the Chiefs could read the writing on the wall. As a consequence, they shifted their emphasis to persuading Johnson to remove the restrictions he had placed on their freedom of movement in fighting the Communists both in the South and the North. In essence, the Chiefs decided on a limited, graduated approach for dealing with Johnson and his strategy for Vietnam.

However, the Chiefs did not all share the same views on how Vietnam should be handled at this time. Gen. John P. McConnell, the air force chief of staff, and Gen. Wallace Greene, the Marine Corps commandant, both believed that the United States had no alternative but to carry out extensive attacks against North Vietnam. But leaders of the army and navy believed that Ambassador Taylor (who had taken over from Henry Cabot Lodge as ambassador to South Vietnam in July) was right when he warned that an attack on the North would provoke such a strong reaction that the weak South Vietnamese government might not survive.

It was against this background that the president met with Ambassador Taylor and some of his advisors (including Wheeler) in September to determine what military steps the United States should take against Communist actions in the South. State and Defense proposed, "among other things, that we resume our naval patrols in the Tonkin Gulf, which had been suspended after the August incident, and that we be prepared to retaliate against North Vietnam in case of an attack on U.S. units or of any 'special' North Vietnamese—Vietcong action against South Vietnam."[39] Johnson approved the plan.

Meanwhile, on November 1, 1964, the Viet Cong attacked the American air base at Bien Hoa. The Chiefs immediately asked permission to launch a strike against the North, but the president disagreed. In effect, the Bien Hoa attack started what amounted to an elaborate dance between the president and the Chiefs. "The response to Bien Hoa typified what would become a pattern in the relationship between the JCS and Lyndon Johnson's administration. The Chiefs tried to use the attack to gain approval for additional actions on the list they had developed less than a week earlier. To keep the Chiefs 'on board,' President Johnson and his closest advisers appeared sympathetic to the JCS recommendation and held out the promise of future action."[40] The Chiefs quickly realized what the administration was up to. In fact, on November 1, General Wheeler had met with McNamara and warned him that the Chiefs were so upset about the situation in South Vietnam that "if the United States did not take action against North Vietnam immediately it should withdraw all forces from South Vietnam."[41] They asked McNamara to send a memo to the president to that effect. "McNamara responded on the president's behalf by promising that LBJ would soon decide to use American military force in Vietnam."[42]

But McNamara was continuing to play games with the Chiefs. For example, on November 2, the president created a study group to again review policy options. Yet the Chiefs were unable to make much of an impact during the early stages of the discussions, which moved so quickly that Vice Adm. Lloyd Mustin could not provide meaningful input from the JCS. Not surprisingly, the Chiefs again recommended against the gradual application of force. However, the president and McNamara remained scared that the use of massive force would antagonize either the Chinese or the Soviets, so targets such as the North Vietnamese MIG fighter base at PhucYen were placed off limits. The Chiefs protested, but to no avail.

McNamara asked the Chiefs to develop a plan for gradually applying force, an approach that they wholly rejected. "The senior military officers did not believe that the United States should commit military force and expend the lives of Americans without fully committing to the policy objective that the intervention was supposed to achieve."[43] The Chiefs reiterated their preference for an intensive air campaign against the North and again asked for permission to destroy the ninety-four targets on their list. They sent their memo to McNamara on November 18, requesting that he send it to the president, but he refused. Equally upsetting was his decision to ignore the Chiefs' call for a clear statement of military objectives in the Vietnam conflict. In good military fashion, they were eagerly searching for a coherent strategy, one that would help them plan military operations in a systematic and coherent fashion, rather than the eclectic approach McNamara and the president seemed to favor. However, when the president raised military issues, McNamara assured him that the JCS had been "working for weeks on this problem."[44] He neglected to point out, however, that he had interfered with their efforts to present their plan to the president.

Johnson was not happy with the Chiefs' performance. On December 30, he complained that "every time I get a military recommendation . . . it calls for large-scale bombing. I have never felt this war will be won from the air. . . . What is much more needed and would be more effective is . . . appropriate military strength on the ground. . . . I am ready to look with great favor on that kind of increased American effort."[45] McNamara made it plain to the Chiefs that their advice was unwelcome and, when given, would not be taken seriously. Thus it is not surprising that they had not suggested a more robust presence on the ground. In fact, there was a proposal for ground troops, but it came out of the blue, and the Chiefs were not asked to comment on it. At the time, the United States placed its primary emphasis on getting the South Vietnamese to fight their own war. Five thousand Americans were working as advisors to the South Vietnamese army, and another eighteen thousand provided operational support. U.S. ground combat troops were not part of the equation at that time.

Rolling Thunder

On February 6, 1965, the Viet Cong launched a major attack on Camp Holloway, an American installation near Pleiku, killing eight Americans and destroying several aircraft. At a subsequent NSC meeting, Johnson's advisors recommended that he respond by attacking four army barracks associated with North Vietnam's infiltration of troops and supplies into the South. The Joint Chiefs also argued for a reprisal, and Johnson himself favored the idea: "I thought that perhaps a sudden and effective air strike would convince the leaders in Hanoi that we were serious in our purpose and also that the North could not count on continued immunity if they persisted in aggression in the South."[46] The president's decision to launch reprisals signaled a major change in the country's policy toward Vietnam. All U.S. dependents were evacuated.

Then on February 10, the Viet Cong bombed a Qui Nhon hotel, killing enlisted American personnel housed there. Everyone in Washington now agreed that some form of response was in order. The resulting operation, Rolling Thunder, would place the Joint Chiefs at odds with McNamara and the president.

The civilians and the military primarily disagreed over whether they should proceed gradually or with a massive air strike. The majority of civilians believed that the United States should begin by attacking carefully chosen targets, an approach that assumed that Hanoi "would 'get the signal' that the United States was serious about the war in Vietnam, and they would cease supporting the Viet Cong." The military, however, continuing to believe that the most effective attacks would employ the principles of mass and surprise, wanted to strike airfields, petroleum storage areas, and industrial facilities throughout the North. "They wanted to hit the North hard and keep hitting it hard. They argued that this was the way to use air power, and that Hanoi would best get the 'message' regarding the seriousness of United States intentions from its own destruction."[47] The differing stances on how the war should be fought were grounded in part on an important generational difference. The vast majority of those in uniform had been taught in their service academies that the best way to fight a war was to engage in an all-out assault on the enemy. The civilians regarded such thinking as outdated; from their perspective, the generals and admirals were still living in the past and did not understand that the United States was fighting a limited war whose limited goals were best achieved using limited means. Not surprisingly, the two sides continued to distrust each other. The civilians believed that if the military had its own way, the United States would soon be in World War III, while the military believed that if the civilians had their way, the United States would lose the war.

Rolling Thunder began on March 2. To a large degree, this entire operation—like many others—was directed from Washington. Washington policy makers reserved the right to call off planned strikes and did so several times. Those serving in Saigon considered the policy to be absurd, as Westmoreland told Wheeler. After all, the weather in Vietnam changed more quickly than people there could inform Washington. "Last-minute orders and counter-orders from Washington continued to confound planning staffs and exhaust pilots who had to remain on almost constant alert."[48] Nevertheless, Wheeler told Westmoreland to make Rolling Thunder work despite operational limitations.

Given the importance of Rolling Thunder to the war effort, Westmoreland and others began to worry about security at the huge U.S. air base at Danang. Up to this point the South Vietnamese had been in charge of security, but everyone recognized that they were not up to the task. A VC unit could easily slip past or destroy any security forces and directly attack U.S. aircraft on the tarmac. As a consequence, Westmoreland, with Taylor's agreement, requested that two Marine battalion landing teams be sent to Danang to protect the base. According to Admiral Moorer, the Marines were "needed immediately before the base was attacked and troops were killed and planes were destroyed." On February 26, the president approved the deployment of a helicopter squadron and two Marine battalions to Danang, a force that was twice as big as the one Taylor had approved. What was most surprising was that the decision was made casually and "without any consideration of the radically changed nature of the American commitment once U.S. ground forces entered South Vietnam."[49] Indeed, it would be difficult to overestimate the enormity of this decision, as the floodgates had been opened. Soon American ground forces would stream into Vietnam. Eventually, more than a half million found themselves there.

Faced with the increasing American commitment to Vietnam, on March 2, 1965, the president ordered Army Chief of Staff Harold Johnson to travel to Saigon to assess the situation. The resulting report was extremely depressing. According to the general, collapse of the South Vietnamese government seemed likely. The only hope was to send more American ground troops. In addition, General Johnson also proposed "expanding the air campaign against North Vietnam; creating a multinational anti-infiltration force along the Demilitarized Zone [DMZ]; and deploying a U.S. Army division, approximately 16,000 soldiers, near Saigon or in the central highlands north of the city." When he met with the president on March 15, Harold Johnson told the president that he estimated that up to 500,000 troops and five years would be required to win the war. All who heard his report—the president, McNamara, and the Chiefs—were shocked. "None of us had been thinking in anything approaching such terms."[50]

During the March 15 meeting, President Johnson also gave the Chiefs a pep talk. Realizing that he needed their support, even if he did disregard their advice, he told them he would do whatever was necessary to save South Vietnam. He loosened some of the controls on Rolling Thunder, permitted officers in South Vietnam a bit more autonomy, and called on the Chiefs to find ways to improve the military situation. In addition, he also told them that he wanted to do whatever was necessary to "kill more Viet Cong." And then in a move that reinforced the importance of body counts, he told them he wanted a weekly report on how many Viet Cong were killed.[51] Killing more Viet Cong was not a strategy; indeed, if that was what the president wanted, the only answer was to send still more U.S. soldiers, sailors, Marines, and airmen to Vietnam. After their March 15 meeting the Chiefs set their staffs to work to "determine how we can increase the Viet Cong (VC) kill rate within the framework of our present posture in Southeast Asia."[52] The JCS was doing exactly what Johnson wanted. The problem, however, was that he had done nothing to explain American goals and objectives in Vietnam beyond promising to get tough in the future and asking the military kill more of the enemy.

The Chiefs were taken by the president's apparent commitment to improving the military situation in South Vietnam, but they split on how to conduct ground operations. As a result, they were unable to devise a proposal to present to the secretary of defense, an action that weakened their ability to influence policy. In the meantime, McNamara tightly held the reins that guided the overall direction of the air war against North Vietnam; the same was true of increases in ground troops. He continued to see the use of military force in Vietnam from the perspective of "graduated response." Rather than significantly increasing the number of U.S. combat troops all at once, McNamara favored using select increases to signal American resolve to Hanoi. The more troops the North sent into South Vietnam, the more the United States would send, so the North would be wise to cease and desist. To mollify the Chiefs, McNamara told them that mining Haiphong's harbor and taking other steps they wanted the president to approve were *not* out of the question. He also told them that "if they supported restrictions on the air campaign in the short term, they would eventually be permitted to place 'very strong pressure' on North Vietnam."[53] The Chiefs soon realized, however, that McNamara was playing the same game of deception with them as the president.

The Johnson administration continued to approach the situation in South Vietnam in a piecemeal fashion. For example, when LBJ met with his advisors on April 1 and 2, 1965, the military pushed for an intensification of the air program and the assignment of greater numbers of American combat forces to South Vietnam. The president claimed in his memoirs that most of his civilian advisors argued against intensifying the bombing campaign because they feared bringing the Chinese into the war. In the end, he decided to continue the " 'slowly ascending tempo[,]' adding strikes if Viet Cong operations increased." Similarly, the president decided that the United States would scale back its operations if "Communist forces reduced their actions." In addition, however, he agreed to "an 18,000–20,000–man increase in U.S. logistic and support forces," as well as the "deployment of two additional Marine battalions (for a total of four) and one Marine air squadron." Finally, he also approved a change in the mission assigned to the Marines to permit "their more active use." Forty thousand troops were now assigned to Vietnam, with 35,500 actually in country.[54] By the end of May, the number surpassed 50,000.

The Chiefs were becoming increasingly outspoken about their frustration with the president, who seemed more concerned with avoiding defeat than developing an overall strategy. They were well aware that he really wasn't interested in their opinions—his primary goal was to keep them on board. For example, Hugh Sidney noted that "one high general late at night in a Washington men's club told a disturbed group around him that the NSC session seemed more an occasion for issuing orders to the military, or a least for informing them of decisions that had been made, than a deliberative affair where alternative actions were weighed and diverse voices listened to."[55] When top generals began complaining to the Senate Armed Services Committee about how Johnson was conducting the war, Mississippi senator John Stennis went to the president. Thereafter, Johnson began including General Wheeler in many of the key sessions, but the result was the same: "More visible consultation calmed the critics, but Johnson went right on taking the crucial measure of events with his four or five most trusted civilians."[56] Johnson simply had no interest in the military's advice. Henry Graff reported a conversation with Bill Moyers, who commented that "President Johnson . . . relies less on military advice than any President since Wilson."[57] The president neither liked nor trusted his senior military officers.

Nothing seemed to frustrate the Chiefs more than the bombing pauses the president ordered as part of his graduated response to North Vietnam. On May 10 the president approved a five-to-seven-day bombing pause while informing both Hanoi and Moscow that he was prepared to begin negotiations on the future of Vietnam. The North Vietnamese did nothing to modify their behavior toward the South; in fact, on May 12 they began their summer offensive, which left the South Vietnamese army in shambles. As a result, on May 18 Johnson resumed bombing. He was one of the first to admit that the pause had been "a total failure. It produced nothing."[58]

Given their orders to seek out and kill VC, the country's senior military officers continued to call for more troops. Sitting in enclaves and defending coastal bases was not the way to carry out the president's order. The U.S. military had to find and destroy the enemy where he lived. Westmoreland thus requested an increase in troops from 82,000 to 175,000. CINCPAC endorsed the request, noting that the "situation requires a substantial further build-up of U.S. and Allied forces in RVN . . . at the most rapid rate feasible on an orderly basis."[59] Indeed, McNamara claimed that this cable upset him more than all of the other thousands he received in the seven years he served as secretary of defense. "We were forced to make a decision. We could no longer postpone a choice about which path to take."[60] By any measure, the United

States had reached a critical point in its involvement in Vietnam. The first U.S. combat operation occurred from June 27 to June 30, 1965, when troops from the 173rd Airborne Brigade went into Zone D, northwest of Saigon.

The president, ever concerned about the public response to the growing American commitment to South Vietnam, sought to conceal the depth of American intervention. His secretiveness put the Chiefs in a quandary: they worked for the president, their commander in chief, but they also had an obligation to support the Constitution, which placed considerable authority in the hands of Congress as the American people's representative. In the end, the Chiefs sided with their commander in chief: they slanted their congressional testimony to cast his positions in a positive light.

Calling Up the Reserves

Nothing was more politically sensitive at this time than the question of calling up the reserves. If the United States intended to expand its forces in Vietnam, it had to call upon the these military personnel. But mobilizing the reserves was an inherently political action that would strongly influence domestic public opinion, which Johnson paid close attention to. The president had two options available to him in calling up the reserves: First, he could ask Congress to issue a joint resolution permitting such an action. Alternatively, he could declare a national emergency and activate as many as one million reservists for one year.[61] Declaring a national emergency would have focused public attention on the war instead of on his domestic programs, probably guaranteeing that little more would be accomplished at home. Yet potential congressional opposition to issuing a joint resolution also would be problematic. Johnson wanted both guns and butter: he was not prepared to sacrifice one for the other.

McNamara, however, remembered the critical role reservists played in the 1961 Berlin crisis and believed that the United States had to call them up once again. He was supported by the Chiefs, who asked for a meeting with the president to discuss the issue. They explained their reasoning as he listened to them. He then leaned across the table and said to General Johnson, "General, you leave the American people to me. I know more about the American people than anyone in this room."[62] McNamara then proposed that Johnson go to Congress and ask for the authority to call up 235,000 men in the reserves and National Guard. McNamara also proposed that the overall strength of the regular military be increased significantly so that the United

States could maintain its commitments in other parts of the world while fighting the war in Vietnam. Something had to be done. There was general agreement that Saigon would collapse unless the United States sent additional troops to Vietnam.

Eventually the president approved raising the number of troops in Vietnam to 175,000, and he gave Westmoreland permission to maneuver his forces as he saw fit.[63] But he said no when it came to the reserves. His decision was a major blow, especially to the army, which depended on its reserves. General Johnson could hardly believe the president's continued refusal to call up reserves: "It *came as a total and complete surprise.*" "*And I might say a shock.* Every single contingency plan that the Army had that called for any kind of expansion of force had the assumption in it that the reserves would be called." Concerned by the long-term consequences of the president's decision, the general told McNamara, "I haven't any basis for justifying what I'm going to say, but I can assure you of one thing, and that is that without a call-up of the reserves that the quality of the Army is going to erode and we're going to suffer very badly. I don't know at what point this will occur, but it will be relatively soon. I don't know how widespread it will be, but it will be relatively widespread." General Johnson was prophetic. He understood the army; the president did not. Indeed, the president shocked the Chiefs when he informed them that he had decided not to mobilize the reserves. They grew even more upset when the secretary of defense, who had supported them as their leader in the call for reserves, openly backed the president. "Their civilian superior, Robert McNamara, had abandoned them."[64] Gen. Creighton Abrams, who was serving as Westmoreland's deputy, observed that the increase in troops would consist primarily of privates and second lieutenants, yet it was the career NCOs and mid-level officers typically found in the reserves who were critical to a successful war effort.[65] By not extending enlistments and calling up reserves, Johnson created chaos in the army. Individuals who were being trained to go to Vietnam left the army because their enlistments had expired, only to be replaced by green soldiers who were not trained to do the job.

The president's decision had a profound impact on the military. According to Mark Perry, after hearing LBJ's speech on July 24 announcing he would not call up the reserves, General Johnson, who had a reputation for honesty and integrity, was "almost desperate." He purportedly put on his best dress uniform and informed his driver that he was going to see the president. "On his way into Washington, Johnson reached up and unpinned the stars from his shoulders, holding them lightly in his hands. When the car arrived at the White House gates, he ordered his driver to stop. He stared down at his stars, shook his head, and pinned them back on." Many years later he reportedly regretted his decision. "I should have gone to see the President . . . I should have taken off my stars. I should have resigned. It was the worst, most immoral decision I've ever made."[66]

Deploying U.S. Troops in South Vietnam

When the United States signaled a major change in policy by deciding to deploy forces to South Vietnam, its primary goal shifted from propping up the South Vietnamese government to fighting and defeating the enemy in the South, largely through the use of American troops. As the president himself recognized, "Now we were committed to major combat in Vietnam." Even more important than the initial increase in the number of American forces was his statement indicating that "additional forces will be needed later, and they will be sent as requested."[67]

Having obtained more American combat forces, the Chiefs believed they might have made a breakthrough. They called on the president to undertake a "sustained air and naval campaign against North Vietnam and its communications to its forces in the South—roads, railroads, and waterways—to include a blockade of North Vietnam, as well as land and air actions in Laos and Cambodia to stop the movement of troops and supplies."[68] They constantly pushed for the adoption of such a strategy, but neither McNamara nor the president would support them; indeed, the latter verbally abused the Chiefs. For example, when they entered the Oval Office for a meeting in November, he did not ask them to take a seat. Instead, a field-grade officer was left standing, holding an easel. General Wheeler spoke, then Admiral McDonald, and finally General McConnell. The president then asked Generals Johnson and Greene if they agreed with what their colleagues had said. They said they did.

> LBJ turned away for a moment, then whirled on the assembled senior military leadership and attacked them in the most vile and despicable terms, cursing them personally, ridiculing their advice, using the crudest and filthiest language. They were . . . subjected to the worst side of a "venal and vindictive man." Dean Acheson had spoken of Lyndon Johnson's "swinish bullying boorishness which made his last three years unbearable," and the nation's military leadership was getting an undiluted demonstration of these appalling qualities. . . . Still screaming and cursing, LBJ told the Joint Chiefs of Staff that "he was not going to let

> some military idiots talk him into World War III and ordered them to 'get the Hell out of my office!' "[69]

One can only wonder at the Chiefs' willingness to continue to serve after such an experience.

Meanwhile, Westmoreland carried out his orders to fight a war of attrition. If the Americans could keep the VC and the North Vietnamese on the run and decimate their numbers, it would help win the South Vietnamese people's allegiance and thus stabilize the political situation in Saigon. At least that was the plan. One of the first instances in which American forces were used in this manner was in the Ia Drang Valley in November 1965.[70] In accordance with Washington's policy of attrition, the First Cavalry was deployed to "Find and destroy the North Vietnamese forces."[71] The First Cavalry was assigned an area about the size of Rhode Island and told to go in and destroy the Communists. During the ten-day campaign the Americans demonstrated superior firepower and mobility; however, the Americans were not as superior as they perhaps thought. To quote Gen. David Palmer, "Once on the ground and out of their helicopters, U.S. units were for all intents and purposes immobilized. NVA units maneuvered, attacked, broke contact, withdrew, sidestepped, and continued their march; Americans dug in, defended, and watched the enemy fade away to fight again."[72] In the end, the Americans lost 300 dead while the enemy left some 1,300 behind. Many of the young U.S. personnel (both officers and enlisted) who lost their lives in that battle had been learning their skills on the battlefield; clearly, the president's decision not to mobilize the reserves negatively affected combat readiness. Still, the Americans had proven they would be successful in a head-on clash and had left the battlefield with a favorable kill ratio. The issue, however, was not that simple. The VC and NVA read casualty reports differently than policy makers in Washington because the Vietnamese sympathetic to the Communist cause could accept that ratio far more easily than could the Americans.

In 1966 Westmoreland asked for another 200,000 military personnel, for a total of 410,000 U.S. forces in Vietnam by the end of the year. McNamara called Westmoreland's request, which essentially represented an open-ended increase in U.S. forces, a "shattering blow."[73]

The Christmas Bombing Pause

McNamara, who began to suspect that a military solution was not the answer, considered a negotiated settlement to be the only viable solution. For that reason, on December 2, 1966, he told the president that he had grown "more and more convinced that we ought definitely to think of some action other than military action as the only program."[74] The secretary of defense's suggestion was motivated by more than strictly military factors. For example, his Whiz Kids had convinced him that the war was not "cost effective," a judgment that made little sense to the generals and admirals who were waging the conflict. As far as they were concerned, their most important considerations were saving lives and carrying out the task assigned to them. The better the equipment, the better their ability to carry out their mission, which in turn would result in fewer dead GIs. What did cost-benefit analysis have to do with it? However, in 1965 the Whiz Kids pointed out to McNamara that according to their estimates, the Rolling Thunder's toll "on North Vietnam amounted to roughly $70 million, but that it had cost the United States $460 million to inflict that damage." The issue of cost effectiveness was just one battle in the war for power that was being waged in the Pentagon. "The contest pitted the generals and admirals, the Joint Chiefs of Staff, and other 'hardline' bombing advocates such as 'Oley' Sharp and Westmoreland on one side against McNamara, [his aide John] McNaughton, and the OSD [Office of the Secretary of Defense] civilians on the other."[75] The struggled pitted civilians against professional military officers for control of military operations in the field.

The following February the president met with the JCS to discuss a request by General Westmoreland for more troops. McNamara told the president that they could send "U.S. troops with limited training to 'rear areas.' It was at this point that Army Chief of Staff shot back at McNamara, 'Mr. Secretary, there are no rear areas in Vietnam anymore.' "[76] Throughout the war, the JCS and Westmoreland lived in a different world and fought a very different war than McNamara and his civilian colleagues. It is not surprising that the two camps often spoke *past* one another.

On Christmas Eve the United States instituted a thirty-four-hour truce, including a halt in the bombing of the north that the president extended "for several more days, possibly into the middle of next week."[77] In terms of bureaucratic politics, the pause represented a victory for McNamara and the Whiz Kids. The president had clearly sided with the civilians against the Joint Chiefs, who had repeatedly argued that a pause "would undo all we've done," according to McNamara.[78] The secretary of defense played down the military's concerns, noting that the United States could resume bombing at any time.

Among those arguing that the bombing should begin anew was Admiral Sharp. He reiterated the JCS argument that the enemy was taking advantage of the pause, and he stated that upon its reinstatement, Rolling Thunder should focus on destroying lines of communication between China and North Vietnam.

The Chiefs circulated a memo expressing their view that only renewed bombing would bring the North Vietnamese to the bargaining table. Ironically, the president himself became convinced that the pause was a failure for the reasons cited by the Chiefs. "Throughout the pause in the bombing, Hanoi continued to rush men and supplies toward the militarized zone and into the supply lines through Laos, which were known as the Ho Chi Min Trail. North Vietnam's actions and its words, once again said 'no' to peace."[79] Consequently, the United States renewed its bombing campaign on January 31.

Send in More Troops?

On March 18, 1967, Westmoreland, faced with the rising tide of VC and NVA force levels, sent in a request for 200,000 additional troops. Johnson was stunned. The request set off one of the more explosive battles between the Chiefs and civilians in Washington. The arguments, however, were "clothed in the same old tattered rags of United States troops levels in South Vietnam and the conduct of the bombing program in North Vietnam."[80]

On April 20 the Chiefs opened the battle by recommending that Washington grant Westmoreland's request. They also asked the president to mobilize the reserves and allow the military to pursue the VC and NVA into Laos, Cambodia, and even North Vietnam. In addition, the Chiefs asked that the ports of North Vietnam be mined and that Washington "make a solid commitment in manpower and resources to a military victory."[81] Once again the military was telling the president that it was time to get serious about fighting the war. The graduated response program was not working.

McNamara and a number of civilians were horrified. In May they came back with their own recommendation that the war be scaled back. Troop levels would be held at the current 470,000, with the possibility of another 30,000 troops being added in the future. Furthermore, the civilians argued that Rolling Thunder should be restricted to the southernmost part of Vietnam. Then they dropped a major bomb. Instead of pursuing the goals set forth in NSAM 288—an independent, non-Communist Vietnam and defeat for the Viet Cong—McNamara and the civilians suggested that the United States commit to more modest goals that would enable the South to determine its own future; in addition, if the South Vietnamese failed to help themselves, the United States would end its commitment.

The furious Chiefs condemned McNamara's proposals, arguing that they would prolong the war, and fired their biggest blast at his attempt to change U.S. policy in Vietnam. "They fulminated that '. . . when viewed collectively, an alarming pattern emerges which suggests a major realignment of United States objectives and intentions in Southeast Asia. . . . The Joint Chiefs of Staff are not aware of any decision to retract the policies and objectives which have been affirmed by responsible officials many times in recent years.' "[82] Finally, they argued that the civilian proposals should *not* be shown to the president.

As he often did, McNamara had gone behind the Chiefs' backs and presented his proposals to the president before the Chiefs had an opportunity to comment on them. When they learned what McNamara had done, one source claimed that the Chiefs informed the president "that they would resign en masse if the president approved McNamara's recommendations."[83] According to David Halberstam, John McNaughton claimed that had the president adopted the civilian proposals, there would have been "at least two high-ranking military resignations."[84] With his hawkish military and dovish civilian advisors at each others' throats, the president faced a dilemma. Ultimately, he decided to give Westmoreland additional troops, but nowhere near the number he was seeking. Thus the U.S. policy was more of the same.

In the meantime, McNamara went to Saigon to catch up on the latest developments. He made clear his utter lack of interest in the briefings presented to him by those at the top, including Ambassador Ellsworth Bunker, Admiral Sharp, and General Westmoreland. Phillip Davidson, who gave the intelligence briefing, recalled that "during most of the briefings he read or worked on papers spread out before him; and he asked almost no questions of the briefers. His indifference to the presentations left no doubt that McNamara believed that none of the presenters could tell him anything he wanted or needed to hear."[85] The secretary of defense's demeanor did nothing to improve his relations with the uniformed military. The only issue that he solved during the trip was the question of troop strength, which, as part of a compromise, would rise to 525,000, pending presidential approval.[86]

In August, the fate of Rolling Thunder was being debated in hearings conducted by John Stennis before the preparedness committee of the Senate Armed Services Committee. The Chiefs stated openly that the sole major problem they faced in their effort to fight the war was civilian meddling. Such interference was not only making victory impossible, it was getting soldiers killed. Mark Perry characterized General Wheeler's testimony in the following manner: "In essence, the JCS's cigar-chewing chairman, the Army's 'leading sycophant,' the officer who most represented the new breed of desk general, savaged the administration: the war wasn't being won and couldn't be won until North Vietnam's support of the southern insurgency was broken." McNamara responded in his testimony that it would be impossible to cut off supplies from the North solely through the use of an air campaign. He then attacked the JCS.

> Halfway through his testimony, McNamara looked up and paused, purposely emphasizing his next statement: "There can be no question that the bombing campaign has and is hurting North Vietnam's war-making capability." There was silence in the hearing room, a palpable sense of tension. "A selective, carefully targeted bombing campaign, such as we are presently conducting," he reiterated, "can be directed toward reasonable and realizable goals. This discriminating use of air power can and does render the infiltration of men and supplies more difficult and more costly." His words were almost a shout. While Johnson's policy might be debatable, he was saying, its impact wasn't; it was working. The North Vietnamese were buckling. America was winning the war in Vietnam.[87]

The Joint Chiefs were stunned by McNamara's devastating testimony, which dismissed their crucial contention that the war could be won only by shutting off supplies to the North. Civil-military relations had not been so seriously undermined since World War II.

In a three-hour meeting held on August 25, Wheeler told his colleagues that given McNamara's behavior, he thought they should resign en masse at a press conference the next morning. After the chiefs reviewed McNamara's testimony, Admiral Moorer said he wasn't surprised, and General McConnell said he would follow the majority. "[General] Johnson was the most outspoken proponent of resignation, saying that the military was being blamed for a conflict over which it had little control."[88]

The next day, however, General Wheeler had second thoughts. He called a meeting at 0830 and retained the previous day's rules: no aides, no notes, and a pledge of absolute secrecy. Wheeler argued that what the Chiefs were considering was mutiny. Johnson disagreed, arguing that "no one was really paying any attention to their recommendations." Wheeler responded that if they resigned, the White House would just appoint others to take their places. The Chiefs eventually decided not to resign, but General Wheeler concluded that the relationship between the president and the JCS had to change. Instead of having to work through McNamara, the Chiefs needed direct access to the commander in chief. As a result, Wheeler "insisted that he be included in the President's Tuesday luncheons with McNamara on Vietnam policy and strategy. . . . They were ruled by an icy cordiality that conformed strictly with the requirements of courtesy, but no more."[89]

The disgust the Chiefs felt toward McNamara and his Whiz Kids bordered on insubordination. "Not only was Harold Johnson ridiculing the Pentagon as the 'Department of Deceit,' Wheeler constantly modified the secretary's full name into a more suitable description of JCS feelings, calling him Robert 'Very Strange' McNamara, which brought smiles to the frustrated and overworked JCS staff."[90]

The hawkish Senate subcommittee that was conducting hearings on Rolling Thunder leveled additional criticism at the administration for restricting the bombing campaign and pursuing a policy of gradualism. It also blasted civilians for constantly overriding military advice. Why were they telling the military how to carry out tactical operations? The conclusion of the subcommittee's report must have sounded like the music of heaven to the Chiefs. It argued, "It is high time, we believe, to allow the military voice to be heard in connection with the tactical details of military operations."[91]

McNamara was in deep trouble. Shortly after the subcommittee released its report and the president learned of the Chiefs' response to McNamara's testimony, he approved fifty-two of the fifty-seven bombing targets that McNamara had previously prohibited the Chiefs from attacking. McNamara had lost the president's confidence; his resignation was now only a matter of time.

The Tet Offensive

Of all the battles in Vietnam, the Tet Offensive stands out as the most important. On January 31, 1968, in the northern part of Vietnam, the VC launched a full-scale attack involving some 84,000 troops, of whom approximately 45,000 were killed by the end of February.[92] Militarily, the United States achieved a major victory by eliminating the VC as a further significant threat; psychologically, however, the Communists had won a victory in the United States.[93] From this point on, regardless of the strategy employed, the American people refused to accept the attendant sacrifices and costs. It was only a matter of time before the United States would be forced to accept a negotiated peace.

The Tet Offensive was larger than anyone had expected. The Communists took cities such as Kontum and Pleiku, attacked Quang Tri, and held the historic city of Hue. Westmoreland's attempt to retake Hue led the JCS to believe he was bungling matters: "In fact, the handling of the attack was so confused that Westmoreland himself, in an apparent and controversial fit of frustration, appointed Creighton Abrams to handle the Marine counterattack, which angered Marine commanders responsible for the Hue operation. 'My God, Westmoreland hated the Marines,' a retired colonel William Corson, said. 'That bastard damn near crapped his pants when the Vietcong hit, so he blamed the Marines.' "[94] To the Chiefs, this was a perfect opportunity to convince the administration to call up the reserves. On February 12 and 13 they met with the president, who approved sending a Marine regiment and a brigade of the army's Eighty-second Airborne to Vietnam. Turning to the issue of reserves, the president asked a number of questions to which he demanded answers before making a decision.

On February 28, upon his return from Vietnam, General Wheeler attended a White House breakfast. He told an astonished president that Westmoreland needed 205,179 more troops. In addition, he informed Johnson that the situation within Vietnam was worse than people in Washington realized. " 'Pacification is at a halt,' he said. 'The Vietcong can roam at will in the countryside. General Westmoreland has no theater reserve and needs one badly.' "[95] Consequently, the president requested a full-scale review of U.S. policy toward Vietnam, and he asked Clark Clifford, who would take over as secretary of defense on March 1, to head the committee.

The Chiefs were overjoyed when they heard about McNamara's retirement. They were getting rid of a man they detested "not only for his 'Whiz Kids,' his operations analyses, and his omniscient attitude, but because they felt deeply that his tenure had harmed the national defense of the United States."[96] Looking at Clifford, the Chiefs thought they were getting someone who shared their views and who would be much easier to work with than McNamara. In short, they felt a great sense of relief that "Mr. Very Strange" was gone and they could now start anew. Clifford was a breath of fresh air. In contrast to McNamara, he asked the JCS for its opinions and not only was he respectful and honest, he seemed to value their views, even if he did not agree with them. For example, he demonstrated his respect for the Chiefs by not attending their meetings uninvited, as McNamara had done. Coming only when invited was an important matter of protocol to the Chiefs.

Clifford's first task was to answer the questions the president had asked about the Wheeler-Westmoreland request. However, Clifford's first meetings with the Chiefs did not go well. He asked them some of the same questions that the president had: Would 205,000 men be enough? If that would not be enough, how many more would we need? The Chiefs could not provide answers. The only answer they knew was more and more troops and bombing targets. And that upset Clifford. As he recalled in his memoirs, "The military was utterly unable to provide an acceptable rationale for the troop increase. Moreover, when I asked for a presentation of their plan for attaining victory, I was told there was no plan for victory in the historic American sense."[97] In the Chiefs' defense, it should be noted that McNamara had not permitted them to conduct the type of studies necessary to answer such questions: "If blame had to be assessed, it lay with the president and his civilian advisers in the State Department and OSD. It was the civilian advisers who had convinced the president of the feasibility of carrying out a limited war, it was the civilians who had sold him on 'gradualism'; and it was the civilians who through the president, placed the United States forces on the strategic defensive—a 'no-win' concept."[98]

When the White House began to focus on its future strategy, the president decided to pursue a policy of "Vietnamization," which meant turning over to the Vietnamese as much of the war as possible. American forces would continue to be involved, but the signs of an eventual disengagement were already evident. According to Davidson, "American forces would provide the shield behind which this enhancement would take place, and they would be withdrawn when the RVNAF [Republic of Vietnam Air Force] and the GVN [Government of Vietnam] could defend themselves. The air strategy would support the ground strategy. . . . For the first time in the war, the United States government had devised a strategy which was coherent, integrated and above all, attainable."[99] Westmoreland then learned that instead of the 200,000 troops he had requested, he would receive only about 30,000 for support services. However, the administration did change its policy toward reservists, as Clifford announced in May that 24,500, mostly from the army, would be called to active duty. "Of these, about 9,000 were earmarked for eventual deployment to Vietnam."[100] From now on, the major focus would be on the South Vietnamese. The war would be theirs to win or lose, and the Americans could not—and would not—save their country for them.[101] To implement this new strategy, the president announced that Westmoreland's deputy, Creighton Abrams, would take over command of the Vietnam War in June.

After more than five years in office, the president was feeling besieged by military problems in Vietnam, the increasingly strong feeling that the war was unwinnable, public demonstrations against the war, and race riots that required his attention. The president had had enough. His health was not good (he had been hospitalized twice for surgery while in the White House), and he was tired of fighting the political battles at home. He decided that not only would he announce that he would *not* be a candidate for the presidency in 1968, he would also introduce another cease-fire—even if the Chiefs did not like the idea.

The president dropped his bomb in a speech he made on March 31. Turning to the subject of Vietnam, he announced that he had "ordered our aircraft and naval vessels to make no attacks on North Vietnam, except in the area north of the demilitarized zone, where the continuing enemy build-up directly threatens allied forward positions, and where the movement of their troops and supplies are clearly related to that threat." Turning to his future, the president stated that "I shall not seek, and I will not accept, the nomination of my party for another term as your President."[102] The Johnson years were drawing to a close, much to the Chiefs' relief.

As one might predict, the North utilized the bombing pause to resupply their forces, a matter of major concern to the Chiefs. Johnson asked General Wheeler if "the time is limited when we can continue to keep the area above the 19th [parallel] 'off limits' without being hurt?' 'Yes, Sir,' he [Wheeler] said. 'They are moving men and equipment south rapidly.' We discussed all the pros and cons of resuming bombing. I decided to hold off a few more days."[103] Three days later the North Vietnamese announced they were ready for negotiations. Held in Paris, the talks between the United States and Hanoi ran from May until late October. Then, on October 31, the president announced the cessation of all bombing of the North.

Abrams decided to discontinue Westmoreland's policy of search and destroy. Instead, he began to insist that the military implement the policy of pacification—something that was supposed to have been implemented two years earlier but was instead ignored by the military in Vietnam. However, this policy was strongly supported by his new secretary of defense.[104] "Abrams would insist on hamlet protection, not enemy destruction, as the definitive mission. As a consequence, population security, not body count, was going to become the measure of merit." In implementing this "new" strategy, Abrams ordered that no heavy artillery or rockets be fired into an inhabited area unless he gave his personal permission. By the end of 1968, the situation appeared to be improving. A Marine general assigned as a MACV operations officer claimed that "we were wearing out the NVA."[105]

Thus, as President Johnson left office at the beginning of 1969, the United States, locked in seemingly fruitless negotiations with the North, continued the bombing pause, and Abrams vigorously pursued a policy of Vietnamization, a policy that appeared to be having a positive impact. Overseeing its full implementation, however, would be the newly elected president Nixon.

CONCLUSION

Presidential Leadership Style and Violations of Service/ Military Culture

It is hard to know where to begin in discussing Johnson's leadership style. It is also impossible to separate his leadership style from his and his secretary's violations of military culture.

Both men (McNamara especially) violated almost every aspect of military culture. They repeatedly lied to, misled, and ignored the Chiefs. Indeed, McNamara's decision sometimes to leave them out of the Tuesday lunches revealed just how little he respected them and their opinions. Many critical military decisions were thus made without the Chiefs' input; had they been given the opportunity to attend the meetings on a regular basis, they would have at least understood what was decided and been able to offer some input into the decisions, even if they might have disagreed with the final results. Such actions as omitting senior military officers from such meetings are not unheard of in civil-military relations, and the president has the right to choose whatever kind of leadership style he feels appropriate. Having risen through a bureaucracy that can be impolite on many occasions, military officers are usually immune to insults. However, both McNamara and the president demonstrated their disrespect for—and even loathing of—their subordinates on several occasions, which certainly undermined the possibility of working together smoothly. Consequently, they gradually lost the Chiefs' respect and trust, and the president's power of persuasion eroded to almost nothing.

To make matters worse, the president operated in a leadership vacuum. The Chiefs were well aware that they could not expect the president to mimic their bureaucratic style; however, they expected some sort of structure in their relationship. Their only option was either to send memos through McNamara, or, when that did not work, to try and send memos to the president through back channels. However, even if they were lucky enough to get their memos or plans to the president, they were more often than not left in policy limbo. Decisions were sometimes not made, while in other instances the Chiefs were left wondering exactly what was expected of them. Too often the result was organizational chaos.

McNamara's decision to bring his Whiz Kids with him to the Pentagon further complicated matters. Although the Chiefs certainly recognized McNamara's right to have a separate source of information, they objected to the disdainful attitude held by McNamara and the Whiz Kids, who lacked knowledge about the military and its operation. Being instructed on how to fight the war by someone who knew nothing about war was hard to swallow. Indeed, the military especially hated being told to carry out body counts and then being criticized for doing so as if it had been the army's idea in the first place.

Then there was the question of civilian meddling. As noted previously, no military officer objected to civilian involvement at the strategic level. However, although the Chiefs recognized the president's right to participate and they understood his concern over potential involvement by the Russians or Chinese if the United States went too far in retaliating against North Vietnam, they became uneasy when meddling occurred at the operational level (not to mention the tactical level). The fact is that McNamara and the president interfered at both levels, something that is guaranteed to demoralize almost every officer.

The Chiefs never once questioned the supremacy of civilian control, but they were constantly upset by the president's refusal to devise a strategy for Vietnam. Clark Clifford himself was justifiably angry at senior military officers who really had no idea of how to get the United States out of Vietnam; however, as noted above, neither Johnson nor McNamara had permitted them to carry out such long-term planning. The president's primary attention was on creating his "Great Society." One can understand his priorities, but it is also important to remember both that fighting the Vietnam War was a full-time occupation and that he made a mistake in the beginning by not working with the military and ordering the Chiefs to come up with a broad-based plan.

The president's decision to accept McNamara's idea of graduated response, in spite of opposition from the Chiefs, pushed them to advocate "bombing the North Vietnamese into the Stone Age" or sending masses of troops to the country. Perhaps no approach would have saved the South Vietnamese government, given its corruption and lack of public support. But both McNamara and the military should have been forced to focus on a fundamental strategy as early as 1964.

Also noteworthy during the Johnson period was the Chiefs' inability to speak with one voice, which weakened them. First there was the question of whose service could do the best job. For example, could airpower sufficiently be applied to a conflict like Vietnam? Then there was a reemergence of the feud between the Marines and the army, as exemplified by the ongoing battle between Generals Westmoreland and Lewis Walt over how to conduct the ground war in Vietnam. Although this writer has not seen any evidence of an effort by Johnson or McNamara in particular to split the Chiefs on the basis of service loyalty, one can only wonder if the Chiefs would have been more effective in dealing with the president and the secretary of defense if they had presented a unified front.

Changes in Service/Military Culture?

At one point during the Johnson administration, the Chiefs believed that presidential interference was so pervasive that they were not even being permitted to run the war at the tactical and operational levels. Believing that they could not accept responsibility for the consequences of Johnson's decisions, they came very close to stepping down. Subsequent statements by some of the participants, especially General Johnson and Admiral McDonald, suggest that they later believed they erred in not resigning. However, the fact that they came close to doing so profoundly affected military culture, even though the idea that one should resign if he or she cannot execute an order in good conscience was already part of the culture. As Perry argued, "But if Wheeler set the precedent for military loyalty to civilian control in his refusal to resign, his actions also became the test of military silence in the face of civilian incompetence. Since Wheeler's tenure, it has been impossible for a JCS member to assent silently to policies with which he strongly disagreed."[106] Johnson's successors would always have to remember that senior military officers who believed they were being ignored on key issues during a crisis could, and perhaps would, resign, or speak out forcefully against the administration's policies.

7
THE MILITARY AND RICHARD NIXON

Nixon was the closest we've come to fascism.
—Admiral Elmo Zumwalt

If Johnson turned Kennedy's seminar approach to decision making into chaos, Nixon made Eisenhower's formalistic "chief of staff" model into the most centralized and highly structured management style employed by any president to date. This was especially true of foreign policy and matters of national security. For practical purposes, security policy was made in the White House; the rest of the National Security Council was involved only when Nixon needed its support. Unlike Eisenhower, who enjoyed the give and take of NSC attendees arguing the problem at hand, Nixon was not interested in debate among his subordinates.

Under Nixon, the Chiefs were policy implementers. They rarely became involved in the formulation of policy. For example, Adm. Elmo Zumwalt faced the wrath of the White House when he refused to obey the president's direct order to throw a number of black sailors out of the U.S. Navy for protesting their treatment on ships at sea. Furthermore, because Nixon took a secretive approach to policy, he often placed them in difficult situations. For example, Henry Kissinger ignored the Chiefs' superior, Secretary of Defense Melvin Laird, and spoke directly to them regarding policy on Vietnam, warning them to keep the conversations private.

NIXON'S LEADERSHIP STYLE

Nixon did not trust the machinery of government. To quote William Safire, who worked as a speechwriter in the Nixon White House, "[H]e used *government* and *bureaucracy* as 'half words,' which were complete only when preceded by the expletive *damn*, as in *damn-government* and *damn-bureaucrats*."[1] Similarly, Nixon told Joan Hoff-Wilson that a president should "never rely on his cabinet . . . no [president] in his right mind submits anything to his cabinet . . . it is ridiculous . . . boring."[2] Nixon believed that policy formulation occurred most effectively when it was rationalized to the maximum possible extent. In his mind, the bureaucracy obstructed this kind of policy making: each bureaucratic fiefdom would pursue its own bureaucratic interest, even if it contradicted what the president considered to be the national interest. Nixon's goal was to limit the bureaucracy's involvement by barring it from policy formulation and, whenever possible, restricting it to implementing policy. The bureaucracy's job was to enact presidential decisions, not to deliberate and provide him with policy options. Although senior policy makers would disagree with each other in front of Nixon (in spite of his dislike for such behavior), they often played a marginal role. At most, they might try to persuade him to slightly modify or delay implementing a decision he had already made.

To maximize rationality in the policy process, Nixon endeavored to place the White House at the center of all important aspects of policy. Thus, he took two important steps to gain better control over policy: First, he expanded the size of his staff from the 292 it had been under Johnson to 583 by the end of his first term.[3] Second, his administration created a system of six special committees that operated out of the NSC. Chaired by the president's national security assistant, these committees comprised "the Vietnam Special Studies Group, the Washington Special Actions Group (to deal with international crisis), the Defense Programs Review Committee, the Verification Panel (to deal with strategic arms talks), the 40 Committee (to deal with covert actions), and the Senior Review Group (which dealt with all other types of policy issues)."[4] To assure maximum control, these committees "reached down into the departments and agencies, absorbing key personnel," and they were overlapping and interdepartmental. The latter were generally chaired by assistant secretaries, who received their assignments from the White House. Consequently, many departments were marginalized. To cite only one example, Secretary of State William Rogers "was not even informed in advance of the administration's most innovative foreign policy initiative—the opening to China, which Nixon visited in February 1972."[5] Furthermore, the president walled himself off from the rest of the government, protected by what Greenstein called a "Berlin Wall" in the form of his senior policy assistants.[6] The immediate effect was a stronger White House: "The difficulty of communicating with the president produced dissatisfaction with White House decision-making procedures, . . . in the short run it . . . enhanced the clout of the White House aides who coordinated the processes and saw the president on a regular basis."[7] However, Nixon eventually paid a price for isolating himself from both the bureaucracy and Congress, as his bungling of Watergate would demonstrate.

Given Nixon's distrust of the bureaucracy, not to mention his own introverted, secretive personality and his need to control policy, it is not surprising that politics in Washington during his administration acquired an even more Machiavellian cast than was normally the case. The Nixon White House believed that the government's task was to get the job done. If that meant cutting out of the action the people who would normally be in charge of the task at hand, so be it. Bypassing the head of an agency and dealing directly with his subordinates, who were ordered not to inform the secretary or director of what was transpiring, was also acceptable behavior when obtaining information or implementing a policy favored by the White House. Toward this end, the Nixon administration made extensive use of back-channel communications, which, as Kissinger observed, were useful in circumventing the bureaucracy.[8] Placing primary emphasis on getting the job done, the Nixon White House downplayed ethical issues: the end justified the means.

The Chiefs thus found themselves in a difficult situation when dealing with Nixon's administration. Trained to follow the chain of command, military officers resisted the idea of not informing their senior officer when given an order that the superior officer would oppose. They felt similar discomfort when the White House became involved in personnel issues or tried to tell the military how to fight a war. Just as upsetting to them was the secrecy pervading the Nixon White House. Having overseen secret operations on a routine basis, the officers balked when all the information they needed to operate successfully was withheld or not provided in a timely fashion. For example, when Nixon decided to turn the bulk of the fighting in Vietnam over to the South Vietnamese, the plan was presented to the generals as a fait accompli. Lastly, the Chiefs' relationship with Nixon was further complicated by his readiness to criticize them for policy failures, even when they were following proper procedures.

Despite the difficulties, senior military officers did have the benefit of usually knowing what Nixon expected of them. And, in contrast to the Johnson White House, Nixon asked for their advice on fighting the war in Vietnam. The Chiefs did not always get what they wanted, but they felt that the president had at least heard them, which was quite a step forward when one considers the previous administration.

A key player in Nixon's managerial approach was former Harvard professor Henry Kissinger, who would accumulate more power over issues of foreign relations and national security than any special assistant before or since.

President Richard M. Nixon (center) meets with the Joint Chiefs of Staff. Secretary of Defense Melvin Laird is seated just to the president's left and Admiral Thomas Moorer just to the president's right. (Richard Nixon Library)

While Nixon waited to assume the presidency during the transition period, Kissinger conceived of the interdepartmental groups and prepared for the NSC's expansion, which he would oversee. And Kissinger complemented Nixon in that he too was suspicious, secretive, and determined to accomplish his goals regardless of the cost. He was also highly pragmatic, albeit conservative. Furthermore, when it came to the game of politics, Kissinger, like his boss, could be ruthless. General Westmoreland, who was serving as army chief of staff, wisely perceived how Kissinger's ascendancy to power in the White House affected national security policy:

> As President Nixon came into office, new personalities and a new modus operandi entered into the conduct of White House affairs and the war in Viet-Nam. For the first time all policy in connection with the war centered in a person other than the President, the President's adviser on national security affairs, the erstwhile Harvard Professor whom I had known for a number of years, Henry Kissinger. No longer did initiative come from the American command in Saigon; it came from the White House and Dr. Kissinger. No more were there overly sensitive reactions

> to timid subordinates in the State and Defense Departments, but fearless, skillful amalgamation of divergent opinions to come up with strong, definitive conclusions to present to the President.[9]

There was a new sheriff in town, a fact that the military recognized very quickly.

Kissinger understood the low morale that the Chiefs carried with them into the new administration, and he decided to reinvigorate them, "even if it meant using more hawkish officers . . . as a lever against those who advocated a faster disengagement."[10] He was prepared to employ such officers whenever and wherever possible.

The new administration included Lt. Col. Alexander Haig, Kissinger's young, dynamic, and smart assistant. Haig's influence was considerable, and it would grow exponentially. Indeed, he was soon promoted to colonel, and after that his rise was nothing short of "meteoric. He was promoted quickly to brigadier general and then major general, skipped the grade of lieutenant general and four years later, in January 1973 was promoted by the president to full general—four stars."[11] One might consider Haig's appointment as Kissinger's assistant to be a plum for the military; he battled vigorously to protect the army whenever he felt it was under attack, but given the manner in which Nixon's administration operated, his primary loyalty was to the White House and Kissinger.

Another key player in the new Nixon administration was Melvin Laird, the secretary of defense. The former leader of the House of Representatives was considered to be a smart, shrewd, and consummate politician. One senior military officer called Laird "a political animal to the marrow of his bones. . . . He could use one line on the JCS, a somewhat different one with the service secretaries, and a third version in dealing with key members of Congress, many of whom were close personal friends."[12] As far as the military was concerned, he hit a home run in his first meeting with them by clearly stating that he would work with them as a team and would welcome their advice and consul.

> In the history of the JCS, the Laird introduction of January 22, 1969, stands out as the primary example of just how a civilian leader can both dampen military mistrust and gain military allegiance for controversial foreign policy initiatives that run counter to traditional military beliefs . . . Indeed, the Laird meeting proves the point: of all the secretaries who have served in the Pentagon, Laird remains among the most respected, not because he agreed with military programs and policies (he often didn't), but because he was willing to compromise on JCS positions and accord the chiefs the respect they thought they deserved.[13]

Yet Laird's relationship with Kissinger and Nixon would be rocky. Kissinger believed Laird was out to get him from the beginning, while Laird objected to Kissinger's effort to assume total control over security policy, especially as it related to Vietnam. Kissinger considered the secretary of defense to be a dove, and he sometimes tried to utilize members of the Chiefs, whom he considered more hard-line, to circumvent Laird, a solid supporter of the policy of Vietnamization. The secretary saw the beleaguered country as a bottomless pit that devoured scarce military resources and tore apart the army. Thus, the key to any policy was to turn the fighting over to the South Vietnamese as soon as possible. Indeed, "from his first visit to Vietnam, Laird 'was pushing the idea of Vietnamization,' said General Goodpaster."[14] Laird did share at least one of Kissinger's traits: he was equally adept at playing secretive politics; for example, he kept in close touch with Gen. Creighton Abrams, who was in command of American forces in Vietnam, using back-channel communications or calling him by secure phone when necessary.

The problem was as simple as it was difficult to resolve. For his part, Kissinger believed that as the president's personal representative "he had the right to deal directly, and if need be secretly, with anyone in the government." Not surprisingly, Laird pointed out that he was a "Constitutional official and as a critical link in the chain of command he was the conduit through which all dealings with his subordinates must pass, and that he could not tolerate those subordinates being given orders outside the chain of command or engaging in activities that he knew nothing about." Indeed, when Kissinger asked Zumwalt to set up a back-channel communications system, the latter answered that he preferred to receive all White House orders via the secretary of defense. "He said he would not operate that way, nor would the President, who considered each member of the Joint Chiefs to be a military adviser to him and who intended to go directly to each of us when he wanted undiluted military advice."[15] According to Zumwalt, he ignored Kissinger and instead informed Adm. Thomas Moorer, then chairman of the Joint Chiefs, of whatever Kissinger happened to tell him. When Zumwalt became chief of naval operations, he passed such information to Laird or his executive assistant.

Like everything else in the Nixon administration, the relationship between Laird and the Chiefs was unorthodox. Laird, a consummate politician, had difficulty accepting the Chiefs' belief that they were apolitical. Indeed, there were times when he believed some of them were playing politics to get into good graces with the White House. But any problems in his relationship with them stemmed less from any political behavior on their part than from his views on the situation in Vietnam: he was strongly opposed to any widening of the war; in fact, he wanted the United States to exit as soon as possible.

Kissinger (and Nixon) decided that he could not be trusted. As a consequence, Kissinger often went directly to one of the Chiefs for information. Not surprisingly, this infuriated Laird, and he let the Chiefs know that he did not appreciate them speaking privately with Kissinger. Some, like Zumwalt, made sure that the secretary was kept fully informed of their contacts with the White House, while others, such as the future chairman of the Joint Chiefs, Admiral Moorer, were more willing to play Kissinger's game. Contacts that bypassed the chain of command, especially those concerning the ongoing war in Vietnam, would create constant conflict between the secretary and the Chiefs throughout Kissinger's White House tenure.

ENDING THE VIETNAM WAR

When Nixon was running for office, he claimed that he had a plan to bring the war to a quick conclusion. The Chiefs were initially encouraged. Finally, after all they had been through in the last eight years, an anti-Communist president was prepared to do what it took to "win this damn war!"[16] The problem was that Nixon really did not have a "plan" to end the war, although Kissinger had begun to focus on the problem. Nixon later wrote, "During the transition, Henry Kissinger, whom I had chosen to be my national security adviser, began reviewing all the possible policies toward Vietnam and distilled them into a full spectrum of specific options, with massive military escalation at one extreme and immediate unilateral withdrawal at the other."[17]

When constructing his Vietnam policy, Nixon engaged in considerable "play acting." He soon decided, for example, that one of the keys to getting the North Vietnamese to pay attention to him was to give them the impression that he was mad enough to use any means necessary to bring an end to the conflict. H. R. Haldeman quoted him saying, "I want the North Vietnamese to believe I've reached the point where I might do *anything* to stop the war. We'll just slip the word to them that, 'for God's sake, you know Nixon is obsessed about Communism. We can't restrain him when he's angry—and he has his hand on the nuclear button' and Ho Chi Minh himself will be in Paris in two days begging for peace."[18]

In the meantime, Kissinger found no consensus in official Washington on what to do about Vietnam. A Rand study that he commissioned indicated the existence of two broad approaches: Those who fell in Group A (the JCS, MACV, the State Department, the American Embassy in Saigon, and some members of the CIA) believed that the United States was winning. The Viet Cong and North Vietnamese were in retreat; thus, the United States should

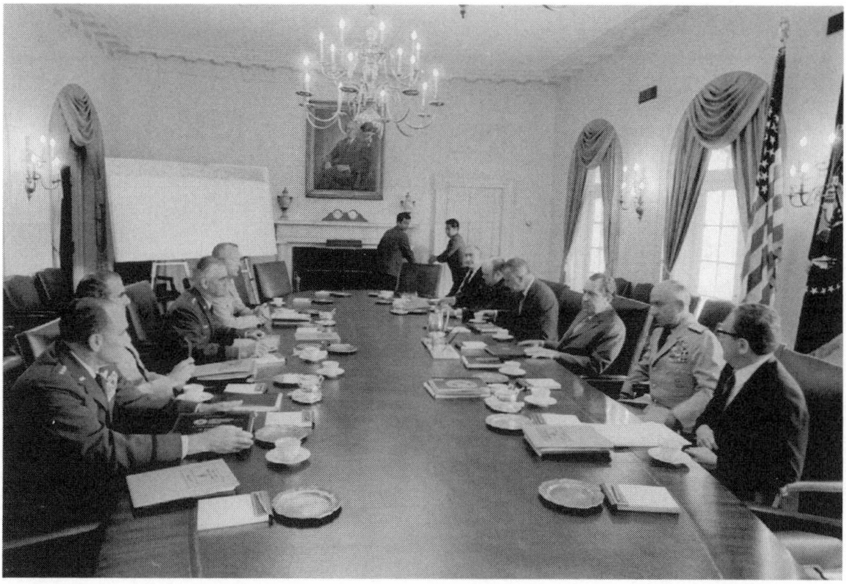

President Nixon (seated on the right in the middle of the table) meets with the Joint Chiefs of Staff. Admiral Moorer is on his left and Henry Kissinger is to Moorer's left. (Richard Nixon Library)

retain a large force in South Vietnam, Laos, and Cambodia. Group B included the secretary of defense and most of his staff, as well as some in State and the CIA. They believed that military escalation would lead only to military failure and increased domestic opposition.[19] Far from being cast in black and white, the opinions of Group A and Group B differed only in degree. "Nobody believed that the war could be won in the foreseeable future, and even MACV and the embassy in Saigon doubted the RVNAF's long-range capability to defend the country against *both* the VC and the NVA without United States combat support. Furthermore, neither of the American agencies in Saigon held high hopes for the GVN's ability to win the hearts and minds of the South Vietnamese people in the near future."[20] In short, everyone recognized that regardless of the approach taken, the United States was in for a protracted conflict. The new administration was sure of one thing, however: the United States was not going to suffer a defeat in that far-off land.

The more the generals and admirals examined Nixon's administration in their attempts to understand it, the less certain they became. They wondered whether this new regime was simply posturing, as had Johnson's. Would it continue to send American GIs into combat without the support of the American people? On the bright side, Laird was certainly not an elitist like the know-it-all McNamara, and the Whiz Kids had been shown the door. The new secretary of defense indicated that the individual services themselves would be responsible for designing their force structures; furthermore, to discover what kinds of weapons they needed, he would rely upon them, not a bunch of young systems analysts who knew nothing about fighting wars.

Laird told the Chiefs that if they wanted new weapons, the United States had to withdraw from Vietnam—the sooner the better. The money being used to pay for the war could and should go toward purchasing new weapons. The new administration could not be expected both to pay for the war and purchase the new weapons that all of the services desperately needed. Mark Perry noted how this financial limitation actually worked to the secretary of defense's benefit: "The payoff for Laird was immediate: he had gained the JCS's support of his program for an early withdrawal from Vietnam without threatening the new spirit of cooperation between the JCS and himself."[21]

Nixon's Strategy

The administration's strategy was relatively simple. Instead of continuing the Johnson administration's efforts to destroy the enemy through combined diplomacy and attrition, Nixon and Kissinger decided to place greater emphasis on military force, which would be backed up by diplomacy. The two men were convinced that the North Vietnamese (who were the major enemy after the Viet Cong suffered tremendous losses in the Tet offensive) would never come to the negotiating table unless they believed the United States was serious about its threat to use force. They definitely did not want a replay of the Korean situation. The initial result of Kissinger's search for a strategy was his National Security Study Memorandum 1, which was titled "The Situation in Vietnam." General Wheeler brought NSSM1 back to the Chiefs. In their first meeting under the Nixon administration he stated that he believed the new administration "was intent on solving the problem in Vietnam, beginning with a full assessment of where we stand on the war."[22] In essence, the document asked the JCS to examine all aspects of the Vietnam War and provide the White House with their best advice.

At the NSC's first meeting four days later, Wheeler reported that everything was being done in Vietnam "except the bombing of the North."[23] A few days later, Kissinger met with him and Laird, the latter of whom argued that the public would not support renewed bombing of the North. Wheeler then maintained that as an alternative the United States should consider bombing

NVA troop concentrations in Cambodia, something the chiefs had long wanted to do. The North Vietnamese had expelled the Cambodians from the border region with Vietnam and were using it as a sanctuary for garrisoning troops and stockpiling weapons, medical supplies, food, and clothing.

On January 30, 1969, Kissinger went to the Pentagon, where he met with Laird and Wheeler. The meeting showed that in spite of their efforts to work together, Laird and Wheeler had significant differences of opinion. Wheeler maintained that U.S. forces within South Vietnam were "fully committed"; thus, the only effective responses to a renewed North Vietnamese attack would be operations in the Demilitarized Zone (DMZ) or bombing of the North. Laird, however, argued that renewed bombing would lead to public protests in the United States.[24]

In mid-February, the North Vietnamese launched attacks throughout South Vietnam. An infuriated Nixon believed Hanoi was testing him. He could respond by resuming the bombing of North Vietnam or by moving forces into Laos, Cambodia, or the DMZ. The rest of the world, however, would probably view the use of force in these areas as an excessive response.[25] Nevertheless, Nixon had to do something, especially because "he had charged his predecessors with weakness in reacting to Communist moves."[26] The next day, Nixon decided to bomb the Cambodian sanctuaries, but he held off at the suggestion of his advisors. He did make clear, however, his intent to respond. The JCS recommended that the United States bomb both Cambodia and North Vietnam. Laird opposed their proposed course of action, fearing that they would "do the one thing we don't want to happen, they will expand the war."[27]

Bombing Cambodia

Although an attack on the Cambodian sanctuaries could undermine the negotiations the United States was conducting with the North Vietnamese and could lead to renewed public opposition at home, it also had a number of advantages:

> It would punish the North Vietnamese who had numerous logistical base areas and headquarters in Cambodia. It would inflict no damage or casualties on the Cambodian people who had been evicted long ago from the border areas by the North Vietnamese. The bombing might be done secretly without arousing the fury of the doves at home. . . . Finally, the extension of American operations outside South Vietnam

was a forceful hint to Hanoi that the United States might not continue to fight the war in shackles, and that the new administration would not be bound by the restraints which had so hampered Lyndon Johnson.[28]

On March 15, the issue arose again as the Communists fired five rockets into Saigon. Nixon then ordered B-52 bombers to attack immediately the Cambodian sanctuaries. Kissinger again asked him to delay his order, which he did, until a meeting could be held the next day in the Oval Office. This time, Laird and Wheeler were singing from the same page of music, advocating the attacks (in a number of meetings with his colleague, Wheeler had argued that such an offensive operation would provide an opportunity to wipe out the NVA's headquarters). Destroying the enemy's headquarters would facilitate the United States' withdrawal from Vietnam by diminishing the threat faced by the South Vietnamese. The president approved Wheeler's plan and sent him and Laird back to the Pentagon to compose a list of targets.

On March 18, 1969, B-52 bombers struck Cambodia. According to Nixon, the attack was a great success. "We received reports that our bombs touched off multiple secondary explosions, which meant that they had hit ammunition dumps or fuel depots. Crew members observed a total of seventy-three such explosions in the target area, ranging up to five times the normal intensity of a typical secondary explosion."[29] In fairness to Nixon, all strikes were within five miles of the Cambodian border, and each of them had been approved by the White House.

The secrecy of the bombing operation haunted the Chiefs. No one except those directly involved knew they were taking place: the Cambodians were unaware of the attacks because the area was totally occupied by the North Vietnamese, who were also unlikely to complain because they had long maintained that they were not in Cambodia. According to Nixon, his administration chose to keep the bombings secret to avoid creating a public uproar and putting Cambodian leader Prince Norodom Sihanouk in a difficult position. If the bombings were public knowledge, he would have to oppose them because his country was officially neutral.[30] In fact, according to Kissinger, U.S.-Cambodian relations improved in the aftermath of the bombing campaign.[31]

Such secrecy forced the Chiefs to keep a second set of books for the bombings in Cambodia. One file would be a "cover naming targets within South Vietnam, the true file listing the real targets in Cambodia."[32] And the whole process was kept on a close-hold basis. "In the Pentagon only the secretary of defense, the JCS, a handful on the Joint Staff, and the service DCSOPS [Deputy Chief of Staff, Operations] were privy to the secret arrangements."[33]

According to Gen. Bruce Palmer, who was Westmoreland's deputy, the military faced a hopeless situation. They had to lie publicly about what they considered a "legitimate wartime operation." Consequently, he reported, "General McConnell, the Air Force chief, began grumbling about the operation, labeling the effort to conceal the bombing 'stupid' and the other chiefs present chimed in."[34] Importantly, the decision to keep the operation hidden from the public eye had a major impact on Laird's dealings with the White House. He had argued against both the operation and the secrecy surrounding it. From then on his relationship with the White House became increasingly adversarial.

Troop Withdrawals and Vietnamization

Troop withdrawal was a key component of the Nixon strategy. He knew that withdrawals were critical if he hoped to deal effectively with public opposition to the war. "Americans needed tangible evidence that we were winding down the war, and the South Vietnamese needed to be given more responsibility for their defense."[35] In mid-March Laird sent a memorandum to Nixon suggesting that 50,000–70,000 troops be withdrawn in 1969.[36] On April 10, with Nixon's approval Kissinger issued NSSM 36, which ordered the secretary of defense to prepare by June 1 " 'a specific timetable for Vietnamizing the war.' The plan was to cover 'all aspects of U.S. military, para-military, and civilian involvement in Vietnam, including combat and combat support forces, advisory personnel, and all forces of equipment.' "[37] In the meantime, Defense was ordered to formulate a long-range plan on the withdrawal of additional troops, which Kissinger requested on April 10. The idea was to bring home as many of the combat forces as possible, leaving only support and advisory troops in country.

The Chiefs and Laird could not agree on how best to proceed. The Chiefs—and MACV—wanted the withdrawals to be carefully balanced between combat and support forces. They also wanted forces outside of Vietnam, which they considered vital to the country's defense, to be considered support, not combat forces. The secretary of defense's office, however, considered the forces outside of Vietnam to have been ineffective; withdrawing them would have little adverse impact on the war. Similarly, the Department of Defense (DOD) argued for a more rapid reduction of maneuver forces such as infantry and armor than the Chiefs thought was wise. DOD maintained that this would permit American forces to provide the South Vietnamese with more air, artillery, and logistical support. The Chiefs countered by arguing that, if anything, the combat efficiency of the South Vietnamese forces was "declining in relationship to that of U.S. troops in combat."[38]

Kissinger made the situation facing the Chiefs even more difficult when he reportedly approached Wheeler suggesting that the NSC and the JCS work together in "sharing foreign policy and military information outside the government's usual lines of communication." For example, at a White House meeting, Kissinger supposedly told Wheeler that neither he nor the president believed that Laird could be trusted. "Within days, the president himself reiterated Kissinger's point, saying that he hoped Wheeler would be 'frank' in his appraisal of Laird's views." Needless to say, this kind of conduct put Wheeler in a very difficult position. He worked for Laird, even though he knew full well that Nixon was the commander in chief. According to Wheeler, Kissinger again approached him a month later and told him that Nixon

> wanted a "more open policy" on Vietnam, a policy that, he explained, the Secretary of Defense "doesn't seem to agree with." Kissinger intimated that Wheeler's support "in this matter" was "certainly appreciated," and that a means had to found to "communicate the president's concern directly to the men in the field"—a euphemism. He meant that White House officials wanted to run the war without passing orders through Laird. Indeed, Wheeler soon realized that the White House was not only intent on bypassing Laird in the chain of command, it wanted to obtain information on Laird's programs at the Pentagon.

Wheeler at first assumed this was just another example of bureaucratic infighting, but in time he began to realize that the White House really believed that Laird was attempting to sabotage the administration's policy in Vietnam. According to Perry, Wheeler refused to pick up on these "hints" and the White House eventually dropped the issue but kept looking for another route. They apparently found it in Lt. Gen. John Vogt, one of Kissinger's former students, who passed on to him what the JCS and Laird were up to while he was serving as the JCS director. Then, in May, "Kissinger reportedly ordered Haig to wiretap the phone of Colonel Robert Pursley, Laird's military assistant."[39]

Drawing up a withdrawal plan proved to be a difficult challenge for the Chiefs, who knew the war was lost. The writing had been on the wall since 1965, when Johnson's refusal to call up the reserves sealed their fate. Nevertheless, the withdrawal of troops would be hard for the military to take. Going home without victory suggested that the troops had died in vain. It was a hard pill to swallow. Kissinger observed that "it was clear the military approached the subject with a heavy heart. Deep down they knew it was a reversal of what they had fought for. However presented, it would make victory impossible and even an honorable outcome problematical."[40] But withdrawal was a reality they could not ignore. The South Vietnamese, who could not expect the Americans to continue to fight their war forever, would have to save themselves.

Laird bludgeoned the Chiefs with reminders that the U.S. military itself was in a sorry state as a result of Vietnam and could not fight two wars simultaneously as Pentagon directives required. He constantly pushed them to submit lists for additional withdrawals. According to one source, he occasionally angered them by his insistence that they plan further and further into the future. In fact,

> At the beginning of one particularly memorable session, Laird actually ordered the Chiefs to closet themselves in the tank until they had come up with a full schedule of withdrawals, a marathon session that lasted three full days, leaving the JCS officers at once exhausted and exhilarated. In each debate with the JCS, he laid out his only option: agree to a schedule of accelerated withdrawals or come up with a smaller budget; bring the boys home or cut outlays for new weapons.[41]

The Chiefs were caught between a rock and a hard place: while the White House prodded the Chiefs to use aggressive military force in Vietnam, their boss let them know that if they pushed hard for the use of more military force in Vietnam, their budget would suffer.

On May 14 Nixon announced a new policy toward Vietnam. In the past, the United States had insisted that North Vietnamese troops leave the South six months prior to a U.S. withdrawal. Now, however, Nixon was calling for "mutually phased withdrawals" of troops from both sides. The North Vietnamese ignored his offer, which represented a significant modification of U.S. policy. In any case, the president decided that the United States would no longer wait for the North Vietnamese to withdraw. On June 8 he met with South Vietnamese president Nguyen Van Thieu on Midway Island and informed him that the United States planned to withdraw 25,000 troops beginning in July. He assured Thieu that the withdrawals of American troops "would be timed so as not to undermine South Vietnam's stability or political viability, and that the United States would not be party to the imposition of a coalition government on the Vietnamese."[42] The Midway meeting led to the creation of the Nixon Doctrine, which the president outlined on Guam on July 25, 1969. In essence, Nixon told the world that in the future the United States would avoid, if at all possible, becoming involved in local wars.

His doctrine did not mean that the United States would assist other countries; on the contrary, the Americans would continue to provide military assistance, but the country concerned would have to defend itself without the assistance of American troops.

The second aspect of Nixon's new policy was pacification, an idea that had been around for a long time, but had never been the primary focus of U.S. policy. A senior U.S. general described "pacification [as] nothing more or less than an overall program to remove the reasons for revolution."[43] On November 3, 1969, Nixon gave the concept center stage in one of his most successful speeches. In his talk, which he deemed "the most effective of my presidency,"[44] he chastised antiwar demonstrators, arguing that the United States would not agree to an immediate withdrawal while at the same time emphasizing that the United States would not betray the South Vietnamese. Unfortunately, the United States was dealing with a corrupt government that was not seriously interested in creating the kind of society that would remove the causes for revolution. Consequently, the challenges appeared insurmountable: "Successful Vietnamization required an almost total restructuring of the South Vietnamese society, government and armed forces, for these flaws prevented the South Vietnamese from achieving the goal of Vietnamization."[45] Kissinger himself understood the problem. Indeed he had told Nixon privately that given the resources available, there was no way the United States could win the war in the two years that some had predicted. Indeed, he noted that as U.S. troops began to withdraw, the North Vietnamese would only become more emboldened.[46]

Kissinger believed that Washington's only hope lay in applying maximum pressure on the North so that it would be forced to agree to U.S. terms despite ongoing withdrawals of American forces. To that end, the Chiefs called for the mining of North Vietnamese ports and harbors, the institution of a naval blockade, and a resumption of the bombing of North Vietnam, including a number of nonmilitary targets. The plan, which was called Duck Hook, was to commence November 1.

Of particular interest was the decision of the acting chairman of the Joint Chiefs, Adm. Thomas Moorer, to have the JCS staff draw up these plans without the knowledge of Secretary of Defense Melvin Laird. Kissinger's private discussions with Moorer had been more fruitful than those he had had earlier with General Wheeler. Initially, Nixon decided against the plan, fearing an outburst of public demonstrations.

The withdrawal plan may have been politically expedient, but it created major problems within the military, especially the army. Morale went down as disciplinary problems increased. Soldiers did not want to fight once they realized that the United States had adopted a "no-win" strategy. Why put one's life on the line when it was only a matter of time before the United States would leave South Vietnam? Who wanted to go down in history as the last soldier killed in Vietnam? In Europe some units began publishing antiwar newspapers, and problems associated with drugs, which were relatively cheap and available in South Vietnam, increased. In 1970, for example, 65,000 Americans were on drugs in Vietnam, compared to only 8,440 the year before, 11,068 drug arrests were made, and hard drugs appeared for the first time. Fragging (the use of fragmentation grenades by disgruntled soldiers against officers or senior noncommissioned officers who tried to send them out to fight) was up three times when compared with the previous year, and discipline problems such as insubordination, mutiny, and refusal to obey orders went up from .28 per 1,000 men in 1969 to .32 in 1970.[47] Among the host of problems, perhaps the "most disturbing of all were confirmed incidents of soldiers in the war zone who refused to fight, turned on their officers in open rebellion, or even deserted."[48] It was also at this time that the Chiefs learned that eighteen months earlier a company of American soldiers led by Lt. William Calley had massacred more than 350 men, women, and children in a small hamlet known as My Lai. And, as will be discussed below, such problems were not limited to the army. According to one source, the Marine Corps was hit even harder than the army by disciplinary and morale problems. As Ricks put it,

> The Marines were arguably the most devastated of all the services. Calling the early part of the seventies a debacle for the Marines, Jeffrey Record noted in *Proceedings* that, "the Corps registered rates of courts-martial, non-judicial punishments, unauthorized absences, and outright desertions unprecedented in its own history, and, in most case, three to four times those plaguing the US Army."[49]

Sanctuaries

One of the key problems in implementing Vietnamization was the presence of enemy sanctuaries just across the border in Cambodia and in the portion of Laos through which the Ho Chi Minh Trail passed. For example, according to one author, fourteen major North Vietnamese bases were located in Cambodia, some of which were only thirty-five miles away from Saigon. The United States had bombed the havens, but they continued to function. Recognizing that the lack of security posed an obstacle to successful pacification, the Chiefs were determined to reduce the North Vietnamese threat by striking at their logistical assets regardless of where they were located: "As long as they remained 'off-limits' to Allied forces, it was as if a loaded and cocked pistol was being held to head of South Vietnam."[50]

On February 16, 1970, Nixon held a meeting that included Laird, Acting Secretary of State Elliott Richardson, Richard Helms, Acting Chairman of the JCS Moorer, and Kissinger to discuss possible responses to Communist advances in Laos. The general consensus was that the United States should respond with air strikes. General Wheeler told Kissinger that B-52 attacks would be preferable in this instance because they were more accurate than fighter bombers. The president decided to follow Wheeler's suggestion but to conduct the operation in secret. Three B-52s attacked Laos on the night of February 17–18.

Then on March 18 Gen. Lon Nol removed Cambodian president Prince Sihanouk from office while he was in France. The general then asked the United States for assistance in dealing with the large number of North Vietnamese troops in his country who were marching on the capital of Phnom Penh. The White House was determined to respond. If Cambodia collapsed the port of Sihanoukville would again be available to the Communists and "*all* of Cambodia would become a major base area outflanking United States and Allied forces in South Vietnam."[51] Because Nixon had planned the withdrawal of another 150,000 troops by the spring of 1971, South Vietnam would fall soon thereafter unless something was done to destroy the enemy sanctuaries. On March 27, the United States recognized the new government.

On April 4 Laird sent the president a long memo arguing that the U.S. effort in Vietnam was "large and costly. He recommended a fixed monthly rate of withdrawal and a reduction in B-52 and tactical air operations in proportion to our withdrawals. Laird's military proposals all assumed that the enemy threat would decline in parallel with U.S. withdrawals. The opposite was by far more probable."[52] Given Laird's opposition to the Cambodian operation, one source reports that the White House established back-channel communications straight to the military. "He [Nixon] 'was not,' he insisted, 'going to let Laird kill this by pulling out too fast.' "[53]

Prior to Nixon's April 21 meeting with Laird, Kissinger had asked Westmoreland to evaluate the Cambodian operation's chances for success. Westmoreland responded that "they could be effective, but not decisive without American support."[54] Thus, when the president met with Laird, he told him that "we must play a tough game" to gain breathing space.[55] Nixon then postponed the withdrawal of additional U.S. troops for three months.

The NSC met the next day to discuss three possible options. State and Defense preferred doing nothing, Kissinger favored an attack by South Vietnamese forces only, and the Joint Chiefs, General Abrams, and Ambassador Ellsworth Bunker argued for "using whatever forces were necessary to neutralize all the base areas, including American combat forces."[56] Laird, in particular, seemed upset over the way the Defense Department had been left out of the planning process. Ultimately, Nixon decided that South Vietnamese forces supported by American airpower should attack an area known as the "Parrot's Beak."

On April 24, Nixon met with Admiral Moorer and Helms and Robert Cushman from the CIA; Laird, however, was not present. The president told them he wanted to talk about a combined U.S.–South Vietnamese attack against Fishhook, a hook-shaped portion of the Cambodian border, as well as Parrot's Beak. "Helms and Moorer were both strongly in favor of an attack on the Fishhook sanctuary. They felt it would force the North Vietnamese to abandon their effort to encircle and terrorize Phnom Penh. The destruction of valuable supplies would gain valuable time for Vietnamization."[57] Significantly, Kissinger claimed that he thought excluding Laird was wrong, so after the meeting he called him and said that the meeting was only "a military briefing of options, including an American attack on Fishhook."[58]

Two days later, Nixon met with his key advisors—Laird, General Wheeler, Rogers, Helms, and Kissinger—for the purpose of "merely listening to a briefing" provided by General Wheeler on Operation Fish Hook.[59] No decision was announced at that meeting, but as soon as it concluded, Nixon ordered Kissinger to issue a directive authorizing an American attack into the Fishhook area. The president later claimed that he made his decision to attack "acting on the recommendations of the Joint Chiefs of Staff," not the Department of Defense.[60]

The next morning while Kissinger was chairing a meeting on how to implement the directive, both Laird and Rogers called asking if the directive they had just seen meant that the United States was going to invade Fishhook. Kissinger said yes, and when both men protested, he suggested they talk to the president, which they did that same day. Laird expressed concern about casualties, while Rogers worried about the impact the operation would have on his testimony before the Senate Foreign Relations Committee that afternoon. Nixon withdrew the directive for twenty-four hours to ease Rogers's problem on the Hill, and Kissinger sent a back-channel message to Ambassador Bunker asking for his and General Abrams's views on the matter. Both responded that they favored attacks on Fishhook in parallel with the one on Parrot's Beak.

On April 28, the president reiterated his intention of proceeding with attacks on both areas. The next day roughly 8,700 South Vietnamese troops attacked Parrot's Beak. On April 30, the president publicly announced the onset of attacks on Cambodian sanctuaries, arguing that the incursions would be "limited, temporary, and not directed against any outside country, indispensable for Vietnamization and to keep casualties to a minimum."[61] The next day some 15,000 U.S. soldiers attacked Fishhook. "Preceded by a B-52 attack, fighter-bomber sorties, and heavy artillery preparation, the tanks moved north and the infantry units began to move west and south. The great battle was on, except—there was no great battle. They [the North] fled to the west leaving the Americans and the South Vietnamese their supplies and base area."[62] "Within a week after the offensive began, there were 31,000 American and 19,000 South Vietnamese troops in Cambodia."[63] By May 3, the battle was over. The Americans and South Vietnamese destroyed tons of North Vietnamese weapons, munitions, and supplies, but they were unable to find the elusive North Vietnamese headquarters—their real target. By June 30 they had left the country.

The operation was militarily successful: the North Vietnamese had been thrown off balance, pressure on the Cambodian government had been relieved, and the bases in the border areas were destroyed along with their supplies. According to Kissinger, the attack gained the United States about fifteen months by disrupting North Vietnamese military planning and operations.[64] Equally important, the invasion was a morale booster for many of the troops serving in Vietnam. Admiral Zumwalt's son, who served close to the Cambodian border and was only a few miles away from the sanctuaries, later wrote, "I realize that invasion was, and continues to be, highly controversial, but for those of us who served in Vietnam, it was long overdue. In Ha Tien, I had seen with my own eyes trucks drive up to the Cambodian–South Vietnam border to unload weapons for infiltration into South Vietnam. Our men, and the South Vietnamese, were being killed every day with those weapons and I thought this activity inside Cambodia should not go unpunished."[65]

A Change in Command

On July 1, 1970, General Wheeler retired as chairman of the Joint Chiefs of Staff. The military considered him to be "a fine chairman, who literally gave his life for his country. The great responsibilities and pressures of the job broke his health and he died not long after he retired. He was highly respected and had the ear of the President, but he was overshadowed by such men as . . . Kissinger."[66] His successor, Admiral Moorer, had been acting chair for some time already. Considered by the White House to be the perfect candidate, Moorer was hawkish on Vietnam and outspoken to a fault. Indeed, Perry was not far from the mark when he noted that "perhaps the only real surprise is that he wasn't drummed out of the Navy for speaking his mind, which he often did—and apparently with little thought, taking any and every opportunity to call a fellow officer who disagreed with him 'a dirty bastard,' or 'an unshaved peacenik,' a phrase he used with disarming frequency during the height of the Vietnam War."[67] Moorer, who operated in a much more secretive manner than his predecessor, made little effort to inform his fellow Chiefs of what was happening at the White House. He would occasionally be as Machiavellian as Kissinger.

Having been deeply involved with the White House on Vietnam when he served as chief of naval operations, Moorer clearly understood that Nixon did not trust the military. The new JCS chairman also was fully aware of the existence of the back-channel system in the Pentagon's basement that was under twenty-four-hour guard and reported directly to Kissinger, thereby totally bypassing Laird.

Lam Son 719

The problem posed by the sanctuaries persisted. In December 1970 the related question of cutting the Ho Chi Minh Trail was again raised because the North Vietnamese were working overtime to resupply their forces in Cambodia. On December 23, after getting the support of Moorer, the president approved in principle the idea of cutting the trail, which in this case meant sending troops into Laos. The United States also had intelligence suggesting that the North Vietnamese were planning an attack on the northern part of South Vietnam and would thus make extensive use of the trail as well as bases in Laos. Because of the scheduled withdrawal of the American military, this was the last time that enough U.S. forces would be available to make a difference.

On January 25, 1971, the president met with his advisors. Admiral Moorer reviewed the details of the operation, and when asked about possible resistance, Moorer maintained that "if the enemy fought—and it probably would—American airpower would isolate the battlefield and inflict heavy losses that would be difficult to recoup. If it did not, its supply system would be destroyed."[68] The rules for this engagement differed from those in the past. For the first time since 1965 U.S. ground troops would not be involved. They were forbidden to enter Laos. Advisors could not even accompany the South Vietnamese units to which they were assigned.

Planning for the Laos operation also differed from the past. On this occasion, for example, almost all of the Chiefs were cut out of the action. The only one who played a pivotal role was Moorer, and although the White House liked his aggressive, anti-Communist nature, he was a pilot who had never served in Vietnam. He knew almost nothing of ground operations and the complexities associated with that kind of warfare. The only person among the Joint Chiefs who could have addressed the subject authoritatively was Gen. William Westmoreland, who was the army's chief of staff. General Davidson noted that "he has told me on several occasions (as late as 1987) that he was *not* consulted about the operation until after it had been launched."[69]

The plan, which was drawn up by General Abrams and approved by the JCS (i.e., Moorer), called for a three-phased operation. During Phase I, 9,000 U.S. troops took up positions south of the DMZ. While U.S. ground forces would not cross into Laos, they would provide helicopter, fighter-bomber, and artillery support. During Phase II, one South Vietnamese division would move toward the key village of Tchepone in southern Laos. In Phase III, 17,000 South Vietnamese troops would seize the North's logistic base in the village. Laird agreed with the plan to then cut the Ho Chi Minh Trail, feeling that it would remove pressure on U.S. efforts to implement Vietnamization. Nixon approved the plan on January 18. It turned out to be a disaster.

Suffice it to say that the South Vietnamese did not do their job for a number of reasons. First, the politicized nature of the South's military meant that some senior generals could not control some of their subordinates, who, when not clearly inept, occasionally did exactly as they pleased. To make matters worse, President Thieu refused to order some units to carry out their missions because he depended on two of them as his palace guard and he did not want to run the risk of alienating key officers. When he did become involved in operations, he did so to their detriment. In addition, the South Vietnamese army suffered from its so-called "home guard" nature; because the troops served in a particular area they were not mobile and thus could not be used to back up main-force units. Communications security was also lacking, as many units sent messages in the open, enabling the enemy to read them. In short, "Lam Son 719 demonstrated that, while Vietnamization had made progress, the South Vietnamese government and its armed forces had deep flaws which made final success of the concept years, probably decades away. Above all, the operation showed ARVN's complete dependence on the United States forces. Without United States support, there would have been no Lam Son 719."[70] Kissinger was correct when he stated that this operation, the last in which American troops even simply played a supporting role, was a "watershed."[71] The only positive result of the operation was that it delayed an invasion by the North for a year.

As time passed, internal military problems continued to mount. For example, in 1971 the number of general and special courts-martial was 26 percent higher than in 1969 and 38 percent greater than in 1970. In 1971 fragging incidents were at 1.75 per 1,000 men deployed in Vietnam, compared to .35 in 1969 and .91 in 1970. Furthermore, convictions for offenses such as insubordination, mutiny, and refusal to carry out orders in Vietnam also continued to rise, hitting .44 per 1,000 men in 1971, compared to 0.28 in 1969, and .32 in 1970. Indeed, the drug problem became so serious that the president issued a directive ordering that the problem be given "immediate and urgent attention."[72] The U.S. military was sick and getting sicker.

The Radford Affair

It was at this time that one of the more bizarre affairs in American civil-military relations came to light: the case of Yeoman Charles Radford. Radford was a young sailor who had been assigned to work in the White House JCS Liaison Office, and in this capacity he had been furnishing secret NSC documents to the JCS. When Radford's wrongdoing came to light, some asked whether he should be court-martialed. Nixon decided against such an action, fearing that it would expose Moorer's access to the documents and force his favorite "hawk" to retire. Instead, to get Radford out of Washington, he was transferred to Oregon.

The case is notable for demonstrating just how unethical the Nixon administration had become in the face of inexcusable behavior. Everyone appeared to be spying on everyone else, including the Chiefs, who received critical help from Radford. Given the increasingly secret nature of the White House's foreign policy, these documents (many of them carrying the notation "eyes only") helped the Chiefs predict the White House's plans for national security and foreign policy. Without the papers, the Chiefs could only react to Kissinger's next policy. Moorer was convinced that Haig was passing everything he found of interest to Westmoreland so that the army would be on top of things. He couldn't do any less for his service—he had to know what the administration was thinking. Admirals Rembrandt Robinson and Robert Welander, who were the JCS representatives while Radford was in the White House, were put in a difficult situation. Indeed, the whole world of national security policy under Kissinger and Nixon was one of conspiracy on top of conspiracy. As Zumwalt observed:

> In sum, it was clear to me that Radford had done some things he clearly should not have done and that Moorer did not know he had done them;

> Moorer had never even met Radford. That left Bob Welander pretty much in the middle, but I had little disposition to think of him unkindly in the light of what I knew about what went on in the White House basement: Robinson believing that Kissinger expected him to keep us informed; Robinson making a point of seeing to it that Moorer and I got everything that Westy got; Welander, convinced that Haig was keeping Westmoreland fully informed; Kissinger telling me he distrusted Haig; Haig telling me and others he distrusted Kissinger; Haldeman/Erlichman trying to bushwhack Kissinger; Kissinger and the President using Moorer to help them make plans without Laird's knowledge and therefore pretending to keep Moorer fully informed while withholding some information from him too.[73]

It was a world that Machiavelli would have loved. Probably the most important legacy of the Radford affair was the greater respect that Kissinger developed for Moorer. The JCS chairman was not the country bumpkin that Kissinger and the president had assumed he was. Able to play the game of conspiratorial politics as well as they could, Moorer would have to be taken more seriously in the future. Still, Moorer would never significantly influence policy formulation. That was the White House's prerogative, and it was a privilege Kissinger guarded very closely.

Bombing North Vietnam into the Stone Age

As 1972 began, American and South Vietnamese military authorities warned of a coming offensive by the North. Few thought the South could stop the NVA. By March Abrams warned that a major offensive was beginning and that the United States must address it in some manner. He asked for permission "to launch strikes against several nettlesome antiaircraft sites in the Panhandle.[74] Nixon said no for the time being.

On March 30, 1972, Gen. Vo Nguyen Giap sent his armored columns across the seventeenth parallel. Despite having known that a North Vietnamese offensive was in the offing, the South was nevertheless surprised. Initially, everything went the North's way. But as soon as the skies were clear, B-52 bombers began pounding its forces. Soon the big aircraft were used to bomb the key port city of Haiphong. In early May, in spite of opposition from Laird (known in the Pentagon by the nickname "Chicken Hawk") and Rogers, Nixon authorized the mining of northern harbors, including previously untouchable Haiphong Harbor. As the president later explained, "In order to have the necessary military impact, I was convinced that the bombing, which had begun in the southern part of North Vietnam, would have to be brought to the enemy's heartland around the Hanoi-Haiphong area."[75] In spite of Laird's objections, Moorer was not afraid to stand up to his boss as he once again strongly supported the president's decision to apply greater pressure on North Vietnam. He also pushed the idea of mining Haiphong. "The JCS, Moorer announced at a meeting at the White House, 'is 100 percent behind me on this; we have to go after them.' It was advice that Nixon wanted to hear, even though a full-scale American response might ruin the U.S.-Soviet summit scheduled for May."[76] Moorer was the kind of military officer Nixon felt comfortable with: he did not ask questions, he supported the president, and if anything he was a bigger hawk than Nixon. Thus Nixon resumed the bombing campaign that had been dormant since the end of Rolling Thunder in 1968.

In terms of military effectiveness, Operation Linebacker was very different from Rolling Thunder. Instead of dropping bombs here and there, its purpose was nothing less than to devastate North Vietnam enough so that Hanoi would pull back its troops and make concessions at the talks in Paris. Equally important, Nixon told Moorer that the JCS was to run the operation without White House interference, and he removed many of the bombing restrictions that Washington had placed on targets around Hanoi and Haiphong. Nixon, did, however, decide to temporarily refrain from mining Haiphong Harbor. He feared that such an action would complicate his relations with other countries, especially the Soviet Union.

But the situation in the South began to deteriorate to the point that Moorer begged Nixon to mine Haiphong Harbor. He reportedly took the unheard of and insubordinate step of telling Nixon that the JCS was so convinced that mining Haiphong was critical that it "was ready to walk out the door unless Nixon did it." Moorer felt so strongly about the importance of mining Haiphong that he openly challenged Laird on the topic. On May 7 at an NSC meeting, Moorer reiterated the Chiefs' position. "One former JCS aide said that he pleaded with Nixon to 'let us make these bastards pay for the American blood they've spilled.' " Laird was convinced that mining would destroy any chances of a summit with the Russians—something the president wanted very badly. As a result he tried to interrupt Moorer, who was speaking passionately and who ignored him. Moorer later commented, "Hell, someone had to say something. Here we'd been taking it for so long. If we hadn't done something, we'd still have men in prison there."[77] Nixon decided to hand operational control over to Moorer; however, the president did set some parameters:

> Like Johnson, I restricted our bombing to military targets. Charges that we were systematically bombing North Vietnam's dikes were enemy propaganda. . . . But unlike Johnson, I did not retain personal control over target selection. Since a bombing campaign was a military operation, I put Admiral Moorer, Chairman of the Joint Chiefs of Staff, and our military commanders in Vietnam in charge of conducting it. There were bombing restrictions within a twenty-five to thirty-mile-deep buffer zone and within ten miles of Hanoi and five miles of Haiphong. But even within these areas, field commanders could hit certain types of targets—such as power plants, munitions dumps, and air bases—without approval from Washington.[78]

On May 8 Nixon finally agreed to the mining of Haiphong Harbor, which the JCS had been requesting for more than seven years. By July North Vietnam had been almost completely cut off from Russian and Chinese assistance; Kissinger reported that as early as June 9 more than 1,000 railroad cars were backed up on the Chinese side of the border with North Vietnam.[79] When the campaign ended on October 22, 2,346 U.S. aircraft strikes had delivered 17,876 bombs totaling approximately 150,000 pounds.[80] North Vietnamese dead may have exceeded 100,000.[81]

Moorer felt vindicated. North Vietnamese attacks in the South came to a stop, and the Russians did not cancel the summit. Most important to Moorer, the incident served to convince Nixon that he had found his Patton—a two-fisted fighting man who would stand up to his country's enemies. In July, Moorer was reappointed for another two-year term as chairman of the Joint Chiefs.

By December 1972 the North Vietnamese disinterest in a negotiated settlement was obvious, particularly to Kissinger, who had been Washington's primary negotiator. They appeared to be stalling, drawing the talks out as long as possible, presumably to improve their position in the South. The administration decided that it had to reexamine its military options.[82] Kissinger argued that the United States could follow two possible courses: deliver a massive blow with the goal of ending the war quickly or let "matters drift into another round of inconclusive negotiations, prolonged warfare, bitter national divisions, and mounting casualties."[83] Not surprisingly, Nixon chose the first alternative, motivated more by foreign policy considerations than military reasons. He told the Chiefs, "I don't want any more of this crap about the fact that we couldn't hit this target or that one. This is your chance to use military power effectively to win this war, and if you don't, I'll consider you responsible."[84] The Chiefs understood: he wanted to make the North Vietnamese cry "Uncle."

On December 18 the United States began one of the most punishing air campaigns of the war. By December 26 Hanoi expressed its desire to resume negotiations, and on December 30 the United States halted the bombings. North Vietnam lay in ruins. "There were no more legitimate military targets in North Vietnam to strike. In addition, the United States raids had destroyed North Vietnam's ability to defend itself against further attacks from the air."[85] By January 13, 1973, the North had agreed on a basic document, and two years later Saigon fell. A major chapter in American civil-military relations closed.

The Zumwalt Affair

One of the stranger, yet incredibly important events that took place during the Nixon administration involved Adm. Elmo Zumwalt, who was a surprise appointment as CNO. To remove Zumwalt from Washington, Moorer had sent him to Vietnam to run the inland navy. His naval predecessor there had hardly spoken with the army, and relations between the two services were abysmal. Nor was much being done to train the Vietnamese Navy. Zumwalt completely turned matters around, quickly establishing excellent relations with General Abrams and making the South Vietnamese Navy into one of the best trained and led military forces. Indeed, Abrams was so impressed that the next time Laird visited South Vietnam, he took him aside and told him that Zumwalt should be the next CNO, an action that deeply impressed Laird. When it came time to appoint a new CNO, Laird insisted that Zumwalt's name be added to the list of candidates. Chosen for the position, Zumwalt jumped over a number of other officers superior to him. He became CNO on July 1, 1970, and served until June 19, 1974.

Zumwalt was chosen primarily because he intended to change the way the navy operated and bring it into the twentieth century. The secretary of the navy told Zumwalt that he and Laird wanted the new CNO to bring the navy "into the modern age." He also told Zumwalt that he had not been Moorer's first choice, which was not surprising, given that he was one of the traditionalists who opposed radical modernization.[86] According to Perry, after John Chafee told Moorer about Zumwalt's appointment, Moorer reportedly returned to his office and kicked the wastebasket across the room.[87]

Zumwalt, who would go down in history as one of the great military reformers, obtained a number of his ideas on how to run the navy from watching General Abrams, a man whom he called "the most impressive military man I ever have been professionally associated with."[88] Zumwalt took Abrams's concern for the troops serving under him to heart. From the very first day as

CNO, he made it his goal to change the U.S. Navy, which he believed was living in the past, especially in regard to racial matters. Black sailors who went into the commissary could not find suitable toiletries. When they went into navy exchanges they could not find the kind of clothes they wanted to wear when off duty. More important were problems with the promotion and pay of black sailors, which also affected their families. The list went on and on.

The matter came to a head on October 12, 1972, onboard the USS *Kitty Hawk* (CVA 63). The ship was on its way to take up station in the Gulf of Tonkin when a young black sailor was summoned for questioning about a fight that had taken place in Olongapo City in the Philippines a few days earlier. The specific charge was that he had assaulted and refused to obey the orders of a petty officer. He brought nine friends with him to the questioning session, where angry words were exchanged. On their way back to their quarters the black sailors beat up a white mess attendant. From that point on until 0500 the next morning, the ship's men engaged in a series of clashes that were serious enough that three sailors had to be evacuated to onshore hospitals for medical treatment. Twenty-six men, all black, were charged with one infraction or another.

If that were not enough, four days later a group of about a dozen sailors on the USS *Hassayampa* (AO 145), which was docked at Subic Bay, told the ship's executive officer that they would remain ashore when the ship sailed at 1600. They also threatened to beat up white sailors unless some money that they claimed had been stolen from them was returned. That afternoon, seven white sailors were beaten, two of whom had to be hospitalized.

Then on November 3 racial problems erupted on the USS *Constellation* (CVA 64), which was undergoing training exercises off the California coast. In Zumwalt's mind the incident on this ship was particularly upsetting. Aboard the *Kitty Hawk* and *Hassayampa* there "had been, fundamentally, spontaneous outbursts of anger, nasty evidence of past racial injustice and of present institutional inability to cope with it, but tactically simple to bring under control" (222). The situation on the *Constellation* was more complex. In short, black sailors on the *Constellation*—many of whom were recruits with only minimal training—were convinced that they were being openly discriminated against. For example, due to a shortage of bunks, the captain decided to transfer 250 sailors off the ship. A rumor swept the ship suggesting that blacks would be the only ones transferred. Although the rumor was false, the damage had been done. Then, while conducting air operations, sixty black sailors "congregated on the forward mess decks and commenced harassing Caucasian sailors who were eating" (224). The blacks continued to occupy the mess decks, and "the black spokesmen were loud, obscene, and threatening, and drowned out any attempt to reason with them" (225). When the ship returned to port, 144 men, including a few whites, were taken to a barracks to meet with officers. On November 6 the *Constellation* again went to sea, but by this time Washington and the rest of the country were fully aware of what had happened.

Zumwalt had to decide how to handle the situation. A number of ex-navy personnel, including a number of senior admirals, were contacting Secretary of the Navy John Warner and demanding that Zumwalt take a hard line and restore order. Zumwalt pushed the new secretary to let him take action, but Warner, apparently trying to avoid a confrontation, held back. After he finally consented, the sailors who were standing around on the pier next to the ship and refusing to board it were bussed to barracks and held in disciplinary status.

In a November 10 speech to a group of flag officers, Zumwalt described the problems on the three ships as "not the cause of racial pressures; rather, they are manifestations of the pressures unrelieved" (235). As a remedy, he emphasized the importance of addressing discrimination in the navy. A day later, Zumwalt received a phone call from Kissinger. According to the CNO, "Kissinger all but shrieked at me. . . . Kissinger really had only one thing to say: the President (as Commander in Chief) wanted the *Constellation* protesters to receive dishonorable discharges immediately if not sooner" (239–40). However, a significant obstacle stood in the way of carrying out the president's order. Military discipline is governed by the Uniform Code of Military Justice (UCMJ), and neither Zumwalt nor any other military authority could give sailors a dishonorable discharge for being absent on leave for a few hours or for giving the black power salute, which had particularly upset Nixon. Zumwalt thus experienced a strong reaction to Kissinger's phone call:

> As you might suppose, that conversation shocked me. Even though a professional military man has been prepared by training, by habit, and by conviction to obey unhesitatingly the orders of his superiors, including specifically orders he disagrees with, he cannot but be taken aback when his Commander in Chief, of all people, relays to him a peremptory, angry, illegal order such as that which had just been given me. The fact that it was clearly illegal spared me the pain of an internal conflict between conscience and duty: conscience and duty both dictated that I not obey it. However, that same fact grievously eroded my confidence in and respect for my Commander in Chief. (241)

Kissinger also apparently ordered Laird to fire Zumwalt. Fortunately for Zumwalt, Laird had enough power on Capitol Hill to stand up to Kissinger.

"He told Kissinger that if Kissinger wanted me fired he should try firing me himself. Kissinger was not up to knocking that chip off the shoulder of a man Laird's size."[89] It is perhaps indicative of Nixon's attitude toward the military that he never forgot nor forgave Zumwalt's defiance. For example, when Jim Schlesinger took over as secretary of defense in the twilight of Nixon's term, he told Zumwalt, "You should be aware that the President thinks that the JCS are 'a bunch of shits' and that you are 'the biggest shit of all.'"[90]

A New Secretary of Defense

When Nixon began his second term in January 1973, Laird resigned. Elliot Richardson, a Boston intellectual who had extensive diplomatic experience, became the new secretary of defense. Unlike McNamara, Richardson went out of his way to assure the Chiefs that he respected them and expected them to play an important role in U.S. security policy issues, including the defense budget and weapons systems. He was prepared to fight for their weapons systems, even though he and they knew that he would not get everything they needed to rebuild the military. They were especially happy to have a secretary whose openness would help bring an end to the destructive four-year battle between the White House and the secretary of defense that had continually placed them in the middle. Indeed, the military felt like a new page had been turned in the Joint Chiefs' relationship with the secretary of defense. Unfortunately, Richardson's tenure would be short-lived; because of the Watergate scandal, Nixon decided to move him to the position of attorney general and replace him with James Schlesinger.

Upset at having lost an ally like Richardson, the Chiefs greeted Schlesinger's appointment with little enthusiasm. It was no secret that Schlesinger and Kissinger had feuded over foreign policy, which the Chiefs feared would ignite a new war between the Pentagon and the White House. With memories of McNamara and his heavy-handed managerial style still fresh in their minds, they also feared that Schlesinger would gut the Pentagon, just as he had eviscerated the CIA during his tenure there. Schlesinger's views on defense issues were equally troublesome. As an intellectual fascinated by high technology, he caused the Chiefs to wonder if he would understand the nuts-and-bolts kinds of problems they faced on a daily basis. Finally, there was his personality: he was aloof, self-confident, and too certain of the accuracy of his own views.

Schlesinger had two goals. In addition to revising U.S. strategic policy, he wanted to undo the Vietnam legacy. The military, especially the army, had to be rebuilt; its morale was at rock bottom, and its weapons systems were aging and falling apart. Unfortunately, his first meeting with the Chiefs proved disastrous. Appearing in the tank with flowcharts, position papers, statistical analyses, and color slides, he proceeded to lecture them for the next two hours on the importance of technology, while several of them became glassy-eyed. Yet Schlesinger soon redeemed himself in the Chiefs' eyes. Several weeks after his confirmation he told the press, "There has been a fair amount of abuse in using the Department of Defense and the military services as a whipping boy for all the frustrations of Vietnam and all the idiocies committed by civilian leadership." He added, "A democratic nation gets about the kind of military establishment it deserves, and if we continue to abuse these fellows and treat them this way, it is going to have consequences."[91]

The military's top leadership positions had completely turned over by June 30, 1974, when Moorer retired. The appointment of Gen. George S. Brown, a former air force chief of staff, as his successor brought in a very different officer and symbolically refocused the attention of the JCS away from Vietnam and toward the post–Vietnam era. Brown's appointment "also lowered the JCS's high public profile. Brown was an affable, capable officer who eschewed the aggressiveness of Taylor, Wheeler, and Moorer. His task was clear: to return stability to the armed forces and rebuild the nation's gutted arsenal."[92] In addition, Brown worked well with his colleagues, as he exhibited more openness with them and made certain that each of them had enough time to make his points in meetings in the tank.[93]

The JCS could not avoid involvement in the Watergate affair, not because they were direct participants but because the Chiefs were inevitably implicated in the events surrounding Nixon's resignation. Indeed, as Perry described it, his resignation involved the Chiefs in what ranks as one of the stranger events in JCS history.[94] During a meeting with Schlesinger, Brown was cautioned to make certain that " 'any emergency order coming from the President' be shown to the other chiefs 'and the Secretary of Defense' before its execution." Brown was shocked and called a closed meeting of the Chiefs within an hour. He began by noting, "I've just had the strangest conversation with the Secretary of Defense." The other Chiefs felt insulted—as if they would do whatever the president told them even if the order was illegal. The real implication was that Nixon might try to use the Chiefs to stay in power, and that they would blithely do whatever he ordered. Fortunately, for all concerned, the Watergate scandal ended when Nixon decided to resign in early August. "The JCS was relieved: Schlesinger's words of caution had been unnecessary, and no officer had been publicly tarnished by the Nixon White House. The military had, in fact, maintained a dignified silence during the crisis."

CONCLUSION

Presidential Leadership Style

The Chiefs were dismayed by Nixon's secretive style and the willingness he shared with Kissinger to deceive subordinates, to cut critical players out of the policy process, and to lie both to the public and to those who formulated policy. Furthermore, his administration lacked the methodical bureaucratic processes that characterized Eisenhower's administration. The NSC counted for little, as did any respect for established procedures. When Kissinger told Zumwalt that he would deal directly with any officer he felt like talking to, he was directly attacking a key aspect of military culture: the chain of command. Believing that bureaucratic structures stood in his way, Kissinger used the Chiefs solely for his own purposes.

The Chiefs were also upset by the president's failure to provide clear guidance and orders. Instead, he pushed them to do one thing while their superior, the secretary of defense, argued for the opposite. The official U.S. policy often remained a mystery to the Chiefs. Indeed, it appeared to be whatever Kissinger or Nixon decided it was, and they might or might not decide to tell the Chiefs the truth.

Violations of Service/Military Culture?

Nixon did not trust the Chiefs, and they knew it. As a consequence, the White House maintained a strong grip on issues of national security, placing much of the power in Kissinger's hands. When both Wheeler and Zumwalt thwarted his attempts to violate the military chain of command, Kissinger went after Moorer and convinced him to cooperate by dealing secretly with the Nixon administration. Moorer may have agreed to the arrangement, but the White House was guilty in taking the initiative to undermine the chain of command. The administration also demanded that the Joint Staff send policy papers directly to Kissinger without showing them to the secretary of defense. Laird was also unaware of the existence of the back-channel communication systems that the Pentagon had been forced to set up in its basement for Kissinger's use. Then there was the bombing of Cambodia, shrouded in secrecy at the president's behest, and thus making the Chiefs part of a cover-up. Conversely, all of the Chiefs except Moorer were excluded from the planning for the Lam Son 719 attack. Kissinger and Nixon knew full well that they were violating military culture when they committed such acts, but they did not care. They wanted to accomplish the job, even if it meant breaking the rules of military culture.

Nixon demonstrated his willingness to interfere in internal military personnel matters when he tried to have Zumwalt discharge a number of black sailors whose behavior had aroused his ire, but whose actions did not warrant such a harsh response under the Uniform Code of Military Justice. Nixon did not care what the UCMJ said, he was the president and he wanted the men discharged. Zumwalt's decision to stand up to Kissinger and Nixon cost him another tour as chief of naval operations, but he believed that the problems facing the navy at that time were so serious that he had to stand firm, even if he earned the enmity of the president and Kissinger.

The military also violated its own culture during the Nixon era, as illustrated by the Radford incident. Having a sailor in the White House work as a "spy" for the Chiefs was unacceptable behavior on the part of the military. However, given Kissinger's own behavior, an argument could be made that the Chiefs depended on such information to forecast what kind of military action the White House was considering next.

From the Chiefs' perspective, the Nixon administration was not entirely devoid of positive aspects. For example, when it came to deciding how to attack both Cambodia and North Vietnam, Nixon listened to the Chiefs (even though he managed to further alienate his secretary of defense by not letting him know what he planned to do until the decision had been made). Moorer may have been most prominent, but the Chiefs believed their advice was finally being taken seriously. Since 1964 they had been arguing for an operation akin to Linebacker, and when Nixon heeded their advice and unleashed American airpower, North Vietnam was devastated. Moorer felt vindicated, even though the attack only delayed the fall of South Vietnam for a year or so.

Changes in Service/Military Culture?

During the Nixon era at least one significant change in military culture occurred that encompassed the strategic, operational, and tactical levels of conflict: the emergence of the so-called "Vietnam Syndrome." Members of the military, especially the mid-level officers, who had been out in the jungles fighting the war and seeing soldiers die day after day began asking themselves why the United States had become so deeply entangled in Vietnam. The more they examined the issue, the more many of them became convinced that the extensive U.S. involvement resulted from what the military calls "mission creep." The military enters combat on day 1 to achieve objective A, but soon finds its task gradually enlarged to include objectives B, C, D, and so on. Vietnam, which served as a prime example of such an open-ended commitment, led to a new consciousness of the importance of avoiding military conflict unless political leaders could determine and articulate their objective, commit overwhelming force to achieve that end, and recognize when it had been achieved.

Thus, the Vietnam Syndrome significantly altered civil-military relations. Senior military officers became engaged in a higher level of activism when politicians considered deploying troops, planes, or ships around the world. One author noted the importance of Vietnam's legacy, writing, "JCS officers now claim that Vietnam proved that those who argue that the military is a tool for civilian policy makers, that officers should not have a role in determining policy, do so at their peril."[95] In fact, the Chiefs would soon voice their views directly to the president, even if those views were sometimes unwelcome.

8
THE MILITARY AND GERALD FORD

The complicated, jury-rigged arrangement and detailed management from the Joint Chiefs of Staff endangered and nearly destroyed forces on the island.
—*Admiral George P. Steele*

Gerald Ford became president at a very difficult time. He not only replaced a man who had been forced to resign because of misdeeds while in office, he also faced a military that was feeling the ill effects of Vietnam and, like the nation it represented, looking for a way to reclaim its honor and respect. Rebuilding the military, both physically and psychologically, would take much longer than the two and a half years that were allotted to Ford. Nevertheless, he was able to start the healing process when the SS *Mayaguez* was seized by Cambodian pirates.

FORD'S LEADERSHIP STYLE

Gerald Ford was not supposed to become president. When Vice President Spiro Agnew resigned, Nixon picked Ford to replace him. Then, in the aftermath of Watergate and Nixon's resignation, Ford suddenly found himself in the Oval Office. His primary goal was to provide leadership that would help the country move beyond the terrible, traumatic last two years. Thus on September 8, 1974, a month after Nixon resigned, Ford granted the former president a "full, free and absolute pardon" for whatever crimes he may have committed while in office.[1]

Ford was only too aware that Nixon's secretive leadership style was one of the main factors that led to the Watergate affair. Determined to avoid repeating his predecessor's mistakes, he decided not to have a chief of staff, who would isolate him from his subordinates. Instead, Ford sought an arrangement that would permit several senior White House aides to have independent and almost unrestricted access to him. The primary value of this "spokes of the wheel" approach was that it "projected an aura of openness and accessibility, a perception that was essential to Ford's desire to establish the distinctive characteristics of his administration." The experiment would be short-lived, however, because within a month, Ford recognized the danger of having a number of highly competent, type-A personalities all competing for his attention in the White House. Consequently, on September 21, he asked Donald Rumsfeld to become assistant to the president. In practice this meant that although a number of senior officials would still have access to the president, Rumsfeld would be "first among equals." In fact, Ford said that his goal was to "have a chief of staff who is an expert manager and one who does not seek on his own a high identity—in fact, one who purposely avoids that."[2] With far too many tasks to accomplish in the time allotted each day, the president needed someone to oversee his schedule and determine who would be granted access to him. Ford believed that in Rumsfeld he had found a manager who would be both efficient in making the best use of his time and open in permitting the maximum number of individuals access to him.

Ford also wanted his subordinates to feel free to express their opinions without feeling bound by bureaucratic loyalties. Kissinger described the new White House atmosphere in his memoirs, "Bureaucratic rivalries ended at the door of the Oval Office because Ford simply would not listen to them. I never heard him make critical comments about associates, nor would he have welcomed them from others."[3] Ford also disliked Nixon's overbearing White House staff, which had accumulated far too much power at the expense of departments and agency heads. As he explained, "I wanted to reverse the trend and restore authority to my Cabinet. White House aides with authority are necessary, but I didn't think they had the right to browbeat the departments and agencies. Nor did they have the right to make policy decisions. I decided to give my Cabinet members a lot more control."[4] Indeed, in an interview Ford gave after he left office, he expressed his belief that a clash of different opinions helped him reach important decisions: "I don't know what style President Nixon used, although I believe he liked to digest written reports before making decisions. But I like to hear a verbal presentation and to hear the different viewpoints expressed. I was always at ease at NSC meetings. I liked to hear the discussion on the various points of view. I don't mind contention. At some meetings the discussion got very frank."[5]

The military welcomed Ford's approach. Instead of working for two deities at the same time, with Kissinger giving them orders that they were instructed

President Gerald Ford (right center) meets with the Joint Chiefs of Staff in the White House. Future secretary of defense Donald Rumsfeld is seated to the president's right. (Gerald R. Ford Library)

to keep secret from the secretary of defense (who was ordering them to do the opposite), they would have clear lines of authority and the chairman would feel free to speak his mind. If Kissinger wanted something from them, he would have to go through James Schlesinger, who remained as secretary of defense. In addition, the chairman had the authority to go directly to the president if he felt the issue was sufficiently important. The key to Ford's leadership style was that he made clear to General Brown, Secretary Schlesinger, and Kissinger that he wanted an open and free discussion of different options: no more pre-cooked deals by Kissinger and Moorer behind closed doors. The president would soon have an opportunity to test his "open approach" to decision making.

Kissinger remained a major player in the new Ford administration. If anything, he emerged from the Watergate scandal with "his reputation not only undamaged but enhanced. He was depicted in the press as the indispensable man, 'Super-K,' who had kept the nation's foreign policy intact while

Watergate raged on."[6] Indeed, Ford said that one of the first things he did after Nixon left the White House was to call Kissinger.

> As soon as I returned to the EOB [Executive Office Building], I telephoned Kissinger. I thought it urgent to tell him right away how I felt about him. "Henry," I said when he came on the line, "I need you. The country needs you. I want you to stay. I'll do everything I can to work with you." "There will be no problem," he replied in his deep, accented voice. "Sir, it is my job to get along with you and not yours to get along with me."[7]

During the early days of the Ford administration, Kissinger continued to act both as secretary of state and the president's national security advisor (Nixon had appointed him to both positions on September 22, 1973). He would be a force to be reckoned with, but he would not be able to bully the rest of the government the way he had under Nixon.

Ford and the Chiefs

Ford went out of his way to establish "an early close relationship with his Chiefs, which contributed notably to the success of the *Mayaguez* operation."[8] His relations with the Chiefs would be amiable throughout his short time in office. However, as would become obvious several months later, he disliked Secretary of Defense James Schlesinger for both personal and policy reasons.

With the writing already on the wall when he took over as president, Ford was to witness the final collapse of South Vietnam. Bitter over the White House's conduct toward Vietnam, Congress had prohibited any military action "in or over Vietnam" in 1973.[9] Then appropriations for Vietnam were reduced by 50 percent every year after the signing of the Paris Peace Agreement that same year. For example, the Senate Armed Forces Committee cut the administration's $1.4 billion request for fiscal year 1975 to $1 billion. Then the Senate Appropriations Committee cut out another $300 million. The situation became so dire that South Vietnamese president Thieu wrote a letter to Ford on March 22, 1975, pleading with the president to provide the South Vietnamese with badly needed aid and to use B-52s against the North's troop concentrations. Ford was so alarmed by the letter that he sent the army chief of staff, Gen. Fred C. Weyland, to survey the situation in Vietnam. When he returned, Weyland recommended the immediate appropriation of $722 million in aid and the use of B-52s. Having concluded that South Vietnam would collapse without this assistance, he warned, "What is at stake in Vietnam now is America's credibility as an ally. We must not abandon our goal of a free and independent South Vietnam."[10] Congress, however, was unmoved and neither allocated the money nor approved the use of the B-52s. On April 30, 1975, South Vietnam surrendered to the North, effectively ending the war.

The Military Budget and General Brown

Given his negative reputation among members of Congress, Schlesinger was aware that if the military had any hope of getting a budgetary increase in the antimilitary post–Vietnam climate, it lay with the likeable Gen. George Brown. "In the end, it was Brown's job to clear the path, reassuring Congress that Schlesinger really was a good manager, really did understand all the problems that Congress faced, and really was concerned with the political unpopularity of major defense spending increases."[11]

In the beginning, everything seemed to be in order. Congress shared the month-old administration's desire to make a new start and heal the country. The representatives appeared to like Brown, and they listened to his articulate and sensible arguments. However, the good-natured Brown stepped on a political land mine of monumental proportions on October 10, 1974. Speaking at a Duke University seminar he responded to a student's question by saying, "Jews own, you know, the banks in this country, the newspapers. You just look at where the Jewish money is in this country." Considered by his colleagues to be not the least bit anti-Semitic, Brown was the last person in the government from whom one might have expected such a comment. Both the president and Schlesinger called on Brown to apologize, which he did. Nevertheless, the JCS was devastated: Brown's ability to carry the Defense Department's budgetary ball on the Hill by himself was severely undercut. When pressed, Brown claimed that what he was really referring to was the extent of the American commitment to Israel, something that grated on many JCS officers. During the Yom Kippur War, the United States had sent desperately needed conventional arms to Israel, and "this reprovisioning of Israel so angered some JCS officers that they believed Congress owed them a program of one-for-one weapons replacements."[12] It did not matter what Brown meant to say, what mattered was what he said. This comment would haunt him the rest of his life.

Secretary of Defense James Schlesinger meets with the Joint Chiefs of Staff and their chairman, General George Brown (center on left side of table), at the White House. (Gerald R. Ford Library)

THE MAYAGUEZ INCIDENT

Throughout his two and half years in office, Ford faced only one major military crisis: the capture of the SS *Mayaguez* in international waters by the Cambodian Khmer Rouge. The merchant ship, which flew the American flag, was captured in the Gulf of Siam only days after the U.S.–backed South Vietnamese government collapsed. With U.S. credibility and prestige at rock bottom, Ford couldn't ignore the memory of the 1968 seizure of the USS *Pueblo* by North Koreans. At that time, despite considerable bluster and threats, the United States did nothing but express its "outrage" and wait for the North Koreans to release the imprisoned crew, many of whom were tortured. The crew gained freedom only after the United States was forced to make a humiliating apology for acts that it had not committed. Ford intended to send a message to the North Koreans, the Cambodians, and anyone else who might be considering similar actions that the United States was not to be trifled with.

Thus, he shared Kissinger's strong belief that the United States must stand up to military threats after Vietnam. John Robert Greene correctly observed that "the *Mayaguez* incident offered a perfect opportunity: the Ford administration could use it to prove that America—and Ford—was still tough."[13] The United States would meet force with force.

Day 1: Monday, May 12, 1975

Fired upon and boarded by sailors from the infamous Khmer Rouge, the *Mayaguez* was seized at 0300 Washington time. The ultra-left-wing group that had just taken control of Cambodia claimed that its territorial sea boundary extended ninety miles from the country's coastline and included outlying islands. The *Mayaguez* was not the first vessel captured by the Khmer Rouge: Ten days earlier several Thai fishing boats had been seized, and eight days previously a number of South Vietnamese boats had been taken. The Khmer Rouge had even stopped and detained a Panamanian ship for thirty-six hours.

After it was fired on, the *Mayaguez* sent out a distress call that went first to Indonesia and then to the Pentagon's National Military Command Center, which received the message at 0512. During the next two hours a series of additional communications were received. Gen. David Jones, the acting chairman of the Joint Chiefs of Staff, also was notified. The White House's Situation Room had received the message in the meantime, and Brent Scowcroft, the president's deputy national security advisor, was alerted when he arrived there at 0700. President Ford did not learn of the seizure of the *Mayaguez* until he had his morning briefing with General Scowcroft at approximately 0730. Kissinger did not get the news until about 0830. He and Scowcroft then met with Ford at roughly 0920 to discuss the matter.

The National Military Command Center relayed news of the crisis to Adm. Noel Gayler, who was commander in chief of U.S. forces in the Pacific (CINCPAC). He immediately launched air reconnaissance flights to locate the missing ship. A few hours later the navy reported that it had probably found the ship, but it was not certain.

Ford decided to call an NSC meeting immediately because he believed that it was critical for the United States to act swiftly; if the nation did not, the ship would soon be in a Cambodian port and, as happened in the case of the USS *Pueblo,* the crew would be removed and rescue would become almost impossible. "There was no time for a slow 'bubbling-up' of the analysis through the many layers of the bureaucracy."[14] The meeting, which convened at 1200, was attended by Ford, Kissinger, Scowcroft, General Jones (for General Brown, who was in Europe), Deputy Secretary of Defense William Clements, CIA Director William Colby, Deputy Secretary of State Robert Ingersoll, Richard Smyser, who was the NSC officer in charge of East Asia, as well as White House Chief of Staff Donald Rumsfeld. Given his leadership style, the president wanted to hear as many voices as possible, because he intended to handle this matter personally. Too much was at stake: confidence in the American presidency had been shattered only nine months previously and the United States had been humiliated by a third-rate Communist country. Ford wanted to be sure that the matter was handled correctly, and not left to some lower-level bureaucrat or military officer to bungle. Kissinger was even more adamant than the president in favoring a strong response. Ford later recalled that "Kissinger leaned forward over the table and with emotion stressed the broad ramifications of the incident."[15]

Unfortunately, poor intelligence would haunt the decision makers throughout this incident. Indeed, the intelligence briefing that the president received would turn out to be wrong in every respect. For example, the briefer stated that the *Mayaguez* was moving under her own power to the port of Kompong Som at a speed of ten nautical miles an hour. Accordingly, Schlesinger believed that "when I left the Pentagon, the ship was already only about ten miles out."[16] In fact, twelve hours later, the White House learned that the *Mayaguez* had not moved; she was dead in the water where she had been captured. As a consequence of the mistaken intelligence the first meeting was primarily devoted to identifying what kinds of pressures the United States could bring to bear on the Cambodian government to get it to release the ship, presumably tied up in Kompong Som, and its crew. Among the potential obstacles to the successful application of military pressure was the Thai government, which had just asked the United States to vacate its large air base after the conclusion of the Vietnam War. Ford, however, was unmoved by the request. As he explained in his memoirs, U.S. fighter aircraft "would have to use Thailand as a jumping-off point; the Thais wouldn't be very happy about that, but until *Mayaguez* and her crew were safe, I didn't give a damn about offending their sensibilities."[17] In a nutshell, Ford was not about to stand back and let diplomatic niceties get in his way. The crew would be rescued one way or another.

Still sensitive to the debacle in South Vietnam and the fall of Cambodia, Schlesinger was less willing than Ford and Kissinger to advise the use of force. Consequently, "he proceeded cautiously, answering questions while offering little in the way of suggestions." General Brown, who had direct access to the president, could have neutralized Schlesinger and his tendency to avoid confrontations whenever possible. However, Brown was absent from the meeting, and his stand-in, General Jones, did not have the same access to the commander in chief; thus, "anything the generals and admirals had in mind would first go through Schlesinger's ambivalent filter."[18] When the secretary of defense argued that the Pentagon should get its act together before deciding what steps should be taken to try to rescue the ship's crew, Jones supported him. But Schlesinger would eventually find himself at odds with Ford and Kissinger over how the matter should be handled.

At the NSC meeting, the participants agreed on two objectives. First, the United States had to get the ship and its crew back; second, it had to do so in a way that would demonstrate the United States would not put up with such roguish behavior. The country would use whatever force was necessary to protect its national interests, which included the right of innocent passage. Toward that end, the president ordered the Pentagon to come up with some options. Most important, remembering the battle he and Nixon had fought with Congress, Ford added, "I can assure you that, irrespective of the Congress, we will move."[19] Unconcerned with what members of Congress thought about the executive-legislative balance of power, he believed that the president had an inherent right to move quickly even without congressional approval, especially if the United States was dealing with a murderous regime such as the Khmer Rouge. Time was of the essence.

The first NSC meeting ended in some confusion, however. The NSC staff (and General Scowcroft) believed that the JCS had been asked to provide written options for a subsequent NSC meeting later that day. But General Jones and the JCS staff had the impression that the president had neither requested specific proposals nor specified a deadline for their presentation. Furthermore, the JCS believed that the situation was so fluid that providing specific options would be almost impossible. To begin with, the JCS was still uncertain of the *Mayaguez*'s exact location. Second, there were no U.S. warships in the Gulf of Siam. Third, the nearest land-based air assets were in Thailand, and the JCS was not aware of the president's willingness to use them regardless of any diplomatic problems it might cause. Fourth, the closest U.S. ground forces were Marines stationed in Okinawa. Finally, the United States had no idea of the other side's intentions. "General Jones was reluctant to offer premature options that would inevitably be based on 'soft' or inadequate information. The result was that the JCS did not present an options paper to the White House on Monday afternoon."[20]

On his own authority, Schlesinger ordered the military to find the ship. He authorized the use of force to stop the vessel if it was not already at Kompong Som, and he even approved the use of mines if they became necessary. The president ordered the USS *Coral Sea* to move to the region and sent a strong diplomatic note to the Cambodians—a procedure made more difficult by the lack of diplomatic relations between the United States and Cambodia. He also publicly threatened the Cambodians with unspecified "reprisals" if the crew was not released, called the ship's seizure an act of "piracy," and demanded an apology and the release of the crew.[21]

The tight control that Ford maintained over the operation actually complicated matters. By 1975 communications had advanced to the point that the president could talk directly to the pilots on the scene. To many this was an important breakthrough, because as information passed up the chain of command in the past, important information could be stripped away to the point that the key decision maker would not have the precise information that he or she needed to make a critical decision. Now, however, if the president decided to have a plane attack he could contact the pilot directly; Ralph Wetterhahn wrote, "Once the forces got into Cambodian waters, Ford would be able to top LBJ by telling the combatants not only what to shoot at but also when to squeeze the trigger." The problem, however, was that the "person with the least on-scene knowledge and barest information was making the call simply because the system could do it, not because he brought about the best result."[22] Since the president had become the on-the-scene commander, admirals and generals, not to mention more junior personnel, had to wait for him to issue an order, which stifled initiative at the tactical level.

Day 2: Tuesday, May 13, 1975

Tuesday did not begin on a very promising note. The previous day, Scowcroft had asked Maj. Gen. John Wickham (Schlesinger's military assistant) for an assessment of the military situation. At 0100 Tuesday morning Wickham reported that the F-4 fighters based in Thailand could reach the ship and fire across its bow. Scowcroft then called the president and told him that the ship was under way, but it was only fifteen minutes out of Kompong Som. He told the president that he didn't think the fighters could get to the ship quickly enough, but suggested that they try to stop it. "Ford gave the order to proceed, concluding, 'It doesn't seem to me there is any other alternative, Brent. But dammit, they hadn't better sink it now! . . . That would be the ultimate in stupidity.' "[23] However, no sooner had Ford given the order to proceed when information came in suggesting that the *Mayaguez* had changed course and was anchoring off of an island called Koh Tang. To make the point that the *Mayaguez* had better stay where it was, an A-7 fired into the water near the ship. In the meantime, Ford spoke with Schlesinger at 0552 for about an hour. The president repeated his concern over the similarity of this situation and the *Pueblo* incident. He also ordered Schlesinger to make sure that no Cambodian vessels were permitted to move in either direction between the island and the mainland.

The second NSC meeting, held on Tuesday at 1022, included the same attendees as the first meeting, two additional advisors to the president, and Under Secretary Joseph Sisco, substituting for Kissinger and Ingersoll, both of whom had traveled to Kansas City. During the meeting, the president reiterated his order to interdict all ship traffic between the island where the *Mayaguez* was located and the mainland. He also ordered that a battalion of 1,100 Marines from Okinawa be sent to Thailand, in spite of protests from Bangkok over the use of its facilities for an attack on Cambodia. Having decided that the Marines would attack the *Mayaguez* by helicopter, he then ordered the USS *Hancock* to sail with an amphibious unit from the Philippines. Unfortunately, preparations for the attack were marred by the crash in Thailand of a helicopter carrying eighteen air policemen and five crewmen, who thus became the conflict's first casualties, but unfortunately not the last.

Differences between Kissinger and Schlesinger soon came to the fore. Schlesinger was opposed to military action, especially because it might involve sinking Cambodian boats. He also feared that the use of force to retake the ship might injure the crew (which could still be on board), and he was worried that the Cambodians might scuttle the *Mayaguez* in retaliation. Kissinger countered that the Pentagon, suffering from low morale after Vietnam, was unenthusiastic about the whole operation and should simply follow orders. Furthermore, he blamed communication lapses on "doubts of the Secretary of Defense" and went to far as to claim that these doubts about the operation "compounded the trauma of the military."[24]

At 2010 that evening three Cambodian patrol boats tried to leave Koh Tang, in spite of warning shots from American fighters. They appeared headed toward the mainland port of Kompong Som. One of the boats was sunk and one returned to the island, but the third continued toward the mainland. Scowcroft told the president, who then ordered the third boat destroyed. Scowcroft passed the order on to General Wickham. An hour later General Wickham called back to say that one of the pilots who had been ordered to destroy the boat reported that it appeared to have "a group that looked like Caucasians huddled in the bow."[25] Wickham then asked for approval to disable the boat by hitting it in the rear. Scowcroft contacted the president, who ordered the pilot to do everything possible to dissuade the boat from proceeding to port, but said that it should not be sunk because he did not want to risk killing crew members. The boat continued on and reached the mainland. The president then called for a third NSC meeting to be held on May 13 at 2240.

At the evening meeting, Kissinger, who had returned from Kansas City, again insisted that the United States take action. As he had previously, Schlesinger pointed out the inherent dangers, but the president sided with Kissinger. He favored unleashing air strikes against the port of Kompong Som for two reasons: First, by knocking out Cambodian naval assets on the mainland, the president hoped that Cambodia would be unable to interfere in whatever action the United States decided to take against Koh Tang. Second, the president felt that an attack on the mainland would signal to the Khmer Rouge that they would pay a heavy price for their act of piracy.

When the president asked General Jones how long it would take the *Coral Sea* to get on station. Jones replied, "It is making twenty-five knots." The president, who had served aboard aircraft carriers, responded, "That is not flank speed. . . . Flank speed is thirty-three knots." Out of his element, the former bomber pilot could only offer that "the navy says that is the best they can make."[26] Realizing that he was up against a president who knew something about the navy, Jones wanted some protection from future presidential questions related to maritime matters. Consequently, Adm. James Holloway, the chief of naval operations, accompanied him to all future NSC meetings concerning the *Mayaguez* incident.

When the president asked General Jones about the options available to the United States, Jones responded with five.[27] First, the United States could seize the *Mayaguez* by May 14 or as soon as the USS *Holt* arrived on the scene. The second option was to attack the island of Koh Tang, which carried the same risk as the first option—the *Mayaguez's* American crew members could be killed, wounded, or subject to other reprisals. Third, the United States could launch a coordinated attack against the island and the ship on May 16. The fourth option was to bomb Cambodian ships that had been involved in the operation against the *Mayaguez*. The fifth option involved attacks on the Cambodian mainland twenty-four hours after striking Cambodian ships. Jones noted that the Marines and the USS *Holt* would be in place within fourteen hours but that the USS *Coral Sea* would not be in position for another twenty-four hours. Rumsfeld, who had been a naval aviator, pointed out that aircraft could be launched while the ships were still hours away, a fact that did not appear to have dawned on the others at the meeting.

After listening to the various points of view, Ford ordered the State Department to ask the UN secretary-general for assistance in obtaining the crew's release. The JCS was asked if it could undertake the attack on the afternoon of

May 14 (Cambodian time), but Jones argued that too many pieces of the puzzle were missing: not all of the ships or troops would be in place. The plan's three parts were to take place simultaneously. First, some Marines would land on Koh Tang while others from the USS *Holt* recaptured the *Mayaguez*. Second, mainland targets would be attacked to ensure that the Cambodians did not reinforce their forces on the island. (B-52 bombers on Guam were also placed on alert for possible use against Cambodia.) Finally, small boats would not be allowed to travel between Koh Tang and the port of Kompong Som.

After the third NSC meeting, the JCS met in the Pentagon to flesh out the operation's details. Among those providing input was Adm. Noel Gayler, who was CINCPAC. From the military's standpoint, the most critical factor was the coordination of all of the various forces in time for an attack. The military planners believed that waiting until May 15 (Washington time) would increase the chances of success, but they decided that they could move one day earlier, as the president had ordered.

Day 3: Wednesday, May 14, 1975

At 1248 Washington time, General Jones briefed Admiral Gayler and other subordinate commanders on the Tuesday NSC meeting. In the process, he provided guidance for them concerning the military operations that had been planned to recover the crew and the ship.

The fourth and final NSC meeting on the *Mayaguez* was held at 1530 to review the plans for attack. Vice President Rockefeller, Kissinger, Jones, Scowcroft, Press Spokesman Ron Nessen, and Admiral Holloway were present. The key issue at this meeting was the appropriateness of attacking the Cambodian mainland. The vice president and Kissinger were strongly in support of sending a message to the Cambodians; Schlesinger did not want any bombing; and the Joint Chiefs agreed to bombing but wanted to use fighter aircraft, rather than B-52s. Ford sided with Rockefeller and Kissinger. He "ordered that the three operations be set in motion immediately and that four air strikes against mainland targets be conducted from the *Coral Sea*." Aware of Schlesinger's opposition to bombing the mainland, Kissinger maintained that "Ford added that the air strikes 'should not stop until we tell them.' "[28] At 1645 the president approved the plan and ordered the military to carry it out. Although the president was the commander in chief, he expected his orders to be issued through the military chain of command. Accordingly, Admiral Holloway left the room to issue the execute order. CINCPAC was told to seize the *Mayaguez*, conduct a Marine helicopter assault on Koh Tang, and destroy any Cambodian ships or boats that attempted to intervene. "CINCPAC is also ordered to conduct strikes from the USS *Coral Sea* against targets in Kompong Som complex, with the first time on target to be 8:45 pm to coincide with estimated capture of *Mayaguez*."[29] The navy would have its first opportunity to engage in a boarding operation since 1826. The problem, however, as one of Admiral Gayler's aides explained, was that "this action had a lot of *ifs* in it. It wasn't like going in and taking people out of Phnom Penh."[30]

Ford then called a meeting with congressional leaders to brief them on the action he had ordered the Pentagon to take. Senator Byrd told the president that while the War Powers Resolution did not require him to consult with Congress before he took such an action, he thought it would have been better if he had done so. However, Ford refused to acknowledge Byrd's point, responding instead, "As Commander in chief, I have the duty. . . . I acted on the basis that this was the proper exercise of my responsibilities. I believe it was the right decision."[31]

As noted above, one of the problems involved in having the president direct such an operation—as opposed to providing broad guidance and leaving the details to the military personnel on the spot—was that Washington was not always aware of all the issues involved in carrying out such an operation. And in the case of the operation to free the *Mayaguez*, a major problem arose from Washington's failure to understand what only those in the immediate area were aware of: the time of first light. The Marines' attack on Koh Tang was scheduled to begin at sunrise, but daylight at Koh Tang actually arrived twenty-six minutes before the official sunrise. As a result, when the Marines attacked, they did so without the advantage of surprise and in the full light of morning. The 150–200 well-entrenched Cambodians—far more than had been estimated—were waiting for them. The result was disastrous. "In the first hour, fifteen Marines were killed, and eight helicopters—one of which carried all of the radios for the command—had been shot down; only one hundred and thirty one Marines and five air force personnel actually landed on the island. As one general noted, 'We were lucky all of the Marines did not get killed.' "[32] Fortunately, when the forty-eight Marines clad in riot gear landed on the *Mayaguez,* they found it deserted.

The first air strike against Kompong Som was launched, but Kissinger ordered the planes to wait until he had a chance to speak with the president about a radio broadcast from the Cambodian minister of information. The broadcast, stating that Cambodia was prepared to release the *Mayaguez* but not mentioning the fate of its crew, was picked up, translated by the Foreign Information Broadcast Service, and immediately relayed to Washington. The president was informed of the minister's statement while the Marine assault on Koh Tang was in progress and while he was preparing to hold a state dinner for the visiting Dutch prime minister, den Uyl. Because no official diplomatic channels existed for communicating with the Cambodians, Ford ordered Press Spokesman Ron Nessen to issue a statement acknowledging receipt of their broadcast and calling on them to "issue a statement that you are prepared to release the crew members you hold unconditionally and immediately."[33] In the meantime, the planes assigned to attack Kompong Som began running low on fuel; thus, they had no choice but to turn back and drop their bombs in the sea.

After a navy reconnaissance pilot saw thirty Caucasians in a fishing boat waving white flags, the USS *Wilson* quickly brought onboard the crew of the *Mayaguez*, which, unbeknownst to Washington, had been released by the Cambodians before the Marines secured the *Mayaguez*. However, it was not until that evening that all of the Marines (except for three missing in action) were taken off of Koh Tang. At midnight (Washington time) the president received the information that the crew was safe and the ship had been recovered. The fight to recover the *Mayaguez* had ended, but the battle over U.S. air strikes against Cambodia continued.

Although the first wave of aircraft had not dropped their ordnance as a result of orders from the White House, the second and third did. The second wave hit the airfield on Ream, cratering the runway, while the third hit the naval base there, as well as Kompong Som naval facilities, "damaging a fuel storage area, two warehouses and the railroad marshaling yard."[34] However, the fourth wave was never launched. As a result, Schlesinger's standing with the president would suffer when Ford asked why the strike hadn't taken place as ordered.

Not until an NSC meeting was held after the return of the *Mayaguez* and its crew did Ford learn that only two of the four strikes he had ordered had been carried out. General Jones began the briefing by noting that "the first (strike) was armed reconnaissance. They did not expend ordnance." He did not mention, however, that the planned first strike did not occur because Kissinger had placed a hold on the execution order. When he heard that the first attack had not been carried out, "Ford's face reddened. Kissinger asked Jones, 'How many aircraft were used all together?' 'About thirty-two to forty,' came the answer. Schlesinger added, 'Not the eighty-one that had been on the carrier.' "[35] Ford was furious. He wanted his orders carried out, and he wanted the Cambodians punished. Walking out of the meeting, he motioned to Kissinger and asked him for his recollection of the presidential orders.

Kissinger confirmed the president's understanding, but he also failed to mention that he had asked Scowcroft to put the first attack on hold while the president looked at the Cambodian statement. Ford then returned to the meeting only to learn that the fourth strike had not happened either. He angrily ordered Schlesinger to prepare a report detailing what had happened and explaining why.

Schlesinger prepared the report, but it failed to adequately explain why Ford had been told that the first strike was completed when it wasn't or why the fourth strike was never carried out. In his book *A Time to Heal,* Ford recalled the matter, writing,

> [There was] some high-level bumbling at the Defense Department. The first strike never took place, although we were told it had been "completed." The Navy jets dropped their bombs into the sea. It's possible that communications problems may have contributed to the misunderstanding. It's also possible that the planes in the first wave—which I had delayed for twenty minutes—may have run low on fuel. They may have been forced to jettison their ordnance in order to return to *Coral Sea*. What is harder for me to understand is why the fourth air strike—and I had specifically ordered four—was never carried out. I hadn't told anyone to cancel that attack. Apparently, someone had, and I was anxious to find who had contravened my authority.[36]

Kissinger laid the blame on Schlesinger, noting that "the President had ordered all-out strikes at the NSC meeting, and, in the absence of the Chairman of the Joint Chiefs of Staff, there was no military officer sufficiently close to him to transmit the orders unambiguously through the chain of command. This gave the Secretary of Defense—who is actually, in our system, not directly in the chain of command—what turned out to be a decisive voice."[37] The president's order was communicated to subordinate commands at 1248 on May 14, as noted above.

Ford never did learn why the fourth wave did not carry out its orders. "The explanations I received from the Pentagon were not satisfactory at all, and direct answers kept eluding me."[38] He decided not to push the matter, however. Despite the dead Marines, the mission ultimately achieved success: the United States had both the ship and the crew back. Kissinger, who had major turf, policy, and personality battles with the secretary of defense, suggested privately that Ford blamed Schlesinger (implying that he must have personally cancelled the air strike because he was opposed to the idea of hitting the

Cambodian mainland). Kissinger also claimed that "although no heads rolled then, Ford never recovered confidence in the Secretary of Defense."[39]

THE FIRING OF SCHLESINGER

At Schlesinger's instigation, a story appeared in the press that claimed he had put American military forces on alert just prior to Nixon's recent resignation, the clear implication being that the secretary of defense had helped avert a coup d'état. Ford, who brought the issue up directly with Schlesinger, wrote that "Schlesinger never admitted to me that he had been the source of these reports, and right after our conversation, I released a statement that 'I have been assured that no measures of this nature were actually undertaken.'" Months later, Ford said he learned that the story was born during a lunch Schlesinger had with some reporters on August 23, 1974. The angered president ordered Under Secretary William Clements to find out what had happened. Clements confronted General Brown.

> "What in the hell is this all about?" he asked.
> "Nothing," Brown replied. "There was no alert."
> "Are you sure?"
> "Absolutely. I have checked at headquarters. There are no recorded messages coming out of the Secretary of Defense's office. Furthermore, if there had been a call, it would have been referred back to the National Military Command Center here at the Pentagon. We have no record of that. I've checked every record, and it's all pure fabrication."
> "You've checked it yourself, George?"
> "Yes. There's no question."
> Shaken, Clements walked upstairs and entered Schlesinger's office. He mentioned the "scare" stories in the press, said they had obviously emanated from Schlesinger's lunch with reporters, then asked, "Why did you say all this?"
> At first Schlesinger didn't reply. Finally, he looked up and said, "I don't know."

Ford condemned Schlesinger's actions: "For the Secretary of Defense to speculate to the press that our military commanders—men who are controlled by civilians under the Constitution—might take some unilateral and illegal action at a moment of grave national crisis was to stab our armed forces in the back."

The Chiefs had felt similarly maligned when Schlesinger warned them not to carry out an order unless he and the other Chiefs had seen it.[40]

Ford would have selected someone else as secretary of defense when he assumed office, but he decided to retain all of the cabinet officers in their positions to demonstrate stability and continuity in the aftermath of Nixon's resignation. Ultimately, however, Ford informed Schlesinger on November 1 that he planned to replace him with Donald Rumsfeld. Schlesinger was upset and refused Ford's offer of a different position in the administration. A number of reasons—and not just the *Mayaguez* and military alert incidents—had led to their parting of ways. Ford, who could not stand Schlesinger on a personal basis, confessed "that his aloof, frequently arrogant manner put me off. I could never be sure he was leveling with me." In addition, the secretary of defense fought continuously with Kissinger, could not get along with Congress, and opposed a number of security policies favored by the president. Ford concluded that "I had been remiss in not getting rid of him. I don't enjoy firing people, but I didn't see any alternative."[41]

CONCLUSION

Presidential Leadership Style

During Ford's brief tenure as president, only one major military operation occurred: the freeing of the *Mayaguez*. It is true that the collapse of South Vietnam took place on his watch, but there was little he could have done to avoid it. Furthermore, his interactions with the military were limited in that instance.

Ford's open style of dealing with subordinates, including those in the military, was evident in the four NSC meetings discussed above. Although he had serious reservations about Schlesinger, he did not seem put off by the secretary's dissenting view on the policy that the United States should follow in its effort to recover the *Mayaguez*.

Violations of Service/Military Culture?

There is no doubt that many officers objected to Ford's decision to direct the tactical operation to recapture the *Mayaguez*. In addition to taking a personal interest in the matter, the president was motivated by political reasons to ensure that the operation was conducted according to his wishes. In the end, he would have to bear the consequences of taking on Congress and infuriating the Thai government in order to deal with the crisis. In addition, its outcome would be critical not only for military morale (which had hit rock bottom after the Vietnam War), but for the public image of the president. This was a perfect opportunity for him to make a positive contribution toward healing the divisions of the past. As Wetterhahn noted with regard to the difference between first light and sunrise, mistakes were made that might have been avoided if tactical issues were handled at the local level. Had Ford won in 1976, it is unclear whether or not he would have interfered in future military operations.

Although Ford interfered in a major military operation, he went out of his way to protect one aspect of military culture. He did not permit the military to become politicized during a period of domestic turmoil; hence his strong reaction to the story about Schlesinger's attempt to ensure that the military did not come to Nixon's aid during the Watergate affair. Indeed, the story was the straw that broke the camel's back. Ford's action was deeply appreciated by the generals and admirals that Schlesinger had angered when he asked Brown to be sure that they did not follow any orders unless he and the other Chiefs had seen them.

The question of the fourth air strike remains a mystery, but is important insofar as military culture is concerned. Refusal by the military to obey a direct presidential order in a combat situation is almost unheard of and cause for great concern. Based on the foregoing, my suspicion is that Schlesinger had a hand in cancelling the strike—which would explain why nothing came out in the report that the president ordered Schlesinger to prepare. If Kissinger's reading of the situation was accurate, Ford's lack of trust in Schlesinger thereafter probably stemmed from the cancelled strike. To his credit, Schlesinger apparently accepted far more autonomy on the part of the Chiefs than McNamara had. Furthermore, the Chiefs were undoubtedly relieved at Ford's more open style, which significantly lessened Kissinger's ability to entangle them in political issues as he had when Admiral Moorer was chairman. Throughout the *Mayaguez* incident they were treated as expert military advisors. They made no attempt to become involved in political matters, which undoubtedly pleased the president.

Changes in Service/Military Culture?

Little change occurred in military culture during Ford's presidency, perhaps because he was in office for only two years. Still trying to recover from the Vietnam War, the Chiefs tended to focus on internal military problems such as drug use and the restoration of discipline.

All in all, the Chiefs found Ford an easy person to work with. He respected them and their expertise. They did not like his micromanaging style, but they enjoyed working with him. He asked for their opinions and took them seriously. They also appreciated his willingness to give clear and concise orders. They may have disagreed with some of his actions, but they knew what they were supposed to do. From a military standpoint, one cannot ask for more than that.

9
THE MILITARY AND JIMMY CARTER

Right now, we have a hollow Army.
—General Edward C. Meyer

Jimmy Carter faced a daunting challenge when he became president. The military, particularly the army, continued to experience major problems as a result of the Vietnam War. Gerald Ford had begun the process of rebuilding the armed forces, but much, much more remained to be done: worn-out equipment had to be replaced, morale had to be restored, and the entire military had to be modernized. Otherwise, the Chiefs did not believe the United States could possibly maintain its defenses at a level matching those of the Soviet Union. Because many believed that Carter was not prepared to stand up to the USSR, he was politically vulnerable on issues relating to the military.

Although he understood the military's problems, Jimmy Carter also understood the desires of those who had helped him win the presidency. They wanted more domestic spending on social programs, and he had promised during the campaign that he would pay more attention to those needs by cutting unnecessary military programs such as the controversial B-1 bomber program. Furthermore, Carter also understood that the condition of the U.S. economy would prohibit him from spending vast amounts of money on both domestic and military programs, because it would raise inflation to completely unacceptable levels.

Because Jimmy Carter had graduated from the U.S. Naval Academy and spent seven years on active duty in the navy serving on submarines, the Chiefs hoped that he would understand why they needed help in rebuilding the American armed forces. Additionally, they viewed national security as the president's primary responsibility. Unfortunately, they would soon learn that Carter intended to keep his election campaign promises; not only would he *not* give the military the money it sought, but he would actually *cut* its budget! Carter's relationship with the military would be difficult at best.

CARTER'S LEADERSHIP STYLE

Carter's leadership style is difficult to categorize. In terms of personality, Carter was a micromanager. Like Kennedy, he resisted the idea of a chief of staff; he viewed the presidency as the hub of a wheel, an arrangement that would provide him maximum opportunity for direct contact with officials and advisors.[1] In a certain sense, Carter believed he represented the "general will," a political leader who would assert the public interest.[2] He would make the major decisions.

At the same time, Carter wanted to be a collegial leader. Thus he had his national security advisor, Zbigniew Brzezinski, restructure the complex system that had been established in the White House during the Ford and Nixon administrations. Rather than the myriad committees that were omnipresent under his predecessors, Carter wanted a system that would permit cabinet-level participation in decision making. Two standing groups were created to deal with national security matters: The first, chaired by a cabinet-level officer, was the Policy Review Committee (PRC), which "examined foreign policy problems on an issue-by-issue basis."[3] The other was the Special Coordination Committee (SCC), chaired by Brzezinski and responsible for such issues as arms control, crisis management, and intelligence activities. The SCC would play the key role in security/operational matters.

Carter's collegial leadership style suffered from a number of problems. Usually, a collegial leader creates a give-and-take environment in which a meeting's participants are prepared to state their views and argue vigorously, even if the president disagrees with them. Subordinates understand that the leader wants—indeed, demands—contrasting viewpoints before he or she makes a final decision. For example, Ford created such an environment when he dealt with the *Mayaguez* crisis. But Carter's definition of collegiality was different. His actions suggested that he was "first among equals" to the degree that he often paid little attention to others. As John Burke wrote, "Carter's faith was in himself, and the impression he would create."[4] Thus, although he took an interest in his colleagues' views, "Carter had great difficulty in accepting criticisms from others and admitting his own mistakes." Such traits contributed to the failure of collegiality during his presidency. To make matters worse, he had a tendency of "suddenly taking the initiative of intervening in an important foreign policy matter" without even consulting his colleagues. He did so when he made human rights a key part of U.S. foreign policy and left "[Cyrus] Vance and Brzezinski with the embarrassing and difficult task of making the best of it or trying to modify the policy."[5] Although many admired the president's strong sense of morality and his efforts to do what was right, his failure to consider the political consequences of his actions had a significant adverse impact on the bureaucracy and his presidency.

When a carefully negotiated and widely supported policy memorandum goes to the president, the participants generally know where they stand. When the president approves it, they know who is in charge of implementing the policy and what it means for other policies. Such was not the case with Carter. Because issues were not staffed through the bureaucracy in advance, no one knew exactly what the president intended when he raised them. For example, his subordinates did not know who would oversee implementation of his human rights policy, or how the policy would affect everything from the use of mines in warfare to trade relations with countries that were violating human rights. What was needed, as Alexander George and Eric Stern noted, was "an effective central coordinating mechanism for the organization and management of the policy process."[6] Instead, his decision-making approach led to bureaucratic chaos. Everything was left open to clarification, which in Washington means a license to fight to change the proposed policy.[7]

Carter also had a tendency to involve himself in the minutiae of policy matters. An engineer by training, he had the mental capability to understand the majority of issues put before him. The problem, however, was that instead of sitting back, listening to the experts, and then making a decision after discussing the issue with them, he often made groups such as the PRC irrelevant. He was not only president; he was a State Department, Pentagon, or CIA desk officer as well. Consequently, "his desire to get involved in details, evaluate a range of alternatives, but ultimately to make his own judgement caused him to utilize a variation of multiple advocacy with undesirable consequences. His policy seemed to lack direction and consistency."[8]

During its early years, the Carter administration had very little structure. The president relied on small meetings such as the Thursday lunch sessions attended by Vance, Brzezinski, and Secretary of Defense Harold Brown. The attendees would discuss policy issues and often formulate solutions without involving the president. Brown recalled that

> the first couple of years the Thursday lunches were very informal. We just talked about things. Then, what happened is staffs—the NSC staff, Defense, State—began to see them as a way of getting issues resolved that they had been unable to resolve at a staff level. And so big agendas

National Security Advisor Zbigniew Brzezinski (left) speaks with General John Vessey (center), chairman of the Joint Chiefs of Staff, and his fellow chiefs. (Jimmy Carter Library)

> began to be created and we actually resolved things, but we also lost something. We lost the free interplay and it became more than it had been—a staff driven exercise. When that happened, the agenda items for the Thursday lunches would provide part of the agenda for Friday.[9]

No clearly established manner for resolving important issues existed, and no one knew precisely what role they should play. Carter viewed Vance as his primary foreign policy advisor, but it soon became clear that Brzezinski also played a key role. Indeed, the president frequently sided with the latter, which contributed to Vance's eventual resignation.

The Thursday lunches at least meant that the key players were interacting. But what if an important issue arose when Vance was out of town? What if two of the players disagreed? Equally important, what about the thousands of policy decisions that had to be made every day? Must the bureaucracy, whether it oversaw social, education, economic, or military issues, wait until the president had a chance to read its memo on a topic that should be decided at a lower level? The foreign policy and national security agenda quickly became overloaded. Carter tried to rectify this somewhat chaotic situation by forming task forces to handle specific issues, but he never established the kind of regularized mechanisms that Eisenhower employed. Nor did he ever impose an overall concept on foreign or national policy, the majority of which was carried out on an ad hoc basis.

The Carter administration's style of decision making was anathema to the Chiefs. Clear lines of authority, carefully staked-out position papers, and broadly based input were essential ingredients of a policy proposal. Generals and admirals, who did not normally make policy on the spur of the moment, expected the president to solicit their advice before making important decisions, even if that advice went through Secretary of Defense Brown. They had not anticipated serving a president who proposed policies that would significantly affect the military without first considering their views. But that is exactly what the Chiefs encountered when they first met with him.

BUDGETARY ISSUES

The Legacy of the Nixon/Ford Years

The era of the Nixon administration was one of budgetary retrenchment. Defense spending decreased, and Washington changed its strategy from having a military capable of fighting two and a half wars simultaneously to one able to fight one and a half. The downward trend began to change during the Ford administration, which recognized "that during the previous ten years American defense spending had declined by about 7 per cent, while that of the Soviet Union had continued to increase by about 3 or 4 per cent each year."[10] The discrepancy in spending by the two countries prompted the Chiefs and others who supported a larger military budget to argue that increasing U.S. military expenditures would send a clear signal to the Soviets and the rest of the world that the United States was once again able to meet its obligations around the globe.

The Chiefs were right in one respect. The U.S. military was in a sorry state. Take, for example, the navy. The number of general purpose ships (excluding aircraft carriers and strategic nuclear submarines) had fallen from 840 in 1968 to only 450 in 1975. The Ford administration had agreed to increase spending 6 percent a year in real terms to expand the navy to 540 ships by the 1980s. His administration also intended to upgrade ground forces by adding three extra divisions and implementing a structural reorganization. Finally, strategic forces also would be upgraded: the Trident SLBM (submarine-launched ballistic missile) program would be modernized, production of the B-1 bomber would proceed, and development of the MX missile would continue. As Phil Williams explained, "[T]he Carter Administration inherited a fairly comprehensive programme to modernize and strengthen both conventional and nuclear forces."[11] Given this background, the Chiefs understandably believed that Carter would continue Ford's modernization program in spite of his statement during the election campaign that he intended to reduce the military budget. Because Carter came from a military background, few of the Chiefs doubted that he would ignore his campaign promises (like so many other politicians) and come to their aid when he entered office.

Carter Meets the Chiefs

The Joint Chiefs' first meeting with President-elect Carter was nothing short of a full-scale disaster. According to Carter, his goal at this meeting was to "understand our defense organization, its capabilities and weaknesses, my proper role as Commander in Chief of the Armed Forces—and my myriad special responsibilities in the control and potential use of atomic weapons."[12] If this is what was intended, it was not the result. The meeting raised serious questions about Carter's understanding of the Chiefs' role and their methods of operating.

Carter began the meeting by personally greeting each of the Chiefs and their deputies.[13] The Chiefs then presented a briefing that covered everything imaginable. Designed not only to impress the new commander in chief, the presentation also was intended to make him believe that the Soviets were just around the corner and that, unless the United States worked hard to regain its military might, the red flag of Mother Russia would soon be flying over the U.S. capital. Carter listened attentively and asked a few questions. When the formal part of the briefing ended, Gen. George Brown, the chairman of the Joint Chiefs of Staff, summarized its key points and noted the budgetary figures the Chiefs expected to receive based on the Ford administration's plans. Indeed, he observed that this was the minimum amount they needed in order to carry out their job. "He noted that during the last two years of Ford's tenure, Congress had increased defense appropriations that reflected Soviet defense outlays, but added that in the military's opinion, the increase would have to continue until the United States was able to meet its worldwide obligations."

Carter thanked Brown for the briefing, said he would study the figures they had just given him, and noted his belief that the briefing would serve as a good precedent for the future of civil-military relations. He expressed both

The Joint Chiefs of Staff meet with President Jimmy Carter over lunch in the White House. (Jimmy Carter Library)

his own and his aides' understanding and appreciation of the JCS commitment to a strong defense. After asking a number of questions about the JCS claim that the Soviets had an edge over the United States, Carter dropped a bomb that stunned the Chiefs. "By the way," he asked, "how long would it take to reduce the numbers of nuclear weapons currently in our arsenal?" Not knowing what Carter had in mind, Brown broke the president's questions into a variety of different categories. "No, no," Carter said, "I guess I want to ask what you think it would take to cut the missiles, how we could cut the number of missiles." Brown still did not understand. Finally, the president said, "What would it take to get down to a few hundred?" The room became totally quiet as the JCS officers looked at one another, wondering where Carter was coming from. This was the first they had heard of this massive cut, and he had not even asked them for their opinion. The new president had made one thing very clear—he had his own ideas on how to run the Pentagon, and one of them was to negotiate deep cuts in the U.S. and Soviet strategic systems while cutting the military's budget.

When the meeting ended, General Brown went to the secretary and argued that these cuts would be extremely difficult to carry out. Weapons systems—including nuclear systems—are carefully balanced between different kinds of weapons; reducing one system inevitably has an important effect on the other weapons. In speaking to Secretary Brown, the chairman maintained that the JCS was committed to building a military in accordance with the guidance they had received from the Ford administration. The secretary responded that the promises of the Ford administration no longer counted for much: Carter was the new president, and he intended to cut the military's budget by as much as $7 billion, just as he had promised in his election campaign. Some of the military's most prized weapons systems would have to be cancelled, and judging by the way the president was talking, that was only the beginning. Rather than working with the Chiefs, Carter seemed to take no interest in their views, rendering them superfluous. The Chiefs felt a growing bitterness, which helped fuel Ronald Reagan's campaign against Carter four years later.

To prove that he was serious, one of Carter's first acts as president was to order Bert Lance, the head of the Office of Management and Budget, to work with Harold Brown to find the $7 billion he intended to save from the defense budget. With the budget already in a mess because of inflation, their undertaking proved to be very difficult. In the end, they were able to come up with $3 billion. However, Carter believed that the Pentagon constantly engaged in chrome plating, or in other words, exaggerating costs, adding unnecessary items to weapons systems, and building weapons of dubious utility. In addition, "Carter was convinced that weapons duplication was costing at least $50 billion per year, a problem he blamed directly on the JCS." It should be noted that Carter's complaint was partially valid. Rather than work together to focus on joint acquisitions for weapons, each of the services tended to go its own way, thereby costing the American taxpayer billions of dollars. One of Harold Brown's assistants complained that "the country continues to buy four independent tactical air forces, one for each service."

Carter and the Army

If Carter carried out his planned reductions, the army believed it would be particularly hard hit *not only* in terms of weapons, but also in its ability to carry out its missions overseas. And nowhere was that more evident than in the case of U.S. troops in South Korea. Rumors circulated among senior army officers that Carter intended to make good on his campaign promise to withdraw U.S. forces from Korea. What was unusual, and perhaps unexpected, was that he meant exactly what he had said: "Thereafter his mind was made up. As president-elect, he refused a CIA briefing on Korea. As president, he was undeterred by the expressed concern of South Korea that removing the American military would trigger an invasion of South Korea by the heavily armed and erratic leadership of North Korea. Nor did it matter to him that his own national security team was opposed to such a move."[14]

In February 1977 Gen. John Vessey, the influential army commander of U.S. forces in Korea, received a back-channel message from General Brown informing him that the president had sent the JCS a copy of Presidential Review Memorandum 13, a draft plan for a troop withdrawal.[15] Carter asked their opinion on which of three schedules for withdrawal was preferable. Characteristically, he did not request their views on the appropriateness of the withdrawal. In fact, as Gen. John Singlaub noted, the memorandum was dated January 27, 1977, indicating that it had been drafted as soon as the administration took office and could not have been sent to the Pentagon for comment. Despite the manner in which Carter had cast his request, the Chiefs responded with a memorandum arguing that all three options entailed " 'a grave risk' and therefore were unacceptable, given the North Korean buildup."[16] Not surprisingly, Secretary Brown quickly informed them that their answer was not acceptable and that their duty lay in choosing one of the three options the president had suggested. They chose option 3, which called for a phased withdrawal over four or five years. If they couldn't stop things, at least they could delay them as long as possible in the hope that Carter might change his mind.

On May 12, 1977, believing that the deployment of U.S. troops in South Korea was an unnecessary drain on the U.S. budget, Carter signed Presidential Directive 13, which announced the withdrawal of the combat forces. The State Department and the staff of the National Security Council responded by opposing the withdrawal, and U.S. ambassadors to China and Japan warned that a withdrawal would adversely affect U.S. allies in Northeast Asia.[17] Army commanders were shocked. They had been asking for an increase in troops, but instead the president was cutting forces. How could they fight a war in Asia if their major forces were withdrawn? General Singlaub, the third-ranking officer in Korea, spoke out publicly and was recalled to the United States to meet with Carter, who fired him. (He assumed another position, only to find himself in hot water again over something he was quoted to have said, and he then retired.) General Vessey had publicly supported him after he had spoken out against the withdrawal and thus also drew the wrath of Carter, who refused to approve his nomination as army chief of staff when his tour in Korea ended. (Vessey was offered the position of vice chief of staff in the hope that he would turn it down, but he took the job under Gen. Edward "Shy" Meyer and performed outstandingly; President Reagan later nominated him to become chairman of the Joint Chiefs of Staff.)[18]

Ultimately, as happened frequently with Jimmy Carter, the contentious policy was never implemented. On July 20, 1977, Brzezinski announced that Carter had suspended the withdrawal of U.S. troops from Korea. The intense outcry against the policy had led Carter to have second thoughts; in addition, credible intelligence data suggested that the North was building up its forces and thus posing an increasingly dangerous threat to the South.[19]

Carter and the Air Force

While the army focused its bitterness on Carter's handling of Korea, the air force expressed anger at his stance on the B-1 bomber. When asked during his election campaign if he would build the B-1 bomber, Carter responded that there was "a gross waste of money in the Pentagon" and that the B-1 was very expensive. He noted that he would have to closely examine the project before any money was spent on it.[20] In his memoirs, Carter was even more frank, noting, "If I had absolute power, the answer would have been simple: do not build it, because it would be a gross waste of money. My problem was that I would have to win that argument not merely in the Oval Office, but also in the public arena—indirectly with the American people, and then directly with a majority in Congress."[21] He did not anticipate, however, just how much influence the military would have with Congress or how this issue would haunt him right into the next election campaign.

The major argument in favor of the B-1 was that the B-52s were wearing out. The air force argued that it would be better—and less expensive—to build the B-1 than to modernize the B-52s. Gen. Russell Dougherty, the SAC commander, was among those making the case for the new bomber:

> There is no weapons delivery system that is more important, more critical, or offers more deterrent utility with the total mix of our strategic forces than the B-1. A penetrating bomber can always be adapted to utilize and exploit any advantages of a standoff missile, while . . . being able to extract high levels of damage against deep targets, including those requiring a high order of accuracy and yield to achieve reasonable damage levels.[22]

Skipping the B-1 in favor of a follow-on stealth aircraft (whose secret development appeared promising) might make sense, but Carter did not make this argument; nor is there any indication that he tried to convince the Chiefs that he would support a follow-on aircraft. Also, although cruise missiles were frequently touted as possible replacements for manned aircraft, they remained unproven.

Secretary Brown found himself in a difficult position when it came to the B-1. He knew that the president disliked the project, and in the final analysis, Carter was his boss. However, Brown was smart enough to realize that he could not run the Pentagon without the support of the service chiefs, especially the air force generals. In the meantime, Carter asked the military to carry out another study of the utility of the B-1 bomber. Striving to be evenhanded and balanced, the military issued a neutral study showing that both the B-52 and the B-1 could penetrate with equal effectiveness for the next ten years. "After that time, however, the B-52 would be less effective. But there were still questions about how long the B-1 would be an effective penetrator."[23]

On June 30 Carter announced that he was cancelling the project because it was too expensive. "Within twenty-four hours of Carter's decision, the JCS issued a strong protest to the president through channels."[24] In such cases, service chiefs usually fight very hard for their subordinates' programs by lobbying Congress to restore money to the budget. Gen. David Jones, chairman of the Joint Chiefs of Staff, undoubtedly believed that the B-1 bomber was a project desperately needed by the air force and deserving of the White House's support. To everyone's surprise, however, in spite of expressing his strong opposition to the president's action, General Jones made it very clear that he (and the air force) did not intend to lobby Congress for that weapon system.

General Jones was bitterly attacked by all sides. Fellow military officers in particular asked how he could idly sit by while the president cancelled one of the military's most critical weapons systems. Jones told Representative William Chappell that the commander in chief had made a decision with which he did not agree, but as long as he was chief of staff, the air force would not lobby for it—period. As James Locher noted, "There was absolutely no ambiguity about where Jones stood. . . . When the decision was made, he decided to fully support the commander-in-chief and not be party to a civilian effort to overturn the decision in Congress."[25] Jones's belief that the air force lost the fight with the president over the B-1 did not satisfy his colleagues. To those who soon called for him to resign in protest, he responded, " 'That thought never occurred to me,' . . . 'Why should I put myself on this pedestal and say that I have all the answers for this nation?' "[26]

Finally, on February 22, 1978, the Carter administration won. The House voted 234 to 182 to eliminate $500 million from the first two production models of the B-1.[27] However, the president paid a heavy price for this victory. His cancellation of the B-1 turned the JCS and the air force against him. Some members of Congress also began to cite the program's cancellation as proof that he was soft on Communism and putting the United States at risk. Carter was not alone in being attacked because of the bomber's cancellation. Some officers began to question the leadership of Secretary of Defense Brown. "Brown's response, that he had urged Carter to continue funding the program at a reduced rate, didn't help: JCS officers were not inclined to believe him, especially when they recalled his 1962 recommendation that McNamara eliminate funding for the B-70, the Air Force's dream bomber of the 1960s."[28]

Carter alienated members of the air force not only by cancelling the B-1 program, but also by failing to consult with them before he announced his decision; he had similarly shocked the army with his proposed withdrawal of American forces from Korea. Although one can only speculate, the army and the air force probably would have reacted in a more subdued fashion if the president had given the impression that he valued their views and had made an honest effort to negotiate with them. As it was, a large number of air force officers began looking for ways to circumvent him, which included behind-the-scenes deals with members of Congress. A retired air force officer told Mark Perry that "Carter's decision on the B-1 was just a disaster for him. . . . It really made him a lame duck with us [on the U.S. Air Force staff] long before his other decisions made him a lame duck with the American people."[29]

Carter and the Navy

The U.S. Navy also was upset with Carter because of the reductions he was making in the ship construction plan that Ford had approved. Having been delegated additional duties, the navy wanted Carter to agree to the construction of a 90,000-ton Nimitz-class aircraft carrier. If the navy hoped to get back to the 600-ship level, the construction of such a ship was critical to the admirals, who believed that the heart of naval power was the carrier task force (a carrier and six or seven additional ships). Admiral Holloway, the chief of naval operations, led the fight for the carrier and even succeeded in getting the House Armed Services Committee to include $2.1 billion for it in the budget. Then Carter unexpectedly vetoed the defense bill.

The navy brass did its utmost to convince Congress to override the president's veto, but without success. When Admiral Holloway retired in July 1978, tradition called for him to have a face-to-face meeting with Carter in the Oval Office. "Holloway, who advocated a nuclear carrier, was denied the visit."[30] Holloway's successor, Adm. Thomas B. Hayward, attempted to calm the storm by privately ordering senior naval officers not to speak out against the president's action. But the navy officers remained extremely angry at the president, who was supposed to be one of them but was instead tearing the heart out of their most prized program. Hayward himself was upset, especially after a variety of naval officers criticized him for refusing to publicly stand up to the president. "But those orders evoked such anger in the Navy that Hayward's private memo to flag officers one week later was an exercise in ambiguity that avoided clear support for the president. In truth, the Naval brass clearly supported an override of the president's veto with nothing less at stake than naval superiority—not mere equivalence with the Soviet fleet."[31]

The situation did not improve during Carter's last year in office. The navy, now saddled with the need to keep ships in the Indian Ocean and Persian Gulf, required more resources. It wanted to bring four battleships out of mothballs, modernize them, and equip them with long-range cruise missiles. Its sailors were living on starvation wages and in substandard housing when ashore.[32] However, Carter believed in a smaller navy, and in May 1980 he rejected budgetary increases for shipbuilding that were modest when compared to Moscow's shipbuilding program. Furthermore, he made clear that he did not want to expand F-18 production, that he opposed money for two new 688-class nuclear submarines, and that he intended to cut back the number of new guided-missile frigates from six to four.[33]

By the time of the election in 1980, Carter had succeeded in alienating all three services and their supporters. He was having a hard time escaping the Republican charge that he "was soft on defense" because, in a certain sense, he was. The country needed a bigger and more robust military, but that would require reallocating the money he had earmarked for some of the social programs that he and his political supporters believed were vital for the country.

Carter and the Soviet Invasion of Afghanistan

Two days after Christmas 1979, the Soviets invaded Afghanistan. Carter was devastated. He had planned to use cooperation with the Soviet Union on arms control, which was at the heart of his national security policy, to justify cutbacks in U.S. defense commitments and to "restore the American role of moral leadership throughout the world in behalf of human rights." At the very least, his policy of detente was now dead. In the eyes of many Americans, the Russians had shown their true colors, something that the seemingly naive president appeared to be just learning. One author suggested that if Carter had understood power politics—instead of living in a moral world of his own—"he might have been able to prepare public opinion for the failures and events beyond his control that undermined his foreign policy." But, as the same author noted, "then he would not have been Jimmy Carter."[34]

The charge of political naïveté, as well as Washington's perception that the Kremlin's invasion of Afghanistan posed a real danger, would haunt Carter for the rest of his administration and beyond. His ability to argue in favor of cutting the military through arms control evaporated. As he recalled in his memoirs, "The worst disappointment to me personally was the immediate and automatic loss of any chance for early ratification of the SALT II treaty." Moscow's action also reminded Washington of the importance of the region to U.S. vital interests and brought into question whether the Soviet invasion was a limited action or part of a larger move into Iran or Pakistan. To again quote Carter, "If the Soviets could consolidate their hold on Afghanistan, the balance of power in the entire region would be drastically modified in their favor, and they might be tempted toward further aggression."[35] The result was an administration policy aimed both at making "Soviet involvement as costly as possible" and at strengthening "our position in the Persian Gulf and South West Asia."[36]

It was now incumbent on President Carter to show strength to convince the American people and the U.S. military that he was not the "wimp" that many thought him to be. He had to prove to the American public that he was prepared to stand up to the Kremlin's naked aggression in Afghanistan. Thus he told a joint session of Congress in January, "Any attempt by any outside power to gain control of the Persian Gulf region will be regarded as an assault on the vital interests of the United States of America and such an assault will be repelled by any means necessary, including military force."[37] The Soviets had made a major mistake: "it seems clear that the Soviet leaders committed a blunder of historic proportions when they misjudged the depth of the U.S. reaction to their aggression in Afghanistan. Jimmy Carter and Cyrus Vance represented an important but often invisible dimension of U.S. attitudes toward the Soviet Union. They believed deeply in the importance of dialogue and mutual accommodation between the two superpowers on vital issues of peace and international security."[38]

The Soviet invasion of Afghanistan had two important effects on the U.S. domestic scene. First, it forced the president to put more money into the defense budget. Second, combined with his cancellation of the B-1 bomber, his effort to remove U.S. troops in Korea, his refusal to fund a new aircraft carrier, and his presumed naïveté about the Soviets, the invasion helped cost him a second term as president.

Carter and the Military Budget, 1980

Members of Congress began confronting the administration over the military budget. In January 1980, for example, "member after member of the House Armed Services Committee, some gently and other acidly, told Secretary of Defense Harold Brown . . . that the Carter Administration's new military budget was too little, too late."[39] Many, including conservatives from his own party, considered the 5.4 percent increase in appropriations (adjusted for inflation) to be insufficient. Then, at a White House breakfast for Republican legislators in February, Carter was told that his budget was "very inadequate and totally unrealistic." The Pentagon, in contrast, was proposing a budget of $158.7 billion, a 14 percent increase over the FY1980 budget and an amount considerably higher than that advocated by the White House.[40]

Carter saw the writing on the wall. He could not continue to hold the line on his 5.4 percent increase. His proposed budget of $146.2 billion represented an increase of $16 billion, or about 12 percent. This meant that defense spending would be one of few items in the budget that would increase in "real" terms. In the end, however, even this increase failed to address the magnitude of the problem. For example, the Pentagon estimated the price of gasoline would rise at roughly the same rate as the previous year. As one budget expert noted, "They are already higher: its fuel bill in fiscal 1981 will be $4.5 billion higher than estimated."[41]

The Chiefs were getting restless. On March 1 General Jones told the House Budget Committee the military would need "substantial" increases above and beyond those proposed by Carter. Once again the Chiefs would try to use their influence on the Hill against the White House. Reports were coming in to the Congress suggesting that the American military was in a mess. Congressman Jack Edwards, the ranking minority member on the House Defense Appropriations subcommittee, remarked that "only 56 percent of the Air Force's hottest fighter, the F-15 Eagle, were ready for combat at any one time last year, and only 53 percent of the Navy's F-14 Tomcat fighter were ready. The percentages for forward-deployed aircraft, such as F-15s based in Europe, were not much better. . . . About 70 percent of the planes should be ready to go at any given time."[42]

In spite of continued attacks on his defense budget, Carter refused to roll over. In May he sent a letter to Chairman John Stennis urging the Armed Services Committee to remove $6.2 billion in hardware purchases that the House had added to the defense bill. He also asked Stennis to say "no to taking capital ships out of mothballs, no to stepping up F-18 production, no to extra submarines and frigates and, of course, [and] no to resurrecting the B-1 bomber" in order to save $3.1 billion.[43] By the end of the month, the Senate and the House had reached a compromise that Carter assailed as being overly burdened by defense spending. Senate Budget Committee chairman Ernest F. Hollings, the prime mover behind the compromise, was enraged. He accused the president of the " 'height of hypocrisy' and 'outrageous, deplorable conduct' for assailing a compromise congressional budget plan as too defense-heavy." Then the House Armed Services Committee summoned the Joint Chiefs to testify on Carter's projected budget figures. The committee chairman, a Democrat like Hollings, "threatened to subpoena them if the Pentagon tried to block their appearance."[44]

The Chiefs Speak Out

The Chiefs testified on May 30. If Carter was expecting them to fall into line behind the administration, he was in for quite a surprise. In one of the more unusual expressions of military dissatisfaction with presidential authority, the Chiefs made it clear that they were not satisfied with the president's budget. The army chief of staff flatly stated, "Right now, we have a hollow Army." And he continued, "I don't believe the current budget responds to the Army's needs for the 1980s." When Gen. Robert Barrow, the commandant of the Marine Corps, was asked if the budget was adequate, he answered, "In a word, no." Gen. Lew Allen, the chief of staff of the air force, commented that "increased defense spending is required to meet the increased danger." Adm. James Watkins, who was substituting for Admiral Hayward, responded that if Carter's five-year program for the navy was followed, "[W]e would come close" to meeting the danger, but he added that he was skeptical about that happening.

General Jones, who had just been reappointed chairman, was still feeling the heat from the numerous officers he had upset when he refused to fight Carter on the B-1 bomber. This time, Jones stated, " 'I would not vote against the defense part' of the compromise budget resolution now before Congress." Admiral Watkins argued that the situation was so bad that salaries for U.S. servicemen and -women would have to be increased by $3 to $5 billion. He welcomed the additional $1 billion that the president had pledged to spend, but then observed that it was "nothing more than a step in that direction."[45] General Jones remarked that in light of the Soviet invasion of Afghanistan the military budget should be increased to 6 or 7 percent of the country's GNP, instead of the current 5 percent. Such a public disagreement was almost unheard of. Richard Halloran observed, "In the 33 years since the Defense Department was created, individual chiefs on rare occasions have publicly differed with the decisions. But seldom, if ever, in the memory of Pentagon observers, have the Joint Chiefs collectively split with the President on the military budget, as they did in an understated way today."[46] Although Carter may have been upset, Jones noted that the military also worked for Congress, adding that "what the chiefs did Thursday . . . is the only way to preserve civilian supremacy and maintain discipline within the military at all levels."[47]

Carter had done what few presidents had succeeded in doing. He had united the Joint Chiefs of Staff—against him! He was angry that they had complained publicly and that they had lobbied so hard for more money for the armed forces. But he had an election coming up in less than four months, and he was determined not to go into that election with a reputation of being anti-defense.

Consequently, Carter reversed himself on military pay, and by August it appeared that he would agree to the congressionally approved pay raises. He responded similarly to the issue of the navy's nuclear aircraft carrier. After first vetoing a bill because it contained funding for the ship, he approved the next one with a similar appropriation. Furthermore, although he had slowed down the pace set by President Ford on development of the MX missile, he was now calling for full speed ahead in its development and deployment.[48] And so the military began to benefit. By November 1, Congress had passed an 11.7 percent pay raise with better benefits and bonuses. Indeed, the military soon found itself in the middle of what one writer called the "biggest peacetime modernization program ever funded."[49] Jimmy Carter had gotten the word; not only were the Chiefs lined up against him, but Congress and most Americans seemed to agree that the country's defenses had fallen behind the level needed to stand up to an increasingly aggressive Soviet Union. And Carter, in a last, desperate attempt to pull out the 1980 presidential election, understood that he had no choice but to approve the budgetary increases.

THE IRANIAN RESCUE ATTEMPT

If the military found much to complain about in Carter's budget, they had nothing but praise for the way he handled an operational matter as complex as the attempted rescue of American diplomats held hostage in Iran. He was the opposite of President Johnson: he wanted to understand their plans, but he left operational matters up to the military.

November 4, 1979, began as a normal working day in Tehran. The chargé d'affaires, the political counselor, and a security officer had gone to the Foreign

Ministry in an effort to gain more security for the American Embassy. While they were gone, a crowd of about three thousand began forming around the embassy, and by noon they had taken over. The unthinkable had happened. Some seventy American diplomats, Marine guards, and other personnel had been seized by a group of rebellious students, and their lives appeared to be in danger.

The Special Coordination Committee convened on November 6 to discuss a number of questions, including what would happen if Iranian oil were cut off, how the attorney general should handle the large Iranian exile group in the United States, and whether military action should be considered. At a second SCC meeting held the same day, Brzezinski suggested that the group look at three possible military responses: a rescue operation; a retaliatory action if any or all Americans were killed; and a military attack on oil fields in southwestern Iran. The Pentagon was lukewarm to such ideas, as "Brown and General Jones quite correctly stressed the difficulties involved in undertaking any of these tasks, while Vance and Christopher were notably cool to any serious consideration of military options."[50] After all, the embassy was located in the heart of a heavily populated portion of Tehran.

A visibly shaken Carter met with the NSC that afternoon. In his account of the crisis, *All Fall Down,* Gary Sick reported that "when President Carter entered the Cabinet Room, his face was grim and there was none of the usual banter or small talk." In response to a question concerning a possible rescue mission, Secretary Brown, who attended the meeting with General Jones on the Pentagon's behalf, commented that the Department of Defense had examined that option but did not believe the chances of it succeeding were very high. Jones then discussed the problems involved. A variety of other topics were addressed, but by the end of the day the president directed that military contingency planning should proceed on two tracks: first, the Pentagon was to devise a rescue plan "in the event it was needed"; second it was directed to devise options for a punitive military strike "in the event the hostages were harmed."[51] Planning of the options proceeded on two levels. A small group of DOD representatives met privately with Brzezinski in his office (although military issues were also discussed in SCC meetings, the concern with secrecy was so great that they were normally only dealt with at the end of such meetings, and then only by senior officials from State, Defense, the JCS, the CIA, and the NSC). The second group, composed of select military officers, met inside the Pentagon to plan the actual operation.

On November 8, the military reported back to Brzezinski outside of the SCC framework to discuss a possible helicopter assault on the embassy compound. The hostages would be flown to an airfield not far from Tehran, where they would be picked up by larger aircraft. The operation would be extremely difficult because of problems related to logistics and the lack of sufficient intelligence on the whereabouts of the hostages.

In the meantime, the special operations section of the Pentagon was a beehive of activity. General Jones met with Col. Charles Beckwith, who had been chosen to lead the ground assault. Jones informed Beckwith that whatever was decided would have to go through Brzezinski to the president for his approval. Military planners were forbidden from having any contact with State Department personnel because of their opposition to a military option. As Colonel James Kyle observed, "The Chairman then summarized our task, underlining secrecy. He told us that it was essential to organize the JTF [Joint Task Force], develop the plans, select the force, conduct the necessary training, deploy the force and its equipment, and execute the mission all in an environment of airtight secrecy."[52]

While threats toward the hostages emanated from the confusing situation in Tehran, the president and his advisors continued to discuss a variety of military options. On November 23, Brzezinski, Secretary Brown, General Jones, CIA director Adm. Stansfield Turner, and the president met to discuss possible military actions that included mining Tehran's harbors and conducting an air strike on Iran's domestic petroleum facilities. Secretary of State Cyrus Vance was strongly opposed to any military action—"unless the hostages were physically harmed."[53]

When evaluating the possible options for freeing the hostages, the United States had to take into consideration the recent Soviet invasion of Afghanistan. In particular, Washington became increasingly concerned about the impact that a U.S. military (or diplomatic) action could have on the Kremlin's position in the region. The USSR, which bordered Iran, had shown considerable interest in Tehran in the past; an American attack on Iran could push Tehran closer to Moscow. Weak in the region, Washington believed that the only way to project power in the Persian Gulf was by sending in an aircraft carrier. But the general consensus was that attacking Iranian oil fields or mining its harbors would be counterproductive unless the hostages were killed or seriously harmed. Thus, Washington would have to carefully calibrate its actions.

As the military worked on a rescue plan, helicopters soon emerged as the key to any successful rescue effort. They would bring the rescuers in and then extract both the rescued and the rescuers. Unfortunately, the military did not have the proper combination of helicopters and pilots to carry out an operation of this type. The navy's RH-53D helicopters, which had been used to clear mines and hunt submarines, were the only ones that appeared capable of doing the job, but the navy pilots were completely unqualified to fly this kind of mission. Colonel Beckwith recalled that the problem wasn't caused simply by a lack of training: "We were looking for aces, daredevils, barnstormers, guys who flew by the seats of their pants, hot rodders, pilots who could pick it up, turn it around on a dime and put it back down with a flair. These Navy pilots didn't believe in taking the risks we knew were required of the pilots flying into an enemy-held city."[54] Even with special training the navy pilots could not adapt to the kind of flying required in a rescue attempt, so all but one of them were returned to their parent units. As Colonel Kyle, who was in charge of the helicopters and the aircraft for this mission, explained, "Not only did these crews have no one with a Special Operations background and experience in night low-level tactics, but there was only one pilot with any in-flight refueling experience. In all, fairness, I knew the Navy pilots' concern stemmed from the fact that this was a totally unfamiliar ball game to them." According to Beckwith, Marine pilots were chosen to replace the navy aviators because the J-3 or director of operations then in the JCS was a Marine lieutenant general. Better pilots were available, but "there were those in the JCS who wanted to make sure *each of the services had a piece of the action*."[55] The rescue attempt would be a new experience for the Marines as well. They would have to lift off from an aircraft carrier, then fly at 1,500 feet though canyons where Iranian radar could not detect them. A minimum of six helicopters would be required to carry out the rescue mission—anything less and the mission would have to be aborted.

By the dawn of 1980, the failure of the diplomatic route was becoming increasingly obvious. Because of the chaotic situation within Iran, the various overtures attempted by the United States had no effect on bringing about the release of the hostages. As a result, attention increasingly turned to the rescue option.

On March 22, 1980, the president received a full briefing on the proposed mission.[56] General Jones led off with a detailed discussion of the rescue mission, noting that although U.S. intelligence had improved during the five months since the hostages had been seized, it was still impossible to fully ascertain where all of the hostages were located. The United States had a good idea of where everyone was, but the possibility always existed that someone could have been moved. Consequently, the rescue team would have to have enough time to search all of the buildings in the embassy compound.

Jones expressed his confidence that the hostages could be rescued if the rescuers could get inside the compound without being spotted. Brzezinski argued that extracting the hostages would be the easiest part of the mission. "Getting the team to the embassy without discovery and preparing the exit route was much more complex than the confrontation with the students."[57]

Jones told the president that the rescue effort was planned to unfold sequentially and could be aborted at any time if necessary. He also told the president that because nights in Iran were becoming increasingly shorter, the rescue team had to make its move in the near future.

The plan itself called for eight helicopters to rendezvous with three C-130 aircraft in the middle of the Persian Gulf during the first night.[58] The planes and helicopters would fly very low—under Iranian radar—to a point called Desert One. There the helicopters would be refueled and loaded with troops that had been flown in by the C-130s. Once they had refueled the helicopters, the C-130s would leave Iran while the rescue team hid in a remote site in the mountains above Tehran. They would remain in hiding during the next day.

Assuming that the team was successfully inserted and that it remained undetected the following day, the actual rescue mission would begin on the second night and use local vehicles to avoid detection. Once the hostages had been freed, the helicopters would swoop down, pick them up, and take them and the rescue team to the waiting C-130s at an abandoned airfield near Tehran. The helicopters would be left behind, and the airplanes would fly the hostages out of the country under heavy U.S. air cover.

Before proceeding further, the military requested the president's permission to fly in a small aircraft to make sure the field known as Desert One could handle C-130 aircraft. Carter agreed.

> I authorized the flight of a small airplane to the site for a close visual examination of the desert sand—to see how smooth and firm it was. This exploratory flight had to be made when the weather and moonlight would be conducive to success. We all understood that I was not making a full commitment to proceed further with a rescue attempt; at the same time, I wanted the long-standing training operations and planning to continue.[59]

By the end of March, everyone involved understood that while the president had not given his final approval, he was actively considering a military rescue operation.

On April 2 Carter was informed that the small plane had flown hundreds of miles into Iran at a very low altitude and had landed in the desert at a potential rescue staging site. The pilot reported that the location "was an ideal place—a smooth and firm surface, adequately isolated with only a seldom-used country road nearby."[60] The president then gave the go-ahead to assemble a team that could be sent to Iran and attempt a rescue.

On April 7, President Carter informed his close advisors that the time had come for the United States to get tough and take firmer steps in dealing with Iran. He ordered the State Department to break relations with Iran and to institute full-scale economic sanctions. When the possible recourse of military action was discussed, the idea of a naval blockade again came to the fore. As Brzezinski noted, the time for action was drawing near. "The meeting of April 7 was the curtain raiser for the decisive meeting of the NSC held on Friday, April 11."[61]

The April 11 NSC meeting took place at 1130. Secretary of State Cyrus Vance was represented by Deputy Secretary Warren Christopher. Carter told the assembled group that "we could no longer afford to depend on diplomacy. I decided to act." But the volatility of the situation required that the United States proceed carefully; those occupying the embassy pledged to "destroy all hostages immediately" if the United States acted against Iran.[62]

General Jones began the meeting with an updated briefing on the current status of the mission. When it came time to "sign on" for the mission, everyone present voted in favor, with one exception—Warren Christopher, who knew that Vance had serious misgivings about the operation. Vance later noted that his deputy secretary "was aware of, and shared, my strong views against the use of military force in Iran, but he was not fully briefed on the rescue operation, which had been kept a tightly held secret. Christopher properly declined to take a position on the rescue mission and argued that there still remained important political and diplomatic options to consider before we resorted to military force."[63] Brown maintained that Christopher's objections were not "impressive" and instead argued in favor of the military option. Brzezinski took a similar position and spoke very positively about the capabilities of the Delta Team. Stansfield Turner was positive, but cautioned, "The conditions inside and around the compound are good now, but they could change any day." For his part, Carter said that he would " 'explore the rescue option' very tentatively, that he still had a lot of questions. 'I'm going to think and pray about it over the weekend.' "[64]

Vance Resigns

When Vance returned to Washington, Christopher told him about the April 11 meeting. Vance reported that he felt "stunned and angry" that such an important decision was made during his absence. When he went to the president to lodge a complaint, Carter told him that the decision was a very difficult one, "the hardest since he had become president," and he offered Vance an opportunity to present his views to the NSC, an option that Vance seized upon.

Vance could not sway his colleagues. By April 17, Vance later wrote, "I knew I could not honorably remain as Secretary of State when I so strongly disagreed with a presidential decision that went against my judgement as to what was best for the country and the hostages."[65] He told the president that regardless of the mission's eventual success or failure, he did not feel he could continue to serve in good conscience. Carter urged him to stay, but he soon realized that Vance was intent on leaving the administration.

Vance wrote out his formal resignation later a few days later, took it to the White House, and handed it to the president. Carter "took his letter and said he would keep it. We discussed the fact that my general views and political philosophy were very close to his, and that there was no serious difference between us on major issues of American foreign policy."[66] Vance agreed to delay his resignation until the mission had been completed.

Planning the Rescue

The next meeting was held on April 16 in the White House Situation Room. In addition to Generals James B. Vaught and Philip Gast, who played key roles in planning the mission, the on-scene commander, Col. Charles Beckwith, was also present. The group reviewed the plans for a rescue operation. Carter asked questions about the operation and listened attentively to the military's explanation. The military introduced Beckwith and told the president that the Joint Chiefs of Staff believed that he should lead the operation. Carter then turned to General Jones and said, "David, this is a military operation and you're going to run it." Beckwith was satisfied: "[T]he situation was handled perfectly. From Desert One, Jim Kyle and I, back to General Vaught in Egypt, back to General Jones at the JCS, back to the President. It was clean, simple and direct. A precedent had been set that night in the White House. I hope future American presidents, if faced with a similar situation, will follow."[67] Carter's only qualification was that he wanted to avoid collateral damage. Beckwith responded that "if Delta gets in a firefight, it has to be able to use whatever force is necessary to protect American lives. The President understood this and accepted the provision as the basis of engagement."[68] Beckwith not only appreciated the president's statement that he would stay out of operational matters, he also was impressed by the president's personal comment to him: "I want you, before you leave for Iran, to assemble all of your force and when you think it's appropriate give them a message from me. Tell them that in the event this operation fails, for whatever reason, the fault will not be theirs, it will be mine."[69] He also cautioned Beckwith to keep his mission simple.

The group headed by Brzezinski met daily as the military planning continued. The president "was very emphatic in insisting that every effort be made to avoid wanton killings and he requested General Jones give this his personal attention."[70] The danger of a major confrontation with civilians in Tehran was real. If, for some reason, the students in the embassy grounds received advanced warning, "the bloodshed would be unacceptably high, so the operation was designed as a series of independent stages, capable of being terminated at any point if the mission was compromised."[71] The students did not have military training, so they probably would not pose a serious military threat. However, there was always the danger that they would kill the hostages. Furthermore, an inept defense of the embassy compound by the rescuers could make it difficult to bring in the helicopters, which were critical to the mission's success.

On April 18 Hamilton Jordan flew to Europe where he met a secret contact with excellent access to those in charge in Tehran. His contact told him that it would "be a long time before your people come home." After the president had read Jordan's report, he called Secretary of Defense Harold Brown and said, "Harold, my last remaining doubt about the mission has been removed. Tell Colonel Beckwith to proceed."[72] Then on April 23—just one day prior to the start of the raid—the president informed the Pentagon that he had decided against attacks on other targets as long as the rescue operation was under way.

The Operation

At 1020 on April 24, General Jones informed Brzezinski that the weather was good and that the eight helicopters were flying to Iran.[73] Two hours into the flight and already in Iranian air space, one of the pilots was forced to land his helicopter when a warning light indicated the possible failure of a rotor blade. He and his crew were picked up by one of the other helicopters. The aircraft then continued on their way and soon found themselves in the midst of a sandstorm. In order to ensure secrecy, the helicopters were observing strict radio silence, which meant that they could not maintain visible contact, and they became separated. After finally flying out of the storm, they soon ran into another that was even worse.

Four hours into the flight another helicopter began to experience a problem with its flight instruments. The pilot returned to the carrier. Ironically, as a result of radio silence, he did not know that he was only twenty-five minutes away from the landing zone when he turned around. Then, to further complicate the rescue attempt, another helicopter began to have hydraulic problems. Despite successfully reaching the landing zone, the helicopter would be impossible to repair in the desert. The team was now left with only five helicopters. Beckwith, who had stated from the beginning that he needed at least six helicopters to carry out the mission, decided that he had no choice but to abandon the mission. His decision was relayed up the chain of command until it reached the president. Carter concurred.

Preparing to withdraw, however, one of the helicopters collided with one of the C-130s. The latter, which had been carrying gas to refuel the helicopters, immediately burst into flames. Eight crew members died and five were wounded. "The remaining helicopters were abandoned in the inferno of fire and exploding ammunition, and the force withdrew on board the C-130s. The rescue operation, which had been developed in elaborate detail and rehearsed over a period of months, collapsed in ignominious failure and human tragedy within its first hours."[74]

The stunned president offered to call the families of the men killed and wounded, but Secretary Brown persuaded him to leave this task to the army. Shortly after the Delta Team returned, Carter did something that endeared him to everyone who took part in the aborted mission. At 1100 on Sunday, April 27, Beckwith received a secure phone call from the JCS advising him that the president would be arriving that afternoon. General Vaught and General Jones arrived first and had lunch with the members of the Delta Team. In addition, the Marine pilots, drivers, and the Farsi-speaking translators were present. When Carter arrived, Beckwith wrote, he

> was accompanied by Dr. Brzezinski, Dr. Brown and two secret service agents. When the President came over to me, I apologized for the mission's failure. Walking to the hangar where the men had assembled, he put his arm around me.
>
> General Vaught climbed up on a platform and gave a short Knute Rockne speech. The troops were lined up in military formation, but wore civilian clothes. When he was finished, General Vaught introduced President Carter.
>
> He spoke softly and sincerely.
>
> No matter what happened, he appreciated what these men had done for their country. Then he expressed his concern for the hostages, who, you could see, still commanded his full attention. We needed to continue, he stated, to help him find a way to get them released.

> After this short message, he told me he wanted to meet and speak to each person individually. The President then walked through the formation, shaking each man's hand. He spoke to most for a minute, and to some longer. . . .
>
> Before he returned to his helicopter, the President told me in a gentle voice, "I have been remiss in not knowing more about Delta Force. I am very impressed with what I've learned about them and what I've seen today. I didn't know we still had people like this, people who would sacrifice everything for their country. Colonel Beckwith, I am very proud of these men."[75]

What the colonel did not mention was that Carter almost broke down when Beckwith apologized for not carrying out the mission successfully. Like Beckwith, each man that the president spoke to apologized for not being able to complete the mission.[76] It was hard to tell who had impressed whom the most.

Lessons of the Rescue Attempt

Numerous criticisms have been leveled at the rescue mission, including poor planning, insufficient familiarity with flying in desert conditions, and a failure to conduct a full-scale practice raid, but the real problem lay in interservice cooperation. The special operations forces (i.e., the Delta Force) had to rely on helicopters that first were flown by navy officers who were used to clearing mines and then by Marine pilots who had limited experience flying in sandstorms. In addition, the helicopters themselves were not really suited to this kind of mission; they had been used only because they were available. Beckwith discovered

> that the choppers, when they had been put on Nimitz, were not accompanied by any of our maintenance people. It was like having your neighbor knock on the door and ask you to take care of his dog while he's gone, but then not give you any dog food. The carrier provided their own maintenance to the Sea Stallions. These mechanics and their officers had no idea what the choppers were going to be used for. Who knows how they were handled?[77]

Clearly, not everyone involved in the operation was singing from the same sheet of music. Indeed, Beckwith probably put it best when he commented, "In Iran we had an ad hoc affair. We went out, found bits and pieces, people and equipment, brought them together occasionally and then asked them to perform a highly complex mission. The parts all performed, but they didn't necessarily perform as a team. Nor did they have the same motivation."[78] Shortly after the failed rescue attempt, Senator Strom Thurmond echoed Beckwith, suggesting, "We need to be more joint. . . . We need to do much more in being an integrated fighting force in the days ahead."[79]

CONCLUSION

Presidential Leadership Style

Carter's domestic orientation complicated his relations with the military, but his indecisiveness and mercurial nature tended to exacerbate conflict. The Chiefs never knew what to expect from him. He would suddenly decide on one approach or another without prior notification. When making major decisions, he ignored the bureaucracy, including the Pentagon. Thus the military never could be certain of either what he wanted or what exactly was the nation's policy.

Violations of Service/Military Culture?

The Chiefs expected Carter to be understanding of the problems they faced in their attempts to rebuild the military in the aftermath of Vietnam. However, from his very first meeting with them, when he asked how he might reduce the nuclear arsenal to a few hundred missiles, they knew they had a problem. The president was not interested in their opinions. For example, without first consulting them about the wisdom of removing troops from South Korea, he ordered them to devise a withdrawal plan. Similarly, Carter took little interest both in the Chiefs' views on the B-1 and in the navy's perspective on its shipbuilding program, which he slashed without prior consultation.

Like most Americans, the Chiefs found Carter's surprise at Moscow's invasion of Afghanistan even more incredulous. They believed that if he had listened to them, they could have predicted Soviet behavior; but again, he was not interested in their views. Probably nothing upset the Chiefs more than the thought that the president had no respect for them.

However, the Chiefs did approve of the manner in which Carter handled the attempt to free the hostages in Tehran. Despite his reputation as a micromanager, he left the operation to the military, thus providing them with the autonomy they preferred. Then, when the operation failed, it was Jimmy Carter who took the blame, an act of honor that many found impressive. Finally, the military also appreciated that "he was not nearly so bellicose or willing to expend American lives as Johnson nor as duplicitous as Nixon."[80]

Changes in Service/Military Culture?

No major changes occurred in military culture during the Carter administration. As they had previously, the Chiefs used their friends on the Hill to counter the president's attempts to eliminate or reduce the budget for programs they considered critical. They even went so far as to publicly challenge the president, arguing as General Meyer did that the United States had "a hollow Army." Once they had decided that the president would not pay any attention to them, the Chiefs felt no compunction about taking the debate to Congress, which also had responsibility for national security affairs. By the end of his administration, Carter had alienated the Chiefs and the rest of the U.S. military to the degree that only 1 percent of military officers later stated that they preferred him over Reagan.[81]

10
THE MILITARY AND RONALD REAGAN

The politicians mumble generalities; then they say the military is cautious. A lot of people believed that the military is eager to go out and shoot somebody, or that it should be; that's what they expect from the military. The modern military is not like that at all. In my experience, the civilians in the government were more eager to go shoot somebody than was the military.
—Admiral William Crowe Jr.

Ronald Reagan was different from most modern Republican presidents. Where they had placed a premium on a highly centralized form of government in which they were deeply involved, he had little interest in the details of policy, preferring to allow his subordinates to run policy with a minimum of guidance from him. When he did provide guidance it was in the form of broad, if not sweeping, statements.

Under Reagan, service in the military became something positive again. The military believed he had done wonderful things to restore their morale and improve their image throughout the country. They also loved him for what he said: Reagan made no secret of his admiration and respect for members of the military. For this they were grateful. At the same time, his leadership style left much to be desired from the Chiefs' perspective. Although the president established distinct lines of authority, his orders and policies sometimes left his military subordinates wondering what he meant. Similarly, he occasionally asked them to carry out diplomatic assignments that were so open-ended, so vague, that the officers were uncertain of what they were supposed to do; in such cases, they paid a heavy price. Reagan did provide the military services with money—far more than they had obtained in many, many years. Yet, he did so in such a chaotic fashion that one could argue that the additional funding did the military more harm than good in the long run.

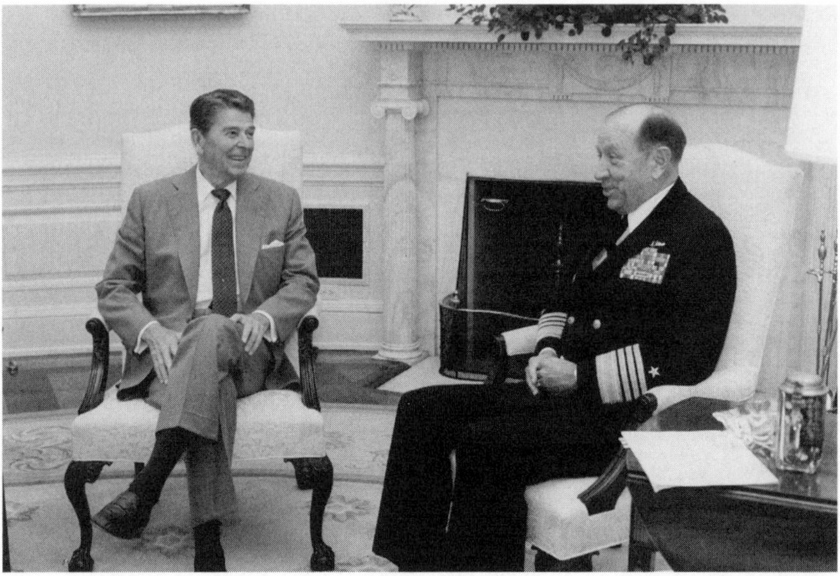

President Ronald Reagan speaks with Admiral William Crowe, chairman of the Joint Chiefs of Staff. (Ronald Reagan)

The armed forces also suffered from service parochialism at the expense of military efficiency, a situation for which they had only themselves to blame. The result would be dead soldiers, sailors, and Marines—men who did not have to die, but whose deaths would serve as a major impetus to change. Indeed, by the early 1980s service parochialism had become so bad that Congress finally stepped in. People on the Hill (and a few in uniform) were sick and tired of the primacy of service parochialism. Forcing the military to become a more jointly organized entity would not be easy, however. Legislators would fight a tooth-and-nail battle with the military before a new joint structure emerged in 1986.

REAGAN'S LEADERSHIP STYLE

Alexander George and Eric Stern observed that during Reagan's first six years "the system was relatively decentralized, undermanaged, and characterized by chronic and exhausting extremes of personal, ideological, and bureaucratic conflict."[1] Rather than witness bureaucratic battles similar to those that Brzezinski had fought against Vance under Carter, Reagan initially decided to weaken the authority of the NSC advisor. Richard Allen, who was Reagan's first NSC advisor, did not have direct access to the president during the first half of his administration; instead, he reported directly to Meese. Change was clearly required by the time Judge William Clark became NSC advisor, so he began reporting directly to the president.

Reagan's particular approach to politics had a number of important ramifications. First, his reliance on broad generalities meant that the bureaucracy did not receive clear instructions. Eugene Wittkopf noted that the president "had strong views on the basic goals of public policy but left it to others to implement his broad vision."[2] He would meet with his advisors (but often only with the chief of staff), give them a general idea of what he wanted, and then rely on them to implement policy. Reagan did not want to be involved in the details of the policy implementation process.[3] He seemed to believe that all he had to do was to make public statements and the bureaucracy would faithfully implement them. Difficulties arose, however, when his subordinates did not understand what he meant in regard to a particular policy; such a failure of understanding would have major implications for U.S. policy toward Lebanon. In many cases, it was left up to them to not only implement his policies but to try to figure out what the president intended in the process. The result too often was confusion as each bureaucracy fought for control of policy.

Second, Reagan was a hands-off president. He did little to enforce order on the bureaucracy, whose infighting he was often unaware of. Unlike Carter, who was accused of being overly involved in policy implementation (with the exception of the Iranian hostage rescue mission), Reagan did not know what was happening outside of his office. According to Richard Neustadt, he "was unconcerned about details except to be told what to know by the time he needed to know it."[4] Donald Regan spoke about this tendency when he argued that the president knew nothing about the funds the U.S. government had received from the Iranians and diverted to the Nicaraguan Contras.[5] Reagan's apparent astonishment at hearing what Lt. Col. Oliver North had been up to should have come as no surprise, because "in the Reagan staff system, there was relatively little direct presidential involvement. Few decisions flowed to the presidential level for action. There were no established mechanisms for making sure that disagreements were brought to the President's attention."[6] Indeed, in contrast to a president like Eisenhower, Reagan often did not even attend NSC meetings, where he could have refined his policy preferences and resolved bureaucratic differences of opinion.

Finally, though sometimes he was not aware of doing so, Reagan often changed policy in midstream, which had major implications for U.S. foreign policy. One cannot assign the Marines in Lebanon job A on day 1 only to change it to job B on day 10 and assume that they will be able to carry out the new task with the existing weapons, equipment, rules of engagement, and manpower.

The Chiefs and the President

The Chiefs were of two minds regarding Ronald Reagan. On the one hand, Reagan fought hard to regain the respect for the military that had been lost during the Vietnam era. He tapped a strain of the public mood that wanted a strong, vibrant, and efficient military and that no longer regarded "patriotism" as a dirty word. Indeed, Reagan went out of his way to play up the American armed forces, to try to make them something that every American would adulate and admire. And the military appreciated his efforts.

On the other hand, the Chiefs found Reagan difficult to work with. His lack of precision, regardless of whether the subject was operational orders or the military budget, created havoc in the Pentagon. As a highly structured and highly bureaucratized organization, the military places a high value on predictability and clear, concise instructions—neither of which were high on Reagan's list of priorities. The White House's willingness to put tremendous amounts of money into the American military was greatly appreciated, but the Chiefs would have preferred to have the funding allocated in a systematic, structured fashion.

The Chiefs and Caspar Weinberger

Given Reagan's tendency to delegate authority, the Chiefs understood from the beginning of the Reagan administration that their key contact would be the newly named secretary of defense: Caspar Weinberger, the former head of the Office of Management and Budget. Unfortunately, Weinberger's first meeting with the Chiefs appears to have been nothing short of a catastrophe.[7] He first met with the Chiefs in the tank on January 15, 1981. Like Secretary Laird, Weinberger shook the hands of all the Chiefs and their deputies. He then invited them to be full partners in the new Reagan administration, observing that it was his hope that the JCS and his office would "find some common ground on the important issues that face the nation." He also informed the Chiefs that "you will have full access to my office and to the president."

In response, General Jones, the chairman of the Joint Chiefs, noted diplomatically that he was certain that the Chiefs looked forward to the opportunity

President Reagan with senior military officers. Secretary of Defense Caspar Weinberger is on the president's left, and General David Jones, chairman of the Joint Chiefs of Staff, is on the president's right. (Ronald Reagan Library)

to work with Reagan. They were concerned how the new administration would react to them after they had served the Carter administration. During his tenure, the JCS had endorsed the SALT II treaty and approved his decision to cancel the B-1 bomber; Reagan, who had opposed both policies, had castigated the Carter administration for the decisions. " 'In a lot of ways we were lame ducks,' [General] Meyer later reflected. 'We had been there under Carter. So this was a new start. We didn't know what to expect.' "

Once the Chiefs had finished with their presentation, everyone expected the meeting to end. However, Weinberger surprised the Chiefs by going into a detailed explanation of the Reagan administration's defense policies. He said that the administration was "committed to 'defense growth' and 'more defense dollars' to meet 'the growing menace of Soviet expansion.' " He then told the Chiefs that one of their first tasks was to "close the window of vulnerability," arguing that unless the United States began a major defense buildup—especially of nuclear weapons—Washington would find itself "in grave peril."

Although most observers doubt that Jones really believed the Reagan administration's rhetoric about a "window of vulnerability," he thanked the secretary for his comments. In any case, protocol, as well as bureaucratic politics, demanded that he show deference to the secretary, who would bring additional, badly needed resources to the Pentagon. Toward this end, Jones noted that the Chiefs were in favor of a number of key initiatives such as the B-1, the navy's Trident program, and an improvement in the army's readiness. Just before the Chiefs adjourned the meeting, Weinberger made a suggestion. "Since we are required to remedy our vulnerability in the strategic area, . . . I suggest we resolve the MX basing debate and vulnerability of the rest of our ICBM force here and now." The Chiefs and their deputies were stunned. One does not normally solve an incredibly complex question such as a basing mode for the MX—one that had been debated for four years under Jimmy Carter—in a few minutes. Weinberger suggested that the United States should put the MX missiles on "ships." "The room was dead silent. The Air Force's Lew Allen had turned to face Jones, his hand over his mouth, his eyebrows up, questioning. . . . No one seemed more surprised than CNO Hayward, who looked straight at Weinberger in apparent disbelief, his jaw slack." Weinberger broke the silence by asking if anyone at the table supported his great idea. The room stayed silent. "Weinberger was sitting there looking as if he had just proposed something that would save America from the communist hordes, and the silence seemed to indicate that they all agreed with him." All eyes were focused on General Jones. In what must go down as one of the more courageous (or foolish) acts of Jones's career, he "looked straight at Weinberger and said, 'Well, I think this is the kind of idea that *Reader's Digest* would like.' " Everyone was stunned. "Weinberger stared at Jones, his anger apparent. 'That happens to be where I get my medical advice,' " he said, and got up and stomped out of the room.

The episode foreshadowed how little respect the Chiefs would have for Weinberger on military issues. They appreciated his support on topics such as withdrawing the Marines from Lebanon, but no one in his or her right mind would consider putting an MX on a navy ship. The missile would probably sink the ship; besides, the navy already had missiles on its submarines. Another consequence of the meeting was that Weinberger left the tank with a deep and abiding dislike of Jones. " 'Weinberger just hated Jones,' Meyer later recalled. 'Really despised him.'. . . The personal animosity between Weinberger and Jones soon became the talk of the Pentagon. 'Jones just thought Weinberger was as crazy as you could get and tried at every turn to add some rationality to Weinberger's proposals.' "[8] In his memoirs Weinberger greatly understated the nature of his relationship with Jones, noting simply that "I recommended that he be allowed to serve out his term, and the president agreed. I thought it might appear that we were politicizing this most important position in our military if the new president changed chairman as his first act. Jones was an able man, but I never felt that he was quite as comfortable with me as his successors were."[9] Indeed, the secretary of defense would try unsuccessfully on more than one occasion to have Jones fired (Jones would be permitted to finish up his four years as chairman [in addition to four years as chief of staff of the air force]). For his part, Jones realized that however little Weinberger understood about the military, he was a genius when it came to finding sacks of money. Weinberger and Jones would eventually clash over military reform; in a somewhat ironic twist, Weinberger completely opposed the reform, while Jones played a critical role in shepherding it through Congress.

Like the president, Weinberger believed in delegating authority. Although he would continue to be responsible for obtaining funding, the secretary felt that the Chiefs ought to play a more prominent role in spending the money: "I also believed that the Joint Chiefs of Staff, the officers who had risen to the top of their very difficult professions, should have a larger role in budgeting (including planning budgets) and in selecting the weapons and organizing the training necessary to carry out strategies and policies determined as a result of *joint* efforts by the Secretary of Defense, the Chiefs and others."[10] Although Weinberger probably believed that he had expanded the Chiefs' role in purchasing weapons, the Chiefs felt that they ended up having very little autonomy in this critical area. They could suggest weapons systems, but the new process would prove to be unsatisfactory to them.

Reagan's Defense Policy

In most political systems, including the American, the military waits until the civilian government agrees upon a particular strategy or doctrine and then uses that as its guidance to build the necessary force structure. Depending on the doctrine chosen by the government, the military may place greater emphasis on the ability to fight a nuclear war or a conventional war. Such radically different kinds of wars require different kinds of weapons systems, training, and troops. Traditionally, in the United States, the Chiefs go to the secretary, the president, and Congress with proposals for the new weapons systems that will meet the requirements of the administration's doctrine. Prior to the Reagan administration, for example, the Nixon administration promulgated a strategy in which the Pentagon was required to have the capability to fight one and a half wars. In practice, this meant being able to defeat the Soviets in Europe while fighting a lesser war elsewhere. Working with this requirement, the Pentagon proceeded to create the appropriate mix of weapons.

The Reagan administration had a different approach. Reagan's view of the world was one in which the United States lagged far behind the Soviets. Believing that reversing this situation was of vital importance, he wrote,

> Pentagon leaders told me appalling stories of how the Soviets were gaining on us militarily, both in nuclear and conventional forces; they were spending fifty percent more each year on weapons than we were; meanwhile in our armed forces, the paychecks were so small that some married enlisted men and women were eligible for welfare benefits; many military personnel were so ashamed of being in the service that as soon as they left their posts, they put on civilian clothes.[11]

The Chiefs concurred. On February 5, 1981, Adm. Thomas Hayward, testifying before the Senate Armed Services Committee, stated that " 'the trends of the last decade have led us to this point where even a slim margin of superiority' over Soviet forces 'has to be set aside. . . . Your country is overexposed and underinsured. Our margin of comfort is totally gone.' "[12]

The new administration wanted not only to increase the domestic appeal of the military, but, more important, to change American strategy so that the United States would have clear military superiority over the Soviet Union. Reagan said of the Chiefs, "I . . . asked them to tell me what new weapons they needed to achieve military superiority over our potential enemies. I knew reversing the effects of years of neglect would be expensive and difficult. But during the campaign the people of America had told me nothing mattered more to them more than national security."[13] Strangely enough, members of Congress weren't the only ones who reacted with concern to the president's drive for military superiority: General Jones himself questioned it in a roundabout manner.

> "I have never used the word inferiority. That is too absolute in the implication that some Soviet advantages can be meaningful. They can be meaningful only if we allow them to be so . . . if we feel inferior . . . if we feel in a crisis that they could intimidate us. I have no doubt that we can deter the Soviets," he continued. "You can hold all kind of war games that show some difference in outcome but in any calculation there is some unprecedented devastation on both sides."[14]

What is interesting about Jones's comment is his rejection not only of the term "superiority," but of the belief that a country could fight and win (in any meaningful sense) a nuclear war without suffering terribly.

Reagan and Weinberger, however, were convinced that a nuclear war could be fought to a successful conclusion. In addition, they believed that it was critical that American armed forces be able to fight as many wars in as many parts of the world as necessary. As one writer explained, "They seek to replace it [the one and a half war] by a giant 'one-war' strategy, to be conducted against the Soviet Union on a series of widely separated fronts on and along the vast Eurasian land mass. The Soviet Union is to be deliberately and concurrently engaged not only in Europe but also in the Persian Gulf, Northwest Asia, and on the high seas."[15] A careful examination would reveal that the new administration's policy had "little to do with military strategies or concepts, but rather with sheer quantities," thus leading one observer to quip that "we've got a national military strategy called M-O-R-E."[16] Weinberger wanted a more combat-ready army, the B-1, and a six-hundred-ship navy, promises Reagan had made in his campaign for the presidency, but that was only the beginning. To really carry out the president's strategy, the military would need more of everything.

From the military's point of view, Reagan was unrealistic when he expected that the armed services could successfully address the kind of universal threat he perceived. As one journalist noted, even though the administration planned to greatly increase the resources it provided to the military, they would still fall far short of those the military would need to deal with such a threat. "These increases, while welcome and long overdue, fall far short of satisfying the ambitious military objectives of the new strategy. The three carrier battle groups to be added to the present 12-group fleet and the expansion of land-based tactical airpower from 36 to 40 wings equivalents are but drops in the bucket of requirements for a prolonged, multi-front war with the Soviet Union."[17]

Paying for the Buildup

While the entire administration and most citizens seemed to agree that the military had been neglected and was in need of modernizing, some questioned how much was enough. When David Stockman, who was the director of the Office of Management and the Budget, attempted to address the question, he quickly learned that the only answer was more. Stockman recalled attending a budget meeting that did not include a JCS representative. According to his account, Weinberger commented,

> "Defense, . . . is not a budget issue. You spend what you need." The only problem was there was no tribunal of wise men who could objectively

> and precisely quantify the "need." In fact, DOD arrived at the conclusion that it needed a quarter of a trillion dollars per year for defense by means of a subjective and approximate process. The theory was that you started at the top by defining broad national security objectives such as deterring a nuclear attack. Then as you moved down the pyramid, you determined missions and capabilities, then force structure, weapons, and resources, then procurement rates and operating tempos. At the bottom of the pyramid was a vast array of clerks counting up how many repair kits, screwdrivers, and paper cup dispensers would be needed to deter a Russian first strike.[18]

In reality, Stockman was playing with a very weak hand. The president's personal prestige was at stake because of his public show of being deeply committed to a significant increase in defense spending. The budget was Stockman's problem—defense was sacrosanct.

How much was Weinberger requesting? Within two months of his arrival at the Pentagon, he asked that the budget for fiscal years 1981 and 1982 be immediately increased by $32.6 billion over Carter's previous request; $6.8 billion of the increase would be applied to FY 1981, with the remainder allocated to the FY 1982 budget.[19] Thereafter, the military budget was slated to increase at the rate of 7 percent per year. The Reagan administration was requesting an increase of $1.3 trillion from 1981 to 1986.[20]

The budgetary explosion created a number of problems, the first of which stemmed from the federal government's accounting methods. The government pays part of the cost of a weapon the first year, another the second, and sometimes pays the largest part only three or four years down the road. As Rick Smith explained, "The $7.3 billion set aside in 1983 for two aircraft carriers will not be entirely spent until 1991. In effect, Congress gives the Pentagon a huge line of credit every year to spend over several years." Smith further noted, "That backlog had reached the enormous sum of $270 billion in early 1987, assuring that no downturn in actual spending would occur until the 1990s."[21] The following year, budget analysts warned, "Today's high-technology weapons are so expensive that President Bush will not have enough money to operate them and still pay for the all the new ones that President Reagan has ordered but not paid for."[22] This was the so-called "bow wave" effect—the need to pay bills for weapons already on order but not yet paid for.

Another problem was that Weinberger and Reagan were primarily interested in acquiring expensive new weapons, whose purchase normally accounts for only part of the military budget. Behind every bow wave lies a "stern wave"—the rising costs involved in operating and maintaining the new weapons systems—which was also getting out of hand. These less-glamorous expenditures, such as operations and maintenance, training, fuel, and sustainability, were equally important, yet these parts of the budget received short shrift. The percentage of the military budget spent on weapons acquisition increased from 26 percent in 1981 to 38 percent in 1987, which seriously hampered the military's ability to operate. As early in Reagan's tenure as 1982, the *Washington Post* noted

> a growing body of evidence in both public and secret reports that the Pentagon has not set aside enough money in Reagan's five-year defense plan to operate and repair all the weapons that have been ordered. The Congressional Budget Office estimated that it will cost 36 percent more to operate the army's new M1 tank than the M60A3 it will replace. Analysts figured the M1 would burn four gallons of fuel every mile, compared with two for the M60A3, and that mechanics will just throw away faulty components on the M1 rather than fix them.[23]

The Chiefs and Military Spending

The Chiefs viewed the increased funding as a mixed blessing. Weinberger's request that they tell him how much they needed was well received; Colin Powell remembered, "This was Christmas in February. This was tennis without a net. The chiefs began submitting wish lists. The requests initially totaled approximately a 9 percent real increase in defense spending."[24] For the first time in the history of the JCS, the Chiefs could argue for a spending increase without facing opposition from either Congress or the executive. Consequently, the military could now replace many of its outdated weapons systems, which it had been unable to upgrade because of the antimilitary attitude of the post–Vietnam era. And the military went on a buying spree. During the first two years of the Reagan administration, the services' requests were "packed with everything you can think of."[25]

In spite of this largesse, some in the military voiced caution. General Jones, for example, worried that the massive buildup would only be temporary. He would have been much happier to have had a smaller, but predictable increase in the defense budget over a longer period of time. Indeed, Jones found himself in the rather odd position of being forced to defend " 'real growth' instead of 'getting roller-coasted' by the unwieldy outlays proposed by Weinberger."[26] Little or no conceptual framework lay behind this massive buildup, which was simply a case of enormous purchases of new and especially high-cost items with little consideration of their impact on the country's overall military structure and readiness.

In fact, Jones's concern was soon validated. By fiscal 1983, the military budget had increased 25 percent above inflation. Within five years, the Pentagon's budget would double. But because the vast majority of money was being spent on new weapons, the military increasingly found itself facing greater difficulties; for example, by 1984, "after . . . $632 billion of the Reagan military buildup, there are 25 percent fewer Army units certified as ready for combat than there were in 1980." And the problem was not limited to the army. Gen. Richard L. Lawson, deputy commander in chief of the European Command, told Congress in 1985, "Battalion field training days, aircraft flying hours and ship steaming time are well below the level where we can feel confident. . . . Some munition stocks, most notably air-to-air missiles, naval munitions and specialized, high-technology munitions are well below our required stockage, to the point where they could be classified as 'war stoppers.' "[27]

By 1985, it was clear that the Pentagon's budgetary problems were becoming very serious. The danger that General Jones and others on the JCS had warned of had come to pass. Senator Sam Nunn, a man who was sensitive to the JCS and military needs, was becoming exasperated with Weinberger. Arguing that "we're trying to force the Pentagon to come to grips with budget realities," Nunn stated that "there is not enough money in sight to complete the '$150 billion to $200 billion in new starts' on the weapons programs that Congress had already approved, much less take on new ones."[28] Furthermore, although Weinberger's confrontational approach with Congress may have worked at the beginning of Reagan's first term, when there was a consensus on the Hill and in the country in general about the need for a military buildup, as time passed, members of Congress increasingly became irritated with Weinberger's refusal to compromise. After all, Congress, not Reagan and Weinberger, controlled the Pentagon's purse strings.

Rationalizing the Military Budget

By 1984 something had to be done. The government's coffers didn't hold enough money to pay for both the military buildup and the weapons systems that had already been ordered but not yet paid for. Even Republicans on the Hill were worried. They believed they would be lucky if they could "hold the rate of buildup to 3 or 4 percent annually after inflation, much slower than in Reagan's first term when the Defense Department won an average annual increase of 9 percent."[29] Weinberger had been very successful in raising money for the Pentagon: when he left office after seven years, he could boast that under his leadership the defense budget had increased "from $180.7 billion in fiscal 1982 to $274 billion in fiscal 1987."[30] By resigning as secretary of defense just in the nick of time, Weinberger avoided the consequences of his spending spree.

Cleaning up the budgetary mess fell to Frank Carlucci, who took over as secretary of defense in 1987. He recognized Congress's concern over the military budget, and he understood that he had no alternative but to abandon Weinberger's confrontational approach to the Hill. In contrast to Weinberger, who tried to save money by slowing production rates and stretching weapons programs, Carlucci pushed for a cut in the rate of budgetary growth. Indeed, when he went before Congress in February 1988, Carlucci presented a budget that called for only a 2-percent real increase in defense spending.[31] Where Weinberger had planned to request a $332 billion budget, Carlucci agreed to a $299 billion budget. Ultimately, Congress passed a $300 billion budget packed with $4.3 billion worth of pork.

By the time the Reagan administration's efforts to boost military strength finally ended, the Pentagon believed that the president had been only partially helpful. The Chiefs were happy to have the MX, the B-1, the Trident, and the new carriers. Indeed, William Crowe Jr., who took over from General Vessey as chairman of the JCS on October 1, 1985, and inherited the problems created by the spending spree of the early Reagan years, argued that the military was wise to spend the money during the early years of the administration, even if part of it was spent unwisely.

> The munificent military budgets of Reagan's first years apparently precipitated a tremendous internal debate in the Defense Department. It was the time of milk and honey; more money was available than Defense could spend wisely. The question was: Should we spend it anyway even if not wisely, knowing that in five years we won't have it? And the decision was deliberately made—Yes! Spend everything we can for just as long as we can get it. So they did spend it, and not all of it wisely either. But they knew from their bureaucratic experience that five years later it would not be there, and sure enough they were right. It wasn't. In retrospect it is difficult to criticize the decision.[32]

But, as noted above, many living in the very ordered military environment recognized early on that the largesse that Reagan was piling on the armed forces would cause them problems in the end. A Marine general summarized the problem:

> "If you could tell me tomorrow" what the Corps would get over the next three to five years "and leave me alone, I could restructure inside and get you a better program," said Lt. Gen. Charles H. Pitman, chief of Marine aviation. "If you don't do that, I've got to fight for everything. If we could go to a three-to-five year [budget] program that meant something, then these contractors could quit sending their guys over to see me. Somebody has to take charge—set goals and make decisions."[33]

As a result, the military's financial problems were greater when Reagan left than they were when he arrived. To quote one analyst at the Defense Department, "We're in for creeping embarrassment, just like the 1970s. It's already happening. The Army is smaller than when Reagan came in, the Navy has had to retire ships and the Air Force has fewer air wings." And to make matters worse, military preparedness had also declined. In fact, it was beginning to look like the entire military budget would be needed just to keep the weapons systems operational.[34] Reagan's legacy in military finances would be a mixed one.

LEBANON

If there ever was a case in which the military argued against being sent to war, it was the deployment of Marines to Lebanon. The Pentagon, joined by Weinberger, opposed the operation from the beginning, doing everything it could within the parameters of military obedience to convince Reagan that the mission was a bad idea.

Why Lebanon?

In June 1982 the Israelis invaded Lebanon in an effort to drive out Palestine Liberation Organization (PLO) terrorists. The PLO was trapped, so the United Nations raised the question of evacuating them. The Israelis refused to permit UN involvement, so the United States, France, and Italy agreed to form a multinational force (MNF) to "interpose itself between the warring factions and to see to the safe evacuation of Arafat's fighters."[35] At the same time, Reagan announced that Marines were being sent to Lebanon to serve as a buffer between the Israeli Defense Forces (IDF) and the PLO. They also were expected to protect Palestinian civilians in the refugee camps.

Secretary Weinberger and the Chiefs strongly opposed the operation. General Vessey talked at length about the operation, especially about the rules of engagement, with the president. Reagan assured Vessey that he would not permit the Marines to be caught in a PLO-Israeli crossfire. "But even more important, Reagan promised the JCS that the Marine unit would only be in Beirut as long as it took to carry out its mission—in any event, no longer than thirty days."[36] Vessey and Weinberger continued to oppose the operation, but they were "overruled by Reagan, who was repulsed by Israeli use of cluster bombs to clear Beirut of obstructions, such as Palestinian women and children."[37]

Having come ashore on August 25, 1982, the Marines presided over the departure of the PLO, which took seven days. "By September 1, the JCS had begun to relax. The Marines were not being subjected to the crossfire that everyone had feared; in fact, they were actually welcomed by PLO civilians and Shiite Militia as neutral liberators, the only troops that stood between the PLO and their traditional enemies."[38] The JCS then began to push the White House to withdraw the Marines, as their job was completed. The president agreed and announced that they would leave; on September 10 they began to redeploy to their ships. However, on September 14, Lebanon's president was assassinated. The IDF immediately moved into West Beirut to subdue the Shiite militia, and then on September 16 and 17 seven hundred Palestinian refugees at the camps of Sabra and Shatilla were massacred by Lebanese Christian militiamen while Israeli forces not only stood by but helped the attackers by sending up flares.[39]

President Amin Gemayel immediately requested the reconstitution of the MNF and asked that it remain in Lebanon until the Lebanese Armed Forces (LAF) could take over the security of the capital. Not surprisingly, both Weinberger and the Chiefs opposed sending in the Marines yet again. Weinberger

> still objected, of course, very strongly, because this MNF would not have any mission that could be defined. Its objectives were stated in the fuzziest possible terms, and then later, when that objective was "clarified," the newly defined objective was demonstratively unobtainable. The Joint Chiefs were also strongly opposed to the reentry of a multinational force, because without a clearly defined objective, determining the proper size and armament and rules of engagement for such a force is difficult at best.[40]

Secretary of State George Shultz, who for many years had a conflict-ridden relationship with Weinberger, argued in his memoirs that the secretary of defense was wrong to argue that the Marines needed a clearer definition of their mission. "I said the mission was defined—help the Lebanese get control of and stabilize their situation." Adm. James Watkins, who was the acting JCS chairman at the time, stated that the U.S. contingent would need about 5,000 men. According to Schultz Weinberger maintained that the military would need even more: a division (some 16,000–20,000 troops). Schultz accused the military of being "nervous" while the president was calm. Indeed, Schultz maintained that he wanted to be sure Weinberger was present when the president made a decision so he would have no choice but to carry it out.

> We went back to the President. I again insisted that Cap be present so that he would hear the president's decision firsthand. The president was decisive: the United States would participate in the return of the multinational force to Beirut at the invitation of the government of Lebanon. The president felt that the United States must contribute to a visible, definite, constructive, international effort to help the central government of Lebanon begin to regain control over its own country.[41]

Behind the Chiefs' opposition lay what could be called the "Vietnam-Never-Again Syndrome." To quote Admiral Crowe, "Anytime anyone has proposed the use of force, Vietnam was right there, in the middle of the table. A lot of questions were asked: Why are we doing this? What are the objectives? And most important of all, will the American people support this in a sustained fashion?"[42] Having been burned badly by being forced to fight an open-ended, undefined war in Vietnam, the brass did not want to be put in a similar situation again. The Chiefs' stance was firm, "but at the end of their fifth day of deliberation, the JCS members began to doubt that their opposition would change the president's mind." Vessey decided that because the president was firm in his intention to send in the Marines, the JCS should support his decision, in spite of their clear misgivings.[43] The Marines went ashore again on September 29, 1982. Unfortunately, as in Vietnam, the time and circumstances of their eventual withdrawal were left undecided.

The Second MNF Force

As the premier service for carrying out amphibious operations, the Marines were proud to have been chosen for the job. They had a long tradition of working closely with the navy, which provided logistics, communications, and other services; in addition, unlike the army, the Marines could put in a battalion-sized force immediately, not after a long buildup.

But the Lebanon operation was unlike any normally carried out by the Marines, who were trained to actively and aggressively engage the enemy by hitting the beach and not going on the defensive unless absolutely necessary, and then only as long as it took to reverse the situation and attack. Furthermore, the MNF's sole task was to interpose itself between other forces, but it was not provided with sufficient arms to defend itself against a possible attack. Weinberger characterized the lightly armed force as being "quite insufficient in numbers or configuration to deal militarily with either the Israelis or the Syrians, and certainly not with all of the factional militias of Christians and Moslems who fought each other with great ferocity and had been doing so for many years. Indeed, the second MNF was not designed or intended to deal militarily with *any* other force."[44] Finally, the airport where the Marines had been deployed was indefensible: the surrounding hills were held by potential attackers. And as one of the Marines noted, determining just who the attackers were was very difficult: "The only time you return fire is when you have a clear shot at the bastard, and then make damn sure you aren't going to hit an innocent bystander. Just because you see a weapon is no reason to fire. Hell, every ten year old and up over there walks around with a fucking Uzi machine gun hanging from his shoulder."[45] The situation was hopeless.

In March 1983 the Marines took their first casualty. General Meyer expressed the Chiefs' sense of frustration in dealing with Beirut, reflecting that "the whole thing was just a disaster. . . . It just kept getting worse and worse. By April, I think it was, I knew we were in real trouble."[46] On April 10 the situation worsened considerably as a terrorist bomb destroyed the U.S. Embassy in Beirut. Everyone now understood that Beirut was a very dangerous place.

In an effort to move Lebanon in a more peaceful direction, Reagan held a televised news conference on May 17, the same day that an American-sponsored accord normalizing diplomatic relations between Jerusalem and Beirut was announced. In the process of answering questions, Reagan reaffirmed the American commitment to Beirut: "The MNF went there to help the new [*sic*] government of Lebanon maintain order until it can organize its military and its policy to assume control of its borders and its own internal security." From the Marines' perspective, the president had just changed their mission. Now they were to remain in Lebanon not just as a symbol of American solidarity with the country, but "to take an active role in policing borders and *providing for internal security*."[47] The Lebanese public perceived that the Marines were now in their nation to protect a government that was besieged. The Americans had chosen sides.

The Marines at the airport were reinforced with a mortar unit and eventually some artillery, but the fact was that they were defenseless, not a good position to be in at a time when they were no longer peacekeepers in the normal sense of the term. They increasingly found themselves under fire from various factions, and as Weinberger never tired of pointing out, "[W]e did not, and could not, . . . equip or authorize our Marines to take the kind of normal responsive actions Marines are trained to do to protect themselves in combat. That would include seizing and holding high ground around their basic position and patrolling aggressively to insure that the airport was not only occupied but was fully secured." In his memoirs, the secretary of defense referred to the Marines at Beirut International Airport as a "bull's-eye."[48]

On August 25 Reagan was sent a memo signed by both Weinberger and the JCS arguing that the United States should pull out of Beirut. It is worth noting that the relationship between Weinberger and Schultz continued to be bad. In addition, Robert McFarlane, himself a former Marine and a man who played a major role in creating and implementing Lebanon policy, found himself at loggerheads with Weinberger. So poor was the situation that Weinberger accused the NSC of trying to get the United States into a war. He claimed that the council did not care about the safety of U.S. troops and that its actions reminded him of the old joke, "Let's you and him fight this out."[49] Indeed, Weinberger never tired of pointing out that the Marines were not structured to carry out the mission assigned to them.

Unfortunately for the Marines, the president worried that the rest of the world would see a withdrawal as a sign of weakness, so he decided to keep them in Beirut. Even worse, he reiterated his intention to keep them in a peacekeeping role, not a military role. The latter would have changed their function and rules of engagement by providing them with the kind of weapons and operational latitude they needed to protect themselves. Instead, the Marines were being increasingly harassed by shelling and sniper fire. Consequently, a very fateful decision was made to billet them in the only concrete-reinforced building at the airport in the hopes that the structure would protect them from sniper fire and shrapnel.

By the end of August, the Marines were being attacked and killed. Two died from mortar fire on August 29, and four others were killed by attacks on September 3 and October 16. The Marines became increasingly frustrated with the strict rules that controlled their behavior (e.g., fire only if fired upon). In *Peacekeepers at War*, author Michael Petit captured the tense mood in dialogue between a private and his sergeant over a decision to respond to incoming fire.

> "The Cobras have been launched, and it looks like the colonel is going to authorize the battery to fire live rounds."
>
> "About goddamn time," Chase sneered.

"That's enough," Jacobs said. "The colonel's in a tough political position."

"Fuck politics," Chase practically screamed. "I'm sick of this political trash. We're the ones who are sitting ducks, not the goddamn politicians in Washington."[50]

On September 11, the president authorized American warships to bombard forces attacking Lebanese army positions at Suq-al-Gharb. Believing that such decisions were best made by the person on the spot, the JCS delegated the authority to request fire support to the Marine commander in Lebanon, Col. Tim Geraghty. Geraghty was only too aware of the dangers his men faced if he requested fire support. Robert McFarlane, who was in Lebanon at the time, tried to convince Geraghty to request naval gunfire, but the colonel refused. "Tim Geraghty was quite simply concerned that the MAU [Marine Amphibious Unit] would be ground to dust by Druse artillery if warships at the MAU's disposal attempted to destroy Druse positions overlooking Suq-al-Gharb."[51] Geraghty was not about to place his own troops in an even worse position than the one in which they already found themselves. One week later, however, he relented, ordering gunfire from three American warships, which "expended a total of 338 rounds."[52]

At an October 18 NSC meeting on Lebanon, Weinberger, acting on behalf of himself and the JCS, asked that the Marines be immediately withdrawn and placed aboard the American ships lying offshore. With the information that was available to the military and the CIA pointing to an increased terrorist threat, "Weinberger argued that the military situation on the ground in Beirut had become untenable in the face of the administration's continuing inability to state a clear or cogent foreign-policy goal with respect to Lebanon."[53] In the end, others attending the meeting asked Weinberger during a break to drop the idea, which he did. As a consequence, Reagan was spared the need to decide whether to withdraw the troops or keep them in Lebanon.

The Bombing of the Barracks

Larry Speakes, the White House press spokesman, was probably right when he stated that Sunday, October 23, "turned out to be perhaps the worst day of the entire Reagan administration."[54] At 0622 that day, a large Mercedes truck rumbled down Beirut's main airport highway and turned into the big, concrete-reinforced building that housed the Marine battalion's headquarters and barracks. Eight seconds later, the suicide bomber set off five thousand pounds of high explosives. "The headquarters folded up like a house of cards, killing more than 225 Marines," a number that rose to 241 within a week.[55] It was one of the single worst disasters ever suffered by the U.S. military.

General Vessey immediately dispatched General P. X. Kelly, the Marine commandant, to Lebanon to investigate the situation and report back. He then reviewed what had happened at an NSC meeting and spoke about what kinds of forces were available to retaliate if the president decided to take that option. Perry reported that Weinberger "sat through the briefing without comment. He didn't need to tell any of those who supported the deployment that he had been adamantly against it; his silence was his testimony." Reagan "was stunned."[56]

The Pentagon opposed retaliation, but the White House felt differently. According to McFarlane, Reagan claimed that "this is an obvious attempt to run us out of Lebanon." He further stated his desire to retaliate. However, with very vulnerable Marines still in Beirut, the military believed that retaliation would only exacerbate the situation. Pentagon opposition notwithstanding, the Chiefs were ordered to "submit options for overt military retaliation against identifiable sources of terrorist activity against our forces."[57] Five days later Reagan issued NSDD (National Security Decision Directive) 111, which expanded the rules of engagement for the Marines. According to McFarlane, who had become the new NSC advisor, the Pentagon initially refused to carry out the president's order.

Having spoken with the president, McFarlane claimed that Weinberger told him he "had a request [to strike], . . . but I denied it." Weinberger listed a number of reasons why he denied it: he didn't want to work with the French, and he feared that a number of things could go wrong if the United States retaliated. The angered McFarlane later wrote, "The fact was that a presidential decision had been made and an order given and that should have been that."[58] He reportedly raised the issue with the president, who referred to Weinberger's inaction as "disappointing" but passed on the opportunity to call the secretary of defense on the carpet.

The situation was similarly tumultuous at the Pentagon. Some army officers were forced to defend Vessey against navy officers who were upset by his willingness to send the Marines into Beirut. They believed that he should have continued to oppose the deployment regardless of what the president wanted. They also felt that the whole operation to retrieve the dead and wounded from the barracks had been mismanaged. The decision to place sixteen of the most critically wounded Marines on an air force C-130 bound for Germany stunned everyone. Instead of being taken to a navy hospital in Naples, which was much closer, the men were sent to an air force base in Wiesbaden, thereby ensuring that the air force would share in the glory of the rescue.[59]

To investigate the disaster at the airport in Lebanon, Weinberger formed a commission, which studied the issue and released its findings on December 20, 1983. The commission, headed by Adm. Robert J. Long, a former CINCPAC, concluded that the Marines' rules of engagement had contributed to a sense of laxity; that intelligence support given to them was inadequate; that their commanders on the ground had failed to take adequate security actions; and that they were not sufficiently trained, equipped, or organized for the mission they had been assigned in Lebanon. Most importantly, however, from a political-military standpoint, the commission criticized the inadequacy of a word "such as 'presence' as a substitute for a valid and properly equipped military mission, and the nonsensical emphasis on quite inadequate military operations as a tool of influence."[60] Needless to say, the report angered Schultz and McFarlane. The report also called upon Weinberger to discipline a number of officers who should have taken steps to ensure the Marines' safety.

The Department of Defense responded by creating a single set of rules of engagement for all Marines in Lebanon, shortening the chain of command, and giving the European Command (CINCEUR) a role in strengthening security. On December 27, the president stated that the local commanders, "men who had already suffered quite enough" should *not* be disciplined. Reagan himself accepted the blame for what had happened.[61]

Almost everyone involved, including George Schultz, began to realize that keeping the Marines in Lebanon was a dangerous and unnecessary policy. They must be brought home. Finally, in February they pulled out of Lebanon. Schultz complained that the action was taken too hastily and that it embarrassed the United States. "Our troops left in a rush amid ridicule from the French and utter disappointment and despair from the Lebanese. The Italians left as they saw us departing. The French stayed until the end of March."[62] However, the Chiefs saw the matter differently: the Marines were finally out of a situation that the Chiefs had opposed from the very beginning. They had feared that the failure of the White House to listen to their military advice would be disastrous, and they were right.[63]

OPERATION "URGENT FURY"

Washington considered the small island of Grenada to be of significant strategic value. First, several hundred Americans were studying at St. George's University School of Medicine on the island, and second, the Cubans were in the process of building an airport with an unusually long runway. Many believed that the Cubans would use the airstrip to support their insurgent operations in

South America and elsewhere, because it was far larger than would have been necessary to handle flights of tourists and other normal traffic to the island. Third, the Soviets and the Cubans appeared eager to impose a far leftist regime on the politically unstable island. As President Reagan explained, "On the small island of Grenada, at the southern end of the Caribbean chain, the Cubans, with Soviet financing and backing, are in the process of building an airfield with a ten-thousand foot runway. Grenada doesn't even have an air force."[64] Some feared that the tiny country also "would be used to export revolution and to train Caribbean subversives and would be the first of a number of island dominoes to fall."[65]

At 2100 on the evening of October 19, 1983, Prime Minister Maurice Bishop was murdered, "with the assistance of General Hudson Austin, Commander in Chief of the Armed Forces."[66] Austin closed the airport, put the island under a four-day, twenty-four-hour curfew, and warned that anyone seen in public would be shot, thereby preventing U.S. citizens from leaving the island. His actions put the question of an American intervention on the table in Washington. Weinberger asked the JCS to see what courses of action would be available to the United States, should the president decide to use military force. One of the ironies of the resulting Operation Urgent Fury was that as the Pentagon looked around for forces to be used to seize Grenada, its eyes immediately fell on the Marines who were in ships on their way to replace their fellow Marines in the Mediterranean—including Lebanon. The Chiefs also drew upon army battalions and airborne divisions that were on alert at Forts Bragg and Campbell. The JCS plan called for a quick seizure of the airfield at Point Salinas and of the airport at Pearls, which was operational. The American forces would also seize the two campuses of the medical school and rescue the governor-general and other political prisoners on the island.

The day after Bishop was murdered, Weinberger approved Vessey's recommendation that the Marines be sent to replace those in Lebanon and a carrier battle group led by the USS *Independence* be diverted. The planning, which was being done in an unusually short period of time, was based on almost no usable intelligence about Grenada: among the resources that the United States needed but did not have were a CIA station on the island, maps (other than those prepared for tourists), and a photograph of the island less than five months old.[67] As McFarlane put it, CIA director "Bill Casey didn't have much he could tell us. A couple of Navy Seal teams had been sent in to reconnoiter but had not yet reported back. . . . The best estimate, Casey said, was that there were a couple of hundred Cubans on the island, chiefly airport workers, who probably had some military training as members of the Cuban reserve."[68] Carrying out a combined operation involving the various services against a relatively unknown target would not be easy.

On October 21, Vessey told Weinberger that if the president so ordered, he was prepared to go into action on Tuesday, October 25. In the meantime, the Organization of Eastern Caribbean States, a small group of island nations, asked the United States to intervene, a request that was conveyed early on October 22 to the president in Augusta, Georgia, where he was playing golf. Although he feared that an early return to Washington would tip the press off about the imminent U.S. military action in Grenada, he went back to D.C. on October 23, but only because of the attack on the Marine barracks in Lebanon. The president met twice with the Joint Chiefs on October 24. During the morning meeting he asked each Chief for his views on the operation. All agreed that no alternative existed to the use of force, and they "assured the President that the operation would succeed." When they met again with Reagan that evening, Vessey explained the operation to Congress's minority and majority leaders, who had been specially invited. After they left, the president asked General Vessey "what were the critical decision times for executing and for calling off the operation." Vessey responded that if the operation was to proceed as scheduled, he had to call the Pentagon as soon as their meeting was over and say the prearranged codeword. However, Vessey also informed the president that he could stop the invasion as late as a few hours prior to its start. Then Vessey told the president:

> As soon as I send the message to the Pentagon to go ahead, I'm going home to go to bed. We've given this mission to an operational commander. He has the forces that he believes he needs. He knows that he has the full support of the Secretary of Defense and of you . . . and the Joint Chiefs of Staff. If he needs more help, then he'll call for it, but otherwise, there's nothing you or I can do until these troops have landed unless you decide to call it off between then and now. I'm going home to bed and in the morning . . . wait for the first reports to come in. The President replied, "I'm going to do the same thing."[69]

The plan had been assembled in only four days. Adm. William McDonald, the commander in chief of Atlantic Forces, oversaw its execution. He asked that the press be banned in order to keep the operation a secret. Weinberger, believing that the commander should be supported, "accepted and agreed to the task force Commander's request, with the understanding that we would make every effort to get the press in at the end of the first day."[70] More important, in contrast to the operation in Lebanon, the president left the details of the operation completely in the hands of the military.

The overwhelming numbers of troops and weapons possessed by the Americans made the success of the operation a certainty. However, the attack on Grenada would hardly serve as a model for future joint operations. To begin with, four days had not provided enough time to work out all of the details involved in an operation of this kind, especially because all of the services were vying to be part of the operation despite not all having operated together previously. (Devising the hostage rescue operation had taken months, and even then problems arose when it came to operating in a joint environment.) The left hand of the Grenada assault often did not know what the right hand was doing. For example, the JCS had intentionally not informed the head of their logistics section, Vice Adm. William Cowhill, of the upcoming operation until only twenty-two hours prior to H hour, leaving him almost no time to do anything.[71] Not surprisingly, American forces did not have everything they needed when H hour came along.

The services themselves made little effort to work together. For example, Norman Schwarzkopf, then a major general, was pulled from his position as commanding general of the Twenty-fourth Mechanized Infantry Division and sent to serve as deputy to Admiral Metcalf, the operational command of Operation Urgent Fury. His task was to lend the admiral whatever assistance the army could provide. To quote Schwarzkopf,

> I walked into Atlantic Command the following morning, October 24, and felt about as welcome as a case of mumps. Vice Admiral Joseph Metcalf, a wiry, feisty three-star with a sharp New England accent, immediately started peppering me with questions about what I expected to contribute to the operation. Then Admiral Wes McDonald, the commander in chief of Atlantic Command, arrived, and we all went upstairs to the briefing room. . . . Admiral McDonald singled me out. He walked up and said, roughly, "Now, for chrissakes, try to be helpful, would you? We've a tough job to do, and we don't need the Army giving us a hard time."[72]

His was not exactly the kind of welcome that a two-star army general should expect in a joint operation. Another example of pre-invasion service warfare came on the afternoon of October 22, as army and navy staff officers argued bitterly, "trying to determine which service should be responsible for capturing the island."[73] In good bureaucratic fashion, they decided to divide the job by giving half to the army and half to the Marines. When the question arose of which units should be utilized, the army wanted to send in the Delta Force, but the navy argued for the Seals. Once again, the problem was solved by dividing the island in half. Delta would come ashore at Point Salinas, while the Seals would secure a landing zone for the Marines. Ultimately, neither of these units performed well. The Delta team was pinned down by the Cubans while the Seals were swept out to sea. Adding insult to injury, army helicopters could not evacuate wounded soldiers because the pilots did not know how to land on navy ships.[74]

Perhaps the best-known operational problem of the invasion involved communications. Specifically, an army officer was "so frustrated by difficulties in communicating with Navy ships that he used his AT&T Calling Card on an ordinary pay telephone to call his office at Fort Bragg, North Carolina, to relay his plea for fire support to higher headquarters and finally down to the Navy ships a few miles away from him."[75] Although the incident is frequently cited, General Schwarzkopf's description of his efforts to get Marine helicopters to ferry U.S. Army Rangers ashore is even more remarkable and provides a paradigm of how interservice cooperation should *not* work. Schwarzkopf had some U.S. Army Rangers aboard his ship whom he needed to get ashore quickly to help rescue the students. The general approached the Marine colonel in charge of Marine helicopters and asked if he would take the rangers ashore.

> "I'm not going to do that." "What do you mean, I asked?" "We don't fly Army soldiers in Marine helicopters." I looked at him incredulously. "Colonel, you don't understand. We've got a mission, and that mission is to rescue those students *now*. Your Marines are way up in Grenville securing that area, and your helicopters are right here. The way to get the job done is to put Army troops in those helicopters." "If we have to do it, I want to use my Marines. They'll rescue the hostages," he maintained stubbornly. "How long will that take?" He looked me straight in the eye and said, "At least twenty-four hours." "Listen to me very carefully, Colonel. This is a direct order from me, a major general, to you, a colonel, to do something that Admiral Metcalf wants done. If you disobey that order, I'll see to it that you are court-martialed." He agreed to do it.[76]

One could go on and on. For example, although the army and the Marines fought side by side, they did so under separate chains of command, which caused nothing but trouble for the army's coordination of naval gunfire support and for both services' coordination of air support. Indeed, it would be difficult to disagree with General Powell's assessment when he observed that relations between the services were marred by poor communications, fractured command and control, interservice parochialism, and micromanagement from Washington.[77]

Finally, there was the intelligence failure. Major Mark Adkin, a British officer and staff member of the Barbados Defence Force explained,

> Their most unforgivable blunders had been in intelligence: in knowing nothing about the 400 or so students outside True Blue, in having no proper maps, and all this despite Grenada's having been the center of communist activity in the region for over four years. The horrendous failure on the part of the intelligence community, particularly the CIA, meant that the troops were badly briefed, had no tactical information, and were led to believe it would be a walkover.[78]

Faced with such criticism, General Vessey did his best to justify the services' planning and execution of Operation Urgent Fury, arguing,

> The thing has been hashed and rehashed, and criticized, but the fact of the matter is that we had a very short time in which to do it. If we were going to accomplish the objectives, we didn't have the time to rehearse or do the sorts of things that one usually does in preparing for that type of thing.
>
> For that reason, some things didn't go as well as they might have, and we lost a few people that we shouldn't have lost. On the other hand, I would suggest that nobody in the world would have done it in the period that we did it in and as well as we did it.[79]

Vessey was probably right. There wasn't another country that could have pulled off that operation with so little lead time. As had been the case with the hostage rescue mission under Carter, Reagan had stayed completely out of operational matters and left the details to the military professionals. In both cases, however, the military failed: it aborted the first mission and lost more men than it should have in the second. The simple fact was that the Chiefs had *not* learned the lesson pointed out by those who participated in the raid on Tehran. More often than not, Washington does not have the luxury of deferring action for five or six months while the military gets its act together and trains its troops to carry out the desired mission. Thus, increasing concern that the Tehran raid and Grenada invasion were indicative of future joint operations would mandate a greater commitment to joint operations training and interservice cooperation.

MILITARY REFORM

During the final years of the Carter administration, Gen. David Jones argued in favor of military reform and spoke at length about it with Secretary of Defense Harold Brown. Brown told Jones to make whatever changes he believed necessary, but in Jones's mind the changes he made were not sufficient. He believed more radical change was needed.

Jones raised the idea of military reform with Weinberger in 1981, but the new secretary of defense was not only not interested, he was totally opposed. Gen. Edward Meyer, the army chief of staff, claimed that he too raised the issue with Weinberger and unsuccessfully warned him of the costs of opposing it. "I told him that he would lose, that he better get out in front of it because actually it wouldn't hurt him, it would strengthen his position. But he couldn't see that, or wouldn't admit it."[80]

Because of Weinberger's opposition to military reform, Jones bided his time until he was ready to retire. His first public blast at Weinberger and the military structure under Reagan came in a widely read article published in the *Armed Forces Journal International* only a few months before the end of his tenure as chairman. In his article, Jones argued that after four years as a service chief and four as chairman of the Joint Chiefs, he had learned that the chairman "generally has more influence but less control than a Service Chief." In order to strengthen the chairman's position, Jones recommended three changes. First, he called for the chairman to have a deputy; instead of having the chairmanship rotate when the permanent chair was away, the change would provide continuity and keep action items in the hands of the chair or his deputy. Second, he wanted the Joint Staff to work directly for the chairman. As he put it, "When a Service Chief acts on a Service matter he should receive advice from his Service staff and when he acts on a joint matter he should receive his advice from the Joint Staff . . . [as opposed to relying] almost exclusively on their Service staffs in preparing for joint meetings."[81] His third suggestion was to broaden the training, experience, and rewards for officers serving in joint assignments. Believing that the JCS would only be effective in Washington's bureaucratic battles if it had "the best and brightest" officers from the four services, Jones wanted to enhance the desirability of service on the Joint Staff, which traditionally had not been a sought-after assignment, especially within the navy.

General Meyer subsequently authored another article in the same journal. In it, he called for "major surgery" that would construct a body of full-time advisors: a National Military Advisory Council composed of four-star officers who would serve out their term on the council but not return to their services.

"Meyer envisioned that 'this body of military advisers would examine military departments to organize, equip, and prepare their forces for war.' "[82] Although Jones and Meyer advocated slightly different approaches, they both pushed for greater authority and control for the chairman.

The Investigations Subcommittee of the House Armed Services Committee (HASC) heard testimony from forty-three witnesses during the summer of 1982. When Jones testified before the subcommittee, he elaborated on the ideas he presented in his journal article. He maintained that the chairman should be the president's "principal military adviser." The other Chiefs would serve as the chairman's advisors. Then he argued that the chain of command should run through the chairman rather than the JCS. Another proposal suggested that Congress would have the right to ask the Chiefs for their advice on an issue, thereby legitimizing even further the right of the Chiefs to provide Congress with their independent views on topics of interest. In addition, Jones reiterated his suggestion that the Joint Staff should work directly for the chairman and added that any Chief who disagreed with the chairman would have the right to provide his views directly to the secretary of defense.[83]

As one might expect, the navy defended the current arrangement. CNO Thomas B. Hayward argued that the situation was satisfactory and that there was no reason to change the role of the Joint Staff. And he added, "I am deeply offended by the slanderous criticisms which one frequently hears about the Joint Chiefs being an ineffective group of parochial service chiefs who spend most of their time bickering among themselves, horse trading to preserve what is best for their service."[84] One of the other Chiefs, Gen. Lew Allen, provided testimony touting the benefits of transforming the Joint Chiefs. However, Marine Commandant Robert Barrow was even more negative than Hayward. He argued that "the proposal set forth by General Jones would not improve Joint Chiefs of Staff effectiveness. It would do serious harm to the system."[85] Once again Washington faced a two-to-two split on military reform. As in the case of the Revolt of the Admirals, the Marines and navy believed that the army and air force were trying to gain control of naval operations, a science and art that only an officer who had spent many years at sea could master.

Regardless of whether the services welcomed or resisted change, the recent missions in Lebanon and Grenada had shown that the JCS needed to be transformed. Beirut was burdened by a "long, complex, and clumsy" command structure, and Grenada "also suffered from lack of coordination among several layers of command. In fact, command difficulties seemed to surface in every operation we undertook."[86] By 1985 Senator Sam Nunn began drafting a major reorganization plan to be called the Goldwater-Nichols Defense Reorganization Act (Senator Barry Goldwater worked closely with Nunn on the Senate side, and William Nichols was a key member of the House Armed Services Committee). Adm. William Crowe, the JCS chairman at the time, knew he was walking a thin line. He needed the cooperation of the other chiefs to get anything done, and he was well aware of their concerns and the secretary's strong opposition to any changes in the role played by the JCS. Still, he did not think that a policy of stubborn opposition was the wisest approach. The military would have to compromise if it wanted to keep control of the process.

Crowe believed he had managed to convince the secretary on an intellectual level that he would have more influence if he agreed to consider some changes to the system. Ultimately, however, Weinberger couldn't bring himself to work with the Hill. As he had with the budget, he believed that a sign of compromise would be read by the Congress as an indication of weakness.

> "I always through that Weinberger played it very dumbly," said Crowe. "I had some fierce arguments with him over reorganization. I actually thought I had won at one time. My argument in winning was, 'Look, Cap, it's going to happen, and you can march up and down over here and stomp your feet all you want to, but that's counterproductive. You ought to say, 'Yeah, we want it to happen,' and then try and shape it—if you've got some things you feel strongly about—try and shape it, but get on board. And one time he said, 'Okay, I'll do that.' But he didn't mean it. He just resisted."[87]

Weinberger opposed strengthening the chairman's authority because he feared that his own power would decrease as the chairman's increased. Crowe reported that he tried his best to dampen the Chiefs' opposition; whether they liked it or not, Goldwater-Nichols was coming. On June 24, 1986, for example, Crowe invited Nichols to the Pentagon for breakfast with the Chiefs. " 'This is your last chance,' I told the chiefs, 'the last shot we have at changing anything.' In the congenial atmosphere of the breakfast I thought that the chiefs might succeed in at least moderating some of the more egregious elements."[88]

Unfortunately, the breakfast meeting went poorly. The CNO, Adm. James Watkins, began in a moderate manner to list some of his objections to the act. However, as the conversation progressed, Watkins "threw caution to the winds. Finally in an emotional burst he said . . . 'You know, this piece of legislation is so bad it's, it's . . . in some respects it's just un-American.' "[89] Such an outburst was not the best way to influence a congressman who had fought in World War II, lost a leg, and strongly supported the U.S. military. Even though Watkins retired from the navy shortly thereafter, Crowe reported that he spent the next three years apologizing for the CNO's comment to Nichols, who had taken the first opportunity to leave the breakfast meeting.

The new legislation was signed into law on October 1, 1986. The act made the chairman the president's principal advisor, which meant that he could provide his guidance directly to the secretary of defense and the commander in chief. No longer would he be obligated to provide an opinion based on the lowest common denominator among the chiefs. Other changes included the placement of the sixteen hundred Joint Staff personnel under the chairman and the addition of a vice chairman, whose authority over the other Chiefs would ensure critical continuity when the chair was away on a trip or tied up by another issue. In addition, with the memory of Iran, Lebanon, and Grenada in mind, the act also "directed that the chain of command run from the president to the secretary of defense to the combatant commander. The JCS, including the chairman, were explicitly removed."[90] The combatant commanders would now have considerably more flexibility as well as authority in carrying out their missions.

Given the confusion that commanders had faced in places like Lebanon, the bill also "directed the president to submit an annual report on national security strategy. Second, it instructed the JCS chairman to prepare fiscally constrained strategic plans. Third, the act required the defense secretary to provide written policy guidance, including political assumptions, for preparation of review and contingency plans. The fourth provision directed the under secretary of defense for policy to assist the secretary on contingency plans."[91] To address the tendency of some services, like the navy to play down the importance of joint assignments, the act placed greater emphasis on "jointness." For example, by requiring officers to have a joint assignment before making general or flag rank, the act forced the services to pay more attention to such assignments and make them more rewarding to the officer corps as a whole. Requiring such service for flag rank also meant that the services would be forced to send their best officers to joint assignments.

Both the chairman and the combatant commanders emerged from the legislative process in much stronger positions. In addition, the word "purple" (to refer to a joint assignment) was now something that would enhance an officer's career, which, in turn, would improve unified command in time of war. Having a competent naval officer on staff is critical if an army command must put its troops ashore in hostile territory. He or she is in a much better position to communicate with other naval officers (if nothing else, such an individual speaks the same jargon), just as the presence of an air force officer or naval aviator is critical if a joint commander intends to employ air assets in his battle plan. Only officers such as these fully understand the limits and capabilities of these planes.

CONCLUSION

Presidential Leadership Style

Although appreciating his support and encouragement, the military was constantly frustrated by Ronald Reagan's lack of structure or order, particularly in the case of the military budget. He was willing to provide them with the largesse needed to rebuild the armed forces. But the somewhat-incoherent fashion in which the money was allocated meant that a considerable part of it was wasted. During his two terms in office, the Chiefs would have much preferred a budget that was predictable, or at least logical. Ultimately, one could argue that the armed forces were in equally bad shape when Reagan left office as when he entered, even if some of the equipment and weapons were newer.

The Chiefs also were deeply concerned by his willingness to deploy and keep Marines in Lebanon. He did not follow their advice, which they had formulated on the basis both of their continuing fixation on the Vietnam experience and of their worries about the open-ended nature of the mission. Supported by Weinberger, the Chiefs warned the president that the deployment and the particular rules of engagement were an invitation to disaster. Yet Reagan kept the Marines there until the unexpected happened: 241 (including sailors and soldiers) died as the result of a truck bomb.

The military also loved Reagan's willingness to use the presidency as a bully pulpit to restore the armed forces' image. The president was always ready to heap praise on them, which, in their opinion, others had been far too hesitant to do. Because of that, they forgave many of his other mistakes. They never felt that he was on one side and they were on the other, as they had with some of his predecessors. Military leaders believed he supported them even if he didn't always act according to their preferences.

Violations of Service/Military Culture?

The Chiefs found Reagan and his chaotic administration difficult to deal with. Instead of the carefully ordered and well-structured administration that they would have preferred, they found a chaotic world, especially in regard to budgetary issues. Yet the Chiefs always felt that the president listened to them and respected their opinions, unlike Lyndon Johnson. Although Reagan did not take their advice on Lebanon, he listened. He did heed their guidance on Grenada and permitted them to carry out the operation without political interference, despite the problems they encountered. The respect that Reagan showed the military and the pride that he fostered in military service counted for a great deal.

Changes in Service/Military Culture?

The Goldwater-Nichols Act of 1986 initiated a significant change in military culture by formalizing the chairman's relationship to the president: the chair was now the president's principal advisor on military affairs. As a result, a strong, independent chairman would have greater power than in the past. He could, and some would, demand direct access to the president. As long as the president agreed, he would be able to circumvent the secretary of defense if he chose to do so. As far as the Chiefs were concerned, the act sharply limited their authority to areas such as personnel, logistics, and weapons procurement. As far as direct input into military operations, much would depend on the chairman—how far he was prepared to go in permitting them to have a say in operational matters. In addition, the Hill's direct involvement in drafting the act demonstrated Congress's belief that its members played a major role in national security affairs. Senior military officers would be expected to speak candidly when providing congressional testimony. Finally, the act also endeavored to supplant the current service parochialism with "jointness." Although the legislation would not wipe out parochialism, it marked the beginning of a move toward more joint military culture. Such episodes as a Marine colonel telling an army general that he would not fly army personnel on his helicopters would become a thing of the past. By the end of Reagan's presidency, the U.S. military remained a long way from being a homogeneous culture, but the groundwork had been laid.

11
THE MILITARY AND GEORGE BUSH

The fact is there isn't a general in Washington who isn't political, not if he's going to be successful, because that's the nature of our system.
—*General Colin Powell*

Like his predecessors, George Bush faced a number of challenges in dealing with the military. To begin with, the military had very serious financial problems; indeed, if the armed forces had been a civilian organization, it might have filed for Chapter 11 bankruptcy. The United States had not yet paid for the weapons systems that Ronald Reagan ordered, but any justification for a large military budget disappeared with the Soviet Union's collapse. Many Americans, especially liberal Democrats in Congress, wanted to cut the budget to reap the so-called "peace dividend." The nation was also in need of a new military strategy. Almost all of Washington's weapons, training, force structure, and strategy had been aimed at countering the Russians in Europe or the North Koreans in the Far East. If the military was to acquire the necessary funding from a frugal Congress and remain effective, it had to be reformed and restructured.

Bush also faced two major deployments of U.S. forces in combat, first in Panama and then in the Persian Gulf. Thus, with a drawdown already in progress, the Pentagon would be called upon to marshal its forces to fight wars in two different parts of the world. For a number of reasons, the Bush administration successfully met these challenges, helped in no small measure by the fact that the president's leadership style facilitated the kind of relationship the military hoped to have with a commander in chief.

BUSH'S LEADERSHIP STYLE

With a passion for foreign affairs, Bush played a greater role than Reagan did in making decisions related to national security. Although he did not try to micromanage policies, he expected to be consulted throughout the decision-making process on issues of national importance, such as Panama and the Persian Gulf. Bush allowed his subordinates to work out policy recommendations, but he was closely involved in making the key decisions. However, he also listened to his advisors, all of whom served him very well. Brent Scowcroft played an especially important role as Bush's NSC advisor. Indeed, as John Burke noted, "Scowcroft spent more time with Bush than any other senior official in the administration, and reports indicate that he freely expressed his views to the president, but made it clear to Bush when he was doing so."[1] Equally important, Scowcroft worked well with both Secretary of Defense Richard Cheney and Chairman Colin Powell of the JCS. James Baker probably gave him the highest form of praise when he noted that "unlike some of his predecessors in the job, Brent wasn't hampered by a towering ego, and he never peddled a private agenda."[2]

Bush also differed from some of his predecessors in that he believed in collegiality and was able to make the process work. Unlike Reagan, who was ideologically driven, he gathered the facts and then acted in a pragmatic fashion. Bush was conservative, but he was far from an ideological conservative: he was a problem solver, not an ideologue. Indeed, with the exception of the hardline Cheney (especially when it came to the former Soviet Union), the president's national security advisors reflected his views. Perhaps because he was pragmatic, Bush tended to be reactive, which led Fred Greenstein to observe, "In the absence of a larger direction there was a situation-determined quality to the Bush presidency."[3] Consequently, the president may have "missed opportunities" that arose in foreign policy.[4]

Like Eisenhower, Bush also enjoyed the give and take of policy debates and was not confrontational. For example, on the several occasions when Bush and his national security team debated the decision to go to war in the Persian Gulf, he did not get upset when others disagreed with him. As a result, Bush did a much better job than either Carter or Reagan in "keeping his cabinet officers involved in the policy process."[5] When the time came to make a decision, he had heard and weighed all points of view. His goal was to reach a consensus among his advisors. Although he had spent a considerable part of his life in the world of foreign policy and intelligence and was knowledgeable in these fields, he also believed that a policy that had been worked out with others would probably be more thorough and effective. Bush's approach,

President George H. W. Bush meets with national security advisors during Iraq's 1990 invasion of Kuwait. General Colin Powell, chairman of the Joint Chiefs of Staff, is on the president's left, and Secretary of Defense Richard Cheney is on his right. Next to Cheney is General Norman Schwarzkopf, followed by National Security Advisor Brent Scowcroft. (George H. W. Bush Presidential Library)

unlike Reagan's, also had the advantage of providing a clear understanding of what he wanted to those who would execute his orders.

Finally, Bush allowed the military professionals to handle operational matters, justify the military budget, and work out new force structures and military doctrines. He would become involved—for example, in making a speech or meeting with members of Congress—when Cheney or Powell believed it was appropriate. Otherwise, he believed it was their job to implement policy.

Secretary of Defense Cheney

Richard C. Cheney was a familiar face around Washington. As President Ford's chief of staff, he earned the reputation of being highly efficient, while never letting "the power game . . . go to his head," to use James Baker's words.[6] Cheney was subsequently elected to Congress from Wyoming and obtained a well-deserved reputation as a hardline cold warrior. When Bush failed to win Senate confirmation for Texas senator John Tower as his secretary of defense, the president, supported by Scowcroft, Baker, and others, asked Cheney to fill the position. Cheney knew very little about the military. He received an exemption when he was of draft age, first because he was a graduate student and second because he had a child. Coming into the Pentagon, he decided that his first order of business was to establish his credentials and his authority. He was especially upset by a story that Rowland Evans and Robert Novak had just written suggesting that he was not in control of the building. It was up to him to show the military who was in charge; unfortunately, he did so in a very undiplomatic way.

Gen. Larry Welch, a very quiet, laid-back officer, provided him with the opportunity.[7] In his capacity as air force chief of staff, Welch had spent considerable time trying to work out a basing system for the MX—one of Washington's seemingly eternal and intractable problems. After informing Scowcroft, Welch went to the Hill to discuss possible basing plans with members of Congress. On March 23 *Washington Post* correspondent George Wilson called Welch to ask about his activities on the Hill. Welch "confirmed that he had been 'pulsing the system.' "

When Cheney saw the story in the *Post,* he became irate. At a press conference the next day, he claimed that the "freelancing" Welch was not speaking for Defense. When asked if he accepted such behavior, Cheney replied, "No, I am not happy with it, frankly." He continued, "I think it's inappropriate for a uniformed officer to be in a position where he's in fact negotiating an agreement." The secretary said that when he had a chance to speak with Welch, "I'll make known to him my displeasure." But he added the interesting comment that "everybody's entitled to one mistake."

Welch was stunned. One of the military's most sacred laws is that subordinates are publicly praised but privately criticized. The secretary had blasted him in public for doing his duty. Soon after the press conference, Welch walked into Cheney's office. " 'I'm not a freelancer,' Welch said standing before Cheney. 'I never have been a freelancer. I support the administration's position and have worked harder than anybody in this town to make it come out the way the administration wants it to.' " For his part, Cheney limited himself to saying the issue was "closed."

When Admiral Crowe, who would remain chairman of the Joint Chiefs until October 1, heard the story, he too was angry. The secretary had not given him any advance warning, and he knew that this kind of reprimand would hurt the quiet, devoted Welch. Furthermore, "he had been trying to get the chiefs to be more open, more a part of the defense debate. Now this public lashing would drive them even further away from dealing with the Congress and the press."

When Crowe met with Cheney later that day, the secretary said that he hoped "that blast didn't cause you a problem." He also observed that Welch had not denied discussing the issue with Congress. Extremely upset, Crowe spoke frankly:

> "I just plain disagree with you, Mr. Secretary," he began. "It's not right." Crowe explained the seriousness of the matter. Cheney effectively had accused Welch of willful disobedience of an order, which was in violation of a military officer's oath. "You picked the wrong guy. If you want a chief to slap down, I can give you plenty." Welch, Crowe explained, was the most quiet, buttoned-down and inhibited service chief. In the tank. . . . he was a listener. And of all the chiefs he was the most flexible and "purple" [willing to serve jointly].[8]

Crowe continued to rake Cheney over the coals, but the latter said little.

When Colin Powell mentioned this incident in his memoirs, he noted that he knew that Welch had done nothing wrong. The general had cleared his discussions with Will Taft, who was Cheney's deputy at that time, as well as with Scowcroft. Powell added, "I had spent enough time in this game to recognize the move. Cheney had seized an early opportunity to say, I am not afraid of generals or admirals. In this job, I run them."[9] Both Powell and journalist Bob Woodward noted that a group of air force officers told Welch that they had very good connections on the Hill and would get their friends to demand that Cheney apologize. Welch would have none of it. He argued that a fight between the air force and the secretary was one the service would lose, and he warned he would resign if they carried out their threat.

Cheney acknowledged what he had done in a conversation with Congressman Les Aspin. As Bob Woodward told the story, Aspin confronted Cheney, " 'Jesus Christ, Dick, . . . Welch wasn't doing anything like that, and he always made it clear it was your decision.' Cheney responded with a knowing smile. 'It was useful to do that,' he said. 'Okay,' responded Aspin, 'I understand the agenda.' "[10]

Although Cheney had used an unorthodox approach (insofar as military etiquette was concerned) to make his point, he did not permit it to influence his long-term relations with the Chiefs. After all, he had said that every officer had a right one mistake, and since that incident was now history, there was no reason to let it adversely affect his relationships: when Cheney told Crowe that the issue was "closed," he meant it.

Chairman Colin Powell

Gen. Colin Powell was unique. The first African American military officer to rise to the top military position in Washington, he had been wounded twice in Vietnam. Serving there, he had decided that the United States should never become involved in a major conflict without strong domestic and international support. Furthermore, he maintained, "If you are in the situation in which military force regrettably turns out to be the means by which a political problem has to be resolved, and if a commander in chief has made the decision, I think it should be used in a decisive way."[11] The use of a surgical strike to solve a major political problem struck him as an absurd way to fight and no way to win a war. Powell's reluctance to go to war would frustrate his colleagues on the NSC, especially senior officers from the State Department. He believed that the military had had enough of being sent out to "show the flag"; the result in Lebanon was 241 dead American servicemen. If the president ordered the military to go to war, he would faithfully and loyally carry out the order, but he also wanted to be sure that the president understood the ramifications of such an action and that the troops were not thrown into one "diplomatic" maneuver after another, only to find themselves outgunned, outmanned, and, more often than not, dead.

Powell was nothing short of outstanding in the arena of interpersonal relationships. Bush remarked, for example, "When he briefed me, I found there was something about the quiet, efficient way he laid everything out and answered questions that reduced my fears and gave me great confidence. I admired his thoroughness, and above all his concern for his troops—something that came through again and again." Scowcroft was just as effusive in his praise for Powell: "He managed brilliantly the sometimes awkward relationship between the secretary of defense and the chairman in NSC discussions with the president, serving as an NSC principal alongside his own immediate boss."[12]

Powell became chairman of the Joint Chiefs of Staff on October 1, and in spite of Cheney having actively recruited him for the job, their relationship at times would be difficult. Indeed, Cheney informed Powell of his intention to assert increased civilian control over the armed forces.[13] At one point, when the general complained to Cheney about the latter's effort to bypass him and obtain information directly from the services, the secretary answered that he expected to get information from a variety of sources—not just through the JCS chairman. Powell "told him I understood, as long as we both recognized my obligation, as his senior military advisor, to give him my counsel. Matters could get choppy if we were to operate on military advice or information of which I was unaware. 'Fine,' he said, 'as long as we understand each other

. . . Colin.' "[14] But Cheney demonstrated both that he supported Powell and, in almost all cases, permitted him to take the lead when a military issue was being discussed in the NSC and with the president.

The Chiefs found the relationship more complex. The Goldwater-Nichols Act of 1986 had essentially provided the chairman the latitude to do whatever he wanted, with or without their concurrence. Powell chose, however, to work hard to establish and maintain a positive relationship with the Chiefs, and he carefully and accurately transmitted their views to the president. Rick Atkinson called him the "most politically deft chairman since Maxwell Taylor," noting that Powell referred to "the chiefs, chairman, and vice chairman as the 'six brothers.' By common consent Powell became their proxy and mouthpiece."[15] This happened only because the Chiefs placed considerable confidence and trust in Powell. And they would soon witness their chairman playing a very important role as the president tried to decide whether to invade Panama.

PANAMA

Manuel Antonio Noriega, a brutish, crude, and brutal Panamanian Army officer, became president of Panama in 1981 when the country's president, Omar Torrijos, was killed in a plane crash. Head of the country's military, the Guardia Nacional, by 1983, Noriega "quickly moved to tighten his grip on the force and reassert its position in Panamanian society."[16]

Noriega was a known commodity to Washington because he had assisted the United States throughout his career. "CIA director William Casey and National Security Council aide Lt. Col. Oliver North found Noriega invaluable" (8). The problem, however, was that Noriega became increasingly corrupt and brutal. Gen. Frederick Woerner, who was commander of United States Southern Command (SOUTHCOM), criticized him publicly, angering him. Then in 1987 he "engineered an attack on the U.S. Embassy in Panama City" (13). As a result, the CIA severed ties with Noriega, who responded with increased harassment of U.S. servicemen and women. Although having become tired of Noriega's actions, the Reagan administration decided to do nothing until after the upcoming Panamanian election.

General Woerner, who had to deal with Noriega on a daily basis, was unhappy with U.S. policy; during a visit to D.C. in November 1989 he made his criticism public. He claimed that Washington was "ill prepared" to deal with an upcoming election in Panama, which he believed (correctly, as it turned out) would be staged and controlled by Noriega. Woerner felt "that we should be seriously debating and deciding now what our actions are to be on May 8 given a variety of scenarios. We ought to know what we plan to do even in the event of a reasonably honest election, a grossly dishonest election, a postponed election or any other possible outcome" (42). President Bush was displeased with the general's comment, and he sent a message to Crowe letting him know that as far as he was concerned, the general's credibility was at an all-time low.

By early 1989 Noriega had again stepped up his harassment of American GIs. In February, Panamanian Defense Force (PDF) thugs beat up a navy civilian employee at a police station. Between January 19, 1989, and the end of February, "SOUTHCOM had logged about sixty incidents of harassment by the PDF, bringing to more than one thousand the number of incidents recorded since early 1988" (43).

Surprisingly, the opposition won the Panamanian election, despite Noriega's attempts to rig it. When Noriega nullified the results, Bush became concerned. The United States had to do something, but the president did not want to do anything that would make Noriega a martyr. Bush's subsequent decision to build up U.S. forces in Panama prompted Crowe to wonder why the United States was trying to solve political problems through "military solutions . . . often the first resort rather than the last." Nevertheless, realizing that the president wanted to respond to Noriega's actions, Crowe suggested to Cheney that they reinforce the garrison in Panama with a brigade-size force of 2,000 to 3,000 troops. He felt that the move would send an important psychological message to Noriega. Cheney and Bush agreed, and on May 11, Bush recalled the American ambassador and went on television announcing that "we will not be intimidated by bullying tactics, brutal though they may be, of the dictator Noriega. I do not rule out further steps in the future."[17]

The Firing of General Woerner

Bush's dissatisfaction with Woerner stemmed from more than just the general's public statement about the Panamanian election. Some in Washington felt that he had "gone native" and was not aggressive enough in dealing with Noriega. According to Jim Baker, the final straw came when U.S. election observers asked Woerner about Washington's order to evacuate dependents; he replied that the process was being delayed by a lack of cardboard boxes to pack personal effects. "Senator John McCain of Arizona, a member of the delegation, was appalled by this explanation and later complained to the President that Southcom was part of the problem, not of the solution. . . . Each time a new recommendation for stronger action was considered, Southcom objected. This vignette was the final straw that led the President, at the strong recommendation of Cheney, Scowcroft and me, to replace Woerner."[18] Because Woerner was no longer trusted in Washington, Gen. Carl Vuono was dispatched to Panama to ask him to step down. Woerner, who had spent his whole life preparing for this job, understood the culture, the region, and its politics. He felt, however, that he had been hamstrung: "He had been directed by his military superiors not to pursue a military option, that the presidents he had served would not authorize force. For his pains, he became reviled as 'WIMPCOM commander.' "[19] He quietly resigned his post and bitterly retired from the army.

The Confrontation Builds

According to Bob Woodward, Crowe was livid when he heard about Woerner's firing. As chairman he thought he should have been involved. After all, Woerner, a high-ranking officer, had been carrying out Washington's orders. "Most chilling to Crowe was the indifference that the Secretary of Defense seemed to have about the career of a four-star officer."[20] He too was bitter.

General Maxwell Thurman was about to end his thirty-six-year career and retire from the army when General Vuono called during the first weekend of July and asked him to go to SOUTHCOM. Thurman had a widespread reputation of being married to the service. He was a bachelor "who would call a staff meeting on Christmas Eve night, expecting every officer to be prepared for whatever briefings he might require."[21] Known as a hard-charging workaholic and highly aggressive officer, Thurman was regarded by many to be the perfect choice. He flew to Washington the next day, spoke with Vuono, and agreed to take the post. Vuono then approached Crowe, who approved Thurman's appointment.

By August 1989 Noriega had installed his own government: one that he could control. Bush reacted negatively, stating that "Panama is, as of this date, without any legitimate government"; he added, "The United States will not recognize any government installed by General Noriega." Given Panama's nullified election and subsequent installation of a puppet government, almost everyone in the upper reaches of the U.S. government, Crowe and Scowcroft among them, began to believe that military force was the only way to remove Noriega from office. Very few officials advocated a dovish approach. Indeed, after an NSC meeting in September, Crowe returned to the Pentagon to tell his subordinates, "I am absolutely 100 percent convinced that the only way the situation is going to get resolved in Panama is with military force. You guys better be ready. . . . I can't tell you when it is going to happen and I can't tell you what the trigger is going to be, but I'm convinced that's the only way it's going to be resolved."[22]

With only days remaining before he was to take over as chairman of the Joint Chiefs of Staff, Powell met with Thurman and General Carl Stiner, the former commander of the Eighteenth Airborne whom Thurman had placed in charge of both conventional and special operations against Panama. Noriega was not a new topic for Powell. He had to deal with the Panamanian dictator's outrageous behavior on numerous occasions during his time as NSC advisor. During the meeting, Powell said he wanted to examine all contingencies. Frankly, he had mixed feelings about an operation against Panama, which was not surprising considering his orientation. The use of a surgical strike to remove Noriega had been discussed during the Reagan administration, and some members of the Bush administration now favored such an option. However, Powell thought a piecemeal surgical strike would not solve the problem: an equally brutal and corrupt PDF member would simply replace Noriega.

Thurman, Stiner, and members of their planning staff in Panama returned periodically to meet with Powell, who was especially pleased to learn of their emphasis on large-scale forces. He reiterated his belief on several occasions that "the task force must be fully prepared to 'take down' the PDF which meant plenty of manpower and rehearsals."[23] He also demanded a complete accounting of all aspects of the plan so that he could effectively advise Cheney, Scowcroft, and the president. On November 3 the Chiefs met in the tank and received a briefing on the plan for invading Panama; they agreed to it as written. Thurman, who was haunted by the possibility of a car-bomb attack similar to the one carried out in Lebanon, increased security for American troops in Panama. He had already told Powell that he intended to send American dependents back to the United States because they presented too tempting a target for Noriega.

Worried about the continuing harassment of American service personnel, Washington had instructed the CIA station chief to meet with Noriega during the early part of 1989. The station chief delivered a "blunt" warning from Bush, informing Noriega that if any more Americans were "harmed or harassed in any way, he would be held personally responsible by the President of the United States."[24] The warning worked. Attacks against Americans stopped until December 16.

On December 15 the Panamanian National Assembly, which was Noriega's puppet, passed a resolution declaring war on the United States "owing to U.S. aggression." On the same day, Noriega had himself proclaimed the country's

"Maximum Leader." He also "speculated that some day the 'bodies of our enemies' would float down the Panama Canal."[25]

The Attack on Americans

On December 16, four American servicemen were driving in downtown Panama City when they were stopped at a PDF roadblock just after 0900. When the PDF guards started waving their AK-47 assault rifles in the faces of the car's occupants, the driver panicked and drove off. The PDF guards fired, and one of the bullets hit Marine lieutenant Robert Paz. Another round hit a Marine officer's ankle. The wounded Marines were taken to the military hospital, where Paz was pronounced dead.

At about the same time, a navy lieutenant and his wife became lost while returning to the base. When they reached the same roadblock that had stopped the Marines, they were forced to pull their car to the side of the road. Well aware that the couple had seen the shooting, the guards took them to a nearby PDF office and blindfolded them before taking them to another location. An interrogation began, and the naval officer was beaten and "kicked in the groin and head. He was told he would be killed if he did not provide details about his assignments and his unit." In addition, the officer's wife received a cut on her head after being slammed against a wall. She was then forced to stand against the wall, but eventually collapsed. "The PDF stood over her, grabbing their crotches and taunting her."[26] At one o'clock in the morning the two Americans were released and returned to their base.

Upon hearing of the Paz incident, the military immediately ordered all troops back to duty and advised all dependents to return to their homes. By 1000, SOUTHCOM went to "the highest state of alert, and moved their forces in Panama to their ready positions under Operations Plan 90–2. Soldiers manned defensive positions at Fort Clayton and Fort Amador."[27]

Thurman, who was in Washington at the time, immediately went with Powell to the Pentagon's situation room. After discussing the matter in some detail, Thurman left to fly back to Panama. In the meantime, Scowcroft informed Bush of the Paz killing, which had a major impact on Powell, who "said 'Noriega has gone over the line.' . . . [and] took the position that the killing was an outrage and an affront to the country."[28]

Powell and his assistants met again at 0500 to hear from Thurman, who was back in Panama. Another soldier had been beaten, and Powell now had a transcript of the beaten navy lieutenant's debriefing. Powell then met with officials from the Department of Defense and recommended that the United

States should hit Noriega with all the forces available to it. Some argued that the killing of Paz and the attack on the lieutenant and his wife were not sufficient grounds for the United States to act, but Cheney agreed with Powell. The United States should act and do so forcefully.

Endeavoring to keep the Chiefs in the loop, Powell avoided meeting at the Pentagon. It was Sunday, so the press would have surmised that something big was afoot if the top brass all showed up there. Instead, he invited the Chiefs to his quarters for coffee at 11:30 A.M. When they met, Powell laid out his recommended course of action. "These senior four-stars picked over the plan, commenting on various details. Marine Commandant Gray . . . urged them not to tinker. 'Leave it alone,' he said."[29] And they did.

The key meeting with the president convened at 1400 Powell presented the plan. Bush's first concern was to ensure that this operation would not "backfire as had the attempted rescue of U.S. hostages in Iran during the Carter administration. He also wanted to preclude the interservice problems that arose in 1983 during the intervention in Grenada."[30] The president also asked why the United States did not just "snatch" Noriega, thereby avoiding a full-scale military operation. "Powell said that the massive use of force was in fact *less risky* than a smaller effort. This was the prudent course, he told Bush. The choice, effectively, was pay now or pay later. You go down there to take Noriega out and you haven't accomplished that much because he would be replaced by another corrupt PDF thug."[31] Powell warned the president that "there will be a few dozen casualties if we go. . . . If we don't go, there will be a dozen casualties over the next few weeks and we'll still have Noriega."[32] Powell, Cheney, and Scowcroft agreed that the time for talking had passed: it was time for action. According to Powell, Bush then "gripped the arms of his chair and rose. 'Okay, let's do it,' he said. 'The Hell with it.' "[33]

The decision to act elicited a sarcastic observation from Secretary of State James Baker, who had joined other State Department officials in complaining about the reluctance of Powell and the military to use force in situations such as Panama: "The death of one of its own had finally brought the military around. A telling indicator of the change in the Pentagon came from a general who attended a late-night meeting in the State Department operations center. At one point, he pointedly asked, 'If we decide to use force on this, will you try to tell us how to do it?' After years of reluctance, the Pentagon was finally ready to fight."[34] This debate over the use of force would continue during Desert Shield/Desert Storm and would also affect the military's relationship with the State Department during the Clinton administration.

The decision to invade Panama also illustrated the ways in which Cheney differed from previous secretaries of defense. He asked question after question, and Powell reported that every so often Cheney would call the president to report on developments. But insofar as the chain of command was concerned, it was "clean and clear." According to Powell, "The President talked to Cheney; Cheney talked to me; and I talked to Max Thurman, who talked to Carl Stiner. Thurman and Stiner were the pros on the scene, and our job in Washington was to let the plan unfold without getting in their way."[35] Cheney reportedly altered only the plan to use six F-117A stealth aircraft against Rio Hato, asking, "Come on, guys, how severe is the Panamanian air defense threat?" When the press broke the story about the use of the F-117A, he knew that Congress would criticize the White House and the Pentagon for opportunistically employing the plane to justify its cost. The military returned to the issue and argued that such aircraft would be useful because they would "stun rather than kill the PDF troops at Rio Hato and . . . provide airborne troops assaulting La Escondida and Boquete with the best available night time close air support." When the president was asked to consider the issue, he approved the use of two F-117As in the attack on the Panamanian base at Rio Hato.[36]

As far as this writer can determine, only one instance of "outside interference" marred the operation, and it involved American journalists. Press agencies in New York repeatedly called Scowcroft and asked if an army unit could rescue journalists from their Panamanian hotel. Powell checked with Thurman, who said the reporters were in no danger, and then denied the request, noting that the various media personnel were in the basement and the fighting had already swept past them. Scowcroft called a second time, but again Powell answered no. "Only a few minutes passed before Cheney called. There was no discussion. Do it, he said. No more arguments." Powell then called Thurman and Stiner, reluctantly telling them, "[G]et those reporters out, and I'll try to keep Washington off your backs in the future." The Eighty-second Airborne rescued the journalists, but as Powell noted in his memoirs, three soldiers were wounded, one seriously, and a Spanish photographer was killed. Most important, however, was the manner in which Powell reviewed the issue with Cheney afterward. As Powell described the situation:

> I told Cheney that I did not want to pass along any more such orders. "If the press has to cover a war," I said, "there's no way we can eliminate the risks of war." Cheney called Scowcroft and asked him not to issue any more orders from the sidelines. This was a new, tough age for the military, fighting a war as it was being covered.[37]

Both men respected each other: Powell felt free enough to speak up when he believed a canon of military operations was being violated, and Cheney was prepared to protect his chairman.

For the military, the most important aspect of the Panamanian invasion was that it showed clearly the impact of Goldwater-Nichols. Powell did not have to consult with the Chiefs, although he had been careful to do so. Yet he managed to subordinate the interests of the various services to those of the operation. Thus, instead of dividing Panama up between the Marines and the army, as had happened in Grenada, Thurman and Stiner were allowed to decide who would fight where. For example, the Marines would have liked to divert some of their forces that were returning home from the Far East to be a part of the operation. But because they would take too long to arrive in Panama and delay the operation's schedule, the Marines' offer was politely declined. Tactical problems did arise, most notably when navy seals suffered serious casualties, but not because of service rivalry. In his book on the Panamanian invasion, *Operation Just Cause*, Ronald Cole attributed the greater spirit of cooperation to "the Goldwater-Nichols Act. Under the old system, the Joint Chiefs might have spent more effort on apportioning missions and forces to be employed."[38]

THE PERSIAN GULF WAR

The Persian Gulf War differed from other wars involving the United States. As Michael Gordon and Bernard Trainor explained, "It was the dawn of a new era in which high technology supplanted the bayonet, a war in which one side had a clear picture of events while the other floundered deaf, dumb and blind."[39] It would also be a war that was primarily conducted by the general on the spot—in particular, Gen. Norman Schwarzkopf, although his superior in Washington, Colin Powell, would also play a critical role in ensuring that "Stormin' Norman" Schwarzkopf had the flexibility he needed.

Although signs indicated that Iraq's Saddam Hussein might invade Kuwait, the actual invasion came as a surprise. For example, on July 17, 1990, Saddam publicly threatened both Kuwait and the United Arab Emirates, claiming that they were "shoving a 'poisoned dagger' into Iraq's back by exceeding production quotes set by OPEC."[40] This, he said, led to a decline in the price of oil, Iraq's primary export. Any drop in the price of oil was guaranteed to hurt Baghdad's economy.

Washington was not entirely asleep to the danger of a potential clash in the region. On July 24 Powell called Schwarzkopf in Florida to tell him that if

President Bush and General Powell in the Oval Office, on the phone with General Schwarzkopf during the Gulf War crisis. (George H. W. Bush Presidential Library)

anything happened he would be in charge. After all, he was head of U.S. Central Command (CENTCOM), a command that included Iraq. In this context, Powell asked Schwarzkopf to "come up with a two-tiered response." The first tier would provide a variety of potential responses in the event that Saddam limited his action to a "minor border infraction." The second tier would address a situation in which Saddam went further. "I want to see a second-tier response, how we'd stop him and protect the region."[41]

On the political front, the situation seemed to be improving. On July 25, Saddam summoned to his office the American ambassador, April Glaspie, with only one hour's notice, thus not allowing her sufficient time to get instructions from Washington. When he spoke with her, Saddam criticized a statement that Cheney had made the previous week to the effect that the United States would "stick by its friends in the Gulf." He maintained that this statement was clearly directed against Iraq, and that it was up to the United States to make clear who its friends and enemies were. Glaspie responded by noting that she had "direct instructions from the President to seek better relations with Iraq." She also told Saddam that the United States did not have a position on issues such as the Iraqi-Kuwaiti border dispute, and she asked about his intentions. Saddam replied that "through the intervention of Egyptian President Hosni Mubarak he had agreed to talks with the Kuwaitis."[42] Saddam's words suggested that perhaps a diplomatic solution to the problem existed, which would avert the use of military force.

Glaspie was attacked for not standing up to Saddam by giving him the impression that the United States was prepared to live with his behavior. In truth, this was not a valid charge because Glaspie stated the administration's position: avoid war by finding a diplomatic solution to the problem. As Gordon and Trainor noted, "There were few officials in the American government who understood how far Saddam Hussein was prepared to go to fulfill his ambitions."[43]

Although the diplomatic option appeared viable, Under Secretary of Defense for Policy Paul Wolfowitz argued that the United States should "send a signal" to Saddam that the nation was prepared to back up its diplomatic policy with military force if necessary. In this regard, he suggested the United States should send to the Persian Gulf some warships based at the island of Diego Garcia. Powell, however, wanted no part of the suggestion, asking rhetorically, What for? What can it accomplish? What's the mission? Powell had no intention of permitting his forces to be used just to send a signal—this is the easiest way to get troops trapped in a never-ending military conflict. The signal could easily lead to direct involvement, which in turn would lead to the dreaded "mission creep," as it had in Lebanon, where the original mission was changed again and again. He wanted the mission to have clearly stated objectives, not some vague goal. Sending the pre-positioned ships closer to the Gulf would indicate that the United States was considering committing ground troops, a step the president had not yet decided to take. Powell thought that the two C-135s the United States had sent to the UAE to conduct surveillance would provide a sufficient "signal."[44]

When Schwarzkopf visited Washington at the end of July, Powell asked him to brief Cheney and the Chiefs on the situation and explain his contingency plans. As Powell told it, "I arrived at the tank about the same time as Dick Cheney. The Chiefs rose, and we took our places. Cheney had me lead off. I quickly turned the floor over to Schwarzkopf, whose robust six-foot-three-inch frame and force of personality filled the room. . . . 'What do you think they'll do?' Cheney asked. 'I think they're going to attack,' Norm said."[45] Reading Saddam's mind was difficult, however. The actions he had taken thus far improved his ability to attack Kuwait, but they might be nothing more than a bluff to scare the Kuwaitis. In any case, Schwarzkopf said that the United States could do very little to stop Saddam: only 10,000 military personnel were in the Gulf; most of them were navy, and "CENTCOM had no ground forces nearby." CENTCOM did have a prearranged plan, Plan 90–1002, but it was formulated to fight a war with the Soviet Union or Iran. Most in the tank responded with disbelief to the idea that Saddam would send 100,000 troops into Kuwait when he could successfully invade his neighbor using far fewer men; such a huge force would be "too much for too little."[46] Powell, however, was beginning to think that perhaps Schwarzkopf was right. Perhaps Saddam really was planning to invade Kuwait. Consequently, he suggested to Cheney that he raise the subject with the White House. If nothing else, a warning from the president might persuade Saddam that the United States would seriously consider responding if he moved against Kuwait.

The Invasion of Kuwait

While Washington tried to decipher Saddam's intentions, the latter did the unthinkable. On August 1 Iraqi forces invaded Kuwait, sending hundreds of main battle tanks toward the capital. Powell called Schwarzkopf while he was riding his exercise bike and told him, "You were right. They've crossed the border."[47] When Bush was informed of the Iraqi action, he wanted the United States to respond immediately to show Saddam that he would have to pay a price for his action.

On August 2 the NSC met at 0800. Powell, Schwarzkopf, Cheney, and Wolfowitz attended, as did Robert Kimmit, who represented Secretary of State Baker. Powell introduced Schwarzkopf to the president and asked him to comment on the situation in the Gulf. Schwarzkopf told the president that not much could be done to stop Saddam at the moment, but that options existed to punish him and demonstrate U.S. resolve. The real problem was that "Saudi Arabia had a military of less than 70,000 and only one small unit between the Iraqi units and the vast Saudi oil fields."[48]

Schwarzkopf then discussed his two-tier response approach. The first tier included single retaliatory strikes that would have to be carried out by navy carriers because no air force or army units were in the area. These strikes could be directed at the Iraqi army, as well as a variety of political and economic targets, but they could not be sustained for long periods of time. The second-tier response would take months and involve 100,00 to 200,000 personnel from all of the services. Such a plan depended on Saudi approval, including permission to set up bases inside the country.

In spite of the logistical problems facing the United States the president insisted that Washington respond, saying, "We just can't accept what's happened in Kuwait just because it's too hard to do anything about it."[49] Bush wanted action, but Powell, still afflicted by the Vietnam Syndrome and wishing to avoid another unpopular war, wanted to wait until the president had overwhelming public support for an action against Saddam. Scowcroft, himself a retired air force general, believed that Powell was being far too cautious. The president did not need to have public support before he moved against Panamanian dictator Noriega. He believed he would get such support in the wake of successful military operations.

Cheney, who desired a well-articulated goal and joined Scowcroft in disagreeing with Powell's cautious approach, believed that the United States should "think big." He was thinking not only of removing Saddam from Kuwait, but from power as well. "Cheney's civilian aides had prepared a classified paper advocating that the United States publicly declare the Iraqi invasion to be unacceptable and recalled that every American president since Franklin D. Roosevelt had insisted that the security of the Persian Gulf oil supply was a vital interest." But Powell did not like the plan, calling it "Carteresque." Increasingly frustrated by the chairman's attitude, Cheney wanted Powell to focus on military questions and leave political issues such as whether the United States should use military force to the president. Having finally had enough of Powell's "political comments" Cheney barked, " 'I want some options, General.' 'Yes, Mr. Secretary,' Powell crisply responded."[50]

Faced with the president's desire to "do something" shortly thereafter, Cheney called a meeting in his office of all of his top military and civilian advisors. The skull session provided an opportunity to review all the options so they could make a recommendation to the president. Cheney became more and more incredulous at the limited options available to the United States. As Powell explained to him, the obstacles were almost overwhelming: the country was 6,000 miles away and now that the Iraqis were in possession of Kuwait, the invasion was a fait accompli. The task now was far more difficult than deterring an invasion. The United States (and whoever agreed to help out) would have to evict Saddam's army—one of the largest in the world—from Kuwait and build up sufficient forces to deter him from seizing Saudi Arabia, whose oil resources would provide him with enough control of the world's market to wreak havoc on global prices. But the American response would have to be handled delicately, lest it bring about what the United States hoped to avoid; as Powell told Cheney, " 'We don't have any ground forces and an air strike would be pissing in the wind and might provoke what we don't want—an assault on Saudi Arabia.' It was one of the tensest exchanges the two had ever had." Powell assured the secretary of defense that the Chiefs were developing options. Cheney was upset; there "was no way he was going to let himself become captive of the JCS or Colin Powell."

Consequently, he went outside of normal channels and sent his aide, Rear Adm. William Owens, to ask the navy what to do. His junior aide asked the air force the same question.[51]

Brent Scowcroft began the Friday, August 3, NSC meeting by suggesting that an examination of the United States' long-term interests was in order. He noted that Saddam's action was clearly unacceptable and added that he wanted Cheney, Powell, and Schwarzkopf to travel to Camp David the next day to brief him on the military options. Cheney then turned to Powell and asked him to review the possibilities. Powell listed the units that could be sent quickly to the Gulf. Although he argued that he saw no indication that Saddam intended to invade Saudi Arabia, he agreed that it was important "to plant the American flag in the Saudi desert as soon as possible assuming we get their okay."[52] In accordance with his longstanding belief that the military should not get involved unless Washington had carefully considered the consequences of its impending action, he asked if everyone was sure that going to war to liberate Kuwait was worth the cost. Later, he admitted that asking the question had been a major mistake:

> I detected a chill in the room. The question was premature, and it should not have come from me. I had overstepped. I was not the National Security Adviser now; I was only supposed to give *military* advice. Nevertheless, I had wrestled with the politics and economics of crises for almost two years in the White House, in this very room. . . . More to the point, as a midlevel career officer, I had been appalled at the docility of the Joint Chiefs of Staff, fighting the war in Vietnam without ever pressing the political leaders to lay out clear objectives for them. Before we start talking about how many divisions, carriers, and fighter wings we need, I said, we have to ask, to achieve what end? But the question was not answered before the meeting broke up.[53]

Some at the meeting spoke once again of surgical strikes, a concept he dismissed: "It was the modern military illusion, the brass-balls approach some people wanted to take when the country was in a pinch with a Saddam: let's launch one of those missiles that will show him what we can do, and no one on our side will get hurt. Pure fantasy."[54]

If the United States planned to respond in a more thorough manner, the cooperation of the Saudis would be key. To discover if they would permit the stationing of hundreds of thousands of U.S. troops in the capital of Islam, Powell met with Prince Bandar bin Sultan, the Saudi ambassador in Washington and his good friend. Powell asked Bandar if U.S. troops would be allowed in his country. Bandar, thinking that Washington was considering sending only a couple of squadrons of aircraft, as had been rumored, asked how many troops the United States wanted to send. Powell replied that the number would be around 100,000. Bandar responded, "Colin, now I know you are not bullshitting me," and continued, "Now you know why we did not want a tactical fighter squadron."[55] The prince agreed to raise the issue with his superiors.

At the August 4 NSC meeting at Camp David, Schwarzkopf was called upon to provide an expanded discussion of the two tiers he had previously mentioned. Powell led off, noting that he believed this plan was "doable." "It will achieve the mission of defending or repelling an attack."[56] Powell also explained to the president that it meant calling up the reserves. In his presentation, Schwarzkopf said seventeen weeks would be required to put in place enough forces to deter the Iraqis from moving into Saudi Arabia. He said he was talking about moving 200,000 to 250,000 soldiers, sailors, aviators, and Marines to the region. He added that

> If we wanted to kick the Iraqis out of Kuwait, we'd have to go on the *offense*—and that would take a whole lot more troops and a whole lot more time. I put up a slide that showed my back-of-the-envelope calculation: we'd have to more than double the size of the projected force, pulling at least six additional divisions out of the United States and Europe and transporting them and additional support units to the Gulf. The earliest such an army would be ready to fight was the slide's bottom line. It read, "Time frame: 8–10 months. . . ."
>
> I heard a few people around the table gasp. This was a much larger commitment of forces than they had ever imagined making in the Middle East. It was also more time than they thought would be needed to solve the crisis by force. Both Cheney and Powell completely supported my position.[57]

The bottom line was that if the United States hoped to dislodge Saddam, it would have to make a major commitment. Airpower would play an important role, but the United States would need large numbers of ground forces, known as "grunts," to take the cities and villages.

The following day, the president dropped a bombshell. Powell reported that he was home in his study watching CNN when the president's helicopter landed on the White House lawn. The reporters were pushing Bush hard to respond to the question of whether he would take military action against Saddam. "His face hardened, he began jabbing the air with his finger. '*This will not stand,* this will not stand,' he said, 'this aggression against Kuwait.' "[58] With that statement, Bush had changed U.S. policy. No longer was the United States simply intent on protecting Saudi Arabia; now it seemed as if the president was committing the nation to the liberation of Kuwait as well. Powell knew that the United States was moving ever closer to a military solution.

On August 6 Powell received a call from Cheney informing him that the secretary's recent trip to Saudi Arabia had yielded fruit: the king agreed to have American troops stationed on his soil. Cheney also told Powell that he had spoken with the president, who had given his approval for inserting the necessary force, and had asked him to begin issuing the necessary orders for the deployment to Saudi Arabia. Powell immediately informed the commanders involved that they should begin moving forces to Saudi Arabia.

On August 15 another meeting was held with the president. Powell began by briefing him on the buildup. He said the United States currently had 30,000 troops in Saudi Arabia and would have enough troops within a few weeks to deter Saddam from any movement to the south. By December 5, Powell told the president, the United States would have approximately 180,000 troops in place, which would leave no doubt that Saudi Arabia could be defended. He also told the president that what the military needed "is for you to tell us before that mission is accomplished what you want us to do next—so if we have things in the military supply pipeline, do we stop the pipeline or keep it going, or whatever."[59] Indeed, while Powell recognized that the authorization of a military operation in the Middle East was a difficult political decision that included many factors, most of which were not military, he wanted the president to be as specific as possible so that clear guidelines could be provided to the troops.

When Bush authorized calling up the reserves on August 17, none of the branches of the armed forces could decide exactly how many troops to send, but, as was usually the case, all were out to get as much of the action as possible for their services. Using his authority as chairman to combat interservice rivalry, Powell called Schwarzkopf and asked him to figure out what he needed, telling him, "The services are out of control. *You* sort it out, and I'll okay the units you request."[60]

Few field commanders have cooperated as closely with the Joint Chiefs chairman as Schwarzkopf did with Powell during the Persian Gulf buildup and war. They spoke on a daily basis via a secure phone, not only while Schwarzkopf was in Florida, but when he moved his quarters to the Gulf as well. In addition, they used the fax when they had important written messages or documents to send. As Schwarzkopf tells it, he would give the document that needed to be sent to his aide, who would call Powell's office so that someone would be waiting for the important fax.[61]

On August 23, Powell telephoned Schwarzkopf, who was about to move his headquarters to the Gulf, and in a matter-of-fact fashion concluded the conversation by noting, "On your way, I'd like you to stop here in Washington and give me a full briefing on your offensive-campaign plan—air and ground both." Schwarzkopf claimed that it took a few minutes for Powell's statement to sink in. When it had, he cleared the room and called Powell back. He told the chairman that he had briefed the president on a defensive plan and added:

> I'm following orders to put a defensive force in place, and all of a sudden you guys in Washington are asking me to prepare an offense using that defensive force. Something is wrong here. I can give you my conceptual analysis, but that's all it is—apart from the phase-one air attack, it's nothing I'd recommend, nothing we've actually planned on, nothing I'd act on. I'm afraid somebody who doesn't understand that is going to turn around and say, "execute this offensive."

Powell emphasized the pressure he was under from civilians in Washington. " 'Norman! Trust me. You've to trust me.' Powell exclaimed. 'Do you think I'd ever let that happen? My problem is that I've got all these hawks in the National Security Council who keep saying that we ought to kick Saddam of Kuwait now. I've got to have something to keep them under control.' "[62]

The Dugan Affair

While Powell and Schwarzkopf were busy dealing with senior civilian officials in Washington, Gen. Michael Dugan, who had just taken over as the air force chief of staff, created a significant problem. As an enthusiastic proponent of airpower, Dugan believed that his predecessor had not done enough to publicize its importance. He set out to change that situation by inviting a number of journalists to accompany him on a trip he made to Saudi Arabia; the journey was unnecessary because Dugan was not in the direct chain of command for operations in the Gulf region.

In fact, Schwarzkopf did not want him there, and his trip was approved only after Gen. Chuck Horner, Schwarzkopf's chief of air operations, made a special appeal to him to permit Dugan to visit CENTCOM.[63] Unfortunately, during his flight back to Washington, Dugan began discussing the briefings he had received, almost all of which were classified. His comments were not specific, but he expressed his strong belief that the army would play a secondary role in a Persian Gulf war. He also criticized the navy and, even worse, Israel. He further suggested that a war with Iraq would be a pushover.

Powell could not believe his eyes when he picked up a copy of the *Washington Post* on September 16 and read what Dugan had said. The chairman had been working overtime trying to build a consensus among the services, but now the general's indiscrete comments were guaranteed to create dissension in Washington. When Cheney read the story after being advised to do so by Powell, he exploded and told Powell he wanted to think about it. The next day he called Dugan to his office. He said he was infuriated by Dugan's comments and told him he was fired. Once again Cheney demonstrated that he had both the will and ability to discipline officers who he felt stepped out of line. However, in this case, the vast majority of senior officers—Schwarzkopf and Powell in particular—agreed with Cheney's action. A senior officer simply could not be permitted to say such things and keep his position.

Beginning the Offensive

By the end of September, Cheney and Powell recognized that time was running out. The military would have to decide by October whether to continue to bring in the additional troops and supplies needed for an offensive strategy in the event that sanctions did not work. The president, who was becoming nervous, kept asking if there wasn't some way the United States could attack Saddam, even if only with airpower. Powell suggested to Cheney that they see the president again and lay out their options, which they did on the afternoon of September 24. The chairman began by noting that the military had two possible alternatives. The first was to undertake the offensive. He went through the mobilization schedule and showed when certain units had to be mobilized if they were to be in the proper position in time. The second option was to continue to rely on sanctions. Powell told the president that he recommended that the United States prepare "for a full-scale air, land and sea campaign," saying, " 'If you decide to go that route in October, we'll be ready to launch sometime in January.' "[64]

Scowcroft then called Cheney and told him the president wanted a briefing that would show him what an offensive campaign would look like. Because planning for such an operation was done in Saudi Arabia, Powell called

Schwarzkopf on the phone and asked him to send a team to Washington to brief the president. Schwarzkopf's response was typical. " 'Goddamn it,' Schwarzkopf told Powell over the phone, 'I told you over and over again, we can't get there from here.' But Powell insisted. The White House 'is on my back,' he explained. 'They want to see what we can do.' "[65]

On October 6, one of Schwarzkopf's subordinates, Lt. Col. Joseph Purvis, presented the plan to him. It called for a straight-ahead attack into Kuwait at night all the way to the Kuwaiti capital and then on to Basra.

> "Do you think this will work?" he asked Purvis.
>
> "It's very high risk," Purvis replied. "It may work."
>
> "What would it take to guarantee success?"
>
> "Another corps," Purvis answered promptly. Two or more divisions make up a corps. The Army's XVIII Airborne Corps currently in Saudi Arabia comprised four divisions, but only two were armed with heavy tanks.
>
> Schwarzkopf nodded. "I agree."

Schwarzkopf had no alternative to sending a team to Washington to brief the president, even if the plan was incomplete. However, he told his team to make absolutely clear that in order to be certain of victory, he would need an additional corps. "We don't bullshit the President," he added.[66]

Prior to briefing the president, Schwarzkopf's team, which was led by his deputy, Maj. Gen. Robert Johnston (USMC), briefed the Joint Chiefs and Cheney and Wolfowitz. The proposed attack plan was split into four phases: (1) an air attack on Iraqi command, control, and communications to cut Saddam off from his forces; (2) a massive attack on Iraqi supplies, munitions, transportation facilities, and roads and bridges; (3) an air attack on entrenched Iraqi ground forces of 430,000 men; and (4) a ground attack.[67] Cheney liked the first three phases, but he considered the fourth phase to be inadequate. Commandant Gray was angry that the plan eliminated the Marine amphibious assault and mixed his men in among army units. Indeed, he was so upset that Powell found it necessary to intervene in order to calm him. After the briefing was finished, Johnston took the floor and made it clear to everyone that Schwarzkopf was likewise unhappy with the ground phase. However, if the CINC was ordered to launch an attack in the near future, that was the only option available to him. He reiterated Schwarzkopf's comment that the only way to ensure victory was for him to have another corps.

October 11 was the day of decision. The president and others present approved of the first three phases but, like the Chiefs, they were concerned about the ground phase. Scowcroft, for example, asked why Schwarzkopf had decided to go "right up the middle." "Why don't you go around?" Powell tried to explain that the problem was logistics. "To 'go around,' Schwarzkopf needed an additional corps."[68]

Although the briefers left believing they had made their case, they had not. Cheney thought the plan was bad, while Wolfowitz believed that Schwarzkopf would just use another corps to reinforce a frontal attack. The strategy would be the same. Most damning, however, was the derisive way in which Scowcroft, Richard Haas, and others in the National Security Council dismissed the presentation with a curt " 'Thank you General McClellan,' a snide allusion to Lincoln's reluctant commander of the Army of the Potomac." When Powell made reference to the McClellan statement later that day on the phone, Schwarzkopf responded angrily, " 'Tell me who said that,' he demanded. 'I'll call the son of a bitch on the phone right now and explain the difference between me and McClellan if they're so stupid. If these guys are advising the president of the United States, they ought to know better than to make flip statements like that.' Powell prudently kept the source to himself."[69]

In October, Powell flew to Saudi Arabia. He spent two days grilling Schwarzkopf on his ground-war plan. Both men understood that if they did not get their heads together the strategy would be dictated by civilians who knew very little about fighting a war. The war planners ran through both a one- and two-corps plan. For the latter, Schwarzkopf's planners estimated that they would need two additional heavy divisions and an armored cavalry regiment. They also projected that it would take about eighty days to get the forces to the front. Powell agreed on the need for a second corps. " 'Tell me what you need,' he instructed Schwarzkopf. 'If we go to war, we will not do this halfway.' "[70]

On October 24, Cheney was summoned to the White House, where Bush informed him that he was leaning toward the offensive option. Iraqi forces would be expelled from Kuwait. They agreed that nothing would be announced until after the November midterm elections. Powell suggested that they wait until they had a chance to hear his report when he returned from his Saudi Arabian trip. In the meantime, Cheney made some public hints suggesting that the White House had decided to expel Saddam. When Powell heard these reports he asked an aide, "What's going on?" Once he realized that the White House was serious, he told one person, "Goddammit, I'll never travel again. I haven't seen the President on this."[71] They had talked about the offensive option, but as far as he knew, no decision had been made. He was tired of learning about important administration decisions after the fact.

When Powell returned to Washington he learned that Cheney, who had been upset with Johnston's presentation, had enlisted some of officers on the Joint Staff to devise a plan and then had them brief the president. As far as Powell was concerned, Cheney's plan could not have been worse. Instead of plunging right in the middle of the Iraqi lines, Cheney's plan called for U.S. forces to send a couple of divisions to occupy the western part of Iraq. The idea was that the arrival of such a force would shock the Iraqis and pose a clear threat to Baghdad. If the Iraqis moved forces to the west to engage the Americans they would be sitting ducks for U.S. airpower. It would also protect Israel from Scud missile attacks and close the key road that Iraq used to circumvent the sanctions.[72] In fact, Cheney correctly assumed the generals would reject his plan. Schwarzkopf sent in a scathing criticism, and Powell expressed his dissatisfaction. However, Cheney's real purpose all along had been to get the generals moving. He believed that "the military was again dragging its feet."[73] Interestingly enough, the final strategy did employ a form of the western excursion, primarily to keep Cheney happy, and happy he was because he was convinced that his approach had succeeded in lighting a fire under the military.

On October 31 at a crucial NSC meeting, Powell stated the problem very clearly. " 'Now, if you, Mr. President, decide to build up—go for an offensive option—this is what we need.' He then unveiled the Schwarzkopf request to double the force." The president then formally approved the idea of sending an additional 200,000 troops to Saudi Arabia, as long as the Saudis granted permission. Ultimately, Schwarzkopf received more troops than he had requested. Once the president had made a decision, he believed it was now the military's job to fight the war and they should have whatever they needed and then some. As he put it, "If that's what you need, we'll do it."[74]

On November 8 Bush announced that he had asked his secretary of defense to increase U.S. forces in the Gulf by another 200,000 to ensure that the coalition had enough *offensive* forces.[75] At the same time Cheney told civilians such as Wolfowitz that he had no intention of micromanaging the military. He would watch what happened and ask numerous questions, but he knew enough to let them run the war. Shortly thereafter, Wolfowitz personally told Schwarzkopf that this would not be like Vietnam. He would not have his hands tied by politicians in Washington.[76] On December 19, when Cheney was barraged with various questions about the proposed offensive attack, he noted that he and Powell were in agreement with each other; he also highlighted the ground attack's total dependence on logistical constraints: "We can't force it too early."[77] Once the war began in January, Cheney and the

White House kept to their word and allowed the military to run the show. That is not to suggest that the president and his staff did not ask questions. But when they did, Powell continued to work as a buffer between the civilians and Schwarzkopf.

Importantly, when the controversial question of terminating the Persian Gulf War arose, the military both in the field and in Washington totally supported Bush's decision to end it when he did. Before he made his decision on when to cease hostilities, however, he checked with Powell, who asked for permission to check with Schwarzkopf.[78] Only when the commanding general in the field agreed with the proposed time for halting hostilities did Bush announce that the coalition would cease its attacks.

In retrospect, the Persian Gulf operation benefited from military-civilian relationships that were better than those of other administrations. Cheney actively involved himself in operations and exerted his authority when he felt it was necessary. Powell played a critical, perhaps central role. He worked well not only with the politicians, but with Schwarzkopf, who, given his confrontational personality, probably would have not survived had Powell not been JCS chairman. Furthermore, Powell reveled in the criticism that he was a "reluctant warrior." He believed his stance helped save the lives of troops who civilians might otherwise have willingly put in harm's way without thinking through the consequences. His readiness to defend the troops in the field was made evident when he fought off the White House on the issue of exactly when the war should begin. Schwarzkopf and his fellow military officers were concerned about the weather, which could hamper offensive ground operations. Schwarzkopf told Powell that he could not begin the attack on the twenty-second: it had to be delayed until the twenty-fourth. Some of the civilians in Washington who wanted him to attack on the earlier date were irate. Finally, Schwarzkopf called Powell and told him that the weather had improved and the attack could take place on the twenty-second. Nonetheless, Powell had gone to the mat and defended his field commander against pressure applied by civilians in Washington.

The Gulf War taught the United States at least two important lessons. First, it showed the importance of centralized command structures and the critical need for interchangeable officers from different services, particularly in regard to the air campaign: "The overriding concern is centralized planning and direction, so that air operations make sense as a comprehensible whole."[79] Second, Powell's idea of decisive force played a vital role. Rather than engage in surgical strikes, the United States waited until decisive force was positioned and then attacked.

RESTRUCTURING THE MILITARY

At the same time that the military was fighting wars in Panama and the Persian Gulf, it was also engaged in a restructuring process, which had been initiated for two reasons. To begin with, the ongoing collapse of the Soviet Union was eliminating the very threat the American military had been built to withstand. True, the Soviet military did not cease to exist, but it soon fragmented into fifteen different national units, and although Moscow still had nuclear weapons, the U.S. military and its supporters could hardly argue for more money to stand up against the Soviet threat when others could simply ask, What Soviet threat?

The second reason for restructuring was financial. The Bush administration inherited the fiscal problems created by the Reagan administration's unsystematic spending habits. The Pentagon was so deeply in debt that it was forced to put ships in mothballs, stretch out the construction time for various weapons systems, and cut back on force structure. A *Washington Post* article at the time reported, "Many career budget officers in the Pentagon say there is no way to avoid deep manpower cuts during Bush's first term, given Congress's refusal to increase defense appropriations and the bow wave of bills falling due in the mid-1990s from weapons ordered in the boom years of the Reagan administration."[80]

Powell realized when he became chairman that he would have to conduct some major surgery on the armed forces. Indeed, in his memoirs he said that he "saw it as my main mission to move the armed forces onto a new course, one paralleling what was happening in the world today, not one chained to the previous forty years."[81] Given the increased power he enjoyed as chairman, he knew he could simply order the services to do what he wanted, but he also knew that the process would work better if he and the services reached a consensus. As Powell wrote, "Realistically, I knew that we had to shape the new military as a team" (449).

Powell discussed the issue with a skeptical Cheney, who believed almost to the end that the Soviet Union would not collapse and that hardline forces within the Kremlin would throw Mikhail Gorbachev out. Finally, Cheney began to come around. Furthermore, both Powell and Cheney believed that it would be far better for Powell and the military to design whatever cutbacks were required rather than leave the job to civilian lawmakers. Cheney, in particular, "wanted his hand, not some outsider's, guiding the ax" (439). After Cheney saw Powell's charts that outlined the proposed reductions, he agreed to take them to the president.

Cheney asked Powell to brief Bush on the kinds of reductions he recommended. The president listened to Powell's presentation but was noncommittal. Although Powell knew he should have informed the Chiefs in advance of his presentation to the president, he failed to do so, using as his only excuse "the pressure of time" (440). The next day he made his presentation to the Chiefs in the tank. According to Powell, "I could see the raised eyebrows. I had blindsided them, not a mistake I intended to make again" (440). Powell knew that if he hoped to be successful, he would have to bring the Chiefs along, and as Gen. Carl Vuono, the army chief of staff, had warned him, the key to a collegial atmosphere was to fully and always inform the Chiefs of any plans or ideas he sent to the secretary or the president.

The reductions that Powell proposed must be viewed in the context of the budget battles of the time. A number of members of Congress continued to argue that the end of the Soviet Empire provided the United States with a peace dividend, which meant that the defense budget should be cut and the money saved used for domestic purposes. Cheney, however, fought hard against such efforts. For example, on August 13, 1989, he said that Bush would have no choice but to veto the defense bill and sharply reduce the number of individuals in uniform if Congress cut too much. Several months later the military told Congress that 229,000 active-duty men and women—10 percent of all U.S. military personnel—would have to be trimmed from the payroll if Congress did not appropriate more money.[82]

Aware of the tremendous pressure emanating from Congress, Cheney did the only thing he could. He ordered the services to cut their budgets by $180 billion.[83] He acknowledged that "there is no way I'm going to do what I have to do without force structure reductions, weapons cancellations, contract terminations and base closings."[84] In his guidance he told the services that they should "plan forces for the end of the five-year period on the basis of a reduced threat in Europe . . . reduced Eastern European forces and the near term likelihood that Soviet planners could not count on the offensive use of such forces."[85] The key was that, unlike some other secretaries of defense, Cheney let Powell and the service chiefs decide which forces should be reduced.

The services would be forced to accept tremendous cuts. For example, one account claimed that the Pentagon's next five-year plan "would eliminate three active duty Army divisions, five Air Force fighter wings and 62 Navy ships by 1994 to meet Defense Secretary Richard B. Cheney's demands for deep budget cuts. . . . It would mean a 16 percent reduction in active Army combat divisions, a 20 percent cut in the Air Force wings and an 11 percent cutback of naval vessels."[86]

Although Powell pushed the Chiefs very hard to make the inevitable cuts, he was determined to avoid the "hollow military" that resulted on previous occasions when the armed services were forced to reduce spending. To gain support for the defense budget, Powell argued that the United States had to retain its global power as the sole remaining superpower. In this regard, he said, "We have to put a shingle outside our door saying, 'Superpower Lives Here,' no matter what the Soviets do, even if they evacuate from Eastern Europe."[87] Cheney chimed in, noting in January 1990 that "we need to begin to thinking about a floor under the defense budget." He argued that "despite changes in Eastern Europe and the Soviet Union . . . the defense budget should [not] drop below $311 billion in 1995, a 2 percent reduction after inflation in each of the next several budget years."[88] In February 1990 Cheney issued new instructions to the services that called for a 2-percent budgetary reduction on the part of each service. As in the past, he neither told them what kinds of systems to cut, nor did he "give them . . . advice on how to cut billions of dollars in the new weapons they have ordered for delivery in the 1990s, but which cannot be paid for unless defense spending is increased substantially."[89]

Powell continued to work with Congress to prevent cuts in military forces from taking on a momentum of their own. In May, arguing that DOD had to conduct a full-scale review of everything from weapons systems to personnel levels, training, and strategy, he asked for time to conduct this survey. Indeed, he directed his comments toward the Chiefs just as much as he had toward Congress. Powell observed that "what I'm trying put across to the department is [the military threat] really is different." Turning to the Hill, he warned that "some people in town are trying to put this [budget] in too steep a dive." Severely reducing the budget, he cautioned, would "break this force if you ask us to do it too quickly."[90]

Powell used the phrase "Base Force" to describe what he believed was the smallest possible military force that could fulfill the United States' needs. He "proposed forces capable of performing four basic missions: one to fight across the Atlantic; a second to fight across the Pacific; a contingency force at home to be deployed rapidly to hot spots, as we did in Panama; and a reduced but still vital nuclear force to deter nuclear adversaries."[91] From a conceptual point of view, Powell began to talk not of a threat-based force, but of a *"threat- and capability based"* force.[92] And in his effort to push restructuring of the military, Powell violated one of Cheney's rules—he got ahead of his boss, Secretary Cheney. On May 7 he gave an interview in which he called for a 25 percent reduction in the defense budget. Cheney called him in the next day. Powell later wrote that the secretary of defense questioned his loyalty.

> "I have to know if you support the President. I need to be sure you're on the team." I was taken aback. I made the cautionary count-to-ten

before answering. "Maybe I spoke out prematurely," I said. But what I had told the reporter was writing on the wall. I regretted causing him a problem by speaking out of turn, I said, "but there can't be any question about my being on the team." It was a tense moment, and the air was crackling. We both, however, knew enough to pull back from the brink. And we continued work on the Base Force, and to achieve the 25 percent reduction.[93]

Publicly, Powell continued to defend the military budget by arguing that the United States lived in a dangerous world and had to be prepared to use force when necessary. He cited Panama, the U.S. naval deployment in the Persian Gulf, the evacuation of Americans from Liberia, and U.S. military assistance to President Corazon Aquino during a coup attempt in the Philippines as examples in which the use of American force helped further U.S. interests. And he also continued to press Congress for more time. "What we need . . . is not more insights on how to trim at the margins. What we really need is breathing space; we need time to make the plans work and we need a gradual approach that will not break the armed forces."[94]

Finally, on August 1 it appeared that Powell had finally succeeded on selling his Base Force within the executive branch. For the past eight months he had been shepherding his plan throughout the military bureaucracy. He had fought with the Chiefs and others who did not want to face the facts of a post-Soviet world. But now Wolfowitz and Cheney were "on board," as were most of the Chiefs. On that day first day of August he briefed the president and received his approval. Base Force was now executive policy. The next day the president was going to Aspen, Colorado, to meet with British prime minister Margaret Thatcher, and Cheney, Wolfowitz, and Powell would be going to the Hill to sell Powell's plan. Powell was proud of what he had accomplished. "The changes envisioned were enormous, from a total active duty strength of 2.1 million down to 1.6 million. The strategic heart, the four services I urged, had survived intact. The plan the President was going to propose would effectively mark the end of a forty-year-old strategy of communist containment, a strategy that had succeeded." But then, as noted above, Saddam Hussein invaded Kuwait. And it would overshadow matters for some time to come. For example, when Powell tried to brief congressional leaders on his Base Force concept, what he heard was "yeah, sure, right. But what's going on in Kuwait?"[95]

Powell, however, did not give up. The following February, Cheney and Powell went back again to Capitol Hill to push their idea of a Base Force before the House Budget Committee. They would once again be frustrated, however. Although a number of the questions followed the expected lines,

Congressman Barney Frank diverted attention away from Powell's plan when he asked him a question concerning the role of gays in the military. Powell responded by noting, "I think it would be prejudicial to good order and discipline to try to integrate that in the current military structure."[96]

Discussion of the Base Force would continue into the next administration, but it was already becoming an increasing reality within the armed forces. For example, the Pentagon began to cite the need to respond to "regional contingencies" as a primary concern. The idea was first publicly mentioned in a speech by the president the preceding August, and Powell returned to it in May 1991 when he observed, "You've got to step aside from the context we've been using for the past 40 years, that you base [military planning] against a specific threat. . . . We no longer have the luxury of having a threat to plan for. What we plan for is that we're a superpower. We are the major player on the world stage with responsibilities around the world, with interests around the world." The Joint Chiefs' annual military net assessment also emphasized the importance of the Pentagon's ability to respond to "major regional contingencies," including a renewed Iraqi military threat against Kuwait and a potential North Korean attack on the South. This particular result of the assessment was clearly a manifestation of Powell's thinking, because the Base Force was intended to provide lots of flexibility, allowing for numerous military responses.[97]

Powell believed it was only a matter of time before the United States would have to use force once again in some region of the world. As he remarked in November, "I am absolutely convinced that the United States cannot afford to disengage from its interests around the world. Now, how you apply military force to those interests is something we can examine as a result of the significant changes that have taken place in the last few years."[98] Like it or not, the United States was destined to play a significant role around the world, as Powell acknowledged in a March 1992 interview: "We've heard it again and again: America cannot be the world's policeman. Yet . . . when there's trouble, when somebody needs a cop, who gets called to restore peace? We do."[99] The issue of how and when to use military force would continue to occupy Powell's mind during the Clinton administration, where he would again be seen as a voice of caution when the option of military force was place on the table.

The changes introduced during the Bush administration significantly changed the face of the American military. For example, between 1990 and 1995, 516,000 troops would leave active-duty service. Defense spending (measured in constant 1992 dollars) would rise from $215 billion at the end of the Carter administration to $329 billion under Reagan in 1986 before falling to $283 billion under Bush. Furthermore, the army cut its active divisions from eighteen to twelve, a drop of one-third. The navy was lucky to hold onto 448 of its ships while the air force shrank from thirty-six fighter wings of roughly seventy-two planes each to twenty-six wings. And the Marine Corps would lose four battalions of infantry, four squadrons of F/A-18s and Harrier jets (about ninety-eight planes), and four artillery batteries (about thirty-two guns).[100] The high price that the military would pay was ultimately the cost of Reagan's spending spree during his first two years in office.

CONCLUSION

Presidential Leadership Style

In spite of conflict between the president and the military on several occasions, of all the presidents covered in this book, George Bush's leadership style most closely matched the model the military preferred. First, he was inclusive. He involved the military—or perhaps more accurately, their representative, Gen. Colin Powell—in almost all of his decisions. The bureaucratic intrigues common to the Nixon White House were absent because Bush worked through his national security advisor, who avoided the backbiting, bureaucratic free-for-all that many of his predecessors fostered. The president permitted the Defense Department to run military matters, although no one doubted that he had the final say on all issues of policy. He solicited the military's views, and unlike Lyndon Johnson, Bush gave the Chiefs the feeling that they had been listened to regardless of whether or not he eventually followed their advice. He was prepared to support the Pentagon when necessary, as he did when Congress tried to slash the military budget while the Soviet Union collapsed.

Bush also believed in a clear chain of command running through Secretary of Defense Cheney, Chairman Colin Powell (after October 1, 1989), the various theater commanders, and the rest of the Joint Chiefs. Neither the president nor his assistants attempted to issue orders behind the backs of the secretary or the chairman. Equally important, and partially because of Powell's insistence, Bush gave clear instructions: when the military received an order, it understood what the president expected.

Most important, however, was the fact that Bush, like Jimmy Carter, did not get involved in operational or tactical matters. In contrast to LBJ, Bush provided broad policy guidance and then left it to his professional military officers to devise the appropriate strategy and tactics to achieve those ends. In addition, like Ronald Reagan, Bush also showed considerable personal respect for the armed forces, a trait that the military and its leadership greatly appreciated.

Finally, there was the intangible personality factor. Bush did an excellent job of picking individuals for key national security positions who held their egos under control and were willing to work together as a team. Powell knew he could ignore the Chiefs if he chose to, but he went out of his way to see that their views were represented. Furthermore, probably no officer in the U.S. military could have performed as well as Powell did in acting as a buffer between Cheney, the White House, and Gen. Norman Schwarzkopf during the Gulf War. Cheney himself demonstrated that he was in charge at Defense, but he permitted Powell and Schwarzkopf considerable autonomy on military matters. As Woodward noted, Cheney believed that the only remedy for situations like Lebanon and Grenada "was a clean, clear-cut chain of command—as short as possible."[101] Similarly, it would be hard to overestimate the importance of the role played by Scowcroft. In contrast to Kissinger, he was a breath of fresh air, expressing his views but making no effort to keep the military's ideas from the president; indeed, more often than not, he solicited them.

Violations of Service/Military Culture?

The military felt that Cheney's attack on Welch was uncalled for, and Crowe—and just about every other military officer—objected to the way the secretary of defense handled the Woerner case. If Woerner had to be dismissed, then Crowe believed that he should have been involved in the process. Simply sending General Vuono down to Panama to inform the general that he was being asked to resign was inexcusable. In addition, Powell objected to Cheney's attempt to devise a new strategy for the Persian Gulf War, but, as in other instances, Cheney was not trying to run the war, but to light a fire under the military. From the military's standpoint, dealing with the Bush administration was largely a very positive experience.

Changes in Service/Military Culture?

With the exception of the increasingly important emphasis on joint operations, little change took place in military culture during the Bush administration, thanks in large part to the smooth relations between the Chiefs and the president. Unfortunately, this situation would change dramatically during the next administration. It would be one more characterized by conflict than cooperation.

12
THE MILITARY AND WILLIAM CLINTON

With this President, I could see how such a bad military move could be made. He was so inexperienced he would have us grab a rattlesnake by the tail because that was where the noise was coming from.
—Colonel David Hackworth

If George Bush fostered one of the most harmonious relationships with the senior military leadership, William Clinton engendered one of the most difficult. Clinton was the first president since the end of World War II who had not served in the military; he knew little if anything about the armed forces and had expressed his disdain for them publicly. He would find himself locked in bitter battles with the military's leadership, initially over the status of gays in the military and then over the role women would play.[1] During his administration, Clinton called on the military to conduct operations in four significant conflicts: Somalia, Haiti, Bosnia, and Kosovo, three of which caused military leaders to complain about what they perceived as his lack of leadership.

Although the military always obeyed Clinton, he created a number of serious problems for the services. First, the Clinton White House was anything but a paradigm of order and structure, the kind of bureaucratic world in which the military feels most comfortable. Rarely stating well-articulated foreign policy goals, the president and his civilian subordinates did not fully understand how to use military power most effectively. Consequently, the military often found itself hampered by confusion and interbureaucratic conflict. Second, many military officers felt that Clinton neither respected them nor the many sacrifices they and their families made on behalf of their country. Finally, they resented his attempts to use the military as a laboratory for social engineering. They believed the military was created to fight and win wars, not to carry out experiments. In short, the relationship between Clinton and the military would be characterized more by conflict than cooperation from the day he entered office, although it would improve slightly over time.

CLINTON'S LEADERSHIP STYLE

Clinton, who was undoubtedly one of the brightest, most charismatic presidents to lead the United States in the last sixty-odd years, demonstrated pure genius when it came to getting himself out of a difficult situations. However, in comparing Clinton to Ronald Reagan, Dick Morris argued that Clinton's superior intelligence was part of his problem.

> Reagan was Bill Clinton's strategic antithesis—not least because strategy seemed almost alien to him. His mind was clear and uncluttered. The simplest of axioms governed his conduct. Where Clinton has an insatiable appetite for new notions and constant reevaluating, Reagan simply amassed ammunition to sell the ideas he already had.
>
> And by any political accounting, Reagan was the more successful—if the less fiercely intelligent—of the two.[2]

Of all of the presidents discussed in this book, only Johnson and Nixon were perceived by the Chiefs to have provided worse military leadership than Clinton. One well-known presidential scholar called Clinton's approach to politics "Ad-hocracy in action."[3] He argued that Clinton had little interest in the decision-making process and that he had no time for organized procedures. Rather than ask the bureaucracy to carefully consider a specific problem and present the best possible solutions, he avoided it. Instead, he preferred a fluid approach to policy issues and frequently relied on outside advisors for advice. Often, Clinton would then make a snap decision; only later would he inform the bureaucracy (including the military) of the solution he had chosen.

Clinton's dislike for structure was so strong that Fred Greenstein compared it "to a little boys' soccer team with no assigned positions and each player chasing the ball."[4] Another writer cited a report that the CIA director "had such trouble getting on Clinton's schedule that he called upon retired Admiral Crowe [who often saw the President] . . . to bring up" an issue with him.[5] Even those who managed to gain a meeting discovered that the president always ran behind schedule, probably because "his talent was matched only by his lack of discipline. Meetings went on interminably, largely because the president was always talking." He made everyone wait, including foreign leaders: For example, at one NATO meeting he was twenty minutes late. That meant he was "*very* late. Helmut Kohl and Jacques Chirac were fuming."[6]

The military felt that Clinton focused a disproportionate amount of his attention on domestic policy and did not provide clear instructions. As Sidney Blumenthal put it, "Clinton believed from the start that he would be a domestic policy president."[7] Indeed, he seldom attended NSC meetings, where some of the key decisions in U.S. foreign policy were made. John Burke observed that "during his first 100 days as president Clinton attended only three cabinet meetings. After that it got worse.[8] The simple fact was that Clinton was not as deeply involved in the governmental decision-making process as his predecessor. Taking only a peripheral role in issues such as Somalia, Bosnia, and Kosovo, he relied on his chief of staff to keep him informed.[9] When NSC meetings were held, Clinton's chief of staff usually ran them. Colin Powell complained that the interminably long, nightmarish sessions were more like a college seminar than an organized government meeting. He complained that too many people attended the unfocused meetings and that all of them wanted to talk about the excessive number of topics. "Powell thought of the Clinton team, said one of his friends, as being too much like refugees from academe."[10]

Robert Patterson, a former military aide to Clinton, provided an account of just how chaotic matters were in the administration. When he began his tour in the White House in 1996, Patterson asked for a "wiring diagram," a chain-of-command chart that would show who was in charge of the various issues, something that every military base or command provides each new arrival. In response to his question, he was told, "There isn't one."[11]

Clinton complicated matters by often refusing to make decisions, at least not the unequivocal, clear decisions that the military desired. For example, when he was governor of Arkansas he was asked to sign a full-page newspaper ad urging Congress to support President Bush's policy toward the Persian Gulf War. He promised to consider endorsing the president's policy but never responded in the end. When he was asked later how he would have voted, he answered, " 'I guess I would have voted with the majority if it was a close vote. But I agree with the arguments the minority made.' This effort to avoid taking a clear-cut position became a Clinton trademark."[12] His equivocating approach to decision making created one problem after another for the military leadership. Instead of stepping in at critical points, as had Bush and Carter, Clinton not only vacillated, more often than not he made no decision, leaving the bureaucrats to fight among themselves.

Fundamentally a pragmatist, Clinton always kept an eye on public opinion polls. In the vast majority of cases involving foreign and national security policy, he remained more than prepared to modify policies in light of public and media reactions. As Greenstein observed, in this sense he was a direct opposite

President William Clinton with senior American military officers. General John Shalikashvili, chairman of the Joint Chiefs of Staff, is in the foreground. (Clinton Presidential Materials Project)

of Ronald Reagan. Where Clinton's positions "were ever open to modification," Ronald Reagan "was vague about the details of policies but stood for a handful of broad verities."[13]

The Generals and Clinton

The generals and admirals had reservations about Clinton when he came to office. First, there was the issue of the draft. Like many of his compatriots, Clinton did his best to manipulate the system to avoid being drafted during the Vietnam War. He convinced Col. Eugene Holmes, head of the University of Arkansas ROTC program, to keep a place open for him until he received his draft number, which turned out to be high. Knowing that the chances of being drafted were slight with such a number, he then wrote a letter to Colonel Holmes in which he said that he "loathed the military."[14] Even the manner in which he saluted revealed his distaste for the armed services. They were so sloppy that his aides cringed. According to George Stephanopoulos, "The tips of the fingers would furtively touch his slightly bowed head, as if he were being caught at something he wasn't supposed to do. The snickering got so bad that National Security Adviser Tony Lake came to my office one afternoon to strategize on how to approach the president about it."[15] Many officers took exception to his inability, or unwillingness, to salute properly.

Clinton's first actions in office convinced the military of the correctness of their preconceptions, which justified their wariness of him. He immediately announced that he was going to freeze military pay despite the existence of military studies showing that pay had fallen 20 percent behind the private sector (almost 80 percent of the military made less than $30,000 per year) and that 20,000 enlisted personnel were eligible for food stamps. An army major characterized the announcement as "one more sign that Clinton doesn't care."[16] Two months into the administration Clinton already appeared to not be taking military issues seriously. The majority of Department of Defense positions remained unfilled. "There's a secretary who's getting a pacemaker and a deputy. That's it. The military has some rude things to learn—namely, that this guy doesn't care about them."[17]

Military morale suffered because of a significant reduction in force structure. Like any person pursuing a career in a government bureaucracy, members of the military want to know that tomorrow they will have a job and the opportunity to advance. When major cutbacks are instituted, both of these promises are thrown out the door. If, for example, a person is a helicopter pilot or mechanic and the White House or Pentagon announces that the number of helicopters is being cut, that individual can expect to face one of two prospects: being booted out of the service, often without a pension, or being frozen in his or her position with few promotions in the future. Almost all career members of the military had lived through such cuts during the Bush administration, but such reductions occurred only after careful study of their potential impact on the military's goal of being combat-ready. Clinton, however, appeared motivated by a desire to cut military spending, not by an interest in developing a more effective fighting force. He simply announced that he would reduce military spending. As one Marine lieutenant colonel complained, the Clinton administration was "just making cuts, without examining what future missions would be."

Clinton proposed to cut $120 billion over the next five years; his projected budget for FY 1994 was $263 billion, $10 billion less than that authorized for 1993, and $248 billion for 1997.[18] His fiscal constraints had a variety of adverse effects on the military, ranging from fewer spare parts to units rendered inoperative because of greatly reduce strength. Clinton's budget also had a devastating impact on training: artillery soldiers found they could not fire the requisite number of shells in drills to stay competent; aviators were given less flying time; and the number of sailing days for ships was reduced. Careers, weapons systems, and training were scaled back, as was the quality of life for personnel and dependents. A 1993 article in the *Air Force Times* warned, "Military people also face a Democratic budget plan to cut cost-of-living adjustments for retirees, [and] declining availability of in-house dependent medical and dental care."[19]

Illustrative of the administration's lack of regard for the military was a White House aide's now-famous snub of Lt. Gen. Barry McCaffrey. General McCaffrey, who had most recently served in the Persian Gulf War, encountered the aide in a White House hallway. He said, "Good morning," only to have the aide reply, "I don't talk to the military."[20] Although the president personally apologized to McCaffrey and took him jogging with him, word of what had happened quickly went around the Pentagon. The damage had been done, and the military responded to such slights in a number of ways.

A two-star air force general vented his hostility at an air force banquet in the Netherlands by referring to Clinton as a "gay-loving," "pot-smoking," "draft-dodging," and "womanizing" commander in chief. The air force came down hard on him, and instead of being promoted to a more senior position he was ordered to retire, which he did on July 1. At the Marine command's formal mess night in Quantico, Virginia, officers were warned not to make "any inappropriate remarks during the toast to the president of the United States," which "was to the office, not the man." Most of those present raised a glass but refused to drink from it.[21] And when Clinton flew to the USS *Theodore Roosevelt,* several disrespectful comments scribbled on various bulkheads awaited him, and a comment circulated around the ship to the effect that "maybe we can call this his military service. . . . Three hours is more than he had before."[22] Few precedents existed for such unacceptable behavior by the military toward the president. The fact that it happened illustrated just how poorly the armed forces regarded Clinton.

Despite the military's dislike of Clinton and the chaotic manner in which he made decisions, officers were appreciative of his openness when they were able to meet with him. Their conversations might not change the president's mind, but he always allowed them to voice opinions, a critical trait to senior military officers.

Secretary of Defense Les Aspin

Although few doubted the intellectual brilliance of former congressman Les Aspin, he was a poor choice for secretary of defense. Aspin, who had earned a Ph.D. in economics, had spent a good deal of time focusing on defense issues.[23] Moreover, he had gone head to head with Powell, Cheney, and others over the years and was respected for the depth of his knowledge on issues of importance to the military. Unfortunately, he was neither a manager nor a leader, and certainly not the kind of person to run one of the largest, most complex bureaucracies in the world. Aspin proved far less effective than the coldly efficient Cheney (Powell said he was "as disjointed as Cheney was well organized").[24] He lacked the requisite traits of the key liaison between the military and the president. No one knew when he would come to work, and his meetings often began late and ran well past the allotted time. David Halberstam neatly summarized Aspin's primary problem: "He could not run the Pentagon because he could not run himself."[25] From his very first day, stories about his lack of personal discipline spread throughout the Pentagon—he did not look like a secretary of defense in his rumpled suits, and the military found his schmoozy, arm-on-the-shoulder style too casual. "Military officials told their contacts outside the Pentagon, 'For years [as chairman of the House Armed Services Committee] he sniped at us, and then he came here and put his arm around admirals and generals, and we don't like it.' "[26]

On Aspin's behalf it is worth noting that he was handicapped by his poor relationship with the White House, which contrasted with the open relationship that Cheney enjoyed with Bush. For example, on one occasion, Aspin asked CIA director Jim Woolsey, " 'When you took this job, didn't you think you'd spend a lot of time with the president going over stuff that seemed important?' Woolsey said that he had. 'And have you found that you can't get to him nearly enough on stuff that really matters?' Woolsey said that was also true. 'Same with me,' Aspin said. He later told friends that he had two meetings with the president during his entire tour."[27] Aspin appeared to work well with the Chiefs, probably because he primarily interacted with Colin Powell. And while Aspin would later take the fall for the Somalia debacle, most observers believed that he was carrying out Clinton's orders to the degree that the president was aware of what was happening in that beleaguered country.

Before turning to the most important emotional issue separating Clinton from the Chiefs, it is important to understand that throughout his presidency a fundamental disagreement stood between those in his administration who favored using force around the world and the Chiefs. The latter had little interest in becoming involved in "civil-wars or other unconventional conflicts, preferring, . . . the 'American way of war'—emphasis on massive, prompt, and decisive application of overwhelming force to defeat any aggressor."[28] This approach, however, ran counter to many senior civilians' belief that the United States had an obligation to help build a multinational community by providing military forces when necessary. Don Snider and Andrew Kelly have argued that this belief led to "substantial U.S. military commitments to 'causes' rather than 'interests,' causes that might be better addressed by diplomacy and nongovernmental organizations."[29] The U.S. military could not have stated the problem more clearly. The Chiefs would constantly resist the administration's efforts to involve them in causes, and Powell in particular attempted to dissuade such involvement as long as he was on the scene. He believed that the military should not be employed until the administration had carefully stipulated its reason for using force, its goal (or interest), and its exit strategy. In short, he did not care how necessary the use of force might be for humanitarian reasons. Like many other senior officers of his generation, he did not want another Vietnam or Lebanon.

Homosexuals in the Military

The hostility that many in the military felt toward Clinton escalated when he addressed the issue of gays and lesbians in the services. During a November 11, 1991, press interview, Clinton renewed his campaign pledge to allow homosexuals to serve openly in the military. His campaign's official position paper had said that "Bill Clinton has called for an immediate repeal of the ban on gays and lesbians serving in the United States armed forces."[30] Ironically, the issue did not figure prominently in the election; in fact, Bush did not highlight it, and the gay community paid more attention to the civil rights bill. Clinton could have easily avoided the gay issue by answering media questions with a response similar to Joe Klein's proposed line: " 'Yes, we're going to ask the military to study the situation and come up with a plan'—to be implemented sometime in the next century."[31] When Clinton decided to raise the problematic issue, he may have both overestimated the strength of the presidency and insufficiently understood the military and its culture.[32] He did not even consult the National Security Council about instituting this fundamental change.

Clinton's decision to press ahead on the issue of homosexuals was even more surprising after Colin Powell, whom the president acknowledged was a major political force in Washington, gave him early warning of the potential ramifications. Two weeks after the election, Powell mentioned the topic to Clinton.

> "For whatever its worth," I said, "let me give you the benefit of my thinking. Lifting the ban is going to be a tough issue for you, and it's a culture shock for the armed forces. The chiefs and the CINCs don't want it lifted. Most military people don't want it lifted. I believe a majority in Congress are against lifting the ban too. The heart of the problem is privacy. How can this change be made to work given the intimate living conditions of barracks and shipboard life?" "I know," Clinton said, "but I want to find a way to stop discrimination against gays."

Powell then told Clinton that he had a suggestion.

> "At a press conference when you announce your choice of Secretary of Defense, say right off the bat, 'And I've asked Secretary-designate so-in-so to look into this matter and have a recommendation for me in six months on whether to and how to lift the ban. Give yourself some breathing room. Get it out of the Oval Office. Don't make the gay issue the first horse out of the gate with the armed forces."[33]

Powell said Clinton nodded in apparent agreement with him. But four days after he took office, the new president announced his intention to lift the ban, thus uniting the military against him to a degree that even insiders found amazing. Joining the Chiefs in opposition to Clinton were the Veterans of Foreign Wars, the American Legion, the Retired Officers Association, and the Association of Non-Commissioned Officers.[34] Elizabeth Drew argued that the

Chiefs' primary concern was that the president would also permit "gay culture."[35] They feared that Clinton would not back them up when they wrote rules that the homosexuals opposed. Politically, Clinton had bitten off far more than he could chew.

Recognizing that it would be very difficult to implement such a policy without at least passive support from the Chiefs, Clinton, accompanied by Aspin, met with them on January 25 at the White House. As George Stephanopoulos reported, the meeting was quite an event, as the four service commanders entered the room "in full uniform with their chairman, Colin Powell." Even more important from a political standpoint was Stephanopoulos's observation that "while Clinton was their host and boss, he didn't hold the balance of power in the room. Yes, he was commander in chief, but Clinton's formal powers were bound by the fact that he was a new president, elected with only 43 percent of the vote, who had never served in the military and stood accused of dodging the draft."[36] Clinton was in a very weak position, and he knew it.[37]

Powell told the president that the Chiefs were well aware that gays and lesbians had served honorably in the military—"but not openly."[38] He then mentioned the problem of privacy and suggested that each of the four chiefs provide him with their views on the topic. Emphasizing that they were giving Clinton their personal views, all four spoke in what Stephanopoulos called "uncompromising tones. The crew-cut Marine commander, Carl Mundy, was most vehement; he saw it as an issue of right versus wrong, military discipline versus moral depravity." The Chiefs noted that they had solicited the views of "field commanders, senior NCOs, the troops, service spouses, chaplains—and they had run into a solid wall of opposition to lifting the ban." They also mentioned a variety of problems they foresaw integrating homosexuals on ships, in cramped barracks, and in other intimate situations. Powell suggested that Clinton consider adopting a policy that would stop asking enlistees about their sexual orientation. Homosexuals could serve provided they kept their sexual orientation to themselves.[39]

Clinton responded by underlining the point that gays and lesbians had served and were serving honorably in the military—a point with which the Chiefs agreed. At the same time Clinton said that he did not think they should "have to live a lie." He added that he wanted "to work with you on this." In fact, the Chiefs had played hardball and Clinton knew it. To quote Stephanopoulos, "Their message was clear: Keeping this promise will cost you the military. Fight us and you'll lose—and it won't be pretty."[40]

Powell reported that the Chiefs left feeling optimistic. The president said that he wanted to work with them, and Powell had laid the groundwork for what would be the eventual compromise: Stop asking, and stop pursuing. Gays and lesbians could serve in the military, but they would have to keep their sexual orientation to themselves. Most important, the Chiefs had a very strong feeling that Clinton would not try to force the issue for the time being. However, four days later on January 29, Clinton announced at a press conference that between that date and July 15 the services would no longer ask recruits about their sexual orientation. On July 15 Aspin presented him with a draft executive order on the topic.

Meanwhile, Powell made clear his opposition to gays in the military, arguing that "homosexuality is not a benign behavior characteristic such as skin color."[41] The *New York Times* blasted Powell, charging him with being "defiantly opposed, almost to the point of insubordination." It was not the only newspaper to do so. Commentators suggested a similarity between racial integration and the problem facing gays and lesbians. *Time* magazine called Powell the "Rebellious General," and others argued that he was on the wrong side of the issue and only in his position because Truman had integrated the military. For his part, Powell refused to back down; he later wrote, "I continued to see a fundamental distinction. Requiring people of different color to live together in intimate situations is far different from requiring people of different sexual orientation to do so."[42] As far as defying the president's will was concerned, Powell's spokesman responded by noting that "the chairman, as the principal military adviser to the president . . . has not only a duty but a right and responsibility to express his views and opinions."[43] Powell knew what the 1986 Goldwater-Nichols Act meant in terms of his authority, and he planned to use it, whether or not the press or the current administration liked it.

Clinton was also in a difficult position on the Hill. If he went ahead with his plan to lift the ban, he would be forced to fight a bitter battle with the Hill, particularly Senator Sam Nunn, the Democratic chairman of the Senate Armed Forces Committee. Because any action the president took on the issue was subject to congressional review, and given how strongly Nunn and Senator Byrd opposed lifting the ban, legislation would almost certainly be introduced to restrict gays more than they had been when Clinton first took office. In fact, the House passed a resolution opposing Clinton's position by more than three to one.[44] Furthermore, according to Stephanopoulos, Nunn held the Family and Medical Leave Act hostage to the gay issue.[45]

A number of meetings were held on the topic between January and July. On July 2 alone, Aspin met with the Chiefs three times. The secretary of defense and the White House wanted a "don't ask, don't shout" policy that would permit gays to "quietly acknowledge their homosexuality without flaunting it." But the Chiefs insisted that the principle that "homosexuality is incompatible with military service" be retained in official military documents, because they believe that restricting homosexual speech and sexual conduct would be impossible without that particular language. General Mundy was correct when he said that the Chiefs' position "has been pretty clear from the outset and relatively unchanged from the outset."[46]

Finally on July 19, Clinton announced the new military policy, which had four elements. First, "Servicemen and women would be judged on their conduct and not their sexual orientation." Second, the recently instituted practice of not asking about sexual orientation in the enlistment procedure would continue. Third, if a service member volunteered that he or she was a homosexual, that person would be given an opportunity to "demonstrate that he or she intends to live by the rules of conduct that apply in the military service." Finally, Clinton announced that the Uniform Code of Military Justice would be enforced equally in dealing with heterosexuals and homosexuals.[47]

Although members of Congress posed numerous questions on how the new policy would be applied in a variety of situations, the Senate voted in favor of the policy and made it the law. The change was challenged, but in October the Supreme Court reversed a lower-court ruling and permitted implementation of the administration's policy.

In the end, however, no one was happy. The gay community was furious with Clinton for compromising, while the military resented his effort to interfere in its internal affairs. Clinton admitted that it was a defeat and maintained that if he had worked harder on it during his transition, it would have been handled better.[48] The public was completely confused, as were a number of members of Congress. Most important from the standpoint of civil-military relations, the rank and file of the military never forgave Clinton for trying to foist this policy on them. Clinton and the military would fight other battles in the social sphere, most notably on the role women were to play in the armed forces, and the military would resist. But in the case of women, the Chiefs went along, if only reluctantly. If nothing else, the issue of gays caused the Chiefs to seriously question Clinton's leadership ability. Raising an issue that was sure to get the military to go to battle stations when he could have handled the matter in another way—the one that Powell recommended and that Clinton was eventually forced to accept—was not a sign of good leadership in their eyes.

His leadership style would produce additional confusion and friction when the United States faced a number of situations that required the use of military force. Even though the various crises were ultimately resolved, the military would once again clash with the civilians over the issue of deploying American military forces around the globe.

SOMALIA

Instead of leading to a more stable, democratic government, the 1991 overthrow of the corrupt Somali government of Siad Barre soon plunged the country into a spiral of disintegration, violence, and chaos. Witnessing the widespread starvation and the thousands of Somalis who were dying, the international community decided to provide assistance. The Bush administration first sent food supplies in August 1992, an action that Clinton endorsed.[49] The Pentagon agreed as well, and was even willing to go further. At a meeting of deputies, Adm. David Jeremiah, Powell's deputy, offered, "If you think U.S. forces are needed, we can do the job." According to Halberstam, Powell believed that an operation would work well and save as many as half a million lives, but that the United States should limit its commitment and quickly turn over the operation to the UN. From the Chief's perspective, when compared with the situation in Bosnia, Somalia appeared to be the lesser of the two evils. The primary concern, at least for Brent Scowcroft, was an exit strategy. He feared that if the United States left after a couple of months, the situation would revert back to what it had been just prior to the deployment: " 'We can get in,' he had said at one meeting, 'but how do we get out?' "[50]

On December 9, 1992, President Bush, with Clinton's support,[51] dispatched advance elements as part of a twenty-one-nation force to protect aid distribution, and by the end of the year 146,000 tons of food had been delivered safely. For a while it appeared that the country would return to a sense of normalcy. But the fight between warlords continued despite the presence of outside military forces, and soon Somalia imploded and became a non-state. Rather than attempt to create a civil society, rival clans tried only to maximize their own power. For many Somalis, the clan was their world, and anything that went beyond it was foreign and hostile. The idea of a larger community, not to mention a nation-state, made no sense to them.

The United States had deployed thirty-five thousand service personnel, a force that was large enough to protect itself. However, UN troops were to replace the Americans after they had established control. Nobody anticipated a long-term U.S. deployment: "Bush wanted the departure date to be January 19 in order not to burden a new administration with an ongoing troop commitment in so treacherous a place."[52] Unfortunately, American troops were still arriving as Clinton took office; a withdrawal would have to wait. The actual handover of authority to the UN did not occur until May 1993, when only five thousand U.S. troops remained under the command of the United Nations Operation in Somalia (UNOSOM).

UNOSOM had two purposes: "The first was to persuade or force the warlords—especially General Aideed—to accommodate to a process of reconciliation and shared power. The second would be to set up UN structures and processes to perform adequately and in some reasonable time frame."[53] But another UN force would prove to be a significant problem for the U.S. military: UN Secretary-General Boutros Boutros-Ghali. Boutros-Ghali believed that the UN mandate should be broadened to include efforts to pacify the country, which in practice meant disarming the warlords by collecting all of the weapons in the country, a very difficult undertaking given the availability of weapons provided by the USSR to Somalia in the past. Rounding up the hundreds of thousands of AK-47s—one in every household—without provoking a major conflict would be nearly impossible.

The generals and admirals grew alarmed when they began to perceive that Clinton was sensitive to Boutros-Ghali's more activist approach. The American president strongly advocated multilateralism, and his administration believed that this was a perfect opportunity for the United States to take the lead in helping the UN to rebuild Somalia. Secretary of State Warren Christopher said that "for the first time there will be a sturdy American role to help the United Nations rebuild a viable nation state."[54] However, from the Chiefs' standpoint, that was a recipe for mission creep. Just as in Lebanon, American forces would be sent to a country to carry out one mission, only to have it expanded.

As is often the case, personalities played an important role. Under Bush, the chief American representative in Somalia was Robert Oakley, a professional diplomat. Oakley, who had been ambassador to Somalia from 1982 to 1984, was sent there during the crisis as Bush's special representative. He had created exceptionally good relationships with Mohammed Aidid and the leaders of other factions. His undefinable ability of knowing just how far to push things, how much he could and could not do, contributed much to the successful delivery of food and the establishment of positive relations between Americans and Somalis, including Aidid. But Oakley left the scene when the Clinton regime arrived.

The problem with the new administration, according to Halberstam, was that "the Clinton people were not on top of events."[55] No one from the Clinton team had even gone to Somalia. Aspin, who was getting nervous, had planned to travel to Somalia and had scheduled a trip only to have to cancel at the last minute. In Washington no one understood what was happening in Somalia. Madeleine Albright, the U.S. representative to the UN, testified that a U.S. presence was necessary for "rebuilding Somali society and promoting democracy in that strife-torn land." Under Secretary of State for Political Affairs Peter Tarnoff would also testify on Capital Hill, arguing that "we owe it to ourselves and to Somalia to help UNOSOM succeed."[56] One could only wonder what the administration was thinking when it embarked on an attempt to rebuild a country that had imploded to the point that it essentially ceased to exist.

In March 1993, Oakley was replaced by Jonathon Howe, who was formally designated as the U.S. representative to the UN in Mogadishu. At a time when a diplomat of Oakley's caliber was needed to handle a very delicate diplomatic task, the administration sent a White House insider, a retired admiral who had spent the majority of his life in nuclear submarines. Even worse, Howe worked for the UN, and that meant for Boutros-Ghali, which greatly displeased Aidid. Compounding the danger, Howe knew nothing about Somalia and was not aware of how little he knew. As one person who had worked with him stated, "The worst thing about Jon for that job . . . was not that he was a military man, but that he was the kind of person who, when the political genes were handed out, simply was absent that day—he had no feel for what would be a very complicated political situation."[57] Howe, who considered Aidid's actions to be nothing more than insults hurled at the United States by some rabble rouser from a backwater country, would not tolerate such affronts. A confrontation was inevitable.

Becoming increasingly worried about where the mission in Somalia was headed, the Chiefs began to withdraw American troops gradually until only 4,500 support personnel remained. The 2,600 Marines were replaced by 4,000 Pakistani troops, who neither patrolled as much as the Americans nor were as certain of their rules of engagement. Aidid began to move his heavy weapons back into Mogadishu when he perceived that the UN was attempting to get rid of him.

Convinced that Aidid was behind many of the problems in Somalia, UN officials, prodded by Boutros-Ghali, tried to undercut his authority and limit his activities. On June 5, he struck back, killing or wounding seventy-three Pakistanis. Only the efforts of Italian troops and the American quick reaction force averted worse casualties The next day, June 6, the UN passed a resolution "calling for the arrest and punishment of 'those responsible' for the peacekeepers' deaths." According to Elizabeth Drew, no one in Washington paid much attention to the resolution. In fact, "no one could remember later whether the President was consulted. Aides said later that he must have been told of the need for the resolution. That resolution, and the emotions unleashed by the attack, led straight to the disaster of October 3."[58]

From Aidid's standpoint, Howe's appointment and the UN resolution meant that the UN and the United States were both out to get him. Not only was Howe clearly opposed to him, the U.S. government appeared to be in bed with the UN. As a result, the spiral of violence continued to rise. The UN would use force against Aidid's forces, and the latter would respond, leading to another military action by the UN—and so on.

Howe, according to one source, became "obsessed" with catching Aidid. He reportedly put up notices around Mogadishu offering a twenty-five thousand dollar reward for his capture.[59] During the summer, Howe pressed Washington to send more forces, in particular the highly secret Delta Force and some U.S. Army Rangers, to hunt down Aidid. He was backed by Christopher, Tarnoff, and Albright. Not all supported him, however: "Aspin, Powell and Marine Corps General Joseph Hoar, the head of the U.S. Central Command or CENTCOM, based in Tampa. . . . were all reluctant to send in additional forces, for fear of escalating the mission or having its success measured by whether Aideed was caught."[60]

Aspin seems to have been the only civilian working on Somalia who was worried about the seeming incoherence of U.S. policy. He feared that events were slipping out of control, and he agreed with Powell's assessment that the United States was caught between a rock and a hard place. Events in Africa seemed to be taking on a dynamic of their own. More troops had been requested to protect those who were already there, which was exactly what had happened in Vietnam. After four American soldiers were killed when their Humvee hit a remote-controlled mine on August 8, the Chiefs and Powell recommended that Delta Force be sent to Somalia. Amazingly enough, the decision was made without the high-level consultations that would have commonly occurred in other administrations. To wit, on August 21, Powell called Aspin, who agreed to send the Delta Force and the U.S. Army Rangers even though Gen. Joseph P. Hoar estimated the chance of catching Aidid at only one in four. Lake and Christopher also agreed, and they had an NSC staffer inform Clinton, whom they could not reach that day. "An official said later, 'The President didn't weigh in.' "[61]

In spite of agreeing to send rangers and the Delta Force to Somalia, both Powell and Aspin wanted the United States to get out. In fact, Aspin grew ever more frustrated with the lack of response from the NSC. On August 27 he delivered a major policy speech calling on the UN to devise a more cohesive and "better-focused program of action, to include attention to the need for police, and a coordinated economic-political security approach."[62] But nothing came of it. Then in late September, Powell took the opportunity to speak about Somalia at the last NSC meeting prior to his retirement (the president was not in attendance). He argued that the United States was being sucked into a mission far exceeding that which it had originally agreed to undertake. "He said the commander there, General Montgomery, had asked for reinforcements—primarily tanks and armored personnel carriers." Civilians like Stephanopoulos and David Gergen "looked appalled." Already under pressure from the Hill, they felt that the last thing they needed to do was "to enlarge something that was supposed to be getting smaller."[63] After the meeting, Powell spoke with Aspin, who said he had no intention of sending tanks to Somalia, which would have been interpreted by the media as a further escalation of the conflict.

Then on October 3, the worst possible scenario became reality.[64] Working together, the rangers and Delta Force launched a heliborne attack in an effort to capture Aidid and his senior colleagues. As soon as the helicopters arrived at their destination, one was shot down by a rocket-propelled grenade (RPG). The operation immediately shifted its focus from capturing Aidid to saving the crew of the downed helicopter. Instead of being able to rely on their mobility, the Americans were trapped in an urban environment with high-tech weapons that were useless and no armor. Halberstam hit the nail on the head when he described the battle as follows:

> What took place was urban carnage. By the time the battle was over and relief columns were finally able to fight their way through to rescue the trapped units, eighteen Americans had died, at least seventy-four were wounded, and two helicopters had been shot down. Perhaps as many as one thousand Somalis were killed. But it was in all ways an American disaster, and by the end of the day video clips were being broadcast of a dead American soldier being dragged through the streets of Mogadishu to the cheers of local crowds.[65]

When the president learned what had happened shortly afterwards, he reportedly fumed, "How could this happen?"[66]

He also questioned why the United States had permitted itself to be pushed around by people he referred to as "two-bit pricks." Furthermore, he asked why he hadn't been informed of the problems inherent in U.S. policy toward Somalia and how that policy had shifted without his "*informed approval.*" "He believed that people who were supposed to protect him had not protected him. He had been a little careless, more than a bit disengaged, in fact, but that did not mean he entirely accepted responsibility for what had happened."[67]

When he returned to Washington, he told his advisors that " 'it strikes me as dumb at a minimum to put U.S. troops in helicopters in urban areas where they were subject to ground fire.' He was angry that he hadn't been told about this mission. He compared the situation to Waco, where he said, 'At least I knew what was happening.' "[68] He claimed that he would have never approved the mission had he known that it was to be carried out during daytime.[69]

Although Clinton was upset that he had not been involved in the decision-making process, he had made it very clear to his aides that he did not want to be bothered with foreign policy problems unless the United States was facing a crisis. It is also worth noting that just prior to the battle in Somalia, Powell told Clinton to "get those Rangers out of Somalia."[70]

Blaming Aspin

When the attempt to rescue American refugees in Tehran ended in failure, Jimmy Carter told the Pentagon that although he had not been directly involved in the details of the operation, he personally accepted responsibility, even though the mission commander was ready to accept it himself. Clinton took a different approach, however. David Hackworth, who had spent a lifetime creating and commanding the Delta Force, vented his bitterness over the president's action when he observed, "I don't know which is worse: the attempt to duck responsibility or the image of a Commander in Chief so out of touch that he allowed his foreign policy and military aims to take entirely different paths—both fatally mined."[71]

Attention quickly focused on the secretary of defense. It was Les Aspin who had turned down the request to send tanks on September 25, primarily because he believed the administration wanted to keep a low profile in Somalia. Some viewed his decision as an important mistake (although a JCS study later concluded that the presence of tanks would not have significantly altered the events of October 3). Besides, many in Washington felt that Aspin was doing a lousy job managing the Pentagon, which at times seemed to be an institution running itself, with no one really in charge. When he and Christopher were called to testify on the Hill, neither could articulate a clear American policy vis-à-vis Somalia, because the United States did not have one.

The White House attempted to downplay its role in the entire Somalian mess, which was leading the Chiefs to perceive that "Clinton [was] . . . uninterested in the welfare of America's soldiers."[72] The recent tragic events, which had further weakened the president's already unpopular image in the eyes of many military leaders, reinforced the Pentagon's belief in the Powell Doctrine—the United States should never become involved anywhere unless American security was threatened, which it had not been in the case of Somalia. Most Americans did not even know the United States had troops in Somalia until they saw the CNN reports of the slaughter of American soldiers.

On October 5 Washington decided that U.S. troops would be reinforced in a show of strength, but that the United States would give up any further efforts to capture Aidid. American troops laid low for several months, until it was politically safe to bring them home.

Somalia's Consequences

The events in Somalia resulted in significant changes in U.S. security personnel and policy. Les Aspin, who had gained only limited respect from the military, also suffered from a lack of other allies in Washington: neither Christopher nor anyone in the White House was prepared to come to his aid, and even his former colleagues on the Hill turned against him. The last straw was delivered when "a couple of very important members of Congress gave the President a very strong report. . . . that Aspin would never have the respect on the Hill necessary for a Secretary of Defense"[73] On December 13 Tony Lake told Aspin that the president had lost confidence in him and believed it was time for a change. In a subsequent meeting with the president, Aspin made a strong case for keeping his job, but Clinton told him that the decision had been made. His resignation was announced by the White House on December 15.[74]

The change in personnel was accompanied by a change in policy. For example, when Rwanda sank into an orgy of genocide and the calls came from around the world for the United States to send troops to help pacify the region, the answer was an unambiguous no. Washington wanted no part of another undefined military adventure. As Secretary of State Christopher noted, "The shadow of Somalia loomed large over our internal planning, and Secretary Perry [Aspin's replacement] and General Shalikashvili [Powell's replacement] were careful to heed its lessons and take steps to avoid mission creep. As a result, the Rwanda mission was limited to those tasks for which we had unique capabilities, such as the air transportation of heavy equipment."[75]

PERRY AND SHALIKASHVILI

William Perry, the new secretary of defense, and General John Shalikashvili, the new chairman of the Joint Chiefs of Staff, differed greatly from their predecessors. Perry held a Ph.D. in mathematics from Penn State and had worked for Harold Brown as under secretary for research and engineering in the Pentagon, where he became a well-regarded expert on high-tech weapons systems. In addition to winning unanimous Senate confirmation as the new secretary, he was highly esteemed by everyone in the Pentagon, including the uniformed military; indeed, to this day, many consider him to have been the best secretary of defense the United States has had in recent years. He was a modest man, who did not feel it necessary to show the military he was in charge by blasting one of the Chiefs in public the way Cheney had. As Halberstam noted, "Unlike most civilians, he knew more about the new high-technology weapons than almost anyone in the shop. It was a great source of strength in running the Pentagon, but he never exploited it, never flaunted it in front of the uniformed military as others might have. It was simply there and meant that he could not be fooled about weapons systems, an area that tended to befuddle high-level civilians."[76] Even when he disagreed with the Chiefs, he treated them with respect; they knew they could rely on what the forthright secretary said.[77]

Raised in Poland by parents who were from Soviet Georgia, John Shalikashvili came to the United States as a child. He claimed that he learned English with the help of John Wayne movies. Shali (as most people called him) was drafted by the U.S. Army and sent to Officer Candidate School. Like Powell, he discovered that he enjoyed army life and did well in the post–Vietnam era.

> He was smart, paid great attention to detail, and estimated the strengths and weaknesses of the people around him with considerable skill. He always turned out to be more intelligent and efficient than those above him thought he was going to be, and with his knowledge of languages—German, Polish and Russian—he was particularly valuable during his tours in Europe. There he performed brilliantly as deputy commander of American forces, a three-star slot, during the Gulf War.[78]

In the beginning, the Clinton administration—as well as some of Shali's colleagues on the Joint Chiefs—thought that the new chair's views were closer to Clinton's than to Powell's. Both the Chiefs and Clinton's administration recognized and appreciated that he was no Colin Powell, a man who had the political clout necessary to stand up to the president when he considered it appropriate. They also liked the fact that Shalikashvili believed in greater flexibility in using military force. Early in his tenure, he indicated that he wanted to modify the Weinberger Doctrine, which specified that the United States should become involved militarily only when the vital interests of the United States were at stake. Shalikashvili wanted to drop the word "vital." He could envision numerous situations in which a president would wish to advocate the use of troops even if no threat were posed to the nation's vital interests. He also recognized that the cold war had ended and that the United States would inevitably become involved in what the Pentagon called "Operations Other than War." He did not believe that the chairman of the Joint Chiefs had a right "to put a notice on his door saying, 'I'm sorry—we only do the big ones,' and signed 'John Shalikashvili.' "[79] His ideas about unconventional warfare aroused suspicion among many of his colleagues, many of whom were already deeply distrustful of the Clinton administration and its attitudes toward the military. He had to be careful not to get too close to Clinton if he wanted to maintain credibility within the ranks of the military.

HAITI

Haiti is the poorest country in the Western Hemisphere. Until 1986, it was run by a dictator, who was overthrown and sent into exile. A military junta then took over until free elections were held in 1990. Jean-Bertrand Aristide, a Roman Catholic priest who had been defrocked because of his radical views about liberation theology, was elected president. Serious questions existed concerning his emotional stability, but Washington nevertheless acknowledged him as the country's elected president. Eight months later, however, he was ousted by a military junta led by Lt. Gen. Raoul Cedras. Aristide fled to the United States, where he received asylum.

The Bush administration did very little beyond sheltering Aristide and freezing Haitian assets in the United States, hoping to convince Cedras and his colleagues to restore democracy in that poor country. When Cheney asked Powell what he thought of using military force, he replied, "We can take the country over in an afternoon with a company or two of Marines." Getting out would be the problem: the last time the United States had intervened in Haiti was in 1915, and the Marines ended up staying there for nineteen years.[80] Powell had no intention of supporting an invasion of an economic and political basket case just to restore a questionable democracy devoid of democratic institutions or traditions.

Clinton and Haiti

In the beginning, the Clinton administration hoped to rely primarily on sanctions to apply pressure on Cedras and his colleagues.[81] During the election campaign Clinton had attacked Bush's policy toward Haiti as being inhumane. The Democratic challenger's position "implied a welcome to Haitians fleeing poverty and misery, as well as, in some cases, political persecution."[82] As a result, boats—many handmade and not especially seaworthy—full of Haitians began to move toward the United States. The angry governor of Florida asked how his state was supposed to absorb thousands of Haitians looking for a better life in America. Clinton "didn't need Haitian refugees swarming all over our beaches. He knew how refugees could hurt you."[83] As a consequence, the president reversed his policy, tightened restrictions on entry into the United States, and placed a naval blockade around Haiti while his administration tried to figure out what to do. The resulting combination of sanctions and diplomatic pressure produced the Governor's Island Accord in July 1993. According to this agreement, the Haitian military agreed that Aristide would be returned to power by October 30, 1993.

The Haitian military, however, had no intention of turning over power to Aristide. Cedras and his colleagues believed that the United States lacked the resolve necessary to throw them out of office. Indeed, there were deep splits within the Clinton administration. Tony Lake wanted to use the military to throw out the military and reinstate Aristide, but the Chiefs, supported by Aspin, opposed such an operation. Getting rid of Cedras and his colleagues would be easy, but what then?

The situation in Haiti deteriorated further. In September one of Aristide's advisors was murdered, followed soon thereafter by the assassination of Aristide's choice for justice minister. The message had been sent: if Aristide should go back to Haiti, he too would be killed.

The *Harlan County* Debacle

While the political situation in Haiti worsened, a group of about two hundred American soldiers and twenty-five Canadians boarded the USS *Harlan County,* bound for Haiti. They planned to begin the process of nation-building and training the Haitian military. Unfortunately, no backup plan existed in case the soldiers, who were only lightly armed, ran into trouble. No military force existed in the area to back them up.

When the ship arrived, a mob of more than one hundred men, many of them armed, awaited on the dock; they threatened the ship and, with the American debacle in Africa on their minds, shouted "Somalia, Somalia!"[84] The ship waited for two days while Washington tried to decide what to do next. Unfortunately, Washington remained divided. The hawks wanted to send in the Marines, while the doves, particularly Aspin and the Joint Chiefs, advocated waiting a couple of days while they tried other forms of pressure before sending in the troops.

In the end, the *Harlan County* turned around and headed back to the United States. Its return was a major embarrassment for the Clinton administration. The great power from the north had been forced to retreat—just as in

Somalia! As William Hyland noted, "Haiti was a bitter setback, more so than Bosnia or Somalia. It deeply offended the moralists in the administration, who believed that Haiti was a test case for an American policy of defending human rights and advancing democracy. Haiti was, after all, in the backyard of the United States."[85] Clinton again was irate, and he blamed his NSC staff for putting him in this position. He claimed that the Reagan people were much better at putting a positive spin on things. Look how they managed to get involved in Grenada, thereby keeping Reagan's popularity up. Why couldn't his aides do the same? Stephanopoulos was shocked. He couldn't believe what he was hearing. *"Grenada? That is how we should handle things? Like Reagan? The answer to losing 250 marines in a terrorist attack is to stage an invasion of a tiny country? If you really believe that, then why don't we turn the damn ship around?"*[86] Stephanopoulos concluded that Clinton must have been so angry that he did not realize what he was saying.

Planning an Invasion

By the summer of 1994, rumors circulated in Washington suggesting that the administration was considering an invasion of Haiti. The refugee problem had gotten out of control. During July 3 and 4 alone the U.S. Coast Guard intercepted over 6,000 boat people trying to make their way to the United States.[87] The Pentagon was told to begin making plans for an invasion, which Clinton hoped would be unnecessary; however, if Cedras and his colleagues would not honor the agreement they had signed, the United States would have no alternative but to use military force.

To make sure that Cedras understood the seriousness of the situation, Marine lieutenant general Jack Sheehan, who was helping plan the invasion, was sent to Haiti to speak directly to him. "Sheehan was an impressive figure, six feet five, a combat veteran of Vietnam and bedecked with medals. 'I have two sets of uniforms,' he told Cedras on one occasion, 'my dress uniform and my combat one. You can make the choice of which one I'm wearing the next time we meet.' "[88] By September the invasion plan was complete, although senior military and defense officials continued to be uneasy about Aristide. For his part, Clinton continued to blame his staff for getting him into this mess: "I can't believe they got me into this. . . . How did it happen? We should have waited until after the elections."[89]

On September 7, the NSC met. Clinton, who made a rare appearance, listened as Shalikashvili briefed him on the invasion plan. Stephanopolous described his presentation:

> With his straight back, square shoulders, and short haircut, Shali was the epitome of an American military man—an identity reinforced for my ethnic ears by his clipped Polish accent. Listening to the general detail the pathetic state of the Haitian military, I was struck by his supreme confidence—and slightly apprehensive. *'Isn't this what they always think before the fighting actually starts?'* But his certainty wasn't hubris. The Haitian forces were fierce when facing unarmed women, orphans, and priests, but they'd cut and run at the sight of twenty thousand American troops.

Clinton then thanked Shalikashvili for the briefing and immediately told him, "It's a good plan, let's go."[90]

In the meantime, former president Jimmy Carter volunteered to lead a negotiating team to Haiti in a last-ditch effort to avoid the invasion. Senator Sam Nunn and Gen. Colin Powell joined him. Carter was a wild card, a man who was difficult to control. Clinton had visions of Carter reaching an agreement with which the United States could not live. The bottom line, for Clinton, was that Cedras could not remain in power: he had to go. The negotiating team arrived in Haiti on September 17, only two days before the planned invasion.

The negotiations played out in a fashion similar to a comic opera. Cedras claimed that his forces were prepared to die for their country, while Powell tried to tell him that he would probably get that opportunity given the enormity of the force he would face if the invasion actually took place. To make matters even more interesting, the meeting dragged on and on, to the point where the C-130s carrying the Eighty-second Airborne began to leave Fort Bragg. Clinton even ordered the negotiating team to leave, given the danger they faced from American forces about to descend on the island. While they were discussing matters, Cedras was informed by an aide that the Eighty-second Airborne was on its way. Cedras then capitulated and a date was set for the junta to leave and Aristide to return.

Haiti's Impact

From a military standpoint, the events in Haiti had minimal importance. The United States was up against a highly unpopular junta, whose ragtag army would have been easily defeated by invading American forces. True to Powell's and Shalikashvili's understanding of the role of military force, once Clinton gave the word, the Chiefs made sure that maximum force would have been employed. Haiti would have been overwhelmed in days, if not hours. Unfortunately, the Pentagon would face much more serious problems in Bosnia and Kosovo.

BOSNIA

Bosnia was a case of ethnic cleansing. Three distinct ethnic groups, Muslim Bosnians, Croatian Bosnians, and Serbian Bosnians, had lived there for centuries. The Serbs were determined to take control of vast parts of Bosnia that were inhabited by Muslims, either by forcing them to leave or by eliminating those who stayed. On many occasions the Serbs engaged in what could only be described as genocide; indeed, many believed that their crimes were surpassed in efficiency and magnitude only by Nazi Germany. By the time Clinton took office, the situation had deteriorated significantly, with men and boys being slaughtered daily and women being raped and driven from their homes.

The only solution on the table was the Vance-Owen Plan, named for David Owen, the former British foreign secretary, and Cyrus Vance, the former U.S. secretary of state. The plan broke Bosnia up into "ten cantons; three with a Serb majority, two with a Croat majority, three with a Muslim majority, and one with a mixed Croat-Muslim majority, and one for Sarajevo."[91] Fearing that this agreement would make it appear as if Washington was accepting what the Serbs had done at gunpoint, the Clinton administration refused to accept it, and instead soon began to undermine it. However, the new administration had no alternative to the diplomatic and humanitarian approaches followed by the Bush administration. Furthermore, given the newfound friendship with Russia, Washington did not want to offend Moscow by cracking down on its Bosnian Serb friends. Most of all, no one wanted another Vietnam. Even if the Clinton administration had wanted to intervene militarily, there was little interest on the part of either the Chiefs or Congress for deeper involvement in that beleaguered country. Clinton, meanwhile, did not make it clear to his subordinates what kind of a policy he wanted.

When Clinton asked Powell what the United States could do to help stop the killing, he laid out the same options that he had presented to President Bush, ranging from limited air strikes around Sarajevo to a heavy bombardment of Serb targets throughout the theater. He emphasized that bombing by itself would probably not change Serbian behavior. They could easily and quickly disperse their forces, making it very difficult to spot them from the air. In addition, there was always the possibility that the Serbs would seize humanitarian workers on the ground as human shields.[92] As he had in the past,

Powell never tired of pointing out at high-level meetings that the military should never be used unless the United States had a clear political objective. It was on such an occasion that one of the more interesting clashes on Bosnia occurred.

Powell was explaining the importance of thinking through matters to fully define the goal and exit strategy, when Madeleine Albright, who was then the U.S. ambassador to the UN, "asked [him] in frustration. 'What's the use of having this superb military that you're always talking about if it we can't use it?' "[93] Powell almost had an "aneurysm." From his perspective, soldiers were not some kind of toys to be moved from one place to another. They were human beings and should only be utilized when absolutely necessary—once again revealing the major gap dividing the Pentagon from the State Department and, to a lesser extent, the NSC.[94] The former wanted the military utilized only in *extremis,* while the latter two wanted to make the threat (and actual use) of the military an integral part of American foreign policy. NSC advisor Tony Lake chimed in to note that he thought Powell was right. It was the military's job to ask the difficult questions, the kind of questions that "the military never asked during Vietnam."[95]

At a meeting of Clinton's principal advisors on March 25, Lake argued that given the Bosnian Serb assault on a number of towns, including Srebrenica, where numerous Muslims had taken refuge, the time had arrived for the United States to come up with some new ideas. Powell maintained again that he was against any use of American ground forces. In April the principals and the president held a number of meetings that, unfortunately, were more like seminars: "The long hours spent in the Situation Room, the protracted agonizing, said one high-level official, was a 'bad sign.' He added, 'It wasn't policy making. It was group therapy—an existential debate over what is the role of America, etc.' A month after Lake had begun the new round of meetings to find a new policy, no decisions had been made."[96]

On April 29 Clinton met for two hours with the Chiefs in the Oval Office. Stephanopoulos, Christopher, Lake, Aspin, Sandy Berger, and Leon Fuerth, representing Vice President Gore, also attended. The group reviewed all of the options, including lifting the arms embargo on the Muslims, thereby permitting them to obtain the weapons they needed to defend themselves. Clinton expressed concern about getting sucked further and further into Bosnia, a fear shared by the Chiefs.

At their next meeting, on May 1, the president made a policy decision. Powell again explained the problems involved in trying to hit artillery pieces from the air. The Serbs would just move them, thereby making them very difficult to find. The president's plan, named "lift and strike," provided for the ending of the arms embargo on the Muslims and the initiation of air strikes "if the Serbs took advantage of the interval before the arms reached the Muslims."[97] Christopher then received the dubious honor of going to Europe to obtain Allied approval. However, the trip turned out to be an embarrassment. The Allies, who had troops on the ground, rejected the plan and asked instead why the Americans wanted to limit their participation to air strikes. The minute the planes began to fly, the Bosnian Serbs would probably seize Allied personnel. As Michael Dobbs observed, the United States essentially had offered a "muddle through policy that satisfied no one."[98]

In July the Bosnian Serbs intensified their siege of Sarajevo. The president, who was visiting the Far East, was shocked by the pictures he saw on CNN and called for options, including military ones. Because Powell was in Kuwait, Clinton's request was relayed instead to Adm. David Jeremiah, the vice chairman of the Joint Chiefs. At a principals' meeting on July 13, Jeremiah said that 70,000 troops would be required to take Sarajevo. In addition, because the Sarajevo airport was small, flying in all of the soldiers would be impossible; an overland route would have to be opened up. Christopher, supported by Madeleine Albright, called for the use of ground forces, but Aspin considered the idea a nonstarter because of both the large number of troops required and the potential quagmire that they would enter. A week later Powell proposed several options that used fewer than the 70,000 soldiers suggested by Jeremiah. Nevertheless, the numbers were still too high for some members of Congress.

While the administration mulled over its options in D.C., the Serbian military machine continued to seize town after town and expand its brutal control over Bosnia. In particular, public attention began to focus on Srebrenica, a small mining town located near the border with Serbia. On July 6, 1995, the Serbs began an all-out assault on the village, whose population was swollen with thousands of Muslims who had left their land and sought refuge. On July 11, 1995, the town fell to the Serbs and a massacre ensued, which David Halberstam described: "Now having taken charge of the village, the Serbs started to rid the area of all Muslims. The Serbs might not be good fighters, but they did pogroms very well indeed. They were familiar with the drill, and the entire process had a macabre efficiency." One report claimed that the Serbs "systematically" executed seven thousand Muslim men.[99]

French president Jacques Chirac and Clinton spoke on the phone. The former was outraged, comparing the events surrounding the Serbian taking of Srebrenica to the worst actions of World War II. He insisted that the West had to do something. Clinton agreed, but in response to Chirac's suggestion that the two countries team up to send forces to liberate the city, Clinton answered that he did not think that would make a major difference.

Once again, Clinton was furious, telling his senior advisors that "the United States . . . can not be a punching bag in the world anymore."[100] The sheer barbarism of Srebrenica also had shocked Perry and outraged Shalikashvili, who had been a refugee himself. In the past, when he had spoken to the Europeans they had always responded, "Fine, but where are your ground troops?" Now, however, Shalikashvili used the massacre at Srebrenica to convince the Europeans that the time had come to act and let the Bosnian Serbs know what Western high-tech airpower could do. Bosnia now had the full attention of the American government.

The Bosnian Serbs, however, were not paying much attention to Clinton, Chirac, or anyone else in the West. On August 28, 1995, they launched a "brutal and senseless attack on Sarajevo." Thirty-eight people were killed and another eighty-five were wounded.[101] Within two days NATO responded with devastating bombing attacks against Bosnian Serb positions, even using cruise missiles. The next day, August 31, was "the busiest day of military action in NATO history, with planes ranging across all of northern and Western Bosnia."[102] Bombs and cruise missiles rained down on the Bosnian Serbs until 0500 on September 1 when a bombing halt was declared.

Unfortunately, this bombing campaign was not part of a larger strategy, but simply a response to an action by the other side; thus, it was not used to bring the Bosnian Serbs to the negotiating table. Indeed, the U.S. military opposed making bombing part of a larger policy. No one was more outspoken in his opposition to a bombing campaign than Adm. Leighton "Snuffy" Smith, who was both commander of all U.S. forces in southern Europe and commander of all U.S. naval forces in Europe. Demonstrating little or no enthusiasm for a military campaign in the Balkans, Smith opposed the policy so strongly that Richard Holbrooke suggested he "was edging into an area of political judgements that should have been reserved for civilian leaders."[103] In fact, his opposition was so intense that when Holbrook's military liaison officer at the time, Lt. Gen. Wesley Clark, relayed to Smith the order to reopen the air war, he blew his top at Clark and complained to Gen. George Joulwan, who was commander in chief of U.S. forces in Europe, about Clark's "civilian loyalties." Nevertheless, the bombing resumed on September 6.

On September 11 Clinton attended a meeting of the principals in the White House; his presence, as Holbrooke noted, "made a huge difference, giving our discussion focus and enabling us to reach some important conclusions quickly." Clinton asked if the bombing campaign had reached a point of diminishing returns or was worth continuing. When told that useful targets remained, he responded by saying what he should have said much earlier: "Okay. . . . But I am frustrated that the air campaign is not better coordinated with the diplomatic effort." For the first time the president considered tying the two together. However, as Holbrooke noted in his memoirs, he essentially lacked a mechanism for doing so. The NSC should have been doing that job, but it wasn't. In fact, relations between the civilians and military were so bad that Admiral Smith had ordered General Michael Ryan, his air force commander who was in charge of the bombing, "to have no contact with the negotiating team" led by Holbrooke. (Holbrooke's team played a critical diplomatic role, dealing directly with both the Bosnian Serbs and Serbian president Slobodan Milosevic.)[104] Finally, on September 14 the Bosnian Serbs agreed to cease offensive operations in the Sarajevo region. They also agreed to remove all heavy weapons from the area within a week, to open a land route out of Sarajevo, and to reopen the airport within twenty-four hours. NATO would stand down for seventy-two hours, but bombing would resume if the Bosnian Serbs did not comply. They did.

The Dayton Accords

In an effort to turn the cease-fire into a permanent agreement without recognizing the gains of Serb aggression, a meeting involving the Bosnian Croats, Bosnian Muslims, and a combined Serb-Bosnian delegations was held at Wright-Patterson Air Base in Dayton, Ohio. Discussions began on November 1 and ended on December 14. The resulting agreement gave 49 percent of Bosnia to the Serbs and the rest to the Muslim-Croat federation. The accords called for elections to be held by September 14, 1996. The agreement also called for the arrest of suspected war criminals such as the former president of the Bosnian Serb sub-state, Radovan Karadzic, and General Ratko Mladic, both of whom were considered responsible for the massacre of large segments of the Muslim population.

As a result of this agreement, NATO replaced the UN troops in Bosnia. Twenty thousand American troops, the advance guard of the American contingent of the 60,000-strong NATO Implementation Force (IFOR), crossed the Sava River at the end of December 1995 to take up positions in the northeast quadrant of Bosnia around Tuzla.[105]

At this point a major dispute emerged between the military and civilian leaders. The civilians believed that the only way this agreement would work was if the "military enforced [it] enthusiastically and identified those known troublemakers who were sworn to destroy [it]."[106] The military, and especially Admiral Smith, did not want to put the military in a position in which it would be required to act as a police force. He had no interest in having his forces arrest anyone. The civilians were angered, and they believed that Gen. George Joulwan, who was Smith's superior, did not do enough to get him to support the Dayton Accords by going after war criminals. When the issue was raised with Clinton in November, he agreed with the civilians that "it is best to remove both men." He then looked directly at General Shalikashvili. "I know there has been ambivalence among some of your people—not you, Shali, but some of your people—about Bosnia," he said, "but that is all in the past, I want everyone here to get behind the agreement."[107]

In spite of Clinton's support for the arrest of Karadzic, Mladic, and other accused war criminals, the military in the person of Admiral Smith balked. Smith's behavior would later lead Clinton to call him "insubordinate" for not carrying out his orders.[108] General Joulwan also came in for criticism; indeed the civilians were so upset by the military's refusal to carry out their orders that in the summer of 1997 they replaced him with a young four-star general named Wesley Clark. Given his background as Holbrooke's military assistant at Dayton, the civilians hoped he would be more amenable when it came to dealing with war criminals. A former Rhodes scholar, considered by many to be one of the brightest four-star generals in the U.S. Army, Clark now held one of the most coveted commands in the army. Unfortunately, the position would eventually lead to the premature end of his military career.

NEW FACES IN WASHINGTON AND EUROPE

William Cohen, a former senator from Maine and a moderate Republican, replaced William Perry as secretary of defense in 1997. To the military, he was an unknown. The Chiefs were unsure of where they stood in relation to their new boss and how he would respond to the problems in Kosovo. Compared with William Perry, he was much more relaxed and less aware of military issues. Indeed, he did not seem nearly as interested in defense matters as Perry had been. As Halberstam wrote, "Someone who knew them both said that if Bill Perry wrote his autobiography, virtually all of it would be about his years as secretary of defense; if Bill Cohen wrote his autobiography, after a long and successful career in both the House and Senate, his years in the Pentagon would get one brief chapter."[109]

The relationship of Cohen and the Chiefs with Clark provides an important insight into civil-military relations from the standpoint of the military. Although Cohen had appointed Clark SACEUR (Supreme Allied Commander, Europe), the secretary of defense soon became concerned about him and his actions. From the Pentagon's perspective, Clark was too ambitious. A hard-

President Clinton with senior American military officers in the Pentagon. Secretary of Defense William Cohen is on his right, and General Henry Shelton, chairman of the Joint Chiefs of Staff, is on his left. (Clinton Presidential Materials Project)

driving master of the bureaucracy, he had a reputation for using every avenue open to him to get what he wanted. Also well connected with high-ranking civilians, Clark had been very close to Holbrooke during the Bosnian affair, and now there was concern that he was selling out to the "other side"—the State Department and the White House. After all, he was a general in the United States Army, and his first loyalty (in the minds of senior officers in the Pentagon) was to the secretary of defense. Indeed, Cohen began to warn him that he was too close to civilians outside the Defense Department as early as 1997. He also heard similar comments from Gen. Henry Shelton, who had replaced Shalikashvili as chairman of the Joint Chiefs.

A straightforward question would provoke major battles between Clark and the Pentagon: should the United States pursue an "activist" foreign policy toward Kosovo, including the commitment of ground troops, or should the United States avoid involvement in military operations to the maximum degree possible? Washington was prepared to use airpower if that became necessary, but ground troops? No way. Neither public opinion nor the Hill (Cohen's major concern) would support such a policy. But Clark, and especially Madeleine Albright, believed that backing up U.S. foreign policy with a credible threat of military force was the only way Serbian president Slobodan Milosevic could ever be convinced to stop massacring Albanians in Kosovo.

The Chiefs and Cohen had good reason for hesitating to get involved in Kosovo, especially if it meant deploying ground troops. The Pentagon already faced more than enough problems, including the no-fly zone in Iraq, the always-unpredictable North Korea, the complicated expansion of NATO, and the tumultuous Middle East. In addition, the Vietnam Syndrome also haunted military leaders, who wished to avoid an undefined, open-ended war that would suck them into another form of mission creep. The Chiefs, in particular, worried "that he might be a little too political" (433). The list of desired SACEUR candidates that the army had submitted to the chairman did not include Clark's name, and when General Shalikashvili had asked Army Chief of Staff Dennis Riemer to sign off on Clark's selection as SACEUR, Riemer refused. The only reason Clark was chosen for the position was because Holbrooke, NSC advisor Sandy Berger, and Deputy Secretary Strobe Talbott—and possibly Madeleine Albright—lobbied Shalikashvili on his behalf. From the standpoint of the army leadership, Clark was a questionable choice. After all, what if Clark lined up with the civilians when it came to a major policy position? He could well be the swing vote in the Washington foreign policy community, one that would get the Pentagon involved in a conflict it wanted to avoid. Some asked, "Was he really one of theirs? Was he too political, too likely to grandstand? Did his ambition reach too far?" (394).

In contrast to Clark, General Shelton, the new chairman of the Joint Chiefs, was an old-fashioned soldier. Excellent in dealing with the troops, "crusty, and significantly more laconic, for example, than Wes Clark, Shelton had a worthy combat record and was not likely to break any crockery." He would follow his orders to the letter. He was not about to come up with new policy recommendations. After all, that was not the military's job as Shelton understood it. When Cohen introduced him to the media, he reportedly compared him to Gary Cooper and John Wayne, "tall, straight to the point, not a lot of words" (414).

Partly because of his own actions, Clark found himself in a difficult position. He was caught in the middle of a bureaucratic war between the Pentagon and the high-level civilians on the other side of the river. He later claimed to have received minimal guidance from Cohen; for example, according to Clark's account, when he came back to Washington in September 1997, he asked Cohen directly, " 'Sir, I am within your intent, aren't I?' . . . I knew he didn't want any casualties or problems of course, but he also had directed that I not allow American soldiers to be pushed around. And the U.S. policy was to support those who supported the Dayton Agreement and oppose those who opposed it. 'Just barely,' he said, looking at me piercingly." Clark said he hoped for more guidance, but Cohen did not provide any. The next day he met with General Shelton, who informed him that Cohen was unhappy with his briefing. Clark noted that he was aware of Cohen's unhappiness, but he still did not receive any guidance. Clark left Washington feeling that "I was going to be on my own."[110] Indeed, the situation deteriorated so badly that Cohen and Shelton ordered Clark to provide them with copies of his itinerary prior to coming to Washington. They wanted to be able to take appropriate action if they did not want him to meet with a particular individual.

Clark's position was made even more difficult because he wore two hats: one as CINCEUR (Commander in Chief, U.S. European Command) and the other as SACEUR. The former placed him in command of U.S. forces in Europe, while the latter one placed him in command of NATO forces. As SACEUR, he worked for Javier Solana, the secretary general of NATO. Clark's unenviable task required him to not only keep Washington happy but also to do the bidding of Solana, who put considerable pressure on Clark to solve the Balkan problem using NATO in a more active role.

KOSOVO

The final major military campaign under Clinton occurred in the province of Kosovo. Although primarily populated by Albanians, Kosovo contained some of Serbia's most important and treasured historical sites and shrines. As a result, it was one of the potentially most dangerous pieces of real estate in the Balkans. Hatred between the Albanians and the Serbs had simmered for centuries. The Serbs were determined to keep Kosovo under their control, and Milosevic had made keeping Kosovo part of Serbia a key component of his successful campaign to win the presidency. But the Albanians wanted to return to the arrangement that Marshal Josip Tito had created in 1974, whereby the constitution gave the Albanians considerable autonomy.

Kosovo was not part of the Dayton Accords; it wasn't even mentioned. Consequently, although the accords had ended the fighting in Bosnia, they did nothing to control conflict in Kosovo. By 1997, the Albanian Kosovo Liberation Army (KLA) had been formed and soon had 15,000 to 20,000 troops under arms and was getting weapons from a variety of areas. The KLA began what amounted to a guerrilla war, attacking Serbian police stations and other buildings and individuals they believed supported the Belgrade government.

Enforcing Order in Bosnia

Clark continued his war with the Pentagon while NATO considered what it should do about troop levels in Bosnia to enforce the Dayton Accords. When Clark consulted with the commander of the troops in Bosnia, Gen. Rick Shinseki, the future chief of staff of the army, Shinseki recommended that the United States continue to maintain 10,000 troops in the region. Clark accepted Shinseki's recommendation, which he then passed on. Then, shortly after Christmas 1997, he was informed by his executive officer that the American military representative at the talks had been ordered to disavow his recommendation. Clark claimed he thought he was doing what Washington wanted. He called Shelton, who promised to look into the matter. The next day, however, the American military representative—a three-star general—disavowed Clark's recommendation, an action that made the Americans look silly. As a result, Clark said,

> The episode caused me to review exactly where I stood with NATO and the Pentagon. Responding to guidance, I had adopted a somewhat more active strategy for using NATO forces to assist civil implementation during the last six months. And formulating a strategy wasn't enough—you had to push relentlessly to make it work, including, sometimes, pushing against the judgements of your own subordinate headquarters. Implementation of the Dayton Agreement was going better, despite dire predictions that a more active NATO force might prove dangerous for our troops. In fact, the opposite was the case: the more we pushed against the hard-line Serbs, the less they wanted to challenge us. (105)

Regardless of the correctness of Clark's approach, it put him on a collision course with his colleagues in the Pentagon.

Monica Lewinsky

From the military's standpoint, the most significant impact of the Monica Lewinsky scandal was its creation of even more chaos in Washington. Never a hands-on president, Clinton and his advisors were overwhelmed and trying to find a way to save his presidency. Madeleine Albright, now secretary of state, was more than happy to fill in for the president on foreign policy. The administration's leading hawk on Kosovo, she believed the United States should use military force in the Balkans, beginning with American airpower. Unfortunately, like others in the administration, she could offer no further solution if airpower failed, as the Chiefs feared it would. They saw a potential political alliance between Albright and Clark.

Many in the military considered the Lewinsky affair to be an example of a double standard. If a military officer had been discovered carrying on an affair with a subordinate as had Clinton, it would not only severely hurt his career, as it had in the case of Gen. Joe Ralston, who was denied the chairmanship because he had an affair when he and his wife were separated; the offending officer could even be forced to resign. After all, Clinton was the commander in chief. While military leaders were well aware that he had been elected by the American people, in their minds they could not help asking if he should not be held to the same standard as those serving under him. In any case, the incident reduced the respect many in the military had for the president to an all-time low.

From a political standpoint, the last thing the president wanted was another war. Public support for it was minimal, and he was in a corner. Besides, there were those who would claim that he got the United States involved only to direct attention away from his scandalous behavior.

Milosevic Retaliates

By May 1998 Milosevic began to retaliate against the KLA. The response came in the form of even more brutal attacks on Albanians in Kosovo not only by elements of the Yugoslav Army, but also by private armies that massacred thousands of Albanians, especially young men and boys. Violence escalated and the Albanians were given their martyrs. Clark, who believed that the West could no longer afford to sit on its hands and watch the slaughter continue, spoke with Shelton and Cohen in Washington in June about using the threat of airpower to compel the Serbs to back off. They both agreed. However, no sooner had he returned to Brussels, when Vice Chairman Ralston called and asked the now familiar question, "Wes, what are we going to do if the air threat does not deter him?" Clark responded, "I think that's unlikely, but in that event, I guess we'd have to do something on the ground, directed at Kosovo" (119). The issue troubling military leaders was that the Balkans were of secondary importance to the Pentagon. What if Saddam Hussein did something that they would have to react to? What about Korea? The Chiefs only had so many people in uniform.

By the time the NATO defense ministers met in June, the planning process had reached an advanced stage, but attention was focused primarily on the use of airpower, with very little interest in employing ground forces. In addition, those in Washington and in Europe were worried; force was the last thing they wanted to use, but they needed some means of restraining Milosevic. As a result, NATO decided to run an exercise called Operation Determined Falcon on June 16. "Approximately one hundred NATO aircraft flew through Albania up to the Serbian border and then flew east, within Albanian and Macedonian air space" (120). The operation lit up Serbian radar and sent a message of what Serbia could expect if it didn't back off in Kosovo.

Planning for a full-scale air strike went ahead. Clark designed a plan and took it back to Washington. When he arrived, Shelton was not available, so he went to see Robert Gelbard, the State Department's coordinator for the Balkans. Gelbard took Clark to the White House, where he told Jim Steinberg, the deputy national security advisor, that he had worked out a plan for a limited air operation against the Serbs but that he could not show it to him until he had spoken with Shelton. Unfortunately, Shelton heard that he had been over to see Steinberg before speaking to him, and he was angered by his assumption that Clark had shown the plan to Steinberg. The matter passed the next day when Clark explained what had happened, but it served to underline how suspicious Shelton and others were with regard to Clark's dealings with high-level civilians outside of the Pentagon.

In September Clinton went to the National War College, where he met with the CINCs. According to Clark, the only comment Clinton made to him was "You'll be ready to take care of the Kosovars, won't you?" Clark replied, "Yes sir" (132). After the various military leaders had explained the situation in their parts of the world the president got up and left. The one-hour meeting had been neither stimulating nor useful in the eyes of the military.

If any event solidified Western determination to take action in Kosovo, it was the massacre at the village of Racak. Ambassador William Walker, who was head of the OSCE (Organization of Security and Cooperation in Europe) mission, called Clark to report that he had seen roughly forty farmers who had been shot at close range lying in a ditch. As a result, NATO met in emergency session to discuss what should be done. Madeleine Albright called on "NATO foreign ministers to propose that the Alliance review and update plans to launch military strikes." In a last-ditch effort to avert a military action, however, NATO decided to send Gen. Klaus Naumann, the head of the NATO

Military Committee, and Clark to Belgrade to talk to Milosevic. The Yugoslavian leader was not impressed. He denied that a massacre had taken place, noting that the Serbian police were investigating the matter. He also refused Clark's request to permit Louise Arbour, who was the chief prosecutor of the international criminal tribunal on Yugoslavia, to come to Serbia, unless she was escorted by the country's justice minister. Then he said he was ordering Ambassador Walker to leave the country, and he made it clear that he would not honor the agreement he had made with NATO concerning the withdrawal of troops and heavy weapons from Kosovo. As Milosevic said, "I told you, General Clark, that we must have the right to defend ourselves."[111] That was the final straw: NATO's credibility was now on the line.

The situation in Washington, however, was much the same as it had been over the last six years since Clinton took office. The White House provided no leadership, no policy, and no focus. The president did not address the deep divide between the military and civilians concerning the use of force. While he was in office, Powell was able to bridge the gap and help focus attention on the critical aspects of military policy. But the military's best-known icon was gone.

In a final attempt to head off the use of force against Serbia, Albright proposed holding a conference that would bring together representatives of the Serbs and Albanians at Rambouillet in France. The conference began on February 6, 1999, but neither side wanted to be there. Furthermore, the Albanians were lost; they had no understanding of the give-and-take concept that is an inherent part of negotiations, nor did they understand the procedures. They also had no idea of who was who at the negotiations. At one point, for example, when Madeleine Albright stood up, "They probably thought, said Dugagjin Gorani, an adviser to the Kosovo delegation, that she was a cleaning woman."[112] Senator Bob Dole, who had championed the Albanians' cause, finally convinced them to sign the agreement on March 18. However, the Serbs refused to sign.

One interesting question that arose during the conference was whether Clark would be permitted to attend. After all he was NATO's military commander. In mid-February, the American delegation convinced the attendees that Clark should be permitted to attend in an effort to bring the Serbs around. However, shortly after that idea was raised, Joe Ralston phoned Clark and told him that "the Secretary of Defense doesn't want you there."[113] Clark was surprised that the United States would not send the chief military officer in NATO to the conference to reinforce the seriousness of the talks. Then Cohen called Clark and gave him a figurative slap in the face: he could go, but he could only talk about the military annex.

The Kosovo Air War

Because the White House was determined to proceed with the bombing plan, the Chiefs went along but would do everything possible to minimize the extent of U.S. involvement. Not only were they concerned about losing assets, they also worried about the lack of a backup plan if bombing proved insufficient. The air force and navy air personnel believed that airpower would be decisive, but like all officers, the Chiefs were paid and trained to imagine the worst-case scenario.

Ultimately, the politicians agreed that the operation would rely primarily on airpower. "That was the strength of America and thus the strength of NATO. Or as Sandy Berger sometimes said privately, that was where the West's greatest advantage lay—an advantage of perhaps one thousand to one in air power, whereas if it was a struggle with ground troops in terrible terrain, the advantage dropped to seven to one and the terms began to favor Milosevic." The bombing began on March 24. Unfortunately, that same day Clinton inserted a critical sentence in his statement announcing the start of hostilities: "I do not intend to put our troops in Kosovo to fight a war."[114] From a military standpoint, the president's ad hoc remark was counterproductive. Telling the other side that minimal force will be used is much less effective than letting him think that everything available will be thrown at him. Ruling out ground troops in particular sent the wrong message to Milosevic: as long as he dispersed and hid his troops and equipment, they would survive because pilots flying at 12,000 to 14,000 feet could hardly distinguish a single armored car from a bus.

By the fourth day of the bombing campaign, NATO's hope that Milosevic would quickly back down evaporated. And because Serb atrocities on the ground were only increasing, Clark was given the authority to move from phase 1, which had focused primarily on air defense systems, to phase 2 strikes targeting lines of "communication, and attacking their choke points, storage and marshaling areas, and any tank concentrations that could be found."[115] Bad weather often proved problematic, however, forcing more than half of the planes to return without dropping their ordnance.

Target Selection

The process of selecting bombing targets produced constant friction between the military and civilians. Not only did Clark and Lt. Gen. Mike Short, who was in charge of the air war, have to negotiate with Washington over what targets to attack, they also had to deal with NATO. Clark and his people, the experts when it came to the air war, wanted to pick the targets themselves but were denied that opportunity. First, Clark and Short had to get the permission of the Pentagon, and then civilian authorities had to approve the proposed targets from a list submitted to the White House. According to Clark, at one point General Shelton called him and asked, "Wes, how soon are you going to get me your Phase II targets? . . . I need to get them across the river for approval."[116] After the war, a study prepared by Adm. James O. Ellis argued that "an otherwise well-executed air campaign had been 'politically constrained.' Among the adverse effects, according to Ellis, were a tendency toward 'incremental war' and excessive concerns about collateral damage."[117] Mike Short was even more outspoken when he maintained that "political restrictions had prevented [him] 'from conducting an air campaign as professional airmen would have conducted it.' "[118] One of the most telling comments came from a pilot who observed that "this has been a farce from the start. We have violated every principle of campaign air power I can think of."[119] Because of the heavy political influence on target selection (Clinton was even involved in some instances), Benjamin Lambeth reported that even Short and Clark battled, as the latter attempted to micromanage the process because of pressure from Washington.[120]

Clark continued to believe that without a credible ground threat, Milosevic could hold out for a long time, and by the third week of the war a consensus had begun to form in Washington that ground forces might be necessary. Clark made a proposal to Shelton, but as he spoke to him he realized that he had no idea how decisions were made (or not made) in Washington. He wondered why Shelton didn't bring him into the decision-making process the way that Powell had with Schwarzkopf in the Gulf War. As in the past, Clark claimed he could not get guidance, suggesting that even Shelton was left out of the decision-making process. On March 31, for example, Clark called Shelton to talk about the ground option. " 'Sir, I need some guidance: how hard should I continue to push?' I expected some measure of support. Instead, he replied, 'Wes, I don't know.' "[121] This was certainly not the kind of answer Schwarzkopf would have received from Powell.

Public opinion fueled the White House's resistance to including a ground option. Public support for the war dropped from "65 percent in late April to 59 percent by mid-May, with opposition to the war rising from 30 to 38 percent during the same period.[122] Some members of Congress also began to complain about the unpopular war.

Clark, convinced that even the mention of the potential use of ground troops would have a major impact in Belgrade, continued his confrontation with Cohen and the Chiefs. Whenever the Pentagon learned that he was trying to raise the issue, the Chiefs or Cohen would move quickly to block him. However, Clark's desire to use ground forces got a boost in April when Tony Blair visited Brussels. Clark explained his idea, and Blair agreed with him. Unfortunately for Clark, Washington began to suspect the existence of some kind of a Blair-Clark axis that Clark would try to use as leverage in his campaign to deploy ground troops. Needless to say, that did not endear him to either the Pentagon or the White House.

Battling over Apache Helicopters

When Shelton asked Clark if he could use Apache helicopters, Clark jumped at the idea and said yes. They could be used in low-level attacks against specific targets. Initially, however, the Pentagon denied his request, noting that their use could be misunderstood by our allies as being a precursor to ground troops. The army had dug in its heels. Clark called Shelton and told him, "[Y]ou should know that I'm having a hard time back here with the Chiefs. The Army Chief just doesn't want to send them in."[123]

During an April 1 video teleconference between Clark and the Chiefs and their chairman, the army representative raised all kinds of objections. And as Clark noted, "When a service doesn't support the use of its own assets in combat, assets developed over two decades and at a cost of billions of dollars, there's no end to the detail of the questions that can be asked. I had been forewarned, but to listen to the Army's questions was still painful."[124] The Apaches were the best and most modern weapons of their kind. They were designed to elude even the most sophisticated antiaircraft systems, and they were the best air-to-ground system the army had. Indeed, their firepower was more accurate than that of fixed-wing aircraft.

Faced with countervailing pressures, Shelton came up with a compromise. He would send the helicopters from Germany to Albania and hold them there while he tried to build a consensus. If one was reached, he would suggest to the president that the helicopters be utilized. Bureaucracies, however, have a way of making life difficult when they want to, and Gen. Dennis Riemer, the army's chief of staff, had no intention of sending the Apaches to Clark: "The army slow-walked the Apaches through the pipeline. Its every move seemed greased with molasses. Clearly someone at the very top had sent out a signal saying there was no rush. Deadline after deadline was missed. Excuses piled up. There was always some reason not to proceed."[125] Then on May 18 Clinton stated publicly that the helicopters probably would not be used. From Clark's standpoint, "My problem was that the Administration had never reached an official decision on the Apaches, so far as I knew. If it had, I wasn't informed."[126] The helicopters were eventually returned to Germany without having been used in combat.

Clark Stay Home!

The NATO summit that convened in Washington on April 23 would turn out to be a watershed event. The Allies agreed that they would do whatever it took to win the war in Kosovo. Clark was initially told by Shelton that Cohen did not want him at the summit, an order that made very little sense. How could NATO make a major military decision if its military commander in chief was not present? Finally, Cohen agreed that he could come, but told him to say "nothing about ground forces. We have to make this campaign work, or we'll both be writing resumes." Clark agreed to the explicit guidance: " 'Yes, sir,' I said. 'I'm not going to spoil the summit. I'm not going to be the skunk at the picnic.' " When he arrived at a reception for senior officials, he started walking toward Clinton and his senior advisors to pay his respects, but "the body language was uninviting. I turned away and halted about twenty feet behind and off to the side of the group." According to Clark, as he traveled back to Brussels, some journalists misinterpreted his words to suggest that NATO was not winning. The next evening Shelton called him, "The Secretary of Defense asked me to give you some verbatim guidance, so here it is: 'Get your f____ g face off the TV. No more briefings, period. That's it.' I just wanted to give it to you like he said. Do you have any questions?" Clark claimed that he later learned that Clinton had seen a transcript of what he had said and found nothing wrong with it.[127] In spite of Clinton's reaction, Cohen's guidance—no more briefings, period—stood.

In Brussels planning continued for the possible use of as many as 225,000 to 250,000 ground troops. Retreating from his original statement prohibiting the deployment of U.S. ground troops, Clinton announced that "all options are on the table."[128] On May 27 Cohen met secretly with his four principal NATO counterparts to consider whether to proceed with a land invasion. "By the end of May, NATO was generally acknowledged by the media to be inching ever closer to some kind of ground operation in the Balkans."[129]

Fortunately, Belgrade's June 3, 1999, capitulation rendered a ground invasion unnecessary. Even though the ground option had deeply concerned Milosevic, airpower could claim the lion's share of credit for the victory.

Evaluating the Kosovo Operation

In retrospect, the major problem with the Kosovo operation was that the military had neither clear guidance for the conduct of the war nor a clear definition of the goal to be achieved (other than to force Milosevic to give up). Civilians saw a relationship between escalating military force and a diplomatic end, but to the Chiefs, White House planning seemed to be a new form of ad hoc planning. According to the guidance that had been approved by the president, the military was supposed to be able to fight two wars in different parts of the world simultaneously. Getting bogged down in the Balkans while having to fulfill existing obligations would seriously burden the capability to fight two major wars at once. As General Ralston said to Clark, "Wes, let me ask you this question, . . . Let's just say we implemented your plan and then something went wrong in Korea, and we had to go to war there. What would we do? We do have 80,000 Americans there and a treaty. So we'd have to do something."[130]

To the Chiefs, Clinton had failed to provide leadership after he had made his statement about not using ground forces. He seemed instead to disappear, even though American aircraft were in the midst of a war. As Halberstam explained, "The President, who by temperament and upbringing did not like the use of force, seemed to shy away from public responsibility for it, loath until much later in the war to make the case for it to the American people."[131] It was not until June 3 that Clinton went through the motions of meeting with the Joint Chiefs as a group.

For his part, Clark knew he had the authority of Goldwater-Nichols behind him, but he also knew that he worked for a secretary of defense who was appalled by his activist approach to policy. From Cohen's standpoint, Clark was there to implement policies decided in Washington or Brussels, not formulate them. Indeed, Cohen believed that Clark was constantly putting him in conflict with the Chiefs, particularly the army chief of staff. Deeply suspicious of Clark, Cohen was convinced that his subordinate was constantly circumventing him, working through Prime Minister Blair or Secretary of State Albright. As a consequence, their relationship could only be called a disaster. On the one hand, Clark believed that he was not getting clear orders, and that left him no choice but to make up policy as he went along. On the other hand,

Cohen despised this upstart four-star who created one problem after another. "Clark told friends that dealing with Cohen was the worst professional experience he had had since his encounter with Jack Hudachek as a young battalion commander. Cohen felt the same way about Clark. 'I rue the day I made him SACEUR,' he told aides as one point.' "[132]

Finally the officer who had led the victorious American military campaign in Kosovo was unceremoniously sacked by Cohen.[133] Shelton informed Clark that he would leave the SACEUR position in April, two months early. The purported reason was that the JCS had to find another position for Ralston, who would otherwise be required by the law to retire, and the White House concurred. Clinton would later claim that he did not understand what was going on and was upset by what happened to Clark. However, as far as the military was concerned, Clinton's action—or inaction—in permitting Cohen to fire Clark smacked of betrayal. Many disagreed with Clark, but he had run the war, and he had won it. Once again Clinton stood on the sidelines and did nothing.

CONCLUSION

Presidential Leadership Style

The Chiefs believed that, in addition to suffering from moral lapses, Clinton failed them by not providing leadership. For an organization that expects the president to be "in charge," an absentee landlord who is more interested in domestic policy and provides little guidance in time of war is anathema. Leaving the military in the dark on what he expected with regard to Somalia, Bosnia, and Kosovo was unforgivable. From the Chiefs' standpoint, he was responsible for deciding what U.S. policy was and then enforcing it throughout the U.S. government. They would rather have an imperfect, but clearly articulated policy than one that was undefined and constantly shifting.

Clinton lacked control of the foreign policy apparatus partly because he had difficulty making decisions. Sidney Blumenthal commented on Clinton's approach to Somalia, Haiti, and Bosnia when he noted, "In all of these international situations, Clinton appeared irresolute, unsure about the use of force, whether in deploying it or refusing to deploy it. He seemed to have miscalculated or, worse, blundered."[134] In addition, his authority was so diminished by his personal scandals and the issue of homosexuals in the military that he could never gain the respect of the Chiefs, who viewed him as weak and indecisive.

Violations of Service/Military Culture?

Whether he intended it or not, from the very beginning of his tenure in office, Clinton sent a message to the military that he despised it; thus, because the president had given the impression that he "loathed those who served, the understanding and respect he would eventually require would never be there." For example, Gen. Ron Folgeman, chief of staff of the air force, reportedly retired before his term was up because he "had simply lost respect and confidence in the leadership that [he] was supposed to be following."[135] One unusually outspoken Marine complained, "Our military's heart and soul can survive lean budgets, but they cannot long survive in an America that would tolerate such a character as now occupies the Oval Office. We are entitled to a leader who at least respects us—not one who cannot be bothered to remove his penis from a subordinate's mouth long enough to discuss our deployment to a combat zone."[136]

The military believed that Clinton's effort to push gay rights on the military was another sign that he neither understood nor respected the military as an institution. He would not listen to Powell, who proposed a more gradual approach to change that policy, nor would he recognize the increasingly conservative nature of the military; at the time, 64 percent of officers considered themselves Republicans, while only 8 percent said they were Democrats (in 1976, only 33 percent were Republicans, and 12 percent were Democrats).[137] New ideas can certainly be introduced into an institution like the military, but only with time and patience.

From an operational standpoint, Clinton provided very little leadership. He gave the Chiefs the impression that he was not especially interested in foreign policy. Although a president may prefer working on domestic reform, national defense remains one of his primary duties and cannot be left to others. A president must adopt a hands-on approach to policy at the strategic level, provide clear guidance, and ensure that the government works together smoothly toward a common goal. Clinton understood neither the complexity nor the importance of bureaucratic structures, and the military is probably the most highly bureaucratic structure in Washington. The military wants to know someone is in charge, and it wants clear and concise orders, even if it does not approve of them. The military may not want to send forces to Somalia, Bosnia, or Kosovo, but if the order comes it wants to know what it is supposed to do. In the case of Kosovo, for example, Clinton provided little leadership, even though it was his task to call together Cohen, Albright, Shelton, and Clark and make certain they understood his policy and his goals. They needed to know who was in charge. As it was, Clark, who had a reputation among senior military officers as an officer who would push the envelope and then act surprised when his superiors got upset, was caught in the middle. If Clinton had told Albright and Cohen what he wanted, Clark's independent streak would have been eliminated or at least controlled, confusion and embarrassment would have been avoided, and Clark would have been permitted to finish out his tour. The same was true of Admiral Smith, whom the president accused of "insubordination." However, it is up to the president to take charge in such cases and not only make his will known but enforce it. Clinton was too detached from the process, and when he made critical decisions too many were made on an ad hoc basis. More often than not, no one knew who was issuing the orders and what they meant in practice. And when force was used, Washington (and NATO) too often interfered in operational matters. General Short was driven up a wall by Washington's constant interference in target selection; too frequently items that he believed should be attacked from a military standpoint (e.g., anti-aircraft batteries) were placed off limits with little or no explanation.[138] Contributing to the problems caused by Clinton's lack of leadership was the absence of regular NSC meetings. In many instances the president need not become involved in policy discussions, but Clinton's absence from the vast majority of NSC meetings dealing with issues such as Bosnia or Kosovo was inexcusable.

One of the values that is pounded into cadets and midshipmen at American military academies is the importance of accepting personal responsibility for one's actions. Although there are those who do not follow that rule, it is a trait that most military men and women expect from their leaders. In this case, from the military standpoint, Clinton failed. Instead of following Jimmy Carter's example of accepting responsibility for the disaster at Tehran (even though it was planned and executed by the military), Clinton consistently blamed his subordinates when something went wrong. Clinton's primary concern seemed to be his public image, and although the Chiefs understood that image was important for a politician, they also believed that a person should accept responsibility for his or her actions. Note Halberstam's comments concerning Clinton's responsibility for Somalia.

> Nor, when Somalia turned into a disaster, had they been pleased. What happened there was like a terrible death in the family for the military, but they had been equally disturbed by the White House response. First, came the preoccupation with spin, about which they were aware, and second, as the White House people prepared to go before the Congress to explain what had happened, they made it clear to the military people who came over to help brief them that the White House wanted to minimize

> its own culpability in the decision to upgrade the mission and go for mission building. The Pentagon people believed that decision had been as much Tony Lake's as Jonathan Howe's but the perception was that the White House wanted to get Lake's fingerprints off it. . . . To them it showed that what was for them a matter of life and death, of young men dying, could become for the White House all too easily a matter of images.[139]

The military neither respected Clinton nor had confidence that he would provide meaningful leadership. In a word, he was the antithesis of the kind of political leader and commander in chief that the military sought. They were happy to see him leave office.

13
THE MILITARY AND GEORGE W. BUSH

We understand that leadership is not an exclusive function of the uniformed services. . . . So when some suggest that we in the Army do not understand the importance of civilian control of the military, well, that's just not helpful and it isn't true.
—General Eric Shinseki

The administration of George W. Bush began quietly, and there was every indication that it would be uneventful in the area of civil-military relations. True, the new secretary of defense, Donald Rumsfeld, made clear that he felt the military was in need of transformation, of becoming more mobile and modern, but this was a line the country's senior military officers had heard many times before. And it was the kind of pressure that they had usually been able to keep at arm's length. In the meantime, the military now had a president who touted their virtues and importance whenever possible; a man who made it clear that he intended to make up for the neglect of the Clinton years by providing the armed forces with increased financial support, assistance that would give it the assets it needed to strengthen its standing as the world's most powerful military.

But then came the events of September 11, 2001. National security in the United States would never be the same: the specter of terrorism both at home and abroad was real, and the need for the American military to fight a new and different type of war *today* rather than tomorrow was critical. In the meantime, in spite of the wars they were being asked to fight, the military was also pressed hard by their new secretary of defense, who had not yet established his vision for defense transformation, to make major structural, attitudinal, strategic, and operational changes. The pressure to change would be applied especially to the U.S. Army, which had two years previously initiated an aggressive, comprehensive effort to transform large, unwieldy forces into smaller, more rapidly deployable units for the twenty-first century. Unfortunately, Rumsfeld either chose to ignore or discount what the army was already doing. Had he made an effort to fully understand the ongoing process, he would have seen that the army was already pursuing the transformation that he favored. He may have disagreed with the pace and some aspects of the policy, but the army and Rumsfeld would have enjoyed a more cooperative relationship than the conflicted one that developed.

Many of the country's military leaders were opposed to the changes sought by Rumsfeld, but the secretary was determined to force them to accept change regardless of their opposition. Those who dared to question the correctness of Rumsfeld's decisions would soon find themselves either shunted aside to new jobs or forced to leave the Defense Department—regardless of whether they were civilians or military officers. The only individuals whose careers would survive and prosper were officers who were prepared to play Rumsfeld's game. In short, the period was marked not only by rapid change, but also by upheaval in the world of civil-military relations.

GEORGE W. BUSH'S LEADERSHIP STYLE

George W. Bush was the first MBA corporate executive to become president, and he let "it be known that he favors a corporate model of political leadership."[1] Not wanting to becoming involved in details, he instead intended to rely on his subordinates to deal with problems and provide answers to his questions. In a sense, he was the opposite of Jimmy Carter, who loved to delve into the minutia of national security policy. Additionally, in contrast to many other presidents, Bush's vice president, Richard Cheney, was deeply involved in many of the administration's key national security issues, especially in the aftermath of the events of 9/11. Furthermore, the decision-making process in the new Bush administration was hierarchical. As Thomas Preston and Margaret Herrmann have observed, "Bush's advisory system is structured more hierarchically (due to Cheney's influence) than might be expected for a leader with low power needs, but it functions in the gathering of information and advice as would be expected given the president's style."[2] Hence, Bush waited for the various departments or governmental entities to provide him with options. The heads of these departments were autonomous, and the president dealt almost exclusively with them. The idea of Kennedy calling up a State Department desk officer and asking him or her for answers to questions would never happen under George W. Bush. However, Bush's proclivity to delegate decision-making authority to his cabinet officials had two serious implications for the country's armed forces.

First, his style invited bureaucratic conflict between the various departments, all of which would try to "steal" as much of the action as possible from others in the bureaucracy. "Bureaucratic infighting and conflicts over the shape of Bush's foreign policy have been quite visible over the past two years, putting administration hardliners like Defense Secretary Donald Rumsfeld and Vice President Cheney against the more moderate Secretary of State Colin Powell."[3] Bush wanted a healthy mix of differing views and attitudes, so he selected a group of individuals with strong personalities (including his vice president) and varying perspectives on how to address the country's problems. Having enjoyed listening to the clash of viewpoints, he would then make his decision. But once he had done so and given the action to one department, that particular cabinet official and his subordinates would attempt to dominate policy, even when it meant keeping other parts of the U.S. government out of the action, regardless of how sound their advice might be. Consequently, unlike Kissinger or Brzezinski, the national security advisor, Condoleezza Rice, served primarily as an advisor. G. W. Bush's approach stood in stark contrast to his father's leadership style, which was to select a number of highly competent officials, none of whom attempted to steal the action on a policy issue. Rather, they proposed a variety of different opinions, but always worked together without letting their egos control their actions.

Second, Bush's leadership style allowed Rumsfeld to dominate the formulation of national security policy. The president admitted that he was not a military expert and expected Donald Rumsfeld, who was in charge of the Defense Department, along with individuals such as the chairman of the Joint Chiefs of Staff and Director George Tenet of the CIA, to advise him on military issues. As far as the Defense Department was concerned, Rumsfeld left no doubt in anyone's mind that the armed forces worked for him. Regardless of Goldwater-Nichols, which made the chairman the president's chief advisor on military affairs, Rumsfeld was determined to decide what role, if any, the Chiefs would play. If he wanted them advise the president, he would say so—although in practice this would not happen very often.

Bush also was a man who wanted quick answers to the country's national security problems; Bob Woodward noted, "Bush's leadership style bordered on the hurried. He wanted actions, solutions."[4] He was not a man who spent hours trying to figure out a solution to a problem. For example, when the terrorists struck on 9/11, he immediately wanted a set of options for responding.

Finally, Bush also was a president who saw problems in terms of "moral blacks and whites," which resulted in a more forceful approach to foreign policy. "Bush's comfort level with a conflict in which 'you are either with us or against us' will be high enough to allow a far more forceful level of participation in policy debates than would normally be expected."[5] Because of this tendency to see the world in terms of strict dichotomies, Bush also more readily used force to address security problems—especially after the events of 9/11—than some of his predecessors. Indeed, 9/11 forced Bush to focus on foreign policy to a much greater degree than he might have wished. It became the major force driving him and his administration. For several years, his primary focus would not be health care or the economy, but how the United States would respond to terror, and what it should do to wipe it out. Furthermore, as Gordon and Shapiro noted, 9/11 also convinced him and the rest of the country's senior leaders to be prepared to act unilaterally. "If Europeans did not agree with the way America decided to respond to the new challenges, that was unfortunate, but it was their problem and the United States would not risk its safety to accommodate dissenting views."[6]

Donald Rumsfeld

Rumsfeld was considered by most to be pugnacious, arrogant, bright, brusque, and very difficult to get along with. He was convinced that he understood the national security problems facing the U.S. military better than the Chiefs. In his eyes, the problem was no longer how to maneuver massive tank and artillery units, but how to make good use of smaller, carefully packaged forces that had been crafted to deal with a specific threat. Furthermore, the president agreed with him. As one of Rumsfeld's biographers explained,

> The two men agreed completely about what kind of transformation of the military was required. The armed forces would have to be lighter, faster, more flexible; the various forces would need to work together more closely and conduct more joint operations; greater use would have to be made of strategic air power; and in general both doctrine and equipment should be brought more fully into line with the galloping technological advances of the age.[7]

With the foregoing in mind, when he first arrived at the Pentagon, Rumsfeld emphasized two themes.[8] First, he argued that the American military "was hidebound and outdated, still equipped and trained and organized to fight old enemies, mainly the Soviet Union." Second, he emphasized the importance of being prepared for surprise attacks, an especially important capability during the post–9/11 period. Terrorists could strike anywhere at any time against the most unlikely targets, and the United States had to be able to respond quickly and effectively.

To address these two issues, Rumsfeld devised a policy that he called "transformation." In order to make that policy a reality, Rumsfeld believed that his first task was to reassert civilian control over the military—control that he believed had been lost during the Clinton administration: "Rumsfeld's primary objective in reasserting civilian control over the Pentagon has been in reigning in a Joint Staff that the defense secretary, according to associates, believed had become too powerful and independent of civilian control, with officers acting at times as though they were not subordinate to their civilian bosses."[9] He began by demanding that commanders "reduce headquarters staff by 15 percent a year."[10] The military would have to understand that they were subject to civilian control, and as far as he was concerned, that meant Donald Rumsfeld's hand would be involved in any area he believed relevant. He also had no compunctions about micromanaging the military down to the tactical level if that would help him transform it. The Chiefs might not like his approach, but he was in charge.

Rumsfeld also believed that he and his civilian advisors understood military strategy, doctrine, structure, and weapons systems better than the generals and admirals he encountered. Indeed, one four-star officer who worked with him called him "an egomaniac cleverly disguised . . . a hip shooter who gives the impression he is not." Another officer stated that "if anyone disagreed with Rumsfeld it was risky because the result might be an 'ass chewing from him.' "[11] Frankly, Rumsfeld distrusted the uniformed military and worked with them only to the degree necessary, relying instead primarily on civilians: "Working with a close-knit group, mostly civilians, he was a mystery to many in the building, especially members of the Joint Chiefs of Staff, the uniformed heads of the Army, Navy, Air Force and Marine Corps."[12] And these civilians shared his lack of respect for the uniformed military. "Their attitude bordered on disdain, many officers thought. Snide comments slipped out frequently, 'You all are screwed up here,' or 'You screwed up there.' Never 'we'—the divide was always there."[13] Furthermore, according to some reports, Rumsfeld's management style bordered on the chaotic. To quote the *Washington Post,* "The . . . senior management team is as indecisive and confused as anything we've seen since Les Aspin."[14]

Not surprisingly, Rumsfeld's approach met with almost unanimous opposition on the part of the uniformed military. Indeed, opposition was so strong that Woodward argued that it bordered on "insubordination."[15] Needless to say, Rumsfeld's first years as secretary of defense would be filled with one conflict after another. He would try to undercut the opposition by appointing only those officers he thought he could dominate, even to the point of perhaps "stepping on the toes of the service chiefs by getting involved in the selection of two- and three-star generals."[16] His interference served only to drive military opposition to his plans underground.[17]

The Chiefs and Rumsfeld

Gen. Hugh Shelton, who was serving as chairman of the Joint Chiefs when the new administration came into office, quickly discovered that Rumsfeld was not interested in what he had to say on critical issues. Rumsfeld even suggested at one point to Shelton that all military advice to the president should go through him, despite the fact that the law made the chairman the president's principal advisor on military matters. Shelton refused. Rumsfeld's attitude shocked the Chiefs; they considered the president to be a "warrior's warrior," who seemed to highly value their contributions and was unafraid to sing their praises to the entire country. But then he installed a secretary of defense who "relegated Shelton and his staff to the status of 'second-rate citizens.' "[18] Or as another senior officer put it, "The fact is, [Rumsfeld] is disenfranchising people."[19]

When the Chiefs sent studies to Rumsfeld on issues he was considering, he tended to ignore them. In fact, military representatives were often excluded from critical meetings of direct concern to them, including discussions of the future of the U.S. armed forces. Indeed, as noted above, Rumsfeld even interfered in internal military personnel questions to the point where he personally interviewed all officers selected for jobs above the rank of two-star general.[20] If the military's nominee for a position answered no when asked if he or she would *unconditionally* support Rumsfeld's transformation policy, the candidate would not get the job (and corresponding promotion).

The Chiefs quickly got the impression that they did not exist as far as Rumsfeld was concerned. For example, instead of turning to them for an examination of U.S. security, he asked Andy Marshall, the director of the Office of Net Assessments. Even his outside consultants, such as Richard Perle, who at that time was chairman of the Defense Policy Board, played a more important role than the Chiefs in designing security policy. One source spoke of closed-door meetings held by the Chiefs "devoted entirely to a scathing discussion of his methods and intentions." The situation was so bad, "some members of the military would later tell interviewers, they feared that the future of the institution to which they had devoted their lives was being shaped without seriously consulting them."[21]

Rumsfeld had little respect for officers like Shelton. He considered them to be dinosaurs who did not understand the new world into which the U.S. military was moving. They were obstacles who would fight his effort to transform the military, especially the army, into the kind of military force needed to deal with terrorism. Indeed, the relationship between Rumsfeld and the military became so tense that, according to Dana Priest, Shelton secretly hoped for a crisis that would give the military an opportunity to show Rumsfeld what they could do, thereby removing his distrust of them.[22]

Myers Replaces Shelton

On October 1, 2001, the president announced that Shelton, who was retiring, would be replaced by the vice chairman of the Joint Chiefs, Gen. Richard B. Myers (who, in turn, would be replaced by Gen. Peter Pace, the first Marine to hold that position). Myers, a fighter pilot and a specialist in space weapons, was very different from Shelton. But what was most important about both Myers and Pace was that their selection "made it clear that the administration wanted obedience, not officers who might make waves."[23] Both officers were intelligent, and Myers, in particular, was committed to the high-tech ideas advocated by Rumsfeld. As one source noted, "He has been a leading advocate of radical changes in the way the military organizes itself and buys its weapons, without alienating advocates who emphasize conventional forces and ways of fighting."[24] Furthermore, from all outward appearances, Myers and Rumsfeld appeared to work well together. But the chairman would pay a price. Although he might be allowed to disagree with Rumsfeld, Myers was "but one member of a Pentagon brain trust of about two dozen that Mr. Rumsfeld now convenes each workday morning to review war planning. "[25]

In October 2002, General Myers informed Rumsfeld that he intended to appoint Lt. Gen. Ronald E. Keyes to be the next director of operations, or J-3. "Not so fast, said Rumsfeld, who in a sharp departure from previous practice personally interviews all nominees for three-star and four-star positions in the military. Give me someone else, Rumsfeld told Myers after twice interviewing Keyes."[26]Then, during a meeting in March 2003, President Bush turned to Myers "with a pressing question: How long would the war in Iraq last? But before General Myers could respond, Defense Secretary Donald H. Rumsfeld put a hand on his arm and said, 'Now, Dick, you don't want to answer that.' "[27]

AFGHANISTAN

The attack on the World Trade Center in New York City and on the Pentagon on September 11, 2001, turned the Pentagon's world upside down:

President George W. Bush speaks in March 2003 at the Pentagon, where he receives an update on the war in Iraq. With Bush are General Richard B. Myers (center), chairman of the Joint Chiefs of Staff, and General Peter Pace, vice-chairman. (AP/Wide World)

"Osama bin Laden abruptly ended Rumsfeld's campaign to reign in the armed forces."[28] The key focus was no longer military transformation, it was now striking back at the terrorists regardless of where they were. Furthermore, the terrorist attack pushed Rumsfeld to the fore as he participated in numerous press conferences detailing the actions the Defense Department was taking toward Afghanistan. As Midge Decter explained, "At that point Rumsfeld's briefings made him the chief public exponent and explainer of the war. And he conducted them with a candor so uncommon to the usual public demeanor of a public official, and at the same time with so much wit and panache, that what came to be known as the 'Rummy Show' was soon playing to ever larger and ever more appreciative audiences."[29]

Soon after 9/11, Bush, like all other presidents of countries that have been attacked, wanted to know what immediate steps the military could take.

"Very little effectively," Rumsfeld answered. Feeling the heat, the secretary of defense turned to Gen. Tommy Franks, who was the commander in chief of CENTCOM, which was responsible for South Asia and the Middle East. Franks had told Rumsfeld that it would "take months to get forces in the area and plans drawn up for a major military assault in Afghanistan." Rumsfeld, however, responded by telling him, "You don't have months." He wanted something done in weeks or days. The problem, Franks tried to explain, was that Afghanistan was on the other side of the world. Furthermore, "Al Queda was a guerilla organization whose members lived in caves, rode mules and drove large sport-utility vehicles." Rumsfeld's response was "Try again."[30]

On September 12, at a meeting at the White House, Rumsfeld suggested that in addition to al Qaeda, the United States should *"go against Iraq."* He was not alone. His deputy, Paul Wolfowitz, had been arguing that Iraq was a major danger to the United States for some time. The two men believed that "they could take advantage of the opportunity offered by the terrorist attack to go after Saddam immediately."[31] In essence, why not kill two birds with one stone?

General Shelton, who had two weeks remaining before Myers took over, completely opposed invading Iraq. He maintained that the only justification for including Iraq would be the existence of solid evidence indicating that Iraq had been directly involved in the events of 9/11. Otherwise, attacking Iraq would only serve to anger moderate Arab states, whose assistance the United States would need. For his part, the president stated that he did not believe this was the time to deal with the Iraqi problem. The goal was to strike hard at the terrorists, not at the government of Saddam Hussein. While Shelton, Powell, and the president opposed attacking Iraq, "Wolfowitz was fiercely determined and committed."[32]

At an NSC meeting on September 13, the president reiterated his desire to take quick action. "This is a new world," noted Bush. "General Shelton should go back to the generals for new targets. Start the clock. This is an opportunity. I want a plan—costs, time. I need options on the table. I want Afghan options by Camp David. I want decisions quick" (62–63).

The meeting at Camp David was held on September 15. General Shelton proposed three options for dealing with Afghanistan: The first was a strike with cruise missiles, which could be initiated and completed very quickly by the navy and air force from hundreds of miles away. But with the al Qaeda camps having been emptied, there were few targets to attack. The second option was to use cruise missiles with manned bombers. Such attacks could be carried on for three or four days, perhaps even ten. Finally, the third option included cruise missiles, bombers and commandos from the army's special forces, and maybe even regular army troops and Marines. Such an operation would require ten to twelve days to set up. Rumsfeld responded to the proposal by taking a swipe at the uniformed military, arguing "the military options look like five or ten years ago." He said he wanted "unconventional" approaches. "Get a group functioning fast. Lift out of conventional mind-set" (88).

The following Monday, Bush informed the assembled group that he had decided on the third option that Shelton had presented. And he added, "Let's hit them hard. We want to signal this is a change from the past. We want to cause the other countries like Syria and Iran to change their views. We want to hit as soon as possible" (98). He called on the Pentagon to present some detailed plans, but questions remained, including what targets the United States should attack in the nonindustrialized country and when ground troops should be inserted. Shelton asked for four days to a week to airlift the troops and supplies closer to the Afghan border; positioning special forces troops would take even longer.

Unfortunately, the planning process did not go well. At a meeting on September 24, the Pentagon announced again that it did not have any meaningful war plans. Not surprisingly, a furious Rumsfeld "beat up on Franks incessantly" but to little avail (129). On September 29 Rumsfeld again told the president of the problem the Pentagon was facing in finding suitable targets. General Myers, who had replaced Shelton, reinforced the point by arguing that during the Gulf War, the United States had been able to attack hard targets: communication centers, early warning radars, command and control centers, and military equipment; now, however, "We've got a military that does great against fixed targets. We don't do so well against mobile targets. You're not going to topple a regime with this target list" (174). Furthermore, the Pentagon was not prepared to put aircraft or helicopters into battle until a base could be found to station combat search and rescue (CSAR) helicopters. To cite only one example of the difficulties involved, assuming the United States could get permission to station CSAR forces in Uzbekistan, it would take 67 deliveries from the C-17s to ferry in the personnel, equipment, and helicopters to get up and fully ready with the search and rescue (185).

Meanwhile, Rumsfeld, who sometimes quoted Al Capone to the effect that "you'll get more with a kind word and a gun than a kind word alone," wanted action from the military.[33] Accordingly, on October 2 Rumsfeld sent the service chiefs, the combatant commanders, and the under secretaries a fifteen-page, top-secret order titled "Campaign against Terrorism: Strategic Guidance for the Department of Defense." In it, Rumsfeld laid down the law, emphasizing that the global war the president had ordered on terrorism would target not only al Qaeda, but all other forces supporting terrorism as well. "In a section on 'means,' Rumsfeld said 'All tools of national power' would be utilized in the war on global terrorism. The department should anticipate multiple military operations in multiple theaters."[34] Weapons of mass destruction were also singled out for attention: states or organizations that harbored or supported efforts by terrorist organizations to get such weapons would also be fair game for attack.

Finally, on October 3 Wolfowitz, who was sitting in for Rumsfeld, announced that the Uzbeks had given the United States permission for CSAR forces to operate from their territory. In addition, the CIA announced that it would provide the special forces and General Franks with the identities, locations, capabilities, and assessments of all of their assets in Afghanistan. In contrast to the Bay of Pigs, the Defense and the CIA were determined to work together.

On October 4 General Myers informed the president that CSAR would be ready to enter Northern Afghanistan by Monday, and that special forces were moving into Oman. Within days after bombing began, ground troops could be inserted. The next day, General Franks joined the discussion via secure video. The president asked him, "[A]re we ready to go?" Franks assured the president that he was. Cruise missiles, heavy bombers, and strike aircraft would hit about thirty-one targets, including the Taliban air-defense system and any groups of al Qaeda that could be located (200). Rumsfeld asked the president for a "go" and Bush replied, "Go. . . . Its well thought through. It's the right thing to do" (204). The only restriction Bush put on the air attacks was that the Pentagon should avoid collateral damage to the best of its ability. On October 7 he signed the papers to begin hostilities against Afghanistan.

The targeting problem remained, however. On October 9 General Myers argued that pilots did not know what to bomb. The planes circled around in the air waiting for the drones to find a target, but they seldom did. "It was an incredible moment, barely imaginable in the annals of modern warfare. After a day of strikes, the airborne might of the United States had been a somewhat helpless giant lumbering around the sky . . . waiting for targets of opportunity" (211).

The issue of nation building soon arose. After all, if the United States was able—as seemed likely—to dominate Afghanistan, it could not simply go home and leave the Taliban to retake control. Yet the president had spoken out against peacekeeping in his election speeches, and the United States did not want any part of telling the Afghans how to live. As Rumsfeld noted, "I don't know people who are smart enough from other countries to tell other countries the kind of arrangements they ought to have to govern themselves" (220). Bush, meanwhile, argued that the United States should attempt to bring in a UN protective force and then leave.

With the CIA playing a significant role in the U.S. operation in Afghanistan, the answer to the question of who should be in charge on the ground wasn't immediately apparent. Consequently, several senior officials—Rice, Powell, and Rice's deputy, Stephen Hadley—told Rumsfeld that it was a Department of Defense operation. The secretary, who played a key role in the attack on Afghanistan, produced a top-secret/close-hold paper that he sent to Wolfowitz, Myers, Pace, and Under Secretary for Policy Douglas Feith. In the document, Rumsfeld called for ideas on intelligence, humanitarian assistance, and other relevant issues. Interestingly, although the Department of Defense took charge and operated within the bounds of its normal bureaucratic secrecy, officials like Colin Powell were kept informed of any plans that might affect the State Department by a process his deputy called "under the blanket," which utilized an informal old-boy network of former and current military officers.

Not until October 19 was the first special forces A-team, "a twelve-member contingent of Army" special operations forces, "deployed in the north."[35] By November 12, General Myers was able to tell the president that the anti-Taliban Northern Alliance now controlled half of the country and had cut the country in two. Remnants of al Qaeda and the Taliban were fleeing to the Pakistan border. The American commitment had amounted to far less than the previously anticipated deployment of 50,000 to 60,000 troops; instead, a heavy use of airpower was combined with only 110 CIA officers and 316 special forces personnel operating on the ground.[36]

The Lesson of Afghanistan

For Rumsfeld the lesson from Afghanistan was "loud and clear." In order to effectively address the new threats facing the nation, the United States required an even greater capability to handle insurgencies around the globe in a matter of hours, rather than taking weeks, or even days, to deploy its armed forces. Rumsfeld insisted the military "get with the program" and make the kind of transformations that would permit him or his successor to deploy significant numbers of troops anywhere in the world very quickly. The United States no longer faced the prospect of fighting a major war whose objective might be akin to that of stopping the Soviet goliath in Europe. Now, speed and lethality were critical capabilities that he believed would be attained only if he pushed the military to transform.

Thus, the United States would place greater emphasis on special operations forces. To make them more mobile, Rumsfeld took them away from the CINCs to whom they had been subordinated so they would no longer be limited by geography. In November 2002 Rumsfeld ordered the Special Operations Command (about 47,000 strong as this point) to come up with "a new war plan for capturing and killing terrorists."[37]

TRANSFORMATION

Rumsfeld was fully aware that 9/11 had taken attention away from his effort to transform the military to meet the challenge of terrorism. But undeterred, he remarked, "Even as we prosecute this war on terrorism, we must be preparing for the next war."[38] In addition to emphasizing special operations forces, Rumsfeld continued stressing to the services the importance of joint operations. Extensive changes would be required. "This means reconsidering some of their doctrine, the way they organize themselves and giving up traditional fiefdoms and future platforms."[39]

In a February 1, 2002, press conference, Rumsfeld articulated a number of goals he hoped to achieve with transformation, which an article appearing in the *Economist* characterized as "the military buzzword for a change from heavy, slow-moving forces to lighter, more agile units, employing the latest information technology to wage computerized warfare."[40] For example, he wanted to protect the U.S. homeland and U.S. bases overseas, project and sustain power in distant parts of the world, deny America's enemies their sanctuaries, protect U.S. information networks from attack, use information technology to link up U.S. forces, and maintain "unhindered access to space and protect our space capabilities from attack."[41]

The difficulties associated with Secretary Rumsfeld's plan were twofold: first, the implementation of his program would require a bigger defense budget; second, many analysts believed that the resulting smaller size of the U.S. armed forces would make fighting two simultaneous wars impossible. Rumsfeld would have to address both of these issues if he hoped to create the kind of military he had in mind.

The Military Budget

Rumsfeld and Bush realized that if they hoped to transform the military they needed more money. According to one expert, the military suffered from numerous deficiencies when Bush entered his presidency; for example, the "Clinton era was the only time since 1950 when the allocation for weapons fell below one-fifth of the defense budget." The money for weapons had been reallocated to the operations and maintenance budget to sustain the high operational tempo of forces around the world under Clinton. As a result, many of the bombers were twenty-five years old and the tankers thirty-seven. This expert believed that "under-provision for replacing aging, worn-out equipment has caused a shortfall of 83% for armored vehicles and of 86% for army helicopters. The Navy fleet, which has already been halved to 300 vessels, should be replaced at a rate of eight a year, but the current building rate is only five."[42] The military budget was key.

Consequently, Bush told a military audience in January 2002 that he would ask Congress for the biggest increase in the military budget since Ronald Reagan's first term. He said he would spend whatever money it took to defeat terrorism around the world. In particular, Bush said he would propose a budget that would permit a spending increase of $48 billion during 2003, a 14 percent increase (in comparison, Reagan's rose 17 percent for FY 1982). If he was successful, the Pentagon's budget would rise to $379 billion in 2003.[43] But this was just the beginning. The administration would try to increase the Pentagon's budget by $120 billion over the next five years, to a total of $451 billion by 2007.[44]

While Bush did not get everything he asked for, he persuaded the Hill to approve a budget of $355.4 billion. The overwhelming vote in favor passed an increase of $34 billion over the previous year.[45] However, for practical purposes, this budget would not help transform the military; in too many areas shortages or problems remaining from the previous administration would have to be overcome.

When the FY 2004 budget came up for debate, Rumsfeld was ready to focus directly on transforming the military. The Pentagon asked for a budget of $399.1 billion, but Congress actually passed a bill in the amount of $400.5 billion. The additional money was to pay for bombers, missiles, transport planes, and a variety of other programs.[46] Equally important as the high level of military funding in the FY 2004 budget was the way the money was to be spent.

In terms of dollar amounts, the air force emerged the biggest winner, with its budget going from $108 billion to $113.7 billion, an increase of 5.3 percent. The navy and Marine Corps received an increase of about 3.1 percent, as their budget went from $111.1 billion to $114.6 billion, and the army's budget rose from $90.7 billion to $93.7 billion, a 3.3 percent increase. Rumsfeld's favorite, the Special Operations Command, increased from $3 billion to $4.52 billion, a 47 percent increase.[47] The majority of the increase in the special oper-

Senator John Warner (R-Va.), chairman of the Senate Armed Services Committee, chats with the Joint Chiefs of Staff before a hearing on the Defense Department's fiscal year 2004 budget. From left to right: General Eric Shinseki, army chief of staff; Warner; Admiral Vernon E. Clark, CNO; General Michael W. Hagee, commandant of the U.S. Marine Corps; and General John P. Jumper, air force chief of staff. (AP/Wide World)

ations budget went to "additional troops, refitted HM-47 Chinook helicopters and new CV-22 tilt-rotor aircraft and . . . submersible vessels."[48]

The greater importance of the special operations forces was also evident in the more independent role they played. In January 2003 Rumsfeld announced a plan that would give them increased authority to better enable them to chase, find, and kill al Qaeda and other terrorists groups. He argued, "The global nature of the war, the nature of the enemy and the need for fast, efficient operations in hunting down and rooting out terrorist networks around the world have all contributed to the need for an expanded role for the Special Operations forces."[49]

Although the army perceived the new budget as a serious blow, the level of funding was only one of a number of problems that the army experienced under Rumsfeld. To begin with, Rumsfeld cancelled the army's new self-propelled artillery piece, the Crusader. The Crusader was a fast-moving vehicle that could fire rapidly and at greater range than any existing weapon. The problem, however, from Rumsfeld's standpoint, was that it weighed over forty tons, which made it too heavy for rapid transport by aircraft and almost all bridges. (In all fairness, however, tanks weigh seventy tons and most modern bridges can bear almost one hundred tons. And even in the Third World, forty-ton howitzers are still better than seventy-ton tanks.) Rumsfeld's supporters also argued that the accompanying thirty-ton vehicle that carried the Crusader's heavy shells made the weapon even more difficult to transport rapidly. Furthermore, the Crusader was designed to stop a Soviet invasion of Europe, not for quick insertion around the world. For Rumsfeld it was not "transformational." Favoring weapons systems that were precise and transportable, the secretary touted "a futuristic system called NetFires that would replace the 40–ton Crusader . . . with a precision-guided missile in a six-foot box that two soldiers could set-up on the battlefield."[50]

The manner in which Rumsfeld and Wolfowitz handled the question of the Crusader made the whole process very difficult for the Chiefs. On May 2, the secretary and his deputy told army leaders they had thirty days to defend the Crusader or to propose alternatives. However, a few days later—without telling the army—Wolfowitz "surprised senior Army officials and members of Congress by informing them of his decision to cancel the program, even though it had been recommended for full funding at $475 million in the president's fiscal 2003 budget."[51] When Gen. Eric Shinseki, the army's chief of staff, appeared before the Senate Armed Services Committee, he testified that "ending the Crusader would create 'a window of risk' for U.S. troops 'until we find a replacement system.' "[52] And a set of talking points, which had been prepared by the army's Office of Congressional Liaison in response to a congressional request before Rumsfeld decided to terminate the Crusader, further argued that "soldiers would die in combat if the system was cancelled." On May 7 Rumsfeld blasted those who lobbied Congress but expressed support for Army Secretary Thomas E. White, whom he said was not party to the action; the secretary felt that "there is no question but that . . . some individuals in the Army were way in the dickens out of line."[53] Needless to say, the incident served to worsen the already bad relationship between Rumsfeld and the U.S. Army.

A New Military Doctrine

Rumsfeld did not limit himself to manipulating the budget and personnel: he also pushed for the introduction of a new military doctrine. Previously, the Pentagon strove to have the capability to fight two simultaneous wars, one on the scale of Desert Storm. Now, however, as an unidentified U.S. government official noted, "The nature of the enemy has changed, the nature of the threat has changed, and so the response has to change."[54] In January 2002 Rumsfeld observed that the country had to scrap the two-war strategy, arguing, "By removing the requirement to maintain a second occupation force, as we did under the old strategy, we can free up resources for the future and the various lesser contingencies which we face, have faced, are facing and will most certainly face in the period ahead." What he meant was that the United States would no longer build armies to confront the armies of other states, who would be foolish to take us "head on." Because the United States was clearly the strongest country in the world, any enemy who wanted to attack the United States would have to do so asymmetrically. To fight such a war, the United States would need "rapidly deployable, fully integrated joint forces capable of reaching distant theaters quickly and working with our air and sea forces to strike adversaries swiftly, successfully, and with devastating effect."[55] To that end, the nation would need modular units that could be selectively inserted to deal with problems; "instead of relying on 10 active duty divisions, this more modular Army would enable commanders to pick from 30 or more battle groups, a dozen of which could be kept on alert for quick deployment." Such an approach would not only lead to a change in military structure and weapons, it would also require a major change in personnel policies. Instead of rotating every two years, for example, soldiers might stay in one unit for three years. "Officials said this would improve combat skills through better cohesion, discipline and technical proficiency on the battlefield."[56]

Considering the danger posed by terrorist groups, Rumsfeld believed the United States could not afford to simply wait for an attack that could very easily involve the use of weapons of mass destruction. As a result, "preemption" entered the U.S. military lexicon. The idea was not particularly new; American officials had contemplated such action in the past. But for the first time, preemption was being openly discussed as an integral part of U.S. national security policy.[57]

Rumsfeld and his colleagues believed that deterrence was no longer a viable defense. It might work against other states, but when faced with terrorists or rogue states such as North Korea, it was useless. Furthermore, no matter how hard the U.S. government worked, a defense against weapons of mass destruction would never be perfect, but consequences of even one such weapon could be catastrophic. Waiting to be attacked was a recipe for suicide.[58]

RUMSFELD VS. SHINSEKI

One of the more ironic aspects of Rumsfeld's efforts to transform the military was his ongoing war with General Shinseki. In fact, the general was ahead of

Rumsfeld's call for transformation. Like most army officers he recognized that something had to be done to meet the new challenges his branch of the services was facing. In October 1999 Shinseki began his own struggle to transform the army "from waging war by slog and slash, calling for new theory and proposing new weapons to create a land force more agile and precise in bringing lethal force to the battlefield."[59] It looked like Shinseki and Rumsfeld would become allies who shared a common goal. However, "when Rumsfeld and Shinseki met . . . , they talked past each other. The secretary wanted new ideas. Shinseki said he had put the Army on the right course. 'It was a dialogue of the deaf,' said a senior Army officer who was briefed on the meeting."[60] Then, shortly after Rumsfeld took over with the intention of making cutbacks in force structure to finance modernization, Shinseki and Army Secretary Thomas White told the House Armed Services Committee that they needed an additional forty thousand soldiers. " 'Given today's mission profile, the Army is too small for the mission load it's carrying,' General Shinseki testified. Added Mr. White. 'I am very nervous about shifting down any further.' "[61]

But Rumsfeld had no interest in working with the army or any other service. He intended to bring about a revolutionary transformation in the armed forces, and especially the army, by himself. Indeed he wanted to scrap a considerable part of it. For example, in addition to criticizing and eventually terminating the Crusader, he cut the Comanche helicopter program in half. Then, aggravating the situation, Rumsfeld announced Shinseki's "replacement"—his deputy, Gen. John Keane—fourteen months before Shinseki's retirement. Shinseki reportedly first read the news in the *Washington Post*.[62] Rumsfeld complained that the army was resistant to change, while army officers argued that he "does not sufficiently appreciate the value of large, armored conventional ground forces. 'Does he really hate the Army?' asked one Army officer, obviously pained by the question. 'I don't know.' "[63]

The Stryker brigades proved another point of contention. The lightly armored vehicle was equipped with the latest, most modern technological equipment. "It is the first building block in the plan of Gen. Eric K. Shinseki . . . for 'transforming' the Army from a heavy, armored force designed during the Cold War into a futuristic, 'Objective Force' built around information superiority on the battlefield."[64] Shinseki planned to use the Stryker to create six army brigades, each with 3,500 men, that would include "wheeled troop carriers, heavy weaponry and high-tech communication equipment. They would deploy anywhere on the globe within four days and fight smart when they got there."[65] The concept appeared to be exactly what Rumsfeld was seeking.

In fact, the army's senior leaders soon began to perceive that Rumsfeld's real goal was to raid their service's budget to pay for other projects. In addition to calls for eliminating the fourth, fifth, and sixth Stryker brigades, a plan was introduced that would delay fielding the Future Combat System brigades, which were to be the centerpiece of the "Army's Objective Force" from 2008 to 2010. And in addition to his plans to reduce the number of RAH-66 Comanche helicopters, as mentioned above, Rumsfeld intended to slash funds for the "non-line-of-sight cannon system."[66]

Rumsfeld and Shinseki would also spar over the question of how many troops would be needed to secure postwar Iraq. Testifying before the Senate Armed Services Committee, Shinseki estimated that "something on the order of several hundred thousand soldiers are probably a figure that would be required."[67] His remark stunned U.S. lawmakers. After Shinseki gave Congress his best advice, an officer from another service noted, "He's always been a. . . . pretty straightforward guy. . . . That's probably a good faith estimate."[68] The next day, however, Wolfowitz, called Shinseki's estimate "wildly off the mark." Wolfowitz claimed that the Pentagon's estimate of approximately 100,000 troops was more accurate because of a lack of ethnic violence in Iraq, the feeling that Iraqis would welcome American troops, and the willingness of others—even those opposed to the war—to help pay for the rebuilding of the country.[69] However, not only was Wolfowitz's criticism of Shinseki inaccurate, "It [was] unusual for a senior Pentagon civilian to so thoroughly reject the testimony of a ranking military officer."[70] Shinseki refused to back down. Testifying in March before a House subcommittee, Shinseki repeated his earlier estimate when asked about the number of troops needed to pacify a post-Saddam Iraq. "It could be as high as several hundred thousand."[71]

Relations between Rumsfeld and Shinseki were so poor that when the latter retired in June 2003, neither Rumsfeld nor Wolfowitz were invited to his retirement ceremony. Furthermore, Shinseki did not mention Rumsfeld by name in his retirement remarks, although he clearly had him in mind when he said, "We understand that leadership is not an exclusive function of uniformed service. . . . So when some suggest that we in the Army don't understand the importance of civilian control of the military, well, that's just not helpful and it isn't true."[72]

By now, the army and Rumsfeld were at loggerheads. A newspaper article observed, "Many U.S. military officers, especially in the Army, view Secretary of Defense Rumsfeld the way most Europeans do—as headstrong, abrasive, and arrogant. Mr. Rumsfeld, in turn appears to view many Army officers as unimaginative."[73] The secretary of defense continued to be abrasive and inconsiderate in his dealings with the Chiefs, who viewed themselves as being on the outside, with Rumsfeld listening only to his civilian advisors and Generals Myers and Pace. Despite including the two generals to give the impression that he was interested in the military's views, he regularly denigrated the armed forces' contributions. For example, in January 2003 Rumsfeld "in a private memo to his top aide, criticized the Joint Chiefs of Staff for generating unnecessary and poorly prepared strategies. 'It is just a lot of people spinning their wheels, doing things we probably have to edit and improve.' "[74] Indeed, Rumsfeld intended to neuter the Chiefs by combining their staff, the Joint Staff, with his staff; thus, the heads of the various services would depend on a staff that he controlled for all of their analyses and position papers. It would effectively mean the end of an independent military voice. When confronted with the contents of his memo at a press conference, Rumsfeld responded, "The Constitution calls for civilian control of this department. And I'm a civilian." And he added, "I have received on occasion from people—military and civilian—work that I was not impressed with and have indicated that. And there have been times when I've sent things back six, seven times."[75] Defending Rumsfeld, General Myers argued that he and General Pace met with the secretary frequently. But others in the military strongly believed that they would not stand up for the armed forces the way General Shelton had during the early part of the administration.

Rumsfeld Sacks White

Army Secretary Thomas White clashed repeatedly with Rumsfeld. He disagreed with the secretary's decision to cancel the Crusader, which White had repeatedly argued was vital to the army's future when he appeared before Congress to testify in support of the president's budget. He also fought with Rumsfeld over the army's intention to invest money in the Stryker brigades. Although service secretaries had disagreed with the secretary of defense in the past, Rumsfeld would have none of it. "He expected the secretaries, who are civilians appointed by the defense secretary, to be agents of change, serving to push the sometimes recalcitrant military branches into shedding old ways of fighting and obsolete weapons systems."[76] As far as White was concerned, the problem was that Rumsfeld believed he and Shinseki, with whom he had sided, were opposed to transformation, which of course was not the case. They were strongly opposed to Rumsfeld's version of transformation because they believed that he did not understand the importance of having an army that could fight against large land forces, nor did he understand the problems the army would face in occupying and pacifying a country like Iraq in the postwar period. Convinced that he had lost his war with Rumsfeld, White resigned on April 25.

While it would be an exaggeration to suggest that the army was at war with Rumsfeld, it was clear that relations were seriously strained. As Ralph Peters, a former army officer and distinguished commentator on national security affairs, put it, "You look at Rumsfeld, and beyond all the rationale, spoken and unspoken, he just dislikes the army. It's just palpable. . . . You always have to wonder if when Rumsfeld was a Navy lieutenant junior grade whether an Army officer stole his girlfriend."[77]

THE WAR IN IRAQ

While Rumsfeld was battling with the army and the Chiefs on one front, the United States was attempting to decide what to do about Iraq. Saddam Hussein had been repeatedly warned by the United Nations to get rid of his weapons of mass destruction (WMD) and to permit intrusive inspections to verify that he had done so. Saddam refused, and in the aftermath of the events of 9/11 some in the administration, especially civilian members of the Defense Department, believed he represented a major danger to the United States. For many in the Bush administration, the issue was simple:

> Should it call off the war after Afghanistan and entrust the continuing struggle against Islamic terrorism to an international policy and intelligence effort? That option would minimize the disruption of the Middle Eastern status quo, please many of America's European allies and all the Arab and Muslim Middle Eastern states. On the other hand, it would leave the war on terror as unfinished as the Gulf War had been left in 1991. Saddam Hussein would continue to build nukes and germ bombs. The Iranian mullahs would continue to sponsor Hezbollah and shelter the remnants of al-Qaeda.[78]

As noted above, Rumsfeld had been convinced since the events of 9/11 that something had to be done about Iraq.[79] He was supported by his deputy, Paul Wolfowitz, who believed that the first Bush administration should have removed Saddam during the first Gulf War. "Now he saw a chance to rectify this mistake."[80] They and their allies believed that if Saddam Hussein were overthrown, the United States would have a reliable ally in the Arab world. Having troops in Iraq would give heart to the Iranian people and perhaps even inspire them to throw off the yoke of the mullahs.[81]

The administration split over how to get rid of Hussein, with Cheney, Rumsfeld, and Wolfowitz favoring the use of military force and Secretary of

State Colin Powell advocating greater use of diplomacy. Powell warned the president that the consequences of a war in Iraq could be disastrous. He favored a policy of containment, which he believed offered the best chance of bringing about regime change. "Powell said the president had to consider what a military operation against Iraq would do in the Arab world. Cauldron was the right word. . . . The entire region could be destabilized. . . . War could change everything in the Middle East." The president was in the middle. On September 2, Powell asked the president if it was his intention to send the inspectors who were searching for weapons of mass destruction back into Iraq. Bush replied that he intended to do just that but that "he was skeptical it would work." Powell went on to argue that while Saddam was crazy and a menace, he had been contained for the past ten years. In contrast, Cheney was for a war with Saddam. "It was as if nothing else existed. . . . That was not the issue, Cheney said. Saddam and the blatant threat was the issue." Indeed, according to Woodward, Cheney and Powell went after each other in what he called "a blistering argument."[82] Then in November, Bush's NSC advisor, Condoleezza Rice, who had supported Powell, "threw in her lot with the Rumsfeld faction against the Powell faction."[83] On October 10 and 11 the House and Senate had given the president overwhelming support, giving him full authority to attack Iraq unilaterally if necessary.

In January Bush gave his State of the Union address, in which he labeled Iraq, Iran, and North Korea the "axis of evil." He blasted the Saddam regime for hiding weapons of mass destruction and warned, "The United States of America will not permit the world's most dangerous regimes to threaten us with the world's most destructive weapons."[84] Two weeks later, Colin Powell delivered a speech in which he cited Bush's address and warned that "the administration was considering a variety of options to topple Saddam Hussein."[85]

The Plan

When CENTCOM commander Gen. Tommy Franks was first told to begin planning for a possible invasion of Iraq in November 2001, he was stunned. According to Woodward, "Franks was incredulous. They were in the midst of one war, Afghanistan, and now they wanted detailed planning for another. Iraq? 'Goddamn,' Franks said, 'what the fuck are they talking about.' "[86] Incredulous or not, it was up to the military to come up with a plan of attack.

Rumsfeld decided to circumvent the Chiefs and work directly with Franks. The two men soon began detailed planning in January 2002 for a possible invasion.[87] The first critical issue was size. The United States had employed close to 500,000 troops during the Gulf War. Now, however, Rumsfeld pushed for a much smaller force. Colin Powell reportedly spoke to Franks expressing considerable concern about going into Iraq with too few troops. Franks responded by noting that he was "first a military officer and that he had no intention of losing a war on his watch." Nevertheless, as far as Powell was concerned, "the guidance to Franks seemed to be: keep it small, the smallest you can get away with."[88] According to Franks, however, he was in favor of using a much smaller force than was the case in Desert Storm.[89] While Franks worked with Rumsfeld and compromised with him when necessary, the country's top generals were deeply concerned. According to two different sources, the plan originally proposed by Franks "called for tens of thousands of soldiers and marines to invade Iraq from Kuwait—along with air-, land-, and sea-based forces to attack from the north, west and south." A total of 250,000 troops, including three divisions of heavy armored forces, would be required.[90] Rumsfeld, however, desiring to forgo the Powell Doctrine's use of overwhelming force to subdue an opponent, wanted the military to fight a different type of war with smaller forces—50,000 to 75,000, according to one source.[91] The secretary of defense argued that the United States could take advantage of its overwhelming lead in technology and thereby eliminate the need for large numbers of troops. In addition, Wolfowitz maintained that the Iraqi army would quickly collapse.

On February 16, 2002, Bush signed a secret National Security Council directive that laid out the "goals and objectives" for going to war with Iraq.[92] However, Franks, who worked for the secretary of defense and not the Chiefs under Title X, did not brief the Chiefs on the plan until March 29. Tension in the meeting was palpable. The Chiefs did not like being cut "out of the action," and they were more interested in pushing the interests of their own services than in working on a "joint plan."[93] The president was briefed on May 11, and in summer 2002 General Myers "issued detailed war plans to his combatant commanders and set up a special planning cell within the Joint Staff." On August 29 the president approved the plan.[94] Rumsfeld was reportedly involved in almost every military decision. Clark, for example, argued that the secretary utilized the deployment order, which gave the secretary "control over each unit and move." Rumsfeld had to approve each unit (or, as the overwhelmed secretary soon decided, batch of significant units), including reserve units. But the time the secretary required to analyze each move resulted in problems. "What followed . . . was an irregularly timed patchwork process that interspersed early-deploying units with those needed later, delayed mobilization, hampered training, and slowed the overall deployments considerably."

Rumsfeld's desire to retain personal control over the process prompted retired U.S. Army general Barry McCaffrey to argue that Rumsfeld "sat on each element for weeks and wanted an explanation for every unit called up out of the National Guard and Reserve and argued about every 42-man maintenance detachment. Why would a businessman want to deal with the micromanagement of the force? The bottom line is, a lack of trust that these Army generals knew what they were doing."[95]

The battle over the total size of the American forces continued to rage. Rumsfeld argued in favor of "a small force and a daring, modern battle plan building on the model of Afghanistan." Not surprisingly, in accordance with the Powell Doctrine, many generals were in favor of a force large enough to overcome the Iraqis with brute strength. It reportedly took "20 drafts of the battle plan to reconcile these contradictory impulses and produce the final strategy."[96] No mention was made of a significant planning role played either by the Chiefs as a group or the army chief of staff as an individual. The process apparently was carried out between Rumsfeld and Franks.

As the United States would subsequently learn, much to its chagrin, allowing the Pentagon and Rumsfeld to plan the war in January 2003 resulted in major mistakes. For example, little thought was given to the post–Saddam phase.[97] Too few troops had been deployed to deal with the many problems the military faced after Baghdad fell. As *Time* explained, "Rumsfeld and Franks so stripped down the invasion force for speed that the occupation army that came out of the other end was too small for the job of peacekeeping."[98] Furthermore, once Saddam had been ousted, the U.S. military faced many unforeseen problems, including looting, difficulties associated with the dissolution of the Iraqi army, violence, and so on.[99] The army's War College Peacekeeping Institute at Carlisle Barracks could have played an important part, but its role had been downgraded; consequently, only a few of its officers were involved.[100]

As far as the actual war itself, army officers on the battlefield complained that they did not have enough forces. Indeed, a number of them, including some in Iraq, blamed Rumsfeld for taking a major risk by not having enough troops on hand when the United States attacked. "That resulted in an invasion force that is too small, strung out, underprotected, undersupplied and awaiting tens of thousands of reinforcements who will not get there for weeks."[101] Many in the military believed that Rumsfeld had used fewer troops for ulterior motives:

> "We will win, but as what cost?" asked a senior Army officer, who spoke on the condition that he not be identified. "It is not a question of expect-

> ing the Pentagon to foresee every change in battle's fortune. However, there is no excuse to artificially insert risk to prove a budget or transformation point. The current plan, he said, is not about winning, but winning a certain way to prove [Rumsfeld's] transformation plans."[102]

In the end, achieving victory turned out to be much easier than the military anticipated, as well as much quicker, requiring roughly two weeks. Furthermore, although the intelligence was not perfect, the new technology permitted American forces to regroup and share data far more quickly. According to General Myers, the war showed that adaptability would be a key to "the new American way of war."[103] Again, however, Rumsfeld's insistence on a stripped-down army created major problems in the aftermath of the invasion. An article in the *Los Angeles Times* noted that "one price of Rumsfeld's lean-force, high speed invasion plan turned out to be an occupying force unprepared for the violence and looting that followed."[104] As General Michael DeLong, USMC, Frank's deputy, put it with regard to the looting and chaos that ensued after the Americans occupied Baghdad, "What most people don't understand was that there was not a lot we could do. The relatively small number of troops we had in Baghdad had to be reserved for fighting, patrolling, and maybe guarding a few of the major facilities."[105]

Many of the problems encountered in the aftermath of the invasion could have been avoided had it not been for the determination of the civilian leadership in the Pentagon to control everything in Iraq. For example, responsibility for post-invasion Iraq was given to the Office of Reconstruction and Humanitarian Assistance in Defense under the supervision of Douglas Feith, the undersecretary for policy on defense and an individual disliked by the military. As Franks reportedly said of Feith, "I have to deal with the fucking stupidest guy on the face of the earth almost every day."[106] Colin Powell and the State Department sent Feith and his colleagues the "Future of Iraq" study, a massive report based on comments and reports from a wide range of "experts on government, oil, criminal justice, and agriculture in Iraq," together with a list of seventy-five State Department Arab experts who had done the study. Defense ignored the study and threw key State experts out of the Pentagon. This led to a major confrontation between Powell and Rumsfeld.[107] The basic problem was that the Pentagon should have been just as focused on the aftermath as it was on the war.

One positive aspect of the Iraq invasion from the standpoint of the Chiefs and Franks was Bush's determination not to get involved in operational matters. As Woodward noted, " 'I'm not picking targets,' Bush said. In the Vietnam War, President Johnson had spent hours reviewing and approving targets.

'I want you to tell us about targets you think you have to hit to secure victory and to protect our troops.' "[108] This was music to Franks's ears.

One might have thought that the American victory in Iraq and the lessons that the army and Rumsfeld learned from it would help overcome the mutual hostility of the two parties and bring them together, but it did nothing of the sort. Rumsfeld interpreted the quick victory as proof that his new approach to military matters—smaller, more mobile armed forces—worked. "The swift victory in Iraq, with relatively low casualties, is seen by Mr. Rumsfeld's supporters as vindication that future wars can be won with more covert operations to gather intelligence, a more agile force, more sophisticated equipment and a willingness to strike first."[109] The ability to strike first was very important to the secretary of defense, who in congressional testimony in September 2002 argued that the United States could no longer wait until "there is proof beyond a reasonable doubt," before it intervened militarily. "Expecting to find that standard of evidence, from thousands of miles away, and to do so before such a weapon has been used is not realistic."[110] And the only kind of military capable of responding in a timely fashion was the small, highly mobile units that Rumsfeld wanted the army to create.

Evidence of Rumsfeld's continuing distrust of the army abounded. For example, he chose James Roche, who had been serving as secretary of the air force, to replace Thomas White. Based on press reports, Roche bore a strong resemblance to Rumsfeld: "He is blunt. He is intellectual. He is not afraid to knock heads. He likes to get his own way. And he believes changing culture is the way to change an organization."[111] The problem for Roche, however, was that his nomination was held up on Capitol Hill because of problems at the Air Force Academy and a questionable leasing arrangement of Boeing tankers while he was secretary of the air force. In any case, his nomination meant one thing: Rumsfeld had enough of the army and was determined to make it change "so that it can fight in the 21st Century."[112]

Then when it came to a replacement for Shinseki, Rumsfeld did something even more outrageous from the army's standpoint. He overlooked the active-duty army generals and instead recalled a special operations officer, Gen. Peter J. Schoomaker, from retirement to active duty. Although surprising to many, Rumsfeld's decision was consistent with his apparent desire to "break the china" by doing things differently than they were done in the past. The *Washington Post* quoted one unidentified senior officer who said, "Rumsfeld is essentially rejecting all three- and four-star generals in the Army . . . undermining them by saying, in effect, they aren't good enough to lead the service."[113] Very few retired generals have been recalled to active duty, among them Maxwell Taylor, who was recalled by Kennedy. Schoomaker immediately ordered army officers to reconfigure their forces into the modules that Rumsfeld was championing; a division's three brigades of 5,500 people would become five specialized units that were smaller, lighter, and more lethal.[114] The restructuring began first with the Third Infantry Division when it came home from Iraq, to be followed by the 101st Airborne Division when it returned in March 2004. Rumsfeld also intended to restructure bases. Instead of a few large bases, Rumsfeld wanted a number of smaller, forward-deployed bases in areas like Qatar, Bulgaria, Kyrgyzstan, and Guam. He believed that bases such as those in Germany that had been created to stop a Soviet advance into Western Europe were no longer important. Indeed, in many cases, Rumsfeld argued that they were irrelevant because it took too long to get forces from these bases to the places where they would be needed. On October 1, 2003, Rumsfeld's new policy was given a new name—the Joint Presence Policy. Under this policy, which synchronizes the overseas rotation plans of navy, air force, army, and Marine Corps units, the commander will have to request capabilities, not specific kinds of weapons or troops. Commanders also will have to specify why they need them (e.g., peacekeeping or combat). Armed with this request, the Pentagon will then select the types of modules or military units that best meet the commander's needs. "This is a fundamental shift of mindset," said one Pentagon planner involved in shaping the policy. For the army, this was an especially difficult task "because we're still fully engaged [in Iraq]."[115] The army did win something of a victory when Rumsfeld was forced to authorize an additional 30,000 troops in January 2004, bringing the army's troop strength to 510,000 on a temporary basis because the army was stretched so thin.[116] The expanded troop strength is planned to last four to five years while the army simultaneously attempts to restructure and serve in a number of hot spots around the world. The army won at least a partial victory with General Schoomaker's appointment as chief of staff of the army. For example, it appears to have been his decision to cancel the Comanche helicopter, although Rumsfeld presumably agreed with it.[117] Schoomaker began to reshape the army in order to "deploy more agile, lethal, adaptable forces."[118] Soldiers are being retrained—primarily to ensure that they have the combat skills that will enable them to fight, regardless of their specialty. Others are being retrained to fill different needs (e.g., logisticians may become military police), while a serious effort is being made to balance the skills present in the guard and regular military.[119] Meanwhile, the Green Berets have been given the task of intelligence gathering in addition to their traditional responsibilities.[120] Finally, in mid-August 2004, the president approved Rumsfeld's plan to withdraw a total of 70,000 troops from Asia and Europe over the next decade.[121]

The navy, on the other hand, was far better positioned to adapt to Rumsfeld's new military. Recognizing Rumsfeld's determination to transform the armed forces, the navy began restructuring its forces:

> Adm. Vern Clark, chief of naval operations, already is executing a plan that will bring fundamental change to the way the Navy deploys and sustains our fighting forces. Based in part on the experiences of Iraq and Afghanistan, Clark's *Fleet Response Plan* is the foundation for a Navy capable of surging new types of strike groups to world hot spots on short notice. He is creating a surge Navy that will provide the president with a nimble yet powerful force to protect U.S. interests in a violent and unpredictable world.[122]

This was also the motivation behind the "Littoral Combat Ship," which was designed to perform a variety of missions, including finding and destroying hidden missiles and intercepting terrorists with small boats.[123]

As this book goes to press, Bush has won a second term. There are many in the military who want Rumsfeld to step down. Many in the army believe Rumsfeld "is responsible for a series of strategic and tactical blunders over the past year. Several of those interviewed said a profound anger is building within the Army at Rumsfeld and those surrounding him." Furthermore, some army officers blame Rumsfeld and those civilians associated with him for the many problems the military has faced in Iraq. To quote one unidentified general, "I do not believe we had a clearly defined war strategy, end state and exit strategy before we commenced our mission. . . . Had someone like Colin Powell been the chairman [of the Joint Chiefs of Staff], he would not have agreed to send in troops without a clear exit strategy. The current OSD [Office of the Secretary of Defense] refused to listen or adhere to military advice."[124]

CONCLUSION

Presidential Leadership Style

The Bush administration's style of conducting a war differed from the Johnson administration's in one critical area. Whereas Johnson and McNamara both attacked the military and attempted to micromanage it, President Bush attempted to stay above the fray while supporting Rumsfeld's efforts to transform the armed forces.

Based on the available evidence, Rumsfeld decided in the beginning of Bush's term that he had no intention of working with the services, who, in his mind, were too ossified. He had no interest in encouraging officers like Shinseki in their efforts to transform the military. He was in charge, had his own plan for radical change, and took steps to achieve it. Making no attempt to hide his disdain for many in the military, Rumsfeld allowed very few officers into his inner circle of decision makers. He was convinced that he and his civilian cadre understood the threats facing the United States far better that those who had worn their country's uniform for many years. They lived in the past, while he was looking to the country's future.

As a result, throughout the administration, Rumsfeld ignored the military. He understood the importance of how things looked to the outside world, so he chose as his chairman and vice chairman officers who would go along with his approach *unconditionally*. Privately, Myers or Pace might ask questions, but when major decisions or public comments were made, they understood who was in charge. In terms of personal authority, General Myers was probably one of the weaker chairmen the United States had seen since the end of World War II.

Violations of Service/Military Culture?

One can make a good argument that Rumsfeld was correct in his belief that the military needed significant changes. Even some in the army agreed with him. Yet, he managed to anger the military with both decisions and the manner in which he reached them. He was not interested in working with the military—he wanted to dominate every aspect of its life. To quote Rowan Scarborough, "Rumsfeld was talking to everyone but the admirals and generals. 'They squandered an opportunity to embrace the building,' a senior officer told me two years later. 'We waited for the cavalry. Mostly they didn't call us. They didn't play like we wanted. We were used to the Clinton administration. All they wanted us to do was keep quiet in public. No criticism.' "[125] And as far as the culture was concerned, he could not care less if he offended senior officers. Indeed, there were times when he gave the impression that he enjoyed putting them down, as illustrated by his dealings with General Shinseki. The fact that the latter believed he had a responsibility to give his best advice to Congress, to speak honestly as he was bound by law to do, was seen by Rumsfeld as a failure to be a team player. To the secretary, Shinseki's view was not only irrelevant, it was disloyal. Rumsfeld knew best, although in the end it became clear that Shinseki's estimate of the number of troops that would be needed to pacify Iraq would turn out to be much closer to the mark than was Rumsfeld's.

The military also found Rumsfeld's willingness—even eagerness—to interfere at all levels especially unsettling. Even Shinseki would have acknowledged Rumsfeld's right and obligation to interfere at the strategic level. After all, he was secretary of defense. But when it came to operational and tactical matters, they objected strongly to his interference. The same thing was true of personnel decisions and structural modifications, areas in which military expertise should have taken precedence. The Chiefs believed that Rumsfeld had the right to ask questions about operational or tactical issues, but not micromanage everything that took place.

The Chiefs also objected to Rumsfeld's idea that civil-military relations were totally one-sided, with Rumsfeld in charge of everything and the military simply complying with his decisions. In their eyes, this opened a dangerous Pandora's box. If the Joint Staff was made subordinate to the secretary of defense, he would have no alternate view to consider. What if the civilian view of how to fight a war was wrong—as has been the case several times since World War II? Doesn't the president deserve to hear the military's perspective? Congress passed a law making the chairman the president's primary military advisor. Diluting his authority by making him one of twenty individuals at a strategy session would undermine his independence—which is exactly what Rumsfeld wanted, but not what Congress intended. In a political sense, the ball was now in Congress's court. The United States had a secretary of defense who was prepared to discipline a senior military officer like Shinseki for giving the Hill his best advice as required by law. Whether or not the Hill will stand up to Rumsfeld on this issue remains to be seen.

There is also the question of whether or not Rumsfeld's transformational steps will last beyond his tenure. Bureaucracies have a strange way of seeming to obey the person in charge even when they are being insulted, as with Rumsfeld, but they generally have the last laugh by jettisoning most of the changes he made as soon as he is gone. Furthermore, what if the transformation is successful and the United States is faced with a major ground war somewhere in the world? It is fine to suggest that the United States is dominant because of its technological superiority, but as Iraq and Afghanistan have shown, the use of a large number of "grunts" remains critical. Thus, the military tends to be conservative. Implementing a whole new way of fighting a war may make sense to the civilian authors of much of the transformational reforms, such as Andrew Marshall and Rumsfeld, but history suggests that things do not change as radically as Rumsfeld seems to believe.

Morale, especially in the army, is also an issue. Wolfowitz tried to smooth things over in October 2003 at a meeting of the U.S. Army Association. He lauded Shinseki for his accomplishments and noted, "If you've been reading the papers lately, you undoubtedly know that we had a difference or two. . . . What the papers fail to report is that I have enormous respect for what General Shinseki accomplished in his four years as chief of staff, moving the Army into the 21st century." However, the article went on to note that Wolfowitz "was conciliatory yet unapologetic, Wolfowitz also reminded his audience that the Army is subordinate to civilian authority."[126] In other words, Wolfowitz was making it clear to the army that while he and Rumsfeld wanted to make up for past differences, they would do so only if the army recognized that Rumsfeld was in charge and was ready to dance to his tune.

In spite of Rumsfeld's behavior, the Chiefs and the rest of the military appreciated Bush's efforts to restore their image through his use of the bully pulpit on numerous occasions. As a strong and unabashed supporter of the country's armed forces, he repeatedly expressed his respect for them and the sacrifices they made for their country. He also took steps to improve their quality of life and made a special effort both to overcome the equipment and weapons problems he inherited from the last administration and to fight for money for research and development in order to help build an armed forces that was second to none.

An argument can be made that Rumsfeld's changes will benefit the military, that the civilian knows something the generals do not. While only time will judge the long-term utility of these changes, the problem is that he has made it clear on numerous occasions that he has little respect for the military leadership, especially that of the army. Furthermore, he has gone out of his way to micromanage the armed forces. Indeed, his leadership style is so invasive and so intolerant of different points of view that some in the military have begun comparing him to former secretary of defense Robert McNamara. Even if he turns out to be right, one cannot help but wonder if his acerbic treatment of the army did not make the transformational process more difficult that it would otherwise have been. As a consequence, the Rumsfeld period has been one of intense conflict, not only against terrorists in Afghanistan and Saddam Hussein's regime in Iraq, but between the military and their civilian superior as well.

Two key questions face the Bush administration in the area of civil-military relations. First is the question of how inclusive and permanent Rumsfeld's reforms will be and what impact they will have on U.S. ability to fight a large, frontal war if that should become necessary. Second, and equally important, is the question of how long it will take to restore morale not only among members of the army, but of the other services as well. Leadership requires more than simply the ability to issue orders. Persuasion is a critical part, but Rumsfeld's ability to utilize it with the military has been obviated by the way he has treated all of the services. He will never get 100 percent cooperation and support until—if ever—he learns that he will gain more from treating them with respect for the years of service they have given to the United States. Indeed, the decision of the Chiefs to support Powell's effort in "seeking a UN-sanctioned force in Iraq" in September 2003 may be only the beginning of their effort to exert themselves.[127]

Changes in Service/Military Culture?

If the conflicts in Iraq and Afghanistan did nothing else, they put pressure on the military to operate in a more joint environment. For example, both campaigns saw special forces troops composed of all the services in combat. Furthermore, all of the services fought together much better than had been the case in either Grenada or in Iran.

It is also worth noting that the army in particular had no problem with making its complaints against Rumsfeld a matter of public record. Indeed, if there has been one change that has taken hold since the end of World War II, it is that the Chiefs will take their complaints to the Hill. Rumsfeld has neutralized the Chiefs by finding two officers to head the JCS who are pliable when it comes to being "team members."

However, it would by wrong to assume that service culture has completely disappeared. For example, as the Marines prepared to redeploy troops to Iraq, they let it be known that as in Vietnam, they intended to take a different approach in administering dangerous areas. Rather than mimic the army and use overwhelming force against insurgents, the Marines said that they would apply what one source called a "Velvet Glove" approach.[128] Hence, in this particular case, service culture remains strong, in spite of greater emphasis on "jointness."

14
CONCLUSION

A democratic nation gets about the kind of military establishment
it deserves.
—James Schlesinger

In the introduction I argued that the military has become an interest group much like other governmental structures in Washington. I also maintained that while conflict between the Chiefs and the president is inevitable, conflict is intensified to the degree that the president's leadership style does not accord with the service or military culture prevailing at the time. Second, I argued that service/military culture has changed over time, moving from a highly service-oriented culture to an increasingly military or joint culture. Third, I asserted that the defense mechanism utilized by the Chiefs to defend what they believe is their prerogative will also evolve. It is now time to evaluate each of these assertions.

INTENSIFYING CONFLICT

Conflict between the president, his senior officials, and the Chiefs proved to be most intense in those administrations in which the presidential leadership style and service/military culture were most at odds. The level of conflict experienced by the administrations covered in this study may be categorized on the following scale.

High Conflict	Moderate Conflict	Minimal Conflict
Nixon	Truman	G. Bush
Johnson	Eisenhower	Ford
Clinton	Kennedy	Reagan
	Carter	Roosevelt
	G. W. Bush	

Note: This categorization is based on the material included in chapters 2 through 13. This notional taxonomy makes no claim of exactitude.

High-Conflict Presidencies

High-conflict presidencies produced a number of areas of intensified conflict. Although individual examples of conflict differed, they shared a number of commonalities. In each case, the president exhibited a lack of respect for the chain of command. Second, the president showed a lack of respect for the Chiefs or their expertise. (However, conflict resulted not just because the Chiefs did not get their way, but because the president or his secretary of defense had no interest in listening to them. When they were able to express their opinions, decision makers such as the secretary of defense, the National Security Council advisor, and the president ignored them.) Third, the Chiefs believed they were lied to or misled in several instances. Fourth, although the Chiefs respected the office of president, they had little respect for the individual holding it. Finally, the Chiefs objected to incidents when the executive interfered in what they considered internal operational, tactical, or personnel matters.

Lyndon Johnson. Johnson clashed repeatedly with the Chiefs over how to fight the war in Vietnam. In the process he violated just about every aspect of military culture imaginable. Although they recognized his authority, they objected to his tendency to micromanage the war, his failure to show the Chiefs respect, his willingness to lie to them, and his effort to keep them out of the decision-making process.

The Chiefs focused upon Johnson's confusing, disordered approach to formulating his Vietnam policy. For example, with the exception of killing Viet Cong, they never did understand what his goal was. Restricted to producing plans for a "graduated response," they balked and advocated massive strikes that they believed would have a far bigger impact on the VC and North Vietnamese. Worried that massive strikes could lead to an expanded war, McNamara made it clear that he did not want any war plans from the Chiefs unless they related to gradual escalation. Thus, it was not surprising that they had not developed any meaningful alternative strategies when Clark Clifford asked them for ideas on how to fight the war. For almost ten years a battle had been waged between those who wanted a graduated response and those who favored massive strikes. No other options had been explored.

Even more upsetting from the Chiefs' standpoint was the lack of respect they received from the president and his secretary of defense. McNamara told them both personally and through his Whiz Kids that he was not interested in what they had to say. He refused to send their memoranda to the president, even while forwarding his own that he had not shown them. How could they do their jobs if they were not part of the decision-making process? They understood politics was a dirty game, but they were deeply upset when their commander in chief misled them, as McNamara did on more than one occasion. The situation deteriorated to the point that the Chiefs and the president had almost no contact.

Concerned that the Chiefs would start World War III, Johnson and McNamara cut them out of the decision-making process and micromanaged the conflict in Vietnam. In most cases, Johnson and McNamara ran the air war: the Chiefs had to get permission for almost every target they wanted to bomb. They understood that the restriction stemmed from fear that the Chinese might intervene, as they had in Korea, but the infuriated Chiefs believed that American GIs were dying as a result of that policy. And when they raised the issue in testimony on the Hill, their boss, the secretary of defense, attacked them. He claimed that gradualism was working and the North Vietnamese were losing the war. His response, coupled with the president's blistering personal attack on them in the Oval Office, so upset them that they came very close to resigning. Considering the degree to which they were ignored and disrespected by Johnson and McNamara, they had little incentive to remain in their positions.

Despite these criticisms, it should be noted that the military had made some major mistakes that fostered the intense conflict between the White House and the Chiefs. The army's battle against VC and North Vietnamese troops in Ia Drang Valley demonstrated very clearly the ineffective folly of Westmoreland's strategy of seeking direct battles with the other side, as if the conflict was similar to the Korean War. When Americans attacked, the VC melted away, and as soon as the Americans left, the VC returned. General Harkins's effort to paint a rosy picture by slanting intelligence reports to Washington not only gave the JCS and the president a false view of what was happening in country, it also led to frustration and eventually hostility on the part of the media, which had a tremendous negative impact on the course of the war.

The Chiefs and political authorities had legitimate policy differences on how to fight the war. The tension that grew between them, however, stemmed less from those differences than from the manner military input was received—or in most cases, ignored. It was clear to the Chiefs that neither the president nor the secretary was interested in what they had to say. Yet they commanded troops fighting and dying in Vietnam, and the president seemed to focus primarily on how to extract himself from the war so he could get back to creating his "Great Society." The Johnson administration represented one of the lowest points in American civil-military relations.

William Clinton. Clinton had problems with the military on almost all levels. From the Chiefs' perspective, Clinton understood neither the military nor how force could and should be used. The chaos the Chiefs found in the Clinton White House did little to build up their confidence in the apparently indecisive president's decision-making ability. Too often the Chiefs could not clearly understand the orders they received, and just as important, they often had no idea who had issued them. An official chain of command seemed nonexistent.

Viewed from the military's perspective, Clinton started off with one hand tied behind his back. First there were the stories about his draft dodging, his "loathing of the military," and his purported drug usage that raised questions about his moral character. Clinton was no sooner in office when he immediately froze military pay and began making budgetary cuts. Most offensive to the military was his effort to have gays openly accepted in the armed forces. Although one may support Clinton and disagree with the Chiefs on this issue, Powell offered sage advice when he warned the president, "Don't make the gay issue the first horse out of the gate with the armed forces." For whatever reason, Clinton did not listen; consequently, he ignited the deep-burning antipathy the military felt toward him. When he was forced to back down on this issue and accept the policy proposed by Powell, the Chiefs formed the impression that Clinton would be a weak leader. Preferring to allow his subordinates and at times international bodies to direct policy, he fulfilled their expectations in many ways. Yet the military's leaders did not relish the opportunity to devise policy on their own. As Wesley Clark learned, even success could not protect an officer who was perceived as playing politics with civilians.

While part of the blame for Somalia must be laid on the shoulders of George Bush, the Chiefs did not believe that the Clinton administration handled matters correctly or stayed on top of the situation. Only Secretary of Defense Les Aspin seemed to be focused on what was happening. Some in the administration, such as Madeleine Albright, wanted a more activist foreign policy that used the military to promote human rights in the chaotic African country. The Chiefs, fearful of the serious dangers presented by mission creep, simply wanted to know where the mission in Somalia was going. When they attempted to fulfill the order to capture Aidid, the operation fell apart in the "Black Hawk Down" incident. Clinton blamed his staff for not informing him of how bad the situation was in Somalia. To the Chiefs, he seemed less concerned with the mission than with the impact of events in Somalia on his poll numbers. Furthermore, sensing a complete lack of leadership, especially when blame was laid on Aspin's shoulders, they wondered why the president did not accept responsibility, a critical trait in military culture.

Next came Bosnia. Clinton came to office amid international outcries over the rampant slaughter of young men and boys in Bosnia by Bosnian Serbs. But the Clinton administration failed to develop quickly a policy to deal with these obvious violations of human rights. Clinton's proposed policy—"lift and strike"—was rejected by the Allies. And when Albright and others raised the question of deploying ground troops, relations between the civilians and the military leaders were so bad that no mechanism was available to explore this option and tie the ideas of a ground and air assault together.

The Dayton Accords offered a glimmer of hope: the Serbs would pull back, NATO troops would move in, and those guilty of crimes against humanity would be punished. Many assumed that the military forces on the ground would carry out the necessary arrests. However, Admiral Smith refused, arguing that it was a task for the police, not a military function. Such insubordination would usually be unthinkable, but the military so questioned Clinton's authority that Smith felt emboldened to ignore the order. The military perceived Clinton as being too weak to impose his will.

Wesley Clark also posed a major problem for the Chiefs. He had close ties to civilians in the Clinton administration, but he was a four-star general working for the Pentagon. He repeatedly lobbied for an activist policy, one favored by Albright and the civilians, in direct defiance of orders from his superiors in the Pentagon. Clark certainly bore a major part of the responsibility for not doing what the Pentagon ordered him to do, but in the end, it was up to the president to enforce order on the foreign-policy bureaucracy. The Chiefs believed he should have stepped in, articulated a clear policy (even one they might not like), and then enforced its implementation. As it was, the lack of presidential leadership often created policy chaos that resulted in wasted resources and shattered lives and careers for some military members and civilians alike.

Clinton's handling of Kosovo also demonstrated the kind of leadership that upset the Chiefs. The president was distracted by the Monica Lewinsky affair, which the military saw as a violation of the Code of Military Conduct, a code that many of them believed should also apply to the commander in chief. They fully realized that the president had been elected by the American people, but to them there were two standards, one for them, and one for Clinton. Meanwhile, the administration did not have a clear policy toward Kosovo. Finally, a massacre at the village of Racak propelled the Allies into taking action, but once again the dispute between the Pentagon on one side and Wesley Clark and the civilians on the other came to the fore. Clark's authority and effectiveness were impeded when he was told not to attend conferences that were part of his area of responsibility as NATO commander.

Clinton's meddling and tactical errors undermined the mission even when the Kosovo air war began. When Clinton issued a statement noting that he did not intend to put ground troops into Kosovo, he left the Chiefs speechless and wondering why a leader would tell the other side that he wouldn't use something in his arsenal. They did not want to put ground forces into Kosovo, but openly saying so made no military sense. Then the White House began trying to micromanage target selection, and the president who was supposedly in charge seemed to disappear.

In short, the Chiefs not only questioned Clinton's character, they objected to his efforts to use the military for social experiments, and they were bothered by his lack of leadership. This feeling was further strengthened when Clinton backed down on the issue of homosexuals in the military. Senior officers expect the president to issue clear and concise orders, even if they do not agree with them. At least then they would understand what they are expected to do. But Clinton did not seem to respect them or the sacrifices they were making. Given the problems facing the United States, they wanted a president who was "in charge."

Richard Nixon. The Vietnam War dominated the Chiefs' relationship with President Nixon. Relieved to be free of Johnson's micromanagement, they were happy to see Nixon, but they soon learned that his unscrupulous actions and his secretive behavior put them in a very difficult situation. He would violate one canon of military culture after another. To begin with, Nixon and Kissinger ignored the chain of command whenever it suited them. The Chiefs were appalled by the White House's efforts to go around their boss, Secretary of Defense Melvin Laird, regardless of the reason. Both Adm. Elmo Zumwalt and Gen. Earl Wheeler refused to comply with Kissinger's efforts to get them to work directly with him. Later, however, Adm. Thomas Moorer, the chief of naval operations and then chairman of JCS, cooperated with Kissinger without informing Laird of what was taking place. Not only did this action violate the chain of command, it also put the chairman in an untenable position: he had crossed over the line and become very political. The chain of command was also broken in the Radford incident, when the White House did its best to keep critical information from the Chiefs, and someone got the idea of using a navy yeoman as a conduit to pass information to the Pentagon.

The Chiefs clashed with Nixon over a host of other issues as well. They were mortified at being forced to lie when he decided to bomb Cambodia. They wondered why they should not take credit for a positive action, one that was hurting the North Vietnamese and saving American lies, and why they should keep two sets of books. Then there was Kissinger's effort, at Nixon's insistence, to get Zumwalt to throw several black sailors out of the service because they gave the black-power salute and refused to reboard their ship. Zumwalt was furious at the commander in chief's attempt to issue such a blatantly illegal order. The Uniform Code of Military Justice governed military behavior, and Nixon's order violated it. Zumwalt flatly refused to dismiss the sailors. Finally, the Chiefs recognized the political necessity of a gradual withdrawal from Vietnam. They knew that it was tearing apart the military, especially the army and Marines. Why should soldiers continue to fight if they knew the United States, which was not interested in victory, was using them as a diplomatic bargaining chip?

It is important, however, to note that the Chiefs appreciated Nixon's willingness to do what they had advocated ever since the United States had gone to Vietnam: bomb extensively. They appreciated his massive attacks on Cambodia, Laos, and then North Vietnam, the operational details of which he had left to the military.

Regardless of their frustration with Nixon's Vietnam War policy, the Chiefs distrusted and disliked Nixon. They could not get over his lies, his deceitful ways, and his many efforts to get them to commit open violations of the chain of command.

Moderate Conflict

While conflict between civilian and military leaders certainly existed during these presidencies, it was not as intense as in the preceding cases. Presidents presiding over periods of moderate conflict occasionally ignored the chain of command, acted indecisively, failed to fully value the Chiefs' opinions, or turned to civilians to provide analyses to the secretary of defense. Ultimately, however, a sense of respect existed between the president and the military. None of the presidents during times of moderate conflict insulted the Chiefs that way that Johnson or Nixon did.

Harry Truman. President Truman's indecisiveness in dealing with the services led to conflict, which in turn led the services to believe that they could and should use their allies on the Hill to fight the administration. In time such actions would become common, but it was a new and unexpected phenomenon under Truman.

Truman inherited a battle-toughened command and was immediately challenged to assert control. The president faced these especially difficult tasks:

fighting a war, pushing through structural change, and forcing the services to accept racial integration. Given Truman's involvement in directing and changing broad aspects of the military, as well as his indecisive leadership style, it is not surprising that conflict flared between him and the Chiefs.

Service unification meant that the president was interfering in what the various military branches, especially the navy and Marine Corps, believed was sacred ground. He was threatening to change roles and missions, something that went to the heart of the military profession. The army wanted to get rid of the Marines, and the air force wanted to gain control of the navy's air assets. To make matters worse, Truman was believed to favor the army. The bitter battle sparked the Revolt of the Admirals, a very public attack on Truman's efforts to bring about service unification. Indeed, the navy and Marines never stopped fighting his efforts to centralize authority in a department of defense, which they feared would be controlled by the army and air force, thus leaving the navy out in the cold.

Truman's effort to advance racial integration also met resistance. He wanted to increase the Democratic Party's appeal to black voters, but the army's job was to fight wars, not engage in social experiments. The army, which regarded unit structuring and personnel decisions as internal military matters, fought the president with the aid of a civilian secretary of the army who strongly opposed integration. In the meantime, the navy and the air force attempted to convince the president that they were taking important steps to integrate their services.

The Chiefs did approve of President Truman's handling of the war in Korea. In this case, he listened to the Chiefs and generally followed their advice. He wanted to be involved when major strategic decisions were being made, but he left operational and tactical operations to them. When the MacArthur affair escalated into an outright challenge to presidential authority, Truman did everything possible to accommodate this American icon. The president feared him for political reasons and did not want a confrontation. In time, however, it became obvious that regardless of how hard he tried, MacArthur would continue to be insubordinate. So Truman fired him, and fortunately for him, the Chiefs all agreed and testified to that effect before Congress.

General Bradley's telling comment that Truman should have fired MacArthur "two years ago" spoke volumes about the manner in which Truman operated. He hesitated in introducing service integration, put up with opposition from his own political appointee, and then acted indecisively. He achieved his goal, but only after bitter political battles that became public. This experience taught the Chiefs to appeal administrative decisions to Congress, and it convinced them that they had every right to turn to the Hill and the media for help if the president was trying to undercut them or their programs.

Dwight Eisenhower. During his time in office, Eisenhower was not involved in a combat operation (after the Korean War ended), unlike his predecessor, Truman, or his successor, Kennedy. As a consequence, it is impossible to know how he would have responded if armed conflict had occurred. Would he have tried to micromanage the war? We will never know. During his administration, he and the Chiefs struggled over doctrine and the military budget. The burning issue of the time focused on determining what kind of military force structure the United States should develop. Eisenhower was primarily concerned with saving money, while the Chiefs wanted what they called a balanced force structure.

The Chiefs were most concerned with the question of whether Eisenhower would listen to them when it came to balancing fiscal problems with the needs of military force structure. In an effort to save money, the president proposed the "New Look" force structure, one that placed primary emphasis on nuclear weapons. The Chiefs understood that Eisenhower was trying to economize, but they also believed they had a right and a duty to field a military that could stand up to the Russians. After all, the United States was now engaged in a cold war that could become hot at any time.

From his perspective, Eisenhower went out of his way to involve the Chiefs. He sacked the old Chiefs, whom he was convinced did not understand the new world, and replaced them with new faces. He explained the economic problem to the Chiefs and asked them to come up with the necessary cuts. Instead, they refused, and came back to him with requests for more money. Even when they appeared to support his approach, they found ways to circumvent it. Eisenhower did not want to interfere in internal military affairs by telling them what kind of force structure to have, but it soon became obvious that the only effective approach was to set a budgetary limit. The Chiefs responded by lobbying their friends in Congress and the media to make their case for more money. Eisenhower fired his new Chiefs only to discover that their replacements were equally committed to their services. They went public in a devastating fashion. Taylor, for example, published an article and a book blasting Eisenhower's New Look strategy for not paying sufficient attention to conventional forces.

From the Chiefs' standpoint, they had no choice but to stand up to Eisenhower. They believed they had tried to work with him and provide him their expert advice, but he ignored them. He was their commander in chief, but they feared that his overemphasis on nuclear weapons exposed U.S. troops to extreme danger. Believing that the future of their services was at stake, the Chiefs genuinely disagreed with Eisenhower's stance that any war would immediately go nuclear. The felt an even stronger need to resist his efforts to bring about greater service integration. He could not even get the air force to sit down with the army. The Chiefs' response was simple: get Congress involved, go public, make the president back down. Eisenhower proved stubborn, and he achieved greater service integration. But as the Kennedy administration would demonstrate, the equally stubborn Chiefs were right to argue for more emphasis on conventional forces.

John F. Kennedy. The Kennedy administration faced problems with the Chiefs in almost every sector. To begin with, Secretary of Defense Robert McNamara brought the "Whiz Kids" into the Pentagon and in the process demonstrated that he and they had little or no respect for the Chiefs or their military expertise. McNamara at times lied to the Chiefs and refused to pass on important policy papers. For their part, the Whiz Kids tried to tell the military what kind of weapons to purchase, placing a premium on cost effectiveness, not on the military effectiveness of weapons. It is not surprising that the Chiefs fought against this political intrusion into an area critical to their ability to fight and win wars.

Kennedy dealt with three military operations while he was president. The first, involving the Bay of Pigs invasion, precipitated a disaster both for U.S. foreign policy and for Kennedy's relations with the Chiefs. The Chiefs, who believed that the action in Cuba belonged to the CIA, felt that they were not in the chain of command and thus not responsible for the outcome. The military was not supposed to be involved, but the president asked them to evaluate the plan. Unfortunately, the president did not understand what they meant when they said the plan had a "fair" chance of success, and they did not make a special effort to explain the term's significance. They argued that an invasion was dependent on an uprising as well as air supremacy and surprise. However, in the end, they gave their support to the invasion plan. Then the president decided to cancel the air strikes—unbeknownst to the Chiefs.

The president was furious with the Chiefs for not speaking up, and they were upset with the way he ran the operation. A clear clash of cultures ensued. They had not felt free to voice their misgivings because another agency had the lead, and indeed, General Lemnitzer later commented that not saying anything had been a major mistake. The military also found it difficult to understand how or why Washington would leave the Cuban invaders without any assistance when such help was nearby. To his credit, Kennedy made a special trip to the Pentagon in an effort to patch up matters.

The Cuban Missile Crisis would prove to be a worse experience from the standpoint of those involved. Kennedy demanded military advice, and the Chiefs provided it, despite not being used to giving such counsel. When they spoke they sounded like political Neanderthals. While an argument could be made to support their proposal to bomb Cuba into submission, the president had to consider the broader political ramifications. Furthermore, at the president's urging, McNamara did something few previous secretaries of defense dared do. He went to the CNO's plot room and tried to tell the navy how to operate its ships. From the military's standpoint, his outrageous behavior was only a sign of things to come.

Vietnam embroiled the administration and the Chiefs in serious disagreements. From the army's perspective in particular, the president was trying to dictate tactical and operational strategy. Senior army officers were not interested; they had fought in Korea, and too many of them assumed that Vietnam would be similar. It was not, and Kennedy pushed hard for the expansion of special forces. Then there was the questionable appointment of General Harkins, and the army's continued insistence on its search-and-destroy approach, despite its futility.

The Chiefs had a rocky relationship with Kennedy. They despised the Whiz Kids and their interference in what they believed to be internal military affairs. The confusion between the president and the Chiefs over Kennedy's expectations during the Bay of Pigs spawned distrust. They tried to be helpful when it came to the Cuban Missile Crisis, but their hawkish recommendations led Kennedy to ignore them. They also resisted Kennedy's attempt to force them to change strategy in Vietnam. From the army's point of view, once again civilians were trying to tell the professionals how to fight a war.

Jimmy Carter. Jimmy Carter also endured a rocky relationship with the Chiefs, although they praised him for his refusal to become involved in military operations. The major focus of conflict between Carter and the Chiefs revolved around his efforts to cut back on the military budget while negotiating arms control agreements with the Russians. At his first meeting with the Chiefs, Carter asked how long it would take to reduce the American nuclear deterrent to "a few hundred" missiles. The Chiefs did not know how to respond. How could they cut nuclear missiles without taking into consideration the impact on overall force structure? To complicate matters, the president did not seem to be interested in their reaction: he was cutting the military and that was that. They became bitter.

Carter then turned on the services, ordering the army to begin plans to evacuate Korea, telling the air force he was cancelling the B-1, and informing the navy he was scrapping plans for a new super carrier. The further embittered Chiefs provided him with their best advice, which he ignored. Then the Russians invaded Afghanistan, upsetting Carter's efforts to seek arms control agreements. The Chiefs soon embarked upon their now customary course of appealing to Congress and speaking out publicly. General Meyer, for example, told the Hill that America had a "hollow" army. The other Chiefs followed suit. Carter tried to save himself by increasing the military budget toward the end of his tenure, but he was never able to overcome the belief on the part of many in the United States that he had let American defenses deteriorate.

Although the Chiefs disliked Carter for cutting the budget and ignoring them, they were appreciative of his willingness to stay out of the Iranian rescue mission. Instead of micromanaging the operation, he asked some questions and then allowed the Pentagon to prepare and run the operation. He merely asked to be informed. In the end, the rescue attempt failed, but it was the military's fault, not the president's. Equally important, he accepted responsibility for the failure. Still, the military's bitterness toward Carter was so great that in 1980 only 1 percent of officers said they favored Carter's reelection.

George W. Bush. Conflict between George W. Bush's administration and the military stemmed from both operational matters and force structure issues. In contrast to most other presidents, however, the tension afflicted the relationship between the Chiefs and Bush's secretary of defense, Donald Rumsfeld. The president remained above the fray and the vast majority of those in uniform appeared to like and respect him.

Rumsfeld came into office as the U.S. military found itself in a period of technological change. The army, for example, was moving from a large, tank-heavy force structured to fight the Russians in Europe to one that had to address the increasing dangers of terrorism. The Chiefs were well aware of the problem, and the army in particular had been working on it, but insofar as Rumsfeld was concerned, the military had not done enough. He believed it was time to take "transformation" seriously.

Rumsfeld quickly projected an image of himself as one who knew all there was to know about such problems, certainly more so than the Chiefs, whom he distrusted—an attitude that was guaranteed to produce conflict. Rumsfeld tried to deal with the issue by appointing a chief and deputy chief of the JCS whom he believed he could command to do his bidding. He also spoke individually with all officers on the promotion list to senior ranks, reserving the right to scratch anyone who did not satisfy him.

The war in Afghanistan and the associated inordinate period of time it had taken to deploy forces where they were needed confirmed Rumsfeld's beliefs that the U.S. military had to be revamped quickly. In particular, he was determined to increase the role played by special operation forces. But to build the force structure he wanted, he had to redirect regular military spending toward the purchase of high-technology items. Anyone who got in his way would be pushed aside.

Rumsfeld primarily targeted the army. In one instance, he and his deputy disingenuously suggested that the army would have thirty days to present a defense for the Crusader, only to announce a few days later that the weapon had been eliminated from the budget. The army's chief of staff, Eric Shinseki, then testified before Congress that failure to fund this weapons system would have a serious impact on the ability of the army to carry out its missions. Rumsfeld had little tolerance for army opposition, and when the secretary of the army agreed with Shinseki, he was forced to resign. Shinseki's own replacement was selected from the retired ranks, a major blow to the hundreds of generals on active duty. But Rumsfeld did not care. In the meantime, officers grew increasingly bitter.

Rumsfeld again argued with the Chiefs over how to configure troops for an invasion of Iraq. Rumsfeld wanted a very small force, while the Chiefs wanted a much larger one that would unleash overwhelming force. In the end, they agreed to a compromise force structure that fell somewhere in between the two plans. When the war preparations commenced, Rumsfeld did his best to micromanage the process. Later, the quick victory convinced Rumsfeld that he had been right, and he used the opportunity to go after the army again. To make sure that they understood who was boss, the man he chose to be the new secretary of the army had been both a naval officer and the secretary to the air force. Major changes would ensue.

In the second term of the Bush administration it is possible that Rumsfeld will be replaced or that he could adopt a different approach to dealing with the military. As it is, conflict between Rumsfeld and the military remains a problem. The Chiefs resent the fact that he ignores them and replaces any officer who dares to speak up. Although Rumsfeld has found compliant officers for the chairman and deputy chairman's job, he has created such a high level of resentment that it would not be surprising if the services, especially the army, worked hard to reverse the changes he instituted once he is gone from the scene.

Minimal Conflict

The presidents who fit into this category were not perfect from the Chiefs' standpoint. Although each of their administrations witnessed conflict, primarily over policy, these presidents accorded the Chiefs a high degree of respect. The commanders in chief respected the chain of command, provided strong leadership (in at least two of the cases), and seriously regarded the Chiefs as military advisors. The president did not always accept their advice, but they left the Oval Office feeling that he had listened seriously to them.

Franklin Roosevelt. Franklin Roosevelt gained extensive experience with the military during a major war. He maintained positive relations with his Chiefs, even when he overrode them on occasion. Roosevelt valued their advice and generally took it, unless he believed diplomatic problems necessitated a different approach. For example, in regard to Operation Torch, Marshall and others were convinced that the Allies should attack the European mainland as early as possible. But Roosevelt, who understood British objections over the lack of troops, equipment, and landing craft, said no. Although Marshall did not agree with his commander in chief and expressed concern that he was paying too much attention to his Allies instead of his own military, he immediately went about carrying out the president's order.

Roosevelt refused to involve himself in the tactical and operational planning that would be done for an invasion such as Operation Torch. Like other presidents he wanted to know what was planned and happening, but he resisted the temptation to micromanage, leaving the military professionals to do their job. The same was true of personnel issues. One can argue that he played a significant, if delicate, role in Marshall's "decision" to remain in Washington instead of going to Europe to oversee Operation Overlord, but, ultimately, he did not order Marshall to stay. Similarly, when Gen. George Patton slapped a soldier and then made an indiscreet statement in England, Roosevelt allowed Eisenhower to handle the personnel matter. One could argue that Roosevelt should have stepped in when disputes broke out among military leaders such as the one that erupted between Nimitz and MacArthur. But that was not his way, and there is no indication that the Chiefs expected him to become involved. What was important to them was that he respected them and did not interfere in what the military considered its internal affairs.

It is also worth noting that Roosevelt used the Chiefs to a far greater degree in the world of diplomacy than they had ever expected. He took them with him to Yalta and Tehran and both solicited and listened to their opinions, which he sometimes accepted.

George Bush. President Bush led the military during much different wars in Panama and the Persian Gulf and also addressed the military's force structure, which was still configured to fight the Russians. Major changes were in order, but implementing and overseeing them would be difficult. George Bush assigned the task to Colin Powell, thereby ensuring that the military could significantly contribute to the process. It was a gesture that Powell and the military greatly appreciated.

The swift and effective war in Panama was handled by the military; Bush wanted to stay on top of the action, but he permitted Gen. Maxwell Thurman considerable latitude in deciding how to fight. It is also worth noting that Thurman was backed up by General Powell, who kept the civilians well informed of what was happening. However, some unpleasant incidents occurred; for example, Carl Vuono's firing of Woerner upset the JCS chairman, Adm. William Crowe, because he had no forewarning.

The Persian Gulf War, a major operation, eventually involved close to 500,000 personnel. Closely involved in all of the decision making, Powell and Secretary of Defense Cheney met regularly with the president, with Powell being permitted to do the majority of the talking. Gen. Norman Schwarzkopf, who commanded the operation, also was brought into the Oval Office. Bush asked some questions, but he expected the military to run the operation. Problems did arise, and at times Colin Powell helped shield Schwarzkopf from civilians who made disparaging comments about his early plans to attack Iraq. The president remained involved, but stayed in the background.

Despite differences of opinion and criticism of the military's plans, the Chiefs felt that they had received the kind of respect they deserved and that the president had brought them into the process; rather than attempt to dictate strategy, Bush had asked questions. He made the important political decisions, such as stopping the war instead of continuing on to Baghdad. While many in uniform would consider that decision a mistake, they recognized that it was a political decision best left to the president.

Ronald Reagan. Reagan would have an opportunity to interact with the Chiefs on a variety of issues: two military operations, a bill that led to a major change in service unification, and an effort to rebuild the military. To the Chiefs, Reagan represented a much-needed breath of fresh air. Not only did he act in a respectful manner toward them, he also went out of his way to make the military respectable again in the public eye; he lavished money on them, at least during his first two years. The Chiefs would have preferred a more systematic disbursement of the largesse that Reagan and his secretary lavished on them in the first two years of his presidency, but they were happy to get what was available.

The deaths of 241 Marines, sailors, and soldiers in Lebanon hit Reagan hard, especially because the Chiefs and Secretary Weinberger had warned him repeatedly that he was putting them in harm's way. The president had heard the Chiefs out, but for political reasons made the decision to keep the Marines there. When the attack came, Reagan accepted responsibility for it. Grenada, meanwhile, was strictly a military operation. Reagan asked questions and listened to the military, but stayed out of operational matters. The problems that arose during the operation were the military's fault.

The 1986 Goldwater-Nichols Act underlined the important role that Congress now played in the arena of civil-military relations. The Iranian rescue mission, as well as Lebanon and Grenada, had demonstrated to the legislators a critical need for more "jointness" in force structure. Although the secretary of defense made Congress aware of his strong opposition to the proposed changes (as did the navy and Marine Corps), Reagan remained above the fray, refusing to become involved in the issue.

Gerald Ford. Ford presided over only one major military operation during his presidency, the recovery of the *Mayaguez.* To make certain that the matter was handled correctly, he intimately involved himself in the operation, which occurred only days after South Vietnam fell. Hence, American military morale was at stake. Although the military would have preferred being allowed by the president to handle the matter themselves, they appreciated his openness. If Ford slighted anyone during the *Mayaguez* crisis, it was his secretary of defense, not the military. The Chiefs were made to feel like team members, something they greatly appreciated. Some officers at the junior level felt that the operation would have run smoother and not cost the lives of some young Marines if it had been handled at the tactical level, but the same problems would have probably arisen if the Chiefs themselves had handled the matter from Washington.

OTHER FACTORS

The preceding chapters have focused on select traits and behaviors that influence the relationship between a president and the military chiefs. The following discussion briefly examines the potential effects of other factors not considered above.

Political Party

This study partially supports the assumption that the Chiefs relate better to Republicans than Democrats. In the minimal-conflict category, there were three Republicans and one Democrat; in the moderate-conflict category, there were three Democrats and two Republicans; and in the high-conflict category, there was one Republican and two Democrats. In short, during most of the last sixty-odd years, Republicans have had a slightly better relationship with the Chiefs than has been the case with Democrats.

It is, however, worth noting that this situation may be changing. The military is becoming increasingly conservative, Republican, and political. As Thomas Ricks observed, "The military increasingly appears to lean toward partisan conservatism. It also seems to be becoming less politically representative of society, with a long-term downward trend in the number of officers willing to identify themselves as liberals. Open identification with the Republicans is becoming the norm—even . . . part of the implicit definition of being a member of the officer corps."[1] The question is whether this politicization and move to the right is temporary. Ricks cites studies that suggest that the change is a result of the end of the draft and what many officers consider to be the collapse of morals in civilian society. If that is the case and it turns out to be permanent, it would have serious implications for civil-military relations in the United States.

Prior Military Service

Many believe that a president with prior military service will have a better working relationship with the Chiefs. Of the presidents in this study, four had minimal or no prior military service: Roosevelt, Reagan (whose military service involved making wartime films), George W. Bush (whose service was limited to the National Guard), and Clinton. Of them, two finished in the minimal-conflict category, one in the moderate-conflict category, and the other in the high-conflict category, respectively. Furthermore, two of the presidents, Eisenhower and Carter, had extensive military service, one as a career soldier and the other as a graduate of the U.S. Naval Academy and as a nuclear submarine officer. Both had problems with the military. In short, prior military service is not a useful predictor of how well a president will relate to the Chiefs.

Change

It is almost axiomatic that a president who decides to make major changes in a short period of time will violate the Chiefs' perception of military culture. Why? Because if the president wants to make such changes he will probably circumvent them. In the high-conflict category, one president tried to introduce major changes (Clinton, who sought to change the roles of women and homosexuals in the military). In the moderate-conflict category, three focused on change: Truman (racial integration, service unification), Eisenhower ("New Look" strategy), and George W. Bush (military transformation). Even presidents in the minimal-conflict category witnessed major changes; however, Reagan stayed above the fray and permitted his secretary of defense to work out the issue of the Goldwater-Nichols Act with Congress.

A president who hopes to introduce change without provoking serious conflict with the Chiefs must involve the senior officers in the process, even if they seem unresponsive. If they believe the change is being imposed on them from outside (as in the reforms being advanced by Secretary of Defense Rumsfeld), they will circle the wagons and work to undo the changes they opposed as soon as the president or the secretary of defense has left Washington.

Valuing Military Culture

Is it worth paying attention to military culture? The answer depends on the president and what he or she expects to accomplish. It can be said, however, that by leaving as much responsibility as possible to the Chiefs, listening to them, and showing them as much respect as possible, the president will minimize conflict and improve his relationship with the Chiefs.

THE CHIEFS' DEFENSE OF THE MILITARY

Historically speaking, the nature of the president's relationship with the military underwent a critical change during the Truman administration. It was under President Truman that the military, particularly the navy and the air force, decided it had a right to turn to sympathetic members of the Congress to buttress its position when senior officers disagreed with the president. At this time, the infamous "leaks" began to appear, and the Chiefs, who regarded the president as a weak, indecisive leader, started to use the media to substantiate their position. Truman, who was intent on creating a more unified military, did nothing to exert control over the various services, in particular the navy, and to a lesser extent the air force.

From Truman on, the Chiefs repeatedly turned to Congress—and the media—in protecting what they considered their service or military rights. Some presidents would try to restrict the Chiefs' access to Congress. For example, Donald Rumsfeld kept most of his senior officers from saying what they thought in front of Congress by threatening to fire them if they did. Nevertheless, the United States has now reached a point where the Chiefs habitually appeal to Congress for protection, especially if the president belongs to a different party than the Senate or House majority. Intimately aware of the importance of Congress to their cause, the Chiefs spare little effort to build up support on the Hill. One need only observe how many members of Congress are invited daily to breakfast with the chief of staff, commandant of the Marine Corps, or chief of naval operations at the Pentagon. Similarly, it is no accident that members of Congress are often invited to visit military installations and ships and to watch exercises. In short, from the perspective of the Chiefs, lobbying the Hill for weapons systems they want, even if the president does not agree with their desire, is a legitimate action.

CHANGING MILITARY CULTURE

During the past sixty years a gradual, but nevertheless significant change in military culture has occurred. During World War II, the military was dominated by service culture: Although everyone in the military wore a uniform and served the country, service orientation dominated military life, creating sharp distinctions and rivalries between the services. An individual was a soldier, sailor, or Marine first, and a member of the broader military family second. Truman, and then Eisenhower, fostered service unification, an action that reached its zenith in 1986 with the passage of the Goldwater-Nichols Act. Like it or not, service on a joint staff became a prerequisite for promotion to general or flag rank. Similarly, a tremendous push for joint operations occurred, especially in the aftermath of Tehran, Lebanon, and then Grenada. Although studies on how individual service members perceive themselves are not available, anecdotal experiences suggest that conversion toward a greater joint-service culture is progressing. To the degree this happens (and it will happen differently in the various branches), civil authorities will face an increasingly unified service.

OTHER STUDIES

My study of the relationship between presidents and the military reaches a number of conclusions that can be compared with those offered by the works cited in the first chapter. All of the presidents discussed in this book would agree with Clausewitz, as I do, that war is always a political undertaking. Yet they differed significantly when deciding the extent to which civilians should be involved in what might be called military matters. No president in the past sixty years has been willing to hand the conduct of war or the military budget over to the Chiefs. During the first Gulf War, even George Bush wanted to be informed of what was happening and why. The same was true of Ronald Reagan and Gerald Ford when they experienced military operations. Different presidents drew the lines between political and military matters at different points, depending on their leadership style and political power.

If anything, this study raises serous questions about Huntington's suggestion that civil-military relations work best if the military is afforded maximum freedom from civilian control. First, as noted above, no president has been willing to leave military matters up to the military. Even those like George Bush and Jimmy Carter, who let the military determine operational details, wished to be kept informed. Providing the military with a degree of freedom may enhance a president's relationship with his officers, but more important is the question of how the relationship is handled. If the president's leadership style does not respect military culture, the likelihood of conflict will increase.

In understanding the evolution of civil-military relations in the United States, works by Feaver and Cohen are useful, unlike those of Lasswell and Janowitz, which provide only limited insight into the matter. Feaver and Cohen recognized that conflict, eternal and omnipresent, can at best be regulated. Toward that end, Feaver's paradigm provides a broad deductive framework that helps us explain how conflict is regulated on the macro-level and even at the mid-level. Similarly, Cohen's study reminds us that politics and conflict between the military and the Chiefs goes on in every polity. Furthermore, as Cohen argued, civilian interference in the military process has occasionally served a positive purpose.

This study has taken a different approach. Its purpose is not to construct an all-pervasive deductive framework; far more modestly, it tries to understand why some presidents have experienced more conflict with the Chiefs than others. The study also seeks to provide the military's perspective and to demonstrate that the military believes that it has a legitimate right to engage the Congress and the media when defending its vital interests from presidential attacks; indeed, the U.S. Constitution and the actions of members of Congress support that belief.

This study has also avoided the normative question of whether the military should avoid involvement in policy formulation. This is a point that Richard Kohn raised in his very thoughtful essay on the topic.[2] This writer would argue that the question of whether or not the military should become involved in policy formulation is a moot point. The fact is that it is involved, and as Powell and other senior officers have noted, the military has become a bureaucratic force in American politics like other institutions within the U.S. government. Most senior officers believe that if they were not actively working with the Congress as well as the media in ensuring that the military's interests and needs are protected, the military would quickly find itself unable to carry out the missions assigned to it. One may rue the day that the military became an active bureaucratic force in Washington politics, and one can argue that the Chiefs' involvement in foreign policy and national security policy is not good for the United States, but I fear that is a reality that we must learn to live with.

Finally, as noted in the introduction, this study does not suggest that the president alone bears the burden of ensuring a positive relationship with the Chiefs. As Henry Kissinger said to President Ford when he asked him to stay on after Nixon's resignation, "It is not up to you to get along with me, it is up to me to get along with you." The Chiefs understand that the president is commander in chief and that he is the one who issues the orders. The key point, however, is that a president has the power to decide how much conflict he or she wants in the relationship. The president can always fire a recalcitrant general or admiral, as has happened in the past, but respecting military culture will help to minimize conflict in the relationship.

NOTES

CHAPTER ONE. THE MILITARY, THE PRESIDENT, AND CIVIL-MILITARY RELATIONS

1. For a discussion of the relevance of Clausewitz to the modern military professional, see Thomas B. Vaughn, "Clausewitz and Contemporary American Professionalism," *Military Review* 62, no. 11 (November 1982): 39–44.

2. For a discussion of the impact of the French Revolution on military structure, see this writer's *Soldiers, Commissars and Chaplains: Civil-Military Relations since Cromwell* (Lanham, Md.: Rowman and Littlefield, 2001), 79–102.

3. Carl von Clausewitz, *On War,* ed. and trans. Michael Howard and Peter Paret (Princeton, N.J.: Princeton University Press, 1989), 81, 87.

4. Ibid., 606, 608.

5. Harold D. Lasswell, "The Garrison State," *American Journal of Sociology* 46, no. 4 (January 1941): 455–68.

6. Raymond Aron, "Remarks on Lasswell's 'The Garrison State,' " *Armed Forces and Society* 5, no. 3 (Spring 1979): 347.

7. Ibid., 348

8. Lasswell, "Garrison State," 455–60.

9. Peter Feaver, *Armed Servants: Agency, Oversight, and Civil-Military Relations* (Cambridge, Mass.: Harvard University Press, 2004), 7. I am indebted to Professor Feaver for generously sharing this work with me while it was still in manuscript form.

10. Samuel Huntington, *The Soldier and the State* (New York: Vintage, 1957), 32.

11. Ibid., 57. This was clearly a play on a phrase from Clausewitz that had a major impact on Huntington.

12. See, for example, this writer's "Commissars in the Red Army," in Dale R. Herspring, *Soldiers, Commissars and Chaplains: Civil-Military Relations since Cromwell* (Lanham, Md.: Rowman and Littlefield, 2001), 103–24.

13. Huntington, *Soldier and the State,* 83.

14. Ibid.

15. Eliot A. Cohen, *Supreme Command: Soldiers, Statesmen, and Leadership in Wartime* (New York: Free Press, 2002), 228.

16. Peter Feaver, "The Civil-Military Problematique: Huntington, Janowitz, and the Question of Civilian Control," *Armed Forces and Society* 23, no. 2 (Winter 1996): 160.

17. Richard H. Kohn, "How Democracies Control the Military," *Journal of Democracy* 8, no. 2 (Winter 1996): 160.

18. Morris Janowitz, *The Professional Soldier* (New York: Free Press, 1960), 9.

19. Morris Janowitz, *Military Conflict: Essays in the Institutional Analysis of War and Peace* (New York: Sage, 1975), 62.

20. Janowitz, *Professional Soldier,* 418.

21. Feaver, "The Civil-Military Problematique," 2, 3, 6, 58.

22. Feaver, *Armed Servants,* 3, 4.

23. Ibid., 7, 68–69, 150. The four patterns of civil-military relations that Feaver singles out are (1) military working with non-intrusive monitoring by civilians; (2) military working with intrusive monitoring by civilians; (3) military shirking with non-intrusive monitoring by civilians; and (4) and military shirking with intrusive monitoring by civilians (119).

24. Personal communication with Peter Feaver, January 2, 2004.

25. Eliot Cohen, *Supreme Command: Soldiers, Statesman, and Leadership in Wartime* (New York: Free Press, 2002).

26. The following is based on numerous conversations with military officers, the author's own thirty-two-year association with the U.S. Navy, and a variety of academic studies. See, for example, A. J. Bacevich, "Tradition Abandoned: America's Military in a New Era," *National Interest* 58 (Summer 1997): 3; John Allen Williams, "The Military and Modern Society," *The World and I* (September 1999): 311; Edgar F. Puryear, *American Generalship: Character Is Everything: The Art of Command* (Novato, Calif.: Presidio, 2002), 1–43; Peter Maslowski, "Army Values and American Values," *Military Review* 70, no. 4 (April 1990): 10–23; Richard K. Betts, *Soldiers, Statesmen and Cold War Crisis* (New York: Columbia University Press, 1977), 157–58; Richard H. Kohn, "How Democracies Control the Military," *Journal of Democracy* 4, no. 8 (1997): 140; Thomas E. Ricks, "The Widening Gap between the Military and Society," *Atlantic Monthly,* July 1997, 66–77; "Cultural Demolition in the Military," *Washington Times,* November 20, 1998; Peter Feaver, "The Gap: Soldiers, Civilians and Their Mutual Misunderstanding," *National Interest* 61 (Fall 2000): 29–37; Gregory D. Foster, "Failed Expectations: The Crisis of Civil-Military Relations in America," *Brookings Review* 15 (Fall 1997): 46–48; and Cohen, *Supreme Command,* 10. See also the articles in Peter Feaver and Richard H. Kohn, eds., *Soldiers and Civilians: The Civil-Military Gap and American National Security* (Cambridge, Mass.: MIT Press, 2001).

27. Cohen correctly argued in his book that politicians (in the four cases he cited) have played an important military role in warfare. As far as the United States is concerned, however, since the beginning of World War II, this role by the president at the strategic level has been accepted as part of the normal process of decision making by the vast majority of senior officers. The problem, however, comes as one moves down the scale to operational and tactical decision making, where the services and the military in general strongly resist civilian involvement. See Cohen, *Supreme Command,* 15–172.

28. Richard E. Neustadt, *Presidential Power and the Modern Presidents: The Politics of Leadership from Roosevelt to Reagan* (New York: Free Press, 1990), 11.

29. Thomas Parrish, *Roosevelt and Marshall: Partners in Politics and War* (New York: Morrow, 1989), 123. Amos A. Jordan, William J. Taylor Jr., and Lawrence J. Korb also note, "The Constitution created a system in which the president and the

Congress were given complementary, at times naturally conflicting, roles in the national security process." *American National Security,* 4th ed. (Baltimore: Johns Hopkins University Press, 1993), 89.

30. Richard H. Kohn, "The Constitution and National Security: The Intent of the Framers," in *The United States Military under the Constitution of the United States, 1789–1989,* ed. Richard H. Kohn (New York: New York University Press, 1991), 86–87.

31. Kenneth W. Kemp and Charles Hudlin, "Civil Supremacy over the Military: Its Nature and Limits," *Armed Forces and Society* 19, no. 1 (Fall 1992): 8; Richard H. Kohn, "How Democracies Control the Military," *Journal of Democracy* 8, no. 4 (1997): 144.

32. Cohen, *Supreme Command,* 241–42.

33. Richard H. Kohn, "Out of Control: The Crisis in Civil-Military Relations," *National Interest* 35 (Spring 1994): 11.

CHAPTER TWO. THE MILITARY AND FRANKLIN ROOSEVELT

1. Fred I. Greenstein, *The Presidential Difference: Leadership Style from FDR to Clinton* (Princeton, N.J.: Princeton University Press, 2000), 22.

2. George C. Edwards III and Stephen J. Wayne, *Presidential Leadership: Policy and Policy Making,* 3d ed. (New York: St. Martin's, 1994), 174.

3. Richard E. Neustadt, *Presidential Power: The Politics of Leadership* (New York: Wiley, 1960), 147.

4. Ibid., 17.

5. William Emerson, "Franklin Roosevelt as Commander in Chief in World War II," *Military Affairs* (Winter 1958–59): 196.

6. Thomas Parrish, *Roosevelt and Marshall: Partners in Politics and War* (New York: Morrow, 1989), 114.

7. Mark Perry, *Four Stars* (Boston: Houghton Mifflin, 1989), 2.

8. Emerson, "Roosevelt as Commander in Chief," 184.

9. Ibid.

10. Eric Larrabee, *Commander in Chief: Franklin Delano Roosevelt, His Lieutenants, and Their War* (New York: Harper and Row, 1987), 17; Emerson, "Roosevelt as Commander in Chief," 184.

11. Emerson, "Roosevelt as Commander in Chief," 184.

12. Ibid., 186.

13. Forrest C. Pogue, "George C. Marshall on Civil-Military Relationships in the United States," in *The United States Military under the Constitution of the United States, 1979–1989,* ed. Richard H. Kohn (New York: New York University Press, 1991), 205. I do not mean to suggest that the militaries were never political or that they did not cooperate with those on the Hill who supported them. As Gen. William Odom pointed out, the navy had a lobby in the nineteenth century and the National Guard was always one of the more effective lobby groups in Washington. The point I am making here is that during the interwar period, most senior officers believed they worked for the president. Personal communication between the author and General Odom, August 22, 2004.

14. Mark Skinner Watson, *Chief of Staff: Prewar Plans and Preparations* (Washington, D.C.: Department of the Army, 1950), 22.

15. Ibid., 22ff.

16. Mark A. Stoler, *George C. Marshall, Soldier-Statesman of the American Century* (New York: Twayne, 1989), 76.

17. Robert Payne, *The Marshall Story: A Biography of General George C. Marshall* (New York: Prentice-Hall, 1951), 145.

18. Parrish, *Roosevelt and Marshall,* 129.

19. Ibid., 422; Payne, *Marshall Story,* 218.

20. Larrabee, *Commander in Chief,* 96.

21. Ibid.

22. Parrish, *Roosevelt and Marshall,* 97–98.

23. Payne, *Marshall Story,* 220.

24. Russell F. Weigley, *The American Way of War* (Bloomington: Indiana University Press, 1973), 318.

25. Parrish, *Roosevelt and Marshall,* 216.

26. Quoted in Larrabee, *Commander in Chief,* 17.

27. Watson, *Chief of Staff,* 79.

28. As cited in Emerson, "Roosevelt as Commander in Chief," 184.

29. William D. Leahy, *I Was There* (New York: Whittlesey House, 1950), 101.

30. Omar N. Bradley, *A Soldier's Story* (New York: Modern Library, 1999), 185.

31. Harry C. Butcher, *My Three Years with Eisenhower* (New York: Simon and Schuster, 1946), 26.

32. Stoler, *George C. Marshall,* 98.

33. Rick Atkinson, *An Army at Dawn: The War in North Africa, 1942–1943* (New York: Holt, 2002), 12.

34. Larrabee, *Commander in Chief,* 136.

35. Butcher, *My Three Years,* 29.

36. Larrabee, *Commander in Chief,* 135.

37. Alex Danchev, *A Very Special Relationship: Field Marshal Sir John Dill and the Anglo-American Alliance, 1941–44* (London: Brassey's Defence Publishers, 1986), 35.

38. Quoted in Payne, *Marshall Story,* 182.

39. Dwight D. Eisenhower, *Crusade in Europe* (Baltimore: Johns Hopkins University Press, 1948), 68.

40. Ibid.

41. Bradley, *Soldier's Story,* 190. As another source put it, "Roosevelt was intrigued by this, largely on political and psychological grounds: GYMNAST, providing early employment to American troops, would boost American morale, give needed battle experience to the armed forces, and encourage the suspicious Russians . . . to believe their Western allies intended to do everything possible at the earliest hour to relieve the intense Nazi pressure on the Eastern Front." Kenneth Davis, *Experience of War* (New York: Doubleday, 1965), 136.

42. Eliot Cohen, *Supreme Command: Soldiers, Statesmen, and Leadership in Wartime* (New York: Free Press, 2002), 200.

43. Atkinson, *Army at Dawn,* 16.

44. Stoler, *George C. Marshall,* 101.

45. Atkinson, *Army at Dawn,* 32.

46. Stoler, *George C. Marshall,* 100–101.
47. Danchev, *Very Special Relationship,* 37.
48. Atkinson, *Army at Dawn,* 288.
49. Perry, *Four Stars,* 5.
50. Ibid.
51. Quoted in Emerson, "Roosevelt as Commander in Chief," 198.
52. Ibid., 297. It should be noted that the president overruled the Chiefs on other issues, including the 1943 plan to mount a campaign to recapture Burma from the Japanese and reopen land communications with China and the October 1944 recall of General Stilwell. See Larrabee, *Commander in Chief,* 15.
53. Atkinson, *Army at Dawn,* 293.
54. Emerson, "Roosevelt as Commander in Chief," 196.
55. Stoler, *George C. Marshall,* 106.
56. Leahy, *I Was There,* 201.
57. Ibid., 309, 310, 314, 315–16.
58. Parrish, *Roosevelt and Marshal,* 515.
59. Davis, *Experience of War,* 111.
60. Payne, *Marshall Story,* 154.
61. Ibid., 155–56.
62. Ibid., 159.
63. Quoted in James R. Locher III, *Victory on the Potomac: The Goldwater-Nichols Act Unifies the Pentagon* (College Station: Texas A&M University Press, 2002), 20–21.
64. Douglas MacArthur, *Reminiscences* (Annapolis, Md.: U.S. Naval Institute Press, 1964), 183.
65. Ibid., 258. See also E. B. Potter, *Nimitz* (Annapolis, Md.: U.S. Naval Institute Press, 1976), 46.
66. Locher, *Victory on the Potomac,* 200.
67. Ibid.
68. Holland M. Smith, *Coral and Brass* (New York: Bantam, 1987), 118.
69. Ibid., 161–62.
70. Ibid., 165.
71. Locher, *Victory on the Potomac,* 200.
72. Stoler, *George C. Marshall,* 119, 120.
73. MacArthur, *Reminiscences,* 230.
74. Potter, *Nimitz,* 325.
75. Locher, *Victory on the Potomac,* 203.
76. Potter, *Nimitz,* 378.
77. Larrabee, *Commander in Chief,* 149.
78. Ibid.
79. Payne, *Marshall Story,* 213.
80. According to Larrabee, Roosevelt paid Marshall the ultimate compliment when he said, "I didn't think I could sleep at ease with you out of Washington." *Commander in Chief,* 150.
81. Stephen E. Ambrose, *Americans at War* (New York: Berkley Books, 1997), 159.
82. Cole C. Kingseed, "Dark Days of White Knights," *Military Review* (January 1993): 75.
83. Quoted in Ambrose, *Americans at War,* 161.

84. Larrabee, *Commander in Chief,* 487.
85. Carlo D'Este, *Eisenhower: A Soldier's Life* (New York: Holt, 2002), 178–82.
86. Ambrose, *Americans at War,* 164.
87. Ibid.
88. Ibid., 167.
89. Larrabee, *Commander in Chief,* 486.
90. Bradley, *Soldier's Story,* 161.
91. Eisenhower, *Crusade in Europe,* 180.
92. Ibid., 224.
93. Quoted in Ambrose, *Americans at War,* 169.
94. Eisenhower, *Crusade in Europe,* 224.
95. Stephen E. Ambrose, *Eisenhower: Soldier and President* (New York: Touchstone, 1990), 215.
96. It is perhaps ironic that many major histories of World War II fail to even mention this event—an event that would help poison army-Marine Corps relationships for years to come. See, for example, Kenneth S. Davis, *Experience of War: The United States in World War II* (New York: Doubleday, 1965), 41ff.
97. Leahy, *I Was There,* 95.

CHAPTER THREE. THE MILITARY AND HARRY TRUMAN

1. Alexander L. George and Eric Stern, "Presidential Management Styles and Models," in *Presidential Personality and Performance,* ed. Alexander L. George and Juliette George (Boulder, Colo.: Westview Press, 1998), 206–7.
2. Sidney M. Milkis and Michael Nelson, *The American Presidency: Origins and Development, 1776–1990* (Washington, D.C.: Congressional Quarterly, 1990), 281.
3. John Burke, *The Institutional Presidency: Organizing and Managing the White House from FDR to Clinton,* 2d ed. (Baltimore: John Hopkins University Press, 2000), 16.
4. Fred I. Greenstein, *The Presidential Difference: Leadership Style from FDR to Clinton* (Princeton, N.J.: Princeton University Press, 2000), 41.
5. Alonzo L. Hamby, "Harry S. Truman: Insecurity and Responsibility," in *Leadership in the Modern Presidency,* ed. Fred I. Greenstein (Cambridge, Mass.: Harvard University Press, 1988), 71.
6. Ibid., 66.
7. See Steve Neal, *Harry and Ike* (New York: Touchstone, 2002), 38–46.
8. As quoted in ibid., 42.
9. Ibid., 107.
10. Michael J. Hogan, *A Cross of Iron: Harry S. Truman and the Origins of the National Security State, 1945–1954* (Cambridge: Cambridge University Press, 1998), 25.
11. Ibid., 25–26.
12. Mark Perry, *Four Stars* (Boston: Houghton Mifflin, 1989), 5.
13. Demetrios Caraley, *The Politics of Military Unification: A Study of Conflict and the Policy Process* (New York: Columbia University Press, 1966), 249.
14. Stephen E. Ambrose, *Eisenhower: Soldier and President* (New York: Touchstone, 1990), 219.

15. David Jablonsky, "Eisenhower and the Origins of Unified Command," *Joint Services Quarterly* (Autumn/Winter 1999–2000): 25.

16. Ibid., 223.

17. Ibid.

18. Ibid., 227.

19. Hogan, *Cross of Iron,* 34.

20. David McCullough, *Truman* (New York: Touchstone, 1992), 476.

21. James R. Locher III, *Victory on the Potomac: The Goldwater-Nichols Act Unifies the Pentagon* (College Station: Texas A&M University Press, 2002), 25.

22. As quoted in Neal, *Harry and Ike,* 86. See also McCullough, *Truman,* 829.

23. Ibid. Or as noted elsewhere, "General Eisenhower has expressed the belief that the Marine Corps should be limited in size and organized in units no larger than a regiment and lightly equipped, for minor operations against objectives in which the Navy is primarily interested, and for employment as interior guards of naval vessels, and for the guarding of shore establishments. He has stated that Marine Corps units as large as divisions should not be in existence. He believes that when a Marine Corps unit reaches the size of a division it is encroaching on an Army function." Quoted in Caraley, *Politics of Military Unification,* 133.

24. E. B. Potter, *Nimitz* (Annapolis, Md.: Naval Institute Press, 1976), 407–8. Gen. Carl Spaatz, the U.S. Army Air Force's chief of staff, "has expressed the view that all land-based aviation other than carrier-type planes should be a function of the Army Air Forces." Caraley, *Politics of Military Unification,* 133.

25. Hogan, *Cross of Iron,* 36.

26. Ibid., 41.

27. Ibid., 42; Caraley, *Politics of Military Unification,* 129.

28. Caraley, *Politics of Military Unification,* 129–30.

29. Ibid., 133.

30. Hogan, *Cross of Iron,* 47.

31. Caraley, *Politics of Military Unification,* 164.

32. Hogan, *Cross of Iron,* 53.

33. Caraley, *Politics of Military Unification,* 145.

34. Locher, *Victory on the Potomac,* 24.

35. Caraley, *Politics of Military Unification,* 151n.

36. Ibid., 176.

37. Ibid., 177.

38. Nathan F. Twining, *Neither Liberty nor Safety: A Hard Look at U.S. Military Policy and Strategy* (New York: Holt, Rinehart, and Winston, 1966), 27.

39. Ibid., 182.

40. Locher, *Victory on the Potomac,* 25–26.

41. Ibid., 26.

42. Paul Y. Hammond, *Super Carriers and B-36 Bombers: Appropriations, Strategy, and Politics,* Inter-University Case Program 97 (Indianapolis: Bobbs-Merrill Company, 1963), 9.

43. Quoted in Townsend Hoopes and Douglas Brinkley, *Driven Patriot: The Life and Times of James Forrestal* (New York: Knopf, 1992), 406.

44. Russell F. Weigley, *The American Way of War* (Bloomington: Indiana University Press, 1973), 376.

45. Hoopes and Brinkley, *Driven Patriot,* 413.
46. Ibid., 423.
47. Ronald H. Cole, Lorna S. Jaffe, Walter S. Poole, and Willard J. Webb, *The Chairmanship of the Joint Chiefs of Staff* (Washington, D.C.: Joint History Office, 1995), 8.
48. Richard K. Betts, *Soldiers, Statesmen and Cold War Crises* (New York: Columbia University Press, 1977), 68.
49. Perry, *Four Stars,* 16.
50. Ambrose, *Eisenhower,* 243.
51. Locher, *Victory on the Potomac,* 266.
52. Stephen Jurika Jr., ed., *From Pearl Harbor to Vietnam: The Memoirs of Admiral Arthur W. Radford* (Stanford, Calif.: Hoover Institution Press, 1980), 148. Radford was especially biting in his criticism of Johnson. "In my long Navy career I met many civilians who served in high places in our government. I became quite well acquainted with many who served as Secretary of the Navy. All were gentlemen, and most were outstanding men who had made a success of their civilian careers but who, when it came to purely professional naval matters, took the advice of their military assistants. Louis Johnson was certainly an exception to this rule" (149).
53. Hammond, *Super Carriers,* 41.
54. Ibid., 51.
55. Quoted in Hogan, *Cross of Iron,* 187.
56. Weigley, *American Way of War,* 377.
57. Perry, *Four Stars,* 14.
58. Richard F. Haynes, *The Awesome Power: Harry S. Truman as Commander in Chief* (Baton Rouge: Louisiana State University Press, 1973), 126.
59. Hammond, *Super Carriers,* 63.
60. Quoted in ibid., 65.
61.Quoted in Locher, *Victory on the Potomac,* 267.
62. Stephen Howarth, *From Sea to Shining Sea: A History of the United States Navy, 1775–1991* (New York: Random, 1991), 485.
63. Richard M. Dalfiume, *Desegregation of the U.S. Armed Forces: Fighting on Two Fronts, 1939–1953* (Columbia: University of Missouri Press, 1969), 81.
64. *New York Times,* June 16, 1945.
65. Dalfiume, *Desegregation of the U.S. Armed Forces,* 102–3.
66. Ibid., 150–51.
67. Morris J. MacGregor Jr., *Integration of the Armed Forces, 1940–1965* (Washington, D.C.: Center for Military History, 1980), 165.
68. Dalfiume, *Desegregation of the U.S. Armed Forces,* 157.
69. Ibid., 159.
70. Ibid., 162.
71. MacGregor, *Integration of the Armed Forces,* 323.
72. Dalfiume, *Desegregation of the U.S. Armed Forces,* 172.
73. MacGregor, *Integration of the Armed Forces,* 325.
74. Ibid., 329.
75. Ibid., 351.
76. Dalfiume, *Desegregation of the U.S. Armed Forces,* 180.
77. Ibid.

78. Ibid., 182.
79. MacGregor, *Integration of the Armed Forces,* 374.
80. Ibid., 379.
81. Ibid., 431.
82. Matthew B. Ridgway, *The Korean War* (New York: Da Capo, 1967), 192–93.
83. Betts, *Soldiers, Statesmen and Crises,* 141.
84. L. James Binder, *Lemnitzer: A Soldier for His Time* (Washington, D.C.: Brassey's, 1997), 176.
85. Ibid.
86. Dean Acheson, *Present at the Creation: My Years in the State Department* (New York: Norton, 1969), 465–66.
87. Harry S. Truman, *Memoirs: Years of Trial and Hope* (Garden City, N.Y.: Doubleday, 1955), 332–33.
88. Mark W. Clark, *From the Danube to the Yalu* (New York: Harper and Row, 1988), 16.
89. Michael D. Pearlman, *Warmaking and American Democracy* (Lawrence: University Press of Kansas, 1999), 293.
90. Ibid., 288.
91. Perry, *Four Stars,* 25.
92. Ibid.
93. Acheson, *Present at the Creation,* 610.
94. Neal, *Harry and Ike,* 182.
95. Pearlman, *Warmaking and American Democracy,* 294.
96. Perry, *Four Stars,* 27.
97. Ridgway, *Korean War,* 36.
98. Ibid.
99. Perry, *Four Stars,* 27. MacArthur put his position as supreme commander in chief on the line when, according to Al Haig, he told his staff, "Gentlemen, we will land at Inchon on September 15 or you will have a new Supreme Commander in East Asia." Alexander M. Haig Jr., "Lessons of the Forgotten War" (lecture, Foreign Policy Research Institute, Washington, D.C., August 14, 2003).
100. David Rees, *Korea: The Limited War* (New York: St. Martin's, 1964), 100.
101. Ibid., 103. See also McCullough, *Truman,* 798–99.
102. Acheson, *Present at the Creation,* 586.
103. Perry, *Four Stars,* 26.
104. Ridgway, *Korean War,* 45.
105. McCullough, *Truman,* 803.
106. Rees, *Korea,* 127.
107. Perry, *Four Stars,* 29.
108. Richard H. Rovere and Arthur Schlesinger Jr., *General MacArthur and President Truman* (New Brunswick, N.J.: Transaction, 1992), 153.
109. Francis Fox Parry, *Three-War Marine* (Pacifica, Calif.: Pacifica Military History, 1987), 197.
110. Ridgway, *Korean War,* 60; Neal, *Harry and Ike,* 187.
111. George C. Mitchell, *Matthew B. Ridgway* (Mechanicsburg, Pa.: Stackpole, 2002), 91.
112. Rees, *Korea,* 75.

113. Acheson, *Present at the Creation,* 609.
114. Ibid.
115. Truman, *Years of Trial and Hope,* 384.
116. Acheson, *Present at the Creation,* 663.
117. Douglas MacArthur, *Reminiscences* (Annapolis, Md.: U.S. Naval Institute Press, 1964), 378; Haynes, *Awesome Power,* 223.
118. Haynes, *Awesome Power,* 224.
119. Ibid., 230.
120. Truman, *Years of Trial and Hope,* 442.
121. Rees, *Korea,* 201.
122. MacArthur, *Reminiscences,* 386.
123. Truman, *Years of Trial and Hope,* 446–47.
124. Haynes, *Awesome Power,* 254 (emphasis added).
125. Neal, *Harry and Ike,* 214.
126. Ridgway, *Korean War,* 234.
127. McCullough, *Truman,* 839.

CHAPTER FOUR. THE MILITARY AND DWIGHT EISENHOWER

1. Fred I. Greenstein, *The Presidential Difference: Leadership Style from FDR to Clinton* (Princeton, N.J.: Princeton University Press, 2000), 55.
2. Robert Cutler, *No Time for Rest* (Boston: Little, Brown, 1965), 313. See also, Greenstein, *Presidential Difference,* 55.
3. John Burke, *The Institutional Presidency: Organizing and Managing the White House from FDR to Clinton,* 2d ed. (Baltimore: Johns Hopkins University Press, 2000), 60.
4. Ibid., 62.
5. Alexander L. George and Eric Stern, "Presidential Management Styles and Models," in *Presidential Personality and Performance,* ed. Alexander L. George and Juliette George (Boulder, Colo.: Westview Press, 1998), 209–10. It is important not to get the impression that everything was done in a formalistic fashion. As Burke noted, he also relied on a good deal of "informal channels of information" when he felt that was in order. *Institutional Presidency,* 65–66.
6. Sidney M. Milkis and Michael Nelson, *The American Presidency: Origins and Development, 1776–1990* (Washington, D.C.: Congressional Quarterly, 1990), 287.
7. Fred I. Greenstein, "Dwight D. Eisenhower: Leadership Theorist in the White House," in *Leadership in the Modern Presidency,* ed. Fred I. Greenstein (Cambridge, Mass.: Harvard University Press, 1988), 82. Greenstein maintained that the chief of staff position was "modeled on those of Eisenhower's military chiefs of staff—for example, General Walter Bedell Smith in World War II and General Alfred Gruenther at NATO headquarters."
8. Lewis L. Gould, *The Modern American Presidency* (Lawrence: University Press of Kansas, 2003), 115.
9. Fred I. Greenstein, *The Hidden-Hand Presidency: Eisenhower as Leader* (New York: Basic Books, 1982).

10. George C. Edwards III and Stephen J. Wayne, *Presidential Leadership: Politics and Policy Making,* 3d ed. (New York: St. Martin's, 1994), 181.

11. Milkis and Nelson, *American Presidency,* 285.

12. Quoted in Richard A. Aliano, *American Defense Policy from Eisenhower to Kennedy: The Politics of Changing Military Requirements* (Athens: Ohio University Press, 1975), 32.

13. Saki Dockrill, *Eisenhower's New-Look National Security Policy, 1953–1961* (London: Macmillan, 1996), 29.

14. Robert R. Bowie and Richard H. Immerman, *Waging Peace: How Eisenhower Shaped an Enduring Cold War Strategy* (Oxford: Oxford University Press, 1998), 97.

15. Charles C. Alexander, *Holding the Line: The Eisenhower Era, 1952–1961* (Bloomington: Indiana University Press, 1976), 29.

16. Stephen Jurika Jr., ed., *From Pearl Harbor to Vietnam: The Memoirs of Admiral Arthur W. Radford* (Stanford, Calif.: Hoover Institution Press, 1980), 318.

17. Greenstein, "Dwight D. Eisenhower," 91.

18. Stephen E. Ambrose, *Eisenhower: Soldier and President* (New York: Touchstone, 1990), 295.

19. Gerald Clarfield, *Security with Solvency: Dwight D. Eisenhower and the Shaping of the American Military Establishment* (Westport, Conn.: Praeger, 1999), 103.

20. Dockrill, *Eisenhower's New-Look,* 30.

21. Clarfield, *Security with Solvency,* 104.

22. Bowie and Immerman, *Waging Peace,* 101–2.

23. Ibid., 103.

24. Clarfield, *Security with Solvency,* 104.

25. Ibid., 110.

26. Samuel Huntington, *The Common Defense: Strategic Programs in National Politics* (New York: Columbia University Press, 1961), 71.

27. *Time,* June 1, 1953, 20.

28. Clarfield, *Security with Solvency,* 112. Hereafter cited parenthetically in text.

29. Ibid., 103. Among the other changes were "Nathan Twining to succeed Hoyt Vandenberg as Air Force Chief of Staff, Matthew B. Ridgway to succeed J. Lawton Collins as Army Chief of Staff, and Robert B. Carney to replace William M. Fechteler as Chief of Naval Operations. Marine General Lemuel C. Shepherd remained Commandant of the Marine Corps."

30. Ibid., 125.

31. Jurika, *From Pearl Harbor to Vietnam,* 318.

32. David L. Snead, *The Gaither Committee: Eisenhower and the Cold War* (Columbus: Ohio State University Press, 1999), 26–29.

33. Aliano, *American Defense Policy,* 37.

34. Alexander, *Holding the Line,* 67. Hereafter cited parenthetically in text.

35. Jurika, *From Pearl Harbor to Vietnam,* 67.

36. Ibid., 321.

37. Bowie and Immerman, *Waging Peace,* 186, 184–85.

38. Clarfield, *Security with Solvency,* 129.

39. Bowie and Immerman, *Waging Peace,* 186.

40. Clarfield, *Security with Solvency,* 130.

41. Dockrill, *Eisenhower's New-Look,* 39.

42. Clarfield, *Security with Solvency,* 134–35.
43. Dockrill, *Eisenhower's New-Look,* 39.
44. Clarfield, *Security with Solvency,* 136.
45. Bowie and Immerman, *Waging Peace,* 189.
46. Ibid.
47. Taking a footnote refers to an action by one of the participants who finds either the material in a joint document unacceptable or does not agree with a policy recommendation. It makes clear to outsiders that the participants lack unanimity.
48. Bowie and Immerman, *Waging Peace,* 195.
49. Ibid., 196.
50. Clarfield, *Security with Solvency,* 148.
51. Matthew B. Ridgway, *Soldier: The Memoirs of Matthew B. Ridgway* (New York: Harper and Brothers, 1956), 288.
52. Clarfield, *Security with Solvency,* 142.
53. Ridgway, *Soldier,* 288–89.
54. Jurika, *From Pearl Harbor to Vietnam,* 326.
55. Bowie and Immerman, *Waging Peace,* 199.
56. Maxwell D. Taylor, *The Uncertain Trumpet* (New York: Harper and Brothers, 1959), 26.
57. Clarfield, *Security with Solvency,* 150. Hereafter cited parenthetically in text.
58. Taylor, *Uncertain Trumpet,* 28–29.
59. Ken Jones and Hubert Kelley Jr., *Admiral Arleigh (31 Knot) Burke: The Story of a Fighting Sailor* (Annapolis, Md.: Naval Institute Press, 2001), 169.
60. Clarfield, *Security with Solvency,* 162.
61. *New York Times,* May 18, 1955.
62. *Time,* May 30, 1955.
63. Clarfield, *Security with Solvency,* 170.
64. Matthew Ridgway, "Keep the Army Out of Politics," *Saturday Evening Post,* January 28, 1956, 34, 72; see also Dockrill, *Eisenhower's New-Look,* 183.
65. Clarfield, *Security with Solvency,* 174; Dockrill, *Eisenhower's New-Look,* 183.
66. Dockrill, *Eisenhower's New-Look,* 183.
67. Ibid., 185.
68. Ibid., 186.
69. This was just the latest run-in between Eisenhower and Wilson. "Colonel Goodpaster recalled that the President was 'quite dissatisfied' with Wilson's management of the military establishment and . . . he was sometimes very critical of Wilson's handling of the Pentagon. During a telephone conversation with Humphrey on 7 December 1956, Eisenhower complained about Wilson, saying that 'I have got a man who is frightened to make decisions. I have to make them for him.' " Ibid., 185.
70. Clarfield, *Security with Solvency,* 175. Hereafter cited parenthetically in text.
71. Thomas M. Coffey, *Iron Eagle: The Turbulent Life of General Curtis LeMay* (New York: Crown, 1986), 338.
72. Lest the reader get the wrong impression, the Soviet Army made the same claim at one point and won control over most short-range missiles because, it was argued, they are just like artillery.
73. Clarfield, *Security with Solvency,* 183.
74. Ibid.

75. Dockrill, *Eisenhower's New-Look,* 187.

76. Jones and Kelley, *Admiral Arleigh Burke,* 179.

77. Dockrill, *Eisenhower's New-Look,* 187–88. Hereafter cited parenthetically in text.

78. Ridgway, *Soldier,* 157.

79. Dockrill, *Eisenhower's New-Look,* 60 (emphasis in original). When a source from the United Kingdom is cited, as in this case, British spelling will be utilized.

80. Andrew Bacevich, "The Paradox of Professionalism: Eisenhower, Ridgway, and the Challenge to Civilian Control," *Journal of Military History* 61, no. 2 (April 1997): 307.

81. Ibid.

82. Ambrose, *Eisenhower,* 376.

83. Ibid., 377.

84. Quotatons in this section from Clarfield, *Security with Solvency,* 195, 197–98.

85. Snead, *The Gaither Committee,* 185.

86. Aliano, *American Defense Policy,* 112.

87. Ibid., 114–15.

88. James R. Locher III, *Victory on the Potomac: The Goldwater-Nichols Act Unifies the Pentagon* (College Station: Texas A&M University Press, 2002), 28.

89. L. James Binder, *Lemnitzer: A Soldier for His Time* (Washington, D.C.: Brassey's, 1997), 231.

90. Jones and Kelley, *Admiral Arleigh Burke,* 190–91.

91. Clarfield, *Security with Solvency,* 230.

92. Ibid., 231.

93. Dockrill, *Eisenhower's New-Look,* 257.

94. Ibid.

95. Ambrose, *Eisenhower,* 507.

CHAPTER FIVE. THE MILITARY AND JOHN F. KENNEDY

1. Alexander L. George and Eric Stern, "Presidential Management Styles and Models," in *Presidential Personality and Performance,* ed. Alexander George and Juliette George (Boulder, Colo.: Westview Press, 1998), 210–12.

2. Ibid.

3. Maxwell D. Taylor, *Swords and Plowshares* (New York: Da Capo, 1972), 200.

4. Lawrence Freedman, *Kennedy's Wars* (Oxford: Oxford University Press, 2000), 40.

5. Carl M. Brauer, "John F. Kennedy: The Endurance of Inspirational Leadership," in *Leadership in the Modern Presidency,* ed. Fred I. Greenstein (Cambridge, Mass.: Harvard University Press, 1988), 115.

6. Taylor, *Swords and Plowshares,* 198.

7. Geoffrey Kemp, "Presidential Management of the Executive Bureaucracy," in *The Domestic Sources of American Foreign Policy,* ed. Eugene R. Wittkopf and James M. McCormick (Lanham, Md.: Rowman and Littlefield, 1999), 159–60.

8. See John Burke, *The Institutional Presidency: Organizing and Managing the White House from FDR to Clinton,* 2d ed. (Baltimore: Johns Hopkins University Press, 2000), 76–77.

9. Fred I. Greenstein, *The Presidential Difference: Leadership Style from FDR to Clinton* (Princeton, N.J.: Princeton University Press, 2000), 72.

10. Ibid., 33. See also David L. Snead, *The Gaither Committee: Eisenhower and the Cold War* (Columbus: Ohio State University Press, 1999), 26–29.

11. Russell F. Weigley, *The American Way of War* (Bloomington: Indiana University Press, 1973), 445.

12. Freedman, *Kennedy's Wars,* 45.

13. Quoted in Weigley, *American Way of War,* 447.

14. Freedman, *Kennedy's Wars,* 45.

15. Quoted in L. James Binder, *Lemnitzer: A Soldier for His Time* (Washington, D.C.: Brassey's 1997), 279.

16. Quoted in Thomas M. Coffey, *Iron Eagle: The Turbulent Life of General Curtis LeMay* (New York: Crown, 1986), 370, 372.

17. Richard H. Kohn, "Out of Control: The Crisis in Civil-Military Relations," *The National Interest* 35 (Spring 1994): 3.

18. Taylor, *Swords and Plowshares,* 254.

19. Trumbull Higgins, *The Perfect Failure: Kennedy, Eisenhower and the CIA at the Bay of Pigs* (New York: Norton, 1987), 38.

20. Freedman, *Kennedy's Wars,* 48.

21. Ibid., 126.

22. Ibid., 127.

23. Richard M. Bissell Jr., *Reflections of a Cold Warrior: From Yalta to the Bay of Pigs* (New Haven, Conn.: Yale University Press, 1996), 177.

24. Lucien S. Vandenbroucke, "Anatomy of a Failure: The Decision to Land at the Bay of Pigs," *Political Science Quarterly* 99, no. 3 (Autumn 1984): 476.

25. Binder, *Lemnitzer,* 259.

26. Arthur M. Schlesinger Jr., *A Thousand Days: John F. Kennedy in the White House* (Boston: Houghton Mifflin, 1965), 238.

27. Binder, *Lemnitzer,* 259–60.

28. Bissell, *Reflections of a Cold Warrior,* 164. Unfortunately, this very qualified statement has often been interpreted as a sign that the Chiefs supported such an invasion. For example, in his acclaimed biography of Kennedy, Robert Dallek noted that "the CIA and the military gave him assurances that the Cuban exiles could succeed without the participation of U.S. forces. On March 10, the Joint Chiefs told McNamara that 'the small invasion force of some twelve to fifteen hundred men could be expected to achieve initial success. Ultimate success will depend on the extent to which initial assault serves as a catalyst for further action on the part of anti-Castro elements throughout Cuba.' " This superficial analysis of the military's role in domestic decision making is all too common. Robert Dallek, *An Unfinished Life: John F. Kennedy, 1917–1963* (Boston: Little, Brown, 2003), 359.

29. Peter Wyden, *Bay of Pigs: The Untold Story* (New York: Simon and Schuster, 1979), 92.

30. Mark Perry, *Four Stars* (Boston: Houghton Mifflin, 1989), 105.

31. Wyden, *Bay of Pigs,* 92.

32. Freedman, *Kennedy's Wars,* 135.

33. Wyden, *Bay of Pigs,* 100; Schlesinger, *Thousand Days,* 242.

34. Schlesinger, *Thousand Days,* 243.

35. Binder, *Lemnitzer,* 262–63.

36. Ibid., 262.
37. Wyden, *Bay of Pigs,* 103.
38. Binder, *Lemnitzer,* 264.
39. Ibid., 263–64.
40. Wyden, *Bay of Pigs,* 149–50.
41. Ibid., 163.
42. Binder, *Lemnitzer,* 265.
43. Wyden, *Bay of Pigs,* 164.
44. Ibid., 266.
45. Dean Rusk, *As I Saw It* (New York: Penguin, 1990), 212.
46. Wyden, *Bay of Pigs,* 205.
47. Luis Aguilar, *Operation Zapata: The "Ultrasensitive" Report and Testimony of the Board of Inquiry on the Bay of Pigs* (Frederick, Md.: Aletheia Books, 1981), 244, 259.
48. Binder, *Lemnitzer,* 269.
49. Ibid., 270.
50. Wyden, *Bay of Pigs,* 125.
51. Higgins, *Perfect Failure,* 124.
52. Wyden, *Bay of Pigs,* 284.
53. Ibid., 243.
54. Aguilar, *Operation Zapata,* 164.
55. Wyden, *Bay of Pigs,* 267.
56. Schlesinger, *Thousand Days,* 295.
57. Dallek, *Unfinished Life,* 367.
58. Wyden, *Bay of Pigs,* 307.
59. Freedman, *Kennedy's Wars,* 146.
60. Wyden, *Bay of Pigs,* 317.
61. Binder, *Lemnitzer,* 277. This statement became the text of a National Security Action Memorandum defining the basis of civil-military relations.
62. Ibid., 286.
63. Weigley, *American Way of War,* 452.
64. Taylor, *Swords and Plowshares,* 263.
65. Schlesinger, *Thousand Days,* 801.
66. Ibid.
67. Robert F. Kennedy, *Thirteen Days: A Memoir of the Cuban Missile Crisis* (New York: Norton, 1969), 9.
68. Robert Smith Thompson, *The Missiles of October* (New York: Simon and Schuster, 1992), 191–92.
69. Kennedy, *Thirteen Days,* 13.
70. Roger Hilsman, *To Move a Nation: The Politics of Foreign Policy in the Administration of John F. Kennedy* (New York: Doubleday, 1967), 204.
71. Freedman, *Kennedy's Wars,* 180.
72. Ibid.
73. Coffey, *Iron Eagle,* 391.
74. Taylor, *Swords and Plowshares,* 269.
75. Freedman, *Kennedy's Wars,* 180–81.
76. Dallek observed, "He saw their counsel as predictable and not especially helpful. His memories of the navy brass in World War II, the apparent readiness of the

Chiefs to risk nuclear war in Europe and their unhelpful advice before the Bay of Pigs, and the army's stumbling performance just a few weeks before in Mississippi deepened his distrust of their promised results." *Unfinished Life*, 554.

77. Freedman, *Kennedy's Wars*, 191–92.

78. Taylor, *Swords and Plowshares*, 271.

79. Kennedy, *Thirteen Days*, 27.

80. Graham T. Allison, *Essence of Decision: Explaining the Cuban Missile Crisis* (New York: Harper Collins, 1971), 128.

81. Freedman, *Kennedy's Wars*, 193.

82. Taylor, *Swords and Plowshares*, 273.

83. Dino A. Brigioni, *Eyeball to Eyeball* (New York: Random House, 1991), 399–400. Although the material available on this incident is sometimes confusing, what is clear is that McNamara was angry and that Admiral Anderson refused to back down.

84. Elie Abel, *The Missile Crisis* (Philadelphia: Lippincott, 1966), 155. He also reportedly told McNamara that he "felt McNamara's actions were unbecoming the secretary of defense." Brigioni, *Eyeball to Eyeball*, 400.

85. Brigioni, *Eyeball to Eyeball*, 400.

86. Ibid., 156 (quote), 562–63. A slightly different portrayal of the admiral's confrontation with the secretary of defense is in Dallek, *Unfinished Life*, 562. In spite of minor differences, the main point is the same, that the navy was extremely upset by McNamara's actions.

87. Quoted in George Anderson, "The Cuban Blockade: An Admiral's Memoir," *Washington Quarterly* 5, no. 4 (Autumn 1982): 84.

88. Schlesinger, *Thousand Days*, 536.

89. Phillip B. Davidson, *Vietnam at War: The History, 1946–1975* (Novato, Calif.: Presidio Press, 1988), 291–92.

90. Freedman, *Kennedy's Wars*, 287.

91. Taylor, *Swords and Plowshares*, 221.

92. Freedman, *Kennedy's Wars*, 311.

93. Hilsman, *To Move a Nation*, 420.

94. Ibid., 421.

95. Schlesinger, *Thousand Days*, 545.

96. Taylor, *Swords and Plowshares*, 232.

97. Ibid., 245–46.

98. Andrew F. Krepinevich Jr., *The Army and Vietnam* (Baltimore: Johns Hopkins University Press, 1986), 64.

99. Freedman, *Kennedy's Wars*, 335.

100. Krepinevich, *Army and Vietnam*, 69.

101. Dallek, *Unfinished Life*, 667.

102. Taylor, *Swords and Plowshares*, 289.

103. Freedman, *Kennedy's Wars*, 369.

104. Ibid., 376.

105. Ibid., 387.

106. Dallek, *Unfinished Life*, 679.

107. Schlesinger, *Thousand Days*, 997. Ngo Dinh Nhu was Diem's brother and a very ambitious politician.

108. Binder, *Lemnitzer*, 285.

109. Kennedy, *Thirteen Days,* 97.

110. Quoted in Richard E. Neustadt and Graham T. Allison, afterword to Kennedy, *Thirteen Days,* 126.

CHAPTER SIX. THE MILITARY AND LYNDON JOHNSON

1. Alexander L. George and Eric Stern, "Presidential Management Styles and Models," in *Presidential Personality and Performance,* ed. Alexander L. George and Juliette George (Boulder, Colo.: Westview Press, 1998), 212.

2. Fred I. Greenstein, *The Presidential Difference: Leadership Style from FDR to Clinton* (Princeton, N.J.: Princeton University Press, 2000), 87.

3. Henry Graff, *The Tuesday Cabinet* (Englewood Cliffs, N.J.: Prentice-Hall, 1970), 3.

4. Doris Kearns, *Lyndon Johnson and the American Dream* (New York: Harper and Row, 1976), 318.

5. John Burke, *The Institutional Presidency: Organizing and Managing the White House from FDR to Clinton,* 2d ed. (Baltimore: Johns Hopkins University Press, 2000), 104.

6. Ibid., 86.

7. George Edwards III and Stephen J. Wayne, *Presidential Leadership: Politics and Policy Making,* 3d ed. (New York: St. Martin's, 1994), 210–11 (emphasis in original).

8. Ibid., 88.

9. Hugh Sidney, *A Very Personal Presidency* (New York: Atheneum, 1968), 203. See also H. R. McMaster, *Dereliction of Duty* (New York: Harper, 1998), 50.

10. Mark Perry, *Four Stars* (Boston: Houghton Mifflin, 1989), 133.

11. Lewis Sorley, *Honorable Warrior: General Harold Johnson and the Ethics of Command* (Lawrence: University Press of Kansas, 1998), 148.

12. McMaster, *Dereliction of Duty,* 62.

13. William Westmoreland, *A Soldier Reports* (New York: Doubleday, 1976), 110.

14. Robert S. McNamara, *In Retrospect: The Tragedy and Lessons of Vietnam* (New York: Vintage, 1995), 238.

15. This writer disagrees with Eliot Cohen's argument that civilians did not impose the "body count" on the generals. He maintains that "the 'body count' and similar quantifiable systems were developed by civilian and military leaders alike, with the latter often embracing them enthusiastically." *Supreme Command* (New York: Free Press, 2002), 183–84. One can criticize the generals and admirals for accepting the idea, but to suggest that the military embraced it "enthusiastically" pushes the argument too far. Yes, the military helped in its development, and some supported it, but the majority knew it was a poor way to measure success in war. Besides, McNamara was in charge, and he wholeheartedly supported it. The military clearly recognized that Washington wanted the body count.

16. Ibid., 238.

17. Phillip B. Davidson, *Vietnam at War: The History, 1946–1975* (Novato, Calif.: Presidio Press, 1988), 401.

18. McNamara, *In Retrospect,* 238.

19. Davidson, *Vietnam at War,* 403.

20. Westmoreland, *A Soldier Reports,* 83.
21. Davidson, *Vietnam at War,* 406.
22. Deborah Shapley, *Promise and Power: The Life and Times of Robert McNamara* (Boston: Little Brown, 1993), 414.
23. Thomas Moorer, "Lesson Learned from the Air War over Vietnam," *Proceedings of the U.S. Naval Institute* 113, no. 7 (August 6, 1987): 21.
24. McMaster, *Dereliction of Duty,* 163.
25. McNamara, *In Retrospect,* 105; also quoted in McMaster, *Dereliction of Duty,* 58.
26. McNamara, *In Retrospect,* 107–8.
27. McMaster, *Dereliction of Duty,* 68.
28. Ibid., 72. Taylor had become chairman on October 1, 1962.
29. Westmoreland, *A Soldier Reports,* 86.
30. McMaster, *Dereliction of Duty,* 70, 76–79.
31. Ibid., 85–86.
32. Ibid., 91.
33. Perry, *Four Stars,* 133, 134.
34. Lyndon Baines Johnson, *The Vantage Point: Perspectives of the Presidency, 1963–1969* (New York: Holt, Rinehart and Winston, 1971), 113.
35. Davidson, *Vietnam at War,* 320 (emphasis in original).
36. McNamara, *In Retrospect,* 134; also quoted in Johnson, *Vantage Point,* 115.
37. McMaster, *Dereliction of Duty,* 126, 127, 128.
38. McNamara, *In Retrospect,* 138, 139.
39. Johnson, *Vantage Point,* 120.
40. McMaster, *Dereliction of Duty,* 175.
41. Ibid.
42. Ibid., 176.
43. Ibid., 186.
44. Ibid., 187.
45. McNamara, *In Retrospect,* 165.
46. Johnson, *Vantage Point,* 125.
47. Davidson, *Vietnam at War,* 339.
48. McMaster, *Dereliction of Duty,* 233.
49. Ibid., 232.
50. McNamara, *In Retrospect,* 177.
51. McMaster, *Dereliction of Duty,* 249.
52. Ibid., 272.
53. Ibid., 254.
54. Johnson, *Vantage Point,* 140–41.
55. Sidney, *Very Personal Presidency,* 204.
56. Ibid., 206.
57. Graff, *Tuesday Cabinet,* 50.
58. Johnson, *Vantage Point,* 233.
59. David M. Barrett, "The Mythology Surrounding Lyndon Johnson, His Advisers, and the 1965 Decision to Escalate the Vietnam War," *Political Science Quarterly* 103, no. 4 (1988): 26–27.
60. McNamara, *In Retrospect,* 188. See also Michael R. Beschloss, *Reaching for*

Glory: Lyndon Johnson's Secret White House Tapes, 1964–1965 (New York: Touchstone, 2001), 348–49.

61. See Douglas Kinnard, *The War Managers* (Hanover, N.H.: University Press of New England, 1977), 119.

62. Sorley, *Honorable Warrior,* 201.

63. Bruce Palmer Jr., *The 25-Year War: America's Military Role in Vietnam* (Lexington: University Press of Kentucky, 1984), 41.

64. Sorley, *Honorable Warrior,* 212 (emphasis in original), 216.

65. Ibid.

66. Perry, *Four Stars,* 156.

67. Johnson, *Vantage Point,* 153.

68. Palmer, *25-Year War,* 42.

69. Sorley, *Honorable Warrior,* 223.

70. This battle has been immortalized in the book by Harold Moore and Joseph L. Galloway, *We Were Soldiers Once . . . and Young* (New York: Harpertorch, 1992). It was subsequently made into a movie of the same name.

71. Dave R. Palmer, *Summons of the Trumpet* (Novato, Calif.: Presidio Press, 1978), 95.

72. Ibid., 97.

73. McNamara, *In Retrospect,* 221.

74. Ibid., 223.

75. Davidson, *Vietnam at War,* 389–90.

76. Barrett, "Mythology Surrounding Lyndon Johnson," 115.

77. Johnson, *Vantage Point,* 237.

78. McNamara, *In Retrospect,* 235.

79. Johnson, *Vantage Point,* 239.

80. Davidson, *Vietnam at War,* 461.

81. Ibid., 462.

82. Ibid., 463.

83. Ibid.

84. David Halberstam, *The Best and the Brightest* (New York: Ballantine, 1992), 644.

85. Davidson, *Vietnam at War,* 464.

86. The president approved this number after talking with McNamara and Generals Wheeler and Westmoreland on July 13, 1968. Johnson, *Vantage Point,* 379.

87. Perry, *Four Stars,* 161, 162.

88. Ibid., 164.

89. Ibid., 165, 169. See also Bruce Palmer, *25-Year War,* 44.

90. Perry, 172.

91. Davidson, *Vietnam at War,* 464.

92. Johnson, *Vantage Point,* 383.

93. A former North Vietnamese colonel admitted that Tet was a devastating military defeat for the Communists. Bui Tin, *Following Ho Chi Minh: Memoirs of a North Vietnamese Colonel* (Honolulu: University of Hawaii Press, 1995), 61–63.

94. Perry, *Four Stars,* 183.

95. Clark Clifford, *Counsel to the President* (New York: Random House, 1991), 486. It is worth noting that when General Abrams came back to Washington shortly

before being appointed Westmoreland's successor, he was asked if he needed more troops. Unaware of Westmoreland's request, he replied, "Oh, no sir, Mr. President, we've got plenty of troops." "This was a bombshell, at least for those who knew how military lash-ups were supposed to work. The idea that Abrams, a four-star deputy in a theater of war, would not have been informed by his commander of so crucial a matter as a request for a massive troop augmentation was almost unimaginable." Lewis Sorley, *Thunderbolt: General Creighton Abrams and the Army of His Times* (Washington, D.C.: Brassey's, 1998), 222.

96. Davidson, *Vietnam at War,* 510.

97. Clifford, *Counsel to the President,* 493–94.

98. Davidson, *Vietnam at War,* 515. In regard to the Chiefs discussion of resigning, Cohen argued that "they had no arguments to use, no alternative, no offer, no 'professional judgement' that applied to the War." *Supreme Command,* 179–80. Factually, Cohen was correct; however, as noted in the text, the Chiefs had not been permitted to seek an approach other than escalation because of McNamara's strict control. In this writer's opinion, it is unreasonable to expect an organization such as the Joint Staff to devise an alternative strategy when "gradualism" was clearly the only one that the administration would consider.

99. Davidson, *Vietnam at War,* 530–31.

100. Kinnard, *War Managers,* 122. As Kinnard put it, "They were called to active duty despite complaints."

101. As Johnson explained, "I wanted the South Vietnamese to carry a heavier share of the burden of fighting for their country. . . . As each day passed I became increasingly confident that these people whom we had pledged to help were not only willing but able to do more." *Vantage Point,* 423.

102. Ibid., 435.

103. Ibid., 504.

104. " 'As a concept,' said Ambassador Diem, 'Vietnamization began in 1965, not in 1968, but Americans never got around to implementing it because they expected early victory without Vietnamese participation.' " Sorley, *Thunderbolt,* 256.

105. Ibid., 233, 239.

106. Perry, *Four Stars,* 207.

CHAPTER SEVEN. THE MILITARY AND RICHARD NIXON

1. William Safire, *Before the Fall: An Inside View of the Pre-Watergate White House* (New York: Doubleday, 1975), 315.

2. Joan Hoff-Wilson, "The Corporate Presidency," in *Leadership in the Modern Presidency,* ed. Fred I. Greenstein (Cambridge, Mass.: Harvard University Press, 1988), 170.

3. Sidney M. Milkis and Michael Nelson, *The American Presidency: Origins and Development, 1776–1990* (Washington, D.C.: Congressional Quarterly, 1990), 313.

4. Alexander L. George and Eric Stern, "Presidential Management Styles and Models," in *Presidential Personality and Performance,* ed. Alexander L. George and Juliette George (Boulder, Colo.: Westview Press, 1998), 213.

5. Milkis and Nelson, *American Presidency,* 314.

6. Fred I. Greenstein, *The Presidential Difference: Leadership Style from FDR to Clinton* (Princeton, N.J.: Princeton University Press, 2000), 107.

7. George C. Edwards III and Stephen J. Wayne, *Presidential Leadership: Politics and Policy Making,* 3d ed. (New York: St. Martin's, 1994), 183.

8. Henry Kissinger, *White House Years* (Boston: Little, Brown, 1979), 722.

9. William C. Westmoreland, *A Soldier Reports* (New York: Doubleday, 1976), 386.

10. Mark Perry, *Four Stars* (Boston: Houghton Mifflin, 1989), 211.

11. Bruce Palmer Jr., *The 25-Year War: America's Military Role in Vietnam* (Lexington: University Press of Kentucky, 1984), 98.

12. Ibid., 89.

13. Perry, *Four Stars,* 217.

14. Lewis Sorley, *Thunderbolt: General Creighton Abrams and the Army of His Times.* (Washington, D.C.: Brassey's, 1998), 258.

15. Elmo R. Zumwalt Jr., *On Watch: A Memoir* (New York: Quadrangle, 1976), 309–10.

16. Samuel Zaffiri, *Westmoreland: A Biography of General William C. Westmoreland* (New York: Morrow, 1994), 328.

17. Richard Nixon, *Two Foreign Policy Classics: Real Peace; No More Vietnams* (New York: Touchstone, 1990), 210.

18. H. R. Haldeman, *The Ends of Power* (New York: Times, 1978), 82–83.

19. Jeffrey Kimball, *Nixon's Vietnam War* (Lawrence: University Press of Kansas, 1998), 92–94.

20. Phillip D. Davidson, *Vietnam at War: The History, 1946–1975* (Novato, Calif.: Presidio Press, 1988), 589.

21. Perry, *Four Stars,* 219.

22. Ibid., 213.

23. Kissinger, *White House Years,* 239.

24. Ibid., 240.

25. Davidson, *Vietnam at War,* 591.

26. Kissinger, *White House Years,* 243.

27. Perry, *Four Stars,* 230.

28. Davidson, *Vietnam at War,* 593.

29. Nixon, *Two Foreign Policy Classics,* 219.

30. Ibid. In his defense of the administration's secrecy policy, Kissinger added that it also avoided placing the Chinese and the Russians in a position where they would have been forced to condemn the U.S. action, and perhaps take additional actions that could have damaged bilateral relations. Kissinger, *White House Years,* 249–50.

31. Kissinger, *White House Years,* 249–50.

32. Westmoreland, *A Soldier Reports,* 389.

33. Palmer, *The 25-Year War,* 96.

34. Ibid.

35. Nixon, *Two Foreign Policy Classics,* 2l6.

36. Kimball, *Nixon's Vietnam War,* 138–39.

37. Jeffrey J. Clark, *Advice and Support: The Final Years, 1965–1973* (Washington, D.C.: Center of Military History, United States Army, 1988), 348.

38. Ibid., 349.

39. Perry, *Four Stars,* 221, 222.

40. Kissinger, *White House Years,* 272.

41. Perry, *Four Stars,* 223–24.

42. Sorley, *Thunderbolt,* 262.

43. Dave R. Palmer, *Summons of the Trumpet* (Novato, Calif.: Presidio Press, 1978), 219.

44. Nixon, *Two Foreign Policy Classics,* 225.

45. Davidson, *Vietnam at War,* 607.

46. Kissinger, *White House Years,* 284.

47. Davidson, *Vietnam at War,* 631.

48. Perry, *Four Stars,* 224. See also Bruce Palmer, *25-Year War,* 84; Davidson, *Vietnam at War,* 616.

49. Thomas E. Ricks, *Making the Corps* (New York: Simon and Schuster, 1997), 136.

50. Dave Palmer, *Summons of the Trumpet,* 229.

51. Davidson, *Vietnam at War,* 625 (emphasis in original).

52. Henry Kissinger, *Ending the Vietnam War* (New York: Simon and Schuster, 2003), 143.

53. Kimball, *Nixon's Vietnam War,* 202.

54. Kissinger, *White House Years,* 487.

55. Kissinger, *Ending the Vietnam War,* 146.

56. Kissinger, *White House Years,* 490.

57. Kissinger, *Ending the Vietnam War,* 155–56.

58. Kissinger, *White House Years,* 496.

59. Kissinger, *Ending the Vietnam War,* 158. Interestingly, Kissinger noted, "To my astonishment, both Rogers and Laird—who, after all, were familiar with their elusive chief's methods by now—fell in with the charade that it was all a planning exercise and did not take a position. They avoided the question of why Nixon would call his senior advisers together on a Sunday night to hear a contingency briefing." Ibid.

60. Nixon, *Two Foreign Policy Classics,* 230.

61. Kissinger, *Ending the Vietnam War,* 162.

62. Ibid., 627.

63. Kimball, *Nixon's Vietnam War,* 210.

64. Kissinger, *White House Years,* 986.

65. Elmo Zumwalt Jr. and Elmo Zumwalt III, *My Father, My Son* (New York: Dell, 1986), 112.

66. Bruce Palmer, *25-Year War,* 90.

67. Perry, *Four Stars,* 209.

68. Kissinger, *Ending the Vietnam War,* 196.

69. Davidson, *Vietnam at War,* 641 (emphasis in original). To be fair, both Laird and Moorer have claimed that Westmoreland was consulted and that he approved of the operation. See Kissinger, *White House Years,* 1005.

70. Davidson, *Vietnam at War,* 654. The preceding description of the battle and South Vietnamese deficiencies is taken from Davidson, 651–55.

71. Kissinger, *Ending the Vietnam War,* 204.

72. Davidson, *Vietnam at War,* 661.

73. Zumwalt, *On Watch,* 375.

74. Kimball, *Nixon's Vietnam War,* 300.

75. Richard Nixon, *RN: The Memoirs of Richard Nixon* (New York: Touchstone, 1990), 590.

76. Perry, *Four Stars,* 236.

77. Ibid., 237.

78. Nixon, *Two Foreign Policy Classics,* 261.

79. Kissinger, *White House Years,* 1301.

80. Kimball, *Nixon's Vietnam War,* 324.

81. Dave Palmer, *Summons of the Trumpet,* 254.

82. Kissinger, *Ending the Vietnam War,* 408.

83. Ibid., 411.

84. Davidson, *Vietnam at War,* 727.

85. Ibid.

86. Zumwalt, *On Watch,* 46.

87. Perry, *Four Stars,* 132ff.

88. Zumwalt, *On Watch,* 34. Hereafter cited parenthetically in text.

89. Ibid. It is interesting that in his memoirs, Kissinger has nothing to say about this incident. He presumably did not attach as much importance to it as Zumwalt did.

90. Ibid., 506.

91. Perry, *Four Stars,* 249.

92. Ibid., 251.

93. It is also worth noting that Schlesinger made another appointment at this time that would have major ramifications for civil-military relations. He appointed Gen. David C. Jones as Brown's replacement as chief of staff of the air force. Jones would become one of the most important—and surely the most controversial—officer in the history of the JCS.

94. Perry, *Four Stars,* 257–59.

95. Ibid., 243.

CHAPTER EIGHT. THE MILITARY AND GERALD FORD

1. Fred I. Greenstein, *The Presidential Difference: Leadership Style from FDR to Clinton* (Princeton, N.J.: Princeton University Press, 2000), 116.

2. Roger B. Porter, "Gerald B. Ford, A Healing Presidency," in *Leadership in the Modern Presidency,* ed. Fred I. Greenstein (Cambridge, Mass.: Harvard University Press, 1988), 210, 212.

3. Henry Kissinger, *Years of Renewal* (New York: Simon and Schuster, 1999), 188.

4. Gerald R. Ford, *A Time to Heal* (New York: Harper and Row, 1979), 132.

5. Richard G. Head, Frisco W. Short, and Robert C. McFarlane, *Crisis Resolution: Presidential Decision Making in the Mayaguez and Korea Confrontations* (Boulder, Colo.: Westview Press, 1978), 110.

6. John Robert Greene, *The Presidency of Gerald R. Ford* (Lawrence: University Press of Kansas, 1995), 119.

7. Ford, *Time to Heal,* 30.

8. R. Gordon Hoxie, *Command Decision and the Presidency: A Study in National Security Policy and Organization* (New York: Reader's Digest Press, 1977), 336.

9. Kissinger, *Years of Renewal,* 478.

10. Greene, *Gerald Ford,* 137.
11. Mark Perry, *Four Stars* (Boston: Houghton Mifflin, 1989), 260.
12. Ibid., 261–62.
13. Greene, *Gerald Ford,* 144.
14. Head, Short, and McFarlane, *Crisis Resolution,* 108.
15. Ford, *Time to Heal,* 276.
16. Kissinger, *Years of Renewal,* 552.
17. Ford, *Time to Heal,* 276.
18. Ralph Wetterhahn, *The Last Battle: The Mayaguez Incident and the End of the Vietnam War* (New York: Plume, 2002), 37.
19. Kissinger, *Years of Renewal,* 554.
20. Head, Short, and McFarlane, *Crisis Resolution,* 111, 112.
21. Ron Nessen, *It Sure Looks Different from the Inside* (New York: Playboy Press, 1978), 118–19.
22. Wetterhahn, *Last Battle,* 45–46.
23. Greene, *Gerald Ford,* 146.
24. Kissinger, *Years of Renewal,* 558–59.
25. Greene, *Gerald Ford,* 147.
26. Wetterhahn, *Last Battle,* 99.
27. The following discussion of these options is taken from ibid., 100.
28. Kissinger, *Years of Renewal,* 565.
29. Head, Short, and McFarlane, *Crisis Resolution,* 273.
30. Roy Rowan, *The Four Days of Mayaguez* (New York: Norton, 1975), 177 (emphasis in original).
31. Ibid., 180.
32. Greene, *Gerald Ford,* 149.
33. Nessen, *It Sure Looks Different,* 126.
34. Head, Short, and McFarlane, *Crisis Resolution,* 138.
35. Wetterhahn, *Last Battle,* 259.
36. Ford, *Time to Heal,* 284.
37. Kissinger, *Years of Renewal,* 573.
38. Ford, *Time to Heal,* 284.
39. Kissinger, *Years of Renewal,* 573.
40. Ford, *Time to Heal,* 322, 323. Schlesinger's warning to the Chiefs is the incident referred to in the previous chapter.
41. Ibid., 323–24.

CHAPTER NINE. THE MILITARY AND JIMMY CARTER

1. Alexander L. George and Eric Stern, "Presidential Management Styles and Models," in *Presidential Personality and Performance,* ed. Alexander L. George and Juliette George (Boulder, Colo.: Westview Press, 1998), 215.
2. Erwin C. Hargrove, "The Politics of Public Goods," in *Leadership in the Modern Presidency,* ed. Fred I. Greenstein (Cambridge, Mass.: Harvard University Press, 1988), 231.

3. John Burke, *The Institutional Presidency: Organizing and Managing the White House from FDR to Clinton,* 2d ed. (Baltimore: Johns Hopkins University Press, 2000), 124.

4. Ibid., 122.

5. George and Stern, "Presidential Management Styles and Models," 218, 219, 221.

6. Ibid., 222.

7. This writer was in the Department of State when Carter made his famous (or infamous) statement about human rights. Six months of chaos followed as everyone tried to determine how the statement would affect the policy process and the constant turf battles.

8. George C. Edwards III and Stephen J. Wayne, *Presidential Leadership: Politics and Policy Making,* 3d ed. (New York: St. Martin's, 1994), 443.

9. Alexander Moens, *Foreign Policy under Carter: Testing Multiple Advocacy Decision Making* (Boulder, Colo.: Westview Press, 1990), 40.

10. See Phil Williams, "Carter's Defense Policy," in *The Carter Years: The President and Policy Making,* ed. M. Glenn Abernathy, Dilys M. Hill, and Phil Williams (New York: St. Martin's, 1984), 86.

11. Ibid., 87.

12. Jimmy Carter, *Keeping Faith: Memoirs of a President* (New York: Bantam, 1982), 39.

13. For most of the information and all of the quotations presented in the following discussion of Carter's first meeting with the Chiefs, see Mark Perry, *Four Stars* (Boston: Houghton Mifflin, 1989), 265–67.

14. Fred I. Greenstein, *The Presidential Difference: Leadership Style from FDR to Clinton* (Princeton, N.J.: Princeton University Press, 2000), 143.

15. John K. Singlaub, *Hazardous Duty: An American Soldier in the Twentieth Century* (New York: Summit, 1991), 382.

16. Ibid., 383.

17. Williams, "Carter's Defense Policy," 99.

18. The preceding discussion is based on Singlaub, *Hazardous Duty,* 425.

19. According to General Wickham, South Korean morale was hurt by the withdrawals that did occur during the Carter administration. John A. Wickham Jr., *Korea on the Brink: A Memoir of Political Intrigue and Military Crisis* (Washington, D.C.: Brassey's, 2000), 120.

20. Nick Kotz, *Wild Blue Yonder: Money, Politics and the B-1 Bomber* (New York: Pantheon Books, 1988), 140.

21. Carter, *Keeping Faith,* 81. Interestingly, Carter's quote doesn't mention efforts to persuade the military, which gives one the impression that the president neither cared nor worried about military opposition to his cancellation of the B-1.

22. Kotz, *Wild Blue Yonder,* 154.

23. Ibid., 163.

24. Perry, *Four Stars,* 268.

25. James R. Locher III, *Victory on the Potomac: The Goldwater-Nichols Act Unifies the Pentagon* (College Station: Texas A&M University Press, 2002), 42.

26. Perry, *Four Stars,* 269.

27. Kotz, *Wild Blue Yonder,* 14.

28. Perry, *Four Stars,* 269.

29. Ibid.

30. “Washington’s Naval Battle,” *Washington Post,* September 4, 1978.

31. Ibid.

32. One senior officer remarked to the author that, as an executive officer of a ship at the time, he quite honestly could not recommend reenlistment to sailors because of the disastrous economic conditions facing them, especially if they were married and had children.

33. “Sinking the Navy,” *Washington Post,* May 31, 1980.

34. Hargrove, “Politics of Public Goods,” 245, 247.

35. Carter, *Keeping Faith,* 473.

36. Cyrus Vance, *Hard Choices* (New York: Simon and Schuster, 1983), 389.

37. Zbigniew Brzezinski, *Power and Principle: Memoirs of the National Security Adviser, 1977–1981* (New York: Farrar, Straus, Giroux, 1983), 443.

38. Gary Sick, *All Fall Down: America’s Tragic Encounter with Iran* (New York: Penguin Books, 1986), 342.

39. “House Armed Services Panel Sees the New Military Budget as Too Little, Too Late,” *New York Times,* January 30, 1980.

40. “Advocates of More Defense Spending Press Carter to Increase ’81 Budget,” *Washington Post,* February 1, 1980.

41. “Of Budget Cuts, Military Money, Inflation and Moonbeams,” *Washington Post,* March 1, 1980.

42. “Shortages of Parts Hamstring Warplanes,” *Washington Post,* March 17, 1980.

43. “Sinking the Navy,” *Washington Post,* May 21, 1980.

44. “Carter Accused of ‘Hypocrisy’ on Arms Budget,” *Washington Post,* May 29, 1980.

45. “Joint Chiefs of Staff Break With Carter on Budget Planning for Defense Needs,” *Washington Post,* May 30, 1980.

46. “Joint Chiefs Dissent on Carter-Brown Military Budget,” *New York Times,* May 30, 1980.

47. “Low-Key Military Leader Makes No Apologies, No Changes,” *Washington Post,* June 1, 1980. It is also worth noting that Carter was furious with Meyer. According to Perry, Carter was so mad that Brown called Meyer into his office “and demanded a public apology. Meyer, remembering Johnson’s experience as Army Chief . . . told Brown that he would resign or be fired, but he would not retract his statement. ‘You know, we have a responsibility to the Congress, too, we don’t just serve at the behest of the Secretary of Defense,’ he said. Brown backed down and the statement stood.” Perry, *Four Stars,* 301.

48. “Carter: Shifting, Shoring Up Position on Defense,” *Washington Post,* August 19, 1980.

49. “Arms Readiness: Glass Half Empty, Half Full,” *Washington Post,* November 1, 1980.

50. Brzezinski, *Power and Principle,* 482.

51. Sick, *All Fall Down,* 250, 253.

52. James H. Kyle, *The Guts to Try* (New York: Ballantine, 1995), 39.

53. Sick, *All Fall Down,* 275.

54. Charlie A. Beckwith, *Delta Force* (New York: Avon, 1983), 249.

55. Kyle, *The Guts to Try,* 95 (emphasis in original); Beckwith, *Delta Force,* 249.

56. The following discussion of the March 22 meeting is taken from Sick, *All Fall Down,* 235–37.

57. Ibid., 335.

58. Eight helicopters would give the team the capability to continue the mission even if two of the helicopters were damaged or completely destroyed.

59. Carter, *Keeping Faith,* 501. See also Sick, *All Fall Down,* 337.

60. Sick, *All Fall Down,* 335.

61. Brzezinski, *Power and Principle,* 492.

62. Carter, *Keeping Faith,* 506.

63. Vance, *Hard Choices,* 409.

64. Hamilton Jordan, *Crisis: The Last Year of the Carter Presidency* (New York: Putnam, 1982), 251.

65. Vance, *Hard Choices,* 410.

66. Carter, *Keeping Faith,* 513.

67. Beckwith, *Delta Force,* 285–86.

68. Kyle, *The Guts to Try,* 223.

69. Beckwith, *Delta Force,* 10.

70. Brzezinski, *Power and Principle,* 495.

71. Sick, *All Fall Down,* 345.

72. Jordan, *Crisis,* 267.

73. Although a wide variety of sources discuss the operation, most of the following account of events leading up to the accident is taken from Sick, *All Fall Down,* 348–49. Sick's analysis of the operation from beginning to end provides one of the best perspectives from inside the White House.

74. Ibid., 349.

75. Beckwith, *Delta Force,* 316–17.

76. Jordan, *Crisis,* 282.

77. Beckwith, *Delta Force,* 315.

78. Ibid., 326.

79. Locher, *Victory on the Potomac,* 48.

80. Ibid.

81. Perry, *Four Stars,* 277.

CHAPTER TEN. THE MILITARY AND RONALD REAGAN

1. Alexander L. George and Eric Stern, "Presidential Management Styles and Models," in *Presidential Personality and Performance,* ed. Alexander L. George and Juliette George (Boulder, Colo.: Westview Press, 1998), 222.

2. Eugene R. Wittkopf and James M. McCormick, eds., *The Domestic Sources of American Foreign Policy* (Lanham, Md.: Rowman and Littlefield, 1999), 209.

3. John Burke, *The Institutional Presidency: Organizing and Managing the White House From FDR to Clinton*, 2d ed. (Baltimore: Johns Hopkins University Press, 2000), 146–47, 155.

4. Richard E. Neustadt, *Presidential Power and the Modern Presidents* (New York: Free Press, 1990), 276.

5. Donald T. Regan, *For the Record: From Wall Street to Washington* (New York: Harcourt Brace Jovanovich, 1988), 38–39. Regan spent two years as Reagan's chief of staff.

6. John Burke, *The Institutional Presidency: Organizing and Managing the White House from FDR to Clinton,* 2d ed. (Baltimore: Johns Hopkins University Press, 2000), 146.

7. The following account of Weinberger's first meeting with the Chief is taken from Mark Perry, *Four Stars* (Boston: Houghton Mifflin, 1989), 279–83.

8. Ibid., 283.

9. Caspar Weinberger, *In the Arena: A Memoir of the 20th Century* (New York: Regnery, 2001), 293.

10. Caspar Weinberger, *Fighting for Peace: Seven Critical Years in the Pentagon* (New York: Warner, 1990), 43 (emphasis in original).

11. Ronald Reagan, *An American Life* (London: Arrow, 1991), 234–35.

12. "Lehman Wins a Budget Battle," *Washington Post,* September 8, 1983.

13. Reagan, *American Life,* 235.

14. "Buildup," *Washington Post,* November 30, 1982.

15. Jeffrey Record, "A 3-War Strategy," *Washington Post,* March 22, 1982.

16. Quoted in Samuel Huntington, "The Defense Policy of the Reagan Administration, 1981–1982," in *The Reagan Presidency,* ed. Fred I. Greenstein (Baltimore: Johns Hopkins University Press, 1983), 88.

17. Record, "A 3-War Strategy," *Washington Post,* March 22, 1982.

18. David A. Stockman, *The Triumph of Politics: Why the Reagan Revolution Failed* (New York: Harper and Row, 1986), 283–84.

19. Weinberger, *In the Arena,* 47.

20. Hedrick Smith, *The Power Game: How Washington Works* (New York: Ballantine, 1988), 174.

21. Ibid., 208.

22. "Pentagon Is Bracing for Two 'Waves': Rising Costs Threaten Weapons, Readiness," *Washington Post,* November 13, 1988.

23. "The Birth of a Spending 'Bow Wave,'" *Washington Post,* November 28, 1982.

24. Colin Powell, *My American Journey* (New York: Random House, 1995), 258.

25. Perry, *Four Stars,* 288.

26. Ibid., 284.

27. "Military's Readiness, Command System Criticized," *Washington Post,* March 5, 1984.

28. "Inside the Defense Department," *Washington Post,* July 8, 1985.

29. "Military Budget Showdown Looms for Reagan, Congress," *Washington Post,* December 16, 1984.

30. "Champion of the Military and of Reagan," *Washington Post,* November 3, 1987.

31. "Debate Begins Today on Restructuring Defense—$33 Billion Cut in '89 Must Be Followed by $200 Billion More over 3 Years Carlucci Warns," *Washington Post,* February 18, 1988.

32. William J. Crowe Jr., *The Line of Fire* (New York: Simon and Schuster, 1993), 241ff.

33. "Pentagon Is Bracing for Two 'Waves': Rising Costs Threaten Weapons, Readiness," *Washington Post,* November 13, 1988.

34. Ibid.

35. Eric Hammel, *The Root: The Marines in Beirut, August 1982–February 1984* (New York: Harcourt Brace Jovanovich, 1985), 15.

36. Perry, *Four Stars,* 306.

37. Edmund Morris, *Dutch: A Memoir of Ronald Reagan* (New York: Modern Library, 1999), 463–64.

38. Perry, *Four Stars,* 307.

39. Morris, *Dutch,* 464.

40. Weinberger, *Fighting for Peace,* 151–52.

41. George Shultz, *Turmoil and Triumph* (New York: Simon and Schuster, 1993), 108, 109.

42. Deborah Hart Strober and Gerald S. Strober, *Reagan: The Man and His Presidency* (New York: Houghton Mifflin, 1998), 291.

43. Perry, *Four Stars,* 309.

44. Weinberger, *Fighting for Peace,* 154 (emphasis in original).

45. Michael Petit, *Peacekeepers at War: A Marine's Account of the Beirut Catastrophe* (Boston: Faber and Faber, 1986), 41.

46. Perry, *Four Stars,* 310.

47. Hammel, *The Root,* 82, 82–83 (emphasis in original).

48. Weinberger, *Fighting for Peace,* 157.

49. Ibid., 159.

50. Petit, *Peacekeepers at War,* 124.

51. Hammel, *The Root,* 218.

52. Ibid.; Robert C. McFarlane, *Special Trust* (New York: Cadell and Davis, 1994), 251; Reagan, *American Life,* 446.

53. Hammel, *The Root,* 279.

54. Larry Speakes, *Speaking Out: The Reagan Presidency from Inside the White House* (New York: Avon, 1988), 189.

55. Perry, *Four Stars,* 312.

56. Ibid., 315.

57. McFarlane, *Special Trust,* 267, 267–68.

58. Ibid., 270–71.

59. Ibid., 318.

60. Weinberger, *Fighting for Peace,* 163–64.

61. Ibid., 165.

62. Schultz, *Turmoil and Triumph,* 231.

63. Caspar Weinberger's famous six criteria (or tests, as he called them) for utilizing military force were heavily influenced by his frustration over the handling of the Lebanese situation. Weinberger, *Fighting for Peace,* 441–42.

64. Ibid., 105.

65. Mark Adkin, *Urgent Fury: The Battle for Grenada* (Martinsburg, W.Va.: Arcata Graphics, 1989), 110.

66. Ronald H. Cole, *Operation Urgent Fury* (Washington, D.C.: Joint History Office, Office of the Chairman of the Joint Chiefs of Staff, 1997), 11.

67. Ibid., 118.

68. McFarlane, *Special Trust,* 263.

69. Cole, *Operation Urgent Fury,* 39–40.

70. Weinberger, *Fighting for Peace,* 115.

71. Adkin, *Urgent Fury,* 132.

72. H. Norman Schwarzkopf, *It Doesn't Take a Hero* (New York: Bantam, 1992), 246.

73. Perry, *Four Stars,* 320.

74. Ibid., 321.

75. Smith, *Power Game,* 197.

76. Schwarzkopf, *It Doesn't Take a Hero,* 254 (emphasis in original).

77. Powell, *My American Journey,* 292.

78. Adkin, *Urgent Fury,* 336.

79. Strober and Strober, *Reagan,* 281.

80. Perry, *Four Stars,* 299. Ironically, Weinberger's memoir avoids mention of the reform process, one of the major civil-military events during his time as secretary of defense.

81. David Jones, "Why the Joint Chiefs Must Change," *Armed Forces Journal International,* March 1983, 65, 72. The article was published in a slightly different form with the title "What's Wrong with Our Defense" in the November 7, 1983, issue of the *New York Times.* From Jones's perspective, expecting a staff working for one service to provide genuinely "joint" advice was unrealistic; the body had to be a joint staff made up of officers from all services.

82. Locher, *Victory on the Potomac,* 65. Locher's book, by far the best to date on the Joint Chiefs of Staff and its evolution, details how the 1986 reform was passed.

83. Ibid., 69–71. Although the secretary of defense opposed a reorganization of the JCS, at least two very influential senior military officers who had served on it—Meyer and Jones—were strongly in favor of giving the Chiefs more authority.

84. Ibid., 70. When asked if he agreed with any of the changes suggested by Jones or Meyers, Hayward responded, "Not one—except that I do agree we need to strengthen the role of the JCS." Ibid., 71.

85. Ibid.

86. Crowe, *Line of Fire,* 150.

87. Locher, *Victory on the Potomac,* 380.

88. Crowe, *Line of Fire,* 158.

89. Ibid., 159. Locher also wrote about the event, buttressing Crowe's suggestion that the remark infuriated Nichols. Locher, *Victory on the Potomac,* 423.

90. Locher, *Victory on the Potomac,* 440.

91. Ibid., 441.

CHAPTER ELEVEN. THE MILITARY AND GEORGE BUSH

1. John Burke, *The Institutional Presidency: Organizing and Managing the White House from FDR to Clinton,* 2d ed. (Baltimore: Johns Hopkins University Press, 2000), 170.

2. James A. Baker III, *The Politics of Diplomacy: Revolution, War and Peace, 1989–1992* (New York: Putnam, 1995), 25.

3. Fred I. Greenstein, *The Presidential Difference: Leadership Style from FDR to Clinton* (Princeton, N.J.: Princeton University Press, 2000), 170.

4. Burke, *Institutional Presidency,* 174.

5. Ibid., 164.

6. Baker, *Politics of Diplomacy,* 22.

7. The incident is described in Bob Woodward, *The Commanders* (New York: Pocket Star Books, 1991). The quotes that follow appear on pages 44, 46, and 47.

8. Ibid., 48. For whatever reason, Crowe failed to discuss this incident in his memoirs, although it was common knowledge inside the Pentagon at the time. See William J. Crowe, *The Line of Fire: From Washington to the Gulf; The Politics and Battles of the New Military* (New York: Simon and Schuster, 1993).

9. Colin Powell, *My American Journey* (New York: Random House, 1995), 406.

10. Woodward, *Commanders,* 49.

11. "Strategy for Sole Superpower Pentagon Looks to 'Regional Contingencies,'" *Washington Post,* May 19, 1991.

12. George Bush and Brent Scowcroft, *A World Transformed* (New York: Knopf, 1998), 23, 24.

13. Woodward, *Commanders,* 82.

14. Powell, *My American Journey,* 425–26.

15. Rick Atkinson, *Crusade: The Untold Story of the Persian Gulf War* (New York: Houghton Mifflin, 1993), 123.

16. Thomas Donnelly, Margaret Roth, and Caleb Baker, *Operation Just Cause: The Storming of Panama* (New York: Lexington, 1991), 7. Hereafter cited parenthetically in text.

17. Woodward, *Commanders,* 56; Donnelly, Roth, and Baker, *Operation Just Cause,* 47.

18. Baker, *Politics of Diplomacy,* 184.

19. Donnelly, Roth, and Baker, *Operation Just Cause,* 51.

20. Woodward, *Commanders,* 68.

21. Donnelly, Roth, and Baker, *Operation Just Cause,* 52.

22. Ibid., 64, 65.

23. Ronald H. Cole, *Operation Just Cause: The Planning and Execution of Joint Operations in Panama, February 1988–January 1990* (Washington, D.C.: Joint History Office, Office of the Chairman of the Joint Chiefs of Staff, 1995), 18.

24. Baker, *Politics of Diplomacy,* 188.

25. Cole, *Operation Just Cause,* 27.

26. Donnelly, Roth, and Baker, *Operation Just Cause,* 94, 95.

27. Ibid., 96.

28. "The Conversion of Gen. Powell, Incidents Led JCS Chief to Reverse Opposition to the Use of Force," *Washington Post,* December 21, 1989.

29. Cole, *Operation Just Cause,* 28. According to Woodward, Powell said, "'My recommendation is going to be that we execute BLUE SPOON. I want to make sure that we're all agreeing.' He went around the room once again for final recommendations. All four chiefs said they were with him." *Commanders,* 143.

30. Cole, *Operation Just Cause,* 29.

31. Woodward, *Commanders,* 144 (emphasis in original).

32. Baker, *Politics of Diplomacy,* 189.

33. Powell, *My American Journey,* 425.

34. Baker, *Politics of Diplomacy,* 189.

35. Powell, *My American Journey,* 429.

36. Cole, *Operation Just Cause,* 31.
37. Powell, *My American Journey,* 432.
38. Cole, *Operation Just Cause,* 73.
39. Michael R. Gordon and Bernard E. Trainor, *The General's War* (Boston: Little, Brown, 1995), x.
40. H. Norman Schwarzkopf, *It Doesn't Take a Hero* (New York: Bantam Books, 1992), 291–92.
41. Powell, *My American Journey,* 460.
42. Woodward, *Commanders,* 191.
43. Gordon and Trainor, *The General's War,* 22.
44. Ibid., 18.
45. Powell, *My American Journey,* 461.
46. Woodward, *Commanders,* 200, 201.
47. Schwarzkopf, *It Doesn't Take a Hero,* 295.
48. Woodward, *Commanders,* 206.
49. Quoted in ibid., 209.
50. Gordon and Trainor, *The General's War,* 33, 34.
51. Woodward, *Commanders,* 214, 216.
52. Powell, *My American Journey,* 464.
53. Ibid., 464–65 (emphasis in original).
54. Woodward, *Commanders,* 220.
55. Gordon and Trainor, *The General's War,* 40.
56. Woodward, *Commanders,* 229.
57. Schwarzkopf, *It Doesn't Take a Hero,* 301–2 (emphasis in original).
58. Powell, *My American Journey,* 466 (emphasis in original).
59. Woodward, *Commanders,* 265.
60. Schwarzkopf, *It Doesn't Take a Hero,* 323 (emphasis in original).
61. Ibid., 326.
62. Ibid.
63. See Tom Clancy, with Chuck Horner, *Every Man a Tiger* (New York: Putnam, 1999), 287–90.
64. Powell, *My American Journey,* 479.
65. Atkinson, *Crusade,* 110.
66. Ibid.
67. Woodward, *Commanders,* 289.
68. Atkinson, *Crusade,* 111.
69. Ibid., 111, 112.
70. Ibid., 113.
71. Woodward, *Commanders,* 297.
72. See Gordon and Trainor, *The General's War,* 144–45.
73. Ibid., 141.
74. Woodward, *Commanders,* 305, 306.
75. Powell, *My American Journey,* 489.
76. Woodward, *Commanders,* 335.
77. Schwarzkopf, *It Doesn't Take a Hero,* 395.
78. See Gordon and Trainor, *The General's War,* 413–16.

79. Merrill A. McPeak, *Selected Works, 1990–1994* (Maxwell AFB, Ala.: Air University Press, 1995), 225.

80. "Cheney Warns Defense Bill Risks a Veto—Unrequested Arms May Force Troop Cuts," *Washington Post,* August 13, 1989.

81. Powell, *My American Journey,* 436. Hereafter cited parenthetically in text.

82. "Pentagon Says Troop Strength Might Decline by 10 Percent—Effect of Across-Board Budget Cuts Described," *Washington Post,* November 9, 1989.

83. "Playing the Numbers on the Defense Budget," *Washington Post,* December 3, 1989.

84. "Administration Seeks Defense Spending Cut—Cheney Says Soviet Threat Has Diminished," *Washington Post,* November 18, 1989.

85. "U.S. Military in Europe Being Reshaped—Cheney Is Presented with Options for Eventually Halving Troop Levels," *Washington Post,* December 17, 1989.

86. "Pentagon Drafts Major Cuts in Force Weapons—250,000 Troops, Hundreds of Planes, 62 Ships May Be Eliminated," *Washington Post,* November 28, 1989.

87. "The Conversion of Gen. Powell—Incidents Led JCS Chief to Reverse Opposition to the Use of Force," *Washington Post,* December 21, 1989.

88. "Pentagon Could Change '91 Budget, Cheney Says—Possible Treaties, Aircraft Review Cited," *Washington Post,* January 31, 1990.

89. "Memos Indicate No Revamping of U.S. Forces—Cheney's Guidance Puts Onus on Services," *Washington Post,* April 14, 1990.

90. "Powell Says Defense Needs Massive Review," *Washington Post,* May 7, 1990.

91. Powell, *My American Journey,* 451–52. Stephen J. Cimbala defined "the Base Force [as] the minimum force with which the United States could continue to function as a global superpower." "The Role of Military Advice: Civil-Military Relations and Bush Security Policy," in *U.S. Civil-Military Relations: In Crisis or Transition,* ed. Don M. Snider and Maranda A. Carlton-Carew (Washington, D.C.: Center for Strategic and International Studies, 1995), 89.

92. Powell, *My American Journey,* 451 (emphasis in original).

93. Ibid., 455.

94. "Powell Resists Deeper Pentagon Cuts," *Washington Post,* June 23, 1990.

95. Powell, *My American Journey,* 458, 463.

96. Ibid., 547.

97. "Strategy for Solo Superpower—Pentagon Looks to 'Regional Contingencies,'" *Washington Post,* May 19, 1991.

98. "For the Record," *Washington Post,* November 27, 1991.

99. Colin Powell interview, *McNeil-Lehrer NewsHour,* March 1992.

100. "For U.S. Forces, Cuts Mean a Sweeping Rearrangement," *Washington Post,* December 8, 1991.

101. Woodward, *Commanders,* 151.

CHAPTER TWELVE. THE MILITARY AND WILLIAM CLINTON

1. The role of women in the military during the Clinton administrations is not covered here for reasons of space. Furthermore, although many senior officers were

concerned about the role of women, their resistance paled in comparison to the military's opposition to the issue of homosexuals in the military.

2. Dick Morris, *Power Plays* (New York: ReganBooks, 2002), 1.

3. John Burke, *The Institutional Presidency: Organizing and Managing the White House from FDR to Clinton,* 2d ed. (Baltimore: Johns Hopkins University Press, 2000), 180.

4. Fred I. Greenstein, *The Presidential Difference: Leadership Style from FDR to Clinton* (Princeton, N.J.: Princeton University Press, 2000), 186.

5. Burke, *Institutional Presidency,* 188.

6. David Halberstam, *War in a Time of Peace: Bush, Clinton, and the Generals* (New York: Scribner, 2001), 207, 329.

7. Sidney Blumenthal, *The Clinton Wars* (New York: Plume, 2003), 60.

8. Burke, *Institutional Presidency,* 182. Burke goes on to note that "between 1 January 1999 to mid-March 1999, Clinton would attend thirteen fundraising events and host seven foreign heads of state, but meet with his cabinet only once" (183).

9. Alexander L. George and Eric Stein, "Presidential Management Styles and Models," in *Presidential Personality and Performance,* ed. Alexander L. George and Juliette George (Boulder, Colo.: Westview Press, 1998), 245.

10. Halberstam, *War in a Time of Peace,* 246.

11. Robert "Buzz" Patterson, *Dereliction of Duty* (New York: Regency, 2003), 51. Such "wiring diagrams" are not only used in the military. Every unit of the U.S. government, from the State Department to the Department of Agriculture, has one.

12. Thomas H. Henriksen, *Clinton's Foreign Policy in Somalia, Bosnia, Haiti, and North Korea* (Stanford, Calif.: Hoover Institution, 1996), 6.

13. Greenstein, *Presidential Difference,* 187.

14. George Stephanopoulos, *All Too Human* (Boston: Little, Brown, 1999), 75; "Feeling Snubbed by Administration, Military Views Clinton with Growing Distrust," *Baltimore Sun,* March 21, 1993; "The Commander in Chief," *Washington Post,* April 4, 1993.

15. Stephanopoulos, *All Too Human,* 132. Eventually, one of Clinton's military aides took on the job of teaching him how to salute.

16. David H. Hackworth, "Rancor in the Ranks: The Troops vs. the President," *Newsweek,* June 28, 1993.

17. "Feeling Snubbed by Administration, Military Views Clinton with Growing Distrust," *Baltimore Sun,* March 21, 1993.

18. "Joint Chiefs Warn Congress Against More Military Cuts," *New York Times,* May 20, 1993.

19. "The Mood of the Military," *Air Force Times,* June 14, 1993.

20. Patterson, *Dereliction of Duty,* 90. Another source has the aide commenting, "We really don't want people in uniform over here, unless it is absolutely necessary." "Feeling Snubbed by Administration," *Baltimore Sun,* March 21, 1993. Gen. Tommy Franks commented in his memoirs, "I had never been invited to the Clinton White House, but colleagues had described a palpable coolness toward military officers." Tommy Franks, *American Soldier* (New York: Harper Collins, 2004), 230.

21. Hackworth, "Rancor in the Ranks." A popular bumper sticker at the time read, "First Hillary, Then Genifer, Now Us."

22. A. J. Bacevich, "Clinton's Military Problems—and Ours," *National Review,*

December 13, 1993, 36. See also Elizabeth Drew, *On the Edge: The Clinton Presidency* (New York: Simon and Schuster, 1994), 87. The author can attest to the fact that derogatory comments by military officers about Clinton and his administration were common at the time, in spite of orders from the top to show the commander in chief the respect his office warranted.

23. This writer had the honor of being assigned to the House Armed Services Committee for two years when Aspin was chairman.

24. Colin Powell, *My American Journey* (New York: Random House, 1995), 578.

25. Halberstam, *War in a Time of Peace,* 246.

26. Drew, *On the Edge,* 357.

27. Ibid., 153.

28. Stephen J. Cimbala, introduction to *Clinton and Post–Cold War Defense,* ed. Stephen J. Cimbala (Westport, Conn.: Praeger, 1996), ix.

29. Don M. Snider and Andrew J. Kelly, "The Clinton Defense Program: Causes for Concern," in ibid., 11.

30. Drew, *On the Edge,* 43.

31. Joe Klein, *The Natural: The Misunderstood Presidency of Bill Clinton* (New York: Doubleday, 2002), 45.

32. This writer can remember many conversations with new administration officials on this topic. And what was most striking was not so much their point of view, it was their incredible lack of any kind of understanding of how the military operated, including the kinds of problems that such a change would have for the way it operated. As one senior official put it to this writer, "It is simple, the president told them to do it, so they should do it. It's their problem."

33. Powell, *My American Journey,* 564. In his memoirs, Clinton noted that Powell was "opposed to my proposal to allow gays to serve in the military, even though during the Gulf War, which made him a popular hero, the Pentagon had knowingly allowed more than one hundred gays to serve, dismissing them only after the conflict." Bill Clinton, *My Life* (New York: Knopf, 2004), 450.

34. "Feeling Snubbed by Administration," *Baltimore Sun,* March 21, 1993.

35. Drew, *On the Edge,* 46.

36. Stephanopoulos, *All Too Human,* 123.

37. According to Sidney Blumenthal, Powell viewed Clinton "essentially as an interloper who had deposed the benefactors of Powell's sterling career." *Clinton Wars,* 60.

38. Powell, *My American Journey,* 571.

39. Stephanopoulos, *All Too Human,* 123–24; Powell, *My American Journey,* 572.

40. Stephanopoulos, *All Too Human,* 124, 123.

41. Blumenthal, *Clinton Wars,* 53.

42. Powell, *My American Journey,* 573 (*New York Times* quote), 574.

43. "Clinton and the Military: Is Gay Policy Just the Opening Skirmish?" *Washington Post,* February 1, 1993.

44. Clinton, *My Life,* 485.

45. Stephanopoulos, *All Too Human,* 126.

46. "Aspin, Joint Chiefs Fail to End Impasse on Gays in Military," *Washington Post,* July 3, 1993, and "Colin Powell: The Debate is Over," *Washington Post,* July 27, 1993.

47. "Clinton: Policy in Military Is 'Sensible Balance,' " *Washington Post,* July 20, 1993.

48. Clinton, *My Life,* 486, 468.

49. Thomas H. Henriksen, *Clinton's Foreign Policy in Somalia, Bosnia, Haiti and North Korea* (Stanford, Calif.: Hoover Institution, 1996), 9. Much of the background material on the situation in Somalia prior to the attempt of American forces to seize Aidid is based on Henriksen's and Halberstam's excellent studies.

50. Halberstam, *War in a Time of Peace,* 251, 252.

51. Clinton, *My Life,* 550.

52. Halberstam, *War in a Time of Peace,* 254.

53. James L. Woods, "U.S. Decisionmaking during Operations in Somalia," in *Learning from Somalia: The Lessons of Armed Humanitarian Intervention,* ed. Walter Clarke and Jeffrey Herbst (Boulder, Colo.: Westview Press, 1997), 161.

54. "Christopher, in Unusual Cable, Defends State Dept," *New York Times,* June 16, 1993.

55. Halberstam, *War in a Time of Peace,* 254.

56. Henriksen, *Clinton's Foreign Policy,* 11.

57. Halberstam, *War in a Time of Peace,* 256. Sidney Blumenthal made a similar point, noting that some of Clinton's national security advisors "lacked practical strategies for the new international politics or failed to carry themselves with authority vis-a-vis American allies and others." *Clinton Wars,* 60.

58. Drew, *On the Edge,* 320. According to Halberstam, Bob Oakley's view of the Clinton team was that they were "nice people. . . . well intentioned, but no one was really in charge." *War in a Time of Peace,* 258.

59. Drew, *On the Edge,* 320. The military's after-action report suggested that "in the future if a native is going to be asked to risk his life, the incentive offered had better be worth the risk." Ed Wheeler and Craig Roberts, *Doorway to Hell: Disaster in Somalia* (Tulsa, Okla.: Consolidated Press International, 2002), 196.

60. Drew, *On the Edge,* 321.

61. Ibid., 322. In his memoirs, Powell called it "a recommendation I would later regret." *My American Journey,* 584.

62. Woods, "U.S. Decisionmaking during Operations in Somalia," 164.

63. Halberstam, *War in a Time of Peace,* 261.

64. This event was memorialized in Mark Bowden's well-known book, *Black Hawk Down* (New York: Signet, 2001), which also appeared as a movie under the same name. In this writer's opinion, this is one of the very best books ever written on a military operation.

65. Halberstam, *War in a Time of Peace,* 262.

66. Ibid., 262; Drew, *On the Edge,* 317.

67. Halberstam, *War in a Time of Peace,* 262–63.

68. Drew, *On the Edge,* 317.

69. Clinton, *My Life,* 533.

70. David Hackworth, *Hazardous Duty* (New York: Avon Books, 1996), 189. According to Powell, he told Clinton that "we could not substitute our version of democracy for hundreds of years of tribalism. 'We can't make a country out of that place. We've got to find a way to get out, and soon,' I said. The President admitted that he had not focused enough on the UN resolution back in June that had put us on a collision course with Aidid." *My American Journey,* 588.

71. Hackworth, *Hazardous Duty,* 189.

72. Bowden, *Black Hawk Down,* 379.

73. Drew, *On the Edge,* 358.

74. Clinton ignored his firing of Aspin, noting only that he "had resigned not long after the day of Black Hawk Down." *My Life,* 576.

75. Warren Christopher, *In the Stream of History* (Stanford, Calif.: Stanford University Press, 1998), 468.

76. Halberstam, *War in a Time of Peace,* 329.

77. For once, the Chiefs and Clinton were in agreement. Clinton argued that Perry "would turn out to be one of my best appointments, probably the finest secretary of defense since General George Marshall." *My Life,* 576.

78. Halberstam, *War in a Time of Peace,* 320–21.

79. Ibid., 391.

80. Ibid., 268.

81. Christopher, *In the Stream of History,* 175.

82. Henriksen, *Clinton's Foreign Policy,* 22–23.

83. Dick Morris, *Behind the Oval Office: Getting Reelected Against All Odds* (Los Angeles: Renaissance Books, 1999), 5.

84. See William G. Hyland, *Clinton's World: Remaking American Foreign Policy* (New York: Praeger, 1999), 61.

85. Ibid., 62. Hyland noted that an ABC–Washington Post poll showed that 45 percent of the populace disapproved of Clinton's handling of Haiti.

86. Stephanopolous, *All Too Human,* 273 (emphasis in original).

87. Christopher, *In the Stream of History,* 278.

88. Halberstam, *War in a Time of Peace,* 279.

89. Stephanopolous, *All Too Human,* 305.

90. Ibid., 306 (emphasis in original).

91. Halberstam, *War in a Time of Peace,* 198.

92. Powell, *My American Journey,* 576.

93. Ibid.

94. Albright also mentioned this incident in her memoirs, complaining that "time and again he led us up the hill of possibilities and dropped us off on the other side with the practical equivalent of 'No can do.'" She also noted that "in the face of all his medals and prestige, I found it hard to argue with Powell about the proper way to employ American force." It is also worth noting that the two of them joked about their disagreements later. See Madeleine Albright, *Madam Secretary* (New York: Miramax Books, 2002), 182n2.

95. Michael Dobbs, *Madeleine Albright: A Twentieth-Century Odyssey* (New York: Holt, 1999), 360.

96. Drew, *On the Edge,* 150.

97. Ibid., 155.

98. Dobbs, *Madeleine Albright,* 361.

99. Halberstam, *War in a Time of Peace,* 315.

100. Ibid., 331.

101. Ibid., 348.

102. Richard Holbrooke, *To End a War* (New York: Random House, 1998), 110.

103. Ibid., 118.

104. Ibid., 144, 145.

105. Henriksen, *Clinton's Foreign Policy,* 19.

106. Halberstam, *War in a Time of Peace,* 362.

107. Holbrooke, *To End a War,* 316, and Clinton, *My Life,* 684.
108. Halberstam, *War in a Time of Peace,* 349.
109. Ibid., 412. Hereafter cited parenthetically in text.
110. Wesley K. Clark, *Waging Modern War* (New York: Public Affairs, 2001), 98–99. Hereafter cited parenthetically in text.
111. Albright, *Madam Secretary,* 394; Clark, *Waging Modern War,* 161.
112. Halberstam, *War in a Time of Peace,* 421.
113. Clark, *Waging Modern War,* 169–70.
114. Halberstam, *War in a Time of Peace,* 423. In his memoirs, Clinton ignored his use of this language. *My Life,* 850.
115. Benjamin S. Lambeth, *NATO's Air War for Kosovo* (Santa Monica, Calif.: Rand, 2001), 25.
116. Clark, *Waging Modern War,* 178.
117. Andrew J. Bacevich, "Neglected Trinity, Kosovo and the Crisis in U.S. Civil-Military Relations," in *War over Kosovo,* ed. Andrew J. Bacevich and Eliot Cohen (New York: Columbia University Press, 2001), 156.
118. Ibid.
119. Lambeth, *NATO's Air War for Kosovo,* 235.
120. Ibid., 190.
121. Clark, *Waging Modern War,* 229.
122. Lambeth, *NATO's Air War for Kosovo,* 47.
123. Clark, *Waging Modern War,* 227.
124. Ibid., 232.
125. Halberstam, *War in a Time of Peace,* 466.
126. Clark, *Waging Modern War,* 319–20. See also Blumenthal, *Clinton Wars,* 640.
127. Ibid., 269, 270, 273.
128. Halberstam, *War in a Time of Peace,* 475.
129. Lambeth, *NATO's Air War for Kosovo,* 47–48.
130. Clark, *Waging Modern War,* 312.
131. Halberstam, *War in a Time of Peace,* 461.
132. Ibid., 456.
133. Blumenthal, *Clinton Wars,* 650–51. See also Eliot Cohen, *Supreme Command: Soldiers, Statesmen and Leadership in Wartime* (New York: Free Press, 2002), 204.
134. Blumenthal, *Clinton Wars,* 63.
135. Patterson, *Dereliction of Duty,* 89, 93.
136. "Please Impeach My Commander in Chief," *Washington Times,* November 9, 1998.
137. "Sharp Divergence Found in Views of Military and Civilians," *New York Times,* September 9, 1999. See also Ole R. Holsti, "A Widening Gap between the U.S. Military and Civilian Society," *International Security* (Winter 1998/99): 5–42, and Mark J. Eitelberg and Roger D. Little, "Influential Elites and the American Military after the Cold War," in *U.S. Civil-Military Relations: In Crisis or Transition?,* ed. Don M. Snider and Miranda A. Carlton-Carew (Washington, D.C.: Center for Strategic and International Studies, 1995), 34–67.
138. Based on a conversation between the author and General Short, September 12, 2001.
139. Halberstam, *War in a Time of Peace,* 417–18.

CHAPTER THIRTEEN. THE MILITARY AND GEORGE W. BUSH

1. Fred I. Greenstein, "The Changing Leadership of George W. Bush: A Pre- and Post-9/11 Comparison," in *The Domestic Sources of American Foreign Policy,* ed. Eugene R. Wittkopf and James McCormick, 4th ed. (Lanham, Md.: Rowman and Littlefield, 2004), 359.

2. Thomas Preston and Margaret G. Herrmann, "Presidential Leadership Style and the Foreign Policy Advisory Process," in ibid., 376.

3. Ibid.

4. Bob Woodward, *Bush at War* (New York: Simon and Schuster, 2002), 256.

5. Preston and Herrmann, "Presidential Leadership Style," 370.

6. Philip H. Gordon and Jeremy Shapiro, *Allies at War: America, Europe, and the Crisis over Iraq* (New York: McGraw Hill, 2004), 62.

7. Midge Decter, *Rumsfeld: A Personal Potrait* (New York: Harper Collins, 2003), 130.

8. This section is taken from Woodward, *Bush at War,* 22–23.

9. "Rumsfeld's Style, Goals Strain Ties to Pentagon," *Washington Post,* October 16, 2002.

10. "Pentagon Staff to Be Trimmed by 15 Percent: Bureaucracy an Adversary, Rumsfeld Says," *Washington Times,* September 11, 2001.

11. Woodward, *Bush at War,* 23.

12. Ibid. See also "Rumsfeld's Style," *Washington Post,* October 16, 2000.

13. Dana Priest, *The Mission: Waging War and Keeping Peace with America's Military* (New York: Norton, 2003), 24.

14. "No. 3 Civilian Ruffles Feathers at the Pentagon," *Washington Post,* December 8, 2002.

15. Woodward, *Bush at War,* 22.

16. "Rumsfeld on High Wire of Defense Reform: Military Brass, Conservative Lawmakers Are Among Secretive Review's Unexpected Critics," *Washington Post,* May 20, 2001.

17. It is worth noting that at least one four-star general reacted positively to Rumsfeld. As Tommy Franks put it, "I had heard the rumblings of discontent from a few colleagues, who accused him of being 'out in left field' when it came to the practicalities of national defense. Maybe so, but my earliest session with him convinced me that he would be good for the military. Popularity is never as important as respect." *American Soldier* (New York: HarperCollins, 2004), 232.

18. Priest, *The Mission,* 23.

19. "Rumsfeld on High Wire," *Washington Post,* May 20, 2001.

20. "Rumsfeld Taps Retired General for Army Chief," *Los Angeles Times,* June 11, 2003.

21. Decter, *Rumsfeld,* 136, 124.

22. Priest, *The Mission,* 34.

23. Based on a conversation with a four-star officer intimately familiar with the selection process at that time. As another source put it, "The Goldwater Nichols Act gave the chairman broad power to advise the president separately from the secretary. Myers, however, agreed not to go around Rumsfeld." Rowan Scarborough, *Rumsfeld's War: The Untold Story of America's Anti-Terrorist Commander* (Washington, D.C.: Regnery, 2004), 121.

24. "Joint Chiefs Pick Is at Home in Battles Real or Diplomatic," *Los Angeles Times,* August 24, 2001.

25. "Rumsfeld Seeks Consensus through Jousting," *New York Times,* March 19, 2003.

26. "Rumsfeld's Style," *Washington Post,* October 16, 2002.

27. "Rumsfeld Seeks Consensus through Jousting."

28. Priest, *The Mission,* 38.

29. Decter, *Rumsfeld,* 145.

30. Woodward, *Bush at War,* 43, 44. According to Tommy Franks, he shared Rumsfeld's frustration. As Franks put it, "For ten days, the first words the Secretary spoke in virtually every conversation concerned the Special Forces. 'When is something going to happen, General?' 'I do not see any movement, General Franks.' 'What is the situation with those teams, General?' The variations were few and subtle: 'Can you predict *when* something is going to happen?' 'Where *are* the teams, General?' " *American Soldier,* 296 (emphasis in original). Indeed, Rumsfeld's constant questions led Franks to suggest to Rumsfeld that the latter no longer had confidence in him. Rumsfeld responded that he had his "complete confidence" (300).

31. Woodward, *Bush at War,* 49 (emphasis added). See also Ivo Daalder and James M. Lindsay, *America Unbound: The Bush Revolution in Foreign Policy* (Washington, D.C.: Brookings Institution, 2003), 104. This charge is repeated in Bob Woodward, *Plan of Attack* (New York: Simon and Schuster, 2004), 23, and Michael DeLong (Franks's deputy), *Inside CentCom: The Unvarnished Truth about the Wars in Afghanistan and Iraq* (Washington, D.C.: Regnery, 2004), 21. As far as the president was concerned, he reportedly told his national security advisor on September 12, 2001, "We won't do Iraq now. . . . we're putting Iraq off. But eventually we'll have to return to that question" (26).

32. Woodward, *Bush at War,* 61. Hereafter cited parenthetically in text.

33. "Rumsfeld's War," *Newsweek,* September 16, 2002, 1.

34. Woodward, *Bush at War,* 189. Hereafter cited parenthetically in text.

35. Daalder and Lindsey, *America Unbound,* 107. The authors make the mistake of assuming that rangers and special forces were the same. Most special force soldiers are ranger qualified, but they generally operate in separate units.

36. Woodward, *Bush at War,* 314.

37. "Rumsfeld Gives 'Blank Sheet' to Update Special Operations," *Washington Times,* November 21, 2002. One of the strongest indications that Rumsfeld's words were hitting home was the willingness of the Pentagon's smallest service, the U.S. Marine Corps, "to relieve some of the burden on overtaxed Army and Navy Special Operations forces by offering to take on more command tasks, overcoming past resistance to assigning Marines to the Special Operations Command." "Distancing Tradition, Marines Eye Role in Special Operations," *Washington Post,* November 17, 2002. In simple terms, the Marines had "gotten the word," either get into the special operations game or become irrelevant.

38. "Rumsfeld Cites Terrorism in New Call for Military Reform," *Washington Post,* February 1, 2002.

39. "Rumsfeld Outlines Transformation Priorities," *Defense News,* October 21–27, 2002, 38.

40. "Transformed?" *Economist,* July 20, 2002, 3. For a more in-depth discussion of transformation, its advantages and disadvantages, see Thomas G. Mahnken, "Transforming the U.S. Armed Forces, Rhetoric or Reality," *Naval War College Review,* www.nwc.navy.mil/press/Review/2001/Summer/art6-su1.htm; Andrew L. Ross, Michele A. Flourneoy, Cindy Williams, and David Mosher, "What Do We Mean By 'Transformation,'" www.new.navy.mil/press/Review/2002/winter/art2-w02.htm; and James Jay Carafano, "The Army Goes Rolling Along: New Service Transformation Agenda Suggests Promise and Problems," *Backgrounder,* no. 1729, February 23, 2004.

41. "Transforming the U.S. Military," Pentagon briefing, February 1, 2002, manuscript.

42. "Transformed?" *Economist,* July 20, 2002, 9.

43. "Bush Seeks Major Defense Boost," *Washington Post,* January 24, 2002.

44. "A Nation Challenged," *New York Times,* February 2, 2002.

45. "Bush to Sign Defense Spending Bill," *Los Angeles Times,* October 23, 2002.

46. "Both Houses Back More Military Spending," *New York Times,* May 23, 2003.

47. "Pentagon Plan Seeks Annual Budget Boost of $20 billion," *Washington Post,* January 31, 2003.

48. "Bush Plans to Seek $14 Billion Hike in Defense Budget," *Washington Post,* December 15, 2002.

49. "Revamp of Special Operations Forces Planned," *Washington Post,* January 8, 2003.

50. "Rumsfeld Mulls Missile to Replace Crusader," *Washington Post,* June 23, 2002.

51. "Rumsfeld Backs Army Secretary. Crusader System to Be Dropped Despite White's Lobbying," *Washington Post,* May 8, 2002.

52. "Rumsfeld Defends Decision to Recommend Killing the Crusader," *Washington Post,* May 17, 2002.

53. "Rumsfeld Backs Army Secretary," *Washington Post,* May 8, 2002.

54. "Bush Developing Military Policy of Striking First," *Washington Post,* June 10, 2002.

55. "Remarks by U.S. Secretary of Defense Donald Rumsfeld to the National Defense University," Fort McNair, January 31, 2002, manuscript copy.

56. "Rumsfeld Turns Eye to Future of Army Mobility, Cohesion Sought for Units," *Washington Post,* June 8, 2003.

57. M. Elaine Bunn, "Preemptive Action: When, How, and to What Effect?" *Strategic Forum,* no. 200, July 2003, 1.

58. Ibid., 2.

59. "Rumsfeld's Design for War Criticized on the Battlefield," *New York Times,* April 1, 2003.

60. Scarborough, *Rumsfeld's War,* 119.

61. "Troops-Cut Plan Faces Wide Opposition: Civilian Service Secretaries Join Officers to Argue Against Reduction in Forces," *Washington Times,* August 13, 2001.

62. "Army Holds Its Ground in Battle with Rumsfeld," *Los Angeles Times,* November 29, 2002.

63. "Rumsfeld's Style," *Washington Post,* October 16, 2002.

64. "Army Shows Off Its New Strykers. Vehicles Termed Key to Planned Transformation," *Washington Post,* October 17, 2002.

65. "Army Holds Its Ground," *Los Angeles Times,* November 29, 2002.

66. "Rumsfeld Plan Has Army Officials Crying Foul," *Defense News,* October 21–27, 2002, 36.

67. "Wolfowitz Criticizes 'Suspect' Estimate of Occupation Force," *Washington Times,* February 28, 2003.

68. "Army Chief Says 200,000 Troops Needed to Keep the Peace," *Los Angeles Times,* February 27, 2003.

69. "Pentagon Contradicts General on Iraq Occupation Force's Size," *New York Times,* February 28, 2003.

70. "Wolfowitz Criticizes 'Suspect' Estimate," *Washington Times,* February 28, 2003.

71. "Shinseki Repeats Estimate of a Large Postwar Force," *Washington Post,* March 13, 2003. It is worth noting that in June after the defeat of Iraqi forces, 165,000 American and more than 40,000 coalition troops were in Iraq. "Rumsfeld Taps Retired General for Army Chief," *Los Angeles Times,* June 11, 2003.

72. Associated Press, June 11, 2003. "William L. Nash, a retired Army major general and veteran of the first gulf war and the Bosnia mission, said of General Shinseki, 'He is as fine a soldier as I've every served with, and his key characteristics are loyalty, and professional competence." "Rumsfeld's Design for War Criticized on the Battlefield," *New York Times,* April 1, 2003.

73. "Rumsfeld and All the Army's Men," *Washington Times,* March 27, 2003.

74. "Rumsfeld Criticizes Top Staff," *Washington Times,* January 24, 2003.

75. "Wolfowitz Criticizes 'Suspect' Estimate," *Washington Times,* February 28, 2003.

76. "Army Secretary Resigns: Leadership Vacuum Seen," *Los Angeles Times,* April 26, 2003. Rumsfeld also pushed what some have called a "modular" military. By this Rumsfeld meant creating units that could be selectively inserted to deal with problems. For example, "instead of relying on 10 active duty divisions, this more modular Army would enable commanders to pick from 30 or more battle groups, a dozen of which could be kept on alert for quick deployment."

77. "Rumsfeld Army Leaders in Discord," *Boston Globe,* September 1, 2003.

78. David Frum, *The Right Man: The Surprise Presidency of George W. Bush* (New York: Random House, 2003), 195–96.

79. According to Philip Stephens, British prime minister Tony Blair agreed to support Bush, but got the latter to agree to work through the UN. Stephens reported that Rumsfeld and Vice President Cheney did everything they could behind the scenes to get the United States to act unilaterally in spite of Bush's agreement with Blair to go through the UN. *Tony Blair* (New York: Viking, 2004), 205, 214–15, 216, 218.

80. Ivo H. Daalder and James M. Lindsay, *America Unbound: The Bush Revolution in Foreign Policy* (Washington, D.C.: Brookings Institution, 2003), 104.

81. Todd S. Purdum, *Time of Our Choosing: America's War in Iraq* (New York: Times Books, 2003), 16.

82. Woodward, *Bush at War,* 332, 345, 346, 348. Karen Kwiatkowski, a retired air force officer who served in the Pentagon at the time action against Iraq was being considered, argued that the Pentagon manipulated intelligence information to justify an invasion of Iraq. "The New Pentagon Papers," www.salon.com/opinion/feature/2004/03/10ospmoveon/print.html.

83. Frum, *Right Man,* 200.

84. Ibid., 239.

85. Jeffrey Krames, *The Rumsfeld Way* (New York: McGraw-Hill, 2002), 202.

86. Woodward, *Plan of Attack,* 8. According to Franks, his language was more circumspect when Rumsfeld called him on November 25, 2001, and told him that the president wanted to look at options for Iraq, including the potential use of military force.

87. Clark claims that planning began in January, but based on Woodward's and Franks's accounts, the president, Rumsfeld, and Franks were already working privately on such a plan in December. Wesley Clark, *Winning Modern Wars* (New York: Public Affairs, 2003), 9; Woodward, *Plan of Attack,* 1–4; Franks, *American Soldier,* 328–35. See also "Rumsfeld Seeks Consensus through Jousting," *New York Times,* March 19, 2003.

88. Woodward, *Plan of Attack,* 80.

89. Franks, *American Soldier,* 329, 333.

90. Purdum, *Time of Our Choosing,* 97–98; Scarborough, *Rumsfeld's War,* 45.

91. "Rumsfeld and All the Army's Men," *Washington Times,* March 27, 2003. Purdum uses the figure "fewer than 100,000 troops." *Time of Our Choosing,* 98. See also "Secretary of War," *Time Magazine,* December 29, 2003–January 5, 2004, 87–88.

92. Scarborough, *Rumsfeld's War,* 45.

93. Woodward, *Plan of Attack,* 118–19. Throughout his memoirs, Franks expresses frustration with the Chiefs, who, he believed, were often more concerned with their services' parochial interests than with working together to win a war. *American Soldier,* 207, 277–78.

94. Scarborough, *Rumsfeld's War,* 45–46.

95. Clark, *Winning Modern Wars,* 17.

96. "Rumsfeld Faulted For Troop Dilution," *Washington Post,* March 30, 2003.

97. "Rumsfeld and All the Army's Men," *Washington Times,* March 27, 2003.

98. See, for example, James Follows, "Blind into Baghdad," *Atlantic Monthly* (January/February), 2004, 52–74.

99. "Secretary of War," *Time Magazine,* December 29, 2003–January 5, 2004, 88.

100. Franks put the best face possible on planning for post–Saddam Iraq, but he ignored many of the problems—the looting, the lawlessness, the instability—that most observers believed were a result of a force structure that was too small to occupy and rebuild Iraq.

101. For a discussion of the army's view of peacekeeping, see Lyle J. Goldstein, "General John Shalikashvili and the Civil-Military Relations of Peacekeeping," *Armed Forces and Society* 26, no. 3 (Spring 2000): 387–411.

102. "Rumsfeld Faulted for Troop Dilution," *Washington Post,* March 30, 2003.

103. "Rumsfeld's Support Is in High Places," *Los Angeles Times,* April 2, 2003.

104. "For All Sides, War Evolved Not Quite According to Plan," *New York Times,* April 20, 2003.

105. "Pentagon Reform Is His Battle Cry. Donald H. Rumsfeld with New Political Clout Won in Iraq and Afghanistan, Intensifies His War on the Military Establishment," *Los Angeles Times,* August 17, 2003.

106. Woodward, *Plan of Attack,* 281. Franks made similar comments about Feith in his memoirs. *American Soldier,* 330, 545.

107. Woodward, *Plan of Attack,* 282–84.

108. Ibid., 331.

109. "After the War, New Stature for Rumsfeld," *New York Times,* April 20, 2003.

110. Ibid.

111. "Analysts: Roche to Change U.S. Army Culture," *Defense News,* May 12, 2003, 17.

112. "Air Force's Roche Picked to Head Army," *Washington Post,* May 2, 2003. Roche would eventually withdraw his name for consideration for the post, primarily because of a scandal over a deal he made with Boeing and because of a sexual scandal at the Air Force Academy. "Roche Bails Out as Pick for Top Army Job," *Los Angeles Times,* March 11, 2004.

113. "Retired General Picked to Head Army; Rumsfeld's Choice of Schoomaker Expected to Rankle Many in Uniform," *Washington Post,* June 11, 2003.

114. "Chief Hope to Quicken Army's Shift," *Washington Post,* October 3, 2003.

115. "Pentagon Plans for 'Global Surge,' " *Defense News,* September 18, 2003.

116. "Army Expansion Could Last 5 Years," *Washington Post,* January 30, 2004; "Army Will Add 30,000 Soldiers over 4 Years," *Los Angeles Times,* January 29, 2004.

117. "Army Cancels Comanche Helicopter," *Los Angeles Times,* February 24, 2004; "Army's Comanche Decision Preceded White House Review," *Defense News,* March 22, 2004, 4.

118. "Army Retraining Soldiers to Meet Its Shifting Needs," *New York Times,* March 11, 2004.

119. Ibid.

120. "Green Berets Take on Spy Duties," *Washington Times,* February 19, 2004.

121. "Kerry Criticizes Bush's Plan to Withdraw Troops," *Los Angeles Times,* August 19, 2004, and "U.S. to Cut Forces in Europe, Asia," *Washington Post,* August 14, 2004.

122. "Adm. Vern Clark: A Visionary Naval Chief," *Seapower,* October 2003, 3. See also "U.S. Navy Forces Shrink Again in 2005 Budget," *Defense News,* January 12, 2004, 18.

123. The air force would be one of the winners in this new military structure. Repackaging air force assets to meet Rumsfeld's new criteria was not difficult.

124. "Dissension Grows in Senior Ranks on War Strategy," *Washington Post,* May 9, 2004.

125. Scarborough, *Rumsfeld's War,* 113.

126. "Defense Official Moves to Ease Strained Relations with Army," *Washington Post,* October 9, 2003.

127. "Powell and Joint Chiefs Nudged Bush Toward UN," *Washington Post,* September 3, 2003.

128. "The Risk of Velvet Gloves," *Washington Post,* January 19, 2004. See also "Marines to Offer New Tactics in Iraq," *Washington Post,* January 7, 2004, and "Marines Plan to Use Velvet Gloves More than Iron Fist in Iraq," *New York Times,* December 12, 2003.

CHAPTER FOURTEEN. CONCLUSION

1. Thomas Ricks, *Making the Corps* (New York: Simon and Schuster, 1997), 280. Ricks's comments are based on a wide variety of surveys conducted with military officers. See also Michael Desch, "Explaining the Gap: Vietnam, the Republicanization

of the South, and the End of the Mass Army," in *Soldiers and Civilians: The Civil-Military Gap and American National Security,* ed. Peter Feaver and Richard H. Kohn (Cambridge, Mass.: MIT Press, 2001), 305, 308, 311–12, and Ole R. Holsti, "Of Charms and Convergences: Attitudes and Beliefs of Civilians and Military Elites at the Start of a New Millennium," in ibid., 27.

2. Richard H. Kohn, "The Erosion of Civilian Control of the Military in the United States Today," *Naval War College Review* (Summer 2002): 1–38, www.nwc.navy.mil/press/Review/art1-su2.htm.

INDEX